SOLDIERS

ARMY LIVES AND LOYALTIES
FROM REDCOATS TO DUSTY WARRIORS

RICHARD HOLMES

Harper
Press

Harper*Press*
An imprint of HarperCollins*Publishers*
77–85 Fulham Palace Road
Hammersmith, London W6 8JB

This Harper*Press* paperback edition published 2012

1

First published in Great Britain by Harper*Press* in 2011

A catalogue record for this book
is available from the British Library

ISBN 978-0-00-722570-5

Set in New Baskerville with Bulmer and Caslon Openface display
by G&M Designs Limited, Raunds, Northamptonshire
Printed and bound in Great Britain by
Clays Ltd, St Ives plc

MIX
Paper from
responsible sources
FSC
www.fsc.org   FSC™ C007454

CONTENTS

LIST OF ILLUSTRATIONS

Cartoons of the Yeomanry Cavalry by Giles on pages 102 and 106 reproduced by permission of the Trustees of the Suffolk and Norfolk Cavalry

PLATE SECTION

The Prince of Wales, later Edward VII, Duke of Saxe Coburg, and Duke of Connaught in military dress. © *Popperfoto/Getty Images*

Young Prince of Wales (later Edward VIII) at his headquarters in WWI. © *Mary Evans Picture Library*

Clement Atlee in uniform during the First World War. © *Illustrated London News Ltd./Mary Evans Picture Library*

William Cobbett, engraving by F Bartolozzi, 1801. © *Hulton Archive/ Getty Images*

Sir Redvers Henry Buller © *Hulton Archive/Getty Images*

John Churchill, Duke of Marlborough, by Sir Godfrey Kneller © *Hulton Archive/Getty Images*

A soldier, called Major John André (oil on canvas). *Presented by the Trustees of the Estate of Miss Evelyn Syme. Huntington Library and Art Gallery, San Marino, CA, USA* © *Bridgeman Art Library*

Execution of Major John André (colour litho). © *Peter Newark Military Pictures/Bridgeman Art Library*

Travers Clarke with H.R.H. Duke of York and officers at RAOC Headquarters. *The Trustees of the Imperial War Museum, London (HU81798)*

Lieutenant General Sir John Cowan. *National Library of Scotland, Edinburgh (119) L.718*

Field Marshall Sir William Robertson, 1910. © *Hulton Archive/Getty Images*

Captain James Jack in the trenches at Bois Grenier, 5th January 1915. *The Trustees of the Imperial War Museum, London (Q.51567)*

'An early lesson in marching', by Thomas Rowlandson. © *Mary Evans Picture Library/Reform Club*

'Heroes recruiting at Kelsey's, or Guard-Day at St James's' by James Gillray. *Courtesy of the Warden and Scholars of New College, Oxford/Bridgeman Art Library*

Harrow OTC recruits, drilling in 1927. © *Hulton Archive/Getty Images*

The King's Shilling c. 1770 (oil on canvas). © *National Army Museum, London/Bridgeman Art Library*

Listed for the Connaught Rangers, by Lady Butler (Elizabeth Thompson). © *Bury Art Gallery and Museum, Lancashire/Bridgeman Art Library*

Sergeant McCabe at the Battle of Sobraon. © *Peter Newark Military Pictures/Bridgeman Art Library*

WWI recruitment poster for the Tank Corps by Alfred Leete. © *Onslow Auctions Ltd./Mary Evans Picture Library*

A tank bringing in a captured naval gun at the Battle of Cambrai. *The Trustees of the Imperial War Museum, London (Q.6354)*

Padre writing field postcards for wounded men near Carnos, 1916. *The Trustees of the Imperial War Museum, London (Q.4060)*

Repatriation ceremony of Private Lee O'Callahan. *Courtesy of the Princess of Wales's Royal Regiment*

Soldiers of the King's German legion and Greek Light Infantry from *Costumes of the Army of the British Empire, according to the last regulations 1812.* © *National Army Museum, London/Bridgeman Art Library*

A private, drummer, piper and a bugler of the Black Watch, 42nd Foot, *c.*1912. © *Hulton Archive/Getty Images*

Officers and men of the 3/3rd Gurkha Rifles, 75th Division, in the line. December 1917. *The Trustees of the Imperial War Museum, London (Q.12936)*

Men of the Chinese Labour Corps at Proven, 1917. *The Trustees of the Imperial War Museum, London (Q.2762)*

British troops being transported to the front during the Korean War, 1950. © *Hulton Archive/Getty Images*

Hannah Snell, engraving by Maddocks. © *Mary Evans Picture Library*

Dr James (Miranda) Barry (1795?–1865), assistant surgeon. © *Mary Evans Picture Library*

WAAC recruitment poster, *c.* 1916. © *Onslow Auctions Ltd./Mary Evans Picture Library*

ATS recruitment poster, 1942 © *Archive Photos/Getty Images*

WAAC Corps training for a public display, June 1919. © *Hulton Archive/Getty Images*

Ambulance drivers of the First Aid Nursing Yeomanry, *c.* 1943. © *Archive Photos/Getty Images*

Officer of the 11th Hussars. © *Malcolm Greensmith Collection/Mary Evans Picture Library*

Military fashions cartoon by Henry Heath, *c.*1830 © *Mary Evans Picture Library*

The Yeomanry Cavalry cartoon by Giles. *Courtesy of the trustees of the Suffolk and Norfolk Yeomanry*

A bugler and drummer of the Royal Artillery during the Crimean War, 1856. © *National Army Museum, London/Bridgeman Art Library*

A mortar section of 3 Para. *Courtesy of Captain Euan Goodman*

'Loyal Souls, or A Peep into the Mess Room at St James' by James Gillray. *Courtesy of the Warden and Scholars of New College, Oxford/ Bridgeman Art Library*

FOREWORD

RICHARD HOLMES WAS a professional in several fields. As an author he never failed to fulfil a contract, so it is ironic and tragic for his many readers that an untimely death prevented him from completing the final touches of this his last book. However, we are lucky that he left it in such good shape that only the odd addition has had to be made. This was typical of the man whose sense of duty meant that he always did what he promised. The trouble was that he frequently promised too much.

I was an unlikely friend to Richard Holmes, he an academic and I with not an A level to my name. It was a chance remark and a question that led us to be companions astride our horses, first in France and then in other parts of the world. Our love of the horse and history forged a friendship which coped with late nights, hangovers, and a good deal of snoring. To spend weeks on end in the company of this extraordinarily well-informed man was to me a great joy. On those days the modern world was far away, and only occasionally did outside communication interrupt our imagining of another age and another battle. Reading the pages of this book, I felt increasingly that he was beside me at the camp fire, enjoying a mug of local liquor, telling one more anecdote, one more yarn. On those trips we were a happy band; Richard's repartee and amusing turn of phrase were an important part of the expedition even when things went wrong – 'we have a bijou problemette'. Where there was Richard, there were also smiles and laughter.

Richard played many roles in his life but soldiering was at the heart of it. From those early days when he joined the Territorial Army and when he studied the Franco-Prussian War at university, he had a fascination for the history of warfare – but then so do many others. He was unusual in that his power of recall was quite extraordinary in its breadth and detail. While on a tour of a World War One battlefield, he stayed at a French nobleman's house. After the introductions, he remarked in his particular style of French, that it was a pleasure to meet the descendants of a family who had fought against the English at Crécy. The family were astonished at his knowledge of French history, and could not do enough for him and his companions. His other notable quality was the way he made his subject so interesting to the reader or listener. One of his obituarists described how he captured the imagination of a group of sceptical soldiers to whom history was unimportant. It was this skill that made him such a brilliant teacher, and there are many of us who reacquired an appetite for military history through his involvement with the army's Staff College. He had the trick of making that interest and knowledge relevant to today's operational theories. There were 1,300 people at his memorial service; well over a hundred were senior officers who had sat at his feet at some stage or other. He became the professional head of the Territorial Army at a critical moment, and his passionate defence of that organisation – which played such a large part in his life – marked him out as a fine and selfless leader. The army and the country have much to be grateful to him for.

Richard was at his best on the very ground where a battle was won or lost. He had a good eye for ground and was able to describe in a matter-of-fact way what had occurred at a particular spot. He always related his account to the various hills, valleys, and ridges in front of us, so that you could almost smell and hear the action. His stories of the personalities involved and their unusual habits brought that element of humanity to the story, quite often causing a great deal of mirth. Written notes tended to be just a few headings; it was invariably the way he answered questions that held the crowd.

The soldier, with all his qualities good and bad, was a passion for Richard. He was deeply moved following his two visits to his regiment in Iraq where they had a particularly testing time. *Dusty Warriors* is his homage to the soldier of today and to the regiment which adopted him – a Territorial – as their Colonel; he was rightly proud of this unusual accolade. This book shows his devotion to the profession of arms at a very personal level. He much regretted that during his life he had not undergone that test of courage, and *Dusty Warriors* was, in a strange way, his penance.

Soldiers is a typical Holmes product, full of detail usefully comparing modern soldiering with the echoes of the past. His technique of bringing perspective to the events of today through the prism of history is always leavened by that inimitable wit for which he was renowned. Having been a private soldier in the yeomanry at an early age he acquired an inner knowledge of how the dynamics of the barrack room worked; this always made him instinctively sympathetic to the plight of the 'Tom'. His trilogy, *Redcoat, Sahib*, and *Tommy* are masterpieces of the social history of the British Army but *Soldiers* adds spice to the mix. Although many will be aware of the 'lives and loyalties' of the British army, few of us are able to describe them in such an amusing and readable way.

As I write this, I am about to embark on another ride in the Borders; we are calling it the Reivers' Ride and the choice of country and period were Richard's. He was once more to be our companion and resident historian, as we fundraise for his favourite charity ABF, The Soldiers' Charity, a charity for which he raised well over a quarter of a million pounds underlining, perhaps, this book's theme: that all soldiers deserve our sympathy, praise, and ultimately a 'hand up'. In the weeks before his death, it was this expedition which provided some sort of goal. He will be much in our thoughts as we relive the English victory at Flodden or Cromwell's annihilation of the Scots at Dunbar. Jessie and Corinna, his daughters, will be with us for part of the ride, making it all the more poignant. I, for one, will miss those tales – perhaps even excerpts from this book – which would have been so much better heard than read, but the time lords will have to work their magic before I can enjoy that old familiar voice.

Evelyn Webb-Carter

INTRODUCTION

IT IS USELESS to deny it. I have loved Tommy Atkins, once a widely used term for the common soldier, since I first met him. And love is the right word, for my affection goes beyond all illusions. I know that he is capable of breaking any law imposed by God or man, and whenever I allow myself to feel easy with him, he smacks my comfortable preconceptions hard in the mouth: it is his nature to do so. Antony Beevor, cavalry officer turned best-selling historian, thought that 'the British soldier's unpredictable alternation between the odd bout of mindless violence when drunk, and spontaneous kindness when sober, is one of his most perplexing traits.'[1] Another former officer described trying to find some soldiers who were late for duty one Sunday afternoon. He was tipped off that they had been seen entering the house of a local civilian:

> The door was answered by a small, rather timid man who invited us in. 'We're looking for some soldiers', my colleague explained, giving their names. 'Oh yes, they're here,' the man told us, 'upstairs, screwing my wife.' A few moments later, nine rather shame-faced soldiers appeared with the fattest and ugliest woman I have ever seen. She was quite clearly drunk and farted noisily as she came into the room … Later I asked one of the boys what he could conceivably have found attractive in the woman. 'The more gopping the slag is, Sir,' he replied, 'the better she is at it.'[2]

The same author identified the moment he decided to resign his commission:

> At 2 a.m. the Duty Officer's phone rang and I lifted it, half asleep, 'Guardroom Sir, we've got a tech stores man down here – he says he's beaten up his wife.' I got there in a few minutes to find a very drunk man who had apparently ended an argument with his

pregnant wife by kicking her in the stomach. He had got drunk, he told me, because he was fed up with the job and 'Anyway, that kid's not mine.' Neither the wife nor unborn child was seriously injured; but that night I decided to leave the Army.[3]

Some men look back on their time in uniform with huge satisfaction. One First World War veteran, Sergeant Adolphus 'Dolph' Jupe of the Hampshire Regiment, thought that:

I suppose that in our life we give our hearts unrestrainedly to very few things. I had given mine to the battalion and bore its three stripes on my arm with greater pride than I have ever experienced since. We had worn a proud uniform for over five years and with many others I was disconsolate at its putting off. For the sufferings, the sacrifice and the heroism of a million men of our generation whose bones lay at rest across the sea, had raised the prestige of our race to a height never before achieved, and even upon us, however faintly, was reflected the glory of their achievements.[4]

But another, Bombardier Ronald Skirth, like Jupe a wartime soldier, declared that:

My abhorrence of war equated with a detestation of the war-machine – the Army of which I was a member … it personified everything I despised. I was a cog in that machine, vastly more powerful than myself, so I was compelled to live a hypocrite's exist-ence[5] … By the time the war ended, my prejudices had become so unreasoning and so deeply embedded that I resolved never to accept any honours, promotions, benefits or even monetary advan-tages from an Authority I both detested and despised.[6]

Author Colin MacInnes, who served in the Intelligence Corps in a later war, hated the whole thought of killing or being killed, but disliked military service itself almost as much:

Three-quarters of military discipline is mindless, obsolete and wastefully self-frustrating – apart, of course, from being highly irri-tating. No one can serve in any army for years without being to some extent an inbred malingerer and scrounger, irredeemably slothful.

Conversely, several of the National Servicemen interviewed by Trevor Royle for his book *The Best Years of their Lives* thought that military service had changed them for the better. 'I sometimes wonder how different I'd have been without the discipline of National Service,' asked one. I mean, what did a Teddy Boy graduate to? 'Most if us *did* feel proud to be part of an army which had only recently won the war', admitted another. 'I feel sorry that modern youth cannot experience such feelings.'[7]

Tommy Atkins certainly has a capacity for extraordinary gentleness. Guardsman Gerald Kersh was abed in a Second World War Nissen hut when the rest of his squad of potential officers returned, heavy-footed, from the cinema:

> Everybody clumped in … I breathed regularly, and kept my nose under the blankets. Then I heard a Potential Officer of a Rifle Brigade Sergeant say: 'Take it easy. Have a little consideration. Man asleep here.'
>
> Something clicked above my head. Looking out of the narrow slit of one partly-raised eyelid, I saw the Rifle Brigade Sergeant take my greatcoat off its hook, open it, shake it gently and approach me. He covered me with it, and then everybody went to bed.
>
> It was not that I was ill, it was not that I was fragile and in need of protection. I was asleep.[8]

He has a harsh edge too. The capture of Goose Green in the Falklands by 2 Para in 1982 was a remarkable feat of low-level dogged courage, and earned a posthumous Victoria Cross for its commanding officer, Lieutenant Colonel H. Jones. Ken Lukowiak, who fought there as a private, admitted that one of his comrades carried a couple of pairs of dental pliers 'to acquire gold', and a handful of his comrades looking at a pretty girl's photograph were soon speculating about her propensity for vigorous anal intercourse.[9] The gallant victors neither expected nor received kid-glove handling, as Lukowiak, chided by Colour Sergeant Frank Pye for obeying an order to clear up after the battle, assures us:

'What the fuck are you doing, you stupid cunt?' said Frank.

'If I told you I was sweeping the floor, Colour, would you believe me?'

'Don't get fucking gobby with me, you crow, or I'll fucking drop you.'

'Sorry, Colour.'[10]

Nor are officers always chivalrous gentlemen, as Lieutenant Colonel Edward Windus observed in 1761 when telling his colonel why he had thrown Lieutenant Meredyth out of the regiment:

> When sober, he cannot keep away from a billiard table, or when drunk, out of a bawdy house, where he is very apt to draw his sword upon friends or foes, though he seldom meets any of the former there, or anywhere else. In short, he has made himself despised by the people of Cork, and this place; as much as he was disagreeable to his brother officers.[11]

Like a rich and time-worn tapestry, Atkins shuns easy analysis. There is an appetite for alcohol, sex, and casual violence. This is then interwoven seamlessly into a personality indelibly coloured by self-sacrifice, comradeship, generosity, humour, a tenderness for other men that owes little to sexuality, and the fiercest of pride in the primary group. A thick braid of decency is folded around the darker strands of self-indulgence, even though it can never quite conceal them. Whatever the controversies of the occupation of Iraq, Steve Brooks, who served there as an officer with the Princess of Wales's Royal Regiment, firmly believed that he was doing the right thing:

> I have found that soldiers are simple people and in general are apolitical – not amoral. As such I deployed to Ulster to stop children having to walk to school between picket lines under a hail of missiles, to Kosovo to prevent ethnic cleansing of a population, and to Iraq to secure democracy for a people who deserved the right to it. By looking at the basic scars of Saddam's regime I knew that we were doing right by the common man.[12]

Yet the judge advocate in the trial of officers and soldiers court-martialled for alleged involvement in the death in army custody of an Iraqi civilian, Baha Mousa, maintained that evidence within the Queen's Lancashire Regiment had been impossible to secure because of 'a more or less obvious closing of the ranks'. After his release from prison, former corporal Donald Payne, who had pleaded guilty to the inhumane treatment of Mousa, maintained that he had seen several of his comrades 'forcefully kick and/or punch the detainees,' and added that 'he had previously covered up the extent of abuse by British troops out of misguided loyalty.'[13] Part of the difference between the behaviour of two groups of soldiers, in Iraq at different times and places, is circumstantial. It owes a good deal to local mood, regimental and small-group culture, and the tone set by commanders, senior and junior alike. In a deep and abiding sense there is less real difference than we might hope for. Atkins retains the chameleon-like ability to be both hero and villain.

Rudyard Kipling, the first writer to get to grips with the British private soldier, could be penetratingly honest about the man's complexity. His own research was carried out in the 1880s with the help of soldiers of the Northumberland Fusiliers and the East Surreys at Mian Mir – the great military cantonment outside Lahore. This allowed him to glimpse a world rarely seen by middle-class outsiders:

> The red-coats, the pipe-clayed belts and the pill-box hats, the beer, the fights, the floggings, hangings and crucifixions, the bugle-calls, the smell of the oats and horse-piss, the bellowing sergeants with foot-long moustaches, the bloody skirmishes, invariably mishandled, the crowded troop-ships, the cholera-stricken camps, the 'native' concubines, the ultimate death in the work-house.[14]

Alongside his heroes, like Captain Crook O'Neil of the 'Black Tyrone', stand tragic figures like Private Simmons, mercilessly bullied by Private Losson, who eventually shoots his tormentor and duly hangs for it. In the poem 'Cells', the narrator, locked up yet again for being drunk and resisting the guard, regrets that 'my wife she cries on the barrack-gate, my kid in the barrack-yard' but knows that 'as soon as I'm in with a mate and gin, I know I'll do it again.'[15]

It was a portrait drawn from life, as we can see from Horace Wyndham's description of a commanding officer's orders – the meting out of summary jurisdiction – in an infantry battalion at Aldershot in the 1890s:

> At first sight, one would scarcely imagine that the pasty-faced, feeble-looking youth in the centre had, a few hours ago, required the united efforts of four of the regimental police to carry him, striking, blaspheming and madly drunk, from the canteen to the guard-room … The burly scoundrel at the end of the row is now to answer as he may for making a savage assault on a non-commissioned officer. He has 'ex-Whitechapel rough' writ large all over his evil countenance, and although he knows perfectly well that trial by court-martial will be his fate, he does not appear to be in the least concerned thereby.[16]

William Roberston was the only man in British military history to rise through the ranks from private to field-marshal. When he arrived to join the 16th Lancers in 1877, the orderly officer warned him that he was entering a world where private property no longer existed: 'Give your watch to the sergeant-major of your troop, my lad … for it is unsafe to leave it lying about, and there is nowhere you can carry it with safety.' His barrack room was peopled with folk

> addicted to rough behaviour, heavy drinking, and hard swearing … treated like machines – of an inferior kind – and having little expectation of finding decent employment on the expiration of their twenty-one years' engagement, they lived only for the present … These rugged veterans exacted full deference from the recruit, who was assigned the worst bed in the room, given the smallest amount of food and the least palatable, and had to 'lend' them articles of kit which they had lost or sold.[17]

This deference was enforced with the aid of unofficial punishment. In 1836 a private of 1st Foot Guards told the Royal Commission on Military Punishments that his battalion had company courts-martial, in which soldiers judged their own kind. Offences like 'thieving from his comrades or … or dirty tricks' could result in a man being sling-belted, held down trouserless across a bench and lashed with the leather sling of a musket. It was a disgraceful punishment, and a man thus treated was thereafter 'never thought anything of'.[18]

When Roberston joined the army, every military offence, no matter how trivial, was regarded as a crime, for which the offender was flung in the unit's guard-room until he could be dealt with by his commanding officer. The guard-room

> in the case of the cavalry barracks at Aldershot, was about fifteen feet square, indifferently ventilated, and with the most primitive arrangements for sanitation. No means of lighting it after dark were either provided or permitted. Running along one of its sides was a sloping wooden stage, measuring about six feet from top to bottom, which served as a bed for all the occupants, sometimes a dozen or more in number ... no blankets (except in very cold weather) or mattresses were allowed, except for prisoners who had been interned for more than seven days. Until then their only covering, besides their ordinary clothes – which were never taken off – consisted of their cloaks, and they had to endure as best they could the sore hips and shoulders caused by lying on the hard boards.[19]

Life in military prisons was infinitely worse. Flogging remained despite having been abolished in the army generally in 1881. By 1895 the cat-o'-nine-tails was rarely used, and had been replaced by the birch, which was applied across the bare buttocks so sharply that most victims cried out with pain. In 1895 Private Jones of the 16th Lancers, found guilty of idleness at the crank and reporting sick without cause, received eighteen strokes, and the eighteen-year-old Private Dansie of the Duke of Cornwall's Light Infantry was awarded eighteen strokes in Dublin Military Prison for repeated idleness. At Gosport, assaulting a warder brought Private Murphy of the West Riding twenty-five strokes.

Not all violence has been formal. From the very beginning, the process of converting civilian into soldier was entrusted to NCOs who used fists or sticks to help things along. In 1738 an ex-soldier maintained that his comrades had to

> stand to be beat like dogs; which, indeed, is generally the case if a man does not speak or look contrary to some officer's humours. I have known men beat with canes and horse-whips till the blood run

from their heads into their shoes, only for speaking in their own defence, and very often laid in irons in some dungeon afterwards … These frequent liberties taken by certain officers, in extending their authorities to use unsufferable severities, is the reason of the best men's avoiding the army, and good recruits being so difficult to get.[20]

It could mean death for a man to strike back. When guard was being mounted in the English enclave of Tangier in July 1677, one drummer was late with his stroke. Captain Carr promptly hit him, and the drummer went for his sword, almost as a reflex. He was sentenced to hang, but the garrison commander, well aware that he had few enough soldiers as it was, commuted the sentence so that the drummer had to stand at the foot of the gallows with a rope round his neck until the crime was expiated.[21]

Until relatively recently some soldiers would rather accept an illegal whack than undergo due process that would leave its mark on their official record. Young Spike Mays, who joined 1st Royal Dragoons as a band-boy in 1924, found that a moment's inattention earned him 'a cut across the backside' from the bandmaster's stick.[22] When Lieutenant Peter Young transferred from his infantry battalion to a newly raised Commando unit in 1940, his NCOs assured him that soldiers far preferred this sort of discipline. Beevor described the army at what he thought was

the tail end of an illegal, though quietly ignored, system of justice as old as the army itself. In many regiments, a sergeant would offer the miscreant a choice: either 'accept my punishment' – usually a thump administered behind the vehicle sheds – 'or the company commander's' – which almost certainly meant a fine. 'I'll take yours, sarge,' was the usual resigned reply.[23]

He would certainly have drawn the line at striking the blow himself, but in May 1780 the thoughtful Captain John Peebles, commanding the grenadier company of the Black Watch, confided to his diary 'I knocked down Norman McKay on the parade not so much for being drunk as swearing he was not, and though he deserved it I am sorry for it, for we should never punish a soldier in a passion.'[24] Peebles was neither a thug nor a martinet. When he returned home in February 1782 he made a moving farewell address to the men of his company, stressing the 'satisfaction and pleasure' of having been their commander, and commending them for 'that good name you are so justly possessed of whether in quarters or the field.' He remembered that he 'could hardly make an end of this little speech, my voice faltered, and my knees shook under me.' Evidently 'the poor fellows were affected too.' He promptly ordered them 'five gallons of rum to make a drink of grog in the evening,' effectively giving them nearly half a pint of rum a head, a gift no doubt destructive of the very sobriety he had urged upon them.[25]

Continuity and change lie at the very heart of my story. Israeli historian Martin van Creveld, has argued that different forms of military organisation were 'ultimately rooted in political, social and economic structures … each of them was also partly the product of the technology then in use.'[26] The British army that came into being with the restoration of the monarchy in 1660 has evolved in myriad ways since then, with these political, social, economic and technological pressures all playing their part in the process. I have no doubt that the Duke of Marlborough, who oversaw the army's transition from a scarlet puddle of 'guards and garrisons' in the late 1600s to the world-class force that helped dash the dynastic ambitions of Louis XIV, would recognise, in the tired heroes of Helmand, the descendants of the men he led to victory at Blenheim over three hundred years ago. They wear loose camouflage fatigues, not red coats with bright facings; their professional knowledge would leave Marlborough's men dazzled, and their rationality and scepticism would mark them off from an age coloured by belief and deference.

And yet their social organisation is so recognisably similar that we may doubt whether, in the British context, technology has really shaped structures quite as much as it has elsewhere. The major combat arms, infantry, cavalry, and artillery, have retained forms and terminologies that the men who fought at Blenheim – or Waterloo or the Somme, for that matter – would readily grasp. Lieutenant colonels, leading their regiments into action, have lost nothing of their pivotal importance in the hierarchy, and the death of Lieutenant Colonel Rupert Thorneloe of the Welsh Guards, killed in Afghanistan in the summer of 2009, underlines the risks they still run. Regiments, with their elders and distinctive markings – as characteristic of the army as an ancient Briton's woad, the cicatrices of an African warrior or a junker's duelling scars – are still an enduring feature of the army, usually much misunderstood and endemically under threat, but thudding on like the beat of a distant drum.

Formal and informal structures continue to intermesh. Most modern soldiers would recognise the close and comradely world prescribed in the 1800 *Regulations for the Rifle Corps*, which stipulated that every corporal, private and bugler should select a comrade from a rank differing from his own. Comrades were to berth, drill and go on duties together, and comrades could not be changed without the permission of the captain.[27]

Although the technology would doubtless baffle a Wellingtonian footsoldier, Colour Sergeant 'Stick' Broome's description of extracting the wounded Private Johnson Beharry from a Warrior armoured vehicle in Iraq shows the same bonds of comradeship that have helped hold men together for three centuries:

> We hit the ground, and we came under contact from small arms immediately. Woody and Erv went left, myself and Cooper started to pull Beharry out of his seat. This was the first chance I had to see the badly lacerated face of Bee ... I pulled him out with the help of big Erv and Jim Cooper and put him into my Warrior with his head in my lap.[28]

There is much in common between a rifleman like William Green of Lutterworth, whose 'disposition to ramble' took him into the army, and Dorset shepherd Benjamin Harris, carried away by the understated glory of a green jacket, and the likes of Lance Corporal Wood and Private Ervin. A modern recruiter would squirm at the Duke of Wellington's assessment of the army of his own age:

> A French army is composed very differently from ours. The conscription calls out a share of every class – no matter whether your son or my son – all must march; but our friends – I may say it in this room – are the very scum of the earth. People talk about enlisting from their fine military feeling – all stuff – no such thing. Some of our men enlist from having got bastard children – some

for minor offences – many more for drink; but you can hardly
conceive such a set brought together, and it is really wonderful that
we should have made them the fine fellows they are.[29]

It remains true that the majority of infantry soldiers are recruited, as
they always have been, from boys whose civilian futures do not seem
bright. The modern army's growing tendency to cream off the clever-
est of its recruits for its technical corps has accentuated the process.
In 1942 the army's adjutant general, responsible for its manpower
policies, admitted that the infantry 'received in effect the rejects from
the other arms of the service'.[30] It is still easiest to recruit at times of
economic depression. Just as Wellington could scarcely have beaten
the French without the aid of men who had chosen to serve rather
than starve, so the army of the early twenty-first century has been
saved from a manning crisis by the shortage of jobs elsewhere.

In Scotland the issue has become heavily politicised, with Scottish
National Party backbencher Christine Grahame maintaining that
many Scots recruits were in fact 'economic conscripts ... turning to the
Army as a way out of poverty and deprivation, brought on by the failed
policies of London Labour'.[31] The predictable furore aroused by these
remarks cannot alter the fact that Scotland's economic plight was a
spur to recruitment from the army's very earliest years. As historian
Stephen Wood wrote of the Scottish soldiers who signed on to fight in
Marlborough's wars: 'Many would be enlisted while drunk or have the
edges of their doubts blunted with alcohol; some would enlist as an
alternative to gaol, or starvation, or domestic responsibilities.'[32]

It is evident that economic compulsion was not restricted to
Scotland. In 1859 Lieutenant General Sir George Weatherall, the
adjutant general, told the Royal Commission on Recruiting 'there are
very few men who enlist for the love of being a soldier; it is a very rare
exception ... they are starving, or they have quarrelled with their
friends, or there are cases of bastardy, and all sorts of things.'[33] In
1877 the sergeant major of the 77th Foot asked a Geordie recruit if
he had served in the army before, only to be told 'No. Aw were niver
hard enough up, to list, afoor.'[34] Robert Edmondson, who signed on
as a private in the late 1880s, suggested that up to 80 per cent of the
army was drawn from the unemployed, adding 'Empty pockets and
hungry stomachs are the most eloquent and persuasive of recruiting

sergeants.'[35] The First World War made comparatively little difference, and in 1926 *The Times* reported that 60 per cent of recruits from the London area were unemployed when they signed on. When Spike Mays arrived at Canterbury to begin his basic training, he was received with a cheery greeting from Mitch, a fellow recruit 'Wotcher, mate. Ain't 'arf 'ungry. Could scoff a scabby-'eaded ape.'[36]

There were always some genuine enthusiasts. Joseph Gregg, who was to take part in the charge of the Light Brigade, wrote, 'My father was a soldier at the time of the battle of Waterloo ... As a boy, I always had a desire to see a battlefield, and made up my mind to enlist in a cavalry regiment.'[37] Herbert Wootton, who joined up on the eve of the First World War, agreed that he too

> was very keen on becoming a soldier. I had two uncles, both regulars, who served through the South African war of 1899–1902. As a youngster I was thrilled with their stories. I became a keen reader of G. A. Henty's books on war, and later read Rudyard Kipling's books. I loved to be in the company of old soldiers.[38]

Captain Doug Beattie's assessment of his own predilection for a military career (he signed on as a 16-year-old in 1981) has many answering echoes:

> I suppose soldiering was in my blood. My dad was a serviceman. My grandfathers had fought in World War Two, one with the Royal Artillery, the other with the Irish Fusiliers. I entered the world in England, a result of the posting system of the army that dad – then a colour sergeant in the Royal Ulster rifles – was subject to.[39]

Wellington's point about conscription is fundamental to understanding the British army. For most of its history it was recruited by voluntary enlistment, although economic necessity, judicial compulsion, and the gulling of drunken youths all blurred the definition of what a real volunteer might actually be. For example, an Englishman in eighteenth-century Atholl observed a poor fellow running to the hills as if for his life, hotly pursued by half a dozen human blood hounds. Turning to his guide, the gentleman anxiously inquired the meaning of what he saw. 'Och,' replied the imperturbable Celt, 'it's only the Duke raising the royal Athole *volunteers*.'[40]

In the British experience legal compulsion has been the exception not the rule. The first Military Service Act was passed in early 1916, as a response to losses in the first eighteen months of the First World War. This represented a sea-change in public policy. Conscription was in force from 1916 to 1919, and again in 1939–60; from 1948 this was in the guise of National Service. It was only during these years that the army was in any sense a genuinely national force, its members, serving and retired, strewn so liberally across society that there was no escaping them.

As a young Territorial private in the early 1960s I hitch-hiked in itchy battledress, getting lifts, without any real effort, from lorry-drivers who asked knowing questions about my 'mob'; mothers whose boys had recently completed their National Service; and men whose conversation slid onto sangars and bocage, desert roses and PIATS – the well-burnished argot of folk who had done it, which I, most demonstrably, had not.[41] It was a world full of men who understood the difference between a brigadier and a bombardier, a battalion and a brigade. They knew that you stepped off with the left foot and that although you assiduously called a warrant officer 'sir', you did yourself no favours by imagining that you might salute him.

In the early twenty-first century, as in the first decade of its existence, the army now constitutes a tiny proportion of the population; all the signs suggest that this proportion will decrease still further. About one in seventy of us has a close family member who has served or is still serving, and regular soldiers themselves account for just 0.087 per cent of the population. For good or ill, Britain is almost wholly demilitarised. Now, as the success of the charity Help for Heroes and the moving unofficial ceremonies that greet the bodies of those being repatriated in the Wiltshire town of Wootton Bassett demonstrate, there is a sympathy for servicemen and women that has little direct connection to the conflicts in either Iraq or Afghanistan. But as Horace Wyndham complained over a century ago, 'Outside the pages of "popular fiction" the soldier as he really is, is scarcely heard of, and over his life hangs a veil of reserve that is but seldom lifted.'[42]

Changes in the system of military honours and awards, instituted towards the end of John Major's administration, mean that acts of bravery are now rewarded with medals whose significance is scarcely grasped by the population as a whole. Successive changes in the regimental system, however good the case in their favour, have replaced the names and badges so familiar to my father's generation with terminology that the nation has not taken readily to its heart. Somehow 1 Mercian (Cheshire) does not have quite the ring of the Cheshire Regiment. Things that loom large in a soldier's intimate life – like the length of a tour or operational duty; the duration of rest and recreation ('R and R') during it; and the quality of single accommodation and married quarters – are rarely discussed in the press. In contrast, there are frequent articles about the poor quality of equipment. Steve Brooks, writing of his time in Iraq, resented this:

> I hate nothing more than civvies taking the piss about the latest article in the *Mail* or the *Mirror* about *the* army where the rifles don't fire and radios don't work. Yes, comms are shit, but we are the calibre of soldiers ... to work hard for comms ... like all aspects of soldiering we had to fight for comms to remain effective.[43]

Not all the news is bad. The growing number of parades marking units' return from overseas is welcome evidence that the army is beginning to emerge from beneath the cloak of invisibility that has shrouded it for so long. This cloak was woven in the long-running campaign in Northern Ireland. It is salutary to recall just how costly this was in terms of human life. In 1972, its worst year for casualties there, the army lost 102 officers and men killed in the province, and on 27 August 1979 two bombs at Warrenpoint left eighteen soldiers dead. There is a strong case for saying that the most serious damage that the IRA did to the army was not by killing its soldiers, but by attacking isolated uniformed soldiers outside the province which led the services to ban their members from wearing uniform in public, except on clearly specified occasions. I had grown up in a world full of uniforms, but by the time I attended Staff College in the 1980s things were very different. Most officers avoided the uniform ban by slipping on a civilian jacket over their military sweater, and downtown Camberley abounded with well-trimmed men in their early middle years. The subterfuge would have been unlikely to fool even the dimmest hit squad, but it was another step on the road to self-effacement. My first arrival as a staff officer at Headquarters Land Command at Wilton (wafted in by a gust of self-importance, for I had contrived to become a colonel) drew a polite rebuke from the MOD policeman on the gate. I had broken the rules by wearing uniform, and should take care to keep it covered up in future.

Reversing the uniform ban has not proved easy. In March 2008, shortly after the Government had commissioned a study that was to recommend that servicemen should be able to wear their uniforms as a matter of course, the station commander of Royal Air Force Wittering ordered that uniforms were not to be worn off-duty because of 'persistent threats and abuse' in nearby Peterborough.[44] In January that year, 200 soldiers had their aircraft diverted, because of bad weather, from RAF Brize Norton to Birmingham. They were told to change from uniform to plain clothes on the tarmac before passing through public areas because, as a ministry spokesman put it 'For security reasons, the MOD wishes to reduce the military profile on flights carried out on its behalf at civilian airports.' There have been numerous cases of discrimination against service personnel in uniform. In November 2006 an army officer was refused entry into Harrods on the grounds that he was in 'combat dress'; in September 2008 a hotel refused a room to a wounded soldier, who was forced to spend the night in his car; and in late 2009 four soldiers attending the funeral of a comrade killed in action in Afghanistan were banned from a Maidenhead nightclub: 'You can all come in,' said the helpful doorman, 'apart from the squaddies.'

My regard for the soldier stems from a lifetime's study as a military historian and almost as long a reserve infantry officer. For more than forty years I have read about soldiers, taught them at Sandhurst and Staff College, listened to them grumble or exult, watched them ply their trade in the Balkans and Iraq, visited them in hospital at Selly Oak and seen them arrive in flag-draped coffins at Royal Air Force Lyneham. It should already be very clear that this portrait will show Tommy Atkins warts and all. At one extreme there are those who prefer their pictures to have blemishes air-brushed out. Many years ago, a military reviewer was pained that the psychologist Norman Dixon (a former Royal Engineer officer, wounded and decorated for his work in bomb disposal) should 'write so cynically about his former profession' in his important book *On the Psychology of Military Incompetence*. One of the few adverse reviews of my own book *Firing Line* appeared in the *British Army Review*. The converse is also true, for there are perhaps as many who focus on an image of unrelieved savagery, or who see the army as a boss-class tool for turning nice boys into layabouts and killers.

This is not a chronological history of the army and its achievements. There have been many published in my working lifetime, with Correlli Barnett's *Britain and Her Army* (1970) wearing its judgements well even where recent scholarship has advanced our detailed knowledge. Allan Mallinson's *The Making of the British Army* (2009) is the most recent easily accessible account. This book is instead a social history of the soldier. Its organisation is thematic rather than chronological, and its preoccupation not with big battles or frontier scrimmages, but with the myriad routine observances of military life. It is the story of a man as ancient as a redcoat in Charles II's Tangier garrison and as modern as the gate-guard on Camp Bastion. It also concerns the women who followed him, anxiously watched his progress from afar or, more recently, soldiered with him. Given the immense change in Britain over the past three centuries, it would be inconceivable for the soldier not to have changed too. What surprises me, as I get ready to endure the fug of our first barrack room, is not how much he has changed: but how little.

I

POLITICS AND POSITION

CHAPTER 1

CHUCK HIM OUT, THE BRUTE

WRITING JUST AFTER the First World War, Field Marshal Sir William Robertson maintained that 'the army is not popular in the sense that the navy is. The latter usually enjoys full public support, the army seldom does except in war, and consequently it labours under considerable disadvantages in order to prepare for war, and from this it has followed that our wars have so often been a case of muddling through.'[1]

To the high Victorians, the British soldier was Tommy Atkins. The nickname probably originated in an 1815 War Office publication showing how the *Soldier's Pocket Book* should be filled out, giving 'Private Thomas Atkins, No 6 Troop, 6th Dragoons' as its exemplar. By 1837 Atkins was a sergeant, and could sign his name rather than scrawl a mark. We are sometimes told that the name was chosen by the Duke of Wellington. He remembered the pivot man of the grenadier company of his regiment, the 33rd Foot, dying in Flanders in 1793 with the stoic words 'Never mind, Sir, it's all in the day's work.' However, Wellington did not become commander-in-chief of the army till 1827, so it is very unlikely that he would have been consulted. In 1883 the *Illustrated London News* showed 'Pte Tommy Atkins returning from Indian Service', and in 1892 Rudyard Kipling dedicated his *Barrack Room Ballads* to 'T.A.' The collection included 'Tommy', Kipling's visceral condemnation of society's predilection for 'makin' mock o' uniforms that guard you while you sleep', which concluded:

For it's Tommy this, an' Tommy that, an' 'Chuck him out, the brute!'
But it's 'Saviour of 'is country' when the guns begin to shoot;
An' it's Tommy this, an' Tommy that, an' anything you please;
An' Tommy ain't a blooming fool – you bet that Tommy sees![2]

Ambivalence about the redcoat long predated Kipling. To the Georgians he was Mr Lobster, a nickname stemming from a 1740 dialogue between 'Thomas Lobster, soldier, and Jack Tar, sailor', in the political news-sheet *The Craftsman*, a periodical so offensive to Prime Minister Robert Walpole that he had its publisher arrested every six months as a matter of course. The conversation redounded little to Mr Lobster's advantage, for while he was weighed down by firm discipline and a heavy pack, plied his murderous trade at close quarters and was commanded by popinjays who had bought their commissions, his apple-cheeked interlocutor cruised the rolling main, defending Britain's maritime prosperity, and returned to a grateful nation enriched by prize money. Nearly a century later Portsmouth's ladies of the night made their own preferences clear:

Sailors they get all the money
Soldiers they get nought but brass.
I do love a jolly sailor
Soldiers you may kiss my arse.

Part of the reason for the nation's long-standing suspicion of her soldiers can be traced to the circumstances prior to the regular army's formation in 1661. Britain had just emerged from a long civil war, and had had quite enough of soldiers, whether they had fought for king or Parliament. Moreover, in 1655–7 Oliver Cromwell had instituted direct military government in England and Wales, through major generals presiding over twelve regions, answerable to the lord protector himself. Although the proximate cause of the experiment was a series of royalist plots, Cromwell believed that the nation's morals needed urgent reform. The major generals, their troops of cavalry funded by a 10 per cent 'decimation tax' on royalists, stamped out seditious and ungodly pastimes like horse-racing, plays, bear-baiting and cock-fighting, and closed unruly ale-houses. They also punished those guilty of licentiousness, blasphemy, and swearing.

Although the rule of the major generals was unpopular, the scars left by the Civil War were far deeper. As historian Charles Carlton has observed, 'No standing army' was a Restoration slogan driven by 'fear of soldiers, not because they killed people, but because they turned society head over heels'.[3] Oxford scholar Anthony Wood thought that his fellow undergraduates who went off to be soldiers were 'debauched' by the experience. Although Bulstrode Whitelock, Cromwell's ambassador to Sweden, was on the winning side when he told his hosts of the horrors of civil war, he believed that his fellow-countrymen were heartily sick of 'seeing servants riding on horseback and masters in great want'.[4]

Although most of the New Model Army's officers were not much different from their cavalier opponents – Lord General Fairfax was a peer's son and Lieutenant General Cromwell a country gentleman – enough of them rose from humble beginnings to high rank to cause affront. Cromwell's assertion that 'I had rather have a plain russet-coated captain that knows what he fights for and loves what he knows, than that which you call a gentleman and is nothing else' struck a jarring chord within a stratified society used to obeying its natural leaders.[5] Amongst the reasons for the long-standing practice of the purchase of commissions, which disappeared only in 1871, was a desire to ensure that officers were gentlemen rather than enthusiasts.

Part of it was about national identity. The Civil War was not simply an English phenomenon, but had extended across each of the three kingdoms ruled by Charles I. It was at its most bloody in Ireland, where its agonies reflected long-standing religious frictions, and each new episode, from the revolt of 1641 to the Cromwellian pacification of 1649–53, simply added fresh horrors, with new heroes and martyrs, to a list that was long enough already. The Scots seemed to have prospered from their early alliance with Parliament, but their war soon turned sour. There was a bitter conflict within Scottish society: part clan feud, part power struggle, part confessional dispute. Alongside this there was an external war which saw Scots royalists suffer appallingly in their invasions of England in 1648 and 1651. So many were sent off as bondsmen to the West Indies after their defeat at Worcester, that merchants complained there was no profit in shipping them out. Suspicion of the soldier was writ large enough in England, but in Ireland and Scotland it was seared on the national consciousness.

The ripples of antimilitarism curled out across the Atlantic. Many Americans were ambivalent about their own Continental Army, without which the War of Independence could not have been won. After the Revolution, the State of Pennsylvania made its feelings clear by affirming in its constitution that a standing army was 'dangerous [and] ought not to be kept up'. Americans did not simply dislike British soldiers, but regulars in general. 'The general instinct to disparage the professional soldier,' writes Lois G. Schwoerer, 'which was discernable at the opening of the seventeenth century, had become by the eighteenth century a political and constitutional principle of enduring significance.'[6] In 1812 President John Adams warned, 'Nothing is more important than to hold the civil authority decidedly superior to the military power.' The point was not lost on the opponents of President George W. Bush's foreign policy. A 2007 polemic lamented that 'the conservative fawning over the military displays an attitude that would have infuriated those first generations of Americans who actually built this country.'[7]

When Charles II was restored in 1660 he found himself the proud possessor of not one army but two, though he had scarcely the money to pay for either. First, there was the remnant of the Parliamentarian New Model Army under the command of General George Monck, soon to become Duke of Albemarle. In the Declaration of Breda, which set out the conditions for his acceptance of the throne, Charles had agreed to 'the full satisfaction of all the arrears due to' the New Model Army, whose officers and men 'shall be received into our service, upon as good pay and conditions as they now enjoy'.[8] In practice, though, an 'Act for the Speedy ... Disbanding' made provision for paying off the army, with a sweetener of a week's bonus pay from the king's own pocket. There was also a sensible relaxation of apprenticeship rules, so that discharged officers and men could practise civilian trades as they pleased. There were concerns, however, that pay arrears were too eagerly converted into ale, so in December 1660 discharged officers and soldiers were banned from coming within twenty miles of the capital. That month only Monck's own 'Coldstream Regiment' of foot and his regiment of horse remained.

Next there was Charles's own tiny army, raised in the Low Countries amongst exiled royalists. Much of this was stationed in the English enclave of Dunkirk, where life was complicated by the fact that the garrison included both royal troops, like Lord Wentworth's regiment of foot guards, and former Cromwellian soldiers. The guards were brought back to England, and most of the rest were posted off to be part of the garrison of Tangier, which came to the English Crown in 1661 as part of the dowry of Charles's wife, the Portuguese princess Catherine of Braganza, or sent to Portugal to support Charles's father-in-law, John IV. A smattering of plots culminating, in January 1661, in a rising in London led by the cooper Thomas Venner, encouraged Charles to proceed with earlier plans for the formalisation of a royal guard.

A new regiment of foot guards was raised by John Russell. He had commanded Prince Rupert's guards in the Civil War; Wentworth's regiment, at first dispersed amongst garrison towns, was soon amalgamated with it. In February 1661 Albemarle's regiment of foot was mustered on Tower Hill and formally disbanded before being immediately re-engaged. The two senior regiments of foot guards, today the Grenadier Guards and the Coldstream Guards, both claim histories which pre-date the regular army's formation: Monck's regiment had been raised in 1650 and the royal guards in 1656. However, the peculiar circumstances of the Coldstream's transfer to royal service made it junior to Russell's 1st Guards. One would be pressed to notice the fact, however, for the Coldstream motto is 'Nulli Secundus' ('Second to None') and, despite Grenadier mutterings about 'Second to One' or 'Better than Nothing', the Coldstream has never been known as 2nd Guards.[9]

Charles's little army had cavalry too, with three troops of Life Guards, and a single New Model regiment of horse, Colonel Unton Crooke's, that had somehow escaped disbandment. This moved to London, where it became the Royal Regiment of Horse Guards. It is generally known, from the colour of its coats, as the Horse Guards Blue or more simply The Blues. In addition, there were twenty-eight garrisons elsewhere, larger ones at seaports like Portsmouth and Hull and smaller outposts like the castles of St Mawes and Pendennis, their Cromwellian officers now replaced by reliable royalist gentlemen with local interests. The cost of guards and garrisons exceeded Charles's total income. Parliament was reluctant to fund a standing army, and there were fears that the soldiery would soon become, as Lord Treasurer Southampton put it, 'insolent and ungovernable'.

Charles's motives in raising the army were threefold. First, at a time when monarchs were on the move a good deal, he would be personally vulnerable without reliable troops for close protection. Second, it was evident that an army, however small, was needed to underpin his foreign policy. Furnishing overseas garrisons is a recurrent theme in the army's history. It is no accident that the Dunkirk garrison predated the Restoration, and it was run down partly by the direct dispatch of units to the new garrison of Tangier. Third, the army created jobs, and Charles had been restored to a throne resting on the shoulders of men who felt entitled to them. Some royalists had accompanied Charles into exile, and far more had endured life under the Protectorate, often ruined by having to 'compound' with the new authorities for their 'delinquency'.

In 1662, when Parliament decided to raise money to pension royalist ex-officers, it found that no less than 5,353 gentlemen, mostly former captains and subalterns, were entitled to a share. Ex-NCOs and men petitioned local magistrates for pensions, supporting their claims, where they could, by fulsome testimonials from former commanding officers, setting out the 'many dangerous hurts' they had received. Those who could manage it got jobs not just for themselves, but for their children too. Winston Churchill, father of the future Duke of Marlborough, was a West Country gentleman and lawyer turned captain of horse. He spent the 1650s living, with his growing brood, in the genteel poverty of his Parliamentarian mother-in-law's house. But in 1660 he found himself the delighted recipient of royal favour, with an augmentation ('Faithful but Unfortunate', announced his new motto) to his coat of arms, a knighthood, a series of sinecures and a seat in Parliament. His daughter Arabella and his son John both obtained minor posts at court, and after the former had attracted the roving eye of James, Duke of York (she went on to bear him four children), young John was given an ensign's commission in 1st Guards.

Charles's little army survived, and by his death in 1685 had taken on some of the characteristics which still define it. It was the monarch's own, its officers 'trusty and well-beloved' gentlemen bearing royal commissions whose wording has changed little over the centuries, with a fresh document marking successive promotions.

CHAPTER 2

KING'S ARMY

MANY OFFICERS AND men have felt comfortable in vesting the moral responsibility for their actions in the monarch's person. Waterloo veteran Colonel Francis Skelly Tidy told his daughter: 'I am a soldier and one of His Majesty's most devoted servants, bound to defend the Crown with my life against either faction as necessary.'[1] Sergeant Sam Ancell, who fought in the 58th Regiment in the 1779–83 siege of Gibraltar, announced:

> Our king is answerable to God for us. I fight for him. My religion consists in a firelock, open touch-hole, good flint, well-rammed charge, and seventy rounds of powder and ball. This is the military creed. Come, comrades, drink success to British arms.[2]

In 1914 Dora Foljambe, married to a keen Territorial, with a brother in the King's Royal Rifle Corps, a brother-in-law in the same battalion and two sons in the regular army, was delighted to see that the government had apparently shrunk from using the army to enforce Home Rule in Ireland. She told her daughter, married to yet another rifleman, that

> I am very glad this did happen as it shows the feeling in the army against being used as a political tool – for one party against another – if there is to be civil war the army must break up or stand in a body for the King, it is impossible they should fight side by side with the [Irish] Nationalists who cheered every Boer victory in the South African war. Our army is not made up of paid levies.[3]

Writing in 1972, Lieutenant Colonel John Baynes affirmed that the monarch's

> immense significance to the armed forces must first be strongly emphasised ... This link with the Head of State is not merely symbolic, but reflects a close loyalty to the person of the Queen as well as to her office. No firmer guarantee of the British soldier's exclusion from politics exists than his personal dependence on the authority of Her Majesty.[4]

Robert William Lowry's commissions lie before me. His appointment as ensign in the 47th Foot, dated 7 June 1841, is signed by Queen Victoria (black ink over a pencil cross reminding the young monarch where she should put her name), though by the time he became a lieutenant colonel on 18 February 1863 the queen entrusted such work to the army's commander-in-chief, her uncle, George, Duke of Cambridge. He later became the epitome of conservatism, telling the officers of Aldershot garrison, assembled to hear a lecture on cavalry, 'Why should we want to know anything about foreign cavalry? ... We have better cavalry of our own. I fear, gentlemen, that the army is in danger of becoming a mere debating society.'[5] But he had commanded a division in the Crimea, fighting bravely in the shocking bludgeon-match at Inkerman, and was, as William Robertson recalled, 'a good friend of the soldier and extremely popular with all ranks of the army.'[6] When he signed Robert Lowry's new commission he was interested not only in military reform, but in maintaining (though with diminishing success) that he was directly subordinate to the monarch rather than to the secretary of state of war.

His rather deliberate 'George', with a curlicue swinging round from the last letter to encircle his name, looks restrained on a document rich in stamps and seals. Both commissions are made of robust parchment, folded in four, with the holder's name on an outer fold, and fit neatly in the inside pocket of an officer's tunic. Lowry's second commission is almost exactly the same size as my own – though that was produced almost a century later. When Cambridge was eventually prised out of office in 1895, after a tenure just short of forty years, Victoria resumed signing commissions on her own behalf. Declining health and the flood of new commissions necessitated by the army's expansion for the Boer war (1899–1902) made things difficult but, borne on by a powerful sense of duty, she struggled hard against having a signature stamp until she was at last persuaded that it would not be misused.

With the exception of Queen Mary and her sister Anne, all British monarchs who ruled 1625–1760, had fought in battle. Charles II received his baptism of fire at twelve at Edgehill in 1642. His brother, James II, had also participated in the Civil War, and was a lieutenant general in the French service during the Interregnum. He accompanied the royal army to the West Country to face William of Orange in 1688 although, racked by nose-bleeds, he was not an inspiring commander. William himself was an accomplished general. His invasion of England in unreliable autumn weather, in the face of a well-posted royal navy and an army whose internal collapse could not be confidently predicted, betokened extraordinary self-confidence. He beat James (also present in person on the field) at the Boyne in 1689, where he was clipped by a cannon-ball that came within an inch or two of changing history.

The first Hanoverians came from a Germanic tradition of soldier-kings. The future George I had fought the Turks as a young man and served as an Imperialist officer in the War of Spanish Succession. His eldest son commanded the allied army in the victorious battle of Dettingen in 1743. The first two Georges took a close interest in the day-to-day running of the army. During their reigns it was still small enough for them to know all senior officers by name and repute. When Lieutenant General Lord George Sackville was court-martialled for failure to charge as ordered at Minden in 1759, George II personally struck his name from the roll of the Privy Council. The king also penned an order, which was read at the head of every regiment in the service, saying that such conduct was 'worse than death to a man who has any sense of honour'. Prince William, Duke of Cumberland, the king's second son, was wounded at Dettingen, narrowly beaten by Marshal Saxe at Fontenoy, and then broke the Jacobites at Culloden in 1746. Defeated in Germany in 1757, he was disgraced on his return home. Opinion on 'Butcher Cumberland' has now softened somewhat. His style of command was uncomfortably Germanic; he was easily impressed by severe officers like Lieutenant General Henry 'Hangman' Hawley. He backed the seedy and idiosyncratic James

Wolfe, victor at Quebec in 1759. The attractive old Huguenot warrior, Field Marshal Lord Louis Jean, Lord Ligonier, always thought Cumberland a good general.

George III had a military brood. His eldest son, the Prince of Wales or 'Prinny' (later George IV) was no soldier, although in later life he came to believe that he had served with Wellington in the Peninsula. 'So I have heard you say, Sir', the Duke would observe when the Regent recounted another martial triumph and turned to him for support. Prinny's younger brother Frederick, Duke of Albany and York, was not a successful field commander, for the French thrashed him in both 1793 and 1799. However, he was a serious-minded commander-in-chief of the army from 1798 to 1827. There was a brief gap in 1809–11, after he had been forced to resign when it transpired that his mistress, Mary Ann Clark, had been dabbling in the sale of commissions. George III's fourth and seventh sons, Edward, Duke of Kent, and Adolphus Frederick, Duke of Cambridge, both became field marshals, although they never held command in the field. His fifth son, Ernest Augustus, Duke of Cumberland, lost an eye at Tournai in 1794, later commanded the Hanoverian army and succeeded as King of Hanover in 1837.

The third son of George III, Prince William, broke with family tradition by joining the navy at the age of thirteen, and fought at the battle of Cape St Vincent in 1780. Captain John Peebles saw him in New York during the American War, and reported that he was 'a very fine grown young man, smart and sensible for his years … & sufficiently well grown, a strong likeness of the King … he was in a plain Midshipman uniform, and took off his hat with a good grace.'[7] Commissioned lieutenant in 1785 he was a captain the following year. Prince William served under Horatio Nelson in the West Indies, and the admiral reported that: 'In his professional line, he is superior to two-thirds, I am sure, of the [Navy] list; and in attention to orders, and respect to his superior officer, I hardly know his equal.'[8]

Created Duke of Clarence in 1789 by his reluctant father, to avoid political embarrassment, William sought active command during the Napoleonic wars, though without success. He managed to get involved in a skirmish near Antwerp in early 1814, narrowly avoiding capture thanks to the efforts of Lieutenant Thomas Austin of the 35th Foot. When George IV died without legitimate issue in 1830, Clarence ascended the throne as William IV. His simple, approachable style gained him many supporters, but his intervention in military affairs was not a success. Coming from a highly centralised service, he had no feel for the army's innate tribalism. He insisted that soldiers should wear red, and sailors, blue, resulting in light cavalry (traditionally clad in what had begun as workmanlike blue) becoming redcoats. Most of them gladly reverted to blue in 1840, although the 16th Lancers, perverse as ever, retained red to become the 'Scarlet Lancers'.

In her youth Queen Victoria appeared in a prettily modified version of a general's uniform, and took military duties very seriously. She had a passionate interest in regimentalia, especially where it concerned the Scots regiments so close to her heart. In 1877 she told the Duke of Cambridge that projected amalgamations would create insuperable problems as far as tartans were concerned, for 'to direct the 42nd to wear the Cameron tartan, or my own Cameron Highlanders to wear that of the Black Watch, would create the greatest dissatisfaction, and would be unmeaning.' She went on to warn against the compromise of using the 'Royal Hunting Tartan ... which is a sort of undress Royal Stewart, [and] will not be appreciated by the Highlanders, nor considered advisable by the Queen'.[9]

Her husband Prince Albert was colonel of both the 11th Hussars and the Rifle Brigade. He ensured that two of the equerries allocated to their eldest son, the future King Edward VII, were upright men who had won the Victoria Cross in the Crimea. Albert, had he lived longer, might have ensured that the prince received a proper military education. As it was, young Bertie was commissioned lieutenant colonel on his eighteenth birthday, and in the summer of 1861 was sent off to the Curragh, the great military camp near Dublin, to train with the Grenadier Guards.

The project was not a success. Amongst the visitors to the Curragh was the actress Nellie Clifden, 'a London lady much run after by the Household Brigade' who did not need much persuading to share the prince's bed. Bertie's parents soon found out: Prince Albert wrote him a pained paternal letter, and Victoria always attributed her husband's fatal illness to the shock and disappointment caused by the news. Despite this inauspicious apprenticeship and his reputation for being 'lackadaisical', Edward took a serious interest in military reform, notably in the period of national soul-searching that followed the Boer War. His adviser, Lord Esher, sought to persuade him that he was *de facto* commander-in-chief of the army, an argument strengthened by the abolition of the post of commander-in-chief in 1904. The following year he affirmed that:

> There is always to be developed as time goes on the authority of the King as Commander-in-Chief. I mean in all personal questions. The King should adhere tenaciously to his right to veto any appointment. Gradually it will become clear to everyone that under the *King* a C-in-C was an anomaly.[10]

Edward's heir apparent was Prince Albert Victor. Albert died from influenza in 1892, leaving his brother George heir. George married his late brother's fiancée, Princess Mary of Teck. He had served as a naval cadet with his elder brother and was commissioned sub-lieutenant in 1884. George left the navy on his marriage and lived quietly in York Cottage on the Sandringham Estate, succeeding to the throne in 1910. The couple had six children, five of them sons. Their eldest, Edward (known in the family as David), had served as a naval cadet and midshipman. As an undergraduate at Oxford he had trained in the university Officers' Training Corps. On the outbreak of war in 1914 he was commissioned into the Grenadier Guards, and urged Lord Kitchener to allow him to go to France with his regiment, saying 'What does it matter if I am shot? I have four brothers.' Kitchener pointed out that it was not the risk of death but the possibility of capture that prevented him from serving at the front. General Sir Dighton Probyn VC, the distinguished warrior-turned-courtier, feared that the young prince felt 'disgraced' by his inability to share his generation's risks.

The Prince of Wales spent 1915–16 on the Western Front, occasionally under shellfire, sometimes closer to the fighting than was wise, but scarcely deserving the Military Cross he was awarded in 1916. General Sir Charles Monro tells us that he heard that the prince had gone up the line, early in the morning, with a Grenadier battalion. He set off in pursuit in his staff car, soon caught up with the young man, and ordered him in. 'I heard what you said, prince', said Monro, 'Here is that damned old general after me again. Jump in the car, or you will spoil my appetite for breakfast.'[11] The prince also served in Egypt and Italy, but the same hard rule of no real action applied. He was unquestionably touched by all the suffering he saw. There is a painful account of his brushing the cheek of a badly wounded soldier with his lips. When assessing the complex character of Edward VIII, shot through with self-indulgence and populism, we should not under-emphasise the impact of the war, which saw him snared by a protective privilege he had never demanded and would willingly have discarded.

His brother Bertie's status as 'spare' rather than 'heir' meant that he had been able to embark on a full-time naval career, serving first as a Dartmouth cadet and then being posted to the dreadnought HMS *Collingwood* in 1913. At Jutland three years later *Collingwood* was bracketed by a salvo from *Derrflinger* or *Lützow*. He recalled the excitement of being aboard a great ship shuddering under the recoil of her guns, with water from the splashes of shell-bursts surging across the decks. Bertie transferred to the RAF on its formation in 1918 and, when he succeeded to the throne on Edward's abdication in 1936, he was the only British monarch who had qualified as a pilot. King George VI and Queen Elizabeth had no sons, but their eldest daughter, Princess Elizabeth, was appointed colonel of the Grenadier Guards in January 1942, on her sixteenth birthday. At her first official function officers found her 'charming, and very sincere'. In February 1945 she was commissioned into the Auxiliary Territorial Service as Second Subaltern Elizabeth Alexandra Mary Windsor, and completed her basic training in driving and maintenance at No 1 Mechanical Transport Training Centre at Aldershot. She became colonel-in-chief of the Grenadiers on her accession, and for many years wore the regiment's uniform at the Queen's Birthday Parade. Until 1986 she attended the parade mounted, latterly on her favourite mare Burmese.

Between 1971 and 1976 Prince Charles trained with both the Royal Air Force and Royal Navy, qualifying as both fixed-wing and helicopter pilot. He also commanded the coastal minehunter HMS *Bronington* during the last year of his service. The Princes, William and Harry, both trained at the Royal Military Academy Sandhurst, and were commissioned into the Blues and Royals – a 1969 amalgamation of the Royal Horse Guards, whom we first glimpsed as Colonel Unton Crooke's Regiment, in 1660, and the Royal Dragoons, raised in 1661 for duty in Tangiers. Prince William, denied the chance of operational service by the same concerns that kept the future Edward VIII in limbo, qualified as a Search and Rescue pilot. Prince Harry characteristically affirmed, 'There's no way that I'm going to put myself through Sandhurst and then sit on my arse back home while my boys are out fighting for their country.' He served in Afghanistan, and might have stayed there longer had an unhelpful intervention by the press not drawn attention to his presence, imposing unacceptable risk on those serving alongside him. In 2008 Prince Harry received his medal for campaign service at Combermere Barracks, Windsor from his aunt, Princess Anne, colonel of the Blues and Royals.

As we branch off from the direct royal line, so the undergrowth thickens, with junior members of the ruling house serving on their own account or marrying into military families. Lady Elizabeth Bowes-Lyon, who was to marry the future George VI, lost one brother, in that most traditional of Highland regiments, the Black Watch, at Loos in 1915. She also lost a cousin, also in the Black Watch, at Ypres, Belgium in 1914, and another cousin, this time a Grenadier, at Cambrai in 1917. Centuries earlier illegitimate offspring also played their part in the process. Of Charles II's extensive illegitimate brood, Henry, Duke of Grafton commanded the 1st Foot Guards, lined out along the Bussex Rhine as the Duke of Monmouth's rag-tag men ran in through the mist at Sedgemoor in 1685; he was mortally wounded attacking Cork in 1690. His half-brother Monmouth, on the other side of the ditch at Sedgemoor, had commanded English troops in French service, showing courage that left him briefly when he pleaded with James II for his life, though he had recovered his self-possession when he faced the axe on Tower Hill.

James II's own child, James, Duke of Berwick, one of the four offspring borne him by Arabella Churchill, emerged as a general of European stature. He had already served against the Turks in Hungary when, in 1688, he did more to check the disintegration of the royal army than his father. In French service after 1690, he was largely responsible for wrecking allied hopes in Spain during the War of Spanish Succession. Although his character showed that streak of inflexible cruelty that had marked his father's, he was the most capable of the later Stuarts, and had become marshal of France by the time that a cannon-ball carried him off at Philippsburg in 1734.

William IV's illegitimate son, George Fitzclarence, served in the Peninsula, became the army's deputy adjutant general, and his father eventually made him Earl of Munster. All four of his boys served in the army or the navy; the youngest was killed in the assault on the Redan in the Crimea. Amongst George Fitzclarence's grandsons were twin brothers, Edward, killed at Abu Hamid in the Sudan in 1897, and Charles, who won the VC with the Royal Fusiliers (first raised in 1685) in the Boer War, then transferred to the Irish Guards in its formation in 1900, and finally died as a brigadier-general on 11 November 1914 in the desperate fighting outside Ypres. His name heads the cruelly long list of officers and men missing in the Ypres Salient battlefields between 1914 and mid-1917, graven in stone on the Menin Gate memorial.

It would be easy to develop the theme more widely, but the point is already hammered home. The monarch was at the centre of a wide constellation of military officers, often serving in the regiments of the Household Division, who were familiar figures at many of the court's activities, from official events at Buckingham Palace or Windsor, Royal Ascot or shooting parties at Sandringham. Members of the royal family serve as colonels-in-chief of regiments, and *Court and Circular* announcements still chart the passage of lieutenant colonels as they report at the palace to formally take over command. Although George VI was constitutionally more cautious than his predecessors, he encouraged senior officers to open their hearts to him. Field Marshal Sir Alan Brooke, CIGS (Chief of the Imperial General Staff) for much of the war, found the process very helpful. 'At 3.15 went to see the King,' he wrote on 21 December 1943, 'who kept me for 1¼ hours. He was in excellent form and most interested in all details of conferences and of my visit to Italy. He has a wonderful knowledge of what is going on.'[12] But regimental politics could corrupt even the most scrupulous monarch. In 1946, Field Marshal Montgomery, Chief of the Imperial General Staff, hoped to reduce the Foot Guards by the same proportion as the infantry of the line, but found his plans dashed when the major general commanding the Household Division appealed directly to the king. Nor should the long influence of Queen Elizabeth the Queen Mother be underestimated, especially as far as the Black Watch and the London Scottish were concerned.

The military importance of the monarchy goes beyond the ties of family, friendship, and familiarity. The significance of both the Dukes of York and Cambridge serving as commander-in-chief of the army for such long periods can scarcely be overstated. Moreover, some of the monarch's most trusted servants were military officers, whether at court for short tours of duty as aides-de-camp or equerries, or in key long-term appointments like private secretary and assistant private secretary. The urbane and gossipy Frederick 'Fritz' Ponsonby was grandson of Peninsula veteran General Sir Frederick Cavendish Ponsonby. He served in the Grenadier Guards during the Boer War and the First World War. His court career started as an equerry to Queen Victoria in 1894, going on to be assistant private secretary to both Victoria and Edward VII, and ending up as lieutenant governor of Winsdor Castle till 1935, the year of his death.

His immediate superior in 1901–13 was Francis Knollys, long a civilian, but a former officer in the Royal Welch Fusiliers with good military connections. Both his father, a general and Crimean veteran, and brother served in the Scots Guards. Knollys's successor as private secretary was the honest but humourless Arthur Bigge, better known by his peerage title of Lord Stamfordham. Bigge was a gunner who had served in the Zulu War of 1879, he was the queen's private secretary for the last years of her reign, and then served George V in the same capacity for most of his life. He was succeeded by Clive Wigram, who had been commissioned into the Royal Artillery in 1893 and had then gone off to the Indian army. Wigram made his mark as assistant chief of staff to the Prince of Wales (the future George V) during his 1905–6 tour of India, returned to serve as equerry until George succeeded, and became the king's assistant private secretary, going on to be private secretary between 1931 and his retirement, gaining the peerage that has generally rewarded royal servants of his status, in 1936.

Focusing on Wigram's family is instructive. He was married to the daughter of a paragon of British India, Field Marshal Sir Neville Chamberlain. Their eldest son served with the Grenadier Guards in the Second World War and then commanded its 1st Battalion in 1955–6. He was married to the daughter of another Grenadier, General Sir Andrew 'Bulgy' Thorne, who had made his mark on history while staff-captain to Brigadier-General Fitzclarence, by whipping-in the fine counter-attack that enabled the Worcesters to repair the broken British line on the Menin Road on 31 August 1914. 'The Worcesters saved the Empire', wrote a grateful Field Marshal Sir John French, commander of the British Expeditionary Force.[13] Not only did their eldest son, heir to the family's barony, also serve in the Grenadiers, but so too did their son-in-law, Major General Sir Evelyn Webb-Carter, who commanded the Household Division in 1988–2001. Clive Wigram's grandson, Captain Charles Malet of the Coldstream Guards, has served in Afghanistan, and was an extra equerry to the queen at the time of writing.

Michael Adeane, maternal grandson of Lord Stamfordham, was private secretary to Elizabeth II for the first twenty years of her reign. He had taken over from Alan 'Tommy' Lascelles, unusually a yeomanry (territorial cavalry) officer rather than a regular, and handed over to Martin Charteris of the King's Royal Rifle Corps. It was only with the latter's departure in 1977 that military officers lost what had become firm tenure of this crucial post, although Robin Janvrin, who took over in 1999, had served in the Royal Navy for eleven years. It may be that his successor, Christopher Geidt, represents a definitive break with tradition, having been a member of the Foreign and Commonwealth Office before initially joining the royal household as assistant private secretary in 2002.

CHAPTER 3

PARLIAMENT'S ARMY

A S THE MONARCHY'S power has shrunk over the three and a half centuries of the army's existence, so that of the House of Commons has increased. We can chart this process and its effect on the army through events like the constitutional settlement of 1688, the last royal veto of legislation in 1707, the great reform bills of the nineteenth century, and the 1911 Parliament Act. It has certainly not removed royal influence, but it has transformed the nature of political control. What is less obvious is that, as the process has spun on, the links between the army and the legislature have become progressively weaker, to the point where almost any major professional group is more widely represented in both houses of parliament than the armed forces. In one sense the development is as much social as political, with the army's increasing professionalisation and diminishing size reducing the political visibility and impact of its officers.

Restoration parliaments imposed no control over the army, provided the king was able to pay for it. The 1661 Militia Act gave Charles II command of 'all forces by land and sea and all forts and places of strength', and both Charles and his brother James II proceeded to run the army as what John Childs calls 'a department of the royal household under the command of the king and his nominees'.[1] It had no foundation in common or statute law, and its code of discipline, the Articles of War, stemmed from the royal prerogative. It was not until 1689 that discipline was given the force of statute.

The senior regiment of infantry of the line, the Royal Scots (in existence since 1633 but allowed to claim seniority only from 1661), had fought at Sedgemoor in 1685 as the Earl of Dumbarton's Regiment. It had previously served under Monmouth on the continent, and a poignant story has him looking out from Bridgwater church towards the royal camp and seeing the regiment's saltire colours in the gloaming. He would be sure of victory, he sighed, with Dumbarton's drums behind him.

In 1689 the new government of William and Mary was shipping troops to the Low Countries to fight the French. The fact that the army had not fought for James II the previous year reflected the defection of senior officers and James's failure of will rather than its affection for William. Scots troops were particularly concerned about being sent abroad while English and Dutch units remained in Britain. After serious unrest along the line of march, the Royal Scots mutinied when they reached Ipswich; over 600 of them set off northwards. The deserters were rounded up with little bloodshed, escorted back to London, and shipped thence to Holland. Nineteen officers were tried, and all but one, who was executed on Tower Green, were simply stripped of their commissions.

The Commons at once passed the first of the many mutiny acts. In theory all it allowed the army to do was to inflict capital or corporal punishment for serious offences, thus meeting the demands of the moment, and it was not conceived as a means of asserting parliamentary control. Indeed, there were times during William's reign when it lapsed altogether without bringing about a collapse of discipline. From 1690 to 1878 Parliament passed mutiny acts annually, and as time went on both their scope and intent changed. As late as 1761 it was decided that neither the act nor articles of war deriving from it were binding on the army when engaged in war abroad, although discipline in such circumstances was preserved through similar articles issued under the royal prerogative. In 1803 the Act was extended to include the army within or without the Crown's dominions in peace or war. It was replaced by the Army Discipline and Regulating Act of 1879, itself superseded by the Army Act of 1881 which, just like the old Mutiny Act, had to be passed annually. By this stage it was, as the *Manual of Military Law* announced, the essential means of 'securing the constitutional principle of the control of parliament over the discipline requisite for the government of the army.'[2] This was replaced by the Army Act of 1955, which was in turn replaced by the Armed Forces Act 2006, the current basis for military discipline, whose Section 19 – the catch-all 'conduct prejudicial to good order and service discipline' – has been the bane of the scruffy, ill-disposed or unlucky ever since.

Alongside the assertion of parliamentary control came a gradual shift of power as the army became first a department of state in its own right, and eventually part of a unified Ministry of Defence. The detail does not concern us here, but the salient features are worth noting. 'The Sovereign is Commander-in-Chief,' affirmed the *Manual of Military Law*, 'unless the office is granted away.' Such was often the case. The Duke of Marlborough, the army's captain-general under Queen Anne, commissioned officers on his own authority, telling a delighted Lady Oglethorpe that her boy could have his promised ensigncy in the Foot Guards: 'If you please to send me the young gentleman's Christian name, his commission shall be dispatched immediately.'[3] Sometimes the office was not filled, and sometimes its holders were ineffective, but as we have seen, the royal dukes of York and Cambridge both exercised substantial power.

The secretary at war was a civilian official, who had begun as the commander-in-chief's secretary, based in the army's headquarters which established itself at Horse Guards at Whitehall in 1722. The secretary at war became increasingly important, and in 1793 was made responsible for submitting the army estimates to parliament. Since the Restoration there had been two secretaries of state, peers or members of the House of Commons, initially for the northern and southern departments of Britain, but with their responsibility later refined to cover home and foreign affairs. A third secretary of state had been appointed from time to time. In 1794 the office became permanent, and its holder took charge of the army's efforts in the war against revolutionary France. The secretary at war was now respon-sible to this secretary of state, a system which continued until 1855 when the Crimean reforms shifted all the former's duties to the secre-tary of state for war. Although this minister's effectiveness depended on many factors – not least hitting-power within a cabinet that might not have the army in the forefront of its thinking – he made steady inroads into the influence of the commander-in-chief, and in 1870 was made formally superior to him.

As part of the reforms that followed the Boer War, the office of commander-in-chief was abolished in 1904, and the Army Council came into being. It initially had seven members – the secretary of state, the chief of the imperial general staff, the adjutant general, the quartermaster general and the master general of the ordnance, as well as a finance member and a civil member. In 1906 the War Office crossed Whitehall from Horse Guards to the neo-baroque War Office Building. When the three service ministries merged to form the Ministry of Defence in 1963 the Army Council became the Army Board of the Defence Council, now established in the Ministry of Defence's main building. This solid monolith was built in the 1930s, and Anthony Beevor surmises that the 'muscular, large breasted women in stone' surmounting the entrance date from the days when the Board of Trade had half-tenure. Although the style 'falls short of the totalitarian architecture of that decade ... it is still not a place calculated to lift the spirits.'[4] The Army Board's membership now includes six ministers, one official and five senior generals. The board's executive committee (ECAB in unlovely abbreviation) dictates the army's immediate policy, and comprises its most senior generals under the chief of the general staff, whose office lost its 'imperial' designation in 1964.

This shift of power away from the military and into the hands of politicians was paralleled by changes in the Civil Service. The Northcote–Trevelyan report of 1854 recommended that this should be divided into 'mechanical' and 'administrative' classes, and instituted processes that led to entry by open competition into a service that, until its corrosion by politics over the past decade, was a source of impartial professional advice to ministers. The Fulton Committee's 1968 report judged that the Civil Service was too close to the traditional sources of power within the British establishment, and though its recommendations did not succeed in creating a British equivalent of the French Ecole Nationale d'Administration the process of breaking down formal barriers within the Civil Service, and between it and outside agencies, has continued steadily.

A by-product of all this was the rise of senior Civil Servants within ministries, notably their permanent under secretaries. They tend to remain in post longer than military officers, who serve in the ministry for between two to three years at any one time, and their links with senior colleagues across Whitehall often give them a sense of collegiate expertise which serving soldiers lack. To this must be added the influence of a Treasury, which, long before the onset of the 2008 financial crisis, was both intrusive and pervasive. No balanced assessment of the Ministry of Defence in the first decade of this millennium should ignore the slurry of management-speak that washes across its decks from time to time, and the many officials who have come to regard defence as they might a commercial organisation with the receivers in. It is certainly not a case of 'boots versus suits', for if there are civil servants who believe in the commodification of defence, there are those who work purposefully towards the preservation of military capability in times of real stringency. Conversely, some military officers, especially those 'Whitehall warriors' on a second or third tour of duty, become so wise in 'the ways of the building' that they sometimes forget that men and women in uniform are much more than 'line serials' on a spreadsheet. Part of this book's contention is that soldiers have, across the army's history, been subjected to treatment that has fallen far short of that to which they have reasonably been entitled, and it is not enough to maintain that this all happened in a distant land where things were done differently. We have done it in recent memory and, given half a chance, would still do it today.[5]

The increase of political control over the army, the diminution of the power of its senior officers, and the growing authority of the Civil Service were all products of wider developments. The two great wars of the twentieth century added their own weight to the process, emphasising that what happened on battlefields was only an index of a much broader national effort. Interwoven with all this has been the increasing professionalisation of the officer corps, a process that has ensured that officers are now educated for longer than ever before. The period spent at Sandhurst is now half the length it was in the 1960s, but many more officers are now recruited as graduates.

In the process the army has become estranged from the political nation. From the army's birth until 1945 serving officers sat in both Houses of Parliament. Retired officers, and gentlemen holding commissions in the auxiliary forces, were added, to make a substantial military voice. The close association between officers and legislature had begun under Charles II and accelerated under James II, who saw officers as convenient placemen, deployable either to Westminster or to local councils. James encouraged officers to seek election not because he valued their opinions, but because he wanted their votes.

Those elected in 1685 were told to 'give their attendance to the House of Commons as soon as possible', and James made it clear that they were not to simply to turn up as ordered, but to vote for the court party.[6]

Crossing the inflexible James II was fatal to a man's career. That year Charles Bertie lamented that

> My nephew Willoughby, my brother Dick, and brother Harry – the three battering rams of our family – are all turned out of their employment as captains … and I am also told that my nephew Peregrine Bertie – who is cornet [the most junior commissioned officer in a troop of horse] to his brother Willoughby – is also dismissed, so they have cleared the army of our whole family, which proving so unlucky a trade I would not have us bend our heads much to for the future.[7]

The precedent established by the later Stuarts proved durable. Army and navy officers regularly sat in parliament thereafter. Between 1660 and 1715 up to 18 per cent of MPs were serving officers, and subsequent general elections regularly returned at least 10 per cent. There were 60 military officers in the 558 members elected to the English House of Commons in 1761. Sixty-five were elected to the century's last parliament in 1796. Gwyn Harries Jenkins argues that 'from the late eighteenth century the military formed the largest single occupational group in the unreformed House.'[8] Of the 5,134 MPs who sat in the period 1734–1832, 847 held commissions and of these two-thirds seem to have been career officers. The reform acts of the nineteenth century helped reduce the number of military MPs by making it harder for interest to procure a man's election, at the same time that the army's growing use as an imperial police force made it more difficult for officers to carry out duties that their constituents were now coming to expect of them. Traditionally the Foot Guards had furnished a disproportionately high number of MPs, pointing not simply to 'a close link between wealth, birth and military-cum-parliamentary activity', but to the fact that it was easier for officers quartered in London to get in to the House than it was for their comrades in the marching regiments, scattered across realm and empire.[9] In 1853 the military, with its 71 sitting MPs, had been eclipsed by the law and their 107 solicitors or barristers – the largest profession in the house. By 1898 there were still 41 officers in the house (all but four of them Conservatives) and 165 lawyers.

From 1660 until 1945, when the serving military were no longer allowed to sit in parliament, most military MPs were officers, though there were a handful of exceptions, like Sergeant W. R. Perkins MP, called up for service with the Royal Air Force Volunteer Reserve in 1939. So too were the huge majority of former members of the armed forces who were elected to the Commons. There was one remarkable exception. William Cobbett, born in 1762 to an 'honest, industrious and frugal' labouring family, joined the 54th Regiment in 1784. He had trudged all the way to Chatham to enlist in the Marines, only to be assured by the recruiting sergeant that they were full up. His literacy and steady ways soon brought promotion to corporal, and he went on to be a regimental clerk, using his spare time to study 'Dr Louth's *Grammar*, Dr Watt's *Logic* … Vauban's *Fortifications* and the former Duke of York's *Military Exercises and Evolutions*'. Promoted to sergeant major, at a time where there was only one in each battalion, he took on much of the day-to-day work of running his unit, for the adjutant was 'a keen fellow, but wholly illiterate' and the other officers were distinguished by 'their gross ignorance and vanity'.[10]

Cobbett was discharged on his battalion's return from Nova Scotia in 1791, and at once set about the prosecution of some of his former officers for corruption. The attempt misfired, and he fled abroad to avoid retribution: while in America he wrote pro-British articles under the name of Peter Porcupine. Soon after his return he started the news-sheet *Weekly Political Register*, and in 1802 began publishing *Parliamentary Debates*, forerunner of the modern *Hansard*. Refusal to bribe voters lost him the Honiton election in 1806 and accelerated his shift from Tory to radical. In 1810 the *Register's* furious condemnation of the flogging of militiamen by German soldiers saw him sentenced to two years imprisonment for treasonous libel. On his release he was honoured by a huge dinner presided over by Sir Francis Burdett, a leading champion of reform.

Cobbett deftly changed the format of the *Political Register* from newspaper to pamphlet to avoid tax, and it was soon selling 40,000 copies a week. In 1817 he left for America to avoid prosecution for sedition. After his return repeated attacks on the government culminated, in 1831, in prosecution for an article supporting the machine-breaking and rick-burning of the Captain Swing rioters. Cobbett conducted his own defence and was triumphantly acquitted. He was a major political figure and author. His *Rural Rides* was an affectionate description of an old, honest countryside progressively corrupted by the seepage of poison from the towns. It was first serialised in the *Register* and then published as a book in 1830. Despite repeated attempts to get into Parliament, he would have to wait until the 1832 Reform Act, when he was elected for Oldham. By now he was a confirmed radical, though his beliefs were shot through with a profoundly conservative yearning for a pre-industrial world of honest toil, interlaced with duty, and for political dispute across the class divide to be undertaken 'with good humour, over a pot or two of ale'.[11]

A conflict soon developed between the constitutional theory that an officer-MP required no permission to attend to his parliamentary duties and could express an opinion freely, and the awkwardness of giving military pay to non-serving men who might make statements of which the government or army might disapprove. In December 1880 Major John Nolan, MP for Galway North, was appointed a Conservative whip, although he was on full pay and commanding a battery on its way to India. The Speaker thought that the best solution was for officers to be seconded from the service on election, but, given the fact that MPs were not then paid, this smacked of penalising the peoples' choice. It was felt safest to let the matter run on unresolved, and Nolan left the army in 1881.

The number of military MPs would have doubtless continued to decline had not the two world wars reversed the trend. Members of both houses volunteered on a huge scale in 1914. Twenty-two MPs died: Arthur O'Neill, Unionist member for Mid-Antrim and a captain in the Life Guards was the first MP to die, at Ypres in 1914. They ranged in rank from lieutenant, with 39-year-old Viscount Quenington (Michael Hicks-Beach MP) dying of wounds in 1916 as a subaltern in the Royal Gloucestershire Hussars, to lieutenant colonel, with Guy Baring (elected for Winchester in 1906 while still a serving officer) killed at the head of his Coldstream battalion on the Somme. In the field, a man's politics could be ignored. Willie Redmond, an Irish Nationalist MP since 1884, joined the attack on Messines Ridge in 1917 (at 56, he was too old for front line infantry service). Hard hit, he was carried from the field by two Ulster Division stretcher-bearers who disapproved of his politics but would not leave him to die alone.

In volunteering, many MPs turned their backs on the manicured world of old, comfortable Britain. Tommy Agar-Robartes left beautiful Lanhydrock to die at Loos commanding a company of the Coldstream, and William Gladstone, grandson of the grand old man of Victorian liberalism, set off from Hawarden Castle to perish as a lieutenant in the Royal Welch Fusiliers in 1915. Sir Fredrick Cawley of Berrington Hall, Leominster had four sons and of these, three died. One was a regular cavalryman in 1914 and the other two, both MPs, died at Gallipoli in 1915 and the Western Front in August 1918. Sometimes we remember them for oblique reasons. Major Valentine Fleming, member for South Oxfordshire, died at Arras in May 1917 commanding a squadron of the Queen's Own Oxfordshire Hussars: his son Ian was to be the creator of James Bond.

Distinctions between Commons and Lords are unhelpful, for eleven of the MPs who died were peers' sons, and some would have gone on to inherit the family peerage. Approximately 1500 members of the 685 peerage families in the United Kingdom served in the war, and 270 were killed or died of wounds.[12] The oldest was 82-year-old Field Marshal Earl Roberts, who had won his VC in the Indian Mutiny. He had been the army's last commander-in-chief and was carried off by pneumonia at St Omer in November 1914, during a visit to Indian troops in France. The youngest was 17-year-old Midshipman the Hon Bernard Bailey, youngest son of Lord Glenusk, who perished when the armoured cruiser HMS *Defence* blew up at Jutland. His eldest brother fought with the Grenadiers on the Western Front throughout the war, and was commanding a battalion at the war's end. His second brother, farming in East Africa when war broke out, returned to England at once and the fact that he had been a lance corporal in the Eton College OTC helped him waft into the Grenadiers. He was killed at Givenchy on 10 August 1915, and lies in Guards Cemetery, Windy Corner, not far from Brigadier-General the Hon John Hepburn-Stuart-Forbes-Trefusis, late of the Irish Guards and one of Lord Clinton's sons, who died two weeks later.

The concentric ripples of family and friendship made the relationship between Westminster and the war even more pervasive. Herbert

Asquith, Prime Minister at the start of the war, had four sons. The eldest, Raymond, died with the Grenadiers on the Somme; Herbert served as a gunner officer on the Western Front, and the much-wounded Arthur commanded a brigade of the Royal Naval Division. Anthony, being born in 1902, was too young to serve. All three sons of Labour leader Arthur Henderson fought: the eldest was killed on the Somme, where he lies, with a brisk walk in the lee of Delville Wood between him and Raymond Asquith. Liberal politician Jack Seely, had served in the yeomanry in the Boer War, and been forced to resign as secretary of state for war over the Curragh affair in 1914. He commanded the Canadian Cavalry Brigade on the Western Front, and his son Frank, a second lieutenant in the Hampshires (the family lived on the Isle of Wight and this was the county regiment) was killed at Arras in 1917.

Although the military demand for manpower in the Second World War was much smaller than in the First, twenty-three MPs died on war service, although this includes seven who perished in aircraft crashes, a retired lieutenant colonel who killed himself, fearing that an old wound might prevent his going on active service, and Private Patrick Munro, MP for Llandaff and Barry, who died on a Home Guard training exercise. Sir Arnold Wilson had served in the Indian Army before the First World War, had gone on to become a colonial administrator, and was elected Conservative MP for Hitchin in 1933. The *New Statesman* thought him 'an admirer of Hitler', but when war came he affirmed 'I have no desire to shelter myself and live in safety behind the bodies of millions of our young men.' He joined the Royal Air Force Volunteer Reserve as a pilot officer air gunner, and was killed at 56 over France in 1940. John Whiteley, elected MP for Buckingham in 1937, had served as a gunner officer in the First World War, and died as a brigadier when the aircraft carrying General Sikorsky crashed at Gibraltar in 1943. Peers and their children (for women were now conscripted) also served in large numbers, and relationships within the Westminster village meant that, just as had been the case in the First World War, there were intimate links between the two houses. The Hon Richard Wood, third son of the Earl of Halifax, lost both legs but went on to serve as a junior minister in four administrations, and was ennobled as Baron Holderness. He married the daughter of Lieutenant Colonel Edward Orlando 'Flash' Kellett, MP for

Birmingham Aston, who had been a regular officer before joining the yeomanry: Kellett was killed commanding the Sherwood Rangers in North Africa in 1943.

The cases of Edward Kellett and John Whitely underline the strength of military representation in the parliament of the inter-war years. In 1919, 12 per cent of new Conservative MPs had served in the forces. Between 1919 and 1939, ex-regular officers were, after lawyers, the second largest occupational group in the Commons. There were the very senior: Lieutenant General Sir Aylmer Hunter-Weston was elected Unionist MP for North Ayrshire in a October 1916 by-election while commanding a corps on the Somme. He left the army in 1919, and sat as an MP till 1935. Field Marshal Sir Henry Wilson was elected Unionist MP for North Down in 1921, though he was murdered by Irish nationalists outside his London home the following year. And there were the more junior: Jack Cohen sat for Liverpool Fairfield in 1918–31, and lost both legs at Passchendaele. Ian Fraser, who sat for St Pancras North in 1924–9 and 1931–7, then for Lonsdale in 1940–58, had been commissioned into the King's Shropshire Light Infantry in time to be blinded on the Somme. He crowned a remarkable career by being ennobled as Baron Fraser of Lonsdale, Britain's first life peer, in 1958.

Most striking is the close connection between military service and high office. Winston Churchill had fought on the North-West Frontier, at Omdurman and in the Boer War before entering politics. In 1916, widely blamed for the Gallipoli fiasco, he rejoined the army (having maintained his military status by serving in the yeomanry), and was attached to the Grenadier Guards to learn the ways of trench warfare before commanding 6th Royal Scots Fusiliers in the Ploegsteert sector, south of Ypres, for the first five months of 1916.

Churchill's deputy from 1940 to 1945, and his successor after that year's general election, was Labour leader Clement Attlee. He had been a lecturer at the London School of Economics when war broke out in 1914, and was immediately commissioned into the South Lancashire Regiment. In 1915 he commanded a company on Gallipoli, and probably owed his life to the fact that he was being treated for dysentery during some very heavy fighting. His company was one of those chosen to furnish the rearguard during the withdrawal from Suvla Bay in December, and he was the last but one man to leave. Attlee was wounded in Mesopotamia, so spent 1917 in Britain, and was then posted to the Western Front for the last six months of the war. In the inter-war years he styled himself 'Major Attlee', and his open, collegiate style of leadership reflected the skills needed to command a mixture of wartime volunteers and conscripts in a middle-of-the-road infantry regiment.

Attlee was ousted by Churchill in 1951, and Churchill himself was succeeded in 1955 by Anthony Eden, a classic example of the well-connected officer (Durham landed-gentry, Eton and Oxford) who had a good war. He was commissioned into 21/King's Royal Rifle Corps, proudly known as the Yeoman Rifles and raised by Charles, Earl of Feversham. The battalion was first committed to battle on the Somme on 15 September 1916; Feversham was killed that day. Eden won the Military Cross, became adjutant of his battalion and finally, aged just 21, became the youngest brigade major (chief of staff of a formation then comprising three infantry battalions) in the army. Styling himself Captain Eden he was elected to parliament in 1923. In 1939 he returned, briefly, to the army as a major. He served as foreign secretary from 1935 to 1938, when he resigned over appeasement. He held important posts during the war, lost one of his two sons in Burma, and again served as foreign secretary for part of Churchill's second administration. By the time Eden became prime minister he was already past his best, and ended up resigning in 1957 as a result of the Suez affair. There is a strong case for blaming some of Eden's misfortunes on the strains imposed by two years on the Western Front.

Eden was succeeded by Harold Macmillan, who had served him as both foreign secretary and Chancellor of the Exchequer. A publisher's son, Macmillan was at Oxford in 1914 and was commissioned into the Grenadier Guards. He was first wounded at Loos in 1915 and had been wounded again by the time he was hit in the pelvis as the Guards Division attacked Guillemont on 15 September 1916. This was the same battle that killed Lieutenant Raymond Asquith and Lieutenant Colonel Guy Baring. Macmillan lay in No Man's Land reading Aeschylus in Greek, and then spent the rest of the war undergoing a series of operations. Like Eden, he was marked by his experiences. He could not bear to return to Oxford to finish his degree, for he could never forget that of his first-year group at Balliol, only one other had survived the war.

In 1924 he was elected, as Captain Macmillan, for the industrial constituency of Stockton. He lost his seat in 1929, but returned to the Commons in 1931. Like Eden he was scornful of appeasement and appeasers, and his easy but authoritative style made him a natural choice for high office when Churchill came to power. From 1942 to 1945 he was resident minister in the Mediterranean. He took over from Eden in 1957 and served till 1963, assuring the country that 'You've never had it so good.' Macmillan's concern for social reform, which put him towards the left of the Conservative party of his day, reflected his contact with ordinary folk in the trenches. 'They have big hearts, these soldiers,' he wrote, 'and it is a very pathetic task to have to read all their letters home. Some of the older men, with wives and families who write every day, have in their style a wonderful simplicity which is almost great literature.'

The pattern was broken by Macmillan's successor, Sir Alec Douglas-Home, who had contracted spinal tuberculosis in 1938. He was bedridden for the first two years of the war and unfit for service thereafter. Harold Wilson, Labour Prime Minister 1964–70 and 1964–6, had volunteered for service in 1939 but had, very sensibly in view of his first-class economic brain, been directed into the Ministry of Fuel and Power. Edward Heath, Conservative Prime Minister 1970–74, had been commissioned into the Royal Artillery, rose to the rank of lieutenant colonel, and soldiered on part-time with the Honourable Artillery Company after the war.

Martial prime ministers are the tip of the iceberg. Until the 1960s the front benches were packed with men who had fought in the world wars, and, certainly as far as the Conservatives were concerned, having had the proverbial 'good war' was almost a *sine qua non* of political success. But a man's service record did not determine his political stance. Denis Healey had been at Balliol College, Oxford with Edward Heath (the men remained friends) and was commissioned into the Royal Engineers, serving as military landing officer at Anzio in 1943. He gave a 'barnstorming and strongly left-wing' speech, still in uniform, at the 1945 Labour Party Conference.But although he made a massive dent in the traditional Conservative majority at Pudsey and Ottley that year, he was not elected till 1952.

In 1962 it was estimated that 9 per cent of MPs were former regular officers, and that military representation in the Commons was nearly a hundred times greater than in society more broadly.[13] Conscription endured till 1962 and, until the sharp cuts of 1967, the Territorial Army was over 100,000 strong: both factors helped maintain military experience in parliament. Margaret Thatcher selected all her secretaries of state for defence from former officers. Michael Heseltine, who held the post in 1983–6 was the least martial. Son of a Second World War lieutenant colonel, Heseltine was called up in 1959 in the dying days of National Service and commissioned into the Welsh Guards. From 1945, serving officers were suspended from duty when they ran for parliament, and were required to retire if elected. Heseltine contested the safe Labour seat of Gower in 1959, and was not required to resume service after his defeat. It was not until the appointment of Malcolm Rifkind in 1992 that this chain was broken. No subsequent secretaries of state for defence have had military service, although John Reid, first-rate minister for the armed forces 1997–9 and secretary of state for defence 2005–6 owed part of his affinity with the military to his family ties, for his father had served in the ranks of the Scots Guards.

The passing from politics of the Second World War generation was underscored by the last of the 'good war' Tories. Lord Carrington had been commissioned into the Grenadiers in January 1939, and fought from Normandy into Germany with the Guards Armoured Division where he earned a Military Cross commanding the first tank across the great bridge at Nijmegen. Foreign secretary in 1982, he resigned, with characteristic probity, to acknowledge his department's failure to predict the Argentine invasion of the Falklands. William Whitelaw, ex-Scots Guards and awarded a Military Cross in Normandy, 1944, held a variety of government appointments. He exercised huge influence over Margaret Thatcher, who made him the first hereditary peer created for eighteen years after her victory in the 1983 election. His resignation in 1987, on grounds of ill-health, deprived her of a major steadying influence.

The Parliament whose life ended with the general election of 2010 contained 43 MPs with military service of some sort. Eighteen were ex-regular army officers, ranging from Michael Mates, sometime lieutenant colonel in the Queen's Dragoon Guards, to Andrew Mitchell, who had held a 'gap year commission' between school and university. There were thirteen Territorials, one of them an ex-regular army officer and another a former member of the RAF; seven former members of the RAF; one of the Royal Navy; one who transferred from the Royal Navy to the Royal Naval Reserve; and another naval reservist. One, Rudi Vis, Labour MP for Finchley and Golders Green, had served in the Dutch Armed Forces in his youth. This constituted 6.6 per cent of a house of 646 members. The breadth of the definitions above, which includes both an MP who served in his university's Officer Training Corps forty years ago, and another medically discharged after a brief period of regular training, underlines the thinness of real military experience, though at least two of the Territorials have been mobilised for service in Iraq or Afghanistan.

To enable peers and MPs without military service to speak with more knowledge of the armed forces, Sir Neil Thorne, a Conservative MP and Territorial colonel, founded the Armed Forces Parliamentary Scheme (AFPS) in 1987. 'The whole purpose of the scheme,' he writes, 'is to enable Members of all parties to speak in debates on the Armed Forces from a position of experience'.[14] The scheme lasts a year, during which participants are expected to spend at least 21 of 30 offered days with the armed forces, selecting the service of their choice. They are initially given status roughly aligning them with majors or their equivalents to enable them to spend time with soldiers, sailors, and airmen, rather than to receive the two-star status normally accorded to MPs visiting military units.[15]

The AFPS makes it possible for participants to return, 'at four levels from Major to Brigadier equivalent'. At least one, Dr Julian Lewis, Conservative MP for New Forest East, spent some time at the Royal College of Defence Studies, writing a 10,000-word dissertation that was rated in the top ten for his year. In all about ninety MPs have participated in the scheme. The opinion of serving army officers on its usefulness is divided, with some contributors to the invaluable Army Rumour Service website arguing that anything that brings MPs into closer connection with the services can only do good. The facts that the scheme has flourished despite its lack of official funding, and attracts both peers and MPs who take it very seriously, underline the perceived need to remedy the progressive demilitarisation of parliament.

Political allegiance and holding a senior military position have existed independently of each other at many points in history. Most military and naval MPs still sitting immediately after 1688 were Tories, although they were soon outweighed by Whigs. It was, by then, possible for an officer to be opposed to the government and to enjoy senior command. Major General James Webb won a useful little victory at Wynendaele in 1708, ensuring that a vital convoy got through to Marlborough who was besieging Lille. Webb was a Tory and the Tories were in opposition. His supporters in the Commons at once complained that he had been insufficiently rewarded for the Wynendaele exploit. The credit seemed to have gone to Marlborough's chief of staff, William Cadogan, who sat in the Whig interest for Woodstock – the town adjacent to Marlborough's country estate, Blenheim Palace.

Ministers were assailed by those who shook the tree of patronage to get commissions, promotions, and appointments for family, friends, and clients. As time went on, ministers became more reluctant to intervene save where they could do so with probity. The papers of the hard-working William, Viscount Barrington, Whig secretary at war 1755–61 and 1765–78, show how patronage worked in the high eighteenth century. In 1760 George, Duke of Marlborough wrote asking for 'a troop of Dragoons, or a company [captaincy] in an old regiment for a gentleman whose name is Travell: his father was a very zealous friend to us in the late Oxfordshire election ... he may stick some time unless your Lordship will favour him with your interest to get promoted.'[16] Marlborough's insistence on an 'old' regiment was intended to ensure that Travell did not get appointed to a junior regiment that would be disbanded at the first opportunity, shoving him off onto half-pay. Barrington failed to oblige the duke, for Francis Travell soldiered on unpromoted, and the 1800 *Army List* has him as a half-pay lieutenant in the now-disbanded 21st Light Dragoons.

Barrington was unusually scrupulous in refusing to break the army's rules even when pressed hard. In 1771 he told Lord North, then Prime Minister, that although he valued the influential Scottish Whig Sir Gilbert Eliott just as much as North himself did:

Yet I must not assist you in getting a company for his son.

Two invariable and indispensable rules of the army are that every man shall begin military life with the lowest commission, and that he shall be at least 16 years of age till he shall obtain any ...

Mr. Elliot was not I believe ten years of age when he had a commission of lieutenant & soon after he was most irregularly made a captain. At the reduction [disbandment] of the corps, he was not kept on any list, or kept on half pay ... What shall I say to the friends of Mr Stuart, or Price, or a great many others if Mr Elliot is a Captain before them? I shall be told with great truth that his former commission is a nullity though it still remains in his possession. The whole world will condemn me, and what is worst of all, I shall condemn myself.[17]

There was a growing belief that an officer should not be penalised, in his military capacity, for opinions expressed as a Parliamentarian. Yet there were still some serious upsets. William Pitt the Elder was commissioned into Lord Cobham's Dragoons, with Treasury approval, so that the government could expect the support of his brother, already an MP, and joined his regiment at Northampton. William himself soon became Whig member for that most addled of rotten boroughs, Old Sarum, which had no resident voters at all. He made strident attacks on government policy, causing Prime Minister Robert Walpole, always slow to turn the other cheek, to observe 'We must muzzle this terrible cornet of horse.' In 1736 Walpole duly secured the dismissal of Pitt and several other military and naval MPs who had opposed the government. The move was not popular in the house, but none of the dismissed officers was reinstated. In 1764 Lieutenant General Henry Conway, who enjoyed the prestigious colonelcy of the 1st Royal Dragoons, voted against the government and was stripped of his colonelcy. The opposition at once protested that this was military punishment for political offence, and although George III did not restore Conway 'he never again breached the principle enunciated by Conway's supporters', and Conway himself went on to be commander-in-chief.[18]

By the 1780s it was clear that the espousal of firm political views was not necessarily a bar to either high rank or employment in sensitive posts. Three of the most senior generals in North America, William Howe (C-in-C 1775–78), Henry Clinton (C-in-C 1778–82) and John Burgoyne, who surrendered at Saratoga in 1777, were serving MPs. Both Howe and Burgoyne were Whigs, and had spoken in Parliament against the American war. Howe had assured his

Nottingham constituents that he would not serve against the colonists. When he agreed to do so one told him that: 'I don't wish you to fall, as many do, but I cannot say I wish success to the undertaking.' Howe replied that 'I was ordered, and could not refuse, without incurring the odious name of backwardness to serve my country in distress.'[19]

The social unrest that followed the Napoleonic wars saw the clearest example of politically-engaged officers attaining high rank despite firmly held opinions. Charles James Napier was a scion of a military family: his father Colonel George Napier and brothers George and William were soldiers, and another brother was a sailor. He earned a brilliant reputation as an infantry officer in the Peninsula. The Napiers were all radicals, and in George senior's case experience of revolt in America, Ireland, and France had given him much sympathy for the rebels. For Charles, the process owed much to his wide reading while at the Senior Division of the Royal Military College. In 1839 the government appointed him to command Northern District as a major general. It was a courageous choice, for he was known to sympathise with the Chartists, who constituted the greatest threat to the order he was sworn to preserve, to hate the Corn Laws that kept the price of bread artificially high, and to tell the government precisely what its errors were.

Charles Napier was able to distinguish between personal sympathy with the Chartists and professional determination to keep the peace. He was inclined to the view that 'the best way of treating a country is a good thrashing, followed by great kindness afterwards', and a notion of responsibility to the Crown rather than its ministers also helped him deal with the inconsistencies in his own position. He made it clear that if the 'physical force' Chartists rose, then he would crush them. 'Poor people! They will suffer', he wrote. 'We have the physical force not they ... What would their 100,000 men do with my hundred rockets wriggling their fiery tales among them, roaring, scorching, tearing all they came near.'[20] This combination of genuine sympathy and absolute firmness made him a notable success in the post.

He went to India, where his sense of natural justice (laced with a good slug of ambition) encouraged him to beat the Amirs of Sindh at Miani, going on to rule the newly annexed province with benevolent despotism. He returned home in 1847 after much bickering with the

East India Company's hierarchy. In 1849 that arch-conservative the Duke of Wellington was sure that Napier was the only general capable of rescuing the Sikh War from the head-on enthusiasm of the commander-in-chief in India, Sir Hugh Gough. By the time Napier arrived Gough had sledge-hammered his way to victory, and his subsequent trial of strength with the viceroy, Lord Dalhousie, saw Napier return home under a cloud.

Charles Napier died a general and a Knight Grand Cross of the Order of the Bath, an achievement not prevented by his political views or notorious scruffiness. His brother William, who had also fought with distinction in the Peninsula, was no less radical. When on half-pay in the 1830s, he declined suggestions that he should stand as an MP, and even more wisely refused command of the Chartists' projected 'National Guard'. He was a regular speaker at political meetings, and argued that while the army as an institution might indeed be politically neutral, 'if a soldier does not know and love the social happiness springing from equal and just laws, how, in God's name, is he to fight as the soldier of a free nation ought to fight?'[21]

He was not re-employed between the end of the Napoleonic wars and appointment as lieutenant governor of Guernsey in 1842, and in the meantime had produced his multi-volume *History of the War in the Peninsula*. This remains an extraordinary achievement, not least because of its flashes of tangible affection for private soldiers, such as John Walton, in Napier's company of 43rd Foot on the retreat to Corunna. Walton was charged by determined French horsemen, but

> stood his ground, and wounded several of his assailants, who then retired, leaving him unhurt, but his cap, knapsack, belts and musket were cut in about twenty places, his bayonet was bent double, and notched like a saw.[22]

There was much more to the book than narrative. Napier was convinced that the French army embodied the egalitarian principles of which he approved, while the British was dominated by privilege. 'Napoleon's troops fought in bright fields where every helmet caught some beams of glory,' he wrote, 'but the British soldier conquered under the cold shade of the aristocracy.'[23] William Napier also died a general and a knight, as did his third martial brother, Thomas, who lost his right arm at Ciudad Rodrigo in 1812. Being in the same political camp as the rest of his family, Thomas was delighted to be governor of Cape Colony when slavery was abolished across the empire in 1834.

In the early nineteenth century in the unreformed House of Commons, officers sometimes sat for family-controlled constituencies. Occasionally, as an ingredient of the oleaginous mix of influence and obligation then known as 'interest', they were installed on behalf of a powerful patron, either because he valued their support, or because he believed that possession of a seat in parliament might improve their own career prospects. Lieutenant General Sir John Moore (killed at Corunna in 1808) was the son of a Glasgow doctor who acted as bear-leader to the Duke of Hamilton on his Grand Tour, travelling with the party. Hamilton not only secured John an ensign's commission in the 51st Foot, but then proceeded to have him elected for the family-run Lanark Burghs in 1784–90. General Sir Henry Clinton sat from 1772 to 1784, first for Boroughbridge and then for Newark upon Trent. These were both constituencies controlled by his cousin, the Duke of Newcastle, who devoted almost as much attention to fostering his career as he did to the breeding of his affable Clumber spaniels. His widow married Thomas Craufurd, and in 1802 gave another of her family's pocket boroughs, East Retford, to his brother Robert 'Black Bob', who was to be mortally wounded commanding the Light Division at Ciudad Rodrigo in 1812.

There was much the same pattern in the Irish House of Commons until its disappearance with the Union of 1800. Arthur Wellesley, the future Duke of Wellington, sat for the family borough of Trim, and Edward Pakenham, brother of Wellesley's wife Kitty, for his own family's Longford borough. Galbraith Lowry Cole (Kitty's rejected suitor) sat first for Irish constituencies, and then represented Fermanagh in the British House of Commons, although he spent most of his time commanding one of Wellington's divisions in the Peninsula. He might have discussed politics with several of his senior colleagues, including cavalry commander Lieutenant General Sir Stapleton Cotton, MP for Newark in 1806–1814 and in the upper house as Lord Combermere thereafter.

From the 1790s there were as many redcoats as black in the Commons, for, with the country mobilised against France, it was hard to tell regulars from militia or volunteer officers. About half the members returned in 1790–1820 held part-time commissions. Indeed, Robert Craufurd was nicknamed 'the regular colonel' to distinguish him from the numerous MPs whose colonelcies reflected their local status. William Pitt the younger, out of office as prime minister from 1801 to 1804, raised three battalions of Cinque Ports Volunteers. He modestly referred to them as 'the advanced guard of the nation', drilling them himself as their colonel commandant and expatiating, red-coated in the House, on the virtues of volunteering. There was a similar rash of part-time officer-MPs during the French invasion scare of the 1860s, and in 1869 no less than 130 had connections with the volunteer movement.

While a government could not affect a senior ranking military career, they could influence their income, being in control of the much desired government appointments. All promotion above lieutenant colonel was, until the reforms of the 1880s, wholly dependent upon seniority, and so once an officer had reached this rank even the government's concentrated spite could not stop further ascent. But generals received no pay (getting by on the half-pay of their regimental rank) unless they were given a specific appointment, like command of troops engaged in operations or a governorship, at home or abroad. There were a good deal more such jobs than one might expect: Regency Brighton kept three generals gainfully employed. All of these posts were at the government's disposal, as were regimental colonelcies, a useful source of income until the late nineteenth century.

George De Lacy Evans – 'an obstreperous radical from an Irish landowning family' – had served in the Peninsula, was present at the burning of the White House in 1814, and fought at Waterloo the following year.[24] On half-pay after the war, in 1835–7 he commanded the British Legion that fought for Queen Isabella, the liberal claimant to the Spanish throne, in the first Carlist War. The British Government was anxious to help Isabella against her uncle Don Carlos but was not prepared to do so directly, although it is clear that Evans' officers and men were ex-soldiers, most serving because of the lack of employment at home. But Evans was also an MP, sitting for Rye in 1830 and 1831–32, and then for Westminster from 1833 to 1841 and 1846 to 1865. Although the diarist Charles Greville testily described him as republican, he was impeccably radical, pro-Chartist but (like his middle-class electors, whose opinions he took very seriously) firmly opposed to political reform by force. He was passed over sixteen times for the colonelcy of a regiment, but when Horse Guards was reviewing the long list of generals to find commanders for the Crimean expedition, it settled on Evans to head the 2nd Division. His broad military experience commended him even though his political views did not, and, in the event, he proved one of the war's most capable generals – and returned to radical politics after it.

The dukes of York and Wellington, as commanders-in-chief, did their best to consider claims to commissions, promotions and appointments on their own merits, and in 1827 Wellington told the king, 'The principle is that the pretensions of officers to Your Majesty's favour should be fairly considered, notwithstanding their conduct in Parliament.' He was less scrupulous during his second term as commander-in-chief (1842–52) when 'he made partial sacrifice of the claims of merit to those of political or party interest', and Rowland Hill (commander-in-chief 1828–42) was, in the kindly way that had earned him the nickname 'Daddy', inclined to favour 'Conservative members of Parliament, old friends, the offspring of brother soldiers and unfortunate widows, [who] all found the way open to their solicitations.'[25]

The abolition of the purchase in 1871 and the increasing formalisation of promotion made it harder for politics to influence an officer's career for good or ill, though it has never wholly prevented it. While government could not stop the declining number of officer-MPs from speaking their minds in parliament, it stamped down hard on the public expression of political opinion by serving officers. Redvers Buller was one of the heroes of his generation. His VC, won in a dreadful fight with the Zulus on Hlobane mountain in 1879, was a remarkable achievement even by the high standards of that award. He was less successful commanding British troops in the Boer War, and in the mood of recrimination that followed his recall he was widely attacked. On 10 October 1901 he replied publicly to an outspoken article by Leo Amery. Both Lord Roberts, now the army's commander-in-chief (and, no less to the point, Buller's successor in South Africa), and the Conservative Secretary of State, St John Brodrick, had much to gain from off-loading the blame for initial failures onto Buller. For speaking without authorisation he was summarily dismissed on half-pay and denied the court martial he requested. Buller remained popular in the country at large, and when the Liberals came to power in 1905 they offered him a safe seat, which he was wise enough to decline.

The Buller affair did not stop officers from having political views, although the fate of a general with a VC and close connections to the king made them cautious about expressing them while they were serving. In 1913 it seemed likely that if the Liberal Government persisted in its plan to give Home Rule to Ireland, then Ulstermen would fight to avoid rule from Dublin. Thousands flocked to Unionist rallies, and the newly formed Ulster Volunteer Force drilled hard. Lord Roberts, outspokenly sympathetic to the Unionist cause, recommended Lieutenant General Sir George Richardson, a retired Indian Army officer, as its commander. Captain W. B. Spender, hitherto the youngest Staff College graduate, resigned his commission to serve on his staff. The North Down Regiment was commanded by a retired major general, and Richardson's chief of staff was a former colonel. All these officers were recalled to service in 1914 when the UVF formed the bulk of 36th Ulster Division, whose service on the Western Front has left such an enduring mark on the province's history.

It was evident that using the army to enforce Home Rule in Ireland would be fraught with difficulties, and in September 1913 the king wrote a statesmanlike letter to Prime Minister Asquith, reminding him

> that ours is a voluntary army; our soldiers are none the less citizens; by birth, religion and environment they may have strong feelings on the Irish question; outside influence may be brought to bear upon them; they see distinguished retired officers already organis-ing local forces in Ulster; they hear rumours of officers on the active list throwing up their commissions to join this force. Will it be wise, will it be fair to the sovereign as the head of the army, to subject the discipline, and indeed the loyalty of the troops, to such a strain?[26]

Sir John French, the CIGS, had already assured the monarch that the army 'would as a body obey unflinchingly and without question the absolute commands of the King no matter what their personal opinion might be,' though he added that intervention in Ulster would subject discipline to serious strain, and 'there are a great many officers and men ... who would be led to think that they were best serving their King and country either by refusing to march against the Ulstermen or openly joining their ranks.' He concluded, though, that he would impress on all serving officers 'the necessity for abstaining from any political controversy'.[27]

The so-called 'Curragh Mutiny' of 1914 remains instructive. It was not in fact a mutiny, and the best evidence suggests that while deployment to Ulster would have imposed a severe strain on the army's loyalty, most officers would have obeyed unequivocal orders. Because they then required private means to serve, resignation would not have been as damaging as it would be today, when almost all officers live on pay and look forward to pensions. There remains little evidence of how the army might have behaved even if many of its officers had indeed resigned. In Francis Foljambe's artillery brigade (then the equivalent of a regiment in any other army) all officers but one decided to go, changed into plain clothes and left command in the hands of the sergeant major and the NCOs. Non-commissioned personnel did not have the luxury of being able to send in their papers, and most had joined the army to make a living. Regiments recruited in Ireland would have been in an agonising position, and many of the Irishmen serving across the rest of the army would have found their own loyalty taxed. Most soldiers would have stayed true to their salt, and we would do well to remember that issues that generate heat in officers' messes do not necessarily cause such dissention in barrack rooms.

Lastly, the incident occurred when Jack Seely, secretary of state for war, was a reserve officer with a reputation for personal bravery, and who knew most major players personally. The CIGS was very close to his political master and on good terms with both the Prime Minister and Lord Chancellor. Soon after French's resignation he went off to lick his wounds with Churchill, First Lord of the Admiralty, aboard the admiralty yacht *Enchantress*. It was not a case of political ignorance of the ways and attitudes of the military, rather a crisis that slid out of control, leaving the army's professional head caught between the hammer of government policy and the anvil of military opinion. Few senior officers would necessarily have fared better at the point of impact than Johnnie French.

The army has faced nothing on the scale of the Curragh ever since. Although there have been suggestions that it would have resented being asked to carry out some tasks, like intervention to help enforce majority rule upon Rhodesia/Zimbabwe in the 1960s, all the evidence suggests that the army does as it is told. This is the case even when some senior officers have substantial moral and practical reservations about the task, as was undoubtedly the case with the invasion of Iraq in 2003. It is striking that none of them, well aware of the rules against making public pronouncements, spoke at the time, although some of the evidence given to the Chilcott enquiry makes the scale of their unhappiness evident.

Some officers suffered for the public expression of their views. In 1938 Duncan Sandys, Conservative MP for South Norwood, Winston Churchill's son-in-law and a subaltern in a Territorial anti-aircraft unit, raised issues of national security that reflected his own military specialism. He was then approached by two unidentified men (presumably representing the security service) who warned him that he risked prosecution under the Official Secrets Act. Sandys at once reported the matter to the Committee on Privileges, which ruled that disclosures to parliament were not subject to the Act, although an MP could be disciplined by the house if, in its view, his disclosures were damaging or unwarranted. Sandys' territorial career was unharmed. He was badly wounded in Norway in 1941, retired as a lieutenant colonel in 1946, and as defence minister in 1957 produced the Sandys Review. The First World War case of Sir Henry Page Croft MP was different. He went out with his Territorial battalion in 1914, and was first of the few Territorials to command a brigade. Frank reports on his dissatisfaction with the high command – delivered informally rather than on the floor of the house – caused sufficient controversy to get him recalled in 1916: all his political connections could not save him.

The army's own regulations grew progressively sterner about the need for serving officers to gain formal clearance for their publications. They had once been very relaxed. Lieutenant Winston Churchill published his idiosyncratic *Story of the Malakand Field Force* in 1898. The first edition of *The River War*, his account of the Omdurman campaign, was highly critical of Lord Kitchener's desecration of the Mahdi's tomb and of the poor quality of some military supplies, notably the soldier's boots. Kitchener was furious, and although Churchill left the regular army soon afterwards, he was recommissioned during the Boer War, then became a yeomanry officer and commanded a battalion when Kitchener was still secretary of state for war.

The rules were much stricter after the Second World War. In 1949 the future Field Marshal Lord Carver, then an acting lieutenant colonel, reviewed Field Marshal Montgomery's *Alamein to the Sangro* for the *Royal Armoured Corps Journal*. He unwisely observed that it was 'a high price to pay for a short book', and was nearly court-martialled. Montgomery ordered Carver's director to 'tell him that a junior officer is not allowed to criticise the head of the army'. Later, when Carver had written his own book on Alamein he found it difficult to get permission to publish. Although he was by then an upwardly mobile brigadier, permission was actually refused for a chapter on training and doctrine which was to have formed part of a *Festschrift* to mark Basil Liddell Hart's seventieth birthday 'as it was clearly controversial'.[28]

A more recent case of a serving officer being disciplined for public criticism, this time of his own superiors rather than politicians, is that of Major Eric Joyce. He enlisted into the Black Watch in 1978 and subsequently attended Stirling University, graduating with a degree in religious studies. Joyce became a probationary second lieutenant while at university, attended the Royal Military Academy Sandhurst after graduation, and was commissioned into the Royal Army Educational Corps in 1988. His service took him to Northern Ireland, Germany, and Belize, and during it he obtained two master's degrees. He was promoted captain in 1990 and major in 1992 – the year that the RAEC was amalgamated into the newly-formed Adjutant General's Corps and became the Educational and Training Services branch.

In August 1997 the Fabian Society published a pamphlet by Joyce called 'Arms and the Man – Renewing the Armed Services', maintaining that the forces were 'racist, sexist and discriminatory'. He had written it without getting the permission to publish required by *Queen's Regulations*, telling *The Times* that 'you can't get radical ideas like this into the public domain if you go through the chain of command.'[29] Joyce denied that he was being covertly supported by ministers, but argued that 'what I'm saying is broadly in line with the modernising agenda which the government is promoting.'[30] He went on to launch the *Armed Services Forum*, which was authorised by the military authorities but contained severe criticism of the forces. When at length the army moved to discipline him, he affirmed that it was 'terribly important' that soldiers should be allowed to speak freely. He also condemned the army's obsession with an 'officer class', and argued that *Queen's Regulations*, simply 'a convention', were not legally enforceable.[31] The Conservative opposition saw the Labour Government's hand behind Joyce's continued survival. In December 1998 Keith Simpson MP, a former Sandhurst lecturer, told the Commons that the case 'strikes at the heart of the important principle that our armed forces do not participate in party politics.' He went on to argue that:

> He has his own political agenda. As a serving officer, he has openly been a Labour party supporter and, for the past four months, has been actively seeking to become a parliamentary candidate. Not only has he repeatedly and blatantly broken every agreement that he has ever made, but he has become party politically partisan.[32]

Major Joyce was eventually directed to resign his commission and did so in 1999. He went on to become Public Affairs Officer at the Commission for Racial Equality (Scotland), and, unsurprisingly, a Labour MP after winning the Falkirk West by-election the following year. He served as parliamentary private secretary (PPS) to a number of ministers, and in September 2009 resigned as PPS to Defence Secretary Bob Ainsworth. As one of the few Labour MPs with recent military experience he had been a logical choice for the post, but his letter of resignation went to the heart of his old unhappiness:

> The Conservatives ... think they can convince the public that we have lost our empathy with the Defence community ... I do not think the public will accept for much longer that our losses [in Afghanistan] can be justified by simply referring to the risk of greater terrorism on our streets ... Most important of all, we must make it clear to every serviceman and woman, their families and the British public that we give their well-being the greatest political

priority. Behind the hand attacks by any Labour figure on senior service personnel are now, to the public, indistinguishable from attacks on the services themselves. Conversely, in my view we should allow our service personnel greater latitude to voice their views on matters which make distinctions between defence and politics pointless.[33]

Joyce's resignation was overshadowed by the fact that he had become the first MP to claim more than £1 million cumulatively in expenses. The website Army Rumour Service suggests far more resentment amongst serving officers of an MP on the gravy train, than sympathy for a former colleague with a reformist agenda. His case underlines two hard old truths. First, no government, whatever its persuasion, relishes serving members of the armed forces pointing to political failings. Tony Blair abolished the individual services' directors of corporate communication to reduce the risk of senior officers briefing the press 'off message'. In that climate Air Chief Marshal Sir Jock Stirrup, when Chief of the Defence Staff, declined a 'non-attributable' lunch with the distinguished author Sir Max Hastings, regretting that he could only attend if a civil servant was on hand to take notes of the conversation. When General Sir Richard Dannatt spoke, within a few weeks of his appointment as Chief of the General Staff, of the need to withdraw troops from Iraq, it was immediately clear that he would not, as had been expected, succeed Sir Jock as CDS. Second, the army itself remains profoundly uneasy about criticism from within its ranks, especially when that criticism has an explicit political purpose.

For most of the army's history its officer corps was closely aligned to the social class that sent members of parliament to Westminster. The proportion of serving officers sitting in parliament fell away substantially as the nineteenth century went on, but the two world wars of the twentieth century packed both houses with an unusually high number of folk with wartime service. That generation has now moved on, though in the second decade of the twenty-first century there are again MPs with direct links to the military. Modern wars have never been more political and senior officers are inevitably politically ensnared.

CHAPTER 4

BRASS AND TAPES

A RMIES ARE HIERARCHIES, their structure given daily prominence by costume jewellery and codes of behaviour. Even those
that, in the white heat of revolutionary ferment, destroy the titles and
badges associated with status tend to reinstate them once the tumult
is over. The Red Army, which had gleefully done away with epaulettes
– hated symbol of officership under the tsars – brought them back in
1943 to reinforce its identity at the height of the Great Patriotic War.
Chinese officers, for so long dressed in drab and rankless Mao jackets,
now sport big shoulder-boards modelled, for such are the ironies of
military fashion, on the same tsarist pattern as Russian epaulettes.
Although the detail of rank varies across ages and nations, the most
crucial distinction has been between officers, who hold a commission
signed by the head of state, and other personnel who lack this crucial
document.

For most of the British army's existence there was a rough congruence between social status and military rank, although this never
prevented, on the one hand, the phenomenon of the gentleman
ranker, serving as a private soldier against the grain of his background,
or, on the other, the rise of the humble but talented. A striking example of the former is the Hon. Michael Francis Howard, son of the Earl
of Carlisle and formerly a lieutenant in the Scots Guards and 18th
Hussars, killed as a private at Passchendaele in October 1917.
Conversely, William Cobbett, that steadfast enemy of privilege, admitted that

When I was in the army, the adjutant-general, Sir William Fawcett, had been a private soldier; General Slater, who had recently commanded the Guards in London, had been a private soldier; Colonel Paton, who I saw at the head of his fine regiment (the 12th, at Chatham) had been a private soldier; Captain Green, who first had the command of me, had been a private soldier. In the garrison of Halifax there were no less than seventeen officers who had been private soldiers. In my regiment the quarter-master had been a private soldier; the adjutant, who was also a lieutenant, had been a private soldier.[1]

Samuel Bagshawe, whose papers are a valuable resource on the army of George II, also blurred conventional distinctions. He was a young man with excellent prospects but ran away from his tutor in 1731 after being reproved for extravagant habits, and enlisted as a private in Colonel Philip Anstruther's Regiment of Foot. He spent seven years in the ranks of the Gibraltar garrison, becoming a quarter-master sergeant. Bagshawe eventually restored himself to family favour by writing to his uncle and guardian, begging him to

Imagine a youth who for some fancied distaste flings himself into the sea, in his fall he sees his folly, but when he views the miseries that surround him (though sensible it is owing to compassion alone if he is taken in) with all his might he strives to regain his ship; you may easily conceive the earnest desire I have to repossess a happiness ... which, the more I reflect upon the more I am confounded and the more I hope to recover.[2]

His uncle arranged for him to be bought out of the service. Two years later family connections secured him an ensign's commission, and he died a colonel, a rank gained by raising a regiment at his own expense.

Nonetheless, these exceptions scarcely bend the general rule. Lieutenant General Sir John Keir, writing in 1919, emphasised that Britain was at that moment 'a nation in Arms', with the chance of creating, for the first time in its history, 'a real National Army.' Hitherto, he argued,

The regular army consisted of two main groups, patricians and proletarians. The officers were patricians, or patricianists; the men almost entirely proletarians. Between these two extreme poles of the social system there was no shading off. A gulf separated the two classes.[3]

Some of the army's friends, and even more of its critics, see a similar gulf today: the Irish writer Tom Paulin condemned British soldiers as 'thugs sent in by public schoolboys to kill innocent Irish people'.[4]

The British have never used the American terminology of officers and 'enlisted men', having initially differentiated between officers, standing outside the formed body of the unit, and the 'rank and file' within it. They then preferred officers and 'other ranks', wisely jettisoning the latter term, with its demeaning overtones, for 'soldiers' in the 1960s. The line of cleavage became evident from the regular army's earliest days. Sergeant Nehemiah Wharton was an earnest puritan and former London apprentice who served in Denzil Holles's Regiment of Foot, fighting for parliament in the Civil War. He wrote his last surviving letter before his regiment was destroyed at Brentford on 12 November 1642. When Wharton wrote of 'we officers' he meant both officers and sergeants, drawing his own line between sergeants, with their sashes and halberds, and corporals, armed and equipped just like the men. From 1660, though, the army was clear in its distinction between 'commission-officers', until the end of the eighteenth century, whose ranks began with cornet (for cavalry) and ensign (for infantry), and non-commissioned officers, who then constituted sergeants and corporals.

In Queen Elizabeth's day a captain, be he a white-haired gentleman gravely stepping out at the head of his company of militia, or a braggadocio roaring back from the Spanish war, was an important man. His title derived from the Latin *caput*, head, and the slightly later *captaneus*, chief. His deputy, ready to take his place when the need arose, was the lieutenant, its French root meaning 'place taker'; the same as the Latin *locum tenens* that now describes the replacement for our usual GP. The ensign (corrupted to give Shakespeare's 'Ancient Pistol' his swaggering title) was the infantry company's most junior officer, and carried its ensign or colour, just as his comrade in its counterpart, the cavalry troop, bore its distinguishing cornet or guidon.

The proud Spanish infantry, until its 1643 defeat by the French at Rocroi, was the cynosure of European armies. Its columns, each made up of several companies, were commanded by officers whose title derived from the *colonello* itself, and they too had deputies, lieutenant colonels, to take their place. The major, from the Latin *magnus*, great, and so on to the Italian *maggiore*, was indeed a major figure, who came to rank between the captains and the colonel's stand-in. Until the 1680s his title in Britain was sergeant major, not to be confused with the later non-commissioned sergeant major. Captains and their subalterns constituted 'company officers', and majors, lieutenant colonels and colonels were soon known as 'field officers'.

Above them came officers enjoying more general authority. Initially their most senior had been the captain general, Marlborough's highest rank. Although that term fell out of use in the early eighteenth century, many Gunner messes, such as the Honourable Artillery Company, with its idiosyncratic 'regimental fire' toast, still drink the health of 'The Queen, our Captain General'. Field marshal, Britain's highest military rank, currently in abeyance, was a relatively late arrival. It does not appear in the *Army List* till 1736, and in 1744 John Dalrymple, Earl of Stair, was the first army commander-in-chief to hold it. In the army's early history the rank was granted sparingly, and there were no field marshals from 1773 to 1792, though there was plenty of fighting. Below this comes general, sometimes colloquially 'full general', just as colonels are 'full colonels' to distinguish them from their 'half colonel' subordinates. Next, for just the same reasons that give us lieutenant and lieutenant colonel, comes lieutenant general. This was, perversely, a senior rank to that of major general (the latter having been 'sergeant major general' in the armies of the Civil War). By the end of the nineteenth century one of generals' dress distinctions was oak-leaf braid around the peak of their flat forage-cap; by the First World War this had given them the nickname 'brass hats'. It is now conventional wisdom to see debates over the war's strategy being carried on between the brass hats and the 'frocks' – the politicians in black coats – and one of the blood-and-thunder memoirs written by Brigadier General Frank Crozier was entitled *A Brass Hat in No Man's Land.*

The British were long ambivalent about the rank between colonel and major general. Brigades of horse or foot, two to four regiments of each, could simply be commanded by whichever of their colonels was 'eldest' by date of rank: we can almost glimpse that anxious fumbling with commissions, followed by beams of satisfaction or growls of exasperation. Or they might be headed by a major general, the working rank for brigade command for much of the army's life. Senior colonels stepping up to lead brigades might be invested with the local rank of brigadier to do so, or might receive formal commissions as brigadier general. In 1685 James II introduced a note of confusion by having 'Colonels of Brigades', 'Brigadiers' and 'Brigadiers-General'. The rank had much in common with its naval equivalent, commodore, with brigadier generals resembling commodores of the first class, who looked very much like the admirals they yearned to be, and brigadiers mirroring commodores of the second class, who were most definitely captains briefly 'acting up'. It was not generally substantive, and officers holding the rank gave it up when the relevant appointment ceased.[5] In 1810 Henry Torrens, the adjutant general, described the rank as 'inconvenient and temporary', and thought that the answer was to make more major generals.

While lieutenant colonels and above were promoted by the buggins's turn of seniority, brigadiers were appointed to fill specific vacancies, a process that inevitably caused mutterings. On the march to Blenheim, Marlborough promoted Colonel Archibald Rowe to command a brigade and, with his encyclopaedic knowledge of the seniority roll, saw at once that this might cause difficulties:

> He is the eldest colonel we have here, and a very diligent officer [he wrote], but this will give just occasion for Colonel Shrimpton of the Guards to desire the like commission, he being an elder Colonel than Rowe, so that I desire they [i.e. their new commissions] may be dated of the same day.[6]

Rowe solved the issue of long-term seniority by boldly ordering his brigade, attacking Blenheim village, not to fire until he had struck the French palisade with his sword; he was knocked over by the opening volley.

We remember Reginald Dyer, responsible for the Amritsar Massacre of 1919, as 'General Dyer'. He was a brigadier general, commanding 45th Infantry Brigade, at the time of the shooting of perhaps 380 civilians in the town's Jallianwalla Bagh. On retirement in 1920, he reverted to his substantive rank of colonel. Regulations contained a provision enabling the Army Council to recommend the grant of honorary rank to any officer who had held local or temporary general's rank. It had taken the view that Dyer's action constituted 'an error of judgement', but did not propose to take disciplinary action, and therefore there seemed 'to be no reason why honorary rank should be withheld'. The Army Council asked the India Office to arrange for the publication of Dyer's rank in the *London Gazette*, but the India Office, nervous of bad publicity, duly missed the publication date and the moment passed. When Dyer mounted a campaign for honorary rank he was able to marshal powerful support, but the fortuitous presence in London of General Sir Claude Jacob, Chief of the General Staff in India, revealed that senior Indian army officers were not in favour, least of all in view of the Prince of Wales's imminent visit. The issue split the Army Council, but it no longer backed Dyer, whose application perished quietly amongst the files and ink-pots. Colonel Dyer had already been disabled by a stroke, and died in 1927.[7]

By the time that Reginald Dyer died the rank he craved had expired too. Brigadier generals were spoken of as 'general' *tout court* and their uniforms and badges of rank aligned them clearly with other generals. The army's massive expansion during the First World War, and the burgeoning of senior officers in supporting arms and services, had led to an unprecedented expansion in the number of generals, with a recent survey identifying 1,253. They narrowly included Hugh Garvin Goligher Esq, financial adviser to the commander-in-chief in France, who capitalised on his precedence as temporary brigadier general by getting a uniform run up, and having his portrait painted in it. As part of its campaign to reduce the visible impact of generals and staff officers in the aftermath of the First World War, the army did away with the rank of brigadier general altogether, replacing it on 1 January 1921 with that of 'colonel commandant', as opposed to 'colonel on the staff'.

This compromise soon foundered, and might prove untraceable today were it not for a memorial in the main hall of the old Staff College at Camberley, commemorating officers killed in Ireland in the 1920s. Two brigade commanders, killed as colonel commandants, are included. In 1928 the rank of brigadier reappeared, although it was not substantive till 1946, and its holders looked far more like colonels than major generals. Their red collar tabs lacked generals' gold embroidery, and their epaulettes bore a crown and three stars, the latter so configured as to make it hard for officers from those regiments (like the Foot Guards) wearing oversize stars to squeeze them onto the epaulette. Today British brigadiers are one-star officers but not generals, though those on the staff of NATO's Allied Rapid Reaction Corps style themselves, by convention, 'brigadier general' in multinational correspondence. All of these arrangements applied to the red-coated army controlled by the commander-in-chief.

Rank titles were standardised as armies evolved to become an essential part of the apparatus of the new nation-state in the 'post-Westphalia' world that followed the 1648 treaty ending the Thirty Years War. Absolutist monarchs, with France's Louis XIV (to whom both James II and Charles II looked with envy) as their exemplar, asserted themselves by ensuring central control of the armed forces. Royal iconography gradually replaced the crests or arms of individual noblemen; uniforms took on a prevailing national hue; and cannon glowed with symbolism reflecting the status of their master – their large-scale production in royal arsenals so symbolic of the power of new monarchical authority. Louis had the words 'Ultima Ratio Regum' embossed on his cannon, and until the end of the First World War German field guns bore 'Ultima Ratio Regis', affirming that their sharp yap was indeed the king's last argument. Royal ciphers and armorial bearings graced the new angular fortifications that helped define the period, for a state needed to protect its frontiers against armies or fleets equipped with modern artillery. Fortress gates routinely bear the confident stamp of the king.

In Britain this is most evident in coastal fortifications. Henry VIII's arms still grace the gateways to the south-coast fortifications he built. Portsmouth was declared a Royal Dockyard by King John in 1212, and impressed Samuel Pepys during a visit in 1661; he found it 'a very pleasant and strong place'. When Charles II's queen, Catherine of Braganza, landed there in May 1662 she was less impressed, being offered beer, which she hated, and calling for tea instead. Portsmouth still bears the royal stamp in the form of a crown embossed above the keystone of Nicholas Hawksmoor's Portland stone Landport – the only surviving gate to the city's demolished fortifications. Unicorn Gate, now the main entrance to the dockyard, is distinguished by its crown-collared unicorn. Its lion counterpart, once standing sentry on a gate of its own, has now come to rest at the base of Semaphore Tower. In 1779 the two beasts cost the Exchequer £203. 1 s. 8 d., a small price to pay for such an elegant affirmation of status.

In the fortress warfare that preoccupied engineers from the seventeenth to the nineteenth centuries a trench dug towards an enemy-held fortress from the parallel lines of entrenchments surrounding it, zig-zagging so that shot would not rake murderously down its line, was called a sap, and the man who dug it was called, in what became the Royal Engineers' word for private, a sapper. The engineers long used the rank of second corporal for their one-stripe junior NCO. The artillery had always called its own private soldiers gunners, and it soon scrapped the rank of matross, a kind of sub-private who did much of the heavy work associated with guns and gunnery. A petard was an explosive-filled container, shaped like the hat traditionally worn by Welsh ladies, which was screwed or propped (crown side outwards, as it were) to the gate of a fortress, its name derived from the same root that gives us the French verb *péter* for the emission of a more discreet personal bang. The grade of petardier, a soldier with the unenviable specialism of attaching the petard to the gate, disappeared early on. We still half-remember just how tricky the job was, though, for the petardier risked being 'hoist with his own petard' if its sputtering fuse was too short, or if enemy fire prevented him from scampering back the way he had come. The arrangement of rank applied to the redcoats did not, in the first instance, cover the 'gentleman of the ordnance', the artillery and engineers. They answered instead to the master-general of the ordnance, usually a peer with a seat on the cabinet, through eventually demoted to become a mere member of the Army Board. Until 1716 artillery and engineer officers were in theory a homogeneous group, though it was increasingly evident that their skill-sets were different, and gunner officers, their importance rising with the power of the weapons they controlled, resented their subordination to men preoccupied with running up the very fortifications that they themselves sought to knock down.

In 1716 the two branches were split, with a corps of engineers and a regiment of artillery. The engineers enjoyed their own rank structure, with one chief engineer, two directors, two sub-directors, and six apiece of engineers in ordinary, engineers extraordinary, sub-engineers, and practitioner engineers in Britain. There were three engineers, headed by a director, in Minorca, and two, with a sub-director in charge, in Gibraltar. This system gave rough equivalency with the rest of the army, with the chief engineer ranking as a brigadier and the practitioner engineers with ensigns, but led to endless difficulties. Engineers were not strictly speaking commissioned, although they might purchase or be granted commissions.

On campaign there were never enough of them to go round, and Marlborough (combining, in his august though overworked person, the offices of captain general and master general) was given to granting bright infantry officers warrants to act as engineers. In 1707 Captain Richard King of Lord Orrery's Regiment of Foot was appointed an assistant engineer, with a useful £100 addition to his annual pay. There was also the problem of authority. Badges of rank were far from being standardised, and it might not be an easy matter for a young sub-engineer, supervising an infantry working-party, to persuade a grimy sergeant that he did indeed speak with an officer's authority and it was not yet time for the men to knock off and return to camp. In 1757 the engineers at last adopted formal military ranks, though there long remained a tension between engineers, with their relatively high pay, and the infantry, invariably at the other end of the scale. In late 1915 Sergeant Major Ernest Shephard of the Dorsets was pleased to observe the scribbled work of a trench poet:

God made the bee
The bee makes honey
The Dorsets do the work
And the REs [Royal Engineers] get the money.[8]

The ranks of the Royal Artillery were simpler from the beginning, although the most junior commissioned rank of fireworker, was soon transformed to lieutenant-fireworker and later to second lieutenant. The rank of second lieutenant also crept into the infantry, first replacing ensign in fusilier regiments, and then used by rifle regiments from their formation in 1800. From 1871 it replaced ensign and cornet across the army as the most junior commissioned rank, although the army's incurable resistance to standardisation means that the old ranks crop up from time to time. Dine with the Queen's

Guard in St James's Palace and you will discover that the major commanding it is styled the captain, and his two commissioned subordinates are the subaltern and ensign, although one may actually be dressed as a captain and the other as a lieutenant. The old artillery rank of bombardier survived, and the bombardier was for many years the most junior NCO rank in the Royal Artillery, with corporal above it. When Corporal Ronald Skirth crossed an incompetent officer in 1917 (a process that drearily punctured his service) he found that the conversation had an immediate result on his battery's notice-board:

> As from April 23rd 1917 Corporal Skirth, J.R., reverts to the rank
>   of Bombardier, as a disciplinary measure.
> R. A. Snow, Major
> Commanding 239 Siege Battery
> Royal Garrison Artillery.

'Partly from pique,' he recalled, 'I renounced the privilege of "messing" with the NCOs'. He wrote:

> I told my three friends I would muck in with them. If in future if any
> of them addressed me by rank (which had been their way) I'd kick
> him in the shins. 'My name is Ron,' I said. 'Not Corporal, of course,
> and not bloody Bombardier.'[9]

It was not until after the First World War that corporal disappeared from the Royal Artillery, with the two-stripe bombardier replacing him and the one-stripe lance bombardier close behind.

Non-commissioned ranks were not short of complexities of their own. At first most soldiers held the rank of private sentinel, soon abbreviated to private. John Marshall Deane of 1st Foot Guards and one of the few non-commissioned diarists of Marlborough's time, always preferred the term in full. When his regiment helped storm the strongly fortified Schellenberg on its way to Blenheim in 1704, he recorded that it lost five officers 'killed upon the spot', and another seven wounded: 'we had likewise in our regiment killed upon the spot and died of their wounds 172 private sentinels, besides above a hundred that was wounded and recovered again.'[10] There were at first only two grades of non-commissioned officer. A man's first step was corporal, derived from the Latin *corpus* for the small body of men the corporal led. It was 'a rank which, however contemptible it may appear in some people's eyes, brought me a clear twopence *per diem*, and put a very clever worsted knot upon my shoulder too', wrote William Cobbett.[11] His second, took him to sergeant – dating back to the Latin *serviens*, servant, but widely used in the Middle Ages to describe a mounted man-at-arms who was not actually a knight. Self-styled 'Captain' Peter Drake served in several armies during the War of Spanish Succession. He did this, often without completing the tiresome necessities which should have accompanied his discharge from one army prior to his enlistment into another. He spoke of the 'brethren of the halberd', an archaic weapon with its spiked axe-blade mounted on a long haft, and carried by infantry sergeants. The halberd was useful for aligning ranks, laying firmly across the rear rank of a unit that was beginning to give way, or forming the 'triangle' to which soldiers were tied for flogging. Halberds were officially replaced by nine-foot half-pikes in 1791, although units in North America had laid theirs aside long before.

The half-pike was not to be despised. A sergeant in 3/1st Foot Guards at Waterloo recalled how his comrades put their pikes to good use at the battle's climax: 'the line was held up by the sergeants' pikes against the rear – not from want of courage on the men's part (for they were desperate) only for the moment the loss so unsteadied our line.'[12] The pike went in 1830, and sergeants then carried a shorter version of the infantry musket. When the breech-loading Martini-Henry rifle came into service in 1871 sergeants generally carried a sword bayonet rather than the socket bayonet used by corporals and privates. Soldiers habitually wore their sidearms when walking out. The sword-bayonet, metalwork and leather duly buffed up, sat comfortably on the rear of the left hip, dividing the fringes of a sergeant's shoulder-sash like a bridge-pier splitting the shining torrent. There is a good deal of undiluted dandyism to soldiering, and the small satisfactions of a new step up the hierarchy's long ladder should never be ignored.

The sergeant major, having started life in the officers' mess, reappeared as a non-commissioned officer in the eighteenth century. The rank had been in existence for some time before it was formalised in 1797 to mark the most senior of the NCOs. There was one for each infantry battalion and cavalry regiment, and sergeant majors were branded by a style of dress that put them, rather like their rank, somewhere between officers and sergeants. In William Cobbett's regiment, for example, the sergeant major wore a fur bearskin cap like the officers and men of the grenadier company; Cobbett hated his. In the infantry, sashes and sticks were essentials, the former often in the solid crimson worn by officers rather than the red cut with a stripe in the regiment's facing colour used by sergeants. These sticks began life as a silver-headed cane, evolving over the years into the pace-stick – sometimes used to measure off a regulation pace of 30 inches, but more usually, in its glossy splendour of varnish and burnished brass, carried as a badge of rank, echoing the vine-staff of the Roman centurion. William Cobbett's early promotion to sergeant major, straight from regimental clerk, shows that in these early days, the post was primarily administrative, and the sergeant major spent much of his time closeted with the adjutant, working on the rolls and returns that could wreck a man's career as surely as a bullet.

In 1813 there was more significant change. The old cavalry rank of troop quartermaster, the senior non-commissioned member of the troop, was replaced by that of troop sergeant major. In the infantry the rank of colour sergeant was introduced, squarely between sergeant and sergeant major. There was to be one colour sergeant for each of the ten companies then found in a battalion, chosen from 'the ten most meritorious sergeants in the regiment'. For the next century the colour sergeant was the captain's right-hand man, his position equating to that of first sergeant in an American company. One of the company's sergeants was responsible for its provisioning, and he was known as the company quartermaster sergeant (CQMS). Sergeants on the strength of battalion headquarters, grave and clerkly men concerned with pay and administration, ranked as staff sergeants, a term which still defines the senior sergeants' rank in all arms except the infantry.

It is impossible to dwell too much on administrative detail here, for the quantity of troops and companies within units often changed. The most significant change, though, was the introduction of grenadier and light companies, one of each per battalion, into the infantry, and a compensating reduction to bring the 'battalion companies' to eight. Grenadier companies ('tow-rows') were traditionally composed of the sturdiest men in the battalion, just the fellows for rushing an enemy post or for waiting at the colonel's supper-party, beery faces and big thumbs everywhere. The 'light bobs' of the light company were lithe and nimble and were specially trained in skirmishing – and, said their critics, apt at making off with other people's property. It was common for these 'flank companies' to be swept together to form combined grenadier or light battalions. A commanding officer enjoyed having smart flank companies, but losing the best of his battalion to someone else's command was wholly infuriating. Flank companies, officers and men alike, wore distinctive caps and short coats. While the grenadiers applied symbolic grenades to any vacant surface, the light companies were as fond of the corded bugle – their own badge of expertise. The flank companies went in 1862, as part of the post-Crimea reforms, to muted mourning.

The tactical revolution of the late nineteenth century, a reflection of the increased range and firepower of modern weapons, encouraged armies to seek larger groupings so as to place more combat power in the hands of individual commanders. The combination of cavalry troops into squadrons, not taken too seriously when Wully Robertson was an NCO, became standard towards the end of the nineteenth century. In 1913 an infantry battalion's eight companies were merged into four. These changes required the creation of, first, squadron sergeant majors (SSMs) in the cavalry, and then company sergeant majors (CSMs) in the infantry. In the latter process the four senior colour sergeants in each battalion were promoted, and the remaining four took over the function of quartermaster sergeant. This arrangement remains in use today, and Colour Sergeant Frank Pye, who makes his incisive appearance on this book's first page, was responsible for keeping his company of 2 Para fed and watered in the Falklands in 1982. Promotion from sergeant to company sergeant major now takes a man through the rank of colour sergeant, but during the First World War it was felt that the qualities that made a man a good quartermaster sergeant did not necessarily make him a good sergeant major.

Ronald Skirth, whose account of his wretched time in the army is aptly titled *The Reluctant Tommy*, took over from his battery quartermaster sergeant when the latter contracted typhoid, although he himself was only a junior NCO. 'The Q.M.'s job I would say is the most envied in the whole service', he wrote,

> and so there was both disappointment and consternation when I was appointed temporary, unpaid 'Quarterbloke'... The Q.M. is in charge of stores – clothing, food and equipment and, most important to many, tobacco and rum. I think I made a reasonably efficient QM. Nobody ever 'drew' anything from my stores without a 'chit' bearing the duty officer's signature. Nobody, that is, except ME! It didn't seem right that I should do extra work without financial reward, so I used the opportunity to look after No 1.[13]

Ernest Shephard, in contrast, simply leapfrogged quartermaster sergeant on his way on up. He happily copied the relevant extract from his own battalion's daily orders into his diary:

> Bn Orders by Major Radcliffe DSO commanding 1st Dorset Regiment ... No 8817 Sgt Shephard: Appointed Acting CSM from 25.4.15 vice CSM Searle wounded 24.4.15, and promoted CSM on 1.5.15 vice CSM Searle, died of wounds.[14]

In a process wholly typical of the army's need to find a spare 'line serial' into which to promote a man, he had bypassed colour sergeant altogether, and replaced the three stripes on his arm ('tapes' in soldier's jargon) with a crown on his forearm, leaving his company's colour sergeant (three tapes with a crown above them) in his dusty world of tables: six-foot, and lamps: hurricane. The process of promoting to fill a vacancy echoed William Todd's elevation to corporal in 1758:

> Sergeant William Bennet of our company was broke by the major's orders for being drunk when he should have attended the hospital ... and that James Crawford, corporal, was appointed sergeant and that I was appointed corporal in the room of Corporal Crawford preferred.[15]

When Shephard was promoted his company commander was the 28-year-old Captain W. B. Algeo MC, a clergyman's son from Studland,

Dorset. Their relationship typified the warmest of associations between figures who, at this crucial level, were headmen of their own distinct tribes. But on 17 May 1916 Algeo and the battalion's intelligence officer crossed into a wood on the German side of the lines. There were shots, and they did not reappear. Shephard raced to battalion headquarters, where the commanding officer authorised him to send a follow-up patrol 'but not to go myself on any account, although I wished to do so'. The pioneer sergeant, Sergeant Goodwillie – 'very well liked by the captain' – set off with Sergeant Rogers a little way behind. There was more shooting, and Rogers returned to report that he had lost Goodwillie and could not find the officers. Shephard was distraught:

> The loss of my gallant Captain to the Battalion, my Company and myself cannot be estimated. He was the bravest officer I have ever met, his first and last thought was for the good and honour of the Bn, his Coy and his men. 'An officer and a gentleman'.

We now know that Algeo and Goodwillie were both killed, and now rest, three long strides apart, in Miraumont Communal Cemetery.

The responsibilities of company commander and CSM remain distinct but interlocked. One friend told me of striding across to speak to his CSM who was chatting to the CQMS and the three platoon sergeants. He was greeted with a cracking salute, and the words 'It's all right, sir, you can fuck off: knobber.' It seemed a bad moment for decisive confrontation, so he withdrew to his office, dignity narrowly preserved. When the sergeant major appeared later, the officer cautiously raised the issue of that last word. The sergeant major was aghast. It was the acronym NOBA: 'Not Officers' Business: Admin'. Another officer recalled how his own attempt to tinker with his company's daily programme produced the as-if-by-magic materialisation of the CSM. 'Sir,' announced that worthy, 'you command this company, but I run it.' When the relationship works well there are few finer, as Major Justin Featherstone of the Princess of Wales's Royal Regiment tells when describing the way he and CSM Dale Norman used to conduct after-action discussions in the Iraqi town of Al Amarah, scene of fierce fighting in 2004:

We shared what became termed 'DVD time'. During tactical pauses we would watch a DVD on his laptop and take the time to reflect on recent events and discuss our prevailing feelings, with unflinching and disarming honesty that would surprise anyone who had not shared similar experiences; such a friendship was critical in enabling us to function over such a tumultuous period.[16]

Yet a steady support to his company commander can easily seem a tyrant to his subordinates. William St Clair joined the RAMC at the beginning of the First World War, and spent his time on the Western Front in a field ambulance forming part of the admirable 9th Scottish Division, seeing more action than most. His commitment to winning the war never wavered, but he was bitterly disillusioned with the standard of leadership, especially with a sergeant major who delayed his overdue leave and sent 'passes for new chaps before their turn so that most of the boys are a bit disgusted at his attitude'. Less than two months before the Armistice he wrote:

Ach I am so tired of being away and the atmosphere of our unit is worse now than ever ... It is a weary life this with so much in it that goes against the grain, perpetual discipline that any Tom, Dick and Harry can work against you if they feel inclined ... I do not say it is unbearable, but oh my word, what a glorious day it will be when we are free and need take nothing from any man.[17]

With the creation of the new grade of SSM, a cavalry regiment's original sergeant major had been renamed its regimental sergeant major to differentiate him from these lesser myrmidons. When CSMs appeared in the infantry the same rank title was adopted for the unit's senior sergeant major, although 'battalion sergeant major' would have been a more accurate job description, for in the British infantry the battalion, rather than the regiment, has always been the key tactical grouping. And there was another important change. Towards the end of the nineteenth century, the army took up the navy's practice of emphasising the status of key individuals by awarding them warrants, issued by the Army Council, and looking not unlike officers' commissions. This process had swept up sergeant majors, together with other folk, mostly specialists like the Ordnance Corps'

'Conductors of Stores and Supplies'. Warrant officers were now set apart from the NCOs from whose ranks they had risen. They were generally addressed as 'Mr' by their superiors, and even within the infantry tended to deplore the term 'sergeant-major', though Guards officers call their RSMs 'sergeant major' and CSMs 'companys' major'. For many years RSMs were spoken of as 'the regimental' and addressed, in the comfortable fug of the Warrant Officers' and Sergeant's Mess as 'major', although when stalking their domain they were 'Sir' to all their subordinates. But different tribes still have their own rituals, as a Guards RSM explains:

A sergeant's mess in the Household Division would appear to be much more rigid than in other regiments. We never relax. Warrant officers are always called 'sir' … But everything is kept within the four walls. Any misbehaviour or indiscretion is never talked about outside. That would not happen in a line regiment.[18]

In 1915 an army order brought SSMs and CSMs into the fold by making them warrant officers, though it elevated RSMs and their equivalents to 'Warrant Officers Class One' and created the rank of 'Warrant Officer Class Two' for CSMs. Warrant officers enjoyed valuable legal privileges, for the Army Act freed them from punishment by their commanding officer, and specified that even if they were reduced to the ranks by sentence of court martial they would not be required to serve as a private soldier. When he was a sergeant major, William Cobbett had feared that the officers he so despised would reduce him to the ranks if he crossed them: now, at least, sergeant majors were secure from the vagaries of summary punishment.

After the bruising experience of the First World War German army, the British were persuaded that their enemy's practice of using selected senior NCOs to command platoons had much to recommend it. In 1938 the new rank of Warrant Officer Class Three was created, specifically to allow warrant officers to command infantry platoons or Royal Armoured Corps troops. The transplant failed to flourish. Only commissioned officers were allowed to handle official funds. At this time soldiers were paid in cash, and so WO3s could not pay their platoons, but had to get an officer to take pay parades on their behalf. Moreover, while officer platoon commanders were senior to the CSM, and thus in theory able (though it was seldom a simple business) to offer their men some protection against his voracious need for 'bodies' when fatigues were at hand, warrant officer platoon commanders were his juniors, and their men stood naked before his clip-board.

The rank was placed in abeyance in 1940, although those who held it already were allowed to remain WO3s until promoted or discharged. It has left at least one enduring mark on history. When 4th Royal Tank Regiment was hotly engaged in the Arras counter-attack of 21 May 1940, one of its tanks was commanded by an ex-circus 'strong man', WO3 'Muscle' Armit. He had already destroyed two German anti-tank guns when his own gun was damaged, and the tank was hit several times as he tried to repair it. Eventually he reversed under cover, repaired the gun, whacked the jammed turret hatch open (an achievement for which his former profession had so well prepared him), and returned to the fray. 'They must have thought I was finished,' he recalled, 'for I caught the guns limbering up … and revenge was sweet.'[19]

Portsmouth-born George Hogan lived close enough to the Royal Marine barracks at Eastney to hear the bugles sing out the alarm on the morning of 4 August 1914, summoning married men who lived out of barracks to report immediately. The ever-helpful booklet *Trumpet and Bugle Sounds for the Army* gave words to help soldiers remember the various calls, and alarm was officially: 'Larm is sounding, hark the sound/Fills the air for miles around/Arm! Turn out! And stand your ground.' But young George already knew it as 'Sergeant Major's on the run! Sergeant Major's on the run! Sergeant Major's on the run.' His father was a sergeant-cook in the Hampshires and he thought it 'right and reasonable' to join the regiment as a boy soldier, but it was not easy to get photographed with his father. 'Non-commissioned officers and men were not allowed to walk out together,' he remembered, 'so I left home a few minutes before dad and we met at the photographers.' He arrived in France just five days too late to gain the 1914–18 war medal, and a long career took him on through the Second World War. He was promoted WO3 – a rank he remembered in its infantry guise of Platoon Sergeant Major – and added a laurel wreath to the crown on his cuff.[20]

When officers took to wearing collar and tie with their khaki service dress in the early twentieth century, warrant officers, who already sported officer-style Sam Browne belts, followed suit. In 1915 a GHQ instruction still had them armed with sword and pistol, although there were few enough swords to be seen on the Western Front, save in the cavalry, by this time, and instructions had already been issued for sending them home. Nevertheless, a photograph of the RSM of 14/Welsh in 1917 shows an elegant figure with gently waxed moustache, officer-style cap with the stiffening removed, officer's tunic with baggy 'patch pockets', Sam Browne and empty sword frog. It is only when you see the royal coat of arms on his forearm that you can tell that he is actually the RSM, rather than a much grander rank. Small wonder that newly-commissioned officers made awkward mistakes when confronted with such splendid figures, as the greatest of the war's skits, *The Song of Tiadatha*, tells us:

> Then at last my Tiadatha
> Sallied forth to join the Dudshires
> Dressed in khaki, quite a soldier
> Floppy cap and baggy breeches
> Round his waist the supple Sam Browne
> At his side the sword and scabbard
> Took salutes from private soldiers
> And saluted Sergeant-Majors
> (Who were very much embarrassed)
> And reported at Headquarters
> Of the 14th Royal Dudshires.[21]

In contrast, CSM Jack Williams DCM MM and Bar (his VC still in the future) of 10/South Wales Borderers, serving in the same division as the 14/Welsh, is scarcely distinguishable from a private soldier save by the brass crown on his sleeve. Nothing could make the gulf between the two grades of warrant officer clearer.

The RSM of a battalion was part hero, part villain, and part shaman, encapsulating all the glory of his tribe and the status of his rank. John Jackson worked for a Glasgow railway company and enlisted in the Cameron Highlanders ('a choice of regiment which I never regretted') in August 1914. He fought at Loos with its 6th Battalion, and one of his lasting memories was of RSM Peter Scotland, upright and steady, though his battalion had lost both commanding officer ('our brave old colonel') and adjutant ('cool and unruffled to the last') as well as 700 of its 950 officers and men, reading the roll-call after the battle:

> There were few responses as names were called, though what little information there was about missing men was given by friends … Another good friend, big 'Jock' Anderson was missing, and to this day his fate remains an unsolved mystery, but I have no doubt he did his bit, for Jock was a whole-hearted fighter.

Wounded, Jackson was posted to 1/Camerons on his return to France, and the battalion was paraded by RSM Sydney Axton, 'known through all the Cameron ranks as "Old Joe"':

> As a new draft, we had come out wearing khaki kilt aprons, and I well remember the first order of the RSM was, 'Take off your aprons and show your Cameron tartan.' 'Old Joe' was the real old fashioned type of soldier, a smart man in every way, a terror for discipline when on duty, a thorough gentleman off duty. A man who would sing a song or dance with the best; who knew everything there was to know about soldiering, and took the greatest pride in his regiment. His decorations numbered 9, and included the Military Cross, won on the Aisne, and the Distinguished Conduct Medal, won in the South African War, so that he was a real old warrior. His word was law in the battalion, and he would give an officer a 'lecture' just the same as he would a private soldier, so all ranks looked up to him as a man to be respected. Personally I always got on well with him, my duty bringing me often in contact with him, and I soon learned that his bark was worse than his bite.[22]

Doug Beattie was RSM of 1/Royal Irish in March 2003 when Lieutenant Colonel Tim Collins made his famous pre-battle speech before the entry into Kuwait. Beattie feared that the message 'had been rousing, but also sobering. It pulled no punches', and there was a danger that the men would become morose and reflective. And so they were going to stop thinking about Colonel Collins and start paying attention to their regimental sergeant major. And woe betide any who didn't. I began to bollock them. I yelled at them about the pitiful state of their weapons. I laid into them over their poor state of dress, their abysmal personal hygiene, their failure to salute senior officers, their inability to get anywhere on time. I told them they were a disgrace to their uniform and weren't fit to call themselves soldiers of 1 R IRISH. I accused the warrant officers of running slack companies ... I called the CSMs to me. They sprang to attention ... and marched forward, coming to a halt in a perfectly straight line, shoulders back, chests out. Beyond the earshot of the rest of the ranks I explained what I was trying to do ... It is true that battalions are commanded by their officers. If 1 R IRISH was a car the driving would be done by them. But the engine that powers that car is to be found in the sergeants' mess, with the five men now standing bolt upright in front of me.[23]

Today's non-commissioned hierarchy reflects other changes. The Wellingtonian army selected its corporals from trusted private soldiers known, by that most satisfying term, as chosen men. Chosen men soon became lance corporals ('lance-jacks'), with a speculative etymology linking the word to the seventeenth century 'lancepesade'. The word derives from the Italian *lazzia spezzata* or broken lance, because the soldier in question was a veteran, likely to have broken a spear or two in his day. Initially the post of lance corporal, its holder distinguished by a single stripe rather than the maturity of the full corporal's two, was an appointment rather than a rank: easy come, easy go. Before long 'lance' became a prefix for junior sergeants too. Having lance sergeants was a matter of regimental preference, as First World War headstones demonstrate. The Foot Guards have retained the rank, although it really equates with corporal. Any Queen's Birthday Parade will show that lance sergeants, with their three white stripes, are not quite the same as sergeants proper, whose gold braid tapes earn them the sobriquet of gold sergeants.

A short walk through a military cemetery tells one a good deal about an army's character. A First World War German cemetery abounds with the specific ranks that say much about the man who lies beneath the greensward, even if he was only a private soldier. The rank of *grenadier* and *fusilier* shows that he served in a particular sort of regiment. A *jäger*, hunter, is the same as a French *chasseur*, with keen eyes and quick step, and would have served, flat-shakoed, in a *jäger* battalion. A gunner is a *kanonier*, and different sorts of cavalrymen get a proper job description: *hussar, uhlan, kurassier* or *dragoner*. A *kriegsfreiwilliger* had volunteered to serve in the war, a *reservist* was precisely that, and an *ersatz reservist* had contrived (probably through having a student deferment from conscription) to incur a reserve liability even though he had not done basic training.

In a British cemetery of the same era, in contrast, most unpromoted men are privates. Privates in Foot Guards regiments are described as 'Guardsmen', although this rank was granted retrospectively, for it did not exist till 1922. Although ordinary soldiers in the Household Cavalry were termed trooper, they were still called privates in the rest of the cavalry, and the 1922 change in terminology did not affect those who had died before this date. In consequence, the last British soldier killed in the war was Private George Ellison of the 5th (Royal Irish) Lancers, a Leeds man, buried at St Symphorien, just east of the Belgian town of Mons. The rank of trooper first referred to privates in the cavalry, then spread into the Royal Tank Regiment, and has most recently appeared, as the evocative hybrid air trooper, in the Army Air Corps. Rifle regiments had called their soldiers riflemen very early on, and the notion of 'the thinking, fighting rifleman' was an attractive currency.

Fusilier regiments followed with 'fusilier'. The Royal Corps of Electrical and Mechanical Engineers selected the word 'craftsman' for its private soldiers; and the King's Regiment, coming close to the end of its own independent existence in the 1980s, took up 'kingsman' for its private soldiers. The Queen's Regiment considered 'queensman', but consultation with soldiers about to receive the new designation revealed that they were firmly against it, fearing that inter-regimental debates on the word's precise meaning might have regrettable outcomes.

Rank is one thing and appointment another. In an infantry battalion or cavalry regiment the adjutant remains the commanding officer's personal staff officer, responsible for what became known as 'A' matters: everything to do with personnel and discipline. An unrelenting stream of papers on postings, promotions, honours and awards, courses, and court martials surged across his desk. Adjutants usually held the rank of captain from the late nineteenth century, and the post is now an essential part of that *cursus honorum* that takes an officer to the highest ranks. But for the first two-thirds of the army's life adjutants were sometimes ensigns and then, more usually, lieutenants, generally commissioned from the ranks, because any sensible commanding officer wanted an assistant who understood both drill and paperwork, and an ex-sergeant major was just the man.

It was not easy to make the step up, and sometimes colonels made the wrong call. When the Light Brigade spurred off to its rendezvous with immortality in the Crimea, Cornet John Yates was adjutant of the 11th Hussars. Troop Sergeant Major George Loy Smith of the 11th was not pleased about it:

> Unfortunately for us Colonel Douglas allowed Colonel Lawrenson of the 17th Lancers to persuade him that his quartermaster [-sergeant] would make us an excellent adjutant – although at the time our two senior sergeant-majors were both eligible ... I have heard on good authority that Colonel Douglas deeply regretted this act. If he did not I know the whole regiment did, for a worse rider, a worse drill, a greater humbug never before held the rank of adjutant in the British army. The 17th might well be glad to get rid of him; they certainly got the laugh of us.

Cornet Yates (nicknamed 'Joey' by the troopers) had been standing in for a sick staff officer who returned to duty on the day of the battle, but he still managed to avoid the charge. Smith heard a soldier call out 'There goes Joey', and sure enough 'in the distance could be seen the adjutant galloping back towards the encampment. This caused great amusement and laughter – he had only been with us a month and had made himself thoroughly obnoxious to everyone.'[24] Adjutants were generally ex-rankers until well on in the nineteenth century, for, as Lord Panmure, Secretary at War 1846–52, observed, it was hard to get a gentleman subaltern 'to take the office of adjutant from the arduous character of its duties and the constant confinement it requires to barracks'.[25]

What the adjutant did for an individual unit, so the adjutant general did for the army as a whole. He was based alongside the commander-in-chief in Horse Guards, before crossing Whitehall to the Old War Office, then moving to the MOD's Main Building and eventually having his own headquarters at Upavon in Wiltshire before being swept up into the army's new headquarters, Marlborough Lines near Andover. The best adjutant generals combined regimental experience (giving them an understanding of the impact of bureaucracy on the army in the field) with a sharp brain and a thirst for the administrative flood that drenched their regimental counterparts. Henry Torrens, a Londonderry man, was commissioned under-age into the 52nd Foot in 1793, and did a good deal of regimental duty in the West Indies, Portugal, and India. By 1805 he was appointed assistant adjutant general for the Kent district. Another interlude of regimental duty saw him wounded at Buenos Aires, where a musket ball 'shattered a small writing apparatus which was slung to his side'. He became Assistant Adjutant General at Horse Guards, and then Assistant Military Secretary there, with a brief period in the Peninsula. A major general and a knight, Torrens became adjutant general in 1820. He managed to write a drill-book, *Regulations for the Exercise and Field Movements of the Infantry of the Army*, and played an important part in rebalancing the army as it ran down for a long period of peace. Contemporaries thought that his 'excessive labours' had weakened his health, and he died suddenly in 1828.

Individual armies in the field had their own adjutant generals, their tasks mirroring those of regimental adjutants on the one hand and the army's adjutant general on the other. From February 1916 until the end of the war Lieutenant General Sir George Fowke was adjutant general in France. He had gone to war as the BEF's senior Royal Engineer, and his promotion partly reflected GHQ's discomfort with this big, clever man whose influence had grown inexorably with the importance of engineering. As adjutant general he left the routine of office work to others, but retained a penetrating overview, sharpened by a remarkable memory for detail. The scale and diversity of his branch's work emerges from the digest of administrative routine orders issued to help all officers in the adjutantal line. Fowke's branch warned individuals of the danger of being struck by the propellers of low-flying aircraft; established the grounds for reporting a man 'missing, believed killed'; directed units to send the originals of their war diaries up to the Deputy Adjutant General on the last day of each month, and decreed that the only vehicle allowed to fly the Union Jack was the commander-in-chief's.[26]

A commanding officer was no less dependent upon his quartermaster than his adjutant. Quartermasters were originally ex-NCOs given warrants to act in that appointment. When Charles Jones was reviewing officers' duties in 1811 he observed that the quartermaster of the Blues was unusual in that he held a proper commission, but although quartermasters as a group 'stand, in front, at the head of their class, [they] can never be on a level with the youngest cornet'.[27] It was not a status that always made for comfortable relations between veteran quartermasters and less experienced junior officers. In July 1811, Quartermaster John Foster Kingsley of the 30th Foot was court-martialled at Campo Mayor for taking possession of bullock carts reserved, by Wellington's orders, for ammunition and supplies, and using them for his own battalion's equipment. One of the charges against him was that he had disobeyed the orders of Lieutenant Rae of the Royal Scots, who claimed use of the carts. It transpired that Rae had detained two members of the 30th's cart-escort, alleging that they were drunk and insolent. When Kingsley declined to hand over the carts there was a quarrel in the street: Kingsley not only refused to acknowledge Rae's authority but, when Rae threatened to take the carts by force, pointed out that he too had armed men at hand. If Rae demurred, suggested the quartermaster helpfully, then they should step aside and settle the issue 'in a private manner'. Matters were not improved by Kingsley's offer to return the carts when he had finished with them, for the commissariat official with Rae said 'I would not take your word for you are no gentleman', serving only to remind Kingsley of his position. Moreover, as commissariat officials did not hold commissions themselves, it was exasperating for one to lay claim to status that was by no means evident.

Most of the witnesses supported Rae, apart from Hospital Mate Evans, who was about to be appointed assistant surgeon to the 30th, and had good reason for not antagonising its quartermaster. The court martial found Kingsley guilty on two of the three charges against him, agreeing that Rae was indeed his senior officer. Kingsley was suspended from rank and pay for three months, a modest sentence in the circumstances, and earned a surprisingly gentle reproof from Wellington, who reminded him that 'inconvenience may be felt at some time by individuals' but the general interest had to take precedence. A modern quartermaster, shown the court-martial papers, concluded that he would have done exactly the same in Kingsley's place, and put his own battalion first.[28]

After 1871 quartermasters were granted honorary commissions as lieutenants or captains, and the *Manual of Military Law* emphasised that, even though they still held substantive warrant rank, this made them officers within the meaning of the Army Act. They were invariably promoted from the ranks, usually moving on to be their battalion's quartermaster after having served as its RSM. It was not until after the First World War that they were given full commissions, and not until later that the concept of a 'Late Entry' commission was introduced, enabling commissioned ex-warrant officers to do a wide variety of jobs. The post of quartermaster had never been the only outlet for officers commissioned from the ranks. There was the adjutant's appointment until it became the preserve of mainstream officers. The regimental post of paymaster, once thought highly suitable for an ex-NCO, had become attractive to gentleman officers rather earlier, because it was seen to be 'one of the best appointments in the service' from a financial point of view. Riding masters in the cavalry were commissioned from the ranks, and the post still exists in the Household Cavalry. Later, directors of music (senior to bandmasters, who are warrant officers) and masters at arms in the Army Physical Training Corps were also ex-rankers. However, the concept of the Late Entry commission enabled such officers to do a wider variety of jobs than ever before, perhaps commanding headquarters companies in infantry battalions or furnishing the Royal Army Medical Corps with the non-medical administrative officers it needs.

Doug Beattie was commissioned in 2005 after his tour as RSM of 1/R Irish and twenty-two years' service, and acknowledged that while this gave him the opportunity to stay in the army 'for the immediate future and well beyond', there was a catch. The army thought him 'best suited to a training and logistical role'. After a training job he would then be likely to return to his old battalion where 'I would probably become a welfare officer, looking after the families of those going off to fight.' It was not for him, and he decided to resign. Before his resignation took effect, though, he was posted to Afghanistan, where he won a Military Cross in a burst of desperate fighting alongside the Afghan National Army and police at Garmsir in 2006. Although still determined to leave the army, he was unable to resist the opportunity of helping his own battalion prepare for its Afghanistan tour, and accompanying them when it deployed. 'Soldiering was what I did and what I knew', he wrote. 'It was in my blood.'[29] His unhappiness with the sorts of jobs on offer after commissioning is not untypical. It reflects a slow transition, not yet completed, between old army and new.

It is impossible to overemphasise either the importance of quartermasters or their impact on superiors and subordinates alike. Some might indeed have deserved the description given the quartermaster of a cavalry regiment in the Indian Mutiny as 'old, excessively conceited, disobliging and ungentlemanly ...'[30] Their passage through the ranks will not have imbued them with profound confidence in human nature; they will be older than most officers of their rank, and, although the selection of mainstream officers from a broader background continues to reduce the social differences between quartermasters and their brother officers, they will certainly not be graduates in a largely graduate officers' mess. At their best they are sources of wise advice as well as solid professional expertise, and are often remembered long after most other officers are forgotten.

In his *Sherston's Progress* trilogy, Siegfried Sassoon modelled that 'husky-voiced old campaigner', the gruff but kindly Joe Dottrell, quartermaster of 2/Royal Welch Fusiliers, on its real quartermaster, Captain Yates. He also appears to no less advantage in *The War the Infantry Knew*, the battalion's unofficial history, compiled by Captain James Churchill Dunn, its medical officer for much of the war. Yates met the battalion as it stumbled back from Le Cateau in 1914. 'The Quartermaster had some stew and tea ready, and we had an issue of rum, and, what was still better, some letters from home.' He got the men away, a platoon at a time, to have a bath – 'badly needed' – when the battalion held autumnal trenches above the Aisne. On St David's Day 1916 (sacred to the Royal Welch) he secured, though we can only guess how, 'a leek for everyone's cap.' He saved time and trouble by keeping his transport close behind the battalion on the Somme, though everyone else's was sent further back. When the battalion ran dangerously short of ammunition in the German spring offensive of

1918 'Yates has made up, although scrounging is not so easy as formerly.' When the war ended he not only took home 'a complete Mobilisation Store for a battalion, down to the last horseshoe and strap,' but a complete German mortar acquired by the brigadier and 'innumerable brass shell-cases' that Yates and the adjutant had collected. And at last, when the battalion paraded through Wrexham on its arrival in Britain, he astonished those who had no notion of there having been a Mrs Yates by spotting her amongst the crowd: 'forty years of army discipline were forgotten, he dashed from the ranks, and greeted her heartily and unblushingly.'[31]

The quartermaster's subordinates were headed by the regimental quartermaster sergeant, from 1913 a warrant officer, and included an assortment of storemen, with cooks, grooms, and transport-men often coming under his command too. He had a particular lien on company quartermaster sergeants who, like him, were known as quarter-blokes. Although his post was not the most martial, RQMS T.W. Fitzpatrick of 2/Royal Irish did more than most to save the BEF on 23 August 1914, assembling a scratch force (including the battalion's armourer, Sergeant Redmond, with that useful asset, a newly-repaired machine gun) to hold the Bascule crossroads near Mons. He was awarded a Distinguished Conduct Medal and a commission for the day's work, and ended the war a lieutenant colonel.

As adjutant generals were to adjutants, so quartermaster generals were to quartermasters. Yet there was one big difference. Although a quartermaster general and his Q staff were responsible for accommodation and quartering, supplies of all sorts, remounts and accounting, neither the army's quartermaster general, nor the quartermaster general of a deployed force, would ever have been a battalion quartermaster. Wully Robertson, the BEF's quartermaster general in 1914, had indeed served in the ranks, though he had been commissioned long before he was eligible to be quartermaster. It is a reflection of the army's relationship with its own logisticians that Lieutenant General Sir Paul Travers, who had spent much of his career in the Royal Corps of Transport, was the first professional logistician to become quartermaster general, in 1982. It was not until the late nineteenth century that the army's logistic services were militarised, and even then there was more than a little disdain, on the part of what became known as the 'teeth arms', for the supporting services.

This did not prevent some quartermaster generals from being very competent. Perhaps the most outstanding of them was General Sir John Cowans, in post for the whole of the First World War and according to Asquith 'the best quartermaster since Moses'. He combined regimental service in the Rifle Brigade, into which he had been commissioned in 1881, with a series of logistic staff jobs. He was urbane and tireless, and, unusually amongst officers who had grown up in a small army, had the capacity to think big. He got on well with ministers – not always a simple task in that uneasy world of frocks and brass-hats – and his 'penchant for other men's wives' may have endeared him to Lloyd George.[32]

When Wully Robertson stepped up from being QMG in France to take over as the BEF's chief of staff in 1915, the post went to Ronald Maxwell. But he was replaced in December 1917 because of political pressure, and against Haig's wishes, by Travers Clarke. Maxwell had been good but Clarke was even better, an extraordinary administrator who coped with both the haemorrhaging of resources after the slashing cut of the German 1918 offensive and the unprecedented demands of the mobile warfare of the last Hundred Days. It says something of the way that history is written (for we scribblers prefer warriors to logisticians) that few, even amongst the war's more serious historians, give him the attention he deserves. Major General Hubert Essame likened him to Lazare Carnot, who had done so much to keep the threadbare warriors of revolutionary France in the field, and called him the 'Carnot of Haig's armies'.

Clarke's department worried about the allowances in lieu of billets available to French and Belgian interpreters; the relationship between ammunition parks at corps level and their satellite divisional sub-parks; and the process of compensating landowners for damage to trees and other property. It had a comprehensive policy on the recycling of damaged equipment, advising that 'any boot which is not badly cut in the uppers can be repaired, and if doubt exists it is better to err on the safe side, and class the boot as repairable.' When the Machine Gun Corps was formed in 1915, the QMG's branch had to devise new scales of equipment, so that cavalry machine gun squadrons received, inter alia, two chisels, one plane, one bench vice, and a saddletree-maker (to equip the horses with the packs used to transport ammuntion and the guns themselves). It issued instruction on correspondence, from ordinary letters, through express delivery and on to weekend letter telegrams, which could be sent from France to certain colonies or dependencies provided that they were written in plain English or French and included no code-words.

Rations were a major preoccupation, with a complex shopping list of entitlements and alternatives for man and beast. Men working in arduous conditions could receive extra tea and sugar daily, and two ounces of pea soup or two Oxo cubes twice weekly during the winter months. Indian rations included ghee, ghur, ginger, chillies, and turmeric; and Africans were entitled to a pound and a half of mealie meal per man per day. Transport of all sorts was the responsibility of Q Branch: spares, spark-plugs and speeding all merited entries in routine orders. Finally, the branch even ventured into matters adju-tantal, warning that officers had been seen returning from France to the United Kingdom wearing Sam Browne belts from which the braces and frog had been removed. At least one of the braces should be worn at all times, although (generous concession) the frog need only be worn with the sword itself.[33]

Historically, the quartermaster general of a field army was its commander's chief staff officer, for military operations were so intim-ately concerned with supply and movement that it was natural for the QMG's branch to take the lead. Both Marlborough's chief of staff, William Cadogan, and Wellington's, George Murray, were formally entitled quartermaster general, and Richard Airey, who made his own imprecise contribution to the misunderstandings that led to the Charge of the Light Brigade, held the same title, although he was effectively Lord Raglan's chief of staff. The title chief of staff did not appear till the end of the nineteenth century, and by the First World War he was defined as the commander's 'responsible adviser for all matters affecting all matters of military operations ... by whom all orders to field units will be signed.'[34] The general staff (G Branch) was *primus inter pares*, with overriding responsibility for all orders, operations, communication, censorship and legal issues.

Until the British adopted the NATO staff system in the 1980s, their staff officers had titles prefixed with GSO (for General Staff Officer). A number indicated their ranks, with GSO1 for lieutenant colonels, '2' for majors and '3' for captains. The chief of staff of a brigade had long been its brigade major, assisted, as the First World War went on, by two staff captains, A and Q. Terminology changed, within NATO, to the prefix SO (for Staff Officer) and a number for rank, mirroring the old British system, and then a designation that places the officer precisely within the appropriate general staff branch, with its G prefix: thus SO2 G3 Training is a major in the training branch of a headquarters. The old GOC, for General Officer Commanding, is now replaced by 'commander', and brigade majors, like their equivalents at higher levels, are now chiefs of staff. Adding acronyms stirs that alphabet soup which itself contributes to a military sense of identity by helping form a language all but impenetrable to outsiders. The British commander of the NATO Allied Rapid Reaction Corps is COMARRC, and his chief of staff (with a whiff of the steppe) COSARRC. Chief of staff survives, at least conversationally, unabbreviated, but his deputy is generally clipped down to the unlovely Dee-Cos.

CHAPTER 5

TO OBSERVE AND OBEY

THE NOTION OF a universal hierarchy in the army was slow to evolve. For instance, until 1788 troopers in the Life Guards were 'private gentlemen', initially recruited from that flotsam of gentry left unemployed after the Civil War, and expected to buy their own costly uniforms. In 1678 the separate troops of Life Guards had been reinforced by the newly raised Horse Grenadier Guards who used explosives in battle. Diarist John Evelyn described them at camp on Hounslow Heath as 'dextrous in flinging hand Granados, every one having a pouch full; they had furred hats with coped crowns like Janissaries, which made them look very fierce ...'[1] In contrast to the gentlemen of the Life Guards, however, privates in the Horse Grenadiers were just like private soldiers in the rest of the army. As time went on, service in the ranks, even the ranks of the Life Guards, became less attractive to a gentleman, all the more so because his 1660 pay of £73 a year (then equivalent to the income of 'Eminent Clergymen') was eroded by inflation and by the 1780s an artisan might expect to earn at least as much.[2] By then the Life Guards had become recruited with 'native Londoners with alternative sources of income, whose part-time jobs as private gentlemen simply furthered family business interests'.[3]

The 1788 reform replaced the existing troops of Life Guards and the Horse Grenadiers, with two new regiments: the 1st Life Guards and the 2nd Life Guards. These would now be recruited like the rest of the army, although the grenade badge on officers' cloaks remained as a last echo of the Horse Grenadiers. This induced the Duke of York to write 'I was a little sorry for the Horse Grenadiers because they were to a degree soldiers, but the Life Guards were nothing but a collection of London Tradespeople.' Their regimental custom of addressing their men as 'gentlemen' harks back to an older world, and so too does the Household Cavalry practice of addressing lieutenant colonels and above by their rank rather than as 'sir'. The reform also did away with the old Life Guards rank terminology, where commissioned ranks below captain (just two for the army as a whole) had been cornet, guidon, exempt, brigadier, and sub-brigadier. It left the Household Cavalry with an NCO terminology that still endures. Lance corporals are lance corporals, just as they would be in the rest of the army. But corporals are styled 'lance corporal of horse', sergeants are 'corporal of horse', staff sergeants are 'staff corporals', squadron sergeant majors are 'squadron corporal majors', and the regiment's senior non-commissioned member is the 'regimental corporal major'.

The reforms did nothing about the advantageous double-ranking system enjoyed by Guards officers. Central to its operation was the concept that rank in the army and rank in a given regiment were distinct. In 1687 captains in the Guards were given the army rank of lieutenant colonel. Four years later, the privilege was extended to lieutenants, who ranked as majors in the army. Finally in 1815 – as a reward for the conduct of the Foot Guards at Waterloo – ensigns were granted lieutenancies in the army. When a Guards officer reached the rank of major in his regiment he was at once made a colonel in the army. Formally a Guards captain would style himself 'captain and lieutenant colonel', but the custom of referring to officers by their higher army rank, clear enough at the time, easily causes confusion now.

At Waterloo there was a glut of colonels in and around the farm complex of Hougoumont. The light companies of the 1st, Coldstream, and 3rd Guards played a distinguished part in the defence of the Hougoumont, standing like a breakwater in front of Wellington's right centre. All the company commanders, captains by regimental rank, enjoyed lieutenant-colonelcies in the army. James Macdonnell of the Coldstream was in overall command; Charles Dashwood of 3rd Guards in the garden and farm surrounds; Henry Windham of the Coldstream in the château and farm; with Lord Saltoun of 1st Guards in the orchard. Eventually Lieutenant Colonel Alexander Woodford (and a 'proper' lieutenant colonel in this context), commanding 2nd Coldstream Guards, was sent down with most of his battalion from Major General Sir John Byng's brigade up on the ridge. Although he was now the senior officer in the area, Woodford generously let James Macdonnell remain in command. The burly Macdonnell had already distinguished himself by leading the handful of guardsmen who had closed the farm's north gate after the French burst in. Private Matthew Clay of 3rd Guards 'saw Lieutenant Colonel Macdonnell carrying a large piece of wood or trunk of a tree in his arms (one of his cheeks marked with blood, his charger bleeding within a short distance) with which he was hastening to secure the gates against the renewed attacks of the enemy.'[4] Some called him 'the bravest man in England' for his part in animating the defence, although he always maintained that it was a team effort. He was knighted and ended his days as a general.[5]

Guards officers eventually lost their double rank in 1871, with the reforms accompanying the abolition of the purchase of commissions. It had always been more than just a genteel way of ensuring that the 'Gentlemen's sons' – as Guards officers were known in the Wellingtonian army – enjoyed added status. This had practical advantages: a force made up of several units or detachments was commanded by the senior officer, by army rank, present. As a general's rank came by seniority from the date of promotion to lieutenant colonel, a Guards captain found himself on the roll from the date of his appointment. This increased his prospects of becoming a general early, and a handful of officers did indeed find themselves major generals in the army while still doing duty as captains in their own regiments.

Andrew Wheeler of the 1st Guards was commissioned in 1678, promoted to captain and lieutenant colonel in 1692, became a major general in 1727, and died a regimental captain three years later. More typical was Richard, sixth Earl of Cavan, commissioned in 1744, made captain and lieutenant colonel in 1756 and major general in 1772. He departed to command the 55th Foot as a regimental lieutenant colonel in 1774, and died, by now a lieutenant general, in 1778.[6] Major Charles Jones, author of the *The Regimental Companion* (1811), argued that dual rank 'has often been detrimental on real service, is always a cause of distracting jealousy to the line, and has never … offered one solid advantage'. Ending purchase did not end the concept of dual rank. This situation initiated a long-running joke: a foreign officer in British pay, marching through Portugal in 1810, saw a senior Guards officer astride a donkey:

'What a beautiful mule that is!'
'It is not a mule, my good fellow, it is a jack-ass.'
'Pardon me, it would indeed be a jack-ass in the line, but because it belongs to the Guards it must be a mule by brevet.'[7]

From its earliest days the army had granted promotion as a reward for gallant or distinguished service, and this was known as brevet promotion. It was especially relevant in an age where medals and decorations were not generally available, and could be awarded individually or to a whole group. By the nineteenth century brevet was available, as an individual reward, only to officers who were already captains, and it could not take a man beyond colonel. Captain Garnet Wolseley, commissioned into the 12th Foot in 1852, was repeatedly put up for the brevet promotion for which his harum-scarum courage qualified him. But the military secretary regretted that he had not yet acquired the six years service that brevet rank demanded:

As Captain Wolseley has only been about three years and six months in the service, he is ineligible under the regulations to be promoted to the rank of Major, for which otherwise, in consideration of the services described by Sir Harry Jones, he would have been happy to have recommended him.[8]

Another hero of the Indian Mutiny, Lieutenant Henry Norman, had so many recommendations that all he needed was his captaincy for the honours to kick in. 'On the day of his captaincy,' wrote a delighted brother officer, 'he will be Major, Lieut-Colonel, CB [Companion of the Order of the Bath], perhaps full colonel. He deserves it all and more.'[9] Fred Roberts (who was to die as a field marshal in France in 1914) received his brevet majority on the day that his captaincy was gazetted in 1860, and a brevet lieutenant colonelcy followed almost immediately. Brevets were granted generously and gave commanders a quick and easy way of showing their approval.

The sniper's fire of individual brevets, aimed at individuals, was interlocked with the wholesale bombardment of general brevet promotions that caught up whole batches of officers of similar seniority. In 1810 Henry Torrens assured a colonel that 'It keeps up the spirit of an army to give frequent promotion to a Class of Men who have nothing to look to but the honourable attainment of rank in their profession.' He enclosed an *Army List* showing the impact of a proposed general brevet. It would make 'the Cols of 1803 and 1804 to be Major Generals, the Lieut Cols of 1800 to be Colonels, the remainder of the Majors of 1802 and the whole of 1803 to be Lieut Colonels.' He added a postscript saying that he had just calculated the speed of promotion across the army, and reckoned that a man would be 'tolerably fortunate' to make lieutenant colonel with fifteen years' service, and it would take him ten more years to make colonel and another seven as colonel before he became a major general. This meant that 'the *more fortunate*' of those who had entered the army at 16, could make major general at 51. The last general brevet, he added, had indeed promoted its youngest major general at 51 but its youngest lieutenant general at 75. Torrens understandably added an exclamation mark.[10]

General brevet promotions could mark an event like a Royal Jubilee, or the end of a war. A large promotion followed peace in 1815 'to reward those by whose brilliant service the peace had been achieved'.[11] When the army was being shrunk in the 1820s, brevet rank was used as an inducement to get officers to leave. They could retire with 'Superior Brevet Rank in the Army' and receive the half-pay of that new rank. They could then, if they wished, sell this 'Unattached Half-Pay Commission', an enticing departure from the general principle that one could only sell a commission that had been bought. There were an enormous amount of general brevets awarded in 1846, 1851, and 1854, but the process created a huge amount of elderly generals: the average age of major generals in the 1854 brevet was over 65. Over a twenty-year period half the major generals had not served for ten years, many had not served for twenty, and one had had no service for thirty-five. General brevets were abolished in 1854 and a fixed establishment for general officers was introduced, with rules for promotion and retirement.

A brevet officer usually did duty in his regimental rank, though serving outside his regiment – for instance, as aide-de-camp to a general – would allow him to be employed in his army rank, and to draw the full pay for it. There were certain other advantages. In 1869 it was laid down that captains holding a major's brevet would be allocated cabins in troopships ahead of mere regimental captains; and in 1898 all brevet officers were ordered to wear the badges and appurtenances of their army rank. An order of 1912, however, ungenerously warned that brevet rank did not exempt an officer from passing the appropriate promotion examinations.

The over-generous use of brevets, together with the granting of temporary rank to help officer an army swollen by war, could create anomalies, with a favoured few enjoying temporary and brevet rank well in excess of their regimental rank. The Duke of Marlborough tried to explain that just because an officer had a temporary commission as brigadier, and brevets taking him through major to colonel, he was still not the senior captain in his own regiment, and when all the froth and bubble had gone, he was likely to finish up commanding a company again. 'Besides Colonel Hollins having a commission as brigadier,' wrote the duke, 'does nowise exempt him from his duty as major, and there are older captains in the first regiment to whom it would be a prejudice when they come to roll together.'[12] In 1767, a dispute over command of the Cork garrison between Lieutenant Colonel Tulikens of the 45th Foot and Lieutenant Colonel Cunningham (regimentally a captain in the 45th, but holding his senior rank by brevet) established that 'When corps join either in camp, garrison or quarters, the oldest officer (whether by Brevet or any other commission) is to command the whole.'[13]

Brevet promotion lasted for much of the twentieth century, although it was increasingly discredited. On 26 August 1914, 1st Battalion the Gordon Highlanders formed part of the 3rd Division, holding the line in front of Audencourt at the battle of Le Cateau. Troops in that sector did not receive the order for a general withdrawal, and so, true to the standards of that tough old army, they fought on. At about 7.45 p.m. that evening Colonel William Gordon VC, second in command of the Gordons as a regimental major, noted that his battalion now had a company of Royal Scots and two of Royal Irish fighting alongside it. He immediately took command of the combined force by virtue of his army rank, which made him senior to Lieutenant Colonel Neish, his own commanding officer. The little party began to fall back just after midnight. It eventually collided with a field gun blocking the route, and although the Gordons rushed the piece before it could be fired, nearby Germans immediately stood to their arms and after an hour's battle the British were overwhelmed. The Gordons lost about five hundred men, although a few survivors made their way through the German lines to Antwerp and on to England.

'The fortune of war was hard upon the 1/Gordons', lamented the official historian. 'For the time, they practically ceased to exist as a battalion.'[14] Survivors found the circumstances of the capture extremely galling, and after the war there was a civil action when Gordon sued a Dundee newspaper for repeating a story that he had ordered the men to lay down their arms: he demanded £5,000 and received £500, which was nevertheless a substantial sum. Whatever the truth of the decision to surrender, command arrangements had certainly not made for a quick decision at a moment when time was of the essence. Nor did brevet rank make Major General Hubert Hamilton's task any easier at Le Cateau. His 3rd Division was bearing the brunt of the battle, but when Brigadier General McCracken of 7th Infantry Brigade was wounded, Hamilton had to send for the *Army List* to determine that, although both Lieutenant Colonel Bird of the Royal Irish and Lascelles of the Worcesters were substantive lieutenant colonels, and the latter had gained substantive rank first, Bird had an earlier lieutenant colonel's brevet that gave him command of the brigade.

Brevet rank lapsed in 1952 but reappeared (though only for major to lieutenant colonel) two years later, to increase the field of selection for promotion to colonel, and 'earmark outstanding officers and give them incentive'.[15] It was finally abolished in 1967, although it lingered on into the twenty-first century in the Territorial Army, for specific use in the case of a territorial second-in-command of a unit normally commanded by a regular officer.

Even if no brevet rank was involved, an officer could be granted temporary or local rank, both of limited duration and the latter more fragile than the first. Local rank began by having a specific geographical limitation, like the 'for America only' caveat that made James Wolfe a major general in 1759. When Lieutenant General Thomas Gage, commander-in-chief, formed his command into three brigades, Lieutenant Colonel Robert Pigot (in Boston in 1775) was promoted locally to brigadier general. He was to command his own 38th Foot, together with the 5th and 52nd. It was Pigot's brigade that led the decisive break into the Patriots' redoubt on Breed's Hill (the key point in the battle known as Bunker Hill), and Lord Dartmouth, Secretary of State for the American Department, announced in the *Gazette* that 'the Success of the Day must in great Measure be attributed to his firmness and Gallantry.' It brought him not only one of the first available regimental colonelcies, but promotion to local major general. He succeeded to his brother's baronetcy in 1777, and shortly afterwards seniority brought him the substantive step of major general. Sir Robert was promoted lieutenant general in 1782, three years after his return to England. He did not serve again, but devoted himself to the improvement of his estate at Patshull, work begun by his elder brother, who had consulted Lancelot 'Capability' Brown.[16]

Temporary rank was linked to a specific appointment, but, unlike local rank which was generally unpaid, brought its holder the appropriate pay. The *London Gazette* solemnly deprived Winston Churchill of the temporary lieutenant colonelcy he had been granted in early 1916 to command 6/Royal Scots Fusiliers, and when he returned to politics that summer he reverted to major in the Queen's Own Oxfordshire Hussars. The rules could be very hard. Colonel Charles MacGregor was promoted to temporary major-general to serve as quartermaster-general in India in 1881, bypassing the appointment of brigadier. Although he held the post for four years, and was knighted in the process, he gave it up before seniority had yet made him a major general and so crashed back to colonel, and although he made a dignified protest, the system would not budge. Already mortally ill, he set off home. A *Gazette* of 18 February 1887 duly promoted him to major general, with seniority backdated to 22 January, but he had died at Cairo on 5 February and never knew of it.

The two world wars saw a huge expansion of local and temporary rank with the Second World War seeing the creation of a 'war substantive' rank which was precisely what its name suggests. The youngest British brigadier general in the First World War was Roland Boys Bradford, killed outside Bourlon Wood in 1917 at the age of 24, still only a substantive captain. The youngest major general of the war was the notoriously testy Keppel Bethell, described by one of his staff officers as 'the most insubordinate man I have ever met'. He gained the temporary rank in March 1918 but never rose above substantive captain during the whole war, becoming temporary major in 1915, brevet major in 1916, and brevet lieutenant colonel in 1917. At that time promotion to full colonel came after four years as a lieutenant colonel and Bethell duly became a colonel in 1921, though it took him till 1930, six years before he retired, to get his second star back.

In 1944 Michael Carver took over 4th Armoured Brigade in Normandy, becoming, at the age of thirty, the youngest British brigade commander of the war. He had been commissioned into the Royal Tank Corps in 1935 and took command of 1st Royal Tank Regiment in 1942: his driver remembered him as a 'young, serious and very professional soldier, devoid of messes and batmen'.[17] Carver later made no secret of the fact that 'my attitude to politics and inherited privilege was … left of centre.'[18] One of his first acts was 'to rid myself of the encumbrance of my second-in-command, who served no useful purpose'.[19] He then decided that the commanding officer of his brigade's motor battalion, 2/King's Royal Rifle Corps had 'lost his grip', and decided to replace him.[20] Rightly sensing trouble, he asked another senior officer from the same regiment to visit the battalion to double-check, and then duly sacked the commanding officer. When Carver proposed to lead an attack with the Royal Scots Greys, his divisional commander objected 'Couldn't you send a less well-known regiment?' Undaunted, he moved on to unseat another commanding officer, Sandy Cameron of 3rd County of London Yeomanry, an experienced warrior with bars to both his DSO and MC. 'He greatly resented the decision,' admitted Carver, 'but 20 years later wrote me a charming letter admitting that I had been right.'

Carver was fortunate in gaining a temporary lieutenant-colonelcy after the war, to work for 'a dull, characterless gunner … a dead loss'.[21] He did not get command of a brigade again until 1960, sixteen years after commanding one in battle. But he was more fortunate than Peter Young, just four days younger, who led a Commando brigade in Burma in early 1945. Young did not become a lieutenant colonel again till 1953, when he went off to command a regiment in the Arab Legion. He left the army in 1959, still a lieutenant colonel, granted the honorary rank of brigadier on his retirement to run the military history department at Sandhurst, where he became this author's first boss.

The army still grants temporary and local rank. The former is often awarded to an officer beginning an appointment in the course of which he will get promoted in the normal way of things, but there are times when temporary rank may reflect a wholly exceptional circumstance. In December 2007 Colonel Richard Iron was made a temporary brigadier to serve alongside the Iraqi army, helping develop its counter-insurgency plan for Basra. The British army's run-down in Basra was primarily dictated by the political requirement to minimise casualties. Iron became a unrepentantly controversial figure. He was close to senior Iraqi officers who felt that they had received insufficient help, and he later suggested that the British had deviated from the principles of counter-insurgency that they, of all people, should have understood. He reverted to colonel on his return in 2008, and the following spring was appointed Companion of the Order of St Michael and St George, on the recommendation of the Foreign Office, which has a proprietary interest in this award. Local rank usually reflects a short term expedient. For instance, when 4th Armoured Brigade was preparing to deploy for the first Gulf War, its established 'Transition To War' posts were immediately filled by the grant of local rank.[22]

CHAPTER 6

WEEKEND WARRIORS

THE ASSOCIATION BETWEEN the (full-time) regular army and (part-time) volunteer and auxiliary forces has been long, for there was a militia long before there were regulars. This has been a complex (and often unedifying) association, with militia units being 'embodied' for occasional full-time service in the eighteenth and nineteenth centuries, and the Territorial Army being merged, lock, stock, and barrel into 'a single integrated national army' in 1940. Two of the most irritating acronyms in my own time were STABs ('Stupid TA Bastards') and ARABs ('Arrogant Regular Army Bastards'). The Reserve Forces Act 1996 made it much easier than before to mobilise reservists in situations short of major war, and 13,510 were called up between the invasion of Iraq in 2003 and 1 June 2007. They served in a wide variety of posts, from deputy brigade commanders to private soldiers, sometimes absorbed within regular units, and sometimes serving in composite TA companies.

There were more triumphs than disasters. 1/Princess of Wales's Royal Regiment took a slice of Territorials with it to Al Amarah in 2004. Charlie Curry, a regular captain, describes the integration of a multiple (half-platoon) of Scots Territorials into his company:

We had ownership of them from the start of their mobilisation and they were trained centrally by the battle group prior to deployment. We had teething problems as we whittled down those not physically or mentally tough enough for the job in hand … What remained was a very well motivated multiple commanded by Sgt Steve Cornhill and supported by Cpl Steve Marsh and LCpl Sven Wentzel. These regs would assist in the integration of the multiple on ops, and eventually step back to allow the TA ranks to take the leash. It is worthy of note that other TA soldiers wound up in company HQ and in other multiples within the company. One such individual was Cpl 'H' Hogarth who went into the company signals detachment and manned the ops room throughout the tour … he was a fantastic operator, could effectively run the ops room alone, and could fix anything he turned his hand to – a top lad.[1]

A regular Royal Armoured Corps NCO in the same battle group was also impressed by the Territorials he served alongside. 'At the beginning I thought that because they were part-timers I would be better than them,' he wrote, 'but they soon changed my mind. I would honestly work in any environment with them again, and I made some really good mates.'[2]

The regular army could not have fought either world war without a massive influx of non-regulars, with the TA, with all its strengths and weaknesses, taking the strain before the ponderous engine of conscription could cut in. In terms of Britain's long-term relationship with her defenders, locally recruited auxiliary forces have always been more visible than regulars, who are either away campaigning or mewed up in barracks that have become increasingly forbidding. For most of the army's history, there were more auxiliaries than regulars actually stationed in Britain. In 1935 Lieutenant Colonel J. K. Dunlop wrote that

In these days, most of the Regular battalions are concentrated in one or other of our great military training areas – Aldershot, Salisbury Plain, or Catterick. The Militia is no longer in existence, and there are large areas of the land without any visible sign of the existence of the British Army were it not for the local Territorial Army unit.[3]

Things are different today only in that the TA's geographical 'footprint' of training centres is about one-tenth the size of that in 1935.

Service in the *fyrd*, the Old English word for army, was one of the 'common burdens' shouldered by free men of the Anglo-Saxon kingdoms, who were obliged 'to build fortifications, repair bridges and undertake military service'.[4] I can scarcely think of the *fyrd* save in terms of that dark October day in 1066 when Duke William beat Harold Godwinson on Senlac Hill to seize the crown of England. But it remained a useful asset even to the victorious Normans. Levies from the northern shires stood steady around the great bloc of dismounted knights (all hefting sword and spear beneath the consecrated banners from the minsters of York, Beverley, and Ripon that gave the fight its name) to break the wild rush of King David's Scotsmen at the Battle of the Standard in 1138. An obligation for military service was incorporated in the Assize of Arms of 1181 and the Statute of Winchester of 1285, and embodied into the first militia acts in 1558. In the absence of a standing army, the process of selecting men for military service 'kept the more established householders at home and sent abroad those socially less desirable persons whom deputy [lord] lieutenants and [village] constables wished to be rid of'.[5]

The practice of calling up the most easily spared sat uneasily alongside the theory that the country was best defended by free men with a stake in its welfare. Sir Francis Bacon had argued that sturdy yeomen made the best soldiers: tenants, cottagers, and labourers were too servile; vagrants and vagabonds unstable and unfit. The Trained Bands, formed in 1572 in an effort to modernise the militia, were essentially county militia regiments, controlled by the lord lieutenants (who entrusted the heavy lifting to their deputies). They were composed of freeholders, householders and their sons, taught how to use pike and musket by a small number of professional soldiers – the rough equivalents of Permanent Staff Instructors in today's TA. The quality of the trained bands was mixed, partly because the more affluent strove to avoid personal service but sent servants or hired substitutes to represent them. In 1642 the London Trained Bands numbered 8,000 men in six regiments, named the Red, Blue, Green, White, Orange, and Yellow. They were certainly better than most, partly because of the role they played in providing guards and contingents for the ceremonies of mercantile London. There was an intimate connection between status in the city and rank in the Trained Bands: all the colonels were aldermen. They also gained much benefit from the existence of the city's voluntary military associations, like the 'Martial Yard', 'The Gentlemen of the

Private and Loving Company of Cripplegate', and 'The Society of the Artillery Garden'.

Many of the enthusiasts belonging to these clubs would have read the drill-books of the period, perhaps taking note of Robert Ward's warning in his 1639 *Animadversions of Warre* that drinking was 'the great fault of the English nation' and particularly of English martial culture. Ward was profoundly mistrustful of the Trained Bands, and his observations prefigure the exasperated comments of many regular soldiers who have tried to train part-timers. Their training periods were

> Matters of disport and things of no moment ... after a little careless hurrying over their postures, with which the companies are nothing bettered, they make them charge their muskets, and so prepare to give their captain a brave volley of shot at his entrance into his inn: where after having solaced themselves for a while after this brave service every man repairs home, and that which is not so well-taught then is easily forgotten before the next training.[6]

In 1642 the London Trained Bands were commanded by Sergeant Major General Philip Skippon, newly returned from the Dutch service, who led them out to Turnham Green that autumn to take part in 'the Valmy of the English Civil War' when they helped face off the victorious royalists and save London. 'Come my honest brave boys,' called Skippon, 'pray heartily and fight heartily, and God will bless us.' He soon went off to command the infantry in the Earl of Essex's Parliamentarian army, but the Trained Bands remained a valuable part of Parliament's order of battle thereafter, though they were never wholly comfortable far from their wards and warrens, with mournful cries of 'Home, home' letting commanders know that they had been campaigning too long.

The Cornish Trained Bands, too, were formidable soldiers, though hugely reluctant to serve in foreign parts, that is, east of the Tamar. However, they formed the nucleus of those remarkable 'voluntary regiments' under Sir Bevil Grenville, Sir Nicholas Slanning, Colonel William Godolphin, Colonel John Trevannion, and Lord Mohun that were to form the mainstay of the king's army in the west. 'These were the very best foot I ever saw,' acknowledged the royalist cavalry officer,

Captain Richard Atkyns, 'for marching and fighting ... but could not well brook our horse (especially when we were drawn up on corn) but would let fly at us.' There is more than an echo of Xenophon's wry suggestion to his Greek infantry (peasant farmers and thus horse-haters to a man) that they should pay no attention to Persian cavalry, for nobody he knew of had been killed by a horse-bite.

The King's western colonels were men whose local power under-lines the intimate connection between social standing and the ability to raise troops. This stretched far back into a feudal past and was still important in 1914, when the Earl of Derby raised four battalions of Liverpool Pals, presenting their soldiers with a solid silver cap-badge of the Derby crest. Grenville died atop Lansdown Hill outside Bath in June 1643. 'When I came to the top of the hill,' remembered Captain Atkyns, 'I saw Sir Bevil Grenville's stand of pikes, which certainly preserved our army from a total rout, with the loss of his most precious life.'[7] At his master's side that day, in war as in peace, was the gigantic retainer Anthony Payne. Sir Bevil's eldest son John was a 15-year-old ensign in the regiment, and when his father slid from the saddle Payne swung the lad up into it, and gave him the dead colonel's sword. The Cornishmen, in their fury and grief, surged forward to regain the lost ground. Trevannion was killed when Prince Rupert stormed Bristol shortly afterwards and Slanning, mortally wounded in the same assault, lived long enough to quip that 'he had always despised bullets, having been so well used to them.' The death of the four men was a great loss: 'Gone the four wheels of Charles's wain,' exulted a Roundhead poet, 'Grenville, Godolphin, Slanning, Trevannion slain.' Lest we get too misty-eyed about loyal country-folk and gallant gentlemen, we must remember that social obligation was laced with economic survival. Grenville had already written to his wife, away in their windy house at Stowe in north Cornwall, to tell her that no tenant could stay at home and expect to keep a roof over his head: they were to turn out in his blue and silver livery or pay the price.

There was an older obligation, for service in the *posse comitatus*, the armed power of a county, raised and commanded by its sheriff. It was an expedient resorted to by the royalists early on in the Civil War, though with mixed success. An officer commented that one of its gatherings was 'more like a great fair than a posse', but Sir Ralph

Hopton secured 3,000 sturdy Cornishmen by summoning the county's posse to Moilesbarrow Down outside Truro in October 1642. Like so much else, the notion crossed the Atlantic, and the ranchers and citizens who ride off with the sheriff to constitute the posse in so many westerns are behaving in a way their English ancestors would have understood.

After the Civil War the militia was retained by Parliament, both because it was seen as a defender of Protestant liberties against arbitrary royal government and because so many members of parliament were themselves militia officers.[8] The Militia Act of 1662 charged property-owners with the provision of men, arms and horses in relation to the value of their property, and was the basis for the militia's organisation for the next century. But by 1685 it was being argued by the government's supporters that the militia had performed badly against the Duke of Monmouth. Some, largely, uncritical historians have tended to follow this view, but recent research suggests that accounts of the militia's incompetence are overdrawn. The argument that its failings justified a significant increase in the regular army says as much about James II's wish to increase the size of the army for his own purposes, not least the cowing of domestic opposition, as it does about the value of the militia. The countervailing argument, that a regular army would encourage governments to embark upon expensive and risky foreign war, whereas the militia (offering what the 1980s might have termed 'non-provocative defence') did not, chimed harmoniously with the mood of the late seventeenth century, and there were to be lasting echoes of it, in both Britain and the United States.

The Militia Act of 1757 broke new ground by transferring the responsibility for the militia from individuals to the parish, that keystone of social organisation in so many other aspects, and successive legislation continued in a similar vein. Each county was allocated a quota of militiamen – 1,640 apiece for vulnerable Devonshire and sizeable Middlesex; 1,240 for the West Riding of Yorkshire and 240 each for Monmouthshire and Westmoreland, with just 120 for little Rutland. Lord lieutenants and their deputies were responsible for providing the officers and for overseeing the selection of the men. Able-bodied men between the ages of eighteen and forty-five were liable to serve; though peers of the realm, clergymen, articled clerks, apprentices, and parish constables were exempt. So too were poor men with three or more children born in wedlock, a number reduced to one in 1786. This last adjustment was a blessing for local authorities, for the parish was responsible for looking after the families of militiamen who had been called up. Service was for three years, and was determined by ballot, with potential militiamen being selected from nominal rolls drawn up by village constables.

Constables' lists are an appetising slice through the layer-cake of time and place. The Northamptonshire lists for 1777 show that 20 per cent of men balloted were servants, 19 per cent were labourers, and 11 per cent farmers. The county's traditional industries were well represented, with almost 10 per cent engaged in weaving and framework knitting, and 6 per cent in shoemaking. At the other end of the scale, the county had ten whip-makers and three woad-men, last of a dying breed, two of them in the parish of Weston Favell and one at Watford. Well-to-do farmers tend to have 'Mr' in front of their names, or 'Esq' or 'gent' after it. Although the constable of Edgcote duly logged four men as 'Servants to William Henry Chauncy Esq' he was far too well-mannered to list Mr Chauncy himself. While some constables sent in simple lists, the two constables of the large town of Daventry (assisted by the town's thirdboroughs or under-constables) produced helpful annotations, telling us that Mr Bailey, surgeon, had been balloted six years since; the mason William Watts had eight children; and William Rogers the baker was infirm. The seventeen students at the nonconformist academy there were liable for balloting, although when they were eventually ordained they would be exempt, for the Act exonerated nonconformist ministers as well as clergymen of the established Church. The constable of Whilton was precise in noting the 'poor men with three children' who were guaranteed exemption, and warned that 'Jos Emery, farmer and churchwarden, [has] lost the thumb of his right hand' – no mean disability, for the thumb was used to cock the musket. A balloted man's obligation was simply to provide military service, and most who could afford it paid a substitute to serve on their behalf. Every parish was obliged to meet its quota. As they were penalised for failure, parish authorities who fell short sought volunteers and paid them a bounty.

Militiamen had a training obligation of twenty-eight days a year, and were billeted in public houses during this time. They were not always popular visitors, their presence striking a chord with that deep undercurrent of antimilitarism. In 1795 the testy Lord Delaval complained of the West Yorkshire Militia on his estate: 'disturbance – noise – drums – poultry – intrusions – depredations – profligacy with servants – camp followers – interruptions – marauding – how to be protected – compensation – recompense.'[9] They were subject to the Articles of War when called up, and a range of punishments – from fines to the pillory or flogging – were available for men who failed to appear when ordered out. Militia regiments generally had between eight and twelve companies, with three sergeants and three corporals apiece. Militiamen could be promoted to these ranks, but the system relied on its small permanent staff, which included a regular sergeant major and a handful of regular sergeants. When the Worcestershire Militia formed in 1770 it was allocated Sergeant Major Henry Watkins of the 27th Foot, and two sergeants, Robert Harrison of the 3rd Dragoon Guards and Ezekiel Parks of the 58th Foot. The twenty-five other sergeants appointed were militiamen, and we have no way of assessing their previous experience. Sergeants did not have an easy life, as weapon-handling was never wholly safe. The Worcestershire Militia suffered a serious accident during its 1777 annual training. The men were drilling on Powick Ham when the cartridge pouches of three soldiers caught fire. Two men were 'terribly scorched' and three others 'much injured'.

In time of major emergency the militia was embodied for full-time service. In April 1778, after France had allied itself to the fledgling United States, transforming what had been a family quarrel into a world war, several militia regiments were embodied. The Northamptonshire Militia, led by Henry Yelverton, Earl of Sussex, was ordered to a training camp at Warley Common, near Brentwood in Essex. They marched though its county town with 'repeated huzzas, and (what is the glory of Britons!) with spirits animated to repulse the designs that may be formed by the enemies to their king and country'.[10] The regiment was moved around the southern counties over the next five years, with substitutes and newly balloted men tramping out to join it at Maidstone in 1782. It was disembodied in 1783, and carried out only part-time training till called up again for the French war in 1793. As the Napoleonic wars went on, militia obligations were successively strengthened. By 1815, what with supplementary and local militia and the hybrid 'Army of Reserve' of 1803, most adult males found themselves obliged to serve or pay. The issue of Scots militia was extraordinarily contentious, for the Government feared that it might be putting arms into the hands of its opponents: indeed, a major current of the Scottish Enlightenment was a desire to see a Scots militia as a bulwark against English oppression. The seminal 1757 Act did not apply in Scotland or Ireland, and it was not until 1797 that a Scots militia was raised. The last militia ballot took place in 1829, and when the militia was re-raised in 1852 because of the threat posed by Louis Napoleon's France recruitment was voluntary.

Militia officers were commissioned by lord lieutenants, using parchment documents very similar to those given to regulars. There was a property qualification, though it was first modified by permitting ex-regular army or naval officers to serve without it, and then, when the militia was revived in 1852, substantially reduced. It was not until 1867 that it disappeared altogether, so that at last 'the officers ceased to be necessarily connected with the county or with the landed interest.'[11] These qualifications had been very substantial. The 1793 Militia Act decreed that a regiment's colonel had to have £2,000 a year or be heir to £3,000; a lieutenant colonel £1,200 a year or hopes of £1,800; and so on to an ensign who needed to have £20 a year or to be heir to £200 personal property a year. Both the colonel and lieutenant colonel of a county's regiment had to have half their property in that county. There were sporadic anti-militia riots, notably in 1757 and 1796, largely amongst those who sought to avoid serving. It became evident that the system would only work by bringing 'the county' onside: the militia service would be encouraged by those familiar ties of social and economic obligation. A first attempt to raise a Worcestershire Militia failed in 1758, when the lord lieutenant, the Earl of Coventry, and several of his deputies met at the Talbot Inn, Sidbury, only to find that not enough gentlemen were willing to accept commissions. The attempt was postponed, but failed in successive years. By 1770, however, when the process was repeated at Hooper's Coffee House in Worcester, the outcome was successful, because there were now enough gentlemen prepared to take a lead. The list of officers, headed by the new regiment's colonel, Nicholas Lechmere, was sent to Lord Weymouth, Secretary of State for the southern department. Sending this to Weymouth emphasised that the militia was a civil and not a military matter. This new proposal was given 'His Majesty's Approbation' in just a week. Lechmere was once captain in 3rd Foot Guards, owner of Lidford Park near Ludlow in Shropshire, and the only son of the high sheriff of Worcestershire, Edmund Lechmere MP. His father-in-law was a landowner in Powick, on the little River Teme just outside the city, and he himself went on to inherit his uncle's large estates and, in 1774, to become MP for Worcester. His major, Holland Cooksey, of Braces Leigh, was an Oxford-educated barrister, a justice of the peace and deputy lieutenant of the county.

A lieutenant colonel was appointed shortly afterwards. He was Robert Fettiplace, of Swinbrook Park, just east of Burford in Oxfordshire, happily not too far from the Worcestershire boundary. The son of Thomas Bushell, a substantial landowner of Cleeve Prior in the county, he had adopted the name Fettiplace on marrying Diana, daughter and co-heiress of Sir John Fettiplace Baronet, the previous owner of Swinbrook. In 1775, when Lieutenant Colonel Fettiplace decided to soldier no more, he was replaced by Thomas Dowdeswell of Pull Court near Tewkesbury, eldest son of the Right Hon William Dowdeswell MP and his wife Bridget, youngest daughter of Sir William Codrington Baronet. Lieutenant Colonel Dowdeswell was married to a baronet's daughter, was a JP and DL for his county, and had been a captain in 1st Foot Guards.[12]

A similar pattern extends across Britain, with militia commissions congruent with social standing, and the entire apparatus of raising and administering the militia wholly characteristic of the way the country was run. There was also a very clear Westminster connection. Most regiments of English and Welsh militia were commanded by peers, and the best of them took their responsibilities very seriously. Colonel Lord Riversdale of the South Cork Militia built a barracks for his regiment, on his own land at Rathcormac, at his own expense. When the South Cork was disembodied after the Napoleonic wars and there was little chance of the men finding work, he allowed many of them to join the regular army, although this was officially discouraged. The regiment proved true to its nickname 'The Long Corks' when, at its disembodiment parade on St Patrick's Day 1816, the mens' average height was found to be 5ft 11in. The radical politician and journalist John Wilkes was a committed patriot, and had travelled home from university at Leiden in 1745 to join a loyal association training to defend the capital against the Jacobites. Two years later he became a substantial landowner by marrying an heiress, thus coming within the qualification for senior militia rank. Although he was frequently at odds with the government, and had a highly coloured private life, he was a serious-minded colonel of the Buckinghamshire Militia, though his practice of using his adjutant as second in his duels was an unwise merging of military and civil.

Captains and subalterns, with their smaller property qualifications, were more modest figures. The historian and MP Edward Gibbon served as a militia officer between 1759 and 1770, including a period of embodied service during the Seven Years War. He always thought that the Hampshire captain had taught the historian something of value. The novelist Jane Austen, living at Chawton on the main road from Guildford to the garrison town of Winchester, was familiar with militia regiments as they marched through, or were quartered in the surrounding villages. George Wickham, the closest *Pride and Prejudice* comes to a villain, was a militia officer, eventually posted off to the north to hide his disgrace. Jane's brother Henry served as a captain in the Oxfordshire militia in 1793–1801, and he acted as regimental agent for several militias (the Devonshire, Nottinghamshire, and North Devonshire among them) before his bank failed in 1816 and he resorted to that perennial stand-by of the educated man down on his luck, and became a curate, following in his father's footsteps. Militia officers, like their regular counterparts, were given to duelling, and the Worcester Militia's first training session ended with two subalterns falling out at Stourbridge, 'but fortunately without a fatal termination'.

In many respects the militia's social composition resembled that of the regular army, with poor men officered by richer ones. In 1852 the Marquess of Salisbury observed of one applicant for a commission, that employment by the General Screw Steam Navigation Company was an 'insuperable obstacle' to military advancement. Property qualifications made it all but impossible for a man to work his way through the ranks to a commission, and so the militia was more socially exclusive than the regular army, which always had a significant proportion of ranker officers. In the eighteenth century men were forbidden to shift from the militia into the regular army, for by doing so they left a gap, which the parish then had to fill. During the Napoleonic wars, when there was an ever-increasing appetite for men who could serve abroad, militiamen were offered bonuses to transfer, or sometimes treated so harshly during their embodied service that joining the regulars came almost as a relief:

> The Militia would be drawn up in line and the officers or non-commissioned officers from the regiments requiring volunteers would give a glowing description of their several regiments, describing the victories they had gained and the honours they had acquired, and concluded by offering a bounty. If these inducements were not effective in getting men then coercive measures were adopted: heavy and long drills and field exercises were forced upon them: which became so oppressive that to escape them, the men would embrace the alternative and join the regulars.[13]

Militia officers were offered free regular commissions if they could inveigle specified numbers of militiamen into signing on as regulars. George Simmons, from a family of impoverished gentry, managed to persuade a hundred men of the Royal South Lincolnshire Militia, of which he was assistant surgeon, to transfer into the regular army. He was rewarded with a regular commission in the crack 95th Rifles, and enjoyed a lively time in the Peninsula, ending up as a lieutenant colonel. By the end of the nineteenth century, when service in the militia was wholly voluntary, it had become a way for young men to test their aptitude for military service, and was 'little more than a recruiting vehicle for the regular army, into whose ranks some 35 per cent of its members passed each year'.[14] After the abolition of the purchase of regular commissions in 1871 a young man could still obtain a militia commission, which did not require him to attend Sandhurst. Then, provided he could pass the examination, he could transfer to the regular army: two future field marshals, John French and Henry Wilson, gained their regular commissions this way.

In sharp social contrast to the militia were the volunteers. They were raised in times of great national emergency, like the Jacobite invasions of 1715 and 1745, and the threat posed by revolutionary France saw the first great wave of volunteering. Volunteer units were often middle class, their ranks filled with men who would have bought themselves out of militia service, giving the cartoonist James Gillray the unmissable opportunity of pouring meaty-bottomed tradesmen into tight breeches. Units were sometimes raised by the efforts of great families, in just the way that Bevil Grenville would have understood. Hugh Percy, 2nd Duke of Northumberland, had been (as Lord Percy) a professional soldier: a captain in the 85th Foot at seventeen, he fought at Minden and in North America. Percy left the army as a lieutenant general, and inherited his dukedom in 1786. Responsible, as lord lieutenant of Northumberland, for his county's militia, he also raised the Percy Tenantry Volunteers from his own extensive estates. When he died in 1817 it was reported that the entire force was 'paid and in every respect maintained in arms at the sole expense of this patriotic nobleman'. Infantry companies and cavalry troops were recruited from specific villages: the 1st and 2nd Barrisford Companies came from the parishes of Simonburn, Stamfordham and Kirkwhelpington, and the Guzance and Thirston Company from Felton Parish. The Percy Tenantry Volunteers numbered around 1,500 men, supported by the two three-pounder guns of its Volunteer Horse Artillery, based at Alnwick, the duke's seat.

The Percy Volunteers mirrored the area's social fabric, with bigger tenant farmers officering the local companies, farmworkers shouldering their muskets, and the duke's directing hand on the reins. Volunteer units raised in London were tiny by comparison, and rejoiced in names like the Temple Association, the Hackney Volunteers, the Guildhall Light Infantry, and the Bread Street Ward Volunteers. Often the city's hierarchy led the way, with the same prominent citizens that summoned public meetings to raise volunteers emerging as the new unit's officers. Volunteer officers were often elected by the unit as a whole, and democracy did not always obey the dictates of local hierarchy. It was also noticeable that volunteers, most of whom had to buy their own uniforms, tended to favour cutting-edge light infantry fashion (with no shortage of frogging), sometimes selecting blue precisely because regular infantry wore red, and so there was no chance of a heroic cheesemonger in the Poplar and Blackwall Volunteers being mistaken for a private in the umpteenth Foot. There were different terms of service: the Frampton Volunteers in Gloucestershire were prepared to deal with the French up to eight miles from their home village, but for the Hitchin Association in Hertfordshire just three miles was the limit.[15] The government did its best to bring the volunteers under central control and the 1804 Volunteer Act did at least ensure that all were paid for twenty-one days a year.

If a man's zeal for his country's defence was gratified by turning out as a smart light infantryman, how much more satisfying it was to emerge as a cavalryman with clinking spurs, and sword-scabbard trailing across the cobbles? The problem, even in a horse-using society, lay in the provision of suitable mounts. The Provisional Cavalry Act of 1796, an offshoot of the militia concept, required all those in possession of more than ten riding or carriage horses to furnish, when required, one mounted man, fully armed and equipped. Far more significant, though, was the raising, from 1794, of troops of 'Gentlemen and Yeomanry.' These local troops, officered by landowners, tended to be attracted by cavalry uniforms of the showier sort, light by name if not by nature, and one reason why the 1796 pattern light cavalry sword, with its D-shaped guard and broad, heavily curved blade, remains relatively common is the fact that so many of them were used by the yeomanry.

The Yeomanry Cavalry on manoeuvres by W. B. Giles.

Yeomen were countrymen of respectable standing, tenant farmers or smaller freeholders. The *Spectator* made much of its character Sir Roger de Coverley, that genial baronet so preoccupied with hunters, hares, and partridges. But no less important in the hierarchy of the shires was his neighbour,

> A yeoman of about a hundred pounds a year, an honest man. He is just within the Game-Act, and qualified to kill a hare or a pheasant … He would be a good neighbour if he did not destroy so many partridges. In short, he is a very sensible man – shoots flying – and has been several times foreman of the petty-jury.[16]

The Game Act of 1670 had prevented anyone with less than £100 a year in lands or tenements from killing game, and authorised the seizure of 'guns, bows, greyhounds, setting-dogs and lurchers' that might be used in the process. It was a measure of substantial social control, and was not significantly altered till 1831. In a system that was always more pliable than it seemed, a second-generation yeoman might indeed make the transition to gentleman, or, if harvests failed, thud down into the ranks of the agricultural labourers. A yeoman had more of a stake in the country than most, and one cannot understand the quintessentially British phenomenon of yeomanry without remembering this.

Few volunteer units survived the Napoleonic wars, for there was no longer a need for them. But the yeomanry trotted on, because now the nation was in the grip of widespread unrest, with Chartists and Luddites in the towns and the Captain Swing rioters in the country-side all presenting a threat to the established order of JP, squire, and vicar: one of Swing's threatening letters put 'Parson Justasses' amongst the 'Blackguard Enemies of the People.' There was no doubt whose side the yeomen were on, and in the absence of a proper police force, they were frequently called out in aid of the civil power. On 16 August 1819 a huge crowd gathered in St Peter's Fields, Manchester, to hear the radical speaker Henry 'Orator' Hunt. The local magistrates had decided to arrest Hunt and other leaders. Although the military commander on the spot, Lieutenant Colonel Guy L'Estrange, had some infantry, two guns, six troops of the regular 15th Hussars and six of the Cheshire Yeomanry wisely deployed, the magistrates sent a troop of Manchester and Salford Yeomanry towards the speakers' platform.

The Manchester and Salford was not a wartime-raised unit, but had been formed in 1817 as a response to local unrest. Their commanding officer, Major Thomas Trafford, was a Roman Catholic landowner, and his second in command, Captain Hugh Birley, a mill-owner. Although we risk confusing history with current politics if we call the troopers 'younger members of the Tory party in arms', most were well-to-do tradesmen with an animus against radicals. Trafford apparently told Birley to take a detachment to make the arrests. Some of the crowd maintained that the troopers were drunk, but Birley argued that the yeomanry horses were not used to working together and were frightened by jeers, yells, and the fluttering of banners. After the arrests were made there was a shout of 'Have at the flags', and some of the yeomen slashed at the crowd as they kicked their horses forward to get at the banners. The magistrates ordered L'Estrange to disperse the crowd and rescue the yeomanry, so he sent in the 15th Hussars. Although the regular troopers had been ordered to use the flats of their swords, more damage was done by sword-swipes and horses crashing into people who were themselves trying to escape. The affair, dubbed 'The Peterloo Massacre' in parody of Waterloo, polarised opinion then and now. Perhaps a dozen people were killed and many more injured, though estimates of 700 casualties beggar belief. The magistrates and yeomanry were supported by the government. Trafford was later made a baronet, while Birley went on to partnership with one Charles Macintosh – who had invented a process for waterproofing cloth. Had things been a little different, we might slip gratefully into a Birley on a rainy day.

Although many yeomanry units disappeared in the 1830s and 1840s, individual troops were consolidated into county regiments, and it was to take the TA reorganisation of 1964–5 to remove most of these, with their shoulder-chains and bright forage caps, from the *Army List*. Some regiments were the hunting field in arms. The future Field Marshal Sir John French recalled that when he was adjutant of the Northumberland Hussars:

They were commanded by the Earl of Ravensworth, than whom no better sportsman ever lived. The officers were all good sportsmen and fine horsemen, and to those who can look back fifty years such names as Cookson, Straker, Henderson and Hunter will carry the conviction of the truth of what I say. Two of them were prominent masters of hounds, but my most intimate friend was Charley Hunter, a born leader of cavalry, whose skill in handling £50 screws over five-barred gates I shall never forget.[17]

Others had even more blue blood in their veins. The troops of Gloucestershire Gentlemen and Yeomanry were combined into a regiment in 1834, with the Marquess of Worcester (soon to be the 7th Duke of Beaufort) as its commanding officer. The regiment became the Royal Gloucestershire Hussars in 1841 and, with its roots deep in Beaufort Hunt country, marched past to 'D'ye Ken John Peel'. When the Yeomanry celebrated its bicentenary in 1994, the 11th Duke was regimental colonel. The Oxfordshire Yeomanry was officially disbanded in 1828 but it remained in being, thanks to being privately financed by the Duke of Marlborough. It was restored to the *Army List* two years later, becoming the Queen's Own Oxfordshire Hussars, or Queer Objects on Horseback, with striking facings of (rather trying) Mantua purple. The regiment was closely linked to the dukes of Marlborough and their seat at Blenheim Palace, which provided a striking backdrop for annual camps: the 6th Duke took command of the regiment in 1845 and the 9th Duke in 1910. Amongst its officers on the eve of the First World War was Major Winston Churchill, who was honorary colonel until his death in 1965. He had given a detachment of the regiment a prominent position at his funeral, but its protocol offended the Foot Guards brigade major who pointed out, with some asperity, that this was not how state funerals were done. Major Tim May, the detachment's commander, was characteristically unabashed: 'In the Oxfordshire Yeomanry we always do state funerals this way.'

This was just how jolly yeo-boys were meant to behave, with a faintly cavalier disregard for the formal side of military life and a generous pinch of self-parody. A Yeomanry brigadier detailed one of his colonels to send a subaltern on a wearing and doubtless nugatory mission. 'I shall send Charles', decided the colonel. 'Charles? Charles?' replied the brigadier. 'D'you think he'll go?' Cartoons in officers' messes caught yeomen the way they liked to think of themselves. A portly farmer-turned-trooper in the Suffolk Hussars scrambles up a bosky bank, with his sergeant, mounted, in the lane behind him, anxious for a report:

> No sergeant – no – I don't see no enemy – not to speak of I don't
> – But I do see as John Martin's roots is terrible backward – wonderful backward they is – to be sure!

'Beg pardon, Major,' observes a trooper, drawn up in rank and file, with an easy gesture towards his passing squadron leader. 'You'll excuse my mention on it, but you've got something on your noose.' The first part-time major general since the 1940s was the 6th Duke of Westminster. He had joined the yeomanry as a trooper in 1970, was commissioned in 1973, and went on to command the Queen's Own Yeomanry. He reckoned that 'military zeal is at its best when tempered by a fine sense of humour': a wholly yeomanry view.[18]

The Yeomanry underwent a resurgence when the French invasion scares of the 1850s saw redbrick forts put up on Portsdown Hill to

Yeomanry reconnaissance at its best:
'The eyes and ears of the Army' by W. B. Giles.

prevent an invading army – which might have landed at sleepy Bosham or harmless Chichester – from descending on Portsmouth dockyard. Far more characteristic of the age were the revived volunteers, about as unlike the yeomanry as it was possible to be. They were prevailingly middle class. Some units elected their own officers. They favoured uniforms of 'French grey', and were delighted to be forbidden the gold lace worn by regulars since this reduced the chances of being mistaken for 'the dregs of society'. They seized on innovation: Hans Busk, one of the most prominent leaders of the rifle volunteer movement, set up a model rifle club at Cambridge in 1837. Long before the Boer War gave fresh emphasis to marksmanship in the regular army, volunteers were spending their weekends on the ranges at Bisley in Surrey. The National Rifle Association was founded in 1859 'for the encouragement of Volunteer Rifle Corps, and the promotion of rifle-shooting throughout Great Britain.' It moved to Bisley in 1890 when high velocity rifles made the ranges in suburban Wimbledon unsafe. Volunteers eagerly combined their martial zeal with the bicycle, another great passion of the late nineteenth century, to produce cyclist battalions. There was a Railway Volunteer Staff Corps in 1865 and a Volunteer Medical Staff Corps twenty years later. Cartoonists sniped away ('Wipe the blood off your sword, general?') but the volunteers, in their worthy, whiskery way, somehow went to the heart of Victorian England. They were visible to the community in the way that regulars were not. They appeared unfussy and meritocratic, and embraced the innovation that regulars, with all their noise and pipeclay, seemed to shun. But their officers were not necessarily gentlemen. There was a saying of the 1860s that a greengrocer with a volunteer commission was not an officer but a greengrocer pleased. When aspiring Jewish families wanted to confirm their own rising status they joined the yeomanry. The Rothschilds bought Waddesdon Manor in 1874, and patronised the Royal Buckinghamshire Hussars, soon nicknamed 'The Flying Foreskins'.[19]

The Boer War unleashed a surge of patriotic enthusiasm, and saw volunteers and yeomanry as part of what Kipling eulogised in *The Absent Minded Beggar* where 'Cook's son – Duke's son – son of a belted Earl/Son of a Lambeth publican – it's all the same to-day.' The process of getting part-timers embodied, trained and sent to South Africa was wasteful and inefficient. It was quipped that the 'IY' (Imperial

Yeomanry) hat-badge stood for 'I Yield', and it was clear that the whole busy ant-heap of yeomanry, militia, and volunteers needed kicking over.

As part of the main post-war reforms that took their name from the Liberal Secretary of State for War, R. B. Haldane, the auxiliary forces were reorganised root and branch, and so the Territorial Force, with an establishment of just under 315,000, came into being on 1 April 1908. One of Haldane's strokes of genius was to entrust the TF's administration to County Associations chaired by lord lieutenants. The force's 1909 yearbook lists county chairman like a digest of *Debretts*: Chester: the Duke of Westminster; Derby: the Duke of Devonshire; Essex: the Earl of Warwick; Hampshire: the Marquess of Winchester; Middlesex: the Duke of Bedford; Oxford: the Earl of Jersey; and Warwick: the Marquess of Hertford. There were 115 peers in the association by November 1909.

Many lord lieutenants were also militia colonels, and had been inclined to oppose the reorganisation, but the king made it clear that he backed Haldane. The powerful National Service League feared that if the TF actually worked, the case for conscription would be weakened, and therefore condemned the scheme as inadequate. Some regulars grumbled about the sheer impossibility of part-timers grasping the mysteries of gunnery, and the new TF embodied all the social complexities of the auxiliary forces that composed it. At one extreme the yeomanry was richly decorated with peers and Tory MPs. Brigadier General the Earl of Longford died commanding 2nd Mounted Brigade on Gallipoli in August 1915. They had advanced across a dry salt lake, marching steadily in open order under accurate shrapnel fire. 'Don't bother ducking,' he told his officers. 'The men don't like it and it doesn't do any good.' Not far away that day Lieutenant Colonel Sir John Milbanke, 9th Baronet, with a VC from the Boer War and now commanding the Sherwood Rangers, announced that the regiment was to attack a redoubt: 'I don't know where it is, and don't think anyone else does either, but in any case we are to go ahead and attack any Turks we meet.' He did, and was duly killed.[20]

At the other extreme, when young Alan Harding, a Post Office clerk, sought a Territorial commission he knew better than to approach one of the 'class battalions' of the London regiment, like the London Rifle Brigade or Queen Victoria's Rifles. These were

subscription clubs for all ranks, but Harding slipped instead into 11/
London, the Finsbury Rifles, fondly known, from the location of its
headquarters at the top of Penton Street and the beery ways of its
members, as the Pentonville Pissers. After a good war, Harding transferred to the regular Somerset Light Infantry, and was knighted in
1942, using the name John which his regular brothers in arms had
preferred to Alan Francis. This had not, though, stopped subordinates from maintaining that his initials stood for 'All Fucking Hurry'.
After mobilisation in 1914, middle-class units considered that both
1/8th Royal Scots and 1/8th Scottish Rifles were 'slum battalions,'
and the gentleman troopers of the Westminster Dragoons found their
journey to Egypt aboard the same troopship as 1/9th Manchesters
made an ordeal by, horrid to relate, the Mancunians' predilection for
spitting and swearing.[21]

On the formation of the Territorial Force all officers had their
commissions signed by the monarch. When serving alongside regulars they took precedence 'as the junior of their degree', and were
subject to military law at all times, principles which have not changed
since.[22] Mobilised Territorials served alongside regulars in all the
main theatres of the First World War. At the outbreak of the Second
World War, the Territorial Army was formally absorbed into the regular army. In both world wars, though, the regular army kept a firm
grip on senior appointments. In February 1916 the House of
Commons was told that only 18 Territorials had risen above lieutenant colonel at the front and three at home. In January the following
year Lord Derby, secretary of state for war, announced that four
Territorials had commanded divisions, and 52 brigades. He later
admitted that these figures included officers in temporary command
in the absence of the regular incumbent, and only ten Territorials
were currently commanding brigades.

Assertions were made that it was wholly proper for regulars to have
a controlling interest in senior command. But this is undermined by
the fact that both the Australian and Canadian contingents on the
Western Front, by wide agreement some of finest Allied troops, were
eventually commanded by lieutenant generals John Monash and
Arthur Currie, who were respectively a businessman and an engineer
by profession. Both had 'amateur' major generals amongst their
subordinates. William Holmes, killed commanding 4th Australian

Division in 1918, had never been a regular, though he had joined the New South Wales Militia as a boy bugler and won a DSO in the Boer War. David Watson, a journalist by profession, commanded 4th Canadian Division for the whole of its existence. Andrew McNaughton, a university lecturer in engineering, commanded the Canadian corps heavy artillery and went on to command the Canadian 2nd Army in a later war. Archibald Macdonnell had been a regular officer for just a year before going off to be a Mountie, and led 1st Canadian Division to some of its greatest successes. The British were occasionally prepared to make generals out of civilian specialists, commissioning Sir Eric Geddes, general manager of the North Eastern Railway, as major general in 1916. But not once did they give a reservist permanent command of a division. In view of the success of the Canadians and Australians, who produced real talent (and not a little rancour and incompetence too) from a far smaller recruitment pool, we can see that there was indeed a khaki ceiling with which non-regulars collided.

In September 1939 the Territorial Army was abolished as a separate entity, and its conditions of service were changed so that 'all wartime promotion would be temporary, with no opportunity for substantive advancement and reversion to the pre-war rank at the war's end'.[23] Eventually concessions in the form of timed promotions (which could take an officer to lieutenant colonel after twenty-two years' service) were introduced in May 1945. A few months earlier former TA officers included one substantive major general, Claude Liardet, who had commanded 56th London Division before the war but did not lead it in action; one temporary lieutenant general; seven major generals; and 36 brigadiers. Of the 160 major generals commanding field force divisions between 1940 and 1945 only three were Territorials. Moreover, a sharp cull of TA commanding officers had seen 253 removed in the war's first thirteen months, as opposed to 72 regulars.

There was, in part, good reason for this. The TA was endemically short of officers, despite their selection criteria being lower than for regulars. The lack of soldiers at weekend training and annual camp made it hard for a Territorial officer to feel the full weight of command, and Territorial commanding officers were not obliged to attend the Senior Officers School. There was a wide spread between 'class corps' like the London Scottish and the Honourable Artillery Company, that naturally attracted well-educated recruits, and the majority of units that relied heavily on urban working-class soldiers. These working-class soldiers needed the pay and found the two-week annual camp (often at the seaside) a blessed relief from the daily grind, but it was hard to produce NCOs from amongst this group. Many of the TA's problems stemmed from systemic underfunding. As David French points out in his majestic *Raising Churchill's Army*, 'the Territorials became victims of governments determined to reduce estimates, and a War Office that preferred to see the cuts fall upon the part-time Territorials rather than the regulars.'[24]

Experienced Territorial officers, some of whom had commanded with success during the last phases of the First World War, complained that the regular army, having denied them the opportunity to train and recruit, now blamed them for it. In April 1941, one of the few surviving TA commanding officers in 48th Division discerned 'a very definite set against Territorial officers'. The Territorial acting commander of 26th Armoured Brigade writing in May 1944, doubted if he would even manage to command his own regiment when his current appointment ended. 'I have the ever-present spectre of some suitable Lt Col arriving from way back,' he wrote, 'either a loathsome little tick from the Tank Corps or else an equally horrible cast-off from some cavalry regiment – we've had plenty of experience of them in this war.'[25]

The TA was reconstituted in 1946, and the successive reductions, in 1956, 1961, and 1966 matched wider reductions in defence expenditure and the army's increasing preoccupation with the defence of Germany. The reductions announced in 1965, however, brought about a more radical downsizing, to some 50,000, and even did away with the name, replacing it with the untidy Territorial and Army Volunteer Reserve, or T&AVR. Territorials had at least abbreviated to 'Terriers', and a suggestion that 'Tavvers' might replace it drew little applause. The disagreeable title was eventually discarded after a Conservative victory in 1971 saw the gradual increase of the TA to reflect the perceived importance of home defence against Soviet special forces. From 1981 the TA reached its post-war apogee, providing the bulk of a division to reinforce 1st (British) Corps in Germany, and reaching almost 89 per cent of its establishment of

86,000. With the collapse of Communism, however, numbers shrank once again, first with the 1990 Options for Change review under the Conservatives, and then again with the Strategic Defence Review of 1998 under Labour, which brought the TA down to around 40,000.

The County Associations (a term harking back to Parliamentarian organisations in the Civil War) were Haldane's device for ensuring that the TA would be administered and supplied by bodies that would at one and the same time protect it from the War Office, and take some of the load off commanding officers' shoulders. They would also link the TA to the community and, so Haldane hoped, encourage military training more widely. Over the TA's evolution these associations had come under the same pressure as the organisation they represented, in part because a smaller TA demanded less administrative support, and in part, too, because a regular army anxious to save money on the TA did not always welcome their interference. There were ninety-four associations in 1909, and sixty-six in 1965, with further reductions to produce the ten large regional groupings that exist today. The associations were successively renamed, becoming, from 2000, Reserve Forces and Cadet Associations. Although the RFCAs rightly emphasise their local knowledge, continuity and independence, they are now more firmly under the control of the army's chain of command than ever before.

There can be no doubt that their influence has declined. In 1965 the Duke of Norfolk, chairman of the Council of Territorial Associations, led the opposition to the reduction, and although he commanded substantial support (the attempt to reverse the cuts was lost by a single vote in the Commons) he was no match for a Labour Government whose military advisers firmly believed that the reforms were essential. But in 1990 the cuts imposed by Options for Change would have been more severe had it not been for the personal intervention of George Younger, who had recently been secretary of state for defence and carried great weight within the ruling Conservative party and the army, in which he had served as both a regular and a Territorial. During the debate over the Strategic Defence Review I was assured by one of the TA's supporters that 'the lord lieutenants would never stand it', but it was evident that the wrath of the lieutenancy did not alarm a Labour administration with a massive majority, and in any event there was a palpable tension between Harris Tweed and Hugo

Boss, with the waning power of the old county connections eclipsed by the growing strength of the Whitehall apparat.

Moreover, the office of lord lieutenant itself had changed from the days of Elizabeth I, when its holders were concerned with enforcing the Act of Uniformity and commanding the county militia at a time of real threat. During Elizabeth's reign all who held office for any length of time were peers or heirs to peerages, apart from three who had close relationships with the queen. Forty-six of the 103 lieutenancies were held by peers as late as 1956, all but one of whom (Field Marshal Viscount Alanbrooke in London) had inherited their titles, and a further sixteen baronets. Most were landowners, thirty-two had held the rank of lieutenant colonel or its equivalent, and amongst their military awards were twenty-three DSOs and eighteen MCs. In 2006 there were only eight hereditary peers and three baronets amongst the 99 lord lieutenants, and only six of the total had held senior military rank. The first female lord lieutenant had been appointed in 1975 when Lavinia Duchess of Norfolk took over from her husband, who had died in office: there were twenty-eight ladies amongst the 2006 sample. There was no longer a natural bias towards the land, and only eight rated their main concern as farming or estate management. Some lord lieutenants have run major public companies, and several of the ladies have had an impressive involvement in charities.[26] The lieutenancy makes an extraordinary contribution to public life, but its days of marshalling county opinion are long over.

About 12 per cent of the 2,700 active deputy lieutenants in the United Kingdom held senior military rank, a proportion justified by the need to advise non-military lord lieutenants on their responsibilities towards the reserve forces and cadets in their counties. As evidence of the wholesale shift away from traditional deputies, when most retired brigadiers soon added DL to their post-nominal initials, there is now a conscious attempt to make deputies socially inclusive, and to reflect the ethnic composition of the population.[27]

In one sense it is hard to fault the remorseless progress towards what is often hailed as 'One Army'. Territorial officers are now selected by the same process as their regular counterparts, and pass out from Sandhurst in a parade which culminates (just as it does for regulars) in marching up the steps of the Grand Entrance. Promotion across the whole rank-structure depends on passing the appropriate courses. The TA's representation within the army has increased. When I became a brigadier in 1994 I was the only one in a large TA. Now there is a two-star Assistant Chief of the Defence Staff (Reserves and Cadets), a post held first by the Duke of Westminster in 2004, and there are TA brigadiers at Land Command, Headquarters Adjutant General and the army's district headquarters.

In terms of overall training and efficiency, the TA I left in 2000 was unrecognisable from the organisation I joined as a private in 1964. Its expectation of use had also been transformed. Militia, yeomanry, and volunteers had been concerned with home defence. Haldane's new Territorial Force was so called because it was territorial (designed to defend the national territory) rather than expeditionary. Those of its members who agreed to serve overseas proudly wore an Imperial Service badge on their right breast. In 1914, Territorials had to volunteer to be sent abroad, and by no means all did so. Although those who joined the TA in the inter-war years and after 1946 recognised that they might be called up for foreign service, there was a clear understanding that this would only happen in time of a major national emergency. Indeed, for most of my own time the mechanism for calling up the TA ('Queen's Order') was so ponderous as to constitute a large on-off switch to be pressed only in time of the gravest crisis.

The process of making it easier to use Territorials in situations short of general war began with the 'Ever Readies'. This small group of TA volunteers was set up in 1962 and they agreed to accept a higher liability in return for a bounty. Ever Readies were called up for service in Aden in 1965. There was some controversy: 14 of the 175 selected appealed against call-up, and men argued unsuccessfully that because they had been unable to take their brief leave entitlement in-theatre, they should have it added as paid leave at the end of their mobilised service. The three officers and 120 men who served with 1st Royal Sussex were well regarded by their battalion, and one of the officers, Lieutenant Mike Smith, won the first Military Cross awarded to a Territorial since the Second World War.

The Reserve Forces Act of 1996 did not simply create a small High Readiness reserve intended to produce specialists like interpreters and civil affairs experts, but it made the whole of the TA subject to call-out by the secretary of state, who could use it not only 'when warlike operations are in preparation or progress,' but for the protection of life or property and the alleviation of distress at home or abroad. Since then Territorials have been called up for service in the Balkans, the Falklands, Germany, Iraq, and Afghanistan. Kingsman Michael Davison, a 22-year-old Liverpool builder, won the first Territorial Military Cross since Mike Smith a generation before by dragging a wounded officer to safety in Basra in 2003. The TA is now emphatically a reserve for use, and nobody joining it can be in any doubt of that.

There have been attendant casualties. The problem of ensuring that a reservist did not lose his civilian employment by being called up for full time service long pre-dates the TA. Liaison with employers was one of the tasks laid on County Associations, and since then first the National Employers' Liaison Committee and then SaBRE (Supporting Britain's Reserves and Employers) have striven to persuade employers that there are practical benefits to having reservists amongst their employees, for they acquire transferable skills like leadership and initiative. When the TA was first formed many employers were hugely supportive, granting their employees paid leave to attend annual camp. The Alliance Assurance Company and the Westminster Fire Office even insisted that their employees should be Territorials.

It was always much harder for small firms, who could be seriously inconvenienced by the disappearance of, say, one of two plasterers at a busy time. Shifts in employment patterns have not necessarily helped the TA. Large, British-owned firms tended to take a more supportive view than multinationals with concerns about the uses to which reservists might be put in a complex world. When jobs are hard to come by, employees are disinclined to risk them, and a pattern of TA service that is now very likely to involve occasional periods of mobilisation makes it harder for professionals like lawyers, doctors, or university teachers to harmonise military and civilian identities. The TA, like the militia before it, was able to profit from the fact that many of its officers enjoyed high status in their civilian capacities, and these have been precisely the individuals squeezed most tightly by changing circumstances. Conversely, many of those attracted by the periods of Full Time Reserve Service (essentially short-term, often extendable contracts) made available by the 1996 Act had reached a dead end in their civilian careers.

A 2007 study by the National Audit Office concluded that most reservists joined with the intention of serving on one mobilised tour, but that 16 per cent of those questioned intended to leave within a year, and just under half of this group had been called up. Most Territorials planning to leave blamed personal or family pressure, with a substantial minority attributing their decision to 'lack of support'. There were difficulties where a reservist's military pay fell short of his civilian salary, and in access to medical care after deployment. In particular, reservists were more likely than regulars to suffer from psychiatric problems on their return, not least because of their rapid transition from military life, with its supportive bonds of mateship, to the more humdrum world outside. These difficulties are exacerbated where there seems no clear mandate for the war, and by the practical problem of finding, within the immediate community, somebody who can begin to understand what it was really like in Al Amarah or Musa Qal'h.

The TA remains under-recruited (in 2006 it was 19 per cent down on its established strength of just under 40,000), and the shortfall is at its most severe in the Royal Army Medical Corps, upon which the army relies so heavily. There is a worrying shortage of officers, not least because the very individuals with the qualities needed to encourage folk on a rainy Friday night on Salisbury Plain are exactly those most likely to be most in demand in the pressure-cooker of stressful civilian jobs. In his epilogue to the book marking the TA's hundredth anniversary, Brigadier Greg Smith, then Deputy Inspector General of the TA and shortly to become Assistant Chief of the Defence Staff, argued that one of the TA's most important tasks lay in 'effectively providing the essential link between the army and society'.[28] It does so with increasing difficulty, and part of the price it has paid for increased military efficiency and tighter links with the regular army is to make it harder to retain its foothold in a society with other pressing concerns.

II

GALLANT GENTLEMEN
AND OFFICERS

CHAPTER 7

A NATIONAL ARMY: 1660–1914

For most of its life the regular army was a volunteer force, its members, officers and soldiers alike, having decided to embrace the profession of arms. The decision to join was rarely simple. A man could be led to enlist for many reasons: a fit of pique, a brush with the law, that extra pint of porter, the vision conjured up by an eloquent recruiting sergeant, or unrelenting hardship in an age of social insecurity. Nor was it necessarily easier for officers, who might find family tradition, patriotic obligation or (especially for Scots or Irish youngsters with many hungry siblings but few paternal acres) the lack of alternative gentlemanly employment scarcely less compelling. The army had existed for two and a half centuries before the exigencies of the First World War forced it to adopt conscription, though there had been times, notably during the Napoleonic wars, when the voluntary principle was stretched to its very limit.

The years between 1916–18 and 1939–60, when conscription was in force, do not fit into the broader pattern of Britain's military development. Both world wars saw the transformation of a small, professional force into a massive national army, a process that helps account for early setbacks. It also explains the rise of a style of warfighting in which the British army engaged 'the enemy with the minimum of manpower in the front line and employ the maximum of machinery to generate the overwhelming firepower required to suppress enemy fire and so make possible movement across the battlefield.'[1] The process was cumulative, for the generals and political leaders of the Second World War – most of whom had fought on the Western Front as young men – knew very well that society would never again tolerate the sacrifice of life on such a scale. Their soldiers, who had grown up in the shadow of the Somme, were less deferential than their fathers. Field Marshal Montgomery's predilection for letting metal, not flesh, do the business of battle was firmly rooted not only in his own military experience but also in the culture of the men he commanded.

As I shuffle off to lunch after a morning spent lecturing newly promoted majors on the Intermediate Command and Staff Course, I am struck by that same mixture of continuity and change that characterises the whole of the army. There will be a few names that have been in the *Army List* since there was an *Army List*, with the same regimental connections. Introduce me to a Tollemache and I will confidently expect the cap-star of the Coldstream. The Winchester College–Oxbridge nexus that would once have taken a boy into the Rifle Brigade or the 60th Rifles, might now see him in the Rifles – arguably the most successful of the recent amalgamations. However, there will be many officers with no family connection with the army, who have arrived by way of comprehensive school and redbrick university, or indeed no university at all. There will be some who have risen through the ranks, being commissioned after making their mark as a private or junior NCO. Others will come up the hard way to a Late Entry commission by way of RSM. Whether on operations in Ulster, the Balkans, or Iraq, I have been struck by their grace under pressure; their constant determination to put the interests of their soldiers before their own; and that physical courage that gives this part of the book its title.

This is not uncritical admiration – their moral courage is not always equal to their physical valour. The desire to succeed in one of the most hierarchical of professions occasionally leads an officer to scramble up the greasy pole without much regard for the boot-prints he leaves on the faces of those below him. Lunching with the Louts Club puts one at serious risk of either injury from flying bread-rolls, whizzing like grapeshot around the great breach at Badajoz, or short-onset cirrhosis. Their champagne/burgundy/rosé striped tie was designed to minimise stains from the fluids that might fall upon it.

There can be surprises among the men in terms of their diverse interests and skills. Today's officers are often as cavalier about reading worthy doctrinal manuals as their great-grandfathers were. At its 1917 Christmas party, the Doctrine and Training Branch in France sang a ditty with the words 'We write books and pamphlets/Yes by the ton/ But nobody reads them/No not bally one', and I know how its members felt. Yet I also know a former Grenadier who can recite Chesterton's *Lepanto* word-perfect, and who showed me the Moons of Jupiter; a Royal Signals officer who cuts the most perfect silhouettes; a Para who left the army after a very heavy landing and has become a successful artist; and an infantryman who combined being one of the most-be-medalled officers of his generation with knocking off a doctorate in his spare time and writing five good books. They are often irritating, but rarely less than engaging.

The notion of a 'national' army has changed over time. Back in the seventeenth century, Charles II united the three kingdoms of England, Scotland, and Ireland only in his royal person. The Union of Scotland and England did not take place till 1707, and that of Great Britain and Ireland in 1800. However, even while the three kingdoms had their separate legislatures, there was no easy relationship between the overall size, either of Britain's population as a whole, or of the army that defended it, and the national backgrounds of officers. The eighteenth-century army was dominated, in numbers though not always in influence, by the Scots and Irish. The army in Ireland, right up to 1800, had its own sharply reduced regimental establishment. In 1774, 41 per cent of officers were English, 32 per cent were Irish, and 25 per cent Scottish. In 1776 these proportions were 37 per cent, 33 per cent and 27 per cent, and in 1782: 36 per cent, 28 per cent, and 33 per cent. Foreigners, mainly Americans, made up 2–3 per cent, though this may reflect the fact that Americans serving in British regiments often reported themselves as English. In the mid-1770s a little over half the population of the British Isles was English or Welsh, just under a third Irish, and one-tenth Scots. British line infantry, regardless of any designation its regiments bore, was officered by a rather larger proportion of Irishmen than existed in the general population, and over twice as many Scots, while the English produced just two-thirds of the officers to which their share of the wider population should have entitled them. The proportions of rank and file were rather different, with around 60 per cent English, 24 per cent Scottish, and 16 per cent Irish, so it is not unfair to speak of a predominantly English army that was disproportionately officered by Scotsmen and Irishmen.

Although the English content of the rank and file increased as the nineteenth century went on, with emigration to the United States replacing enlistment into the army as the preferred career choice for so many young Irishmen, the proportion of Scots and Irish officers remained high. Towards the beginning of the century it was said that if you walked into the officers' mess of the 38th Foot (which boasted a Staffordshire connection)and yelled 'Campbell' a quarter of the officers present would turn round. The 22nd Foot had a proud affiliation to Cheshire but had a regimental agent in Dublin. In 1870, 71 per cent of the population of Great Britain hailed from England and Wales, with 17 per cent from Ireland and 11 per cent from Scotland. The birthplace of the 1914 generals is not necessarily an accurate index of their national background. Tommy Capper, killed at Loos in 1915, and William Birdwood, who went on to command the ANZACs, were both born in India. Only 63 per cent were born in England, with 13 per cent coming from Ireland and a remarkable 19 per cent from Scotland. Throughout the period, the minor gentry of Scotland and Ireland generated a disproportionate number of officers. Sir Walter Scott told the Duke of Wellington that

> Your Grace knows that Scotland is a breeding, not a feeding country, and we must send our sons abroad as we sent our black cattle to England; and, as old Lady Charlotte, of Ardkinglass, proposed to dispose of her nine sons, we have a strong tendency to put our young folks 'a' to the sword.[2]

What the *junker* squirearchy of East Prussia was to the German army, so Ireland was to the British. Thomas Bartlett and Keith Jeffrey argue that the high proportion of Irish officers, even at the close of the nineteenth century, reflects a 'shortage of other career options'.[3] Of the five non-royal commanders-in-chief of the army in the nineteenth century, one (Dundas) was Scots, two (Hill and Hardinge) were English, and the remainder, Wellington, Wolseley, and Roberts, were Irish. The latter, although born in Cawnpore, came from a distinguished Waterford family. Wellington disliked being called Irish, observing that one could be born in a stable without being a horse, but much of his political attitude was shaped by growing up as a child of the ascendancy. His brother-in-law Ned Pakenham, killed at New Orleans in January 1815 (wholly unnecessarily, for peace terms had been agreed, but news had not yet reached North America), was Irish. Galbraith Lowry Cole, a divisional commander in the Peninsula was Irish too. He was described by a biographer coming from a class of

> energetic, masterful men, who interested themselves in local and public affairs and as such looked up to and respected by their neighbours; loving sport and country pursuits but with only a tepid interest in literature and art; careless about money, yet acutely aware of the need for it to make life pleasant; having a high sense of honour, but also a high temper and a lack of patience and caution.[4]

This might almost have been written to describe the family of the future field marshal Harold Alexander, born in London but descended from James Alexander, 1st Earl of Caledon, who had built a fine house on the borders of Tyrone in the late eighteenth century. Alexander grew up on the estate, where 'his mother did not care what he did out of her sight', and joined the army because it had never struck him to do anything else, and was commissioned into the Irish Guards in 1911.[5] His contemporary Alan Brooke was born in the French Pyrenees, where his parents spent their winters, but the family home was in Colebrooke, Co Fermanagh, held by the family since Major Thomas Brooke of Lord Drogheda's Regiment of Horse gained it during the Williamite War. Sir Henry Brooke, 1st Baronet of Colebrooke, had three soldier sons fighting in the Napoleonic wars. One took over from Robert Ross, who burned Washington in 1812, another commanded the 4th Foot in Spain and took temporary command of his brigade when its commander was wounded at Waterloo, a battle in which his nephew, heir to the baronetcy, was killed. As David Fraser has pointed out, 'Twenty-six Brookes of Colebrook served in [the First World War]: twenty-seven served in the war of 1939–45: and in those wars, or from wounds received in them, twelve died.'[6]

The Anglo-Irish ascendancy and the Ulster Plantations have provided the army with many of its most distinguished senior officers.

There has been a whole tribe of Goughs, from Hugh, 1st Viscount, who commanded in both Sikh Wars. His chief tactic was frontal assault, and on one occasion, having been told that his artillery had run out of ammunition, he replied gratefully 'Thank God for that. Now I'll be at them with the bayonet.' The future field marshal Gerald Templer and the future general Richard O'Connor were both children of officers in the Royal Irish Fusiliers, while Field Marshal Sir John Dill, whose equestrian statue stands proudly in Arlington National Cemetery, was commissioned into the Leinster Regiment in 1901; he was the son of a bank manager in Lurgan, County Armagh. Yet to judge Ireland's contribution simply by the senior officers it furnished is to miss the point. There was scarcely an engagement in which an Irish officer did not play a notable part, whether or not he happened to be in an Irish regiment. Joseph Dyas, 'a young officer of very great promise, of a most excellent disposition, and beloved by every man in the corps – an Irishman whose only fortune was his sword', was serving with the 51st Foot when he led the forlorn hope against Fort St Cristoval, at Badajoz, in 1811. Private William Wheeler saw him emerge from the first attempt 'without cap, his sword was shot off close to the handle, the sword scabbard was gone, and the laps of his frock coat were perforated with balls.'[7] He promptly volunteered to lead a second fruitless attempt, from which only nineteen men of two hundred survived. Dyas was eventually made captain in the Ceylon Regiment, and ended his days as a resident magistrate in Ireland.

Infinitely more controversial was John Nicholson, born in 1822 to a family of Scots Lowland stock who moved to Ulster in the early seventeenth century. Educated at the Royal School, Dungannon, he gained a commission in the East India Company's army in 1839. Nicholson quickly showed aptitude for political work, and the discovery of his brother's emasculated body in the Khyber Pass did much to harden an already tough character. He believed in the application of what he called 'swift, stern justice', and on one occasion politely apologised to the officers waiting in their ante-room: dinner would be delayed because he had been hanging the Indian cooks. There was something of the wholly unforgiving Old Testament deity in him. When he appeared in the British camp on Delhi Ridge in 1857, black-bearded, grey-eyed, and unshakeably convinced in the righteousness of his cause, one young officer thought that he was 'by the grace of God ... a king coming into his own.'[8] He was only a regimental captain but had just been appointed brigadier general to lead the Mobile Column down from Peshawar. When the British stormed Delhi, he was mortally wounded. As he lay dying, gut-shot in a sweltering tent, he thanked God that he still had the strength to pistol the British commander if he ordered a retreat.

Whatever Charles II's problems, financial or domestic, officer recruitment was not one of them. There was a glut of ex-officers who had fought for his father, as well as former members of the New Model who had adhered to George Monck. The problem was not so much finding officers as in accommodating even a fraction of the claimants on royal gratitude who already had impressive military credentials. John Gwyn had just missed Edgehill, the first major battle of the war, but was at the storm of Brentford a few weeks later, and fought on throughout the first civil war, becoming a captain. He was in arms in the second civil war, and then fought in Scotland before joining Charles II's little army in Flanders, where he was captured at the battle of the Dunes in 1658. Gwyn had lost his commission by 1663 and was then serving as a gentleman trooper. His *Military Memoirs*, a vivid account 'of all the field-fights and garrisons I have been in', were written with a view to gaining the employment to which his service seemed to entitle him. There were thousands of John Gwyns about, but in 1665 only 210 officers in Charles's regiments and another 134 in his garrisons. By 1684 the overall number of permanent commissions had risen to 613. This increase resulted from bringing the Tangier garrison and the Earl of Dumbarton's regiment (later the Royal Scots) onto the English establishment, and the raising of one new regiment, the Royal Dragoons. Even at the height of the Dutch War in 1678 there were still under a thousand officers, many of whom lost their commissions when war-raised units were disbanded. Gwyn was right to stress his royalist background (though we cannot tell what good it did him) because this was an army wholly dominated by old cavaliers. In 1665, 65 per cent of officers had fought for Charles I or been in exile with his son, and only 10 per cent, most of them concentrated in the Coldstream Guards, had served the Protectorate. Rather more, a full 25 per cent, had held commissions in the English brigade in Dutch service.

There was never a homogeneous officer corps. At this early stage, there were three broad groups of officers, a categorisation that would persist until well into the eighteenth century. First came the professionals, whom John Childs calls men 'who were forced to look to their swords in order to earn a living'. Before the regular army came into existence there had been English families like the Cravens, Russells, Sidneys, and Veres who had traditionally sent their young men off to serve on the continent. Much the same thing happened in Scotland. Among the Scottish officers in Russian service in the early seventeenth century we find the names Crawford, Wemyss, and Hamilton. Alexander Crawford assured the tsar that he already had eight years experience as an officer in the Danish and Swedish armies, and was just the fellow to command a regiment.[9] The Hapsburgs, with their long-running wars against the Turks, were always on the lookout for smart young men. Their charmingly credulous acceptance of self-devised genealogy ('Descended from King Arthur: why then, your highness, that must make you a prince') and eagerness to bestow titles of their own, made them attractive employers. Ireland, with its heartbreaking catalogue of rebellion and disappointment, was a fruitful source of officers. Field Marshal Maximilian Ulysses von Browne, one of the most competent Austrian commanders of the Seven Years War, was son and nephew of Irish gentlemen exiled after the failure of Tyrone's rebellion in 1603. Over the years the royal and imperial *Rangliste* included the delightful composites Franz Moritz Graf von Lacy and Laval Graf Nugent von Westmeath. The Prussians could do as well when they put their minds to it, and when an English war correspondent, Lieutenant Colonel Ponsonby, got into difficulties at the battle of Rezonville in 1870 he was saved by *Oberleutnant* Campbell von Craigmillie.

After 1660, though, there was at least a chance that some professionals could serve their own country. Professor Childs' sample of forty-three of these officers shows them to have been a mixed bunch, with eight of them sons of peers, ten born to baronets or knights, and twenty to ordinary gentlemen, with just five from poor backgrounds.[10] Most were second or third sons, underlining their dependence on military service. Until the army's wartime expansion of 1672 there were simply not enough vacancies in the English establishment for all these men, and commissions cost money that they could rarely afford.

Some served in foreign armies (as their fathers or uncles might have done before them) or in overseas garrisons, whose troops were not part of the establishment. Tangier, in particular, was a source of both regular employment and frequent combat.

Two of Tangier's paladins, admirable examples of the professional warrior, were Andrew Rutherford, Earl of Teviot and Sir Palmes Fairborne. We must not be misled by Teviot's title. He was the impecunious fifth son of a junior branch of a great Scots family. Like many of his countrymen, Teviot learnt his trade abroad, becoming a lieutenant general in the French service where he earned a fine reputation for courage. In 1662 Charles made him governor of Tangier and an earl in the Scots peerage, but a misjudgement in the endemic irregular war against the Moors saw him caught outside the city's walls in a savage little battle in which he was killed, with nineteen other officers and nearly 500 men. The 'worthy and brave' Fairborne was the son of Colonel Stafford Fairborne, royalist governor of Newark in the first civil war. This claim on royal patronage was not enough to get him a regular commission though, and he had already helped defend Crete against the Turks before he was made a captain in the Tangier Regiment in 1662. Fairborne spent much of his time as deputy governor of Tangier, not much helped by the fact that his master, the one-eyed William, 2nd Earl of Inchiquin (given the job because of his late father's distinguished service to the royalist cause in Ireland) was incompetent and vindictive. In 1678 Fairborne slipped his eldest son Stafford into the governor's regiment as an ensign. The lad was only twelve, and he would have been gratified by the fact that after eight years in the army, Stafford Fairborne shifted to the navy and died an admiral. Palmes Fairborne was mortally wounded in October 1680, but lived a day or two and so saw his soldiers mount the attack that ended the long siege of Tangier and enabled the English to conclude a three-year peace treaty. In the long term Tangier was untenable and was evacuated in 1684: the Tangier Regiment was taken onto the establishment as the Queen's Regiment. Other professionals served in the English force in Portugal until its disbandment in 1668 or the Anglo-Dutch brigade in the Dutch service, whence several slipped back into the English army.

In contrast, the six regiments of horse and foot on the English establishment were in the hands of 'gentleman officers': the second category of officers. A sample of 188 who served between 1661 and 1685 shows thirty-nine to have been the sons of peers, seventy-three of baronets or knights, fifty-eight of ordinary gentlemen: the remaining eighteen were low-born.[11] It is striking to see that eighty of these officers were first sons, content to serve until they inherited. They were far happier to mount guard in Whitehall or Windsor than to fry their brains in Tangier. Most had bought their commissions. The classic arguments in favour of purchase had yet to be made, but public offices of all sorts – 'places' – were commonly bought and sold, so this practice ran comfortably with the venial tide of the times. A man who desired a first commission or promotion had first to obtain royal approval, and then find an officer prepared to sell, and agree a price with him. A set fee, according to a table laid down in 1667, had to be paid to the secretary at war for each transaction. The paucity of vacancies kept rates high, though the £5,100 paid by one of Charles's illegitimate sons, the Duke of Grafton, for the colonelcy of 1st Foot Guards was very steep: a captaincy in the guards might cost £1,000. At the close of 1663 Pepys, a fast-rising civil servant with excellent connections, reckoned himself worth £800 in cash. Many gentleman officers sat in parliament, beginning that process of military representation at Westminster that we saw earlier. Their regiments did not generally serve abroad, for expeditionary forces were recruited as required. The rigid channelling of royal patronage, via the Duke of Albemarle at the beginning of Charles's reign and the Duke of York thereafter, ensured that there were tight circles of family loyalty and political allegiance, widened only on the three occasions that troops were raised for war against the Dutch or the French.

Gentleman officers were Restoration England loud in all its privilege and affluence, and in contrast to the professionals, they were an unedifying crew. The MPs amongst them were allowed unlimited leave to attend Westminster when the House was sitting. Although regulations specified that only one-third of officers could be absent at any time, in 1679 Henry Sidney found only 'a corporal and three files of musketeers' at Tilbury fort, and 'never a commissioned officer' at Gravesend. Four years later Charles wrote crossly to the governor of Hull, warning him that officers absent without leave would face 'absolute cashiering'. Not that cashiering was always absolute. Captain Thomas Stradling of 1st Guards lost his commission when he encouraged his soldiers to riot in Huntingdon. As he was a Stradling of St Donat's, scion of a martial tribe that had done much for Charles I, he was soon reinstated. In 1678 Lord Gerard, captain of the King's Troop of the Life Guard, accompanied by Lord Cornwallis, one of his officers, beat up the sentries at St James's and then killed a footboy. Cornwallis (his father a royalist who had accompanied Charles into exile) was tried by his peers and acquitted: Gerard slipped abroad for a few months and then resumed his duties. He had bled for the king in the Civil War, and a cousin had been executed for treason under Parliament: Charles was not a man to punish an old friend for a vinous lapse. When Ralph Widdrington was blinded in a sea-battle against the Dutch, a grateful monarch gave him a pension of £200 a year – and a captaincy in the army, which he retained till 1688.

It was rarely a simple matter to get orders obeyed, especially if they were given to a gentleman of ancient lineage. Captain Sir Philip Howard was in the Queen's Troop of the Life Guard, and brother to Charles Howard, the influential reformed Parliamentarian whom Charles had created Earl of Carlisle. In 1678, he fell out with James, Duke of Monmouth, not only one of Charles' illegitimate brood but an experienced soldier to boot:

> To show military discipline, Sir Philip Howard was suspended his employment for not obeying some orders the Duke of Monmouth gave him in which, though his Grace be found in the wrong, it is thought fit the other should suffer for example's sake to show that orders must be obeyed though never so foolish.[12]

In 1673 Charles hoped to make Frederick, Duke of Schomberg, a professional soldier of wide experience in the French and Portuguese service, commander-in-chief of his own army as it prepared for the Dutch War. But some officers behaved appallingly, with a contemporary admitting that they 'daily offer him affronts' on the grounds that he was a Frenchman; in fact his was an old Palatinate family. Matters were not helped by the legal nonsense that prevented him from ordering capital punishment while the army was still on home soil, without officially suspending common law within it. Officers treated him with disdain and men grumbled about the severities of French discipline: the experiment was not a success. The Earl of Feversham,

James II's commander in 1685 and 1688, was less competent than Schomberg, and he owed some of his difficulties to the fact that, as Louis de Duras, Marquis de Blanquefort, he was French-born, though he had come to England in James's retinue in 1663 and lived there ever since. When the test came in 1688 he remained true to his oath, which is more thsn we can say for many of the milords who sent him up as a fop who 'no spikka da lingo'. The gentleman officers drank and duelled, swore and swaggered, abused tavern-keepers, tumbled serving-girls, and set the worst possible example to their men. Even that satisfied royalist Samuel Pepys could not help comparing the quiet disbandment of Parliament's old army to the noisy indiscipline of the king's supporters, who 'go with their belts and swords, swearing and cursing and stealing – running into people's houses, by force oftentimes, to carry away something'.[13] Public dislike of soldiers, already sharpened by civil war and the Interregnum, was revived by such conduct.

We will see more examples of professionals and gentleman officers, though the contrast between them will never be as sharp as it was in those first two decades of the Restoration. The third category of officer – from the local gentry – left a less enduring mark. The Restoration army comprised the six standing regiments, overseas garrisons and expeditions, and individual garrison companies of locally-raised foot that had never been assembled into regiments and remained scattered in castles and forts across the land. Garrison companies were officered by local gentry who did not allow their military duties to weigh too heavily upon them. In the West Country the same tribal connections that had taken Bevil Grenville's lads up Lansdown Hill ensured that the Arundells of Trerice ran Pendennis Castle, and the Godolphins the Scilly Isles as family fiefs. We will not be surprised to find Sir Bevil Grenville's boy John, whom we last saw in his dead father's saddle on Lansdown Hill, created Earl of Bath and made governor of Plymouth.

These categories were never wholly distinct. Professionals were glad to get onto the establishment if they could manage it, and not all gentleman officers were drunken louts. John Churchill was given an ensign's commission in 1st Guards in 1667. The young man went off to learn his trade in the Tangier garrison, and then fought aboard James's flagship at the Battle of Solebay in 1672, gaining a captaincy in the Lord Admiral's Regiment. The following year he accompanied the Duke of Monmouth to the siege of Maastricht as a gentleman volunteer. Not only could he learn more of his trade but, given that the Lord Admiral's was unlikely to outlast the war, there was much to be said for getting into a regiment that would.

Volunteers might be serving officers whose own regiments were not engaged in the campaign, or civilians who hoped that their conspicuous bravery might help ease them into a commission. When the besieged Dutch put in a brisk counter-attack on a captured work, Monmouth dashed back into action accompanied by 'Mr Charles O'Brien, Mr Villiers, Lord Rockingham's two sons, and Captain Watson their kinsman, Sir Tho Armstrong, Capt Churchill, Capt Godfrey, Mr Roe and myself, with the duke's two pages and three or more of his servants …'[14] Mr O'Brien was shot through both legs for his pains, but the little affair did the survivors no harm: O'Brien secured a French commission for a kinsman, and Edward Villiers got an English one, secured a regiment in 1688 and died a brigadier. Monmouth's favourable report to his royal father helped persuade the king to forgive Churchill for the oversight of impregnating Barbara Villiers, Countess of Castlemaine, who was one of his mistresses. Captain Charles Godfrey went on to marry Arabella Churchill, and to serve under Churchill after he had become, as Duke of Marlborough, the most illustrious British soldier of his age.

If John Churchill is the best example of the gradual blurring of boundaries between professional and gentleman officers he is certainly not the only one. As civil war veterans outlasted their military usefulness, a series of wars against first the Dutch and then the French made it increasingly hard to maintain a standing army that only did duty at home and increased the demand for competent officers. Percy Kirke spelt his first name Piercy and probably pronounced it that way. He was the son of a court official and commanded enough interest to get commissioned into the (rather fragile) Lord Admiral's Regiment in 1666 and then to go on into the (wholly more robust) Blues and to serve as a volunteer at Maastricht. He became colonel of the Tangier Regiment in 1682, and was made governor two years later. His behaviour shocked Pepys – there on a fact-finding mission with Lord Dartmouth. Kirke tolerated the drunken behaviour of soldiers and generously offered to find a conveniently sized whore for a vertically-challenged member of Dartmouth's retinue, warning the young man that he needed to strike fast before all the ladies had gone aboard the fleet to accommodate the sailors. Kirke brought his regiment into English service, and was a brigadier for the Sedgemoor campaign. His regiment's paschal lamb insignia and less than mild behaviour to the rebels earned it the nickname Kirke's Lambs. He assured James II that he had no interest in becoming Roman Catholic. If he was to change his religious opinion he had already given the Emperor of Morocco first refusal and would become Muslim. He defected to William of Orange in 1688 and died a lieutenant general, in 1691.

In contrast, Theophilus Oglethorpe, scion of a Yorkshire Catholic family, served under Marshal Turenne in France. He was commissioned into the Tangier Horse, which came onto the English establishment as the Royal Dragoons in 1684, and then moved on to the Life Guards. In 1685, while commanding a flanking force of Feversham's army as it marched west, he stumbled into a smoky little clash at Keynsham bridge. He was so well regarded by Feversham that Churchill, just ahead of him in the hierarchy, feared that he would scoop the campaign's honours. In the event Churchill not only made the right dispositions at Sedgemoor but also profited from the widespread criticism of Feversham afterwards. Whereas Churchill changed sides in 1688, Oglethorpe did not, although the victors courted him assiduously and he knew that opposition to William of Orange must inevitably cost him his commission, and so it did. He is another good example of the well-connected officer with enough money to sustain himself in the army but a keen interest in his profession.

The contrast between Churchill and Oglethorpe in 1688 illustrates one of the dangers of the growing professionalisation of officers. The line of cleavage in 1688 was complex, for personal ambition and genuine political and religious conviction were often so closely interwoven it might have been difficult for a man to tell us just how he arrived at his decision. Although both Charles II and James II were Roman Catholic – the former fully reconciled to the Church only on his deathbed and the latter a proclaimed Catholic – theirs was in theory a Protestant army. Parliament, perennially nervous about Catholic plots that could imperil the whole Restoration settlement, pressed the king to require officers and men to swear the oaths of

Allegiance and Supremacy. In 1667 those who had not taken the oaths were turned out, a process which swept up just two officers in the ex-Cromwellian Royal Horse Guards but seventeen from the four regiments of foot. Some crept back in almost at once and others went off to raise troops to serve in France. When parliament passed the Test Act in 1673, Charles sweetly observed it applied to troops on land and not at sea, and quickly parcelled off lots of infantry to serve aboard the fleet. This royal prevarication could not go on forever, and although Charles used his dispensing power to free some Catholic officers from the Act, after the Popish Plot in 1678 he was forced to order the dismissal of all known Catholic officers and soldiers as well as those who had not taken the oath. Ninety-one soldiers and sixteen officers were dismissed from Monmouth's Regiment of Foot alone.

James, disinclined to take his brother's more serpentine approach, forced the issue. Sir Edward Hales, a baronet from Kent, stood high in royal favour, and was received into the Roman Catholic Church in 1685. As colonel of a regiment of foot, he was obliged to take the oath yet did not do so. His coachman Arthur Godden (collusively acting on his master's orders) brought an action against Hales, who was convicted at Rochester assizes in March the following year. Hales appealed to the Court of the King's Bench, arguing that he had letters patent from the king that dispensed him from the need to take the oath. The judges found in his favour by a majority of eleven to one. The Lord Chief Justice affirmed that it was 'an inseparable prerogative' springing from 'the ancient remains of the sovereign power' for the monarch to 'dispense with penal laws in particular cases and upon particular necessary reasons'. We may now doubt whether James seriously proposed to convert England to Catholicism, as was widely alleged at the time. But his action in favouring Catholics and sacking anyone who crossed him, in the army or any other branch of public life, aroused widespread fear. Worse, it was evident that Lord Tyrconnell, James's lord lieutenant of Ireland, was indeed engaged in the comprehensive catholicisation of the Irish army, which might then come across to coerce England. As the last straw, in 1685 Louis XIV revoked the Edict of Nantes, which had guaranteed freedom of worship to Huguenots; thousands of dispossessed French Protestants duly arrived in England with horrid tales of the rack, breaking-wheel and pyre.

Many officers disapproved of James's policy. Captain Sandys of the Blues gruffly told him to his face that 'I understand Your Majesty well enough. I fear God and honour the King, as I ought, but I am not a man that is given to change.'[15] Many, including those who, like Churchill, knew him well, feared that he was riding for a fall and his destruction must inevitably encompass those of his adherents. Churchill admitted that his own experience of growing up on the losing side after the Civil War had given him a hatred of 'poverty and dependence'. His wife Sarah was the prime confidante of Princess Anne, James's youngest daughter. Anne's sister Mary was married to William of Orange, head of the Dutch state and leader of the European opposition to Louis XIV's dynastic and religious ambitions. The details of the military conspiracy against James II are necessarily vague, for the conspirators took good care to keep their tracks covered. The so-called 'Treason Club' met in the Rose Tavern in Covent Garden, and the 'Tangerines', a loose association of officers who had served there – many of them of a whiggish persuasion in any event – discussed how they might help unseat James. They were kept in contact with the English officers in William's service by one of the latter's lieutenant colonels, John Cutts. He had served as a volunteer against the Turks in Hungary, establishing an early claim to the reputation that was to give him the nickname 'Salamander' – after the mythical creature that lived in fire – by placing the Imperial standard on the ramparts of Buda. Cutts had no private fortune. Indeed, even after he had been made an Irish peer with a seat in the House of Commons and the governorship of the Isle of Wight he was never free of money worries. A professional rather than a gentleman officer by our earlier categorisation, Cutts had much to gain by a radical shift in patronage in England. We talk lightly about the Curragh affair of 1914 being a 'mutiny'. In fact the 1688 conspiracy was a genuine mutiny, which succeeded by depriving the army of its leadership in its hour of greatest need.

Amidst all the smoke and shadow two things are evident. William would never have launched his expedition against the grain of autumn weather, with Lord Dartmouth's royal fleet close at hand, to land in the West Country where Monmouth had been so easily bottled up in 1685, without being certain that James's army would not fight. The stakes were very high, for the French tide lapped at the borders of Holland, and failure in England might compromise all William's ambitions. Second, there was every chance that James's rank and file would indeed have fought. Although we know annoyingly little about the men who plied their pikes and muskets in James's regiments, this was now, with around 20,000 men, a much bigger army than anything his brother had dreamt of. It was well trained, and nothing in its past suggested that it would not follow its officers. Too many officers, however, declined to lead and those who did try to fight, like the Duke of Berwick, one of James's sons by Arabella Churchill, and Lieutenant Patrick Sarsfield (big, brave, and not over-bright) found that too many senior officers had defected to William to give the loyalists the least chance of success. James had been a gallant soldier in his youth, and was eventually to face a lingering death through illness with an uncompromising courage that impressed Louis XIV. But a combination of nosebleeds and the defection of his favourite Churchill, his son-in-law Prince George of Denmark, and even the flight of his daughter Anne from Whitehall, unmanned him: he abandoned his men to their fate.

The army inherited by William and Mary needed radical remodelling. A few of James's supporters (including Edward Hales) followed him into exile, and more, like Oglethorpe and Dartmouth, were imprisoned for plotting against the new regime. Some of William's irregular adherents, like the volunteers who had seized Nottingham, were given the option of joining the regular army, and others were thanked and sent home, rather promptly. Roman Catholic soldiers, many of them Irish, were disbanded, although a few were packed off to join the Imperial army, deserting in droves (often to join the French) as soon as they reached Hamburg. It was more difficult for William to be sure what to do with his officers. He immediately sent all his English regiments off to the provinces; the Foot Guards were exiled to Portsmouth, Tilbury, Rochester, Dover, and Maidstone. The Dutch and German regiments that had come over with him assumed responsibility for the capital. Politically reliable colonels, even if they were men of little experience, were appointed. The untried Lord Delamere took over Lieutenant General Werden's Regiment of Horse and set about turfing out suspect officers and men as well as improving efficiency. But his lordship's lack of knowledge told against him, and he was soon replaced by the veteran Theodore Russell. The experienced Lieutenant Colonel John Coy was given Colonel Richard Hamilton's regiment when Hamilton, an Irish Catholic, was clapped into the Tower. Perhaps most surprising was the resurgence of Colonel Solomon Richards, once lieutenant colonel of Oliver Cromwell's own regiment of foot, appointed by James in September 1688 and then reappointed by William. Richards immediately sacked five suspect officers, but did not last long. In 1698 he brought his regiment away from Londonderry at the beginning of its famous siege, glumly reporting that the place was doomed, and William duly sacked him, not for political unreliability but for incompetence.[16] Charles Trelawney was a Cornishman whose military career, with spells in the English regiment in French service and the garrison of Tangier, was classically that of the cash-strapped professional. He had been Percy Kirke's lieutenant colonel, and took over the Queen's Regiment from him. In 1688 he deserted to William, and returned to his regiment to get rid of his lieutenant colonel, major and eleven other officers.

These measures took some time to take effect. In April 1689 John Evelyn, who had just heard that James had landed in Ireland 'and was become master of that kingdom', feared that 'This is a terrible beginning of more troubles, especially should an army come thence into Scotland, people being generally disaffected here and everywhere else, so that the sea and land men would scarce serve without compulsion.'[17] There were mass desertions, at least as much because of the disruption caused by the new postings and William's decision to send some of his English regiments to fight in the Low Countries while many Dutch remained in Britain. Some units mutinied on their way to Harwich and Ipswich for embarkation. The poor reputation of the English may have encouraged Marshal d'Humières to attack the Prince of Waldeck's allied force at Walcourt that April, but he received a sharp rebuff, not least because the newly created Earl of Marlborough had his English contingent well in hand. A commission 'for reforming the abuses in the army' was appointed in May, but the commissioners discovered that there were by now few Jacobite officers left, although there were abuses aplenty, like incomplete clothing, pay in arrears, and the familiar racket of colonels pocketing the pay for men who did not exist.

William's policy of appointing Dutchmen to senior commands (and giving them peerages, albeit Irish ones) exasperated his senior officers. Friction between the professional and gentleman officers remained. Although some of the former vanished – Hugh Mackay and John Lanier were killed at the shockingly bloody battle of Steenkirk in 1692 and Percy Kirke died of fever – others, like Marlborough and his brother Charles, Salamander Cutts, and Thomas Tollemache were rising stars. Trailing in their wide slipstream were the new professionals, no longer men who had to serve abroad because there were no vacancies in a small force dominated by court interest, but young men, often from the middling gentry or commerce, who sought to make a long-term career in the army. They served alongside men who would have been comfortable enough roistering with Charles II's red-heeled gallants but did not intend to soldier forever.

Although William hated the practice of buying commissions, and would happily have adopted the Dutch custom of promoting men on merit, purchase was by now too deeply entrenched for him to expunge it. It remained central to providing officers for an army that, in the reigns of William and his successor Anne, grew in size and self-esteem to become a force of European stature. It expanded, but not steadily, as wartime growth was usually matched by peacetime contraction. James II's army of around 20,000 rose to some 70,000 in 1709, up to 134,500 in 1762 at the height of the Seven Years War, down to around 40,000 in 1793 and then up to a staggering quarter-million in 1814. In Victoria's long reign it bottomed out at 91,300 in 1839, and then rose again to exceed 200,000 by 1861. By this time, despite the strictures of Liberal politicians and the complaints of economists, the old pattern of expansion and contraction was constrained by the need to defend the empire and fight a series of small wars, some of which, like the Crimean War of 1853–6 and the second Boer War of 1899–1902, had the uncomfortable ability to morph into big ones.

Whatever the system's purely military defects, it did have the political advantage of producing an officer corps which, while far from homogeneous, was composed largely of men with the proverbial 'stake in the country'. Regimental rolls were filled with officers who wanted stability. Charles Clode, writing in 1871, argued that the system attracted 'men of independent means – not merely professional officers,' and added that Wellington had approved of purchase because 'it brings into the service men of fortune and character

– men who have some connection with the interests or fortunes of the country.'[18] The historian Sir John Fortescue maintained that the whole system was economical: for an officer's pay rarely exceeded the interest on the price of his commission; secure: because officers were bound over for good behaviour on the price of their commissions; and convenient: because sales ensured a steady flow of promotion. Across the whole period 1660–1871 about two-thirds of commissions were purchased. In peacetime the great majority were bought, but in wartime it was difficult to ensure a steady flow of young men whose relatives were prepared to disgorge a substantial sum to give the lad an early chance of death or dismemberment. In 1810, for instance, about four-fifths of all commissions – whether on first appointment or promotion – had been given without purchase.

Purchase was never universal. It did not apply in the artillery or engineers, where officers advanced by remorseless seniority, and there were always non-purchase vacancies that could be given to NCOs promoted to adjutants' posts or deserving young men able to generate sufficient interest to get a free ensigncy, perhaps by serving as a gentleman volunteer. Once the system was fully established, vacancies left as a result of death, retirement or promotion were filled by the next most senior officer on the regimental list, so 'a bloody war or a sickly season' helped the impecunious to rise. In William's day the rules had not solidified and abuses were common: Percy Kirke's son, inconveniently also named Percy, was made an ensign at the age of twelve months in 1684, a captain on his sixth birthday in 1689 and by the time he reported for duty he was his regiment's senior captain. He went on to be colonel of the Queen's, like his father and, like him died a lieutenant general. The practice of commissioned well-connected children went on well into the eighteenth century. Lord George Lennox, second son of the Duke of Richmond, was made an ensign at the age of thirteen in 1751 and was lieutenant colonel commanding the 33rd Foot just seven years later at the age of 20. If some officers were too young, others were too old, for there was no way of forcing a man to retire. In 1699 Lieutenant Colonel Sir Francis Compton, who had survived being pistolled in the chest in the first confused clash on Sedgemoor, was seventy years old, three years younger than his colonel, the Earl of Oxford. Compton evidently had some life left in him, for he had just married a 17-year-old.

Although the detail of purchase varied between 1660 and its abolition in 1871, its general principles are so clear that this is a good moment to explain how it worked. A young man purchasing a commission made an investment, and the pay of his new rank provided him with a dividend. As he bought successive promotions his investment increased, and when he eventually retired he 'sold out' and cashed in his shares.The regulation price of his commission might not increase greatly since the initial purchase – in 1766 a lieutenant colonelcy in an infantry regiment cost £3,500 and had only gone up to £4,500 by 1858. But the fact that the purchaser would have to add a non-regulation premium, varying according to the desirability of the regiment in question, meant that that he could expect to make a profit on his investment to support his old age. In 1745 Lieutenant Colonel Cuthbert Ellison sold his commission in the 23rd Royal Welch Fusiliers for £3,500, saying that his poor health was the 'great motion' behind his selling. His estate in County Durham was hopelessly encumbered with debt, but he hoped the proceeds of selling his commission would, with another annuity left him by his uncle, 'support me with decency, in the decline of life.' This 'delightful old hypochondriac' then proceeded to live for another forty years, dying in 1785 at the age of eighty-seven.[19]

Like most investments a commission was never wholly secure. If an officer was killed in action or died of natural causes its value was usually lost, although there were times when a grateful government might waive the rules. In 1780 Major John André, adjutant general to Sir Henry Clinton, commander-in-chief in North America, was caught in civilian clothes carrying letters to Benedict Arnold, a major general in the Continental Army who was about to betray West Point to the British. An American court-martial sentenced him to death as a spy, and George Washington, stiffly adhering to the letter of the law, declined to vary the mode of his execution from hanging to shooting. He died bravely, declaring 'I am reconciled to my death, but I detest the mode.' André commended his widowed mother and his three sisters to Clinton, pointing out that bad investments had left them impoverished, and asking that they might receive the value of his commission. The circumstances of André's capture and death made him a popular hero: the Government gave his family a pension, and George III made his brother a baronet.

The value of a commission was also lost if an officer was cashiered. The word is a borrowing from the German *kassiert*, broken. Its financial implications were serious in themselves, for the sentence usually deprived the victim of the right to hold any office of profit under the Crown. When Lord George Sackville was court-martialled for failure to charge at Minden in 1760, the court found him 'unfit to serve his Majesty in any military capacity whatsoever.' He lost his lucrative regimental colonelcy and was struck from the roll of the Privy Council. None of this, however, prevented him from emerging in 1775 as Secretary of State for North America, where he made a significant contribution to Burgoyne's ill-starred Saratoga campaign. Sometimes an officer would sell out rather than face a court martial that might cost him the value of his investment. In 1833 Captain John Orrock of the 33rd Foot told a friend that 'our senior captain, Jefferies got into a scrape and Colonel Gore has forced him to sell out or stand a court martial; he preferred the former.'[20] In 1858 Captain William du Vernet of the 84th Foot, on campaign in north India, was as Lieutenant Hugh Pearson aptly put it '"up a gum tree" ... under arrest (with a sentry over him) for being drunk while Field Officer of the day.' Du Vernet had a long record of similar misbehaviour, and when the papers in the case were sent on to the commander-in-chief Pearson wrote: 'I think it is all "up" with him.' Although Pearson believed that there was only a slight chance of his being permitted to sell out, du Vernet was generously allowed to do so, creating a vacancy instantly filled by purchase.[21] If an officer was cashiered after a trial, the vacancy was allocated to an officer from another regiment to ensure that there could be no suggestion that evidence against him might have been given by those who stood to profit from his conviction. Even if it did not cashier him, a court martial might suspend an officer from rank and pay for a specified period. While suspended he was unable to purchase if a vacancy became available, and would miss any free promotions, so it was by no means a derisory punishment. In 1779 Lieutenant Thomas Eyre of the 35th, while in drink, beat the surgeon's mate of his regiment with the flat of his sword, and was suspended from rank and pay for six months. He was lucky, because an 'unseemly quarrel' might get an officer cashiered, and a surgeon's mate was scarcely a gentleman's legitimate adversary.

The career of that serious-minded soldier Samuel Bagshawe shows how interest and purchase combined to advance an officer's career at a time when the system was still open to manipulation. He enlisted as a private soldier in 1731 and was bought out of the army by his uncle in 1738. He gained his first commission without purchase in 1740 when the Duke of Devonshire, lord lieutenant of Ireland and the most notable magnate in Derbyshire, where the Bagshawes owned land, procured him a commission in Colonel Andrew Bissett's 30th Foot. This was on the Irish establishment, and so had fewer officers and men on its strength than regiments on the English establishment, but even so a free commission was not to be scorned. Thomas Fletcher, Dean of Down, and Devonshire's private secretary, wrote to Bagshawe's uncle in the approved style:

> His Grace intending to give your nephew a pair of colours, desires you will send him his Christian name in a letter directed to His Grace the Duke of Devonshire Lord Lieutenant of Ireland at the Castle in Dublin.
> I congratulate you upon this, and am Sir
> Your most humble servant
> Tho Fletcher[22]

Just a year later he was promoted to lieutenant, again thanks to the duke's influence, this time in the very desirable Royal Scots. Bagshawe travelled to London in April 1742 in search of preferment, but although the army was being increased for the War of Austrian Succession, captaincies, at £1,500, were beyond his reach. The duke generously secured him a captaincy without purchase, albeit in Colonel John Battereau's 62nd Foot. As this was a 'new corps', recently raised, it faced early disbandment when peace came, and so the duke secured his transfer to the 39th Foot, on the Irish establishment, which had been raised in 1702 and was a copper-bottomed investment.

In 1745 the regiment's majority came up, and the Duke of Devonshire pressed Bagshawe's uncle to stump up the purchase money: a loan of just £800 would suffice, because Bagshawe 'had been so far a prudent manager as to be able to produce the other two hundred himself without troubling you.' This £1,000 reflected the difference between the value of Bagshawe's captaincy, which he was to be allowed to sell, and the majority's full cost of around £2,500. Bagshawe acknowledged that the promotion would be particularly advantageous, admitting (in a sentence through which he wisely struck his pen) that 'I am the youngest captain save one in the regiment.' The project was certainly not proper, for the vacancy should have been offered to the regiment's captains in order of seniority. It collapsed because Colonel Edward Richbell, the regimental commander, was unaware of it, and before he heard that Bagshawe had the money to hand 'the senior captain had borrowed money for the purchase which effectively overturned my scheme'.[23] In 1746 Richbell managed to obtain Bagshawe the appointment of brigade major for an expedition against L'Orient, but his leg was smashed by a roundshot and he was very lucky to survive its amputation. In October 1747, on hearing that the major of the 39th was near death, he pressed Richbell 'to have your approbation and recommendation to succeed him … I can ride sufficiently to discharge the duty and only expect to be continued on the service on those terms.'[24] The application failed, probably because Bagshawe's missing leg raised concerns, and Matthew Sewell, who had held the lieutenant colonelcy in a short-lived regiment raised for the suppression of the '45, was brought back from half-pay to be major of the 39th. The regimental agent warned Bagshawe that Sewell had irresistible interest in his favour. The 39th was stationed in Portsmouth, and Sewell 'has been recommended by the gentlemen of Hampshire, and in particular by Mr Bridges, one of the members [of parliament] for Winchester, who personally asked the king'.[25]

In 1749 Lieutenant Colonel James Cotes of the 39th announced his intention of selling out, and offered Sewell his commission 'on the same terms that I had purchased'. Sewell asked for time to consult his friends, and decided against purchase, though he would have accepted better terms. Cotes then offered to sell to Bagshawe:

> I am to receive £3,360, and to have my personal account and the non effective account of my company made up to the day you succeed me. I am to give the company complete, and if you will take my tent, and field bed on the same terms, that I bought them. My trunk containing two suits of regimental clothes, linen, etc. are at your service.

A regiment's field officers – its colonel, lieutenant colonel, and major – all commanded companies, and the colonel had an officer, called the captain lieutenant, to do the work for him. Here Cotes offers to sell his company and his lieutenant colonelcy, and takes care to specify that the profit he made from the non-existent soldiers in his company whose pay he drew ('the non effective account') should be made up on the day the transaction took place. Bagshawe borrowed £1,000 from his uncle, got the regimental agent to advance him the rest of the money, and duly became a lieutenant colonel. His friend Lieutenant Archie Grant wrote at once to 'most sincerely congratulate not only you but the whole Corps upon your affairs being at last done'. Apparently, Sewell had doubted if the commissions would be signed, and 'seemed very much surprised and disappointed when he heard they were'.[26]

Having become a lieutenant colonel at last, Bagshawe could expect promotion by seniority. His health was ruined by service in India, he fell out with his colonel, and on his return to England he found himself on half-pay, living the life of a country gentleman, but he was still anxious for advancement. In 1758 he told Lord Barrington, Secretary at War, that he believed that he had been unfairly passed over when new regiments were being raised:

> I have done my duty punctually, I have been as ready to serve and I have run as great hazards and I have suffered as much as any lieutenant colonel in the service … I think there are only eight lieutenant colonels who are seniors and there has been eleven junior officers … promoted to the rank of colonel …[27]

Barrington replied that he had indeed considered Bagshawe when 'the regiments were disposed of,' and 'I do not see that any one here has been put over your head, except the Duke of Richmond's and the King's aides de camp, whom his Majesty has always chose without a strict regard for rank.'[28] In 1759, with more troops being enlisted, Bagshawe wrote to the Duke of Bedford, lord lieutenant of Ireland, offering 'to raise a regiment of infantry at his own expense.' By this procedure, known as 'raising for rank', Bagshawe would recruit the regiment and furnish its swords and accoutrements at his own expense, although if the regiment was disbanded in less than three years the public purse would refund the cost of these items. The government accepted the offer, and his commission as colonel was dated 17 January 1760.

No sooner had Colonel Bagshawe set about raising his regiment, the 93rd Foot, than he found himself the target of just the sort of pleas that powerful men had once made on his behalf. Lieutenant Francis Flood was the nephew of Warden Flood, attorney general for Ireland, and Bagshawe thought that part of the agreement for Flood's commission was that his uncle would provide sufficient money for Flood to raise ten men. The attorney general loudly denied that any such agreement existed, and young Flood was soon in financial difficulties, for he could not balance his recruiting account. 'My family is in distress,' he lamented, 'being concerned with a contested election', so no money was to be had there.[29] Financial embarrassment did not stand in the way of young Flood's desire for promotion. When Captain Alexander Joass decided to sell his captaincy to buy the fort major's place at Stirling Castle he quite properly offered it for £1,000, to Captain Lieutenant Woolocombe, the regiment's senior subaltern, who could not afford it. Joass announced that Flood had put in for it, and 'the young man says that his father will give the cash, this I very much doubt'.[30] Flood assured Bagshawe that 'all my senior officers have declined' to buy the captaincy, 'there is no delay on my side, my money being lodged six weeks ago, and my lieutenancy is disposed to Ensign Watts,' and he would be very glad if the commission could be sent along forthwith.[31]

It soon transpired that to Flood's 'inexpressible disappointment' the deal had fallen through, and Lieutenant Ellis, his senior, had bought the captaincy. Almost immediately Flood blithely told Bagshawe that: 'I have been lately married to a young lady in the County of Clare ... and have got a pretty good fortune,' though he would need a little leave to sort out his affairs.[32] There was evidently a misunderstanding over this leave, and Flood was put under arrest by the regiment's unsmiling lieutenant colonel for arriving at the next garrison a trifling six days after his company. He promptly penned a plea to the lord lieutenant, protesting that he had been deprived of Joass's company by the colonel's unreasonable behaviour, and hoped that your Excellency will not suffer such an infringement of that regulation which has so long governed in the sale and purchase of commissions to be made in prejudice to your memorialist who without the interposition of your Excellency's authority is strongly apprehensive of being severely injured in this affair.[33]

This was no help. Flood went onto half-pay when the regiment was disbanded in 1763, came back onto full pay in a newly raised independent company in 1781, joined the 102nd Foot soon afterwards when it was created by the amalgamation of several such companies, and exchanged into the 49th Foot a few months later. So far so good, for he was now in an 'old corps' and safe from disbandment. But he neither managed to buy a captaincy nor to gain one by seniority, and eventually sold out in 1784, a very old lieutenant. Alas for that 'pretty good fortune' from the lady from County Clare.

Bagshawe's career overlapped that of Viscount Barrington, who did much to enforce the existing rules and to make them more stringent. In February 1759 he made it clear that no purchase could take place without the consent of the War Office, and in 1765 a memorandum for the king's use encapsulated the regulations as they then stood. Only commissions that had been bought could be sold; regimental commanders made the crucial recommendation for an appointment in their regiment; officers could not retire on full pay; new vacancies should be filled, if possible, from officers on half-pay; officers on full and half-pay could only exchange with one another if they were of the same rank, and exchanges between officers of different units could only be between men of the same rank, with colonels' consent, and only then if both officers signed to say no 'sweetener' had been given or received. Barrington must have known that the latter condition was widely flouted. Indeed, the unofficial 'non-regulation' additions to the price of commissions remained illegal as long as commissions were bought and sold, and officers all cheerfully signed to certify what all knew to be untrue. At least Barrington, while admitting that George II was 'in general very much averse to a practice injurious to officers of merit who have no money', managed to establish a comprehensive tariff in 1765.

We can also see the importance of half-pay. In the reign of William III it had become a device for putting officers who had been made redundant by the disbandment of their unit or who wished to quit the service temporarily, to move onto what was in effect a reserve list, available for re-employment when another war beckoned. It was a device that helped make it possible for the army to cope with those great fluctuations in size that characterised it during the eighteenth century. Half-pay also came to play an important part in the manipulation of the careers of the well-connected, for an officer on full pay in a sought-after regiment with no promotion vacancies might exchange with a half-pay officer in a less fashionable corps, buy a promotion in it, and then exchange back to his original regiment in his new rank. A good regimental agent could manage the business so slickly that our upwardly mobile hero might not even be put to the trivial necessity of buying a new uniform as he zig-zagged his remorseless way up the *Army List*, but he needed money or influence to ensure a smooth ascent.

Let us see how influence operated for the future Duke of Wellington, the Hon Arthur Wesley, as his family then spelt its name, left cash-poor but interest-rich by the early death of his father, the Earl of Mornington. The tuneful Earl had combined spending more money than his estates brought in (in the great tradition of Anglo-Irish gentlemen) with being professor of music at Trinity College, Dublin. Arthur was commissioned to the 73rd Foot in March 1787, into a vacancy left by the death of an officer in India, where the regiment was then stationed. That December he was promoted lieutenant, another free vacancy, in the new-raised 76th Foot, then slipped sideways into the more senior 41st a month later, and hopped to a lieutenancy in the 12th Light Dragoons just six months after that. He was bought a captaincy in the 58th Foot in June 1791, moved on to a free death-vacancy in the 18th Light Dragoons in October 1793, became a major in the 33rd Foot in the summer of 1793, before being advanced enough money by his elder brother Richard to purchase the 33rd's lieutenant colonelcy in September that year. He spent 1787–1793 serving as aide-de-camp to the Lord Lieutenant of Ireland, earning a useful 10/- a day in addition to the pay of his rank. As he also sat for the family seat of Trim in the Irish parliament for part of this time, he cannot have done much in the way of regimental duty. Indeed, we cannot even be sure what uniforms he bothered to buy. We have a portrait of him as a shock-headed 26-year-old battalion commander with the 33rd's red facings on his coat, but he was certainly a very atypical regimental officer. In 1813 the less well-connected Lieutenant Charles Kinloch of the crack 52nd Light Infantry found himself six steps from a captaincy and there had been no sales for four years. He did have the money to buy a captaincy in the less desirable 99th Foot, then exchanged with an elderly captain in the 52nd who was on the point of leaving the army, no doubt adding to the old gentleman's pension pot in the process, thus vaulting back into his old regiment as its junior captain without having really ever left it.

Barrington realised that very few officers could play the game like this. In February 1766, in the tone of a man weary of repeatedly listening to the same argument, he told regimental commanders that they were to stop making heart-felt pleas for officers to be allowed to sell commissions they had not bought, because the system depended on a supply of free commissions. It was always maintained that:

> Long and faithful service has worn them out, they have families, the eldest in each rank are willing and able to purchase, they all deserve preferment, which in time of peace can scarcely be obtained in any other way … It is no wonder that these arguments have so frequently succeeded, when any one of them would be sufficient inducement, if there were not another side to the question.
>
> Officers who buy are permitted to sell; men who find themselves growing old or infirm dispose of their commissions which are purchased by the young and healthy; and thus what has been once bought continues for ever at sale, especially in time of peace, except now and then in a case of sudden or unexpected death. The consequence often is, that men who come into the army with the warmest dispositions to the service, whose business becomes their pleasure, who distinguish themselves on every occasion that offers, are kept all their lives in the lowest ranks because they are poor.

Barrington did not blame regimental commanders for arguing as they did, but 'their care is extended no farther than to their own corps'. With the army's broader welfare in mind, it was his duty to ensure that there was a reasonable supply of free commissions, accessible by seniority, so that poor but worthy men were not always bought over 'perhaps by the youngest, least steady and least experienced of that corps, and to the great scandal and detriment of the service.' Of course there would be times when the rule would be broken, but 'the poor, though deserving officer should always find at the War Office, a constant assertor of his rights, and the faithful guardian of his interests.'[34]

Barrington's rules applied thereafter. When Captain John Orrock was retiring in 1813 he was delighted that the Duke of York had given him leave to sell:

> But as I only purchased my Ensigncy and my Company the Duke will only allow me to sell what I purchased. Therefore I shall only receive £1350 instead of £1500 as I expected, but I am very well content, having got [a non-regulation] £300 for the exchange makes it up and one year's economy will bring up the remainder.

He began saving money by asking for his gun-dog Ponto to be sent up to town accompanied by a good supply of oat-meal, 'as dog's meat is expensive in London'.[35]

All rules had exceptions. At the battle of White Plains in 1776 the British 2nd Brigade assaulted a steep hill in the face of 'a severe and well supported fire, Lieutenant Colonel Carr of the 35th was hard hit on the way up, and Major Cockburne took over, rallying the men and leading them on to carry the position. His bravery was witnessed by General Howe, who ensured that he received the vacant lieutenant-colonelcy, although he was not next in line, and 'that instance of spirited conduct, as having occasioned the promotion, was a frequent topic of conversation amongst the officers.'[36]

The Duke of York bolted extra armour onto the regulations, decreeing that no officer could be commissioned before he was 16, must serve as a subaltern for two years before becoming a captain, and could not become a major until he had six years commissioned service. There were still abuses. When, in 1804, John Orrock hoped to slip from his ensigncy in the 65th Foot to a free lieutenancy in the 33rd, where vacancies had been opened up by service in India, he knew it was

A matter of favour, because it prevents the senior ensign of the 33rd getting promotion. The only thing that may induce the commander in chief to do it, is that the eldest ensign of the 33rd is a boy at school in England, consequently not any hardship on him.

The argument worked in Orrock's favour, and in his next letter he reported that 'It is now near 11 months since I have been gazetted a Lieut in the 33rd Regiment, which makes it very pleasant as Colonel Gore is exceedingly kind to me and Mrs Gore and Betsy [Orrock's wife] are on the most intimate terms possible, indeed they are just like sisters.'[37] In 1809, the time limits were increased to three years for captain and nine for major, and a major needed eleven years' service before he could become a lieutenant colonel. Promotion examinations were introduced in 1850, and were rigidly enforced after the Crimean War had highlighted failings in training and leadership. In 1858 Hugh Pearson's comrade, Lieutenant Harry Crohan, was prevented from moving into a vacant captaincy for 'not having passed the necessary examination for his company', though he did so soon enough.[38]

Now for a Victorian example of purchase in action. Lieutenant Colonel Edward Cooper Hodge commanded the 4th Dragoon Guards throughout the Crimean War, and in November 1854 he reflected on the cost of his commissions. His was a relatively smart regiment, though not as ruinous as the sharper end of light cavalry, and it demanded substantial non-regulation additions to the official cost of each rank, and commissions in the cavalry were in any case always more costly than those in the infantry. Hodge's cornetcy had been free, thanks to the Duke of York's influence, but it would have cost him £840 had he bought it. His lieutenancy had been £350 on top of the value of the cornetcy, and he had added a non-regulation £250. His captaincy had been £2,035 more than his lieutenancy, with a non-regulation £1,200; his majority another £1,350, with £1,435 extra; and his lieutenant colonelcy £1,600 with another non-regulation £1,400. He calculated that he had paid out £9,620 to become a lieutenant colonel, £4,285 of it in non-regulation payments. Musing, as a man might at the beginning of a war, on the prospect of wounds and death, he was happy to note that a month earlier on 23 October, the rules had at last changed, so if he was killed in action or died within six months of receiving wounds, his mother and sisters would receive the full regulation price of his rank – £6,175. He calculated, by a process that remains a trifle unclear, that the potential loss was £4,445, 'which I shall have paid the country for graciously allowing me to serve her'.[39]

Officers had an obsessive interest in seniority, because as they edged their way up to become most senior of their rank within the regiment, so promotion, with or without purchase, might come within their grasp. The editor of Lieutenant Pearson's 'Indian Mutiny' letters noted that one-third of them contain some reference to his promotion prospects and the way the death or departure of brother officers affected them. News of an officer's death was welcome to some, and Pearson ruefully acknowledged that he owed his lieutenancy to the sudden death from cholera of 'my friend, my chum', Lieutenant Henry Kenny.[40] In 1808 John Orrock was in the process of buying a captaincy in the 33rd Foot and was delighted to report that he had a better than expected bargain because 'Our eldest captain died the other day which makes me ninth captain and I shall get rank from 1st March last.'[41] When Captain Rowland Lewis of the 39th sailed from Ireland for England in the stormy October of 1752 his ship was late in arriving. His colonel, John Adlercron, was relieved to hear that it had eventually reached port, but admitted that it was 'a disappointment to some, who took it for granted that it was lost and, I was informed, were applying for the company.'[42] One officer who kept a copy of the *Army List* to hand and struck off brother officers as they were knocked over was, however, reckoned to be going too far.

Nevertheless, a sensible officer kept an eye on his progress through the regiment, ready to lend a helping hand to a senior who might be contemplating selling out. John Peebles was the senior lieutenant of the 42nd Royal Highlanders in May 1777, when he was told by his commanding officer that the sickly Captain Lieutenant Valentine Chisholm, next above him on the list, might sell out if a non-regulation £50 was added to the price of his commission:

> I thought it was too much. And of the opinion that Mr Chisholm
> should either sell or serve, that he was no longer able to serve he
> should not accept promotion, if he sold the regulation price was as
> much as he could expect in the current state of affairs, however to
> facilitate the matter and make it as well for poor Chisholm as we

could, I agreed to give the £50, 20 of which Lts [John] Rutherford and [Robert] Potts agreed to make up equally betwixt them on the above conditions and Ensign [Gavin] Drummond gives £30, which with the regulation price from Ens Campbell makes up the 600 guineas to Chisholm if I succeed to this captaincy.

Peebles was promoted captain lieutenant on 31 October, Rutherford became senior lieutenant, Campbell bought the vacant lieutenancy and Drummond moved up on the ensign's list. In September 1778 he was promoted captain without purchase, but complained that another captain – 'one Campbell from the 57th' – had been moved into the regiment, 'which I think a great injustice to Rutherford' who might, because there were two captains' vacancies, have expected a double promotion but 'has only got the captain lieutenancy.'[43]

Each promotion above ensign created a chain reaction, as Sir William Howe's North American order book demonstrates. In 1775 Captain Heptune of the 49th Regiment died, and so there was a welcome step up for all:

Capn Lieut James Grant to be Captain
Vice Heptune Dead
Lieut Robert Wilson to be Capn Lieut
Vice Grant Preferred
Ensign Wilm Roberts to be Lt
Vice Wilson preferred
Joseph Wrigglesworth Volunteer to be Ensign
Vice Roberts preferred.

Because Heptune's vacancy had been caused by his death, all these promotions were free, and swept up the senior officer of each rank below captain. But when Lieutenant Lord Borriedale of the 17th Foot sold out, the vacancies were filled by purchase:

Ensign Isaac Cary to be Lieut
Vice Lord Borriedale by Purchase
Robert Ludlow Gent to be Ensign
Vice Cary by Purchase.[44]

Joseph Wrigglesworth would have been serving in North America as a gentleman volunteer, messing with the officers but doing duty as a private soldier, hoping that either gallantry in the field or comradeship at table would leave him well placed when an ensign's vacancy came up. Sometimes the practice concealed fraud, for that gallant officer Lieutenant Colonel James Cockburne of the 35th listed his son William as a volunteer, drawing a private's pay, before gaining him an under-age ensigncy. James Brotherton, a light dragoon officer in the Peninsula, thought that most volunteers were killed in an effort to make their names, 'but those who escaped were well rewarded for their adventurous spirit.'[45] Perhaps the best-known example of the successful volunteer is that of George Hennell, son of a Coventry ribbon manufacturer 'in a moderate way of business' who arrived in Spain in 1812 with a letter of introduction to Lieutenant General Sir Thomas Picton, who attached him the 94th Foot. Two days later he took part in the storming of Badajoz, and led the way up one of the storming ladders, shouting to encourage the men as he did so. He was promptly given an ensigncy in the excellent 43rd Foot. A gentleman volunteer is remembered in one of the classic images of the age. When Major General James Wolfe was mortally wounded at Quebec, Lieutenant Henry Browne and Volunteer James Henderson of the Louisbourg Grenadiers were with him at the end. Henderson is frozen forever in Edward Penny's painting, gesturing helpfully towards Wolfe's victorious firing line which is, alas for accuracy, far closer to the stricken general than was actually the case.

Genuinely close to Wolfe when he died was his adjutant general, Major Isaac Barré, plucked from obscurity by his master, and told that he would have the honour of taking the victory dispatch homewards, duly receiving the promotion that usually came to such bearers of happy news. He now lamented to William Pitt that 'one hapless stroke', had robbed him of his patron, leaving him 'in all the distressful circumstances of an orphan' and a bullet had smashed his nose and left him blind in one eye.[46] One man's misfortune was another's good luck. Wolfe left a thousand pounds apiece to four brother officers, one of whom was Colonel Adolphus Oughton, whose own career is a wonderful example of the manipulation of interest by an officer who worried, as many did, about looking after his family and friends.

Oughton was the illegitimate son of Colonel Sir Adolphus Oughton, Baronet and MP, and Miss Frances Dickinson. The baronet, who had no other children, raised the boy as his own, and when he died in 1736 his friends rallied round to give the 17-year-old Adolphus a cornetcy in his father's regiment, the 8th Dragoons. He bought a lieutenancy when he came into his legacy, and soon moved upwards, first into a captaincy in the newly-raised 61st Foot, and then into the 37th. He remained in the regiment for eighteen years. When Oughton joined it Christopher Green was serving in its ranks, and in 1746, having been sergeant major, he was commissioned without purchase, just two weeks after the battle of Culloden. The regiment had not behaved well at Falkirk in January that year, but at Culloden it stood firm before the plaid torrent, its right-flank platoons slamming the clansmen to a halt short of the line with their volleys, and the platoons on the left shoving with their bayonets as Camerons and Stewarts swirled into them. Perhaps Sergeant Major Green distinguished himself in the carnage on Drummossie Moor. He could scarcely have gained his commission without the approval of that stern old Huguenot Lieutenant Colonel Louis Dejean, who had stood behind the 37th's colours, yelling encouragement in both French and English. Oughton became major in 1747 and lieutenant colonel commanding the 37th two years later, first appointing Ensign Green to the potentially lucrative post of quartermaster and then making him adjutant.

Green was killed as a lieutenant at Minden in 1759 when five regiments of British infantry advanced against the French cavalry and tumbled them to ruin. His widow Britannia was left with four children, three of them boys. The eldest, Nicholas, had been commissioned into the 37th in 1755 and died as a lieutenant in 1769. Charles went off to be an artillery cadet at Woolwich, and Christopher joined the Bengal Artillery as a cadet. Oughton became colonel of the 55th Foot in 1759 and moved on to the 31st in 1762. Three years later he secured an ensigncy for 16-year-old Charles Green, launching him on a career that saw him die a general and a baronet. Oughton was no less diligent where his own family members were concerned: his brother-in-law became an ensign shortly after Oughton married; and in 1763 he found space in the 31st for his stepson, then only twelve years old, promoting him lieutenant in 1766. When Oughton died, a general and a knight, in 1780, he had not only repaid his debt to his old adjutant, but ensured that his own immediate family was well looked after. Samuel Bagshawe had a debt of his own. When he was dangerously wounded before Lorient, a fatigue party of the 39th under Corporal Kirkland carried him from Plomeur Church to the beach. Kirkland was sergeant major of the 39th when Bagshawe was its lieutenant colonel, and then, when Bagshawe raised the 93rd, Kirkland became its adjutant.

It became progressively more difficult for the likes of Bagshawe and Oughton to ply this sort of patronage, and a major plank in the lofty but ramshackle edifice of interest was snatched away when the purchase of commissions was at last abolished. The end of purchase in 1871 was part of a package of army reform that included the linking of the old numbered regiments of foot into the county regiments that formed the basis of a system which has only just definitively disappeared. It also fitted into a much wider pattern of social and political change at the time: the second Reform Act of 1867, the Education Act of 1870, the legalisation of Trade Unions in 1871, the Public Health Act of 1872, and the 1875 Artisan's Dwelling Act which would make slum clearance possible. Purchase had been under sporadic attack for some time, but an 1833 committee reported that it was 'not inconsistent with the constitutional privileges of the country, but wise and beneficial'. However, the army's failings in the Crimea, which seemed – at least according to that most unreliable of barometers, popular opinion – to be epitomised by the Earl of Cardigan – encouraged George de Lacy Evans to demand a select committee to consider the issue. The Earl led the Charge of the Light Brigade having paid a non-regulation £25,000 for command of the 11th Hussars. Lord Palmerston, the Tory Prime Minister, agreed to establish a Royal Commission, which duly reported in 1857. It recommended doing away with the sale of lieutenant colonelcies and the strengthening of promotion examinations, holding that this would eventually 'tend towards the abolition of the purchase system'. The report generated considerable debate, much of it initiated by Sir Charles Trevelyan, co-author of the pioneering Northcote–Trevelyan report into the Civil Service. Eventually Palmerston concluded that while nobody would think of inventing purchase if it did not already exist, it was a fine example of a scheme that might, 'when opinions and habits had become attached to it, work well, although theoretically objectionable'.[47] He decided, for he was after all a Conservative, to leave things as they were.

By the time the issue was revisited just a few years later, Palmerston was dead and the Liberals were in office under Gladstone. His secretary of state for war, Edward Cardwell, included the abolition of purchase in his Army Regulation Bill of 1871, but it failed to get through the Lords, largely because the compensation to be paid to purchase officers would not include non-regulation sums, illegal even though everyone knew perfectly well what went on, and so officers would lose money. However, the case for reform had been strengthened by German victory in the Franco-Prussian War of 1870–71. Cardwell correctly argued that it owed more to 'the professional education of officers than to any other cause'. The government duly forced abolition through by a Royal Warrant of 1 November 1871, and purchase ended at last.

* * *

With the disappearance of purchase went the ranks of cornet, ensign, and second lieutenant in fusilier and rifle regiments. Officers were now to be commissioned as sub-lieutenants and, subject to receiving favourable reports and passing an exam, would become lieutenants after serving for two years. Appointment as sub-lieutenant followed an open competitive examination in general academic subjects. There were fears that the army would be 'officered by a race of weedy bookworms', but 'army entrance tutors' – crammers – often whiskery retired officers who knew just what was required, nursed their charges over the hurdle to a commission, although many of them took several attempts. Garrison instructors were appointed to prepare sub-lieutenants for their promotion exam. However, the system worked so badly that in 1875 the Royal Military College Sandhurst, abolished in 1871, was re-instituted. Crammers, whose work 'defeated the fundamental purpose of the examination as a quantitative assessment of potential', now steered young men through the Sandhurst entrance exam, but it was noticeable that some of the best-crammed, who passed in high on the list, passed out rather lower.[48]

A shift in the educational background of potential officers was also taking place at this time. In 1864 the Clarendon Commission, which had just investigated nine public schools (Eton, Harrow, Rugby, Shrewsbury, Westminster, Winchester, Charterhouse, St Paul's and Merchant Taylors') noted that:

> The number of public school boys who enter the army is not large. Of 1,976 candidates for first commissions within three years, 122 only had been at any of these schools. Of these 102 succeeded and 20 failed ... of 96 who passed the first examination, 38 came directly from school, 58 had intermediate education. The public school candidates for Sandhurst during that same period were 23 out of 375; the proportion who succeeded being also here much above the average. Of 18 who succeeded, 11 came straight from school; of five who failed, only one.[49]

The Taunton Commission, reporting in 1868, looked at endowed grammar schools and proprietary schools. Its conclusions, that education was poorly provided and endowments often misused, led to the Endowed Schools Act of 1869, which instituted notable improvements. Proprietary schools like Cheltenham, Clifton, Brighton, King's College School and Rossall, and endowed schools like Marlborough and Wellington College joined the Clarendon schools in preparing boys for the army. In 1883 a third of the Woolwich and just over a tenth of the Sandhurst entry came from public schools. In 1896–1900 this had risen to over three-quarters and just over one half respectively, and was to climb further into the new century.

A study of the major generals on the army's active list in the summer of 1914, most of them commissioned from Sandhurst or Woolwich in the 1870s or early 1880s, concluded that 89 per cent had attended public school and the remainder had been educated privately. Thirty per cent of the public school-educated generals had attended Clarendon Commission schools – Eton was well ahead, with twelve generals, as opposed to Harrow's seven. Amongst the second tier of public schools, Cheltenham had produced eleven generals and Wellington ten.[50] Several public school headmasters had followed the trail blazed by Dr Pollock, headmaster of Wellington (and later Bishop of Norwich) who had established, in 1895, an 'army class' in which boys in their last eighteen months of school followed a course intended to give them a good pre-professional education. In some

other schools this was called the 'modern department', though Dr
Temple, headmaster of Rugby (and later, capping Dr Pollock,
Archbishop of Canterbury) was not favourably impressed:

> This modern department is exceedingly liable to get filled up with
> a considerable number of stupid boys, because the stupid boys do
> not get on well in their Latin and Greek, and then there is a strong
> temptation both to masters and parents to put them over into what
> seems to be, and what is to a certain extent, a more easy system.[51]

Officers would receive commissions as second lieutenants, now the
universal starting point, regardless of arm of service, after attending
the Royal Military Academy, Woolwich (for the artillery and engineers) or the Royal Military College (for officers of other arms).
Militia officers could sidestep this requirement if they were able to
pass the entrance exam after attending two summer militia trainings.
The future Field-Marshal Henry Wilson made heavy weather of it.
Having failed for Woolwich twice and Sandhurst thrice, he obtained a
lieutenancy in the Longford Militia, and was crammed by Colonel
Wilson at Darmstadt between his two trainings before passing into
Sandhurst, a lacklustre fifty-eighth on the list. There was certainly little
enough connection between the Sandhurst entrance exam and a
man's future career. Winston Churchill got into Sandhurst at his third
attempt despite being crammed by the celebrated Captain James, and
then only with marks so low that he could only be accepted by the
cavalry: to be sure of the cheaper infantry one needed to pass in high.
Very occasionally, if the army was seriously short of officers, youngsters
who did really well in the entrance examination would be commissioned direct without the tiresome need to attend Sandhurst at all.
Young Robert Baden-Powell, who became the hero of Mafeking and
founded the Boy Scout movement, passed in amongst the top six in
1876, and found himself gazetted to the 13th Hussars immediately.

Woolwich, founded in 1741, had always trained gunners and
sappers. In 1798 Colonel John Gaspard Le Marchant was granted
permission to open a military school with a senior department training staff officers and a junior department preparing young men for
commissions in the infantry and cavalry. The junior department
began life at Great Marlow in Buckinghamshire in 1802 but moved

to its new site, at Sandhurst on the London to Exeter coaching road, far enough, at least in theory, from the capital for cadets not to be 'distracted' by its bright lights, in 1812. This was the very year that Le Marchant, by now a major general, was shot dead in the moment of victory at Salamanca. Old College, with its elegant Georgian grand entrance, and the broad stone steps up which the academy adjutant rides his charger on commissioning parades, is the oldest part of the establishment. Both Sandhurst and Woolwich had always been fee-paying: successful graduates of Woolwich were commissioned into the non-purchase arms, while those who passed out highest from Sandhurst were awarded free commissions. However, parents who could afford the difference between the cost of Sandhurst and the price of a commission had often been inclined to opt straight for purchase.

Historian Edward Spiers observes that despite the end of purchase the 'social composition of the officer corps proved resistant to change' and we must now consider what this composition was.[52] Let us begin by jettisoning all those easy clichés. From the very beginning the social pattern of officer recruitment was complex, and was conveniently misrepresented by the opponents of purchase at the time and by the uncritically credulous since. The case of Arthur Wesley, cited above, is an example of how the well-connected could exploit the system, but is in no sense typical. This was not an army that withered, as William Napier maintained, under the cold shadow of the aristocracy. There was nothing in Britain that approached the French 'aristocratization of the army after Louis XIV', culminating in the 1781 regulation that required a potential officer to show four generations of patrilineal noble descent.[53] Nor could any British monarch have behaved like King Frederick William I of Prussia who, as his son Frederick the Great wrote approvingly, 'weeded out from the officers of every regiment such people whose conduct or birth did not accord with the gentlemanly standards of their profession'.[54] It must be said that even in old regime France and Frederician Prussia the rules were broken. The brave and capable François de Chevert, an orphan born in Verdun in 1695, died a lieutenant general (the highest rank below marshal of France) in 1769. Frederick found employment for numerous generals from decidedly non-noble backgrounds, including one who had no idea who his father might have been. When the

50-year-old Private David Krauel was the first man into the Ziskaberg fortification at Prague in 1744 old Fritz at once ennobled him as 'Krauel von Zizkaberg'.

Nothing in the English language resembled the nobiliary particles 'von' or 'de', much misused though these were. Nor is there any meaningful comparison between burgeoning continental aristocracies and the tiny British peerage, where, with rare exceptions, a father's title was inherited only by his eldest son, and most offspring of junior peers had to make do, like Arthur Wesley, with a simple 'Honourable'. One exception was that of the daughters of those Victorian paragons Roberts and Wolseley, who were allowed to inherit their father's peerages by 'special remainder'. There were 154 lords temporal at Westminster in 1687 and still only 171, with sixteen representative Scots peers, by 1714. Across Queen Victoria's reign the total, including designated bishops, the lords spiritual, fluctuated between 421 and 577. A peerage of this size, even if it paid proper attention to perpetuating its line, could scarcely keep the army officered.

An officer's commission dubbed him esquire – a status between gentleman and knight, unless he could lay claim to a higher title. Although any aspirant for a commission had to produce a certificate saying that he was indeed a gentleman, there was no conclusive agreement as to what a gentleman actually was or, indeed precisely who might sign the certificate. In 1762 Lord Barrington, dealing with the question of 'a subaltern, late of the 5th Regiment, named Gillingham', noted that the young man's father was a master brickmaker who had 'intended to breed up his son to his own business, but the young man would not be satisfied without going into the army.' Barrington thought the brickmaker a man 'of very good character'. There was no doubt that his son was a fit and proper person to be an officer in a senior regiment of foot, commanded by Lord George Bentinck, and indeed 'the late King had consented to Gillingham's having a commission in an old regiment'. Barrington was investigating the matter simply because Gillingham's commission had been obtained by illegal trafficking by an intermediary who had broken the rules.[55]

Mark Odintz is right to point out that social status in Britain was 'an amalgam of birth, occupation, wealth and connections', while an eighteenth-century foreigner noted that 'the title of gentleman is commonly given in England to all that distinguish themselves from the common sort of people by good garb, genteel air or good education, wealth or learning.'[56] Families rose and fell, notions of class changed as time went on, and in our eagerness to retro-fit politically based terminology to the past, we risk doing our subject a grave disservice. Most significant for our purposes is the development of those 'middling sort of folk' who could be identified at the Restoration, into the middle class of the late eighteenth century, as defined by John Seed:

> Its constituent elements were distinguished from the landed aristocracy and the gentry by their need to generate an income from some kind of active occupation. And they were distinguished from the labouring majority by their possession of property – whether mobile capital, stock in trade or professional credentials – and by their exemption from manual labour. Their economic activity thus involved the possession and management of material resources and the labour of others.[57]

Class did not mean quite the same thing across Great Britain. The nineteenth-century humorist Jonah Barrington divided the landed society of Ireland into 'Half-mounted gentlemen ... Gentlemen every inch of them ... [and] gentlemen to the back-bone.' Those half-mounted gentlemen, farming a couple of hundred acres, would have ranked as yeomen in England, while in Scotland they would have looked very similar to the cash-strapped sons and tacksmen of Highland lairds, gentlemen in their own estimation but with precious little with which to reinforce their claim to gentility. Major Pierce Butler of County Carlow observed, in 1794, that he had joined the army 'not by choice but from that necessity which flows from the injustice of a feudal system, giving to the first-born all.'[58]

Another difficulty is our fondness for terminology that is gloriously imprecise. Across the period 1660–1914 a large proportion of officers hailed from the 'landed gentry'. Odintz's painstaking examination of the officers of four regiments of foot between 1767 and 1783 identifies 155 of the 268 officers whose backgrounds can be shown as coming from this group. There were also twelve from the baronetage, eighteen from the aristocracy, with twenty-seven middle class (whose fathers were merchants, lawyers, clergymen, government officials or doctors), ten descending from 'poor officers', five rankers and one whose father was a grocer. There was also a substantial contingent of foreigners: thirty-seven of them American and five German. By 1830 the aristocracy (defined to include members of peers' extended families) provided 21 per cent of officers, and the middle classes 47 per cent; the totals for 1875 were 18 per cent and 50 per cent; and for 1912, 9 per cent and 59 per cent respectively. In each of these three sample years landed gentry constituted a steady 32 per cent of the officer corps.[59] We can thus identify a general trend for the proportion of aristocratic officers to decline and that of middle-class officers to grow, reflecting changes in society at large. Even these figures over-represent the impact of the aristocracy, for in 1838 the 462 officers who were peers or members of their immediate family constituted just 9 per cent of the whole officer corps.

This broad trend conceals a rich granularity, not least as there was a close relationship between an officer's background and the regiment he chose to serve in. Aristocrats were not spread evenly across the army but became concentrated in the Horse and Foot Guards. In 1855 the Earl of Malmesbury spoke in the Lords to refute allegations made in *The Times* that the army was dominated by noblemen. He pointed out that even in the Grenadier Guards, with three battalions and about 100 officers, just eighteen 'were connected by blood directly with your Lordships', not he thought an excessive proportion in 'a regiment particularly charged with guarding the throne of an ancient monarchy'. He then looked at the ten most senior regiments of line infantry, and found only seven sons or brothers of peers, four of them, unsurprisingly, in the smart 7th Royal Fusiliers. And in the seven regiments of heavy line cavalry there were only three officers with close links to the Lords. Moreover, General Sir James Kempt, who had died not long before when colonel of the 1st Royal Dragoons, had sprung from what Malmesbury called 'the humblest order of people', though he did not add that during a period on half-pay Kempt had eked out a living working as a clerk for an army agent.[60]

In 1858 Edward Barrington de Fonblanque reckoned that: 'With the exception of the household troops and perhaps a few picked corps, the officers of which belong principally to the titled or untitled nobility, the upper section of the middle class is the most strongly represented in the higher ranks of the army.'[61] He was perfectly correct, because while the overall number of aristocratic officers was falling, their proportion in the Household Cavalry and Foot Guards (excepting the Coldstream) would actually be higher in 1912 than it had been in 1830. On the outbreak of war in 1914 the officers of the Grenadier Guards included Lieutenant Colonel Lord Brabazon, Majors Lord Bernard Gordon-Lennox, the Hon Hubert Crichton, and Lord Loch, and Captains Lord Guernsey and Lord Francis Montagu-Douglas-Scott. By this time it was unusual to find a peer or peer's son in most line infantry regiments. But there were always exceptions, and although the Royal Garrison Artillery was regarded by many as tediously serious-minded, in 1914 its 108th Heavy Battery was commanded by Major Christopher de Sausmarez, a peer's nephew, and one of his two-gun sections was commanded by a baronet.

The Guards did indeed go on active service. They fought in North America, in Spain at the end of the Peninsular War, at Waterloo, in the Sudan in 1882, and in the Boer War. They were subjected neither to the debilitating process of repeated moves about the United Kingdom, nor to virtual abandonment in some imperial outpost. Although serving as a Guards officer was expensive, for commissions, uniforms and messing costs were significantly more expensive than in line regiments, they gave an officer the best opportunity to combine military service and the lifestyle of a well-to-do gentleman. They were wholly unlike the business end of an army that won and secured an empire. Donald Breeze Mendham Huffer's wonderful study of forty-two officers of the 32nd Foot in 1857, the year the regiment distinguished itself at Lucknow, identifies three officers from landed families, eight who were the sons of officers, fourteen whose fathers were middle-class professionals, seven who were probably middle class, and three who had been commissioned from the ranks. This was a good, solid regiment of foot, its officer corps robustly middle class without a nobleman in sight.

The printed Probate Indexes for England, first published in 1858, show a similar trend. A random selection of the first hundred officer fatalities from the Mutiny reveals that 10 per cent of them left estates worth over £5,000, 20 per cent between £1,000 and £500, 10 per cent between £450 and £100, and a remarkable 60 per cent between £450 and £20. This cannot be deemed representative, for no Guards regiments and few cavalry regiments (where one might expect to find wealth most heavily concentrated) served in the Mutiny. Interestingly, the richest of the officers in this sample, who left an estate worth £16,000, was Cornet William George Hawtrey Banks, 7th Hussars. He was recommended for the VC after being 'almost cut to pieces' while 'thrice charging a body of infuriated fanatics', and was indeed decorated when the VC's regulations were modified to permit posthumous awards. Next below him came Lieutenant William Glynne Massey of the 35th Foot, with an estate of £8,000, who had ten years' service and could have afforded promotion, but was evidently content to remain a subaltern in his regiment of choice until a captaincy came up.

At the other extreme, the twenty poorest officers had probate settled at just £20. One was the Hon Henry Handcock, son of Baron Castlemaine of West Meath, an 'aristocrat' as far as social origin is concerned, but one of the seven sons of a father not overburdened with wealth. Another of the 'bottom twenty', though wholly different in background, was Paymaster Henry Donelan of the 84th Foot, commissioned from the ranks in 1854. Four officers in this group were from service backgrounds, one the son of an officer in the East India Company's service, another of an army surgeon, and a third of a commander Royal Navy. The fourth was Colonel Robert Parker Campbell CB, to all appearances one of the army's rising stars, son of a colonel and brother of a lieutenant colonel, both of whom had commanded the 52nd Light Infantry. When he died of disease at Lucknow the governor-general declared that 'the Queen's service possessed no more gallant or promising officer'. Commissioned in 1837, he had bought all his promotions up to major, attaining that rank in 1854. He had become a lieutenant colonel without purchase in March 1855 and a colonel later the same year. Campbell had commanded the 90th Foot at Canterbury and rented the handsome Nackington House just south of the city, but successive purchases seem to have left him impoverished, for his widow immediately moved out of Nackington House and applied for a pension.[62]

So we can see texture that makes a nonsense of sweeping categorisation. 'Aristocratic' did not always mean well-off. At one extreme came Cromartie Sutherland-Leveson-Gower, 4th Duke of Sutherland, the largest landowner in Britain with 1,358,600 acres in Sutherland,

Shropshire, and Staffordshire (and the steam-yacht *Catania* to boot). He was an officer in the 2nd Life Guards from 1870 to 1875 and subsequently commander of the part-time Sutherland Rifles from 1882 until he succeeded his father in 1892. Somewhere in the middle came the family of Robert Molesworth, son of an old Cromwellian, created an Irish viscount in 1716. Three of his sons became regular officers. There was money and interest enough to help Richard, who became the 2nd Viscount, on his way to field marshal, but another military brother, Edward, retired as a major after thirty-eight years' service, and the third, Walter, left as a dragoon captain after twenty; this was scarcely aristocratic influence at its most unbridled.

A notch or two further down came the alliteratively-named Edric Frederick Gifford, 3rd Baron Gifford, who won the VC as a lieutenant in the 24th Regiment fighting the Ashantis in 1874, not long after he had inherited the title. Lord Gifford transferred to the 57th in 1876 (somewhat presciently, for the 24th was to suffer severely in Zululand in 1879) and left the army as a brevet major in 1882 before becoming a colonial administrator. His grandfather, the 1st Baron, was the son of a grocer and linen-draper of Exeter, and the choice of a military career for Edric represents a well-established tendency for families who had risen fast to use the army as a 'confirmer' of their new status. At the bottom of the category came officers like Henry Handcock, younger sons of noble families with small estates. There were 585 peers in 1883. Sixty-six of them had estates with less than 2,000 acres and sixty had no land at all. The 2nd Lord Raglan, son of the commander-in-chief in the Crimea, rubbed along with 95 acres in Monmouthshire.[63]

Just as 'aristocratic' is too broad a category to aid useful analysis, so too is 'landed interest'. By the 1880s most of those officers falling into this category were recruited from amongst what a contemporary called 'yeomen', farming between 100 and 3,000 acres, or 'small proprietors', with up to a hundred acres. While purchase was in force many of them inched their way up the *Army List* by seniority, sometimes profiting from casualties sustained in the Crimea or the Mutiny to get an unexpected step or two up. Sometimes they came to the attention of an influential senior who helped propel them upwards with brevets. William Francis Butler was born in 1838 in a farmhouse in Ballyslateen, Golden, County Tipperary, seventh child of a small landowner who was always short of money and fell on the very outside edge of 'landed interest'. Nominated to a free ensigncy in the 69th Foot in 1858 by a distant relative, William Butler rose slowly by seniority to become a captain in 1872. He might have trudged on like this had he not come within the charmed circle of fellow-Irishman Garnet Wolseley, whose 'ring' of clients constituted an important interest group in the mid-Victorian army. Wolseley, son of a retired major, whose influence gained him his ensigncy, had been commissioned only six years before Butler, but had shot up to captain in less than three years' service (and, crucially, as many shifts of regiment) as opposed to Butler's fourteen, and his spectacularly brave service in Burma, the Crimea, China, and the Mutiny wafted him up to colonel by brevet in 1865. Knighted for his service in Canada, Wolseley was made a major general for the Ashanti campaign but, scenting the way the wind was blowing, let his wife know that, just in case she was asked, the peerage titles Lord Trent or Viscount Cannock would do him rather well.[64] However, he had to wait for his victory over Arabi Pasha in Egypt in 1882 to make him a viscount and a full general.

Butler served with Wolseley on the Red River Expedition of 1870–71 in Canada, and then – a captain at last and so eligible for brevet – in the Ashanti War of 1873–4. Still in Canada when he heard that Wolseley had got the command, he telegraphed: 'Remember Butler. Will sail by first steamer', and he promptly did so, entering the port of Liverpool just as Wolseley was leaving it. In January 1874 Wolseley told the Duke of Cambridge that: 'Captain Butler is in Western Akim endeavouring to raise the people there … he is a very able and energetic officer – just the man for this sort of work, and if he fails, I am sure that no other man could have succeeded.'[65] He did fail, though it was not his fault and he received a well-deserved brevet majority. He then accompanied Wolseley to South Africa (brevet lieutenant colonel) and the Sudan (colonel by seniority 1885). He became a brigadier general almost immediately, was knighted in 1886, commanded south-eastern district as a major general before going off, as a local lieutenant general, to be commander-in-chief in South Africa. Recalled when he expressed a gloomy opinion that, astonishingly, ran contrary to the government's unrealistic but more optimistic policy, he was promoted lieutenant general in 1900 and retired to Bansha

Castle in Tipperary, not far from his birthplace, in 1905. In retirement he was made an Irish Privy Councillor and a Knight Grand Cross of the Bath. Butler was much marked by the sufferings that accompanied the Great Hunger of 1847, and was a committed supporter of nationalist leader Charles Stewart Parnell. His youngest daughter, Eileen, married Ireland's premier viscount to become Lady Gormanston, and she found a poem amongst his papers:

> Give me but six-foot three (one inch to spare)
> Of Irish earth, and dig it anywhere;
> And for my poor soul say an Irish prayer
> Above the spot.

In 1877 Butler had married the painter Elizabeth Thompson, whose full-blooded battle scenes, the best-known of them 'Scotland for Ever' showing the Royal Scots Greys charging head-on at Waterloo, were much in demand. She took on a good deal of her husband's political shading. 'Evicted' has a very clear message, and even the less explicit 'Listed for the Connaught Rangers' shows two Irishmen marching happily enough down a Kerry glen with a red-jacketed recruiting party. One of them, though, throws a rueful sideways glance at a ruined cabin, perhaps the home he had to leave. When William Butler found his six-foot three of Irish earth (may it lie light upon his bones) he had risen to an eminence that belied his humble origins and firmly held political opinions, even if today we remember him best as the husband of Lady Butler.

Many middle-class families set the seal on their status by buying land, sending a son into the army, and sometimes marrying a daughter into an aristocratic family glad of the money. It was a playing board with as many snakes as ladders. The woollen draper William Mawhood (1724–1797) had grave reservations about allowing his boy William into the army, although the lad obtained a free ensigncy in the 17th Foot in 1777 and was bought a lieutenancy in the same regiment just over a year later. Mawhood *père* warned the subaltern, 'For God's and your own sake that your conduct and whole deportment be such as may establish your character, this often does more than money.' Things went from bad to worse, as Mawhood lamented 'and so you have kept a horse, kept a whore, spent your company's money and ruined your constitution: your soul I shall say nothing of.' The young man went onto half-pay in 1785, fled to France to avoid his creditors and married a count's daughter. When his father persisted in his determination to cut the scapegrace out of his inheritance, young Mawhood conspired with his sister to have the old gentleman declared a lunatic to invalidate the will.[66]

Between 1660 and 1914, while the army did indeed contain many officers with aristocratic connections or substantial landed interests, they were never more than a minority, albeit a significant and influential one which, because of the importance of money and interest from promotion, commanded a disproportionate share of regimental colonelcies (founts of interest in themselves) and senior command appointments. The influence of this group shrank, in part because of the wider trends towards making the public service more accountable and accessible, and, as the period went on, officers with this sort of background tended to concentrate in the Guards, both horse and foot. Major landed families often groomed their eldest to inherit the estate, perhaps after a little light soldiering, sent another son into the army as a career and another into the Church or the law. When Arthur Wesley married Kitty Pakenham in his family's Dublin house his clergyman brother, Gerald, officiated, and it was to him that Arthur muttered 'She has grown ugly, by Jove', when his faded bride entered the room. Even this received wisdom needs leavening with caution, because there is abundant evidence of some eldest sons paying more attention than cliché would suggest. The second Duke of Northumberland, whom we have seen raising the Percy Tenantry Volunteers, had a serious career, as Lord Percy, as a regular officer before he inherited the dukedom.

Although two of the dominant figures in the late Victorian army, Wolseley and Roberts, were indeed peers, they gained their peerages by their own efforts. Wolseley, as we have just seen, was the son of a half-pay major, and Roberts of a major general in the East India Company's service, who had begun his own career in the Bengal Artillery, transferring to the British army proper only when the company's forces were absorbed by it in 1858. Neither officer would have judged himself to be in the top quarter or so of regimental officers with broad acres at their backs. Philip Browne had an atypical career, obtaining a free appointment as quartermaster of the 12th

Foot in 1736, buying a cornetcy in the 2nd Horse the following year, and then, in 1745, purchasing the rank of 'exempt [cornet] and captain' in the 3rd Troop of Horse Guards, whence he disappeared onto half-pay in 1746. His quartermaster's post could not have been gained without influence and his Horse Guards commission would have been very costly. He summed up his brother officers as 'private gentlemen without birth or [influential] friends', and the phrase is wonderfully apposite.[67] The army appealed to a wide coalition of scions of lesser, landed families and sons of the growing middle class, keen to make their way in the world, who constituted a majority of officers. Interest, where they could command it, would secure them a step here or there, and the family could often muster enough money for a crucial promotion. John Houlding, that gifted historian of the eighteenth-century army, identified a third category, 'drawn socially from a wide spectrum across the first two groups, and including a significant minority of foreigners, chiefly Huguenots'. Members of this group lacked land or much money, but 'were nevertheless gentlemen well-enough born and educated'.[68]

As the army grew in size and became a more stable career, so it 'bred up a professional class which was dedicated to its service', and from the early eighteenth century this group was notable for constituting military families that played an increasingly important role in furnishing officers.[69] In his study of 23rd Royal Welch Fusiliers' part in the American war, Mark Urban describes a regimental officer corps that typified many at the start of a long campaign, before death vacancies had opened up promotion. Most officers had grown old in their rank: Frederick Mackenzie, the adjutant, had been a lieutenant for about half his forty-four years. Lieutenant Colonel Benjamin Bernard's father John had commanded a company in the 23rd at Fontenoy in 1745, and his own son John was serving as a second lieutenant. Both the regiment's colonel, Sir William Howe, and the Secretary at War, Lord Barrington, recognised the importance of looking after the poor but deserving officers who constituted such an important part of the regiment. Lord Barrington told Major Blakeney, who was anxious to avoid service, that 'Those not capable of doing their duty should dispose of their commissions nor expect to be continued in the army to the detriment of the service, and the prejudice of other officers able and willing to serve.' When Blakeney took the hint, Howe offered the majority at a knock-down price to the worthy Captain Nisbet Balfour, who was still feeling the pain of buying his captaincy, but knew that the majority was too good to miss and wrote that 'I must trust to fortune to clear me'.[70] By the end of the nineteenth century there was a marked tendency for officers to come from families with strong military connections. Of the sample of 1914 generals referred to above 39 per cent had fathers in the army; the next largest professional group was the 12 per cent of generals who were sons of the manse. Twenty-two of the forty-one military parents were generals or admirals, and most of those who had retired at ranks below colonel seem to have done so to claim the family inheritance. Just over half the eldest sons in this sample had followed their fathers into the service, a larger percentage than for any other major professional group. By 1910 a remarkable 43.1 per cent of the young men entering Sandhurst as 'gentleman cadets' had fathers in the service.

The growing tendency of these military families to remain associated with the same regiment is well exemplified by the Gores and the 33rd Foot. This was later known as the Duke of Wellington's Regiment and nine Gores served in it over two centuries. John Gore was commissioned into it when it was raised in 1702 and retired as captain lieutenant twenty years later. Another John Gore was commissioned in 1748 after spending a year as a volunteer, and retired as a major in 1774. His sons Arthur and Ralph both served in the regiment: Arthur was killed as a brigadier general at Bergen op Zoom in 1814, and Ralph went off to another regiment as a lieutenant colonel. Both Ralph's sons followed him into the 33rd; one of them was killed at Waterloo. Sir Ralph Gore, who became 1st Earl of Ross, lost a hand at Fontenoy and brought the regiment out of action at Laufeld in 1747. William Gore served from 1766 to 1794, retiring as a major. At the other end of our time-scale, Major General Sir John Adye observed that 'The persistence of family names in the gunners and sappers is a very marked feature of these two corps and ... my own family may almost constitute a record.' He himself was a fifth-generation gunner, and when he died in 1930 the family had already accumulated 135 years of unbroken service – which was then continued by his son.[71] Francis Davies, a major general in 1914, had been commissioned into the Worcester Militia in 1881 and then transferred to the Grenadier

Guards, the regiment to which his father and grandfather had both belonged.

These broad social groups were neither static nor self-contained. Henry George Hart was a major's son from a Devonshire family. In 1829 he was given a commission in the 49th Foot, and rubbed along until, nineteen years later, having made some money compiling *Hart's Army List*, he managed to buy the regiment's majority. He died a lieutenant general, and his brother, an engineer officer who won the VC in Afghanistan in 1879, reached the rank of general. Henry's son, Arthur FitzRoy, was born in 1844, and was named after the two officers his father admired as the greatest soldiers of the age: the Duke of Wellington and Lord FitzRoy Somerset, the future Lord Raglan. He attended Sandhurst but was too young to take a commission at the end of the course. From here Arthur went on to Cheltenham College, failed the entrance examination to Woolwich, and promptly went back to Sandhurst, thereby earning the distinction of being the only man to pass out a second time. He obtained a free ensigncy in the 31st Foot and purchased a lieutenancy in 1867. The following year Arthur married Mary Synnot, daughter of Mark Synnot who owned the Ballymoyer estate, with over 7,000 acres in Armagh. He served under Wolseley in the Ashanti war, and eventually commanded the Irish brigade as a major general in the Boer War before retiring to live the life of a member of the landed interest and serve as a JP. Slim, ramrod straight, and sharply moustachioed, he looked every inch the Irish landowner he had become – by marriage. His son Arthur Henry Seton Hart-Synnot was educated at Clifton College, commissioned from Sandhurst into the East Surrey Regiment (as the 31st had now become) in 1890 and served as his father's brigade major in the Boer War. A cultivated man and a talented linguist, he learned Japanese and served as an observer of the Russo-Japanese War, and commanded an infantry brigade on the Western Front in 1917–18. His substantial landed interest might put him towards the top of our second category.

The fourth group comprises what Houlding called 'subaltern officers of advanced age and experience promoted from amongst the non-commissioned officers'.[72] These men, typically, rose from sergeant major to become ensign and adjutant, and were often commissioned so late in life that that they would be lucky to get beyond captain.

Indeed, Thomas Barrow, father of George, author of *Lavengro* and *The Bible in Spain,* joined the army in 1783, became a sergeant nine years later and retired as a captain. When fifteen senior regiments of foot were expanded by being given second battalions in 1756, five of the new ensigns in 2nd Battalion 3rd Foot (The Buffs) were provided by commissioning the quartermaster and four sergeants from the 1st Battalion. When this battalion moved on to become a regiment in its own right, as the 61st Foot, in 1758, six of its subalterns had been commissioned from the ranks. One had served for 25 years, three for 19, one for 13 and the remaining one for 11 years.

The eighteenth-century army seemed more prepared to grant cavalry NCOs commissions in the infantry than it was to commission infantry NCOs within their own arm. Mark Odintz suggests that this might have been because they already understood something of those gentlemanly attributes, horsemanship and swordsmanship, or because it was easier for a man from a traditionally 'high caste' arm to impose his authority. It may equally well reflect the fact that the cavalry always recruited a proportion of well set-up young men with a natural affinity with horses. These often came from a yeoman farmer background, and made admirable NCOs, but they would have little chance of surviving as officers in such a costly arm. When the army was reduced on the outbreak of peace, commissioned rankers were usually the first to be sent off onto half-pay, a process encouraged by the fact that they were often amongst the oldest of their rank. However, even in the eighteenth century there were several examples of men who began low and rose high:

John Jeffries, one of the marine colonels of 1741, began life as a gunner: Joseph Guest who was deputy-governor of Edinburgh Castle and a lieutenant general was originally a Yorkshire groom; James Robertson, colonel of the 15th Regiment and a lieutenant general when he died in 1788, was given a commission in a marine regiment in 1740 after spending some years in the ranks.[73]

A more liberal view was taken in the nineteenth century. From 1830 to 1859, 1,016 NCOs were commissioned, a figure that includes both combatant commissions and promotions to quartermaster and riding master; these thousand men represented 18.69 per cent of the non-purchase total of 6,146. There were some years in which the number of NCOs commissioned actually exceeded that of cadets commissioned from Sandhurst. In 1854, for example, with the army expanding for the Crimea, 372 commissions were bought and 319 given free, 50 of which went to Sandhurst cadets and a remarkable 121 to NCOs. Some regiments were veritable nurseries of new officers: between March 1854 and May the following year, the 13th Light Dragoons commissioned six of its sergeant majors, one into a death vacancy, another 'for distinguished service', and two into the regiment as quartermaster: another was sent off as riding master to the 1st Royal Dragoons, and the sixth as adjutant to the 2nd Dragoons. There were some remarkable stories. The Scotsman William Webster joined the 23rd Light Dragoons in 1812 and was a sergeant by the time the regiment was reduced after Waterloo, when, to avoid being discharged he volunteered for the 16th Lancers as a private. Webster was back up to sergeant again in 1818, became sergeant major two years later, and bought his cornetcy in 1827. This is in itself astonishing, for we can only imagine how someone from the ranks could afford something beyond many middle-class families. Perhaps a regimental officer with money to spare gave his sergeant major a leg up. Webster became lieutenant in 1832 and captain in 1847, both without purchase, and when he retired in the latter year he had a remarkable total of 45 years and 3 months service, with 23 years, 9 months on postings abroad, including the regiment's whole scorching tour of duty in India – from 1822 to 1846.

Not all officers commissioned from the ranks had grown grey in the service by the time they laid aside their musket to buckle on a sword-belt. While there are not enough of these men to constitute a group in their own right, they should certainly not be ignored. The orphan John Shipp joined the 22nd Foot in 1797, and became a sergeant very quickly. He was commissioned into the 65th Foot after repeated displays of bravery at the siege of Bhurtpore in 1805, and given a lieutenancy in the 76th three weeks later. Exceptionally, Shipp was allowed to sell out to pay off his gambling debts, and promptly re-enlisted in the 24th Light Dragoons. After making his way up to sergeant-major, he was commissioned again, this time into the 87th Foot. In 1823 he was sent on half-pay after being court-martialled following a dispute with his major, a sad end to a remarkable career.

Charles Robert Cureton was a gazetted lieutenant in the Shropshire Militia in 1806 who, after getting into severe financial difficulties, faked suicide by leaving his clothes on a beach, then enlisted in the 16th Light Dragoons under the pseudonym Robert Taylor, soon becoming a corporal. Wellington's military secretary, Lord FitzRoy Somerset (who had known Cureton as a civilian) had him attached to headquarters as a confidential clerk, and he was commissioned without purchase into the 40th Foot in 1814. He transferred to the 20th Light Dragoons almost at once, was lieutenant and adjutant in 1816, shifted to the 16th lancers in 1819 and made his way on up to become a lieutenant colonel in 1839 and colonel in 1846. Cureton was killed as a brigadier general at Ramnagar in the Second Sikh War.

NCOs who were both brave and lucky might become officers while they still had time enough to make their way. Bernard McCabe, probably the son of Irish immigrants, enlisted in the 31st in 1839, and was a sergeant when the regiment assaulted the Sikh entrenchments at Sobraon on 10 February 1846. He picked up the regimental colour and planted it on the ramparts, was commissioned into the 18th Foot, and promoted lieutenant in the 32nd in 1849. He was mortally wounded as a captain at Lucknow, leading a sortie against the rebel guns. As the British advanced up the slope from the River Alma in the Crimea under heavy fire, Colour Sergeant Luke O'Connor, a 23-year-old Irishman in the colour party of 23rd Royal Welch Fusiliers, saw that Lieutenant Anstruther (bearing the regimental colour) was hard hit. He picked up the colour and, although wounded himself, carried it until the battle was over. He was no less brave in the assault on the Redan, part of the fortifications of Sevastopol, where he was twice wounded. O'Connor was commissioned and became the first member of the army to be awarded the newly instituted VC. When he died in 1915 it was as a retired major general and a knight. William McBean of the 93rd Highlanders had already been commissioned from the ranks and was a 40-year-old lieutenant and adjutant when his battalion assaulted the great breach in the Begumbagh at Lucknow. He hewed down eleven men with his broadsword, earning the VC, and when congratulated on a good day's work replied 'Tuts, it did'na take me twenty minutes.'

William McBean died a major general, his career epitomising that of a brave, well-conducted soldier who had made his way through his own efforts, with a happy ending to his story. Hector Macdonald or 'Fighting Mac' was not so fortunate. Born in 1853, son of a crofter on the Black Isle, he worked in a warehouse in Inverness and served in the local company of Rifle Volunteers, before enlisting in the 92nd Highlanders in 1870. By the time he joined a draft for India the following year, he was doing so well that he was given the local rank of 'salt water corporal' for the voyage, and was a colour sergeant when the regiment fought in the second Afghan War in 1879. His first citation for bravery, in an action involving small detachments of his own battalion and an Indian unit, told how 'The courage and skill with which this party was handled reflected the highest credit on Colour Sergeant Hector Macdonald, 92nd Highlanders, and Jemadar Sher Mahommed, 3rd Sikhs.' He 'again distinguished himself' in another small action, and his conduct in the defence of Roberts's cantonment at Sherpur was so remarkable that he was allegedly offered the choice of a VC or a commission. Whether the question of the choice is apocryphal, he was certainly commissioned, and the men of his company carried him shoulder-high to the officers' mess, before the pipes played 'Cock of the North' as each man marched up to salute him. His battalion went from India to South Africa, and he was captured at Majuba Hill, earning a third mention in dispatches for his 'conspicuous gallantry'.

Hector Macdonald shone in war but made heavy weather of peacetime, when he was just about able to survive on his pay. T. P. O'Connor knew him well, and wrote, 'He was one of those men who ought never to have appeared out of uniform ... He just looked a Tommy, and a Tommy in his Sunday clothes, which is not Tommy at his best.'[74] He went through 'an irregular form of marriage' to Christina Duncan, and although a son, Hector Duncan Macdonald, was born in 1887 the couple never really lived together and his documents still listed his next of kin as his brother William. He transferred to Egyptian service in 1880, commanded a Sudanese battalion, and in 1898 (by now a brevet lieutenant colonel) led a brigade at Omdurman. The war correspondent George Warrington Steevens described him as being 'very gleeful in his usual grim way' as he swung his brigade, with consummate skill, to meet a flank attack. He was appointed CB, made a full colonel and an aide-de-camp to Queen Victoria, but hated all the publicity. When the Worshipful Company of Goldsmiths and Silversmiths presented him with a sword in 1899, he privately admitted that he wished that he had the price of the sword in his pocket. He commanded a brigade in India and then moved on to lead the Highland Brigade in the Boer War after its first commander was killed in a night attack. On catching some shirkers at Paardeberg, he drew his revolver on them: 'Ye dairty hounds, ye know what I should like to do with ye. Now git on, I say, git on, ye dairty hounds.'[75] Macdonald was knighted after the war, and was soon promoted major general and appointed General Officer Commanding Ceylon.

There he fell from grace, and fell hard. Trevor Royle, his sympathetic biographer, suggests that his 'lack of allegiance to the white planter class' meant that he had enemies ready to pounce on him when he committed 'a habitual crime of misbehaviour with several schoolboys', or perhaps exposed himself in a railway carriage. Royle suggests that this 'was not a court-martial offence, by any stretch of the imagination', although the *Manual of Military Law* observes that an officer's behaviour that might bring a scandal on the service should be tried by court martial as 'Disgraceful Conduct' and 'there is no power to award any other punishment than cashiering on conviction for this offence.'[76] The colony's governor granted him leave 'to save public scandal' and he went to London, called on his wife in the 'relative middle class comfort' of Dulwich, and then went to see Lord Roberts, now commander-in-chief, at the War Office. Roberts had been responsible for commissioning Colour Sergeant Macdonald all those years ago, and was not naturally inclined to court-martial senior officers. He wired Colombo that he did not propose to confirm the six months' leave given by the governor 'as he does not desire to remove Macdonald from the ordinary process of law.' On his way back to Ceylon, Macdonald broke his journey in Paris, where he saw in the papers that he was returning to face a court martial. He shot himself through the head at the Hotel Regina in the Rue de Rivoli, using a small-calibre pistol he had bought the day before. His body was brought back for burial in Edinburgh, though a persistent (and wholly incredible) legend has him covertly spirited away to Prussia, where he became Field Marshal Freiherr Anton Ludwig Friedrich August von Mackensen.

Trevor Royle suggests that if 'Macdonald had been a person of influence in high places or indeed of more worldliness, or a guinea or two, then he would have taken legal or political advice and perhaps put a damper on the charges.' His fall was occasioned by 'the icy indifference of a class system that failed to stand by the hero of its own creation in his greatest hour of need'.[77] There is more to it than that. The issue was not one of covert homosexuality, but of a serious lapse of judgement in a public place before civilian witnesses. It would certainly be fatal to an officer's career today, in an age when attitudes to homosexuality are infinitely more enlightened. Brigadier Michael Calvert, who had an outstanding wartime career conducting irregular operations, winning a DSO and bar in the process, was court-martialled for gross indecency in 1951 and had to leave the army.[78] It was not long after the end of the war, and the evidence against him was given by German youths. Calvert was a Woolwich-educated regular Royal Engineer officer whose reputation as a Chindit column commander was still fresh in the public memory, but none of this could save him.

The broader point, on the treatment of ranker officers by brother officers of a more conventional background, merits serious consideration. The Duke of Wellington told the 1836 Royal Commission on Military Punishments that rankers

> do not make good officers ... They are brought into a society to the manners of which they are not accustomed; they cannot bear at all being heated in wine or liquor ... they are quarrelsome ... And they are not persons that can be borne in the society of the officers of the army; they are different men altogether.[79]

Sir Hugh Rose, commander-in-chief in India at the end of the Mutiny, took the same view, and argued that the process of transferring a man with no advantages of background or education to a much superior class was 'a very disadvantageous anomaly'. In the mid-1880s, Wully Robertson, hoping for a recommendation, discovered that his commanding officer 'held the view that promotion from the ranks was not to the benefit of either the man or the state'.[80] Not long afterwards, Sir Redvers Buller, the adjutant general, expressed himself as

> strongly opposed to any scheme which tends to increase the number of candidates for commissions from the ranks ... The gentleman who has enlisted has lost caste, and it cannot fail that a

man who has deliberately adopted as companions men of a lower social and educational standard than himself must ... have lowered his own standard by the associations he has cultivated.[81]

This was not a universally held opinion. Thomas Hitchbone of the 12th Foot had served in the ranks for nineteen years before becoming adjutant in 1771, but could not obtain an ensigncy till 1778 because of the flood of 'gentleman candidates' for every vacancy. He succeeded only because the dying Lieutenant Sweetenham warmly recommended him for the ensigncy that would fall vacant on his death, and 'the whole corps of officers' at once made the same request to the commanding officer, who was delighted to support it. Fear of losing this admirable man to another regiment induced his colonel to make him a lieutenant in 1780. During the Boer War Lord Tullibardine, a regular officer in the Royal Horse Guards, had raised the irregular Scottish Horse, and told a Royal Commission in 1902 that

Some of the most reliable officers I had were appointed through the ranks. They were of all classes, and were promoted purely on their merits. Many of them were not what is termed gentlemen by birth, but I never kept a man who did not behave himself. Perhaps almost the best officer I had in the corps had been a farm hand and was the son of a small farmer in Perthshire, while another had been a footman in civilian life. This last fact was, of course, only known to me.[82]

What worked so well in a wartime-raised irregular unit was less acceptable in the staid ranks of the old army. Just after the 84th had commissioned its sergeant major and quartermaster in 1858, Hugh Pearson told his father that he was delighted to hear that Lieutenant Williams was to become adjutant, because it meant that 'these "rankers" just raised have no chance. I much prefer a gentleman to a man who has risen.' He was not at all pleased when Ensign George Lambert, who had been sergeant major, was appointed adjutant. 'The fellows had all been congratulating themselves on having a gentleman as adjutant,' he wrote, and Williams had actually been doing the duties of one for a fort-night, when the gazette overthrew all his hopes, and conferred a much prized appointment on a puny and undeserving snob. No one yet knows why, or for what he got the Victoria Cross. Certainly it was not for 'distinguished conduct', and I think even he himself would be puzzled to know why he got it.[83]

Lambert had in fact been decorated, while sergeant major of the 84th, for repeated acts of bravery on three dates and distinguished conduct on another two. He bought a lieutenancy in 1858 (which itself dents conventional wisdom about impecunious rankers) and died of natural causes two years later.

It was often argued that soldiers themselves preferred 'gentleman officers'. Rifleman Benjamin Harris of the 95th Rifles wrote:

> I know from experience that in our army the men like best to be officered by gentlemen, men whose education has rendered them to be more kind in their manners than your coarse officer, sprung from obscure origin, and whose style is brutal and overbearing.

He went on to suggest that ranker officers were unpopular because of their concern for detail, and soldiers were 'worried by these little-minded men for the veriest trifles, about which the gentleman never thinks of tormenting him'.[84] When Lieutenant Thomas Blood, himself a ranker, proposed in 1836 that one-third of all officers should be commissioned from the ranks, he argued that such men would know their soldiers so well that they would not be deceived by malingering, thus giving some substance to suggestions that ranker officers were unpopular because they knew too much. The fiercely brave Bernard McCabe seems to have been unpopular with his soldiers because of his strict attention to detail, as evidenced by his conversation with a sentry, a fellow Irishman, who had not challenged him as he walked night rounds in besieged Lucknow:

OFFICER: 'Are you the sentry?'
SENTRY: 'I am, sir.'
OFFICER: 'And why the devil didn't you challenge me?'

SENTRY: 'Because I knew it was you, sir, and that you would be coming this way.'

OFFICER, VERY SEVERELY: 'You should have fired, sir. You are not supposed to know anyone outside your post, especially at night.'

SENTRY: 'Then by Jesus Christ the next time you come the same way at night I will accommodate you. I will shoot you right enough.'

The officer took no further notice and did not trouble the same sentry again.[85]

In fact the sentry was right not to challenge an officer he could recognise, and sentries had quite enough to put up with as it was. Not long afterwards, and only a few miles away, Lieutenant Poole of the 84th was shot dead by a sentry of 5th Fusiliers, 'but he alone was to blame,' thought Hugh Pearson,

It was a dark night, and he wore a large turban round his cap ... He was visiting the sentries, and to do so, had to expose himself to the enemy's fire; in his anxiety to escape their observation by running along a hedge he neglected to answer the challenge and consequently was shot. He lived just long enough to free the sentry from all blame.[86]

In 1900 W. E. Cairns, in a book aimed at future officers and their families, noted that some officers were indeed commissioned from the ranks, but 'the fact remains that men will follow a "gentleman" much more readily than they will an officer whose social position is not so well assured.' Much of his argument, however, concerned the sheer expense of sustaining commissioned rank, and the risk of being forever compromised by using the wrong military tailor: 'the youngster will make a fatally false start if by any chance he go to the wrong outlet for the right article.'[87] At precisely the time that Cairns was writing, Wully Robertson was making his way through the officer ranks and gaining a DSO in the 1895 Relief of Chitral. He made captain that year 'in the course of ordinary regimental promotion, and was unusually lucky in reaching that rank in less than seven years after being commissioned'.[88] Significantly, he had decided to stay in the cavalry on commission, despite its expense (he thought that it required at least £300 a year and a subaltern was paid £120), by choosing the 3rd Dragoon Guards, a regiment that was stationed in India where living was relatively cheap. When he reported for duty he 'received a most friendly welcome from all members of the officers' mess.' He avoided expense 'by retiring early to bed and leading an abstemious life'. This helped him to stay awake during hot Indian days, and to work on qualifying in language examinations: Hindu, Urdu, Persian, Pushtu, Punjabi, and Gurkhali. All this brought him extra payment, which was 'little more than sufficient to pay expenses, but this little was not to be despised for it helped to keep my head, financially, above water.'[89]

A number of factors helped create an environment in which the commissioned ranker found it harder to survive. The abolition of purchase and its replacement by education at the two fee-paying colleges, the increasing number of public school cadets, and the cost of buying necessary equipment and paying mess bills were all practical deterrents to taking a commission. Indeed, it could be hard for even the well-to-do to survive, especially in the cavalry. In the 1850s, Cornet Barrington of the 6th Dragoons, 'a Bachelor of Arts of Oxford, a good oar, a first-class cricketer, a bold rider, and a pleasant companion', was obliged to leave.[90] Two young officers of the 4th Hussars were bullied in 1896 because they had little apart from their pay, and W. E. Cairns cheerfully reported that 'officers have lived in the 10th [Hussars] with an allowance of only £500 a year apart from their pay, but they have rarely lasted long.'[91] In his majestic study of the cavalry, Lord Anglesey suggests that in the 1870s recruits of 'superior education' tended to gravitate towards the cavalry. He noted that the 17th Lancers alone had seventeen such men in 1879, and in 1887 Wolseley was told by a colonel that 'he had in his regiment some thirty sons of well-to-do gentlemen as privates, corporals, etc. and that they had done much to raise the tone of the men in barracks.'[92] However, Sergeant Major Edward Mole of the 14th Hussars thought that their experiments usually ended in tears, for

From three to six months seemed to satisfy them, for they nearly always found the game different to what they expected, and purchased their discharges ... They were not born for the life ...

They soon recognised that without interest at their backs they could hope for nothing, and that in peace time only about one NCO in a hundred gets a commission and then very often by a fluke ... A commission from the ranks is not always an unmixed blessing.[93]

In 1873 John Edward Acland-Troyte, lieutenant in a volunteer battalion and an Oxford graduate, was anxious for a commission in the regular army but, at 25, he was just too old to obtain one by conventional means. He took the drastic step of signing on in an effort to make his way through the ranks, reached sergeant, and was eventually commissioned. He concluded that most of his fellow-NCOs were happy enough where they were:

Can it be imagined that a man of the class our recruits came from would be comfortable in gentlemen's society, and having to conform to 'society manners?'... I do not believe that there was a man of any rank ... during my time who would have taken a sub-lieutenant's commission if it had been offered to him.[94]

Francis Hereward Maitland signed up as a cavalry trooper not long before the First World War. He knew that his family had 'managed to get me through a public school and I am aware that they could not afford to keep up a commission for me'. He coped well enough with the sweat and piss of the barrack room, but there were times when he reflected on what might have been:

Stationed not far from us is another famous regiment. In it are two subalterns who were at school with me. Now and then, straying into civilian clothes, I am able to meet them. Surreptitiously if in the 'shot [Aldershot], quite openly if I go to the Smoke [London].[95]

On the eve of the First World War it was still possible to rise through the ranks, but between 1870 and 1890 only 3 per cent of all combatant commissions were obtained this way, far fewer than in the days of purchase. One of the most impressive men to make his way at this time was Harry Finn, a tailor's son from Kent, who enlisted into the 9th Lancers in 1871 and was awarded the DCM for bravery in the

Second Afghan War. He was commissioned into 21st Hussars in 1881, and in 1898 commanded the left wing of his regiment, now converted into lancers, in its famous charge at Omdurman, emerging as a brevet lieutenant colonel. In 1900 Finn departed for Australia to take on a series of posts that saw him rise to inspector general of the Commonwealth's military forces as a temporary major general. A recent assessment reckons that

> Finn's breezy, informal and direct manner made him well liked by the troops he commanded. He did much to infuse enthusiasm into young and inexperienced troops and set an example of soldierly bearing and conduct. In this way he was prominent among the small group of professional officers who did much to lay the foundations upon which the reputation of the Australian Imperial Force was built.[96]

The fact remains, though, that talent was squandered, and the high cost of living in the army deterred not only potential officers from within its ranks but young men who might have made excellent officers but whose families could not afford it. In 1903 a War Office committee considered the expenses incurred by officers, and concluded that an extremely careful cavalry subaltern could survive on a private income of £300 a year, but that most actually disposed of twice this sum. Officer casualties in the Boer War had forced the army to the desperate measure of sending out some 'ordinary educated young gentlemen, quite untrained'. Even in 1905 untrained youngsters were being appointed probationary second lieutenants. When the First World War broke out there was already a marked shortage of officers, especially in the more expensive arms, and the outbreak of war would immediately compel the adoption of desperate measures.

CHAPTER 8

TEMPORARY GENTLEMEN: 1914-45

O N 1 AUGUST 1914 there were 10,800 officers in the regular army, with just over 2,500 in the Special Reserve, 10,700 in the Territorial Force and a handful in other categories, totalling 24,896, an overall shortfall against establishment of just under two thousand. The Regular Army numbered 236,632 other ranks, a total easily exceeded by the 265,397 officers commissioned during the war. This stark statistic shows, at a stroke, the problem confronting Britain as she embarked upon a war of national survival in which she would confront, for one of the few times in her history, the army of a major power in that conflict's main theatre.

The war should have come as no surprise. Wully Roberston was serving in the War Office just after the Boer War, in an appointment which helped take him 'from being one of the oldest lieutenants in the army in 1895 ... in less than nine years [to] one of its youngest colonels.'[1] He observed that during his time the official estimate of Britain's most probable adversary shifted from France to Germany. Economic, naval and colonial rivalry, coupled with concern for the balance of power in Europe, left out of kilter by German victory over France in 1870–71, quickly outweighed personal and dynastic regard for Germany, and the 1904 Anglo-French entente cordiale was followed by the opening, two years later, of informal 'staff conversations' that saw Britain plan to send an expeditionary force to northern France in the event of war. That force was the product of one of the most significant bursts of military reform in British history. Between 1906 and 1909 R. B. Haldane, secretary of state for war in the new Liberal Government, instituted a range of reforms, creating an expeditionary force of six infantry divisions and one large cavalry division, fusing together the militia and the volunteers to establish the Territorial Force, and setting up the Imperial General Staff. Haldane had foreseen that there would be an enhanced need for trained officers, and the Ward Committee of 1906 recommended that the existing school cadet corps and university rifle volunteer units should be combined into the Officers' Training Corps. The OTCs were established in 1908, and by the end of 1910 there were 19 contingents in the university-based 'Senior Division', and 152 in the 'Junior Division' at schools. Some 27,700 cadets were enrolled at the beginning of 1912, and 830 former cadets had gone on to take Territorial commissions. Haldane had actually hoped that that the OTCs would play their part in a wider national military regeneration, and although he was to be disappointed here, there can be no doubting the contribution made by OTCs.

Wolverhampton Grammar School, with its single cadet company, lost 116 of its old boys in the war, and the school magazine bravely charts the fate of a generation. Second Lieutenant Douglas William Armitage disappeared at Loos in 1915 'tired, cold and hungry, he was last seen fighting with his fists and since then no more has been heard of him.' George Murphy had gone to Birmingham University to read medicine, but joined the infantry in 1914 and was killed at Passchendaele, when 'most of his [machine] gunners were put out of action and he was seen serving a Lewis gun himself until he was shot through the head. It is interesting to recall that Lieutenant Murphy acted as judge in the House Squad Competition in our OTC in 1915.'[2] At the other end of the scale, Eton College OTC was a full battalion strong and had a regular adjutant. Herbert Buckmaster remembered parading with the college's rifle volunteer contingent when Queen Victoria reviewed the public school volunteers in Winsdor Great Park as part of her Jubilee celebrations: there were 3,679 boys on parade, and Eton, with 360, provided the largest detachment. Some 5,650 Etonians were to serve, and 1,150 of them were killed. The war slew masters as well as boys. An old boy of Reading school (Old Redigensian in insider's jargon), Gordon Belcher was an assistant master at Brighton College and a lieutenant in its OTC. He joined the Royal Berkshires in 1914, was mentioned in dispatches that year and awarded the MC early in 1915, but was killed that May. Herbert Lee was a 1911 Cambridge modern languages graduate who went on to teach at Hurstpierpoint College in Sussex, where he helped run the OTC. He played in the masters versus boys football match of 1913. Four of the eleven masters were killed, amongst them Lee, mortally wounded leading his platoon of Suffolks in an attack on the Salonika front in November 1916.[3]

OTC boys did not automatically get commissions. John William Victor Blazey had been in the 1st Eleven at Reading School in 1911: 'A greatly improved bat with plenty of defence, but will have to learn to drive. His slow bowling has not been much needed this year. A good and keen field.' He enlisted in the Royal Berkshires in 1914 and put in for the commission he would have been certain of getting, but, as he wrote from France:

> Seven months training in England was so wearying that I jumped at the idea of coming out here and cancelled the application. And I must say I don't regret it in the least, for on the whole one couldn't wish to run across a better lot of fellows.
>
> It is with deep regret that I heard of the death in action of Lieutenants Hawkins and Giles Ayres, also of Captain Belcher; but it is certain that each one died as an Englishman should, and no greater tribute could be paid to anyone …
>
> I hope the XI will do really well this season, young though the talent may be. It is a noticeable fact that all the casualties connected with the School, so far as I know, have happened to those who were to the front in sport, and every branch of athletics will be hard hit before this war is over, I fear.
>
> Please give my kind regard to all those masters whom I know and tell Mr Crook that my OTC training has served me in good stead.

Blazey was commissioned that summer, and when 1st Royal Berkshires attacked at Loos on 26 September a brother officer 'saw Lieut. Blazey and a little band of men, surrounded by superior numbers of Germans and … there was little hope of them escaping alive.' His battalion lost 288 officers and men that day, and he is commemorated on the Loos memorial to the missing.[4] Blazey's schoolfellow Francis Stephen Arthur Forss was turned down for Sandhurst in 1913 because of poor eyesight (which had not stopped him from being the best shot in the school's shooting VIII) and went out to Australia. He joined the Australian army in February 1915, was made a corporal at once ('Thanks,' reported his father, 'to his training in your excellent OTC') and was soon a sergeant. He worked as a volunteer stoker to help save the torpedoed transport *Southland* and then fought on Gallipoli and the Western Front, surviving the war. Between August 1914 and March 1915, 20,577 officers were commissioned from OTCs, and there were still another 12,290 ex-OTC men serving in the ranks.

For the classic example of an OTC product one need look no further than George Marsden-Smedley, captain of both cricket and football at Harrow and 'probably the most outstanding sportsman' of his generation at that school. He had just matriculated at Trinity College, Cambridge when he was commissioned into the Rifle Brigade, and on 18 August 1916 his battalion attacked the Somme village of Guillemont. Marsden-Smedley charged the machine gun that was holding up his company and shot one of the gunners with his revolver, but was himself shot by a German officer and fell dead on the parapet of the trench. His body was never found, but a small private memorial still marks the spot where he died: 'Lovely and pleasant in life, in death serene and unafraid. Most blessed in remembrance.'[5] R. C. Sherriff found himself outside the charmed circle. Reporting for a commission in 1914 he told the interviewing officer that he had been at Kingston Grammar School. The officer carefully went through the list of schools that had the War Office's approval and to Sherriff's irritation Kingston Grammar, despite its distinction, had no OTC and was not on the list. He joined as a private and earned his officer's stars the hard way, ending the war as a decorated captain in the East Surreys, and using his experience to write the play *Journey's End*, set in a company headquarters dug-out on the eve of the great German offensive of 1918.

Cambridge University OTC, formed from the university's Rifle Volunteer Corps (which had sent sufficient volunteers to South Africa with the Suffolk Regiment to obtain a Boer War battle honour) had a cavalry squadron, a two-gun section of field artillery, a company of fortress engineers, an infantry battalion, and a field ambulance section. It produced a flood of officers, with a cruelly high proportion of dead. When I was an undergraduate at Emmanuel College I gave less thought than I should have done to the memorial stone at the north-east corner of Front Court, in the shadow of Christopher Wren's chapel, headed 'These sons of this House fell in war'. There are 123 names from this small college. Although he was still a student, Kenneth Ashby answered the War Office's appeal for men who owned their own motor-bikes to volunteer as dispatch riders, was hastily made a corporal in the Royal Engineers and, stripes still white on his sleeve, was reported missing on 1 September 1914 during the retreat from Mons. Frederick Lillie, a regular major in the Royal Irish, was killed at St Eloi in the Ypres salient in March 1915. Thomas Knott, only four years out of college when war the war started, was a lieutenant colonel, with a DSO and two mentions in dispatches, when he fell commanding 1/6th Gloucesters at Arras in April 1917. Of the six clergymen who died, one, John Pinkerton, had laid aside his clerical collar to die on the Somme as a lance corporal in the Royal Scots. Another, Roger Ingolby, had served as a trooper in the Alberta Dragoons before accepting a commission in the Royal Dublin Fusiliers. He died when 36th Ulster Division carried the Schwaben Redoubt, in its inimitable style, on the first day of the Somme. There were no less than twelve doctors in the group. One, Wallace Hillbrook, died at Nairobi while serving with the Congo Carrier Corps, and another, Charles Gow, was killed as a regimental medical officer when the Royal Naval Division took Beaucourt on 13 November 1916, just yards away from a fellow 'Emma' man, Lieutenant Alfred Maynard of the same division's Howe Battalion.

These are just tiny *tesserae* that glitter in a huge mosaic, but they hint at the way the war transformed officer recruiting. Young men who would never have thought of military careers, or who might have been deterred by the expense of such a costly profession, answered the call in their thousands. Some joined their local Territorial units, perhaps getting instant commissions on the basis of OTC service or personal recommendation, or serving in the ranks until commissioned into their own units or elsewhere. A few Territorial units, like the 'class battalions' of the London Regiment, that had behaved, before the war, as much as gentlemen's clubs as military units, produced a disproportionate amount of officers. Of the 12,642 other ranks who served in the London Rifle Brigade during the war, 11 per cent of the total at 1,339, were commissioned, a proportion rising to 26 per cent of the original members of 2/London Rifle Brigade. 28th (County of London) Battalion, the London Regiment, better known as the Artists Rifles and numbering the painter Frederic, Lord Leighton amongst its former commanding officers, began the war as a normal Territorial battalion, and went to France early, in October 1914. The following month it was ordered to send fifty selected men as officers to other battalions in the BEF. Some reported for duty wearing their Artists' private soldier's uniforms with a second lieutenant's pip on their shoulder. The battalion was soon converted to an officer-cadet unit, and over the course of the war furnished the army with 10,000 officers. John Lloyd-Jones, who had matriculated at Emmanuel in 1910, began in the Artists Rifles and died in March 1916, of pneumonia and pleurisy, as a captain in the Green Howards. More typically, Siegfried Sassoon, who was to become a distinguished war poet, was a private soldier in the Sussex Yeomanry until a tedious convalescence from an injury incurred when a borrowed horse fell on him and the growing conviction that his unit would never get into the war persuaded him to let an old family friend recommend him for a special reserve commission in the Royal Welch Fusiliers. Like his fellow poet Robert Graves, an officer in the same battalion, Sassoon was pointedly told that his was a permanent commission, albeit in the regiment's reserve battalion, not one of the temporary commissions awarded to officers in the New Armies.

The New Armies, formed in response to Lord Kitchener's urgent demand for troops, were officered from a variety of sources. Long-retired warriors shook the mothballs out of their uniforms and did their best to keep up with boys less than half their age. 6/Cameron Highlanders was commanded by Lieutenant Colonel Angus Douglas-Hamilton, a general's son who had joined the Camerons in 1884. At fifty-two he was a little old for the front line, but at Loos, when the units on either side had fallen back, he rallied his battalion and led it forward four times: 'The last time he led all that remained, consisting of about fifty men, in a most gallant manner and was killed at their head.'[6] One of his men recalled how

Led by our brave old colonel, bareheaded and with no other weapon than his walking stick, we made for the top of 'Hill 70' through a murderous rifle and machine-gun fire, while shells crashed all around us … The white-haired old man who led us was shot dead, and shortly afterwards Capt Milne [the adjutant, and an Indian Army officer], cool and unruffled to the last, paid a similar penalty.[7]

Many New Army units – 'pals' battalions' – were raised by exploiting strong links within urban communities. The mayor of Swansea was amongst the civic leaders offering the War Office a formed battalion of local men, and the Swansea Pals (formally 14th (Service) Battalion The Welsh Regiment) was formed with the powerful support of Sir Alfred Mond of the Mond Nickel Works. H. W. Benson, a regular officer in the East Surreys, but, more to the point, a member of a prominent Swansea family, arrived to take command. Some of his officers had firm local connections. Dyson Brock Williams was a successful solicitor, and had played cricket for both Swansea and Glamorgan: he was appointed major in May 1915. John Stanley Strange of Brynmill, manager of the Old Brewery, volunteered for the battalion immediately and was soon made a lieutenant. The mayor's eldest son, Francis Llewellyn Corker, had joined the Glamorgan Yeomanry as a private in September 1914 but, wondrous to relate, was commissioned into the Swansea battalion. John Henry England had served in the OTC at King's College, Taunton, and was working as a clerk. He enlisted into the Territorials in August 1914, but the recommendations of local worthy Colonel William Watts and the Earl of Plymouth, Lord Lieutenant of Glamorgan, were quite enough to get him a commission with the Pals.[8]

The Oldham Pals (24th Battalion The Manchester Regiment) was commanded by a 'dug out' who had joined the army in 1884 and retired before the war. Most of his officers were found by inviting local men with expertise (or plain aspirations) to a public meeting. At least four of the new officers had been pupils at Hulme Grammar School, two were serving in a Public Schools battalion and another two in a Manchester-raised pals' battalion. One of the latter men, Walter Wall, was a theatrical agent by profession, who turned up to recommend Douglas Marshall, an actor who was then appearing in one of Oldham's theatres. Not only was Marshall taken on as a second lieutenant, but Wall found himself appointed captain.[9] Similar patterns of recruitment applied across most of these units. But perhaps few New Army battalions were quite as distinctive as 16/Royal Scots, raised from players and supporters of Hearts of Midlothian Football Club, with a good leavening of Hibernian, Raith Rovers and Falkirk men. The battalion was raised by Sir George McCrae, Edinburgh hatter and former MP, who proceeded to command it on the Somme, where it struck deep into the German positions on the first day, its penetration commemorated by a fine memorial in Contalmaison. The sergeant major of the company that made best progress was the Tynecastle half-back Annan Ness: the battalion lost ten officers and 566 of its men that day. Some New Army battalions of the Middlesex Regiment and Royal Fusiliers recruited only public school men, and were soon pressed to send their best on for commissioning: 16/Middlesex had lost 900 by July 1915.

It was all too easy to get a commission early on. When the Territorial 2/4th Somerset Light Infantry left for India in December 1914 it had three Mackie brothers serving as subalterns, the last of them having joined the battalion with days to spare. His elder brother James:

> heard the Colonel saying this morning that he wanted one more subaltern so I at once approached him and said that I had a younger brother who would like to join. He jumped at the idea ... I told him that you were not very old and had no experience, but he said that if Father and Mother were willing and Doctor passed you he would take you ... As the Colonel has definitely decided to take you, you need not wait till you are gazetted before you get your uniform but can begin at once.[10]

All three brothers survived the war. Etonian Herbert Buckmaster had served as a private in the Imperial Light Horse in the Boer War – 'we had Texas boys, sailors, cowpunchers, Bulawayo "stiffs" and a certain amount of what my friend Jack White termed "younger sons sent out to be shot" – but had left the army before accepting the commission for which he had been recommended. In 1914 he was married to actress Gladys Cooper, made a good living betting on horses, and mixed in guardee circles. Later in life he reflected poignantly on the dining room of the Carlton Hotel on a pre-war evening:

I can see Percy Wyndham and his wife sitting there. They had just been married. Percy was killed in 1914. I can see Bobs Ashton and Angus Mackintosh both in the Blues and both so soon to die. I can see David Bingham … and Daisy Orr come in and look round. Both David Bingham and Arthur Orr were killed early in the war. I can see Tommy Musgrave of the Irish Guards, who, going over the top, raced a long way ahead of his men and was killed.

In the summer of 1914 Buckmaster could not, at first, lay hands on a commission. The Inns of Court Regiment had trained officers for London Territorial units and, following an appeal to *The Times* from its commanding officer, was hard at work with hundreds of men 'of good education', and was now full up and had a long waiting list. The War Office told him that 'being married and not under thirty' was a fatal objection. Winston Churchill, then First Lord of the Admiralty, promised him an RNVR commission, though it was not quite what he was after. Eventually he went to see someone:

> whom I knew slightly at the War Office … He was courtesy itself and within minutes I was given a commission and told to report to the 12th Reserve Regiment of Cavalry at the East Cavalry Barracks, Aldershot, as early as possible, which I did.

It was not a comfortable mess because it still adhered to 'the pre-war custom of completely ignoring a newly joined subaltern, even when he was a man of thirty and obviously a man of the world'. When news arrived that the Blues had been 'badly cut up' in May 1915 he jumped at the chance to join them, and was amongst friends immediately: on his first night in the trenches he 'dined in a dug out in the trenches of the Hohenzollern Redoubt' with four cronies. In February 1918, after a good deal of front-line service, he was at last gazetted a lieutenant in the Blues Special Reserve, and was delighted to report that he 'was no longer a temporary gentleman'. He used the captaincy that arrived later that year for the rest of his life.[11] The administrative confusion that inevitably accompanied the hasty commissioning of so many men produced the occasional difficulty. Buckmaster's RNVR commission was gazetted on the same day as his army commission. Cecil Moorhouse Slack ('a junior clerk in Reckitt and Sons Ltd') joined the New Army Hull Pals as a private in August 1914 and, at the same time, applied for a Territorial commission. He reported to 4/East Yorks when he was gazetted, only to be told by his father that 'a squad of soldiers had called at my home to arrest me for desertion.' The matter was eventually sorted out and he received back pay for his period of 'desertion'.[12]

There were many who might easily have been given commissions but decided to serve in the ranks. Lieutenant Robert Bridgeman, son of a Conservative politician (instantly commissioned from Eton in the summer of 1914), lay ill in bed at a Casualty Clearing Station, and was rather surprised when Lance Corporal Crawford, 'a tall and rather forbidding figure' told him that

> I know your father very well and would like to write and tell him about you.' He was none other than the Earl of Crawford and Balcarres, chief Tory whip until he succeeded to the peerage who, at the age of 45, had decided on this form of war work … Even if I had been fit it would have been hard to take being saluted by him and called 'Sir.'[13]

Leslie Coulson, a journalist's son, was assistant editor of the *Morning Post* in 1914, and, feeling obliged to follow the patriotic line promoted by his newspaper, enlisted in 2/2 Londons in September 1914, refusing to apply for a commission. 'No,' he said, 'I will do the thing fairly. I will take my place in the ranks.' He later transferred to 12/London, was promoted to sergeant and recommended for a commission, but was mortally wounded when they took Leuze ('Lousy') Wood on the Somme in October 1916. The furious poem 'Who made the Law?' was found on his body.

> Who made the Law that men should die in meadows?
> Who spake the word that blood should splash in lanes?
> Who gave it forth that gardens should be boneyards?
> Who spread the hills with flesh, and blood, and brains?[14]

It became progressively harder for enterprising young men to gain direct commissions, although even in 1915 the right contacts worked wonders. Carlos Paton ('Pip') Blacker was at Eton when war broke out and failed the eye-test on his first attempt to join the army. He went up to Oxford in the autumn of 1914 but could not settle down, failed the army's eye test twice more, and went off to work in the civilian British Field Hospital in Belgium. His younger brother Robin, a naval cadet until his eyesight weakened, had obtained a commission in the Rifle Brigade, by way of an Eton master who was commanding one of its companies. But his battalion seemed unlikely to go to France fast enough, and he negotiated a transfer to the Coldstream Guards, suggesting that Pip should approach the Coldstream too. Pip duly found a 'broad-minded' doctor so as to pass the eye test (a process eased by being left in the room containing the eye-chart for fifteen minutes so that he could memorise the letters), had a short interview with Colonel Richardson Drummond Hay at Regimental Headquarters in Birdcage Walk on 4 July and was posted to the Coldstream on the 15th. Although 'I had passed Certificate A and been a sergeant in the Eton OTC', Blacker found himself on the drill square three times a day, though the 'extraordinarily easy hours' enabled him to spend a good deal of time rowing. He survived the First World War, winning an MC. Having trained as a doctor between the wars he found himself medical officer of his old battalion in the Second World War, when he earned the George Medal. Robin Blacker, 'beside himself' at the news that his old battalion of the Rifle Brigade had been cut to pieces, pressed to be sent to join 1/Coldstream in France. Pip saw him off from Windsor station, and wrote in his diary 'I put the chances at 4 in 10 that I never see him again.' Like Rudyard Kipling's only son Jack, Robin Blacker was reported missing, believed killed, after the Guards Division attacked at Loos.[15]

Alexander Stewart was working on a rubber estate in Malaya when war broke out, and served as a private in the part-time Malay States Volunteer Rifles. When his contract expired in early 1915 he returned to London, and that summer called at the War Office

> with a letter of introduction from my uncle by marriage, Colonel Delavoye CB, one time in the 90th Foot 'Scottish Rifles'.
>
> Shortly afterwards I received an official intimation from the War Office saying that I had been granted a commission in the Cameronians, as an officer in the Special Reserve, and had been

posted to the 3rd Battalion. I was instructed to report to a school for officers in Glasgow on July 1st, 1915.

Stewart believed that he had got a commission easily because he had served in his school's rifle volunteer unit for two years and then in its OTC for a further year. He put in two years with the Territorial City of London Yeomanry, and four with the Malay States Volunteer Rifles. He received about a month's training – 'one portion of which consisted of rising early in the morning and running about the streets of Glasgow without hat, coat or waistcoat.' Stewart later argued that short training was no disadvantage, as

> Successfully leading men in war, like most work in life that does not require any special technical knowledge, depends to a great extent upon common sense and a shrewd judgement of character, coupled with the capability of subverting fear. I think that all the regular officers, anyhow all those I met up to and including the rank of Major, were splendid fellows; but nevertheless I soon came to the very definite opinion that the new 'war officers' were infinitely more capable, led their men better and did their job better than the old pre-war regulars with whom I came into contact.[16]

He took naturally to the life of an infantry officer on the Western Front, attributing his survival to the facts that he carried a rifle as well as a revolver during attacks and turned up his coat collar so as to look as little as possible like an officer, and was always very careful to see that his pipe was 'properly alight' before going over the top: 'I look upon it in the light of a mascot that must seldom be invoked.' The citation for his MC, won at Arras in the freezing spring of 1917, tells how 'He knocked out a hostile machine gun, killing and wounding most of the team, and throughout the attack he handled his company with marked courage and skill.'[17]

When war broke out the courses at Sandhurst and Woolwich were shortened to three months and six months respectively, and fees were suspended. The senior terms at both colleges had just been commissioned, the cadets in the next batch were either given immediate commissions or promoted after a burst of top-up training. By the end of the year there were 323 cadets at Woolwich and 960 at Sandhurst, most of them preparing for regular commissions, although some of the Sandhurst contingent were New Army officers under training. It was evident that neither the attenuated courses nor the wholesale commissioning of young men into the New Armies, Territorials or Special Reserve would make good the immediate shortfall caused by casualties incurred on the Western Front, and in October the army began to commission regular warrant officers and senior NCOs. They were discharged from the regular army and promptly given temporary commissions, a procedure that was to cause some grief at the war's end. RSM Murphy of 2/Royal Welch Fusiliers reckoned that he had actually come down in the world by becoming a second lieutenant. 'There I was,' he complained, 'a thousand men at my control, the Commanding Officer was my personal friend, the Adjutant consulted me, the Subalterns feared me, and now I am only a bum-wart and have to hold my tongue in mess.'[18] Commissioned with him in the autumn of 1914 were RQMS P. B. Welton, who won an MC and was commanding a battalion of South Wales Borderers at the end of the war, and CSM W. H. Stanway, who was commanding a Cheshire battalion within two years of being commissioned and earned both DSO and MC. Harry Carter had joined the South Staffordshire Regiment as a private in 1899, fought in the Boer War, and had become signalling sergeant by 1914. He was commissioned early in 1915 and first became a temporary lieutenant colonel the following year. He ended the war decorated with DSO and bar and MC and bar, in command of 7/South Staffordshire. When L Battery Royal Horse Artillery was destroyed at Néry on 1 September 1914 its battery sergeant major, George Dorrell, and one of its sergeants, David Nelson, were awarded VCs, and a third went to Captain Edward Bradbury, who was killed. Dorrell and Nelson were both commissioned: Dorrell survived the war and retired a lieutenant colonel, but Nelson was mortally wounded as a major commanding a field battery in the German offensive of March 1918.

While ex-warrant officers and senior NCOs could generally become officers without the need for much extra training, it was evident that none of the early stop-gap measures, like the short courses at Oxford, Cambridge, Dublin, Edinburgh and London universities or in the Staff College building at Camberley, or indeed the Inns of Court OTC, producing eighty officers a week by mid 1915, were the real answer to generating a steady supply of officers for a long and bloody war. Not only was training haphazard, but many regular officers were nonplussed at what James Jack, an upwardly-mobile Cameronian (captain in 1914 to brigadier general in 1918), called the 'unsoldierly appearance and manners' of many of the new officers. All too often the new entry were judged by superficialities. General Sir Ian Hamilton, sent off to command the Gallipoli expedition, was shocked to discover that some of his staff had their spurs on upside down, and wore the cross-straps of their Sam Browne belts over, rather than under, the tunic's shoulder-strap. The newly commissioned were bombarded with pamphlets telling them how proper officers behaved. Captain A. H. Trapman's 'Straight tips for Subs', first published in 1915, was full of helpful hints on 'Commissions, Allowances, Kit, Etiquette, Duties and Correspondence'.

The army was faced with two distinct but intimately related problems: giving its new officers sufficient training to enable them to lead soldiers effectively, and socialising them into the ways of the tribe. The War Office decided, in February 1916, that nobody would be accepted for a commission without serving in the ranks, although time in an OTC service would count instead. Officer-cadet battalions were formed in Britain, one of them using the Inns of Court OTC as its nucleus, and a GHQ Cadet School was established in France. These units took men of all ranks who had been recommended for commissions while serving at the front or in Britain. To start with there were wide variations in the quality of training. Norman Collins, who had enlisted in 1915 and become a lance sergeant in the Seaforth Highlanders, had nothing good to say of No 8 Officer Cadet Battalion at Lichfield.

> We are always scrubbing floors, forming fours, etc. doing 160 paces per minute on the square, brushing boots every hour from 5 a.m. until 7.30 p.m. when we are free to write up our notes till 9.30 p.m. [We] are called miscellaneous names by our sergeants, etc. who know nothing, it's a dog's life and several cadets from the firing line want to go back.[19]

Ernest Shephard, a regular company sergeant major in the Dorsets, was sent to the GHQ Cadet School at Blendecques near St Omer in mid-September 1916. All students removed their badges of rank – 'so that a Pte or RSM are on the same footing' – and were issued with brassards marked CSIC for 'Cadet School Infantry Company'. Training included a stint in a quiet sector of the front line near Béthune. 'I felt very glad we came to this part of the line,' wrote Shephard, ever the enthusiast, 'as it is so interesting.' At the end of the course, in mid-November, he was commissioned into the Dorsets and posted, not to his beloved 1st Battalion, but to the 5th. 'Have seen the last of some jolly good pals,' he wrote. 'Certainly of short duration, but in such places as this gather splendid fellows, privates up to RSM in rank, no distinction, none required. The man who passes through the ranks to a commissioned rank is the better for his experience.' When he joined his battalion he found that it been burnt out by the Somme, and so heavily topped up with officers and men as to be 'practically a new Bn.' Captain Ritson, his company commander, had never been under fire before, but 'is a very decent man and anything I say is worked on'. On 30 December Shephard was told to take temporary command of D Company, and was at its head when it took part in a diversionary attack near Beaucourt on 11 January 1917. His company took its objective but, in filthy weather, was sharply counter-attacked. Shephard sent a message warning a flanking company to fall back, because his position was untenable; he was killed when it was overrun.[20] Until the late summer of 1918 it was still possible for an NCO or warrant officer to receive a direct commission into his own unit. John Lucy was a pre-war regular in the Royal Irish Rifles, who had lost his brother Denis, a corporal in the same battalion, in the war's opening campaign. He was commissioned in June 1917 after a brief interview with a general, and was delighted by the way his brother officers welcomed him to their mess:

> My reception was openly warm. Men who had officered me in peace and war rose to meet me and bring me in. My late title of sergeant evaporated in the first breath of an atmosphere easier and more congenial, though not perhaps as openly intimate as that of the troops. 'Come on, old John here you are at last. The first one's on me.' Someone said: 'No, on the mess.' They drank my health in sherry. They each recommended their own tailors – good tailors, who would let you run a long account. I was given the choice of four

good batmen and the offer of the loan of any article of kit or equipment I temporarily lacked.[21]

At the beginning of the war the army needed officers both to replace
those who had been killed or too badly wounded to serve on, and to
create a force of a genuinely world-class standard. From the summer
of 1916 it became evident that the real problem would be in maintaining the army at the size it had reached, and from the winter of
1917 it had become no less clear that, even though conscription bit
down ever harder, the army was bound to decline in size. This process
was matched by the army's growing preparedness to commission men
who seemed to have the right abilities, wholly regardless of education
or social background. George Ashurst had signed on as a special
reservist when he lost his job in a mine office in 1913, and then found
work cleaning engines in a locomotive depot. He was mobilised in
August 1914 and fought with the Lancashire Fusiliers in France,
Belgium and Gallipoli, and by the summer of 1918 was an experienced sergeant:

> While in the reserve trenches I was sent for by the colonel. When I
> presented myself before him the first question was, 'Sergeant, how
> would you like to go in for a commission?' For a moment I stared
> at him to make sure he wasn't joking. Then, thinking quickly I said,
> 'Oh, I can't be an officer, Sir, I haven't got any money.' 'Nonsense,
> sergeant,' said my CO, 'we don't want men of means as officers
> these days; we want men of experience like yourself – men who
> know this job and can lead others the way to go. Don't think about
> expenses, the government will see to it that you have all you require.
> I shall send your name forward to the general.' And, as though to
> show me that that was final, he started to write on some paper in
> front of him.

Ashurst's men persuaded him that this would be a fine opportunity,
for while he was away from the front the war might finish. He was
interviewed by his brigade commander shortly afterwards, and told
that 'it would be absolutely my own fault' if he did not enjoy his time
in officer training. After two weeks' leave he reported at the Officer
Cadet Battalion at Ripon. 'Wounded officers, unfit for further service

abroad, were in charge of the camp, and gentlemen they were,' he wrote.

> The routine was simple and the parades very easy. The most severe penalty for doing wrong was RTU – Returned to Unit – which meant, of course, being sent back to one's regiment in France. Any man who could not behave like a gentleman and conform to the simple rules of the camp certainly deserved RTU.

Ashurst had passed his first exams comfortably and was preparing to 'go down to Cambridge to have the final polish put on me' when the war ended. He could not get too excited about it, because 'the war had been over for me three months before.'[22]

An experience that was enjoyable for a man who had been at war for three years was a good deal less pleasant to a man from a more sheltered background. Alfred Duff Cooper, whose father was a successful London surgeon, had been educated at Eton and Oxford (where, as he recalled, the OTC was known as 'the dog-potters') before going into the Foreign Office in 1913 and remaining there till he was called up in 1917. He reflected, later in life, that this was excellent timing: had he joined up earlier (when he could have obtained a commission without any difficulty) he would probably have been killed, but had he left it much later he would have missed the war altogether. His mother wanted him to join the cavalry, but he declined the suggestion because 'I have always had such a horror of horses.' Cooper had an interview with the regimental lieutenant colonel of the Grenadier Guards, who was 'a Guardsman of the old school. He spoke to me of my mother, whom he had known years ago, and said that he would put down my name and consider my request to join the regiment.' As he was leaving, the regimental adjutant told him that he could consider the matter as 'practically settled.'

Practically settled, that is, without the necessary rite of passage, in this case the Household Brigade Officer Cadet Battalion at Bushey Park. Cooper had rather thought that he would enjoy a little light officer training, but

> My feelings may then be imagined when I found that I was to live the life of a private soldier, clean my own boots and equipment,

make my own bed, sleep between blankets and take part with my comrades in scrubbing the floor of the barrack room ... I have seldom been more utterly wretched than during the first few days of my sojourn at Bushey Hall.

He was saved by a short weekend leave – mid-Saturday to 10 p.m. on Sunday – with dinner at a club. It was not his own, but 'one of those great station-halls of clubs'. However, an imperial pint of champagne and *Alice Through the Looking Glass* to read over dinner lifted his spirits. This was a contrast to life in his seven-man hut:

They are all rankers except one who is a bank clerk and who has somehow escaped military service hitherto. They are as follows. Clay, a shoemaker from Nottingham, a very nice friendly fellow who helps me a lot with my equipment and in other ways. All the men are really nice and helpful. Schofield, a boy of nineteen who speaks broad Yorkshire and knows the whole of the drill-book by heart. He seldom talks on any other subject. Harris, a tall thin dark fellow, who before the war was a window-dresser in Sheffield. He is quite nice. Catley, a common fellow with waxed moustaches, who talks a lot, fancies himself, refers to the 'fair sex', insinuates that he is one of their conquerors, and smokes Virginia cigarettes last thing at night and first thing in the morning. There is no harm in him. Durgan – not a bad fellow, uninteresting and sleeps in his shirt. Jones, a bank clerk, with a splendid cockney accent and a fund of filthy stories which sometimes shock the others but always amuse me.

The course lasted four months, with four days leave in the middle. Cooper spent his leave with the Horner family at Mells in Somerset. He had been at Oxford with Edward Horner, who had joined the North Somerset Yeomanry at the start of the war, transferred to the 18th Hussars in 1915, returned to the front after being severely wounded that year and had been killed in November 1917:

Edward meant so much in my life. I loved no man better. His high courage and fine independence had so splendidly resisted the effects of the war that already he had begun to seem a glorious record of the glorious past. By his death our little society loses one of the last assets that gave it distinction. And I think we have paid more than our share.

Reflecting on his time in the ranks, he thought that

Class is an inevitable adjunct of human nature. The aim of the lawgiver should be to render the relation between classes happy and to facilitate the passage from one class to another. When class, which is natural, degenerates into caste which is against nature, then it becomes an evil.[23]

The officer corps had never been wholly class-based, although, paradoxically, it had actually become more so after the abolition of purchase and the close links between public schools and Sandhurst. Its social structure was transformed during the war. During the whole of the conflict the army granted just over 229,000 commissions, excluding those given to chaplains and medical officers, and commissions granted for 'special duties'. Of this total, nearly 108,000 went to men who had passed out of officer cadet training units, and another 36,700 to those commissioned into the Royal Flying Corps (RAF from 1 April 1918) from its own cadet battalions.[24] It is impossible to be sure how many commissions had been given to serving NCOs and men before training through officer cadet battalions became the norm, but it is already evident that well over half the officers who fought in the war were ex-rankers of some species. Some were genuine pre-war regulars like John Lucy or Ernest Shephard, others were wartime-joined soldiers from traditional 'other-rank' backgrounds, like Duff Cooper's comrades Clay and Catley, and others, like Cooper himself, came from a conventional officer background and served in the ranks as a means to an end.

The War Office's survey of the 144,000 officers demobilised between the end of the war and 12 May 1920 found that almost 60 per cent came from middle-class occupational groups like 'commercial and clerical', 'students and teachers', and 'professional men'. What is more surprising is to find that 1,016 officers had been coal or shale miners, 7,739 railway workers, 266 warehousemen and porters, 213 bootmakers, and 168 navvies. Indeed, not a single one of the industrial groups analysed failed to produce at least a handful of offi-cers, down to the 20 who had been slate miners and quarrymen.[25] Personal accounts confirm the growing social breadth of the officer corps. Robert Bridgeman returned to 3/Rifle Brigade in late 1916 and was delighted to be given command of C Company. He was 'more than lucky' with his officers, for there was 'Percivale Northcroft, an old acquaintance from [6/Rifle Brigade on] Sheppey ... Later Percy Goodson joined, and so did Dixie Read, as did two first-class men, who had been NCOs in the battalion, Tom Fenner and Les Layton.'[26]

Lieutenant Colonel Edward Hermon, an ex-regular cavalry officer, had begun the war commanding a squadron of King Edward's Horse, a Special Reserve cavalry regiment packed with 'gentleman troopers', but in November 1916 was CO of 27th Battalion the Northumberland Fusiliers, badly knocked about on the Somme. He told his wife that his officers were 'very like the curate's egg', they included 'a funny little man called Crichton, a Weslyan minister, who is a good bloke but nothing very much socially'. When Hermon was interviewing candi-dates for commissions one man told him that he was a 'ladies & gents hairdresser' in civilian life.[27] Hubert Essame, a regular subaltern in the Northamptons, who was to become a major general in the Second World War, described an officer corps 'based on mutual loyalty and trust from which distinctions of class had long vanished', though temporary officers were still expected to display the paternalistic style of leadership which had characterised regulars.[28]

Lieutenant Colonel Graham Seton Hutchison observed that the company commanders in his machine gun battalion were the son of a Scottish miner, an ex-regular sergeant, a wool salesman, and a med-ical student, while his adjutant had been a land agent. None of them had been to public school. Sidney Rogerson had been commissioned into the West Yorkshires in 1914, leaving Cambridge without complet-ing his degree. In *Twelve Days* he describes a battalion's tour of duty on the Somme in November 1916, and tells of his battalion's senior officers, just before going up the line, being briefed by the CO, James Jack, who

> had come to us from the Cameronians, but so completely identified himself with us and incidentally endeared himself to us that his alien origin had been completely and quickly forgotten ...

MacLaren is there, the second in command, an officer on the reserve wrenched by the war from the comfortable home in Ontario which he will never see again. A Company is represented by Palmes, a militia captain, who has left a Rhodesian Farm and is destined to die on the same day as MacLaren ... and by his senior subaltern, Arthur Skrett, just joined from Sandhurst. I answer for B Company. Hawley, a senior captain of the regiment, plunged into this grim winter campaign after years of service in the steam-heat of West Africa, has C; and Sankey, a 2nd Lieutenant just promoted from the ranks of the Canadians, is temporarily in command of D Company. Matheson, another promoted Canadian, is acting adjutant.[29]

The same sort of social mixture encountered amongst the officers of a single battalion was replicated at brigade level. Frank Crozier had been a regular officer, but was forced to resign his commission in 1908 after bouncing cheques. The outbreak of war found him helping train the Ulster Volunteer Force, and he went to France as second in command of a battalion of Royal Irish Rifles, succeeding to command in late 1915 and leading it on the Somme. Promoted brigadier general in November 1916 he headed an infantry brigade for the rest of the war. His accounts of his wartime service are, like the man himself, flamboyant and unreliable, and are not a little coloured by the fact that he needed to make money. His snapshot of the commanding officers of the four battalions of his brigade in 1917 goes to the heart of this war-seasoned army. Lieutenant Colonel Freddy Plunkett, RSM of 2/Royal Irish in 1914, had won a DCM at Le Cateau and an MC the following year. After being commissioned he won a DSO and two bars, and would probably have commanded a brigade had heart trouble not prevented it. Lieutenant Colonel Benzie had been a subaltern in the Ceylon Tea Planters' Rifles in 1914, and he too would have become a brigadier had he not been severely wounded in March 1918. Lieutenant Colonel Andrews had run away from school in 1900 to serve as a trooper in the yeomanry in South Africa and had been involved in several revolutions in South America, and Lieutenant Colonel Kennedy had been a lecturer at the London School of Economics.

Their experience of military service had a profound impact on many officers. Sidney Rogerson, an educated man from a comfortable

background, spoke for many when he described the men he served
with, who, in the normal run of things, he would never have met in
civilian life:

> In spite of all differences in rank, we were comrades, brothers,
> dwelling together in unity. We were privileged to see in each other
> that inner, ennobled self which in the grim struggle of peace-time
> is too frequently atrophied for lack of opportunity of expression.
> We could note the intense affection of soldiers for certain officers,
> their absolute trust in them. We saw the love passing the love of
> women of one 'pal' for his 'half' section. We saw in his letters home
> which came to us for censoring, the filial devotion of the 'toughest',
> drunkenest private for his aged mother back in the slums by the
> Tyne at North Shields. We saw the indomitable kindliness of the
> British character expressing itself towards the French children, the
> wretched mangy French dogs and yes, even to the German wounded
> and prisoners … Despite all the propaganda for Christian fellow-
> ship and international peace, there is more animosity, uncharitable-
> ness, and lack of fellowship in one business office now than in a
> brigade of infantry in France then. Otherwise we could never have
> stood the strain.[30]

Lieutenant Colonel Hermon told his wife that 'the British soldier is a
most wonderful person,' adding

> if you had told me that you could lay hands on every man you met
> in the street, clap a uniform on him and that he would behave like
> a stoic and not only in crowds but in small parties, I should have
> said that the whole thing was absolutely idiotic … Anyhow we have
> done it and one is proud that one is a member of a country that
> produces men like the men out here.

Hermon was killed just over a week later, shot through the chest while
taking his battalion over the top near Arras: he ordered his adjutant
'to go on and not wait for him'. Private Gordon Offord 'Freddie'
Buxton, manservant in civilian life and batman in war, told his own
wife that:

I feel I have lost a good master and friend. My heart is broken and I feel I can't write about it. I want to come home and try to comfort Mrs Hermon. I can't rest. I am thinking about her day and night ... We buried him on Wednesday afternoon in the cemetery amongst the ruined village close to the trenches where he was killed, nobody touched him but me. I did him up in two groundsheets and made him look as nice as possible. I buried him in his uniform just as he died ... I lingered by his grave after everybody had gone and prayed that God would comfort his dear wife and children and make me as good and brave as my dear master ... I had to have a good cry Marie love, I couldn't help it.[31]

Both Lieutenant Colonel Hermon's sons fought in the Second World War, and one of Private Buxton's – given a bursary by King Edward's Horse – went to the Imperial Service College and was commissioned into the Royal Artillery.

I had always thought of Desmond Young as Rommel's first biographer, and knew that he had been a brigadier in the Second World War. It transpired that he had been commissioned into the 60th Rifles in 1914, and badly wounded as a company commander outside Ypres in 1915, when his battalion lost 17 of its officers and 333 men. He always remembered that he owed his life to a Welsh miner Lance Corporal Williams who, with another man, had carried him to a dressing station and then turned down his suggestion that they should spend the night with the transport and go back in the morning. 'That's all right, sir,' said Williams. 'I think we'd better be getting back up the line to the company.'[32] Young wrote this account in 1961, but his memory had not failed him: it was indeed Lance Corporal Williams, who was killed in action in late 1916.

Soldiers were sometimes unenthusiastic about ranker officers because they knew too much. Lieutenant Alan Thomas thought that those in 6/Royal West Kents were disliked because 'they knew their job and there was no chance of swinging it over them.'[33] R. K. R. Thornton, a 'gentleman ranker' in 2/5 Glosters, thought that

A bad officer, that is, a bully, is a ———! A good officer, that is a considerate [one], is 'a toff'. 'I'd follow him anywhere.' 'The men's friend'; or simply, but in significant tone, a 'gentleman'.[34]

Men expected bravery: when an officer of 1/13 London ducked on hearing shells explode the RSM told him to keep his head up, and a subaltern of 22/London, cowering in the bottom of a trench before an attack, was shoved over the parapet by his platoon sergeant. They also expected officers, whatever their origins, to behave in a gentlemanly manner. Private Eric Linklater, a former medical student serving in 4/5 Black Watch was in an estaminet when a noisy, drunken officer pursued the hostess, his evident enthusiasm for the task unconcealed by his kilt. Although the sergeants were slum-dwellers in civilian life, they were 'incensed by such behaviour in an officer of their regiment'.[35] An anonymous former soldier, trying to recall the officers he had served under, produced a composite figure: 'Boyish and middle-aged, cool and reckless; a martinet lapsing into an indulgent father; a thwarter becoming an aider and abetter; an enemy melting into a friend.'[36]

Siegfried Sassoon, second in command of a company of 2/Royal Welch Fusiliers in April 1917, found his sense of obligation to his men wholly absorbing. Years later he recalled foot-inspection after a long march, and when he thought of 'those men showing their sore feet, sitting on the straw in a sun-chinked barn and staring up at me with their stupid, trustful eyes, I can still feel angry with profiteers and society people who guzzled their way through the war.' His company's mess

> contained a typical war contrast in Casson and Evans. Casson, aged 23, had been at Winchester and Christ Church; he was a sensitive, refined youth and an amusing gossip. Evans was about the same age, but had not 'enjoyed the same social advantages'. He was very noisy and garrulous, always licked his thumb when dealing cards, and invariably answered 'Pardon?' when any remark was made to him. That 'pardon' became a little trying at times. Equally good when tested, the two merged their social incompatibilities in the end; both were killed on September 26th.[37]

Second Lieutenant Randal Alexander Casson, of Bron-y-Garth, Porthmadoc, is buried in Poelcapelle military cemetery. The body of Second Lieutenant Hywl Llewelyn Evans of the terraced 22 Llandough Street, Cardiff, was never found, and he is commemorated, with

34,924 comrades who died in the Ypres salient after 16 August 1917 but have no known graves, on the Tyne Cot memorial to the missing.

No sooner had the war's last shots echoed away into silence than the army reverted to type. Many temporary officers who sought to stay on were denied regular commissions, and some who had cleared the initial hurdle in 1918–19 found themselves out of a job when the 'Geddes Axe' fell in the mid-1920s. Lieutenant F. G. S. Thomas immediately enlisted as a gunner in No 8 Mountain Battery on the North West Frontier of India, and made an impressive right marker with his splendid physique and the purple and white ribbon of his MC. He was re-commissioned in 1932, and badly wounded as a battery commander in the Western Desert in 1941, winning a DSO in the process. Sandhurst and Woolwich became fee-paying once again, and their connection with public schools was as strong as ever. There was a decline in the percentage of cadets entering Sandhurst who gave their father's occupation as 'gentleman' from 20.5 per cent in 1910 to 9.1 per cent in 1930, but over the same period the percentage of the sons of military professionals rose from 43.8 to 50.8 per cent. The cost of uniforms and equipment, which an officer was expected to meet, added to mess bills, once again made it difficult for an officer without private means to live on his pay. Lieutenant General Sir John Keir warned that the army was automatically shutting itself off from young men who, as the war had so recently shown, could make admirable officers. He cited the case of

> a young man, well-educated, of good physique, a typical leader of men, with the further recommendation that his father has fallen fighting for his country. He is anxious to become an officer. He has everything to recommend him but money. His only means of entering the army is passing through the ranks and possibly wasting some of the most valuable years of his life in sterile routine.

He suggested that expenses could be much reduced if officers were delivered from 'the thraldom of the military tailor' by the establishment of an officers' branch of the Army Clothing Department. Messes should be simplified so that an officer 'has not a six-course dinner forced upon him, nor is he obliged to pay for it whether he partake of it or not'. Instead of regimental bands being supported by officers' subscriptions, there should be 'a good local brigade band', for battalions could get along perfectly well with their drums and pipes, paid for by the government. Finally, he quoted a question asked by an anxious parent: 'I am going to put my boy into the army. He is very keen to get on, and wants to make a real profession of it. What branch of the service should he join?' Happily the young man had a private income of £300–400 a year. 'In that case,' replied Keir, 'it is quite easy to answer your question. Put him into the cavalry every time.'[38]

The Haldane Committee of 1923 maintained that 'it is neither necessary nor desirable to confine the selection of officers to any one class of the community.' However, instead of lowering the fees at Woolwich at Sandhust, or even acknowledging Sir John Keir's recommendations (some of which remain desiderata to this day), the War Office simply asked county councils to provide scholarships to the two academies, just as they did to universities. Both cost £200 a year, about the same as Oxford and rather less than Cambridge, though very much more than, say, St Andrews or Aberdeen. A suggestion that it might be possible to use suitable Territorial officers to serve as regulars was swiped, with predictable vigour, into the long grass, because 'the door might prove inconveniently wide'. The Y Cadet programme was intended to ensure that 13.5 per cent of the officer corps was drawn from the ranks, and between 1922 and 1930, 189 rankers did indeed receive commissions under this scheme. But the high cost of living in the combat arms meant that so many of them joined the Royal Army Service Corps, that the corps had to give up direct recruitment from Sandhurst because its junior officer ranks were fast becoming filled with impecunious ex-rankers. By the mid-1930s the average Sandhurst intake contained only 5 per cent of ex-rankers. University graduates were, rather like militia officers before 1914, able to sidestep Sandhurst altogether. Charles Farrell left Ampleforth in 1937 and went to Christ Church, Oxford, as a university candidate for a regular commission in the Scots Guards. His military training included a month's attachment to 1/Scots Guards, when 'our time was mainly spent at drill on the square as part of a squad under the tuition of a drill sergeant.' He was surprised at 'the Olympian calm and utter military inactivity' that prevailed and, having just returned from visiting Germany, thought that 'the SS regiments I had seen goose-stepping in the stadium at Nuremberg that spring were unlikely to be in a state of summer torpor, but rather on manoeuvres close to the Czech border.'[39]

There was much truth in this. Writing in 1935, J. R. Kennedy, whose views doubtless reflect the fact that he had left the army as a captain in the Royal Artillery, argued that the army had regressed to the Edwardian era. Officers of his own arm were often unable to become adjutants of Territorial regiments unless they had substantial private means, for the allowances were inadequate. Mounted officers in India – including staff officers who rarely appeared mounted – were required to purchase a charger. He cherished the 'vain hope' that 'officers may no longer be required to make themselves ridiculous by putting on spurs to dine, to dance, or to attend mechanised parades.' He argued that the artillery, such a battle-winner in the war, had been subjected to a 'quite incomprehensible' 45 per cent cut when compared with its 1910 establishment, as opposed to the 17 per cent cut across the whole army. Restrictions on publishing amounted to 'suppression of free thought and free expression', and it was still taboo to talk shop in the mess. Promotions to lieutenant colonel in 1933–34 suggested that the Guards did best, with an average age on promotion of 40 years and 5 months, then the cavalry, at 43.6, the engineers at 44.1, followed by the gunners at 48.5 and then the rest of the army:

> There are infantry subalterns who are older than Guards commanding officers; there is a difference of ten years between the service required for promotion to captain in the Scots Guards and the Prince of Wales Volunteers; captains of artillery are promoted to major at the age that majors of the guards are promoted lieutenant colonel, and it is more than ten years before artillery officers are promoted lieutenant colonel.

Generals, he maintained, were too old and tended to circulate between senior appointments. For instance, General Sir Cyril Deverill, just appointed to Eastern Command, had 'commanded both a brigade and a division in France, and since the war has commanded a division and an Indian district, and has also been QMG and CGS in India. It is seventeen years ago that he reached the rank of divisional commander and every subsequent appointment has carried him upwards.'[40] Kennedy was not to know it, but Deverill went on to be promoted field marshal and appointed CIGS in 1936. The reforming Secretary of State for War, Leslie Hore-Belisha, reckoned that, at sixty-four, Deverill was past his best, and moved him on after twenty months in post.

The inter-war army was hamstrung by glacially slow promotion: in 1937 Robert Bridgeman found himself still a regimental captain at the age of forty-one, and it was 'nineteen years but a few weeks from the day I took over my first company to the day I handed over my last'.[41] Small wonder that, as one subaltern observed in 1925, officers 'live on in hopes of either another war or a recurrence of the Black Plague'.[42] Spike Mays enlisted in the Royals in 1924 and found his officers very much of the traditional stamp, though there was little remoteness. The regiment was still mounted, and at morning stables Lieutenant Whittle mucked out with the men: he 'commanded from us solid admiration and respect for a real man, which developed to that unsentimental affection known only to soldiers.' Mays maintained that 'Cavalry officers were the best in the world … They always inspired confidence and respect in their men, although in some cases courage exceeded wit and knowledge … There was friendliness as well as discipline, and both were sure and certain.'[43]

What was less sure and certain was how the army would react to the challenge of another world war. This time there was to be no delay in introducing conscription, which came into force on 3 September 1939, but the army itself, peaking at 2,920,000 in 1945, would never reach the size it had in the First World War, when it stood just below 3,900,000 between August 1917 and March 1918. Part of the reason for the difference was the huge size of the RAF at 950,000 strong in 1945 from just 144,000 when it came into being in April 1918. The army was always handicapped by the fact that it was regarded as the least attractive of the services, and the sort of men who had volunteered so enthusiastically in 1914 found the RAF or the navy more enticing in 1939–40. In July 1942 the army established the General Service Corps scheme, enabling recruits to be properly assessed: only 6 per cent seemed to be potential officers. At the beginning of the war there were some 14,000 regular officers and up to 19,000 Territorials, and just under a quarter of a million officers were commissioned during the war, the higher officer-to-man proportion reflecting the burgeoning of technical posts that were deemed to require commissioned rank. But it was to be true that, exactly as had been the case in the First World War, most of the army's officers were drawn from men who had been civilians when the conflict began.

To start with, the selection process, and the logic that underpinned it, had echoes of 1914. General Sir John Dill, then at Aldershot Command and CIGS from May 1940 to December 1941, told Field Marshal Montgomery-Massingberd that 'men will follow and work better for some lad who is a gentleman than they will for a more experienced WO. It has always been so.' Anthony Eden, secretary of state for war in 1940, thought that the best officers would have received the traditional education of an English gentleman. In 1940 he ruled against following the RAF's example of giving direct commissions to Polish officers, arguing that 'The officer in the Royal Air Force Squadron is first a technician and a commander only second; the army officer must be a leader first and a technician only second.'[44]

Accordingly, at the beginning of the war the potential officer was reported on by his CO and then generally interviewed by his divisional or district commander, a process that tended to encourage the selection of men from traditional officer-producing backgrounds. Adam Stainton was a Wykehamist who reported for military service in September 1939, enlisted into the Oxfordhsire and Buckinghamshire Light Infantry – and was then told to go away till summoned. He read history at Christ Church, Oxford until, having become 'extremely restless' at the prospect of invasion, he accepted an invitation to meet an officer recruiting for the Brigade of Guards. 'We met in a civilised way over the luncheon table,' he recalled, 'and probably the Coldstreamer's main object was not so much to assess our military potential as to see whether we could wield a knife and fork adequately.' He reported for duty at the Guards Depot, then at Caterham in Surrey, in January 1940, and found himself in the potential officers' 'Brigade Squad', 'which I thought was a pity, as it would have been the only time in our service when we could have mingled with ordinary soldiers on completely equal terms'. After two months he was sent to Sandhurst, which had by then been redesignated 161 Infantry Officer Cadet Training Unit, and was a second lieutenant in the Scots Guards by the end of the year. He was serving in Italy in the autumn of 1943 when his father wrote to say that his call-up papers, promised in September 1940, had at last arrived.[45]

Robin Schaefli had been in the OTC at Whitgift School, and when called up into the Essex Regiment in August 1940 he found that half his platoon were classified as potential officers because they had obtained Certificate A through the OTC. Basic training was a great leveller, but

> Very much as I had hoped, I enjoyed the whole process no end ...
> Some just objected to uniforms, uniformity and being told exactly
> what to do and when to do it. I never minded any of this, and even
> more enjoyed the other side of the coin – living and working hard
> with a crowd of others, such as I had never known before, who soon
> became a team and worked up a wonderful spirit. Whatever the
> hardship or discomfort, someone always saw the funny side and we
> had a good laugh. I found that in all kinds of circumstances
> throughout the war.

In his case there was no formal selection process, and 'We potential officers were, if proved good enough in the ranks, waiting for the call to one of the Officer Cadet Training Units (OCTUs) situated mostly in peacetime holiday resorts.' Schlaefli's time at the depot came and went, and with one other exception all his comrades were posted away, and 'we were sent to join the platoon of men for whom there was no posting – those with crime records, psychiatric disorders and flat feet.' Eventually they were both sent to OCTUs, and he concluded that the delay had been caused by his unusual surname and the fact that his comrade was 'suspect because, his father having been a correspondent of *The Times* in Tienstin and his mother a White Russian, he could have been some sort of Red mole'.[46] Norman Craig, called up into the Welch Regiment in May 1940, failed the first fence when his company commander told him, 'Your platoon sergeant doesn't think you are good enough for a stripe – how do you expect me to recommend you for a commission? ... When you can convince Sergeant Bull that you are worth a stripe, I might think again.' He completed his basic training, earned the elusive stripe, and was then interviewed by the second in command of his battalion and the RSM. When he admitted to reading poetry the latter looked at him with 'undisguised contempt', and asked if he played any games. He replied that he had played rugger for the battalion, 'and that raised my stock a little'. The major then asked if his father had any money 'What I mean … is that if you got into a scrape would he help you out with a fiver?' A few weeks later Craig was told to get ready to leave for an OCTU.[47]

That year Command Interview Boards were set up, and by 1941 most candidates passed through them. Each had a permanent president, with two field officers brought in for the day. Gerald Kersh, though writing with tongue in cheek, tells how he found the board's obstacles easy to circumnavigate. When he announced that he was a journalist, the president pounced:

'What do you think of layout?' he asked me.

I suspected a trap. I fenced: 'It depends what you mean by layout?'

The Brigadier said: 'I mean to say' – and his face contorted in a spasm of distaste – 'I mean to say this business of using all this different kind of type; big type, little type, all this different kind of type. What do you think about it?'

I said 'I think it is absolutely disgusting, sir.'

'So do I. To my mind, Mr Kersh, good material doesn't need layout. Poppycock!'

'How right you are, sir!' I cried with fervour, clapping my hands in ecstasy, 'how very right! And how well you put it!'

'Good wine needs no bush, does it?'

'Absolutely, sir – no bush at all, sir.'

He told the board that although he wrote for the *Daily Mirror* he never read it, but took *The Times* instead, and, if given fifty pounds and a fortnight's holiday, he would go on 'a nice long walking tour' – in Wales. He left feeling that 'His Majesty's Commission was as good as in my pocket.' On his way back to the Guards Depot on the train, though, he concluded that being an officer would separate him from his fellow soldiers, and later asked his CSM to remove him from the list of potential officers. 'Some people are worse than bloody women,' groaned Sergeant Major 'Iron' Duke. 'Don't make their minds up. Are you sure now? All right. I'll tell Captain The Lord Hugh Kennedy.'[48]

Boards like this were less than successful. By 1942 up to half the men they sent up to OCTUs failed. Too many of those who passed, subsequently broke down under stress; several of those who failed maintained that they had been rejected because of snobbery, and by mid-1941 complaints resulted in the secretary of state receiving up to thirty parliamentary questions a week.[49] From April 1942 a new system of officer selection was introduced, and it remains in use, with modifications, to the present day. The War Office Selection Board (WOSB, universally pronounced 'Wozbee') embodied the belief that leadership was not an inherited quality, and was based on principles enunciated in J. Simmoneit's 1922 book *Wehrpsychologie*, which had become the basis for officer selection in the German army. Each board consisted of a permanent president supported by experienced regimental officers, a psychiatrist (inevitably known as the 'trick cyclist') and a psychologist. Over three days candidates underwent a mixture of individual tests, 'leaderless tasks', 'group tasks', went over an assault course, were interviewed by the psychiatrist (Gerald Kersh remembered an unedifying conversation as to whether writers saw mankind 'looking *down*, or at least looking *on* from some place *apart*'), discussed current affairs and talked on a nominated subject.[50] Duncan Leitch Torrance was delighted when asked to talk about a horseshoe, because his father was a vet and they had discussed this very subject on his last leave: he passed, notwithstanding an officer's smug reservations about the state of his PT vest. Geoffrey Picot, who had been unhappy as a lance corporal clerk in the Pay Corps, attended a WOSB at Winchester, had the usual difficulties with the psychiatrist (he thought most words in the word association test seemed to concern either war or sex) and was told that although he was 'too slow, too sleepy, too weak, too soft, too dreamy and so forth' to be a field artillery officer, he would do well enough in the anti-aircraft branch, and was accordingly sent off to the OCTU at Llandrindod Wells in February 1943.[51]

Despite the objectivity of WOSBs, it is not surprising that 34 per cent of officers commissioned during the war had attended public schools, for the self-confidence acquired by those who had made their way through the monitorial system could be a real help where group tasks were concerned. Many public school boys who served their time in the ranks commented on the fact that they found, like Adam

Stainton, 'the constant chasing around and the total lack of privacy of the barrack room easier to endure than did a recruit straight from home'. He certainly found Caterham food a good deal better than that served at Winchester College.[52] Overall, WOSBs had a good effect, for they encouraged men who might not normally have thought of themselves as officers to apply for commissions, and did much to persuade unsuccessful candidates that there were objective reasons for their rejection, and it was not all down to old school ties or funny handshakes.

Having passed a WOSB the potential officer then went on to a four-month course at an OCTU, sometimes going to a pre-OCTU first to be brought up to standard, often in infantry training, the essential basis for so much of what was taught. OCTUs themselves were a mixed bag. They were special-to-arm. In 1940, for instance, the Royal Artillery ran: 121 OCTU at Aldershot, 122 OCTU at Larkhill, 123 OCTU at Catterick, 124 OCTU (AA) at Llandrindod Wells, 125 OCTU at Ilkley, and 133 OCTU (AA) at Shrivenham. Robin Schaefli went off to 166 OCTU on the Isle of Man to be turned into an infantry officer, and thoroughly enjoyed it. 'I had never been anywhere so lovely before,' he wrote, 'and was able to cover the length and breadth of it either on training exercises, when we took turns to pretend to be officers; or on Saturday afternoons to play rugger against other service teams in Castletown, Peel or Ramsey.'[53] Norman Craig, also in the infantry, went to 163 OCTU, in a requisitioned holiday camp at Heysham Towers near Morecambe:

The cadets came from a wide variety of regiments and were readily distinguishable by their headgear. The Guards contingent, consisting of a few foot-stamping sergeants and one erstwhile warrant officer of frightening dignity and military omniscience, wore smart round caps with the peaks almost touching their noses. A group of former tank men with dour faces and unsteady legs, had black berets pulled well over the right ear. A handful of pale-faced and long-haired intellectuals from rifle regiments, still dazed by their rejection from a motorised infantry OCTU, wore green side-caps perched very straight on their heads. The ebullient Scots sported their motley range of bonnets and tartan glengarries in any way they chose. The remaining cadets from the miscellaneous county regiments made do with standard forage caps, balanced at varying angles and each with a distinctive badge. Only the shining white capband was worn by everyone, to denote our new-found status and common objective.[54]

It was generally agreed, though, that there was far too much drill, and that in consequence men relearnt what they had already mastered. In 1941 one newly commissioned officer argued that 'the cadets were treated like peacetime recruits, i.e. they were assumed to be stupid and unwilling learners who required to be driven to work.' He might have been pleased to hear that Sir Ronald Adam, the adjutant general, agreed in 1942 that there was too much emphasis 'on training the cadet to be the perfect private soldier'.[55] Geoffrey Picot was turned into a satisfactory anti-aircraft gunner, but warned that his stick drill, the process by which he transferred his swagger stick from 'under the left armpit … [to] the right hand and held horizontal to the ground' was worryingly poor. No sooner had he been commissioned than he was told that there was not now much need for anti-aircraft officers, but a huge demand for infantry platoon commanders: after another course, this time on the Isle of Man, he joined the Hampshire Regiment, and arrived in Normandy on D+2. Having survived the North West Europe campaign, he concluded that 'the infantryman is the king of warriors … The comradeship that arises is very special. It is the brotherhood of those who have mastered themselves and served their team.'[56] From the middle of 1942 there was an increase in the time spent on tactics, but the fact that so much training was carried out in the context of individual arms did little to make officers more comfortable with the combined arms tactics that were so fundamental to success in battle.

Nevertheless, the experience of Stuart Hills shows how well the system was working by mid-war. He left Tonbridge School in July 1942, and found that his headmaster had written on his final report 'If I was back in the army as in the last war as a company commander, I should like Hills with me as a platoon commander, especially in a tight corner.' He was soon called up, and reported to the Royal Armoured Corps' 30th Primary Training Wing at Bovingdon Camp in Dorset on 20th August. Conditions were 'fairly Spartan,' but 'the former public schoolboys among us had perhaps become more used to the privations and discomfort of boarding life', and the school OTC had conveyed some 'rudimentary military knowledge'. That October he moved on to the nearby 58th Training Regiment to be turned into an RAC crewman, first learning to drive tanks and then to fire their guns. He passed WOSB in March 1943, attended pre-OCTU at Alma Barracks in Blackdown, and then went on to Sandhurst, which had become the 100 RAC OCTU in 1942 when 161 Infantry OCTU had migrated to Mons Barracks in Aldershot:

> Sandhurst was to be my finishing school. We started by going over some old ground – general military training, driving and mainten-ance, gunnery and wireless. But then I moved on to more special-ised training on the latest tanks, which in my case were Churchills, and to a week's battle training in Wales. This was the toughest week I had so far spent in the army. It poured with rain and the wind blew a gale the whole time. We camped out for four nights in one of the bleakest spots on the Welsh mountains, with one blanket each, sodden boots and clothes, and had to do all our own cooking. We had to get up every morning at 4 a.m. and did exercises the whole day with live ammunition, and at times it was extremely dangerous. However, our troop sustained no casualties, which was unique.

Geoffrey Picot, who had a very similar experience in Snowdonia, wrote that 'in my eight months of frontline fighting, I was never once as severely physically tested as on that battle course.'[57]

Stuart Hills received his emergency commission in the Sherwood Rangers Yeomanry in January 1944. The regiment had returned home from the Middle East the previous month to prepare for the invasion of Europe, having lost two commanding officers, Lieutenant Colonel 'Flash' Kellett MP and his successor, Lieutenant Colonel Donny Player. Amongst Hills' brother officers was Keith Douglas, one of the war's most talented poets, described by another officer as having 'a grudge against the world in general and particularly of those of his fellow yeomanry officers who had been with the Regiment before the war and consisted of wealthy landed gentry … he was a complete individualist, intolerant of military convention and discip-line'. For all Douglas's apparent resentment of 'that assumption of superiority, that dandyism, individuality and disregard of the duller military conventions that made the regiment sometimes unpopular, but always discussed and admired', he wrote with real feeling about 'this gentle, obsolescent breed of heroes'.

Hills faced one of the challenges common to young officers in that most of the men under his command were veterans and he was not. Three of the four other men in his tank had served in the desert, as had the sergeants commanding the other two tanks in his troop. Had Hills known it at the time, he might have gained comfort from the fact that Arthur Reddish, the machine-gunner and co-driver in his tank, wrote: 'Lieutenant Stuart Hills was straight from Sandhurst and would be facing his baptism of fire, but we had no worries on that score. He had shown enough during the training period to convince us desert veterans that we had a good tank commander. He was quietly confident and fearless but tolerant and a good sportsman.' Their amphibious Sherman tank sank on its way to the beach on D-Day, and eventually they got ashore with 'one tin hat, my revolver and the clothes we stood up in, provoking the jovial beachmaster to say 'This will swing the balance in Montgomery's favour; there'll be consternation in Berlin.' Hills fought in Normandy, the pursuit into Belgium, through the Siegfried Line and on to Bremen, earning an MC on the way but losing many of his comrades, from Keith Douglas in Normandy to Denis Elmore – 'who had shared so much of my life at Tonbridge and in the war over the last eight years' – killed in the very last weeks.[58]

Although procedures for officer selection and training were better in the Second World War than in the First, with the introduction of the WOSB marking a significant point of departure, they took too long to evolve. In both wars the British army was indelibly marked by the fact that it grew from a small peacetime force into a massive national army, and did so without adequate preparation, either for the demands that this would impose on its officer corps, or for expanding that corps to meet the challenges of a war of national survival. The leadership ethos of the peacetime army, stressing the importance of the paternal care exercised by an officer for his men, was passed on into the wartime army with a fair degree of success, even though a large amount of officers no longer came from traditional backgrounds. Failings often reflected weaknesses in training rather than personal inadequacy. In particular, the army's painfully slow development, in both wars, of a properly thought-through combined arms tactical doctrine meant that young officers often found themselves ill-prepared to meet the test of battle. This should have come as no surprise, for a steady flow of doctrine publications had emphasised the importance of common understanding. As the future Field Marshal Lord Chetwode remarked at an Aldershot Command conference in 1923: 'if an army is to succeed, everyone in it must know the action other people on their right and left, or in front of or behind them, will take under certain circumstances. It is fatal not to work to a common doctrine.'[59] Yet Geoffrey Picot, in his first battle as a platoon commander in Normandy, with all the benefits of two distinct bursts of officer training, found himself in 'the direst situation of my life', because his commanding officer, 'seemingly fearless', and waving his revolver, gave all sorts of encouragement, 'But why doesn't he give me some orders? There are six mortars some way down the road. Doesn't he want me to fire them at the enemy? Why doesn't he tell me where the enemy are?'[60]

Doug Proctor, an experienced infantry section commander, argued that character was ultimately an officer's most important attribute:

> During my six years in army service I knew many officers – some good – some bad. The most obvious difference between them was not in their tactical awareness as one might expect, but in the relationships they had with their soldiers. No matter how tactically aware an officer may be, it counts for little unless he can command the trust, loyalty and respect of his men and is able to inspire them. The good officers, without exception, enjoyed that trust, loyalty and respect.[61]

Robert Bridgeman, who had left the army in 1937 and been recalled in 1939, had become a major general and in mid-1944 was made deputy adjutant general. His tasks included reviewing courts martial, and interviewing

> young officers who had committed no crime but had been reported on as unsuitable for commissioned rank, usually, I imagine, because they were incapable of making up their minds. I cannot recall anything I hated so much as these interviews … In he came, nearly always a nice-looking young chap with no personality. I never saw

one who I thought deserved his commission back ... Fortunately there were very few who availed themselves of what can only have been a forlorn hope. There must have been many more who accepted the verdict and in their hearts knew that it was right, but compared with the thousands who passed through the OCTUs and gained commissions, it is a wonder so few fell by the wayside.[62]

A good deal of received wisdom, encapsulated in what we may call the 'Tommy is no soldier' argument, suggests that the officer leadership was patchy in both world wars, and that much of this was the fault of the pre-war officer corps, 'a conservative rural elite who saw the army as a refuge from the industrial world', that promoted new officers in its own image.[63] It is more accurate to see failures as systemic, embodying doctrinal uncertainty (which itself had spin-offs into the procurement of weapons and equipment, especially in the Second World War), endemic under-funding, especially in the inter-war years, and, again most marked in the Second World War, the growing tendency to put the least intelligent and vigorous recruits into the infantry. There is also room for confronting the legend of inadequacy head-on. Sidney Jary, whose account of a platoon commander's life in North West Europe in 1944–45 is one of the best personal narratives of the war, argued that

> Over the past twenty years it has been the custom of some of our younger military writers to extol the professional ability of the Wehrmacht whilst decrying that of our own fighting arms, particularly our armour and infantry. This has perplexed me because it runs contrary to my own experience. My 18 Platoon were better soldiers than any we fought. So was 'D' Company and the whole of 4th Battalion, The Somerset Light Infantry. Admittedly it was a good battalion, but I find it hard to believe that it was unique.[64]

No testimony should stand alone, and alongside this we might cite the much-quoted report by Lieutenant Colonel A. J. D. Turner, CO of 6/ Duke of Wellington's Regiment in Normandy in June 1944, maintaining that his battalion was so ravaged as to be unable to remain in the line. The battalion's shattered state reflected the fact that in fourteen days it had lost 23 officers and 350 soldiers, one company had lost every officer and another had only one left. The report whizzed up the chain of command like a distress rocket, and Montgomery was not pleased: the battalion was disbanded and used to provide drafts for other units. However, its author, who already had an MC, went on to earn a DSO and was eventually to command a brigade. Whatever Montgomery's view at the time, it is clear that the experienced officers who made decisions about Turner's subsequent career did not find his attitude surprising. Most armies would have found a casualty rate like this, amounting to the turnover of three-quarters of the strength of the rifle companies, no less crippling.

This is perhaps the place to leave these temporary gentlemen. Whatever their social background or the inadequacies of their training, they did not flinch from the risk their job entailed. Indeed, knowledge of the risks dissuaded some men, who might have made good officers, from accepting promotion and the danger that came with it. During the First World War 37,452 officers and 664,958 other ranks were killed, with officers making up 5.63 per cent of the dead. Although unit establishments varied greatly, and much depended upon casualties and the rate at which they were replaced, the average infantry battalion might expect to go into battle with 25 officers and 650 men, with officers constituting 3.7 per cent of the unit. In both world wars officer casualties were proportionately greater than those of the men they commanded, and in many cases the ratio was very much higher. On the first day of the Somme, with battalions in good strength, and officers constituting around 3.3 per cent, of the attacking force, they made up 5.16 per cent of the dead and 4.27 per cent of all casualties.[65] Charles Farrell wrote his memoirs in angry response to a *Spectator* article which maintained that in Normandy and Italy whole 'formations had to be pulled out of the front line because they were unwilling to fight.' He noted that in the First World War the Scots Guards had 111 officers and 2,730 other ranks killed, officer dead making up 3.87 per cent of the total. In the Second World War, though, the regiment lost 98 officers to 943 men, with the officers constituting 9.4 per cent of the dead.[66] Geoffrey Picot assessed that 1/Hampshires 'was effectively twice wiped out' between 6 June and 17 November 1944, and Sidney Jary found himself the only officer in his battalion to emerge unscathed from Normandy to north Germany.[67]

CHAPTER 9

SANDHURST: SERVE TO LEAD

D URING THE POST-WAR period, the army was tugged in two directions. What was left of Field Marshal Montgomery's 21st Army Group became the British Army of the Rhine (BAOR), settling down in north Germany to take on many of the characteristics of a new imperial garrison. Across the rest of the world, old imperial commitments remained, although a gradual process of withdrawal, accompanied by a series of counter-insurgency campaigns, eventually saw the evacuation of all but the tiniest of outposts like Gibraltar and the Falklands. In the process there was one largish conventional war, in Korea from 1950 to 1953, and another smaller one in the Falklands in 1982. The army's commitment to Northern Ireland (Operation Banner) lasted from 1969 to 2007, making it the longest campaign in British military history. With the collapse of communism and the end of the bipolar world, the army found itself increasingly engaged in the 'expeditionary warfare' that has come to characterise the last decade of the twentieth century and the opening years of the twenty-first. Conscription ended in 1945 but was rapidly reimposed, as National Service, in 1947, and lasted till 1960, initially for a period of eighteen months, and then for two years. All of this took place against a back-cloth of relative economic decline and substantial social change.

As far as officer recruiting was concerned, although the army had reverted to type after 1918, it could not do so as completely after 1945. Regional WOSBs were closed, and a single Regular Commissions Board was established at Leighton Park, near Westbury in Wiltshire. Its procedures were firmly based on those used at wartime WOSBs. Its remit was gradually broadened to include the selection of all officers; university graduates were initially selected by a less demanding system. With a new title of Army Officer Selection Board (AOSB), it now selects Territorial as well as regular officers: the latter attend the board for four days and the former for a long, and very busy, weekend. Potential officers have to attend a two-day briefing before attempting the main board. Pass rates vary between boards but currently run at around 55 per cent.

In 1947 Sandhurst and Woolwich were merged into a single institution for training regular officers, its name, properly spelt without a comma, now 'The Royal Military Academy Sandhurst' with the motto 'Serve to Lead'. Its two-year course, no longer fee-paying, included both military and academic subjects. There were two intakes a year, and officer cadets, the term that had replaced the traditional 'gentleman cadets', went on to play a substantial part in the running of the academy by constituting the 'cadet government' in their final term. When I taught there in the 1970s there were half-serious suggestions that the academy resembled a public school at which the Corps had got rather out of hand, and there is no doubt that the rigidly controlled first term, when 'the imperatives of the institution govern the timetable of the cadets' lives', was at least as much about the transmission of attitudes and values as about specifically military training.[1] In his 1970 study of organisational response to change, M. Garnier maintained that it was precisely because of its structure – there were then three colleges, Old, New, and Victory, which were not unlike boarding houses – that public school attitudes retained their dominant hold on the British army. Throughout the 1970s and early 1980s, a significant proportion of Sandhurst cadets came from public schools, which educated about 6 per cent of the population. Antony Beevor, a regular army officer before he became a best-selling historian, suggested that: 'The public school, with its mores and hierarchical system, has always been a natural preparation for army life.'[2] General Sir Mike Jackson, CGS 2003–6, was the son of an officer who had been commissioned from the ranks of the Household Cavalry into the Royal Army Service Corps during the war. He had been educated at the independent Stamford School, where 'my experience in the C[ombined] C[adet] F[orce] had a considerable influence in demonstrating the pleasures of soldiering.' He went to Sandhurst in

January 1962, and thought that its colleges were indeed like boarding school houses. Like all his generation he remembered 'the legendary Jackie Lord', the academy sergeant major: 'I will call you Sir and you will call me Sir because I am a warrant officer. But there's one difference: you will mean it and I most certainly won't.'[3]

Until the early 1970s university graduates, whether they joined the army on graduation or had enjoyed paid 'university cadetships', needed to do only a brief familiarisation course at Sandhurst, a process which did not stop one of them, General Sir Roger Wheeler, from becoming Chief of the General Staff. Cadets destined for National Service or short-service commissions in the artillery or Royal Armoured Corps, were trained at Mons barracks in Aldershot, now called Mons Officer Cadet School. Cadets destined for similar commissions in other arms went to Eaton Hall OCS, on the Duke of Westminster's Cheshire estate. Eaton Hall closed when National Service ended, and in 1972 Mons moved to Sandhurst, initially as a college in its own right – part of an academy that offered a variety of courses, depending on whether they were designed for short-service officers, officers who hoped for full careers, graduates or non-graduates. A period of wearying change ended with the adoption in 1992 of a standard, year-long commissioning course, with all those who passed (regardless of gender or academic background) being granted short service commissions, extendable into regular commissions if their reports warranted it.

Ostensibly the structure laid down in 1947 and developed since would appear to have created a meritocracy, where the only route to a commission in the regular army was by way of taking scientifically based tests and going on to complete formalised professional training. But in 1988 R. G. L. von Zugbach, himself a former regular officer, argued that the process reflected 'the dominance of an established cultural pattern'. The candidates' mess at Westbury was 'a replica of the sort of officers' mess to be found anywhere, where the British army serves'. Meals were taken at 'officers' mess timings', with dinner at 8.00 p.m., and the journals available in the ante-room were, like *Country Life, Horse and Hound* and *Tatler*, 'the 'specialised literature' of the upper middle-classes'.[4] He went on to observe that, although detailed records of the social class of applicants were hard to obtain, over the period 1973–77, 54 per cent of applicants had parents with higher professional/managerial backgrounds (19 per cent were service officers), 11 per cent came from lower professional/ managerial and administrative backgrounds, 21 per cent from clerical, salesmen and small shop owners (2 per cent were service other ranks), and 14 per cent from skilled manual backgrounds. No candidates had unskilled manual backgrounds. Zugbach argued that pass rates suggested that the system was not biased against applicants from working-class backgrounds, for the 'skilled manual' group actually achieved a higher success rate than any other, from the small percentage whose fathers were serving other ranks. The 'dearth of candidates' from this background reflected the fact that a boy from a lower middle- or working-class background would generally have little information on serving as an army officer, and would not be drawn to an army career. Antony Beevor, writing in 1990, argued that

> the egalitarian ethos prevalent in most state schools ... has run counter to all notions of elitism. Several schools have apparently given this as their reason for refusing to provide reports on army candidates. Those from the state sector are also deterred by their ignorance of army life. Most public schoolboys obtain a much better idea through relatives or friends and are less put off by the army's class mystique – a phenomenon which by now owes rather more to cinematic cliché than contemporary reality.[5]

It was in great measure to attract grammar school boys that in 1953 the army established its own sixth-form college at Welbeck Abbey in north Nottinghamshire with the specific aim of getting more officers into the technical corps. For many years Welbeck's former pupils went to Sandhurst without attending RCB, but in the period examined by Zugbach, some 14.3 per cent of them were back-squadded (that is, put down a term) while there, while the average for all cadets was 9.59 per cent. Although Welbexians were not wholly confined to the technical arms on commissioning, in 1973–7 they made up over half the candidates destined for the Royal Electrical and Mechanical Engineers, half of those for the Royal Signals, and 1.1 per cent of those going to the cavalry. Zugbach concluded that although Welbexians outnumbered the products of any other single academic institution, their prospects were unquestionably the poorest. In 2005

Welbeck moved to Woodhouse in Leicestershire, and became the Defence Services Sixth Form College, gaining pupils destined for the Royal Navy and Royal Air Force in 2004 and the defence civil service in 2005. Those destined for the army are now required to pass the AOSB, and the early evidence suggests that this produces better results at Sandhurst.

Zugbach's work, and the studies it was based on, pointed to 'an increasing widening of the social base from which officers are drawn', and when he revisited the subject in 1999 he identified a substantial fall in the proportion of Sandhurst cadets who had attended what he termed 'elite public schools'.[6] Overall, though, the officer corps remained largely recruited from public schools. In 2005, 53 per cent of cadets had attended them, leading the House of Commons Public Accounts Committee to worry that the army was still not appealing to people who had officer potential. Zugbach's study portrayed an officer corps dominated by public school boys and, in particular, by public school boys who had chosen to serve in specific regiments. The distinguished military historian Sir John Keegan, a Sandhurst lecturer for many years, was right to compare the process of selecting a regiment with courting. Some cadets fall in love at first sight, before they even go to Sandhurst, with family tradition, regional origin or technical speciality colouring their affection.

Regimental headquarters (called 'home headquarters' by the cavalry) are the offices that support regimental colonels and deal with the detail of the regiment's institutional existence. One of their staff of retired officers will be responsible for liaising with potential officers, and the best of them develop an uncanny ability to keep in touch with schools and families that have done the regiment well in the past, and to identify youngsters who may prove an asset in the future. The Royal Green Jackets, which came into existence with regimental amalgamations in 1966 and was itself amalgamated into The Rifles in 2007, had an uncanny (and no less irritating) ability to find an apparently never-ending supply of bright, self-assured and generally unpompous young men. Other cadets form bonds while they are at Sandhurst, perhaps because they hope to follow a close friend into his regiment, or are so impressed by their platoon commander or platoon colour sergeant that they wish to join his tribe. Regiments have a representative amongst the officers on the staff of Sandhurst, and although there is no guarantee that he will wear its cap-badge, for there are times when a regiment may not have an officer serving there, he will act as a point of contact with the potential officer.

However, the path of true love does not always run smooth. A cadet has to list three prospective regiments. Each will have a limited number of vacancies (say two or three for a two-battalion regiment on each of two annual boards), and some decline to be nominated as second or third choices, though they may well not say as much. Others will establish invisible but adamantine selection criteria. Until relatively recently a nice and efficient cavalry regiment expected its young officers to have a serious interest in one of the field sports, though this requirement appeared nowhere in its literature. Although the reports furnished by Sandhurst to regiments are now not as frank as they once were, because of the fear, in a litigious age, that a cadet's future career might be blighted by a flash of less than objective honesty, regiments will pay careful attention to the cadet's positioning in his platoon, and may take the view that it is better to select too few officers than to accept somebody rubbing along in the bottom third of his intake. They will also send candidates off for at least one 'battalion visit'. When conducted badly, as they sometimes are, these can consist of letting a pack of subalterns loose on the visitor to test his drinking skills, or driving him at high speed across Salisbury Plain in a Warrior. These processes often have the same copious result, especially if the latter takes place the morning after the former. Well-conducted visits, with an opportunity for the cadet to meet some of the soldiers he may one day command, provide the regimental selection board (perhaps consisting of the regimental colonel, regimental secretary, a captain and a major) with valuable evidence when it sees the cadet towards the end of his time at the Academy.

There are sometimes broken hearts. A cadet who sets his sights too high, perhaps by nominating three sought-after infantry regiments and falling just short of getting into any of them, may finish up in a corps, which was not his first love. A candidate who had seemed an obvious choice, and had been on RHQ's list for years, might get back-termed (a fatal objection for some regiments) or simply interview badly on a board when another, perhaps less favoured candidate, came across surprisingly well. There is just a little room for manoeuvre as the marriage-brokers (regimental colonels and perhaps the

Commandant of Sandhurst) try to ensure that, say, a natural infantry-man does not finish up as a logistician. It is generally possible to be rescued from an unhappy marriage by divorce. Mike Jackson did well at Sandhurst, becoming a junior under officer in the 'cadet government'. He was very much interested in joining the Parachute Regiment, but eventually concluded that his flair for languages made the Intelligence Corps a better choice. The corps requires its officers to spend some time with a 'teeth arm' unit so as to gain experience of the mainstream army, and Jackson was attached to the Paras, who reported on him as 'by inclination, character and physique' being better suited to the infantry than the Intelligence Corps.[7] The Intelligence Corps was not wholly delighted to lose him, but in 1970 he transferred to the Parachute Regiment.

Had Mike Jackson not transferred it would have been inconceivable for him to have risen beyond brigadier, for the army was then, and is now, dominated by its teeth arms. Over the period of Zugbach's first study it was not simply a question of the teeth arms in general, but of some regiments in particular. A remarkable 46 per cent of generals came from the Royal Green Jackets, the Foot Guards, the Household Cavalry, the Cavalry and the Parachute Regiment, with the Green Jackets alone providing 8.58 per cent of the army's general officers. A more detailed breakdown of the Green Jackets concluded that

> The cadets show a high proportion of Etonians, etc. and amongst the generals the proportion is very high … The social location is upper middle-class, with some indication that this may spill over into the upper classes rather than downward. The Royal Green Jackets represents a professional elite, taking cadets from high in the Order of Merit [at Sandhurst], rejecting the back-squadded and producing proportions of generals far in excess of the expected share of the ranks concerned. So extreme is this tendency to dominate the senior ranks of the army that the regiment is nicknamed the 'Black Mafia' (black being the colour of the regiment's buttons).[8]

This was an exceptional period, for two successive Chiefs of the General Staff, Sir Roland Gibbs (1976–9) and Sir Edwin Bramall (1979–82) were Green Jackets. By 1999 though, not only had the Green Jackets lost their dominant position, though they remained very influential, but the proportion of public school-educated generals had declined from 100 per cent to 83 per cent, just as the proportion of generals educated at Oxford and Cambridge had shrunk from 50 per cent to 33 per cent. Moreover, the change is more marked amongst junior generals, with 77 per cent of the 1974 major generals public school educated as against 54 per cent of the 1996 sample. Zugbach concluded that 'the graduate from a non elite university background is beginning to displace the [public school] educated officer at the senior levels of the British military system.'9

When Antony Beevor wrote about his old service in 1990 this process seemed to be gaining momentum rapidly, with fears of 'a collapse in the ethos of public service' as more and more young men seemed to regard the army as a poor investment for their time when there were glittering prizes to be won in the City. The economic crisis of the noughties seems to have checked the movement, and there are currently fewer worries about an officer shortfall. I gave up my post on the academic staff at Sandhurst in 1983, and did not return there till 1999 for my first stint on the selection board as colonel of the Princess of Wales's Royal Regiment, the infantry regiment of southeast England. Graduates outnumbered non-graduates, and the range of universities, and the degrees obtained at them, by subject and quality, was very wide indeed. Some familiar public schools still sent us officers from time to time, but the close relationships that had once linked schools to the county regiments from which my own was created in 1992 was a thing of the past. Family connections still mattered, and I was delighted to welcome the grandson of an officer who had been colonel of one of our predecessor regiments when I was a young officer, but secretly relieved that he had interviewed so well that nobody could accuse me of nepotism. A sense of regionality helped, and there was a steady trickle of applicants who had served, either as officers or soldiers, in our Territorial battalion.

Wise regimental boards will try to give serious consideration to candidates who are likely to pass out in the top third of their Sandhurst platoon, were well reported on their battalion visit, and are unequivocally committed to their arm of service. I never worried about the cut of a cadet's suit or the sound of his voice, and was always pleased, when I remembered a nervous young man sitting opposite the board in the upstairs ante-room of the officers' mess at Sandhurst, to see how much he had developed after his first tour of duty.

CHAPTER 10

CHURCH MILITANT

$\mathbb{S}$OLDIERS HAVE TENDED to judge religion by the quality of its advocates, and the concept of army chaplains is an old one. There were regimental preachers on both sides during the Civil War. Perhaps the best known was the Parliamentarian Hugh Peters, an eloquent and strong-minded Puritan who combined giving inspirational sermons with taking messages from the field armies to parliament, raising troops and even laying hands on artillery to conduct the siege of Pembroke in 1648. George Monck argued that one of a general's main tasks was to 'settle an opinion of right in the minds of his Officers and Soldiers: the which can no better way be done than by the Chaplains of an Army.'[1] Chaplains were appointed by regimental commanders, who took care to select men whose opinions agreed with their own. When Colonel John Okey of the New Model Army's dragoon regiment fell out with some of his officers over knotty theological points, he was vexed to find that his chaplain, Mr Close, supported the dissidents. Okey at once dismissed Close, telling him that he might soldier on as a private trooper but not as chaplain. Close retorted that 'if he were not fit to be chaplain to the regiment, he was not fit to ride in any troop.'[2]

Parliamentarian chaplains had to contend with a soldiery holding firm theological views. Despite the fact that preaching was in theory restricted to ordained ministers of a reformed church, some officers and men interrupted sermons, set up their own conventicles, and spoke from the pulpit. Captain Pretty of Ireton's regiment told a chaplain to be silent, saying that he had been drunk on Saturday night and was therefore not fit to preach on Sunday morning, and a trooper of Cromwell's regiment of horse stood up in church when the minister had finished speaking, 'pretending to question something delivered, but indeed fell upon venting to the people the doctrine of universal grace, that no man was condemned for anything but unbelief'.[3] Chaplains enjoyed officer status, were paid about the same as captains of foot, and in the New Model, had commissions signed by the commander-in-chief.

The Restoration army inherited the concept of regimental chaplains, who were expected to 'every day read the common prayers of the Church of England to the soldiers ... and preach to them as often as shall be thought fit'.[4] They were commissioned on the recommendation of the regiment's colonel. Fortresses and garrisons had their own chaplains, generally appointed with the approval of the governor, and the Board of Ordnance maintained a few chaplains to minister to the Royal Artillery.

Contemporaries had sharply differing opinions on the value of chaplains. In 1708, satirist Ned Ward reckoned that the average regimental colonel 'usually keeps a chaplain for the battalion he commands, as he does a led horse, more for show than for service'.[5] The Revd Peter Vatass, chaplain to the 14th Light Dragoons, had been on unpaid leave for 52 years in 1796, without successive colonels feeling his absence too keenly, not least because they pocketed the money allocated for his pay. There were some officers, like Captain Bennett Cuthbertson, who thought that soldiers were 'bumbling rustics of child-like simplicity' who would genuinely profit from the guidance offered by chaplains, whose sermons ought to be readily comprehensible to simple souls and should identify prevalent moral failings.[6]

A committed chaplain would not only read prayers and hold services, but would also conduct baptisms, marriages, and funerals; visit the sick; attend the dying; and offer consolation to the condemned, treating his regiment for all the world like an itinerant parish. However, the army chaplain was exposed to severe temptations, and Ned Ward maintained that although battles and sieges made him unusually devout, as soon as the danger was past he was in his old pickle of profaneness; for no sooner is the storm over, or the regiment marching into winter quarters, but off goes the glass, and up go madam's fine petticoats; 'tis handle your arms, and to the left about as you were ... He is far from being a scandal to his profession: he may drink and wench to the end of the chapter, yet he may plead with the missionary Jesuits in China that he permits himself those liberties with a design to render his person acceptable to the people ... He seldom swears, but when he's full of brandy wine, or good Burgundy, and then the flesh yields to the spirit: and he carries himself in such a manner, as you'd imagine him, by his dress and behaviour, rather an Irish grenadier or dragoon, than the soldier of a crucified master.[7]

There were certainly scandals enough. In 1774 the Revd Robert Newburgh of the 47th Regiment was accused of sodomy, and in 1797 the Revd Mr Blunt of the 33rd Regiment, while at sea on an expedition to the Philippines, got 'abominably drunk, and in that disgraceful condition exposed himself to both soldiers and sailors, talking all sorts of bawdy and ribaldry'. His commanding officer, the future Duke of Wellington, tried to cheer him up, assuring him that 'what had passed was not of the least consequence, as no one would think the worse of him for little irregularities committed in a moment of forgetfulness.' Sadly Blunt could not be consoled, fell into a depression and 'actually fretted himself to death'.[8] Drink was also the undoing of the 3rd Light Dragoons' chaplain in India in the 1840s. Sergeant John Pearman recalled that the night patrol of the officers' lines 'would often come across our parson dead drunk. We would have him carried to his bungalow or dwelling house.'[9]

The chaplain's most spectacular duty was the pre-battle service. Blenheim was fought on a Sunday. The fact that the British wing of the allied army had to wait until the Imperialist wing was ready to attack, gave the thirteen clergymen with the British contingent ample time to complete their business. They prayed, under sporadic artillery fire, on the line of the Nebel brook, before battle commenced in earnest. One of the best-recorded pre-battle services was conducted by Father Francis Gleeson for 2/Royal Munster Fusiliers on the evening of 8 May 1915 – the day before the battle of Aubers Ridge. The Munsters halted at a wayside shrine and formed up on three sides of a square. Father Gleeson, mounted and with a stole over his uniform, gave general absolution and the battalion sang *Te Deum* before continuing its advance to the front: it lost 19 officers and 374 men the next day. Fortunino Matania painted *The Last Absolution of the Munsters* for *Sphere* magazine using information provided by the widow of the battalion's commanding officer, Lieutenant Colonel V. G. H. Rickard, who was killed in the battle.

Gleeson served a one-year engagement as a chaplain from November 1914 to November 1915, departing after seeing his battalion badly mauled again, this time at Loos. He told the army's senior Roman Catholic chaplain

> I am sorry to be leaving the dear old Munster lads, but I really can't stand it any longer. I do not like the life ... though I love the poor men ever so much ... will you please send me the papers regarding my discharge.

However, he went out to France for another year from May 1917 to May 1918. After the war Gleeson incurred the hostility of the Bishop of Cork, an enthusiastic republican who resented his association with the British army. He died in 1959 as a parish priest in Dublin and a member of the Metropolitan chapter. Gleeson's reputation spread beyond his own battalion. Robert Graves, a special reserve officer in 2/Royal Welch Fusiliers, wrote admiringly of Father Gleeson, and maintained that, when the battalion lost all its officers at First Ypres, Gleeson had removed his black badges of rank, taken command of the survivors, and held the line.[10]

Pre-combat services were common in both Gulf Wars and Afghanistan. 'In Afghanistan we did services for groups of soldiers before they went on planned ops,' recalled a senior chaplain. 'I remember a group of non-church-going soldiers coming and asking me if I would bless them before they deployed because they knew they would most likely get into some heavy fire fights, which they subsequently did.' Another chaplain told him of his experience in going forward to a patrol base to visit the troops and hold a memorial service for a soldier who had been killed. No sooner had the service begun than the base came under attack:

I remember him telling me about the incident a few days after it happened. Apart from those in the sangars, the whole company was on parade and it had formed up in an open square, with the chaplain out in front. Whenever the rounds started coming in and landing all around the place (with RPGs exploding, etc.) the chaplain wasn't sure whether he should run for cover or continue with the service. He looked at the OC and the CSM and those standing on parade and apart from a few that had peeled off to the sides to support the sangars the rest stood firm. The mortars and the heavy weapons in the sangars engaged the enemy attackers, while the chaplain carried on with the service. However, when it came to the minute's silence, all firing from inside the base stopped. Later the mortar sergeant told the padre that he had counted the minute and signalled the end by resuming firing, which was needless to say accompanied by a heavy rate of fire from the sangars. To me this just typifies both the role of the chaplain on modern ops and the attitude of the British soldier. Even in the midst of a heavy attack, the desire to remember and pay their respects out-weighed other considerations.[11]

In fortresses and barracks chaplains were able to avail themselves of garrison churches, but on operations they had to make do with what accommodation they could get. In 1761 Corporal Matthew Webb, commanding the 12th Foot's pioneers in a chilly camp in Germany, received 'unexpective orders' to dig a circular trench and to set boughs around it 'to screen the minister and congregation while at divine service it being so excessive cold standing without'. More branches were piled up in the centre, 'where two drums was fixed, one upon the other, for the minister to lay his books upon'. On Sunday 25 October:

Every man had orders to clean themselves for church and soon after 10 o'clock the drum beat and the whole paraded and, the rolls being called, we marched into this new church that we had made where our chaplain read prayers and preached an excellent sermon and took his text from the 27th Psalm, verse the 2nd and 3rd. A'many of our officers being present acknowledged that our work had been to good effect, and the boughs broke off the wind greatly and made it very commodious, as the trench that was dug within the boughs round for the men to sit in, able to hold 1000 men and upwards.

The regiment's chaplain, Thomas Milward Key, had deputised for his father, who had been chaplain since 1733, and formally replaced him when he died in 1760.[12]

In the eighteenth century it was rarely easy to find sufficient clergymen of the required standard, especially as chaplains with livings very often used a proportion of their army income to pay a deputy 'from the Church of England's underclass of unbeneficed clergy, a group that was responsible for a good deal of clerical scandal'.[13] In 1705 a bishop found that one of his parishes was being looked after by a neighbouring clergyman because its vicar was 'chaplain to a regiment of horse in Flanders', and in 1757 Horace Walpole cheerfully asked the Duke of Bedford, lord lieutenant of Ireland, to allow a chaplain leave of absence from his regiment in Cork to see to his parish in England.[14] The recruitment of chaplains was not helped by the steady decline in the relative value of their pay during the eighteenth century. They were encumbered by the need to cover the necessary expenses of living amongst the officers, and the need to provide themselves with a horse and suitable kit when on campaign. Nevertheless, as late as 1790 the chaplain's £121. 13s. 4d. per annum compared very favourably with the income of many clergymen, and was all the more attractive if the chaplain could manage to avoid the expense of doing duty with his regiment. It is small wonder that there were so many absentee chaplains, and in 1759 the governor of newly captured Guadaloupe told Lord Barrington 'Our new friends the French take us for atheists, as we have ne'er a chaplain amongst us nor any sign of public worship.'[15] There was only one regimental chaplain with the Duke of York's force in Flanders in 1793, although four or five deputies eventually turned up, and two years later not a single chaplain could be found to accompany Sir Ralph Abercromby's expedition to the West Indies.

Wise chaplains kept in touch with influential patrons, hoping that ecclesiastical advancement might reward military virtue. The Revd Samuel Noyes, chaplain to Lord Orkney's Foot in the War of Spanish Succession, wrote a series of informative letters to the Archbishop of

York and the Bishop of Ely. Noyes was close enough to the action to see how Marlborough 'exposed his person the whole day in a most uncommon manner' at Blenheim, and sufficiently well connected for Lieutenant General Lumley to tell him that all the senior Dutch generals had been killed or wounded at the storming of Schellenberg.[16] Valuable though Noyes' letters are to historians, their real purpose was to ensure that powerful prelates did not forget him. Nor did they, for he ended his career holding several good livings as well as a prebend's stall in Winchester Cathedral.

In 1796, the patently unsatisfactory nature of the military chaplaincy encouraged the Duke of York to order all chaplains to join their regiments at once or retire from the service. Thereafter, commanding officers were required to certify, twice yearly, that their chaplains were carrying out their duties in person. New regimental chaplains and deputy chaplains were no longer to be appointed, although colonels of regiments were compensated by being allowed to sell an extra commission in their regiment when their current chaplain died. In place of regimental chaplains the Duke established the Chaplains' Department, whose members were appointed to overseas forces at the rate of one to each brigade or static garrison. Units in the United Kingdom had no full-time chaplains, but were ordered to obtain the services of a nearby clergyman who was to be paid by the regiment. The Board of Ordnance had its own small ecclesiastical establishment to minister to the Royal Artillery, and retained it until its disappearance as an independent body in 1855.

Some clergymen had been given the temporary status of chaplain general, to supervise regimental chaplains on specific campaigns: the sharp-tongued Dr Francis Hare, who was to die a bishop (and, indeed, came close to becoming Archbishop of Canterbury) had been Marlborough's chaplain general. In 1796 a chaplain general was appointed to head the new department. The first incumbent, the Revd John Gamble, was an experienced regimental chaplain. He had been the only clergyman to accompany the Duke of York's lacklustre expedition to Flanders in 1793–4 and was rewarded by being made the Duke's domestic chaplain. Although Gamble succeeded in putting his department on a firm financial footing, it remained hard to fill chaplains' posts.

His successor, the Revd John Owen, took over in 1810. He had already served in the Peninsula, where he had been warned that if he moved up with advancing troops he was likely to be killed. Owen steadfastly replied 'My primary duty is now to those departing this life.' As chaplain general he implemented a thoroughgoing reform. Staff chaplains, serving with brigades on operations, received the pay of infantry majors and were entitled to half-pay. Garrison chaplains were less well rewarded, as were the home chaplains appointed to large garrisons within the United Kingdom who formed, in effect, a pool of probationers for the staff chaplain posts. A new selection process ensured that potential chaplains were first approved by the two archbishops and the bishop of London, and then interviewed by the chaplain general before being commissioned. No clergyman holding a living could now be a chaplain, a regulation that caused fifteen of them to resign immediately.

Sadly, neither Owen's determination nor the wisdom of the new policy succeeded in getting sufficient chaplains into the Iberian Peninsula, where Wellington was at grips both with the French and with the advance of Methodism within his army. Methodism had a tradition of appealing to labourers, prisoners and others who felt excluded from the established Church, and its founder, John Wesley, had published *A Word in Season, or Advice to a Soldier*, in 1744. The following year he preached, with little apparent success, to the soldiers of General Wade's army encamped in rainy misery outside Newcastle. Military Methodism was strongest amongst private soldiers and NCOs, although its advance in North America owed much to Captain Thomas Webb, who had lost an eye at the siege of Louisbourg in 1758 and then served as barrack-master at Albany in New York, retiring in 1767. It did not do for an officer to be too zealous. In 1765 Captain John Scott of the 7th Dragoons encouraged Methodists to hold meetings in the regiment's riding school, and actively proselytised amongst the men. His brother officers were unimpressed, and he had to sell out in 1769. Some officers supported Methodism not from religious conviction but because they felt that it had a beneficial effect on soldiers' behaviour. The Duke of Cumberland, when commander-in-chief, had been encouraged to suppress Methodist meetings in the army, but after hearing one soldier-preacher 'engaged in prayer, and earnestly entreating God on behalf of the King and all the Royal

Family,' reportedly said 'I wish to God that all the soldiers in the British army were like these men.'[17]

The soldier-preacher Duncan Wright, who served in Ireland during the Seven Years War, said:

> here there was none to hinder me but the commanding officer, and he did not choose to do it. Though he did not like the Methodists, yet he wanted us all to be very good, as we did not know how soon our valour might be tried by the French. Therefore we had very strict orders against swearing, drunkenness, &c.; but these orders did not effect any great reformation.

One of his officers told him that he 'feared what our enthusiasm would turn to, and mentioned Cromwell, who could preach and pray one part of the day, and kill and plunder the other'.[18]

Wellington, however, saw Methodism as a potential threat to discipline, as he explained to the adjutant general in 1811:

> The meeting of soldiers in their cantonments to sing psalms, or hear a sermon read by one of their comrades, is, in the abstract, perfectly innocent; and it is a better way of spending their time than many others to which they are addicted; but it may become otherwise: and yet, till the abuse has made some progress, the Commanding Officer would have no knowledge of it, nor could he interfere. Even at last his interference must be guided by discretion, otherwise he will do more harm than good; and it can in no case be as effectual as that of a respectable clergyman. I wish, therefore, you would turn your mind to this subject, and arrange some plan by which the number of respectable and efficient clergymen with the army may be increased.[19]

Wellington complained that the Revd Samuel Briscall, attached to his headquarters, was 'the only Chaplain doing duty'. When Wellington first attended one of Briscall's services he warned the young man not to linger over his sermon: 'say as much as you like in five and twenty minutes. I shall not stay longer.' Owen sent four more chaplains to Lisbon, and told Briscall:

You will please to take care that they receive directions ... Be very peremptory in your orders and give every Chaplain to understand that they must immediately obey ... Know from every man how often he does duty on the Sunday on his part of the line. Entreat my Lord Wellington to issue orders for the facilitating of Divine Service, a great deal is in his power. Direct, as I have done, every Chaplain to give a short discourse intelligible and suitable to the men.

The chaplain general agreed with Wellington that 'the Zeal of the Chaplains' was 'the surest obstacle' to the progress of Methodism.[20]

However, Peninsular diarists testify to the fact that many chaplains made a poor showing. Sergeant William Lawrence of the 40th Regiment maintained that 'They used to say that the three scarcest things to be seen in the army were a dead parson, drum-major, or a woman; the explanation of this was that they were none of them often to be seen on a battle-field.'[21] In 1813 Ensign George Bell of the 34th saw an outdoor service ruined before it had begun when the chaplain entered the battalion's hollow square and thought that the big drum, provided to do duty as a lectern, was there for him to stand on. He had already got one foot up on it when he was vigorously tugged backwards by the anxious drummer: 'You'll be through it, sir; the only parchment in camp.' 'No one, of course, could keep his gravity during this scene', wrote Bell.[22]

Corporal William Wheeler of the 51st was in hospital at Fuentarrabia in the summer of 1814, and his ghastly experience of 'the incurable ward' for infected patients convinced him that chaplains failed in their duty to the sick and wounded:

In this house of misery how many fine brave young fellows have died without the assistance of a friend, mother, sister or wife to sooth their agony in their last moment. No minister of religion to cheer the dying sinner.

The people of England little think how her soldiers are neglected respecting spiritual aid, or I believe it would not be so. If they could but hear or see the agony of the dying, their prayers, their despair and the horrid oaths uttered by some in their exit from the world, I am sure that this most of wants would be attended to. It is true there are chaplains with the army who some-times perform divine service, but of what use are they, the service they perform has no effect, for their mode of living do not agree with the doctrine they preach. I have often heard the remark 'That a Chaplain is no more use to the army than a town pump without a handle.' If these Reverend Gentlemen were stationed at the sick depots and made to attend to the hospitals, they would be much more usefully employed than following the army with their brace of dogs and gun, running down hares and shooting partridges, etc.

Although Wheeler had little use for army chaplains, in Madrid two years before he had been charmed by Father Kelly, a Roman Catholic friar:

At first I was not well pleased for I dislike the whole fraternity. He was about thirty years of age and stood about six feet. He had a good open countenance, which in spite of my prejudice to the order I could not but think him a good free hearted fellow ... I soon found he was possessed of all that generosity of soul so common to his country. He was from the 'Green Isle'. He took off his shovel hat and seated himself. In a few minutes we were as well acquainted as if we had known one another before. As I proceeded with the account of the campaigns he seemed to enter into the very spirit of what I was saying. His remarks was so much to the purpose that I could not help observing that he would look well at the head of a Grenadier Company.[23]

Lieutenant George Gleig of the 85th was to be ordained in 1820 and went on to be chaplain general. He too complained that chaplains not only neglected their duties to the sick and wounded, but rarely conducted services for the dead:

Into huge pits dug to receive them the slain in battle were cast, as manure is cast into a trench, and the victims of fever and privations were in a somewhat similar manner disposed of. Even the officers, though interred apart, had no prayers read beside their graves, for this, among other reasons, that the chaplains of the army were very few in number, and of those few not one, so far as I know, cared to make more than a convenience of the service.[24]

Allocating one chaplain to each brigade, with two to four regiments in it, meant that even if all were present they were hard-pressed to cope. One brigade chaplain found that he had to deal with the whole Lisbon garrison, five regiments spread about the city in barracks, convents, and the citadel, as well as a number of regimental and general hospitals: he reckoned on carrying out three to six burials a day. Those chaplains who did indeed visit hospitals often paid dearly for it. One died on active service, another succumbed soon after his return to Britain, and Owen's correspondence with the adjutant general is speckled with requests for sick leave for chaplains suffering from 'intermittent fever' or worn out by work at 'the great depots of the sick'.

Most chaplains arrived in the Peninsula with little idea of how to look after themselves. Briscall was soaked though on his second night in Portugal, and when he reached Lisbon he lamented that while 'turning out into the street for a certain necessary purpose' he had, in his 'great bustle and confusion,' availed himself of the paper in which he had wrapped a £20 note and the money had suffered a nameless fate. The average Oxbridge fellow or country curate was uncomfortable with soldiers, who came largely from a class with which most clergymen had little real contact. Briscall found attending executions a melancholy business, and another chaplain had to minister to five men who had deserted to the French and had been captured when Ciudad Rodrigo was stormed in 1812. Wellington pardoned others who could obtain 'anything like a character' from their former officers, but the unlucky five, all confirmed delinquents, were to be shot. They greeted their sentence with oaths and scorned the chaplain's prayers. Two remained standing after the volley and had their brains blown out by the provost-marshal: it was enough to shock hardened campaigners, let alone a gently-bred chaplain.

Nor was it necessarily easier for chaplains to strike the right balance with officers, their natural associates. If they slipped too comfortably into the happy-go-lucky life of an officers' mess on campaign, with its sporting dogs, heavy drinking, and bawdy songs, they were accused of failing to practise what they preached. But when the Reverend

George Watson persuaded some officers not to attend a ball at Tarbes in May 1814 'as it would be an unjustifiable breach of the sabbath' we may doubt whether his propriety was widely applauded by the revellers.[25]

Post-Waterloo retrenchment hit the Chaplains' Department just as hard as the rest of the army. In 1829 the post of chaplain general was downgraded to principal chaplain, and by 1844 there were only four staff chaplains still serving, with most of the work in garrisons carried out by civilian officiating chaplains. After much squabbling it was agreed that Presbyterian ministers could act as officiating ministers outside Scotland, and in the 1830s discretionary payments to Roman Catholic priests (made briefly, during the Napoleonic wars, to priests ministering to Irish militia stationed in England) were resumed. Given the scale of the Scots and Irish contribution to the army's manpower, both measures were long overdue.

Because of the importance of the regiment in the army's structure, and the sharp differences between regiments, even of the same arm of service, it would have been surprising had religion not contributed to the complex cultural mix. Although regiments did not always draw their men largely from their theoretical recruiting areas, not least because of the wide distribution of Irishmen across the redcoat army and the presence of some Scots Catholics in Highland regiments, the authorities' growing identification of Scots regiments as predominantly Presbyterian, and Irish regiments as predominantly Catholic, 'was not only administratively convenient but it invariably struck deep roots in the culture of these regiments'.[26]

The 93rd Foot, later the Sutherland Highlanders, was raised in 1800 almost entirely from highlanders, and in 1811 numbered over a thousand Scots with just forty English or Irish soldiers. Most of its men were Presbyterian, and its earnest religiosity (it had over 700 communicants in Canada in the 1840s) and high standard of discipline made it wholly remarkable. Most troops embarking for the Crimea were confined to barracks on the night before their departure to prevent last-minute desertions. In contrast, the men of the 93rd were allowed out, and every one of them was in his place the following day. When the 93rd was about to go into action at Lucknow one soldier swore so horribly that an officer was about to send him to the rear, though the curses would not have aroused such concern elsewhere. However, an old sergeant advised the officer to let things be, as the man was fey, doomed to die, and was not to blame for his words; sure enough, he was killed almost immediately. There were certainly some Roman Catholics in the 93rd, for in 1835 a regimental standing order decreed that an officer was to accompany them to church and remain there throughout the service. Officers were to see that no treason was preached from the pulpit, for

whenever it is found that the clergy of the Roman Catholic church are in the habit of using seditious and inflammatory language to their congregation, officers commanding detachments will take their men to the Service of Mass only, marching them off when that is concluded.[27]

When Major General Sir Colin Campbell addressed the Highland Brigade before it advanced at the Alma in 1854, he warned the men:

Remember this: whoever is wounded – I don't care what his rank is – whoever is wounded must lie where he falls till the bandsmen come to attend to him. No soldiers must go carrying off wounded men. If any soldier does such a thing, his name shall be stuck up in his parish church … Keep silence. Fire low.[28]

Campbell's threat might have rung hollow with some of the 93rd, however, because evangelical Presbyterians in the regiment had no sympathy with the established Church of Scotland. In 1848 they had refused to follow their officers into a church with a Church of Scotland minister, and when the commanding officer complained to a sergeant he was firmly told not to interfere. This directness was wholly in the 93rd's tradition. At Balaclava Campbell warned the regiment that there could be no retreat and they must die where they stood. A soldier replied 'Aye, Sir Colin. An needs be, we'll do that', and there was firm approval from the ranks.

We have seen something of the process that converted highlanders from wild and bizarrely dressed potential rebels in the first half of the eighteenth century to stalwart linchpins of Queen and Empire a century later. Things were infinitely more complex for Irish regiments. The reign of James II, echoing folk memories of the fires of Smithfield and the threat of invasion from Catholic Europe, reinforced long-standing prejudices against Catholicism, and many Englishmen equated it with disloyalty. It was not until 1829 that the Catholic Relief Act removed most of the legal restraints on Catholics. Suspicions that most Irishmen were potential rebels were heightened by the great rebellion of 1798 and then again, by the Fenian agitation of the 1860s and beyond. In 1799 the 5th (Royal Irish) Dragoons was disbanded because of accusations that its ranks had been infiltrated by rebels. When the regiment was re-raised in 1858 it kept its old number but lost its seniority. Having been converted into lancers, it was amalgamated with the 16th Lancers in 1922 to form the 16th/5th, the apparent oddness of numbers being explained by the chequered history of the 5th. While the case against the 5th is far from proven, there was no doubt that several regiments were indeed affected by Fenianism: this may have been why the 76th Foot, despite recruiting in Scotland, was posted off to a long tour of duty in the Far East in 1867.

The behaviour of Irish soldiers was inclined to polarise opinion. There could be no doubting their prodigious achievements on the battlefield. In 1810 the 88th Foot, the Connaught Rangers (or indeed, 'The Devil's Own'), threw the French off Busaco Ridge with a bayonet charge. The following year, grim-faced and silent, they took the charnel village of Fuentes de Oñoro, then in 1812 they clawed their way into Ciudad Rodrigo, helped take the castle at Badajoz by escalade, and played a leading part in Wellington's great victory at Salamanca. The British captured five French regimental eagles in the Napoleonic wars. One was taken at Barossa in 1811 by Sergeant Patrick Masterson of the 87th (Prince of Wales's Irish) Regiment, who celebrated with the deathless cry 'By Jasus, boys, I have the cuckoo.' At Waterloo the 27th Regiment (Inniskilling), drawn up in the centre of Wellington's position, suffered 66 per cent casualties, the highest loss incurred by any British battalion that day. Sergeant Major Edward Cotton of the 7th Hussars tells us how its men, 'it may literally be said, were lying dead in square'.[29] The case of the 27th shows how hard it is to make easy assumptions about religion. Perhaps two-thirds of its soldiers were Roman Catholics, and the remainder were Ulster Protestants.

If the Irish got British generals out of trouble in battle, they got themselves into trouble in barracks, camps and on the line of march. Many of them enlisted into the forces of the Honourable East India Company, and Nathaniel Bancroft thought that three-quarters of the men in his troop of Bengal Horse Artillery were Irish:

> They were the first in mischief, merriment and devilment of all description, brave to temerity, never at a loss for an answer or an excuse, no matter how difficult the question or how grave the subject to be discussed ... They certainly ruled the roost in the troop.

One of his Irish comrades:

> although a man of personal courage, was an utter desperado. He was known among his comrades by the *sobriquet* of 'Bullock-horn', in consequence of his back and shoulders having been discoloured and hardened by repeated floggings for making away with his regimental necessaries and drunkenness on duty. After his promotion ... the first day he made his appearance in a sergeant's uniform, he 'tuk,' as he expressed it, 'a drop o'stuff, be way av wittin' the shrtipes an his arum, an' the goold band an his cap'.

He was promptly court-martialled for drunkenness and selling his gold-braid chevrons and cap-band to buy liquor.[30] Sir Thomas Picton had the Connaughts in his division in the Peninsula and admired their fighting qualities, but their endless thieving led him to call them the 'Connaught Footpads'.

When the Irish fought, it was not always against the monarch's enemies. In India in 1885, Colour Sergeant John Fraser of the 5th Fusiliers heard his battalion's duty bugler sounding for 'picket' and 'double', meaning that the duty picket was required double-quick. When he reached the scene he found that men of the 18th Royal Irish were smashing the windows of the garrison's Nonconformist chapel. There was a major fight when the picket arrived, for 'The Irish were annoyed at being interrupted, and we were annoyed at being turned out of barracks to deal with them. These facts provided motives for a certain amount of exuberance on both sides.'[31] Irish charm occasionally assumed political proportions. Lieutenant Kelly of the 40th Regiment, attending Mass in Lisbon like a good Catholic, fell in love with a Portuguese lady and promptly ran away with her, getting the chaplain of a Portuguese battalion to formalise their union. Unfortunately the lady's father was a general, and Wellington found himself embroiled in the resultant dispute, though the happy couple stayed together.

Wellington maintained that, in the Peninsula, despite the large number of Irishmen in his army,

> nobody goes to Mass ... I have not seen one soldier perform any one act of religious worship in these Catholic countries, excepting making the sign of the cross to induce the people of the country to give them wine.[32]

John Owen, chaplain general at the time, thought that Irish soldiers often made their religion a pretext for idleness on Sundays. However, it was not until 1793 that men serving in Ireland were officially allowed to attend Mass, and only in 1806 that this right was extended to the army as a whole. Catholics still had to tread carefully, as in 1811 Private Charles O'Neill of the 28th Regiment was awarded 300 lashes for refusing to attend an Anglican church parade and demanding to be allowed to attend Mass instead. Nor can we necessarily equate attendance at Mass with a man's belief, for until the second half of the nineteenth century, Catholicism in Ireland was not highly clericalised, and 'the practice of the faith was centred not on the scattered priesthood and weekly Mass attendance at a distant chapel, but on family prayer and the local shrine or holy well and the pattern or pilgrimage, in a rural landscape which had not yet lost its sacred character.'[33]

The East India Company was far more tolerant of Catholicism, and Roman Catholic soldiers serving in India were often able to obtain the services of a clergyman paid to minister to the Company's Catholic soldiers. In 1808 one of the Company's Anglican chaplains discovered that soldiers in the predominantly Catholic regiment in garrison at Dinapore had written to an Italian friar, asking him to visit them:

> When he came into the barracks, the Catholics crowded about him by hundreds, and in a tone of triumph pointed out his dress (that

of a Franciscan friar) to the Protestants, contrasting it with that of a Clergyman of the Church of England, booted and spurred, ready for a hunt.[34]

Catholic NCOs played an important role in arranging visits from priests and encouraging their fellow Catholics. In at least one sense their influence was analogous to that of Wesleyan NCOs, for literacy was a sine qua non of attaining sergeant's rank, and a man who could read the scriptures, whatever construct he placed upon them, was likely to be selected for promotion.

George Gleig became principal chaplain in 1844 and at once made it clear that he believed an active and committed chaplaincy to be fundamental to the maintenance of discipline and morale. He argued that officers set a poor moral example to their men, and soldiers were taken away from their villages to live in a world where

> [D]issolute talk, dissolute conduct – immorality, indecency, drunkenness, being considered as the mere outbreaks of youthful spirit … are certainly not discountenanced and condemned as they deserve; – and yet you lament that crime should be so common in the army, and wonder that the defaulters' list should be so extensive, and that the provost prisons should be so crowded, and barrack-cells never without their full complement of occupants. Moreover, you know that the root of most of the soldier's military offences is drunkenness, and yet if you do not entice him to spend his pay on strong liquors, you furnish him [through the canteen] with a very convenient opportunity for doing so.[35]

He argued that all stations with more than two hundred men, home and overseas, should have a dedicated church with its own minister, provided by encouraging the local incumbent to employ an extra curate with a small stipend from the War Office. Gleig not only carried the day, and had the sale of spirits in canteens banned, but was appointed chaplain general, and inspector general of regimental schools to boot. The product of his twin appointments was the chapel-school, a dual-purpose unconsecrated building that became a standard feature in mid-nineteenth century barracks until its eventual conversion into a dedicated chapel in the 1880s.

On the outbreak of the Crimean War Gleig had only seven staff chaplains: two Anglicans were hastily commissioned, and one Church of Scotland Minister and two Roman Catholics were appointed acting chaplains, though with contracts, not commissions. The allocation of one chaplain per division was inadequate from the outset, and the shocking conditions in the Crimea speedily killed one chaplain and incapacitated others. Just as the war highlighted so many failings in the army's structure, thanks in part to the reportage of *The Times*' William Howard Russell, so the shortage of chaplains caused much disquiet. Gleig recruited some assistant chaplains himself, and the Society for the Propagation of the Gospel found no shortage of volunteers. No less than seventy-two Anglican clergymen served in the east during the war, with nine Presbyterians, over twenty Roman Catholics and Peter Batchelor, a Wesleyan Methodist, who first found himself classified as a 'camp follower' before rising to the heights of 'an accredited Wesleyan Missionary'.

In the war's aftermath there were lengthy discussions as to whether military chaplains would be helped or hindered by having the normal appurtenances of commissioned status. The issue was resolved in 1858 when the Chaplains' Department was given a formalised structure with its members enjoying relative rank. Chaplains to the Forces Class 4 (CF4) ranked as captains, CF3 as majors, CF2 as lieutenant colonels, and CF1 as colonels: the chaplain general equated to a major general. Chaplains enjoyed what was, by ecclesiastical standards, comparatively generous pay. A CF4 earned twice the average stipend of a curate, and a CF1's salary equated to the income from the very richest Church of England parish. Timed promotion would take a clergyman to CF1 after thirty years' service; there were allowances to cover the cost of lodgings and a servant, as well as half-pay for the chaplains and pensions for their wives. Two years later chaplains were given a black uniform, and shortly afterwards a general order decreed that they were to be paid the compliments due to their relative rank.

Chaplains were particularly active in promoting temperance, pressing for improved barrack accommodation, and cautioning men against those 'improvident marriages' that so often wrecked two lives – or more. Some helped set up and even run laundry and clothing contracts so that soldiers' wives would have an honest source of income. Good intentions were not always a match for human nature.

The Revd E. J. Hardy, stationed at Plymouth in the 1890s, organised a subscription to pay some wives, left behind when their husbands' regiment had moved to Belfast, to travel to Northern Ireland. Sadly, a number of the ladies pocketed the money and then made alternative arrangements with men of the incoming regiment. Nineteenth-century chaplains understood the importance of 'manly games', and the evangelical Bishop John Taylor Smith, chaplain general from 1901 to 1925, made a point of recruiting keen sportsmen, amongst them the rugby international James Rowland Walkey, who went on to become chaplain-in-chief of the RAF in 1933–9.

There were challenges aplenty. The Chaplains' Department had a High Church bias, and many of its chaplains objected to the work done around barracks by civilian Methodist clergymen. It was not until 1862 that a compromise allowed soldiers to register their religion as Episcopalian, Roman Catholic, Presbyterian or – to include the Methodists at last – as 'Other Protestant'. Occasionally the High Church bias went too far: there were senior officers who disliked what they saw as the ritualistic style adopted by some chaplains. The devout and hirsute Lieutenant General Sir James Hope Grant was a hero of the Indian Mutiny. He had been raised as a Scots Presbyterian and had become an Anglican communicant but could not bear a hint of 'bells and smells', and when commanding at Aldershot in 1873 he sent a Royal Engineers carpenter along to one of the garrison churches to summarily reduce the height of the communion table. In the ensuing spat with Chaplain General Gleig, now two years away from retirement, Grant was backed by the Duke of Cambridge, and went on to warn all the chaplains in his district that they were as much under his command as any other officers, and he expected to have his orders obeyed.

There remained the suspicion that the commissioned rank of chaplains was actually an obstacle to their ministry. At the Church Congress of 1885 a Royal Artillery officer asked:

Did Jesus Chris have any official rank? Did the apostles have any official rank? Were men bound to spring up and salute them[?] How can a man unfold what is nearest to his heart to one who he feels is his official superior and whom he cannot approach without giving a military salute?[36]

Horace Wyndham, writing from the private soldier's viewpoint, believed that chaplains felt 'a certain diffidence about visiting barrack rooms – thinking, perhaps, that in doing so, they would be unduly intruding'. He also suggested that chaplains were better paid and had less work to do than the average Anglican clergyman, and 'in fact in many stations the chaplain's proficiency at tennis is uncharitably ascribed to his having such ample opportunities for practice!'[37] He affirmed that

> The right sort of chaplain is the man who is not imbued with the impression that his duties are confined solely to officiating at two services on Sunday, and that for the rest of the week his flock have no real claim upon him. On the contrary, he will remember that the barrack-room is almost as much his province as is the garrison chapel, and will, accordingly, not be above visiting the men in their quarters … the power for good that – should he be so minded – an army chaplain can exercise is a very real and wide one.[38]

Yet there was no doubting the fact that most Anglican chaplains were set apart, by background and education, from the men they ministered to. Francis Hereward Maitland saw his padre bowled out at regimental cricket. He walked back from the crease lamenting that he 'ought to have bashed it for four', giving the watching soldiery an unmissable opportunity to mimic his Oxford accent: 'Bally hard luck, sir! Absolutely bally, what?'[39]

On Sunday mornings, in home stations and overseas garrisons, regiments fell in at about 10.30 a.m for church parade. Wyndham describes how, in an English regiment, Roman Catholics, Presbyterians, and Wesleyans were marched off to their respective places of worship before the remainder set off to church, in the glory of full dress. Many soldiers enjoyed the tribal ritual, especially in a big garrison town like Aldershot, where there would be quick-stepping riflemen, bespurred cavalry, and infantry of the line in their scarlet tunics, all strutting their stuff:

> With the band at their head, playing a selection of popular melodies, the men step out smartly, and their progress through the streets forms a highly attractive spectacle to the civilian population,

with particular reference to its female portion. This the rank and file appreciate to the full, for the soldier is the most susceptible of all mortals to flattery of even the mildest description.[40]

In fact the rank and file were less warm in their appreciation of the process of getting ready for the parade, with boots and brasses shone up and every chance of being 'crimed' by a liverish sergeant major for lack of attention to detail. Most soldiers spent the rest of the day 'in bed or out of barracks', and Francis Hereward Maitland remembered his Aldershot Sundays as a time of 'infinite boredom'.[41] Wully Roberston thought it only natural that 'the men should resent being hustled about and made to do unnecessary work on the one day of the week observed by everybody else in the country as a day of rest.'[42]

There was widespread agreement that church parade did little for a man's spirituality. Private Frank Richards of the Royal Welch Fusiliers thought that 95 per cent of his comrades 'thoroughly detested' them. He remembered that they had unofficial words for hymns, and 'O God our help in ages past' was transmuted into

John Wesley had a little dog,
It was so very thin,
He took it to the Gates of Hell,
And threw the bastard in.[43]

However, Horace Wyndham thought that most soldiers enjoyed singing, and Acland-Trote believed that they generally behaved 'quietly and properly', and could often be found discussing the sermon after the service. Wyndham went to the heart of the matter when he argued that 'it is not the service that is considered so obnoxious, but the compulsory attendance threat.' Soldiers, he argued wisely, could be led but not driven.[44]

Men resorted to a variety of subterfuges to escape church parade altogether or to attend the shortest service. In one garrison the absence of a Catholic chaplain encouraged numerous conversions to Catholicism until the commanding officer decreed that, as the converts could not attend Mass, they should have extra drill instead. The future field marshal Evelyn Wood served in the Aldershot cavalry brigade in 1867, and recalled that 'Sunday was a show day in stables'.

One young soldier went to his commanding officer and asked to change his religion to Roman Catholic. He eventually admitted, 'Well, you see, sir, a Roman Catholic always goes to Church at eight o'clock, and I think if I was a Roman it would give me a better chance with my 'arness.'[45]

Chaplains' rooms in barracks, where they were available, helped soldiers meet chaplains on more equal terms, and Church of England Soldiers' Institutes, part of the broader trend towards setting up facilities where soldiers could read newspapers and buy non-alcoholic drinks, also gave Anglican soldiers the opportunity to talk to their chaplain. By the end of the nineteenth century army chaplains were informally known by the term 'padre'. This had originally been applied to Roman Catholic missionaries in India, but soon had wider currency. Today's army chaplains are described as 'Padre' on the name badge above the left breast pocket of their combat kit.

In a series of colonial campaigns and the Boer War of 1899–1902 chaplains demonstrated both courage under fire and attention to the wants of the sick and wounded. The brave and headstrong General Sir Hugh Gough, commander-in-chief during the first Sikh War of 1845–6, hoped to get a chaplain promoted to brevet bishop but was gently informed that no such appointment existed. In 1879 the Revd J. W. Adams of the Bengal Ecclesiastical Establishment became the first chaplain to earn the Victoria Cross, for rescuing two cavalrymen who had fallen into a deep, water-filled gully with Afghan pursuers very close behind. The burly Adams seems to have had no reservation about bearing arms, but Sergeant Forbes-Mitchell of the 93rd had seen another clergyman in real trouble when caught in 'a furious charge' by rebels in north India in 1858:

> I remember the Rev Mr Ross, chaplain of the Forty-Second, running for his life, dodging round camels and bullocks with a rebel *sowar* [trooper] after him till, seeing our detachment, he rushed to us for protection, calling out 'Ninety-Third, shoot that impertinent fellow!' Bob Johnston of my company shot the *sowar* down. Mr Ross had no sword nor revolver, not even a stick with which to defend himself. Moral – when in the field, padres, carry a good revolver.[46]

It was never a simple matter for the chaplain general to assert doctrinal control even over Anglican chaplains, and there were repeated but unavailing demands for him to be made a bishop to enhance his powers.[47] Neither Presbyterian chaplains, first commissioned in 1858, nor Roman Catholics, commissioned in 1859, could accept the chaplain general's spiritual authority, and both enjoyed distinct ecclesiastical chains of command. The Roman Catholic Church promoted several former chaplains to be bishops of dioceses with strong military connections, and recognition that military rank was transcended by priestly status undoubtedly helped Catholic chaplains relate more easily to officers and men alike. Father Robert Brindle was a hero of the 1884–5 Gordon Relief Expedition, marching with the men instead of riding with the officers (he used his own pony to carry footsore soldiers), and helping at the oars when 1/Royal Irish rowed up the Nile. He was awarded the DSO, and attempts to procure him a knighthood eventually foundered when it was decided that such an honour was 'inappropriate for a chaplain'.[48]

The First World War saw the Chaplains' Department, along with the rest of the army, expand to an unprecedented degree, growing from 117 chaplains in August 1914 to 3,416 in August 1918. Methodist clergymen, who had hitherto declined commissions, at last accepted them, and in 1918 there were even fourteen Jewish and five Salvation Army chaplains. Jews had been allowed to attest under their own religion from the late 1880s, and the first Jewish chaplain had been appointed in 1892, though only on a part-time basis because the number of Jewish soldiers was relatively small. There was a rapid increase even before the advent of conscription in early 1916, and a commensurate growth in the number of chaplains. The headstones of Jewish soldiers stand out in Commonwealth War Graves Commission cemeteries not only because they bear the Star of David, but because visitors so often honour the practice of placing a pebble on top of the stone. Many of these men came from London's Jewish community, and were members of the Royal Fusiliers, the Middlesex Regiment or the all-Territorial London Regiment. Indeed, the Fusiliers formed three Jewish battalions which wore, as their cap-badge, the menorah with the Hebrew characters for Kadema ('Forward') on a scroll beneath it. Outsiders unkindly quipped that this was somehow an abbreviation for 'No Advance Without Security.'

All Anglican candidates for temporary chaplain's commissions were interviewed by Bishop John Taylor Smith, the Chaplain General, who was a keen Evangelical and was believed to harbour prejudices against Anglo-Catholics. In 1916 the Revd Julian Bickersteth, son of the vicar of Leeds (one of whose brothers was to die as a subaltern in the Leeds Pals on the first day of the Somme) attended a conference in France and admitted that

> I had not realised before how successful the CG had been in appointing men of his own way of thinking. There were quite a few padres there with moustaches, and as they wore khaki collars they looked very much like combatant officers.[49]

In mid-1916 disquiet at the state of the Anglican chaplaincy led to the appointment of Llewellyn Henry Gywnne, bishop of Khartoum, as deputy chaplain general with special responsibility for the Anglicans on the Western Front. Although Gwynne was a close friend of Taylor Smith, shared his Evangelical and missionary background, and was a keen sportsman (he had played football for Derby County), he was far more skilful than the chaplain general in dealing with men. One fellow chaplain thought that:

> Many of us, I think, would have gone under or suffered shipwreck of their faith had it not been for the patient care and guidance of the great and saintly Bishop Gwynne, Father in God to a whole generation of young men ... I have used the word 'saintly' deliberately. For he made it easier to believe in God. He was a commanding figure of that period.[50]

There were eventually seventeen chaplains to each division, usually sufficient to ensure one for each battalion within it, with more allocated to hospitals, and a hierarchy of senior chaplains at corps, army and GHQ.

The effectiveness of chaplains became a major issue after the war, and many diarists or memoirists had their own views. Non-commissioned personnel sometimes argued that the chaplain's commission put him at a disadvantage. Stephen Graham was an educated man who served in the ranks of the Scots Guards. He thought that 'the padres, being officers, lived at ease; and whereas the men had poor food, they ate and drank in the company of officers. I could not help feeling how badly handicapped the padres were.' In contrast, a senior NCO in his battalion had served in the Boer War and left the army after it. He had been ordained after attending theological college, but did not object when called up as a reservist in 1914. His habit of looking out from beneath a lowered brow gave him the nickname 'Creeping Barrage', but 'he was in secret and sometimes also openly, greatly admired because he lived what he preached.'[51]

A number of clergymen of all denominations decided not to serve as chaplains, but either took combatant commissions or enlisted into the ranks: Julian Bickersteth thought that there were four ranker priests in 56th London Division alone. In Highland Cemetery at Le Cateau lies Rifleman Bernard William King of 2/King's Royal Rifle Corps. The cemetery register tells us that he was a vicar's son, an old boy of St Paul's School and a graduate of New College, Oxford and Cheshunt Theological College. He had enlisted early in 1918 'with his bishop's permission', and died at the age of thirty on 23 October 1918, when the war had just three weeks to run. Brigadier General Frank Crozier, whose rumbustious memoirs are not wholly reliable, recalled a Welsh Nonconformist padre blazing away with a rifle from a shell-hole at the fleeing enemy. There was no immediate emergency which might (at least in Crozier's view) have justified this action, and so Crozier gave him lunch and told him that he was miscast as a chaplain. The man agreed and signed on as a private soldier in a Welsh regiment: he did very well, not least because of his spectacular command of colourful language.

We have already seen Robert Graves' tirade against Anglicans and his assertion that Roman Catholic padres were invariably better. This was not an isolated view, for Alan Hanbury-Sparrow, who rose from lieutenant to lieutenant colonel during the war and felt its hard edge, thought that most chaplains, with the exception of Catholics, 'did not seem sufficiently equipped to withstand, without harm to themselves, the arguments of an earnest doubter'.[52] He was just such a doubter: he could not understand why Christ merited particular regard for having undergone crucifixion. Soldiers of his generation died deaths that were no less agonising and often a great deal more protracted without any certainty of salvation. Guy Chapman felt 'a serenity and certitude' streaming from a Catholic chaplain 'such as was not possessed by any of our bluff Anglicans'.[53] Catholics certainly enjoyed two important advantages. The requirement to be on hand to administer extreme unction to those at the point of death encouraged Roman Catholic chaplains to visit the front line at times of danger, and there was a much better chaplain-to-soldier ratio for them than for other denominations.

But if some of them came from working-class backgrounds and found it easy to talk to soldiers, this was certainly not the case with all. Father Willie Doyle MC, much loved by 16th Irish Division and held in high regard even by the Protestants of 36th Ulster Division, came from a big Dublin family, but a comfortably middle-class one. Indeed, the paucity of the Irish hierarchy's response to requests for chaplains meant that the religious orders and diocesan clergy of England supplied the majority, and many of them were the products of public schools and universities. Indeed, some of the most successful Anglican padres came from traditional middle-class backgrounds. Theodore Bayley Hardy, who was to win the VC, DSO, and MC within a year before dying of wounds; Geoffrey Studdert Kennedy MC ('Woodbine Willie'); and Philip 'Tubby' Clayton, founder of the all-ranks club 'Toc H' in Poperinghe, had all been educated at public schools and universities.[54] The close relationship between the Anglican Church and the military establishment is poignantly underlined in the cloister of Salisbury Cathedral, where a row of wooden crosses, brought back from France when they were replaced by War Graves Commission headstones, commemorates sons of the Cathedral's chapter who died in the war.

The effectiveness of chaplains depended more upon personality than purely on social background or even denominational persuasion. The policy of giving one-year temporary commissions to most chaplains often made it hard for them to relate to officers and men who were in it 'for the duration'. Pressure from the high command to promote morale by preaching on the justice of the British cause struck an uneasy note with some chaplains, as well as with some of their listeners, although most senior officers believed that chaplains had indeed done much to sustain morale. Inadequate preparation and poor selection, both common during the first two years of the war, meant that some chaplains never really recovered from the first shock of seeing wholesale death and agony. Some were simply too old or too unfit (although Padre Hardy had been turned down because of his age in 1914 and died in harness at 54) and broke down physically. Others, wrestling with the conundrum of how an omnipotent God could allow such suffering to occur, lost their faith.

There was always a balance to be struck between being, as one chaplain put it, 'Mr God and Mr Cinema'. On the one hand there were times when men desperately needed spiritual solace, and others when a cigarette or a trip to the beach was more welcome. Chaplains, with no command responsibilities, often became, in effect, welfare assistants to their battalions, but the wisest amongst them knew that they had to go much further. The best-regarded were those who were not shy of running a soldier's risks, and were ready to distribute home comforts in the line and to organise recreational events out of it, but remained sure in their faith and were never reluctant to share it. Colonel Walter Nicholson probably assessed chaplains fairly when he said that 'when the padres were good they were very, very good, but when they were bad they were awful.'[55]

The war did not result, as some clergymen had hoped, in a large-scale religious revival. But the Toc H movement, so called from the phonetic alphabet's initials TH, for Talbot House, flourished, and became one of the largest men's societies in the Empire. David Railton MC, who had served as a brigade padre on the Western Front, wrote to the Dean of Westminster suggesting that an unidentified soldier should be given a national burial service in Westminster Abbey, and the idea swiftly gained momentum. In 1916 he had seen a rough wooden cross inscribed with 'An Unknown British Soldier of the Black Watch' in indelible pencil. 'How that grave caused me to think,' he wrote,

> But who was he, and who were they [his folk]? ... Was he just a laddie ... There was no answer to those questions, nor has there ever been yet. So I thought and thought and wrestled in thought. What can I do to ease the pain of father, mother, brother, sister, sweetheart, wife and friend? Quietly and gradually there came out of the mist of thought this answer clear and strong, 'Let this body – this symbol of him – be carried reverently over the sea to his native land.' And I was happy for about five or ten minutes.[56]

In March 1919 the Chaplains' Department, 179 of whose members had died in the war, was granted the title 'Royal', and was reorganised the following year so that an Anglican chaplain general would be supported by a deputy from a different denomination. Pay, which had dropped behind that of combatant officers, was substantially improved, it was made easier for chaplains to be promoted by merit, and rigid retirement ages were introduced. Military chaplains caught more than their fair share of criticism in the anti-war literature of the 1930s, and this did much to create the prevailing belief in the uselessness of most First World War padres.

The department was much better prepared for the Second World War than it had been for the first. There was a good supply of chaplains in the reserve of officers and the Territorial Army, and chaplains were now expected to serve for the duration of the war rather than for a fixed term. However, it was not easy to bring the department up to wartime strength, partly because of the influence of inter-war pacifism. Senior chaplains, so many of whom had served in the earlier war, were well aware of the problems that padres would face, and a number of publications, notably *The Chaplains in the Grand Assault*, by 8th Army's assistant chaplain general, Frederick Llewelyn Hughes, gave valuable practical advice. Training had also improved immeasurably, and the padres of the inexperienced 2nd Army, which was to land in Normandy, spent a week at a chaplains' battle school learning the skills of camouflage, obstacle-crossing and night marches with map and compass.

Courage was always highly valued. Dom Rudesind Brookes ('Father Dolly') had served as an officer in the Irish Guards during the First World War, resigning his commission after it to enter the Benedictine novitiate. He was chaplain to 1/Irish Guards during bitter fighting at Anzio, which resembled some of the worst days on the Western Front a generation before. The citation for his Military Cross tells us that

There are not words strong enough to describe the wonderful and shining example Father Brookes gave to all ranks, and all the officers and men of this Battalion would give testimony to the tireless kindliness, inspiration, and help they all received from his hand. His personal bravery in addition to his priestly qualities gain him the admiration of all. The sight of Father Brookes pacing up and down reading his Breviary under heavy fire has restored the confidence of many a shaken man.[57]

The prompt and reverent burial of the dead had always been important, for although soldiers sometimes deploy a black humour to help them deal with death, the sight of a dead man reminds them forcefully of their own mortality. One of the most profoundly shocking aspects of death in battle is the capricious destruction of the fragile and complex human body by projectile, explosive or fire, or its abandonment to weather and carrion. A. R. C. Leaney described burying members of 5/Dorsets on the Dutch–German border on a wet and dreary day in November 1944:

> It took a long time. I suppose it is not clear to those who have not witnessed or taken part in one of these field burials how much the padre has to do ... The searching of pockets and general preparation of the body, which was usually roughly string-sewn in an old blanket, fell most often to the padre, whose office made others feel, I believe, that what would otherwise seem desecration or intrusion on the privacy of the unfortunate, was thus a reverent and kindly office.[58]

Leslie Skinner was chaplain to the Sherwood Rangers Yeomanry. Some of his problems were as old as war itself. In Normandy, on his way back from looking for a missing sergeant, he was approached by an officer in the Duke of Wellington's Regiment who

> asked me if I would bury two of 'your' chaps killed a week ago in the attack on Cristot. Seemingly 4th/7th [Dragoon Guards] men lying in a ditch ever since. Really unpleasant – crawling. Scrounged some blankets and started to tie them up. DWs officer went away to be sick and did not return until I had finished. DWs had dug graves for me and I read funeral service – then violently sick myself.

Other tasks, however, reflected the hideous realities of armoured warfare:

Only ash and burnt metal in Birkett's tank. Searched ash and found remains pelvic bones. At other tank three bodies still inside – partly burned and firmly welded together. Managed with difficulty to identify Lt Campbell. Unable to remove bodies after a long struggle – nasty business – sick.

Soon afterwards he followed the line of a successful but costly attack:

Went back to start line and then forward along C Squadron axis. Buried the 3 dead and then tried to reach the remaining dead in tanks still too hot and burning. Place absolute shambles. Infantry dead and some Germans lying around. Horrible mess. Fearful job picking up bits and pieces and re-assembling for identification and putting in blankets for burial … Squadron Leader offered to lend me some men to help. Refused. Less men who live and fight in tanks have to do with this side of things the better. They know it happens but to force it on their attention is not good. My job.[59]

Church attendance had fallen off significantly between the wars: in 1911 almost 10 per cent of the population took Anglican communion on Easter Sunday, and this had shrunk to a little over 7 per cent by 1939. Michael Snape argues that 'the promotion of morale based on religious conviction was necessarily hampered by widespread religious ignorance among the army's citizen soldiers.'[60] It was in an effort to meet this deficiency that 'Padre's Hour' originated, in 1942, in 1st Airborne Division, then under the command of Major General 'Boy' Browning, and soon spread across the whole army. It was wholly unlike church parade. Soldiers, usually in company groups (without officers so as not to risk stifling debate) were allowed to sit comfortably and smoke, given a short talk, and then encouraged to ask questions or discuss contemporary issues. Some confident padres spoke about sexual morality, a relevant topic in view of the high rates of venereal disease in theatres like Italy and India, but many did not feel able to take the subject on. One did, however, go as far as to distribute pornography in his unit in an effort to make men less likely to visit brothels and thus to reduce the rate of infection.

It became depressingly clear that wives left behind in Britain were prone to lapse, and one 1946 chaplains' survey suggested that 'after three years' separation, one wife in five was unfaithful.'[61] The task of helping men deal with the consequences of marriage breakdown often fell to padres, and one, writing home from Italy in 1945, recalled:

Took a laddie 50 miles there and 50 miles back to file a petition for Divorce. His wife had a child by another man last summer. He forgave her although she continued to be unfaithful. Then an airman came along and started to terrify the two real children of the family, so they have gone to our own man's parents. Now the wife is pregnant again with another man's child, what a mess.[62]

The padres of the post-war army divided their time between the United Kingdom, the British Army of the Rhine and a series of counter-insurgency campaigns across a diminishing empire. It was wholly in keeping with the mood sweeping the country after Labour's election victory in 1945 that compulsory church services were abolished the following year. Although some traditionalists fought a stern rearguard action, there was widespread recognition that church parade had had little to do with spirituality. Indeed, many, both within the RAChD and outside it, believed that compulsion 'was actually detrimental to the cause and interests of real religion'.[63] Moreover, as padres' duties were now so wide the disappearance of what had once been the major focus of their week made little difference to them.

There were still times when chaplains had their courage, physical and moral, tested. Stanley James 'Sam' Davies was chaplain to 1/ Gloucesters on the Imjin River in Korea in 1951. On the morning of 15 April he officiated at the traditional St George's Day service with 1/Royal Northumberland Fusiliers, and then held a communion service for members of his own battalion. When the Gloucesters' position eventually became untenable, he and the battalion's medical officer elected to stay behind and go into captivity. He was imprisoned at Pi-chong-in on the North Korean–Manchurian border, and endured harsh treatment, including solitary confinement. Padre Davies ended all his services with the couplet:

Faith of our fathers, living still,
In spite of dangers, fire and sword.

In the 1982 Falklands War, David Cooper was chaplain to 2/Para. His burial service for the dead of Goose Green was widely televised, and was extraordinarily poignant for him because, amongst the men he buried, were several whose marriages he had conducted or whose children he had baptised. At Goose Green his hip flask (filled with whisky to give men a nip and so ease 'an unexpected visit from the vicar') was smashed by a bullet, and after the battle his sleeping bag was used to keep a badly-burned Argentinian soldier warm, something he 'didn't mind at all, but thereafter whenever I got into it, all I could smell was burnt flesh'. In his service in Stanley Cathedral after the town's liberation he

> asked our soldiers to remember how they felt at the time, remembering themselves without any sort of veneer as they were facing death, remembering what they were really like and what mattered to them.[64]

Long after he had left the army, and was setting off to Baghdad as director of civil affairs for Aegis, a private security company, he told a journalist just how powerful the ties linking men in a combat unit were: 'It is a bond passing the love of women, a bond stronger than that of man and wife.'[65] With his robust faith, down-to-earth manner and remarkable marksmanship (he was not only a champion rifle shot at Bisley, but is one of the best game shots I have seen) David Cooper is light-years away from the clerical gentlemen of the age of the redcoat.

Across the three and a half centuries of the army's existence, the position of the established Church has been substantially eroded and attendance at its services has dwindled; Britain is unquestionably a secular society. Yet the military chaplain, his ranks widened, from 2005, by the addition of Buddhist, Hindu, Moslem, and Sikh part-time chaplains, still plays a crucial role. In part this is because the non-spiritual aspects of his task remain as important as they were in both world wars. Moreover, chaplains, like medical officers, are in the army but not of it, and a wise padre can provide a commander with a useful sounding-board. Just because soldiers are less formally religious than their great-grandfathers does not mean that they are not spiritual. In 2004, when 1/PWRR took the bodies of Iraqis killed in a vicious firefight back to its base there was widespread recognition that their reception was properly the work of both doctor and chaplain. Padre Fran Myatt, a Liverpudlian who had worked as a club bouncer before he became a clergyman, enjoyed the respect of the battalion, not least because he kept himself in such good physical shape. 'Body of a Greek god', he would say, pointing at himself. And then, gesturing at a more pear-shaped individual, he would add: 'Body of a Greek restaurant'.

Fallen soldiers are no longer buried in the theatre of operations but are repatriated, and where possible some of their comrades will carry the coffin onto the aircraft, and most of them value a service to mark their respect for a brother soldier. For most young men and women death is something that snatches pets and grandparents until it reaches out, on hillside or in desert, to claim someone who was so very like them. At such moments the physical world has few answers, and a chaplain can often help provide consolation. David Cooper maintained that he believed in a God who might not turn away a bullet, but would never turn away a soul in need. In early 2011 the Army Rumour Service website opined that morale was not good in the RAChD. That was a pity, thought one correspondent, for: 'Our Padre in Iraq was top bloke and kept everyone happy.'[66] It is a judgement echoed far more widely than the secularisation of modern society might suggest.

III

RECRUITING A
NATIONAL ARMY

CHAPTER 11

SOLDIER BOYS

THE ARMY IS a huge, rumbling alimentary canal, inexorably processing men, and more recently women, from recruit to veteran. It is by nature a glutton, concerned primarily with the quantity of its diet, and in wartime its appetite for manpower is utterly insatiable. Once a major war ends it reduces in numbers, but no sooner has it reached its new target size than recruiting once again becomes an issue. This has tended to have a stop-go effect as soldiers, so eagerly signed up yesterday, are discharged today and then, as eagerly, courted tomorrow. Moreover, because one easy way of limiting the army's short-term cost is by imposing a cap on recruiting and thus on pay, it has been easy, especially in recent years, to stop recruiting temporarily only to discover that, externally, the army loses its prominence in the employment market and, internally, its age structures become distorted. The business of recruiting has long been about flattery, seduction, persuasion, appeals to manly virtue or patriotic duty, deception and simple bribery, though the blend is complex. Its precise mixture owes much to recruiters, the individuals who persuade a man to leave a life where individual interests matter most and to enter a narrower world where collective values are dominant, and there is usually someone on hand to tell you when to get up – and what to wear.

The song 'Over the Hills and Far Away', with its haunting melody, appeared in George Farquhar's 1706 play, *The Recruiting Officer*, and was revived with slightly different words in the Napoleonic wars:

Hark now the drums beat up again
For all true soldier gentlemen
Let us list and march I say
Over the hills and far away.

Farquhar had left Trinity College Dublin without a degree and became an actor, but quit the theatre after severely wounding a colleague in a stage duel. He then served as an officer in the Earl of Orrery's Regiment of Foot and spent much of his time on recruiting duties, feeding the ravenous army of his day, and so his characters were drawn from life. The play centres upon events in Shrewsbury after the arrival of a recruiting party led by the amorous and swash-buckling Captain Plume, assisted by the hard-nosed Sergeant Kite. The party would have been empowered to set about its work by a 'beating warrant' given to the regiment's colonel, authorising the recruitment of volunteers anywhere save in the City of London 'by beat of drum'. It would typically have consisted of an officer, a sergeant, a corporal, a couple of privates, and a drummer or two. Sometimes recruiting was carried out as part of 'an agreement between the Crown and some nobleman or gentleman, who has undertaken to raise a corps on receiving the nomination of some or all of the officers', a system known as 'raising for rank'. It was last used in 1854 to raise troops for the Crimean war.[1] More often, though, recruiting parties were simply sent out to keep the ranks of an existing regiment filled, and in either case their procedure was the same.

From 1661 to 1783, when recruiters came under the orders of the Director of Recruiting and Organisation at Horse Guards, officers had a direct pecuniary interest in this business of flesh and blood. Regiments received recruiting money from the government, and held it in a fund called the 'stock purse'. At the end of the year the balance in the fund was divided up between the company commanders, and thus officers were concerned 'in keeping down the expense of recruiting, both by obtaining men cheaply, and by prolonging the service of men enlisted, and so avoiding the necessity of obtaining recruits in their places'.[2] The stock fund was not always equal to the demands placed on it, especially in wartime or if a regiment was posted to an unhealthy station like the West Indies, when there were constant demands for extra recruiting money. Officers often overspent, and on occasion the bankruptcy of a regiment's agent (who managed its financial affairs on behalf of its colonel) could lead to officers being held personally liable for repaying money they had never had. In 1752 Lord Mark Kerr had his pay – as colonel of the 11th Dragoons, governor of Edinburgh Castle and major general – stopped until £1,191. 10s. 3½d. had been recovered to establish a stock fund with a new agent.

In 1783 officers lost this direct financial interest in recruiting, and there was already perceived to be something deeply unsatisfactory in a gentleman holding his majesty's commission and drumming up business like a huckster. Thereafter, officers rarely commanded recruiting parties in person. The Irish folk song *Arthur McBride*, of around 1840, describes the adventures of the eponymous hero and his cousin when confronted by

> Sergeant Harper and Corporal Cramp,
> Besides the wee drummer who beat up the camp
> With his row-dee-dow-dow in the morning.[3]

But in September 1752 Corporal Matthew Todd of the 30th Foot, then stationed in Ireland, found himself in an old-style recruiting party:

> Lieutenant Teavil Appleton was ordered a'recruiting with Sergeant Barnsley, Corporal Todd and Drummer Jones for England ... Disembarked the 26th at Liverpool, and marched to Warrington 14 miles. The 27th marched to Castleton 18 miles in the peaks of Derbyshire. 29th marched to Sheffield, 21 miles. Here the sergeant and drummer quartered and I marched, October 4th, to Doncaster, 12 miles. The 5th to Honden, and the 6th to Beverley [where I] received orders to hire a drummer at Hull and to recruit every market day at each place. Here I continued until February 27th 1753 when I was ordered up with the recruits to Sheffield ... Marched into Liverpool on the 15th of March and embarked on the 22nd and sailed for Dublin.[4]

Wise recruiters ensured that they only took on men who came within the strict limits of the current instructions. Those for the 93rd Foot, issued in early 1760, specified that all recruits were to be certified as

Protestant, and 'able bodied, sound in their limbs, free from ruptures, scald heads, ulcerous sores or any remarkable deformity'. A man could not be accepted if unable to 'wear his hair, who is kneed in [knock-kneed] or subject to fits' and all were to have surgeon's certificates. Men of sixteen to twenty were to be at least 5ft 5ins in their stockinged feet, and those between 20 and 35 (the upper limit even for men with previous service) at least 5ft 6ins. 'No strollers, vagabonds, tinkers, chimney sweepers, colliers, or sailors [were] to be enlisted, but such men only as were born in the neighbourhood' and were well-reported on locally.[5] Height limits were reduced as the need for soldiers increased, and a 1794 sample of a hundred recruits for the 98th Foot found four under 5ft 2ins and only five 5ft 9ins or over. In 1806 a man could enlist for 'general service' if he measured 5ft 4ins, but needed to be an inch higher if he wished to choose his own regiment, and taller still if he hoped for the cavalry or Guards. It is no surprise that potential recruits tried to bluff their way past the examining doctor by tricks like gluing buff-leather, naturally skin-toned, to the soles of their feet, just as disillusioned soldiers seeking discharge on the grounds that they were under-height when examined would bend the knees imperceptibly when being measured.

Benjamin Harris observed that 'tall men ... bore fatigue much better than the small ones.' His comrade Thomas Higgins, exceptionally tall at 'six feet one and a half, and ... lank and bony' was

> dreadfully put to it to keep on ... during a short halt of about ten minutes, he was reprimanded by one of our officers for the slovenly state of his clothing and accoutrements; his dress almost dropping from his lower limbs and his knapsack hanging by a strap or two down his waist. Higgins did not take it at all kind being quarrelled with at such a time, and, uttering sundry impertinences, desired to know ... how he was to be very smart after what we had gone through.

When punished with an extra guard he sloped off and was never seen again.[6]

The Royal Artillery tried to recruit good-sized men to ensure that they could work its guns effectively, and in 1776 Captain Georg Pausch of the Hesse-Hanau artillery described British gunners as 'the tallest, strongest, and best-looking troops which can be seen in the entire world'. Two years later he noted that the thirty or so artillery-men killed or wounded at the battle of Freeman's Farm were between 5ft 10ins and 6ft in height. By March 1779 Major General James Patterson's 4th Battalion of Artillery was not only 250 men below its establishment, but recent drafts contained men so scrawny that Patterson called them 'reptiles' and complained that 'such warriors of 5ft 5½ins I never saw raised before for the service of artillery.' When the Board of Ordnance unhelpfully declined to send out carbines for these men, Patterson sarcastically wondered if they could manage to handle cut-down muskets.[7]

The army was already short of men on the outbreak of the First World War and the lower height limit for recruits stood at 5ft 3ins, though the Foot Guards demanded 5ft 10ins. When 1/Grenadier Guards took over trenches in the Ypres salient from the 60th Rifles in November 1914, Major 'Ma' Jeffreys saw that 'Nos 1 and 2 [Companies] had to dig hard as the trenches of the little riflemen only covered them up to their waists!'[8] In the first autumn of the war Alfred Bigland, MP for Birkenhead, was infuriated by the army's rejection of stocky men, many of them miners, who failed to meet this require-ment but seemed perfectly fit for service. He persuaded the War Office to permit the enlistment of 'Bantams', men who were at least 5ft tall. Initially the scheme worked well enough, and the whole of the 35th Division and part of the 40th Division were composed of Bantam battalions like 15/ and 16/Cheshires, raised in Birkenhead by Bigland himself. Although the project began well, and attracted much press comment, by the autumn of 1916 the commander of 35th Division, Maj Gen J. H. S. Landon, was complaining that the replace-ments sent out to his division were not the sturdy but under-height fellows who had been enlisted early on, but were 'physically underde-veloped and unfit men of a low moral standard'. That December the division's twelve infantry battalions were inspected and 1,439 men were rejected as unfit: subsequently more were added to bring the total number of rejects to 2,784, around a quarter of the division's infantry. No more Bantams were accepted, and the division lost its Bantam status.[9]

One of the original Bantams, Private William Boynton Butler, who had joined 17/West Yorkshires in early 1915, earned the Victoria

Cross when, in August 1917, he stood in front of a mortar bomb whose fuse had ignited prematurely until some passing infantry had moved on, and then hurled it to safety: it exploded as soon as it left his hand. On 26 March 1918 Sergeant Albert Mountain, who had enlisted in a Bantam battalion but had later transferred to 15/17th West Yorkshires, rallied his company in the face of an overwhelming German attack. He too was awarded the VC. Both Butler and Mountain were 5ft 1in tall. The British army's current lower height limit is 148 cm (4ft 8ins), although some arms demand more.

As Lieutenant Colonel Edward Windus warned Samuel Bagshawe in 1760, one could seldom rely on junior officers sent off in search of recruits, for 'very young gentlemen are apt to be a little giddy and to mind their country diversions more than their recruiting'. Of the ten men enlisted by Ensign Cook, for example, one had already run off, and seven were Roman Catholics and thus expressly forbidden to enlist. 'One of which, at least,' grumbled Windus, 'must be known by Ensign Cook to be so, as he was a servant of Mr Cook's father, and lived in the house with him.' Another recruit was 'very old and not strong. He acknowledges to me that he was born in the year of the Battle of Almanza [1707], and calls himself 53 years of age.' The wise Captain Bennett Cuthberston warned his readers that

> It very highly concerns the recruiting officer, to depend more on a man's looks than on what he calls himself: the common people are in general so ignorant on this point that it is absurd to take a peasant's word for being only twenty-five when his appearance … bespeaks him to be many years advanced beyond that age.

Cuthbertson thought that men between the ages of 17 and 25 made 'the most tractable of soldiers'.[10] In 1839 it was suggested that men who joined over the age of 25 were 'habitually dissipated and profligate characters, broken-down gentlemen, discharged soldiers, deserters, etc.' Moreover, as only 5 per cent of soldiers were then fit for service at the age of 40, enlisting a 20-year-old gave a better return than taking on a man of 25. When the 13th Foot was inspected at Martinique in 1812, it contained only three men over 55, nine aged 50–55, eight 45–50, twenty-four 40–45, sixty-three 35–40, 137 aged 30–35, 209 of 25–30, 240 aged 20–25, sixteen 18–20 and twelve under 18.[11]

Recruiters were allowed to take younger lads an inch shorter than the rules required if they could be deemed 'likely to grow'. From 1797 to 1814 thousands of orphans between 10 and 15 years of age on parish relief were given military training until they were sturdy enough to sign on. In December 1797 the manpower shortage was so desperate that six regiments of foot were allowed to complete their recruiting with boys of 13–18. 'They are to be well fed,' the regiments were told, 'and for some time to be mere walking drills, after which they are to be exercised with light fusees [muskets], one hundred of which have been sent to each of the six regiments.'[12] Four more regiments were later allowed similar latitude. In January 1811, as the demands of war bit ever harder, regiments were authorised to enlist up to ten under-16-year-olds per company.

Towards the end of the nineteenth century formal age limits for normal enlistment were set between 18 and 25, rationalising what had in effect been standard practice for many years. The cavalry had long declined to take youths below 19, but when the minimum age for the army as a whole was put up to 19 in 1881 an immediate recruiting shortfall forced its reduction to 18 just two years later. However, an official committee reported that youngsters often broke down in service: 'a large proportion of the losses from death and invaliding which occur ... in the first years of a soldier's service is due to the extreme youth of the men that join, who cannot stand the labour and fatigue to which they are subjected ... and therefore either die or break down and return to civil life weakened and with diminished powers for earning their livelihood.'[13] This echoed the complaints of late eighteenth-century inspecting officers that too many units, especially those recovering at home after lengthy foreign service, were composed, like the 27th Foot in 1786, of 'weakly recruits ... too small and slight for any service'. In 1773 the 37th Foot, just back from Minorca, was composed of 'mostly growing boys' who lacked 'strength enough for any very hard service'.[14]

The recruitment of under-age soldiers was a regular feature of army life until, after the First World War, recruits were at last required to produce birth certificates. As it had been a legal requirement to register a birth from 1875, we must conclude that the army, perennially short of soldiers, was anxious to permit a little creativity where birth dates were concerned. In 1892 General Sir Redvers

Buller, adjutant general, was accompanying the Duke of Cambridge on an inspection of recruits:

> We looked at one young fellow who seemed very young. His Royal Highness said to him, 'What is your age?' He said 'Seventeen years and one month'. A sergeant, who was standing near, said 'What is your regulation age?' and the recruit answered '18 years and 5 months'.[15]

However, for most of its history the army legitimately enlisted boys as drummers and bandsmen, so the issue is not straightforward. Such boys were often the sons or orphans of soldiers, and in parallel with the grand military dynasties of officers went the smaller tribes that meant so much to individual regiments. William Sweeney enlisted into the 79th Highlanders at the age of fourteen in 1825, and was probably the son of Terence Sweeney of the 79th, killed in a Glasgow riot. William was discharged to pension in 1846, and all his five sons joined the 79th. One them, Robert William, was born at Stirling Castle Barracks, signed on in Ireland in 1846 at the age of 11, and eventually went on to become one of the first graduates of the Royal Military School of Music at Kneller Hall, reaching the warrant officer rank of bandmaster. Another of William's sons, Donald Spence Sweeney, became band sergeant of the 79th. Donald had two sons, one of them band sergeant in the Cameron Highlanders, as the 79th had now become, and the other was killed as a bandsman in the Camerons on the Aisne in September 1914, and remembered on the Memorial to the Missing at La Ferté sous Jouarre.[16]

Drummers and bandsmen, whatever their age, were not primarily combatants, but both ran a soldier's risks. When Lieutenant Fred Roberts entered the Secunderbagh at Lucknow on 16 November 1857, on the heels of the storming party, he saw a drummer of the 93rd Highlanders:

> he must have been one of the first to pass the grim boundary between life and death; for when I got in I found him just inside the breach, quite dead, a pretty, innocent-looking fair-haired lad, not more than fourteen years old.[17]

Also during the relief of Lucknow, the 12-year-old Drummer Ross of the 93rd climbed to the top of the Shah Najaf Mosque, where, clutching a spire with one hand, he sounded the regimental call on his bugle, followed by other tunes including 'Cock o' the North'. The two youngest-ever winners of the VC were Drummer Thomas Flynn of the 64th Foot, awarded his decoration for gallant conduct at Cawnpore in 1857; and Hospital Apprentice Andrew Fitzgibbon, who accompanied the 67th Foot when it stormed the Taku Forts, at the mouth of the Peiho River in China, in 1860: both were 15 years and 3 months old. Although John Bent of the East Lancashires was 23 when he won the VC as a drummer in 1914, he fits comfortably into the pattern of army brats: son of a regular soldier, he had enlisted at the age of 14 in 1905.

Regiments were not inclined to take on the boys simply because they were short of men, but because they also felt a moral responsibility to look after the 'sons of the brave'. Until after the Crimean War, when regiments went on foreign service they were accompanied by a limited number of families, and those left behind received no official support. In 1785 1,400 children, whose soldier fathers had died in the service or been posted abroad, were begging on Dublin's streets. The Hibernian Society, a philanthropic organisation, had founded the Hibernian Asylum in Phoenix Park, Dublin in 1769, noting that 'great numbers of children had been destitute of all means of subsistence' and that the establishment had been founded 'to preserve children left in such circumstances from popery, beggary and idleness.' The military authorities took on responsibility for the school, now the Royal Hibernian Military School, in 1806 – it already contained over 2,000 children, one-third of them girls.

Three years before, the Royal Military Asylum, also for boys and girls, was established near Sloane Square on the King's Road in Chelsea, on a site to be long known as the Duke of York's Headquarters. It was renamed the Duke of York's Royal Military School in 1892, and thereafter took boys only. The school moved to purpose-built premises on the cliffs at Dover in 1909. When Ireland became independent in 1922 the Royal Hibernian School moved to Shorncliffe in Kent, and two years later the remaining boys transferred to the nearby Duke of York's. The last Hibernian student to leave the school was Cecil Vincent Walsh, who volunteered for the King's Shropshire Light

Infantry in 1931, was commissioned into the Intelligence Corps, served in a Royal Signals cipher unit throughout the Second World War and died as a retired lieutenant colonel in 1989.

Both the Hibernian Military School and the Duke of York's School were explicit about placing male pupils in the army. The former's 1808 warrant, based on that so recently granted to the Chelsea school, gave its aim as 'to place in the Regular Army as private soldiers, in such corps as from time to time His Majesty shall be pleased to appoint, but with their own free consent, the orphans and children of soldiers in Ireland, for ever.'[18] The army's concept of 'free consent' was somewhat elastic. E. Souter, recalling his time at Chelsea in the 1850s, tells how:

> About a fortnight after joining, the commandant, Colonel Cotton, asked me at what trade I would like to be trained; band, drums, tailors, shoemakers, carpenters or shirtmakers. He said that it was the practice to allow a boy to make his own choice, as a lad made better progress at a vocation of his own selection. I said I would like to be a tailor. The colonel then pointed out the advantages of a musical education and the privileges enjoyed by bandsmen in the army. The interview ended with the colonel using his own discretion and sending me to Mr Butley to be trained as a musician.[19]

Both schools were expressly military: students wore uniform, held ranks, were called upon to teach as part of a monitorial system, and were subject to rigid discipline. Teaching standards were not always high and some NCOs were not bright. One boy remembered being reprimanded when the school lined up in alphabetical order. 'Phillips! Phillips!' bellowed the NCO. 'Why aren't you with the Fs?'

The fact that both schools initially took boys and girls caused difficulties, and in 1822 a formidable steel barrier was erected between the sleeping quarters at Chelsea in a, predictably futile, attempt to prevent nocturnal association. One commentator considered the schools to be 'infant regiments, more or less', and what might have been deemed schoolboy larks elsewhere were here military offences. At Chelsea on 30 December 1852, Private Ends Seta was awarded six cuts of the cane and six hours in the 'Black Hole' for answering the commandant in a disrespectful manner. The punishment was repeated the following day when he was accused of kicking and making a noise in the Black Hole, and he received another eighteen cuts for throwing a mug of water out of the Black Hole and calling the sergeant major a fathead. The same year privates Batemen and Barry, both 13, stole the muff from the regimental chapel and cut it in pieces. They were given eighteen strokes of the birch, four days in the Black Hole, and six days' extra drill.

Both schools produced a steady stream of recruits, many of whom relished the prospect of foreign service and what seemed decent pay. Drummer John Hammond of the Royal Berkshires affirmed,

> I am very happy in my regiment. I have been granted effective drummer and now I clear 9½d. a day pay which I think very good for a boy of 15, don't you?
>
> In my regiment we feel it very keenly at not being sent to the war in South Africa. I think it is a shame as the 1st Royal Berks distinguished themselves at Tofrek, on the 22nd March 1885, and were made a royal regiment on the field of battle … As it is, they are bringing the Royal Sussex Regiment from Malta prior to sailing them to South Africa and sending us to Malta to linger in obscurity.[20]

John Holland left the Royal Hibernian to join the Argyll and Sutherland Highlanders in Dublin in 1902, and went to India the following year. He remembered his arrival in Bombay largely because he found himself at the end of a queue of soldiers at the bar. Each said that the man behind would pay, and he was left with the bill. Of the five boys in his contingent, 'one became a musician, and eventually became conductor of the BBC Symphony Orchestra, and one was sent home paralysed with VD.'[21]

The youngest soldier to enlist in the period 1792–1815 was probably James Wade of the 9th Foot who joined at the age of seven in July 1800, and one study suggests that there were 6,000 boys serving in the infantry alone in 1811.[22] In 1833 N. W. Bancroft was 'a very small shaver' attending a regimental school in India, and told the local brigade commander how much he wanted to sign on. 'Yes, my little man, you shall be a little soldier', replied the brigadier. So Bancroft was enlisted as a boy, posted to the band, and began man-service (in the full splendour of horse artillery uniform) when he attained his 18th birthday, seven years later.[23] In 1924 Spike Mays was 16 years and 3 months old when he left his Essex village to become a band-boy in the Royal Dragoons, and commenced his man-service the following year.

The enlistment of limited numbers of boys into non-combatant roles offended neither the letter of the law nor, on the eve of the First World War when children generally left school to begin work at 14, the custom of the age. What was more questionable was the enlistment of under-age youths by military authorities who had a shrewd idea that the recruit's given age was false. In one sense it was a mutually reinforcing conspiracy, for the army needed to fill its ranks, and potential recruits knew that boys' vacancies were limited and that pension rights only began with man-service. The issue became extraordinarily contentious in and after the First World War, when a large number of under-age soldiers were enlisted. For many years it was believed that Private John Condon of the Royal Irish Regiment was the youngest British soldier killed in the war, aged only 14, although there is now some doubt as to whether this was actually his age (some suggest that he was 18, and others maintain that the body buried in his grave is actually that of another soldier). There is no doubt that Rifleman Valentine Joe Strudwick was killed near Ypres in January 1916 at the age of 15, and that there were many 16-year-olds amongst the 6,340 British soldiers killed before they had reached the age of 21.

George Coppard tells us how he managed to enlist in the Queen's Royal Regiment in 1914 at the age of 16:

> I presented myself to the recruiting sergeant at Mitcham Road Barracks, Croydon. There was a steady stream of men, mostly working types, queuing to enlist. The sergeant asked me my age, and when told, replied 'Clear off, son. Come back tomorrow and see if you're nineteen, eh?' So I turned up again the next day and gave my age as nineteen. I attested in a batch of a dozen others and, holding up my right hand, swore to fight for King and Country. The sergeant winked as he gave me the King's shilling, plus one shilling and ninepence ration money for that day.

Coppard actually gave his age as 19 years and 7 months. When, in February 1916 after he had gone to France, his family applied for his release saying that he was under-age and providing his birth certificate, the army replied that the age given on attestation was Coppard's 'official age' and he could not be discharged.[24] This reflected current policy, laid down in September 1915, which affirmed that a soldier under 17 years of age would be discharged on the authority of his commanding officer, but that youths over 17 would be held to serve according to their official age. Coppard, indisputably over 17 when his parents made their request, was retained in the service. But Private James Tait of the East Yorkshires who had joined aged 15½ in 1915, was released the following year when his mother protested, because he was still under 17. Tait signed up again, this time into the Durham Light Infantry, as soon as he was 18.

George Adams enlisted under-age into the Middlesex Regiment and survived Loos, telling his parents of the fate of so many of his comrades: 'I am sorry to say that nearly all the fellows I knew have gone, and Dad, Jack Badrick the bricky who used to work for Harry Rooney has gone as well.'[25] It is small wonder that his parents told the army of his real age soon afterwards. Offered the choice of staying in France or going home, he went home (in part because he thought that the army had not treated him fairly by denying him proficiency pay as a machine-gunner) but signed on again in January 1916. That year, after significant parliamentary pressure, the army changed its official policy. Soldiers under 17 years of age were to be sent home, and those between 17 and 18½ would be repatriated unless they were unwilling, in which case they could be used for duties out of the line. Men between 18½ and 19 were to be held in training or other units behind the lines until they reached the age of 19 and became eligible for front-line service. Given that units would be unaware of a soldier's real age as opposed to the official age on his records, the process of investigation would only be initiated by an external source, usually the boy's parents.

Some under-age boys signed on giving false names precisely to prevent family interference, and others, however illogical it may seem in liberal retrospect, were prepared to take extraordinary steps to get to France. Captain Dunn tells of a band-boy from the Royal Welch Depot who made his way to the front to join 2/Royal Welch Fusiliers, who at once sent him back. The band went out to France officially in February 1919, and although Sergeant-Drummer Dyer 'ruled them with pre-war severity', the boys managed to burn down the band hut and frequently broke out of camp. In April they found their way into an ammunition dump, where one was killed and three others wounded in an accidental explosion probably caused by fiddling with grenades. Dunn thought that the dead boy, buried with full military honours at the age of 15, 'was probably the youngest British soldier to be buried in France'.[26] His comrades, who had gleefully put up blue 'overseas service' chevrons on arrival in France, returned to the depot wearing wound stripes as well.

Given that some young soldiers were executed by the military authorities, the issue of their recruitment and retention continues to generate as much heat as light. Abraham Bevistein, born in Warsaw to a Jewish family that emigrated to England in 1902, joined the Middlesex Regiment, as Abraham Harris, in September 1914 at the real age of 16½. In March 1915 he 'reminded' his mother that his 19th birthday was on 1 May, to prevent anything interfering with his imminent embarkation for France. He was wounded in January 1916, but after returning to his battalion the following month, he reported sick telling his CQMS that he had been shocked by the nearby explosion of a rifle grenade. On 13 February the battalion's medical officer passed him fit for duty, and the quartermaster sent him back to the trenches with a note. Instead of returning to his battalion, under heavy attack at the time, he drifted to a farmhouse, where he warmed himself in front of the fire with soldiers from another unit. A corporal became suspicious, and Private Harris was arrested. On 23 February he wrote to tell his mother:

> We were in the trenches, and I was ill, so I went out and they took me to the prison, and I am in a bit of trouble now and won't get any money for a long time. I will have to go in front of a Court. I will try to get out of it, so don't worry.

He was charged with desertion, remanded for court martial by his acting commanding officer, and tried by Field General Court Martial on 4 March. Private Harris was not represented (by no means unusual in such cases), and his declaration that 'I did not intend to return until the Company came out of the trenches' could scarcely have been more damning. The *Manual of Military Law* explained that 'the criterion between desertion and absence without leave is *intention*', and a man was guilty of the capital offence of desertion if he either intended not to return to his unit at all, or had absented himself 'to escape some particularly important service'.[27] For instance, a man who disappeared so as to miss his regiment's departure on active service was a deserter, not simply an absentee. Harris's platoon commander, Second Lieutenant Arthur Redford (who had joined as a private soldier a few days before him and had then been commissioned) told the court that Harris 'bears a good character', and had 'begged to be allowed to come' to France with the battalion although it 'was intended to leave him behind'. But this was mitigation and did not deflect the court from sentencing Harris to death. Careful research into the files of Harris and Private Martin of 9/Essex, convicted by the same court, suggests that the negative comments of Lieutenant Colonel Ingle of 11/Middlesex (who reported on Harris's conduct as 'indifferent' in general and 'bad' in the field) encouraged divisional, corps and army commanders to recommend that the death sentence be confirmed. The commander-in-chief took their advice, and Private Harris was duly shot at 5.29 a.m. on 20 March 1916. In early April his family received a starkly formal letter notifying them of his fate. The headstone in Labourse Communal Cemetery gives his official age of 19.[28]

Once the war was over, the War Office reviewed the cases of all soldiers executed below the age of 21. They found that one 18-year-old was shot for murder (an offence for which he would have been liable to hanging in Britain); and eight 19-year-olds were executed for purely military offences. However, this reflected only the official age of the men concerned, and even this survey revealed that the youngest man *knowingly* executed was Private William Hunter of the Loyals, officially 20 years and 56 days old, but actually only 17 years, 9 months when he deserted. Passions were understandably aroused by the issue, making measured analysis difficult. Hunter, who had spent two years in the merchant navy, had been twice convicted for absence, and when previously tried by FGCM for desertion the court had not been persuaded of his intention to desert and had convicted him of being absent. A sentence of two years' imprisonment at hard labour was commuted to one year and suspended. Hunter admitted that 'If I had not been arrested I should have stayed absent', and the court duly sentenced him to death, though with a strong recommendation to mercy 'on grounds of extreme youth, service in the field and likelihood of being a good fighting man'. Commanding officer, brigadier, and divisional commander, all supported the death sentence, but his corps commander, Henry Wilson, was worried about his age and recommended that the sentence should be commuted to five years' penal servitude. The army commander, Charles Monro, supported the death sentence – 'The man is very young, but his commanding officer says he is no good as a fighting soldier' – and Hunter was duly shot on 21 February 1916. In this case it was clear that the army was aware of Hunter's real rather than his official age, and two factors led him to the firing party. First, his commanding officer maintained that his character as a fighting man was 'NIL', and second, his brigade commander recommended execution because the battalion's state of discipline was unsatisfactory. An example had to be made, 'and here was a man who was expendable since he had no value as a soldier. In that context his age became immaterial.'[29]

The British army currently sets 16½ as the lower age limit for enlistment; young men and women below 18 require their parents' written consent before they can sign on. In 2003 Britain acceded to the UN Convention of the Rights of the Child (which defines a 'child soldier' as simply being under 18), agreeing that it would not send under-18-year-olds on active service. But in 2005 the Ministry of Defence admitted that over the past two years it had sent fifteen 17-year-olds to Iraq because of pressures prior to deployment. Many of the traditional challenges posed by young soldiers remain. From the army's point of view there is still a palpable tension between the desire to recruit high-quality youngsters as early as possible and the accusation that it is attracting child soldiers who are too young to have made up their own minds. Added to this is the practical difficulty of providing meaningful employment for under-18s who have completed their time in Army Training Regiments but are still too young to go on operations. This has to be balanced against the concern that many school leavers who might otherwise have become good soldiers, will either have entered the civilian job market or gained a criminal record and, in either case, be lost to the army.

For most of the post-1945 period the army drew a disproportionate amount of its NCOs (and in consequence many of its late-entry officers) from 'junior leaders' units, all of which enabled motivated and ambitious school leavers to join the army at the earliest opportunity. In the infantry, for example, these units had been variously termed the Infantry Boys' Battalion, the Junior Infantry Battalion, the Junior Infantry Wing and latterly the Infantry Junior Leaders' Battalion. Junior Leaders' units were all disbanded in the early 1990s, but in 1998 the army recognised that it was missing a valuable source of recruits and opened the Army Foundation College on the site of the old Army Apprentices College at Harrogate in Yorkshire, taking school leavers between 16 and 17 years and 1 month. The success of Harrogate encouraged the army to open its Technical Foundation College at Winchester, also aimed at school leavers.

The Duke of York's Royal Military School has also survived. It became co-educational in 1994, and is now a secondary school open to children whose parents have served in any branch of the armed forces. Until 1999 its headmasters were serving officers, and it has a regimental sergeant major on its staff. The Ministry of Defence part-funded the school till September 2010, when it became an academy while retaining its military traditions. There are parades on Sunday mornings, the most important of them on Remembrance Day and Grand Day (at the end of each summer term), and the school's monitorial system is modelled on the military rank structure, giving substantial influence to sixth formers. The school's military band is larger than any other in the United Kingdom, including the massed bands of the Brigade of Guards. Its distinguished alumni include many servicemen such as General Sir Archibald Nye, vice-chief of the Imperial General Staff during the Second World War and subsequently high commissioner to both India and Canada, as the best-known. But there are also academics and actors, jazz musicians and classical clarinetists, bishops and rugby-players.

Over the past twenty years there has been increased concern that recruits in general, and young recruits in particular, experience severe 'culture shock' during their training, and this results in high levels of failure leading to the early discharge that is now so easy to obtain. In 2003 Charles Kirke, artillery officer turned academic, described modern British youth culture as a process in which 'external frameworks and order have been replaced by the primacy of individual experience and self-expression.' He suggested that modern recruits

> have to make a considerable cultural leap, greater than their fore-bears who came from the most structured youth culture of the past and this leap concerns their basic expectations of life and their deeply held assumptions and attitudes. To make matters more diffi-cult, they have to do this in an environment, the Army Training Regiment, which is controlled by staff who tend to be highly social-ised into the culture that the recruits are trying to join.[30]

Although some young soldiers have always wilted under the impact of recruit training, there is no doubt that the products of a harder, more deferential society found the process less difficult. George Ashurst had been brought up in rural Lancashire, but moved to Wigan with his parents and six siblings. He found that town boys, in comparison to country lads, were 'more forward and lacked discipline and respect'. He was soon involved in petty crime and practical jokes: most of his gang had part-time work before they left school. Ashurst lost his job as a colliery clerk in 1912 and went to join the Lancashire Fusiliers with a chum:

> The recruiting sergeant spoke to the other fellow first and then he turned to me and asked how old I was. I told him I was sixteen and a half years. He said, 'No, you are seventeen and a half. You are mistaken.' 'No, I am not,' I said. 'Oh yes, I am booking you down as seventeen like your pal here. How long do you want to sign up for?' We both said 'Seven years, Sir.' But he said, 'When you get into the army you might not like it, so I will tell you what to do. Join the Special Reserve, which means that you will do six months in the barracks and seven years on the reserve, with just a month's camp every year.' We thought that would be best.

It was wise of the sergeant to suggest that both boys tried the Special Reserve (the descendant of the old militia) first, and indeed many special reservists opted for regular service once their first six months were over. Ashurst soon picked up the ropes:

I soon learned what life was like in the army and that it paid to do as one was told smartly and quickly. At meal times there was no menu to choose from. What it did say on the menu was what you got, whether you liked it or not, and one serving only. If you didn't like the dripping you got with your bread for tea you bought a twopenny pat of butter at the canteen …

I got on very well as a soldier, except for little reminders by the sergeant major that I was a soldier now and 'Take your hands out of your pockets, stick your chest out and your chin in' as I walked across the barrack square. I felt really fit, too, with the cross-country running and the gym exercises we had daily, and I loved the musketry lessons and the shooting on the firing range with the .22 rifles.

Caught by the orderly sergeant playing cards after lights out, Ashurst and three comrades were sentenced to ninety hours' detention in 'cold stone cells with a hard wooden bed and pillow'. They spent their days drilling in full kit, doing PT and polishing latrine buckets and cooking pots. 'It certainly made me keep to the straight and narrow path afterwards', admitted Ashurst. He was promoted to lance corporal at the end of his first period of annual training, just in time for the First World War: he was 19 years old.[31]

By early 1918 half the infantrymen in the British army in France were 18 years old. In his poem 'In Memoriam', Lieutenant Ewart Mackintosh MC, killed at Cambrai in the autumn of 1917, wrote poignantly about the way young officers stood *in loco parentis* to their even younger soldiers: 'You were only David's father/But I had fifty sons …'

He is buried in Orival Wood Cemetery, not far from an 18-year-old infantryman whose parents have had the words 'School, War, Death' inscribed on his headstone. The men of B Company 2 Para averaged 19 years old in the Falklands War of 1982, and three soldiers of 3 Para were not even 18 when they were killed in action on Mount Longdon. Although the British army of 2011 has a smaller proportion of young soldiers than at any time in its history, the average age in an infantry company on active service is strikingly low, as the details of soldiers killed in Afghanistan show with poignant clarity. In 1/Princess of Wales's Royal Regiment's VC-winning 2004 Iraq tour the average age in the Warrior companies was around 20, while the soldiers in Y Company, who manned the battalion's support weapons like mortars and anti-tank missiles, were mostly around 25. There has been a good deal of criticism within the army about the staying power of 'Generation X' or the 'Millennium Kids'. There are also fears that the Army Training Regiments would be deterred by possible accusations of bullying, from ensuring that training was a proper preparation for the stressful conditions that soldiers would soon meet on operations. When I visited the regiment in Iraq, though, I was struck by the way that officers and NCOs alike wanted to tell me just how good the younger soldiers were. Corporal Si Gower, describing a brisk fire-fight in Basra, in which he himself was wounded, said that

> all the troops involved worked extremely hard and very well. They did their jobs with a small amount of guidance from me. All the lads were very young but worked to the best of their ability and produced the goods. As a commander who has been in the army from the dawn of time I would never change my job and I would never change my men.

The battalion's commanding officer, Lieutenant Colonel Matt Maer, thought that the achievement of 'the *PlayStation* generation' was the real surprise of the tour.[32]

CHAPTER 12

THE KING'S SHILLING

UNDER-AGE RECRUITS were not the only problem faced by Georgian recruiters. In 1760 the exasperated Lieutenant Colonel Windus complained that Lieutenant Charles Crawford had behaved in 'an extraordinary manner' by sending certificates signed, not by a Protestant clergyman, but 'by Felix O'Neile ... who keeps a bleach yard at Monstereven.'[1] Lieutenant Crawford admitted that he was not finding it easy, for he was in competition with other recruiters, but was doing as well as he could 'considering the badness of my party and that so small, as a sergeant, and the worst drum in the service'. He did not actually have a copy of recruiting instructions to hand, which did not help.[2] The Catholic Relief Act of 1791 ended the requirement for the recruit to affirm that he was Protestant. A similar law was passed in Scotland in April 1793, though it took some time for all old enlistment forms to be phased out there. Sir James Grant of Grant turned down one Catholic recruit, saying 'I cannot desire you to do an illegal act, although I am convinced many Roman Catholics are good subjects.'[3]

Recruiting parties stood to gain if a man 'passed the surgeon' and was duly enlisted by a magistrate. In 1805 the 'bringer', often a landlord, received £2. 12s. 6d., the recruiting officer 16s., and the recruiting party shared 15s. between them. But if recruits were discharged when they joined their units because they were old or infirm, then 'the officer who enlisted them will have no allowance for them, but will be charged a fortnight's subsistence to carry them home.'[4] Officers could easily run up debts by spending too much money on recruits, especially if they were in competition with other free-spending recruiters, and then discovered that their men were rejected when they reached the regiment. Sergeant Thomas Connolly, writing of the Napoleonic era, wrote of 'recruiting extravagancies' that left Sergeant Major Cutteridge of his regiment a staggering £900 in debt.

Sharp practice abounded. Corporal Todd, recruiting around his home town of Preston in Holderness in 1758, was 'set over a tankard of ale' with a group of friends when a marine sergeant offered him half a guinea a man if he would enlist men for the marines, or 'if I would let him trap some of them,' for the party was now 'merry with drink.' Todd refused, but one of the sergeant's recruiters spotted a young man, a local gentleman's servant, outside in the alley with a girl, called him to the door to shake his hand, palmed him the King's shilling, the token of enlistment, and told the audience that the man had volunteered. The fellow was immediately brought into the pub, and although his master fetched the mayor and other gentlemen in an effort to rescue him, Todd told them that 'the military law was in such force at this time that any man might easily be trepanned [i.e. conned into enlisting].' He suggested to the rescuers that the only way to save the man was to pay the 'smart money' with which a recruit could buy himself out: this then amounted to 'a guinea and a crown', or 26s. The gentlemen paid up at once and took their man away. The sergeant of marines characteristically put the money to good use, and 'called for a crown bowl of punch which we drank share of it and parted'. To be properly enlisted a man had to take the oath of attestation before a magistrate within twenty-four hours of accepting the shilling as a precaution against exactly this sort of practice. Even when Wellington's Peninsula army enlisted local volunteers, mostly deserters or prisoners of war, into the foreign-recruited Chasseurs Britanniques, it was able to meet this strict legal requirement only because the judge advocate general, Francis Seymour Larpent, enjoyed the powers of a justice of the peace.

When the Duke of Gordon was raising his regiment (eventually numbered as the 92nd) in 1794 his exceptionally beautiful wife, 'Bonnie Jean', and their daughters accompanied recruiting parties dressed in uniform. It was said that the duchess placed the King's shilling between her teeth and offered a kiss to any man who would take it. One man duly kissed her and immediately paid his smart money, saying that it was a bargain for a kiss from a duchess, and another flung the coin into the crowd to show that it was the kiss, not the money, that had persuaded him to enlist.[5]

By 1914 officers were empowered to act as justices for the purpose of administering the oath taken by recruits on attestation; the form currently in use requires signature by a 'justice of the peace or commissioned officer', although in practice it is always signed by an officer. Enlistment was traditionally a two-part process. A man 'offering to enlist' was told of the 'general conditions of service in the army', verbally – often very unreliably – until the 1880s, and in writing thereafter. At this time he was given a shilling, which was taken to signify his agreement 'either to complete his enlistment before a justice or, in default, to pay smart money'. The 1913 Army Act changed this so that a man who failed to enlist after accepting his shilling 'has merely broken his bargain', and could neither be arrested as a criminal nor compelled to take the oath before a justice. Even if he did enlist, he was still able to buy his discharge within three months for £10.[6] The ageless lament, best delivered in a fruity regional accent, describes a recruit's efforts to get the money to buy himself out of the army:

Dear Mother. Army's a bugger. Sell the pig and buy me out.
Dear John. Pig gone. Soldier on.

Although it is now much easier for a soldier to leave the army than it was at any time in the past, there are financial penalties to breaking a 'notice engagement', and 'discharge as of right' enables a soldier to leave the army without any penalty only during the first six months of his or her service. There was traditionally very high wastage in the early months of a soldier's service, before the habit of soldiering had set hard. From 1880 to 1882, 5,500 men under twenty-one were discharged, and 7,177 with less than a year's service deserted. One-third of the men who enlisted in the cavalry over an eight-year period in the 1870s had left it before the end of their first year, and another two-fifths had gone before the end of the following year.[7]

In 1758 Corporal Todd watched the marine recruiters hard at work:

They had begun drinking very freely ... and they gave liquor away to any one in the street or that would come in that I soon saw they were all upon the sharp and desired trepanning anyone they could ... therefore I cautioned several of my townsmen to avoid their company. But William Kerby of this town, being intoxicated with liquor, would enlist, so I enlisted him to hinder the sergeant from getting the smart money from him, as he was but a poor labouring man and [I intended to] set him at liberty when he was sober for nothing.

When Kerby's wife appeared, Corporal Todd told her that her husband could go home with her if he chose, provided he returned the shilling he had taken. Although he was anxious to find recruits, 'I would not offer to trap anyone, especially here in my own country'.[8] In 1812, Sergeant Thomas Jackson, a Staffordshire man who had enlisted into the Coldstream Guards from the militia, had moments of self-doubt but did not let them stand in his way:

> I was ordered to attend the several militia stations ... to induce men to join our regiment. I succeeded in bringing to the Guards some thirty or forty men, many of whom never found their way home again. Some of them, after sober reflection, repented, and said by the way, 'Sergeant, you are leading us to the slaughter-house.' I laughed them out of it, but perhaps they were about right. I said I disliked the recruiting service; however, another tour of that kind was worked out for me and another young sergeant, rather of a whimsical nature. It was to take a drum and fife, and attend all the wakes, races and revels, within twenty miles of London. There we had to strut about in best coats, and swaggering, sword in hand, drumming our way through the masses, commingled with gazing clodpolls, gingerbread mechanics, and thimbleprig sharpers. These pranks ended with the summer.[9]

A century before, Captain John Blackadder, a devout Scot serving in the Cameronians, sent back home to recruit, had complained that

> This vexing trade of recruiting depresses my mind. I am the unfittest for it of any man in the army, and have the least talent that way.

RIGHT Three sons of Queen Victoria in full military dress: (from left) the Duke of Saxe Coburg, the Prince of Wales, later Edward VII, and the Duke of Connaught. Though his own military service was not a success, Edward VII took a serious interest in military reform.

BELOW LEFT The young Prince of Wales (later Edward VIII) in the garden of the chateau that was his base during the First World War. He was commissioned into the Grenadier Guards and had hoped to see action, which was, of course, out of the question, though he made strenuous efforts to get to the front.

BELOW RIGHT Clement Attlee, Labour politician and prime minister, in uniform. Major Attlee saw action in Gallipoli, Mesopotamia and France in the First World War.

LEFT Writer, pamphleteer and soldier William Cobbett. After his discharge from the army in 1791 he set about prosecuting his former officers for corruption.

BELOW Sir Redvers Henry Buller: soldier MP and commander-in-chief in the Second Boer War, 1900. Noted for his bombastic attitudes, he was awarded the VC in 1879.

ABOVE John Churchill, Duke of Marlborough, 'the most illustrious British soldier of his age'. He successfully commanded coalition forces in the War of Spanish Succession – an early example of the soldier diplomat.

TOP RIGHT AND RIGHT
Major John André, adjutant general in the British army during the American War of Independence. Major André was caught and executed by the Americans as a spy. Though George Washington refused to allow him to be shot rather than hanged, he died bravely and became a popular hero.

ABOVE Lieut. Gen. Sir Travers E. Clarke (front row, fourth from right) with H.R.H. Duke of York (centre) and officers at an inspection of RAOC Headquarters, in 1922. Clarke was promoted to quartermaster general in 1917. He was an extraordinary administrator who coped with the haemorrhaging of resources after the 1918 German offensive – the 'Carnot of Haig's armies'.

BELOW Lieutenant General Sir John Cowans (right) talking with a fellow officer. Cowans was QMG throughout the First World War – 'the best quartermaster since Moses'. He had the capacity to think big and his 'penchant for other men's wives' may have endeared him to Lloyd George.

RIGHT Field Marshal Sir William 'Wully' Robertson, Chief of the Imperial General Staff from 1916 to 1918. Robertson was the only man in British military history to rise through the ranks from private to field marshal.

BELOW The upwardly mobile Captain James Jack (right) with another officer of the 1st Cameronians, in the trenches at Bois Grenier, 5th January 1915. By 1918, he had been promoted to brigadier general.

ABOVE 'An early lesson in marching', c.1794: cartoonist Thomas Rowlandson pokes fun at middle-class volunteers.

LEFT Recruiting parties easily ran up debts by spending on new recruits, not least in ale houses: 'Heroes recruiting at Kelsey's, or Guard-Day at St James's' by James Gillray.

BELOW Harrow Officer Training Corps recruits, drilling in their famous straw boaters, 1927.

ABOVE *The King's Shilling* by an unknown artist: a recruiting party of an officer, sergeant, drummer and fifer of an infantry regiment in a village street, *c.*1770.

BELOW *Listed for the Connaught Rangers* by Lady Butler. Enlistment was in many cases the only hope of escape from rural poverty.

ABOVE Raising the colours – Sergeant Bernard McCabe at the Battle of Sobraon in 1846. The tradition of the 'Sobraon Sergeant' is still upheld by the Princess of Wales's Royal Regiment.

LEFT 'Smart Men for the Tank Corps': a recruitment poster for the newly created Tank Corps at the end of the First World War.

BELOW A 'C' Battalion tank, its colours proudly flying, with a captured naval gun at the Battle of Cambrai, in the woods east of Ribécourt in November 1917.

ABOVE The army padre's role has traditionally been as much about pastoral care as spiritual guidance: writing field postcards for wounded men near Carnos, July 1916.

BELOW The repatriation ceremony for the body of Private Lee O'Callahan of the Princess of Wales's Royal Regiment, killed in Basra, Iraq in 2004.

ABOVE Foreign friends: soldiers of the King's German legion (left) and Greek Light Infantry (right) from *Costumes of the Army of the British Empire 1812*. Of all the foreign units, the combat record of the KGL was consistently first-rate, while the Greeks were perhaps the most striking, with their *fustanella* kilts. They were considered too volatile to be issued with pistols as well as muskets.

BELOW Private, drummers, piper and a bugler wearing the distinctive Highland uniforms of the Black Watch, 42nd Foot, *c.*1912. The Black Watch has always balanced its proud Scottish roots with a willingness to welcome other nationalities: in 2004 it had soldiers from the US, Canada, New Zealand, Australia, England, Wales, Gibraltar, and Fiji.

RIGHT Officers and men of the 3/3rd Gurkha Rifles, 75th Division, in the line in December 1917. The Gurkhas were retained as part of the British army after the partition of India in 1947 and continue today as the two battalion strong Royal Gurkha Rifles.

BELOW Men contracted into the Chinese Labour Corps at Proven, 21st August 1917. Over the course of the war over 2,000 Chinese labourers were killed by shells or died of wounds.

BOTTOM The road to hell: British troops being transported to the front line in American army lorries during the Korean War, 16 September 1950.

ABOVE Hannah Snell disguised herself as a man and enlisted in the Regiment of Marines in the mid-eighteenth century. She was wounded several times during fighting, but her female identity was only revealed when she was discharged.

BELOW 'Every fit woman can release a fit man': WAAC (Women's Auxiliary Army Corps) recruitment poster c.1916.

ABOVE Dr James (Miranda) Barry was appointed assistant surgeon in 1813, and rose to become inspector of the Army Medical Department. It was only after her death that she was discovered to be a woman.

BELOW 'ATS at the Wheel', c.1942. Princess Elizabeth, now Elizabeth II, joined as a mechanic in 1945.

ABOVE WAAC training for a public display, June 1919.

BELOW Ambulance drivers of the First Aid Nursing Yeomanry, *c*.1943. At the outbreak of the First World War FANY women were among the first units to arrive in France.

LEFT An officer of the 11th Hussars resplendent in the red trousers that gave them the nickname 'Cherrybums'.

BELOW A cartoon by Henry Heath alludes to the difficulty of keeping up with military trends, c.1830.

BOTTOM The Yeomanry Cavalry, by Giles: 'No sergeant – no – I don't see no enemy – not to speak of I don't – But I do see as John Martin's roots is terrible backward – wonderful backward they is – to be sure!'

RIGHT One of the earliest wartime photographs: a bugler and drummer of the Royal Artillery during the Crimean War, 1856.

BELOW The artillery today: a mortar section of 3 Para in the blistering heat of Sangin, Afghanistan in 2006.

'Loyal Souls, or A Peep into the Mess Room at St James' by Gillray.
Some aspects of the army will never change.

Sobriety itself is here a bar to success. I see the greatest rakes are the best recruiters. I cannot ramble and rove, and drink and tell stories, and wheedle, and insinuate, if my life were lying at stake. I saw all this before I came home, and could have avoided coming, but it was in the hopes of enjoying the blessings of the gospel that I brought me to Scotland, more than recruiting; though I do not deny that I had an eye to that also.[10]

Recruiting by beat of drum disappeared after the Napoleonic wars, and instead recruiting sergeants, tricked out in their best uniforms enhanced by bunches of ribbon, positioned themselves at spots likely to be frequented by young men. Horace Wyndham described their appearance around London's Charing Cross in the 1890s:

Tall, smart, and well set-up, with perfectly-fitting uniforms, adorned with plenty of gold lace, glowing buttons and spotless boots, they present an attractive picture to the eye and, from the crown of their circular caps – set jauntily on the side of their close-cropped heads – to the top of their brilliantly polished boots, they comprise a body of men of which any army would be justly proud.

Sometimes their approach was just the same as it would have been a century or so earlier. Fred Milton was a farm worker at South Brent in Devon, and one Saturday he went off with a friend to see the bright lights of Newton Abbot … 'About four o'clock we were spied by a recruiting sergeant,' he recalled, 'and within a couple of hours we found ourselves in the Devons. And I stayed there for twenty-two years.'[11]

In 1782 infantry regiments were given regional titles in addition to their numbers, a process that became much more specific with the arrival of county regiments in 1881. Sometimes soldiers were indeed motivated by a desire to serve with their local unit. In 1847 James Bodell had it in mind to join the artillery, marines or cavalry, but eventually plumped for the 59th (2nd Nottinghamshire) Regiment because he was a Nottinghamshire man. Recruiting sergeants were anxious to find soldiers for their own regiments, and it did not matter to them where a man had actually been born: 'It is all one to Sergeant Kite, as he expatiates on "the advantages of the army" to every one whom fate may chance to throw across his path.'[12] It was widely agreed that the recruiting sergeant's uniform was a major factor in drawing recruits. One recruiter thought 'the more attractive the head-dress, the better class of men you get as a recruit, and I think that applies to uniform generally.'[13] In 1891 Colonel John Russell, commanding the cavalry depot at Canterbury, thought that 'the colour of the trousers of the 11th Hussars is a great attraction.' The 11th wore dark red trousers, and their nickname 'Cherry Bums' was politely bowdlerised into 'Cherubims'.[14]

By the end of the nineteenth century several infantry regiments with distinctive uniforms were actually filled with soldiers who hailed from outside the regiment's recruiting area. In 1883–1900 the sixteen regiments that drew less than 25 per cent of their soldiers from their own areas included the gorgeously kilted Gordon, Seaforth, Argyll and Sutherland, and Cameron Highlanders. Men of the Royal Welch Fusiliers wore a natty fusilier cap in full dress rather than the more mundane infantry helmet. This proved so attractive to Birmingham men, who should by rights have joined the Royal Warwicks, that it was known as the Brummagem Fusiliers, and drew just 18.9 per cent of its recruits from North Wales.[15] Indeed, the wider pattern of recruitment shows that this was now an urban army: the Hampshires typically drew most of their recruits from teeming Portsmouth rather than the farming communities in the north of the county.

Many of those who joined the 95th Rifles were attracted by its dark green uniform. William Surtees had served in the 56th Foot, known as the Pompadours because the purple of their facings was allegedly Madame de Pompadour's favourite – or, more salaciously, the hue of her knickers. In 1802 he joined the 95th and took 'great delight' in the regiment's snappy drill.[16] In 1906 Thomas Painter enlisted at the Royal Warwickshire Regiment's depot, and came under pressure to join it. He refused, as it wore a red uniform for parade and walking out:

> Well, I didn't want to be a pillar-box, you see, red coat. All due respect to the red coat regiments. But I didn't want a red coat. I said 'What's that regiment that has a green jacket?' 'Oh,' he said, 'the King's Royal Rifle Corps, four battalions, plenty of foreign service.' I said 'That's the regiment for me.'[17]

On the eve of the First World War R. G. Garrod was working as a clerk when he saw 'a gorgeous figure in blue with yellow braid and clinking spurs' and before he knew quite what had happened he was in the 20th Hussars. Recruiters whose uniforms were not quite as dashing would do their best to deter youngsters from making their decisions simply on the basis of elegant uniforms. 'I suppose you think yourselves too smart for the infantry,' said a recruiting corporal to three young men who were dead set on joining the dragoons in about 1900. 'Perhaps you're fond of riding though. Well, I hope you're fond of grooming dirty horses. That's what you'll do most of.'[18]

Until well into the nineteenth century, recruiters often wore officer-style dress to enhance the visual impact of their uniform. In 1814 a sergeant of the Royal Sappers and Miners sported gold bullion epaulettes, white breeches, a shako with a gilt plate 'as big as a sundial, and brazen [chin] scales, surmounted by a long slashing feather. He looked like a prince among savages.' The sergeant's crimson shoulder sash was overlaid with ribbons, and on his breast was the 'bang-up', the recruiter's ribbon cockade.[19] Private soldiers accompanying recruiting parties were allowed some latitude in their own plumage, for they were essentially decoys designed to lure the gullible: they too were 'banged-up' with cockades and wore long ribbons trailing from their caps. When Rifleman Benjamin Harris went off to induce men of the East Kent Militia to join the Rifles his sergeant carried his sword low-slung like an officer, an officer's sash and pelisse, and had 'a tremendous green feather' in his shako. Harris dressed 'as smart as I dared appear', and by the end of the day the party had persuaded two officers and 125 men to volunteer for the Rifles – despite their previous pledges to the 7th Royal Fusiliers.[20]

The recruiter's appeal was always much the same. First came ready cash. Until the introduction of short service enlistments in 1870 (twelve years in all, with six with the colours, and six on the reserve) men received a bounty when they signed on. This varied in size from the 5*s*. paid under Charles II to the 'twenty shillings on the drum/For him that with us freely comes' described by Farquhar, and on to the larger sums paid to Napoleonic recruits. Edward Costello, born in Ireland in 1788, joined the Dublin Militia in 1807 and was in Londonderry, already embodied for full-time service, when he decided to join the 95th Rifles. He wrote:

After receiving my bounty of the eighteen guineas (£4 of which were deducted for my kit, which I was to have on joining), the sum allowed at that time to those who volunteered from the militia, I took the mail coach to Dublin, where I found a recruiting party of my regiment consisting of one sergeant, a corporal and six privates.[21]

Enlistment bounty was subject to immediate official deductions: 'All recruits to be furnished with necessaries out of their bounty money,' ordered the 93rd Foot, 'that they may join the Regiment as free from debt as possible.' There were also unofficial erosions. Wily NCOs assured recruits that it was customary for them to buy ribbons for sergeants' wives, to reward the drummer of beating the points of war, and to buy drinks for the whole recruiting party. Private Joseph Donaldson unwittingly caused much merriment when he asked for the money back at his first payday. Benjamin Harris, a Dorset shepherd called up into the Army of Reserve in 1802 and thence drafted into the 66th Foot, admitted that there was a three-day 'drunken riot' and the bounty 'was spent in every sort of excess till it was gone'. When he moved from the 66th to the 95th Rifles (attracted by the uniform) the whole party, recruiters and recruits alike, got roaring drunk in the Royal Oak at Cashel:

When we paraded before the door of the Royal Oak, the landlord and landlady of the inn, who were quite as lively, came reeling forth with two decanters of whisky which they thrust into the hands of the sergeants, making them a present of the decanters and all to carry along with them, and refresh themselves on the march. The piper then struck up, the sergeants flourished the decanters, and the whole commenced a terrific yell. We then all began to dance, and danced through the town, every now and then stopping for another pull at the whisky decanters. Thus we kept it up until we had danced, drank, shouted and piped thirteen Irish miles from Cashel to Clonmel.

In 1799 Winchester, a substantial military centre within easy distance of the key ports of Southampton and Portsmouth, was

a scene of riot, dissipation and absurd extravagance. It is supposed
that nine-tenths of the bounties ... amounting to at least £20,000
were all spent on the spot among the public houses, milliners,
watch-makers, hatters &c. In mere wantonness, bank notes were
actually eaten between slices of bread and butter.[22]

The latter practice paralleled that of frying gold watches on the Hard
at Portsmouth by discharged sailors awash with prize money and
eager to show just how little they cared for moderation.

The bounty was so substantial that a good living was to be made
by enlisting, pocketing the money, deserting at once, and then re-
enlisting. Harris found that one of his first duties was to form part of
the firing party designated to shoot a serial deserter:

> A private of the 70th Regiment had deserted from that Corps, and
> afterwards enlisted into several other regiments; indeed I was told
> at the time ... that sixteen different times he had received the
> bounty and then stolen off. Being, however, caught at last, he was
> brought to trial at Portsmouth, and sentenced by general court-
> martial to be shot.

Brought out for execution before all the troops in Portsmouth, then
about 15,000, the man 'made a short speech to the parade, acknowledging the justice of his sentence, and that drinking and evil company
had brought the punishment upon him'. He was not killed outright
by the volley, and four men were detailed to shoot him through the
head at point-blank range. The entire parade then marched past in
slow time, and 'when each company came in line with the body the
word was given to "mark time" and then "eyes left" in order that we
might observe the terrible example.'[23] This culprit's desertion was as
nothing when compared to that of Thomas Hodgson, executed for
robbery in 1787, who admitted enlisting under a variety of assumed
names no less than forty-nine times, netting the sum of 387 guineas,
more than a busy working man could expect to make in ten years.

The bounty had an irresistible appeal even for those who had been
legitimately discharged. The great military surgeon George Guthrie
took a keen interest in the management of bladder stones. Not long
after Waterloo, he experimented with a patent three-pronged

instrument designed to be inserted up the urethra into the bladder, where it would be extended to catch and then break up such stones. Duly inserted into a soldier's bladder the machine jammed open, and although Guthrie, with characteristic presence of mind, managed to free and extract it, the soldier declared 'You may cut out the stone, Sir, whenever you please, but you shall never put that three pronged thing into me again.' Guthrie duly cut into the bladder via the perineum and removed the stone. The Duke of York immediately granted the man his discharge 'as an especial favour,' but he 'a few days afterwards, enlisted again, for the sake of the bounty.' The surgeon who carried out his routine recruit's examination did not think of looking to see whether the man had been cut for the stone.[24] As far as badly conducted medicals are concerned, however, this was nothing compared with the less than searching inspection in 1745 of John Metcalf, who was allowed to enlist as a musician. He had actually lost his sight after an attack of smallpox at the age of 6, and is known to us as the road-maker Blind Jack of Knaresborough.

George Farquhar's character Sergeant Kite summed up the other advantages of enlistment:

> If any gentleman soldiers, or others, have a mind to serve Her Majesty and pull down the French king; if any prentices have severe masters, any children have unnatural parents; if any servants have too little wages, or any husband too much wife; let them repair to the noble Sergeant Kite, at the Sign of the Raven, in this good town of Shrewsbury, and they shall receive present relief and entertainment.

'Over the Hills' makes much the same points. Recruits 'shall live more happy lives/Free of squalling brats and wives/Who nag and vex us every day,' and 'Prentice Tom may well refuse/To wipe his angry master's shoes/For now he's free to run and play/Over the hills and far away.' Recruiting parties used posters as ground-bait to attract the gullible. A poster for the 14th Light Dragoons came dangerously close to infringing Farquhar's copyright, appealing to 'all you ... with too little wages, and a pinch-gut master ... too much wife ... or obstinate and unfeeling parents.'[25] In 1813 a recruiting party of the 73rd Foot offered recruits 'Five Shillings a Day and a Black Servant', while the 7th and 14th Light Dragoons, tongues firmly in cheek, warned potential recruits that 'the men will not be allowed to hunt during the next season, more than once a week.'[26]

Youthful self-will often had its part in the act of enlisting against the advice of those who believed themselves to be elders and betters. John Lucy and his brother Denis went 'a bit wild' after their mother died shortly before the First World War:

> We were tired of fathers, of advice from relations, of bottled coffee essence, of school, of newspaper offices. The soft accents and slow movements of the small farmers who swarmed in the streets of our southern Irish town, the cattle, fowl, eggs, butter, bacon, and the talk of politics filled us with loathing.

Both joined the Royal Irish Rifles, and found its ranks leavened with 'scallywags and minor adventurers', as well as a few rather strange characters:

> There was a taciturn sergeant from Waterford who was conversant with the intricacies of higher mathematics ... There was an ex-divinity student with literary tastes, who drank much beer and affected an obvious pretence to gentle birth; a national school teacher; a man who had absconded from a colonial bank; a few decent sons of farmers.[27]

John Miller joined the Scots Guards in the 1960s. 'I genuinely believed that the army was a man's life and a man's life was what I wanted. It would get me out of Motherwell' and an 'incredibly dull' job in the office at a local steel works. He chose the Scots Guards because of its fine fighting record, admired its officers because of their 'amazing sense of style', and found in Sergeant Willie McGill 'what they now call a role model. Or even a father substitute which ... is something I have been looking for throughout much of my life.'[28] Some men were simply attracted by the prospect of regular food. In the West Riding of Yorkshire eighteenth-century recruiting sergeants brandished havercakes, the oat (hafer) cakes that were a staple of the local diet, on their swords, demonstrating that recruits would not go short of food. The 33rd Foot, eventually to become the Duke of

Wellington's regiment, earned the nickname 'The Havercake Lads' in this way – and the shoulder-bag in which soldiers carried their rations was christened the haversack for the same reason.

The majority of recruits were unemployed when they enlisted. Even in 1925, when the dole was available for the out-of-work, 60 per cent of London recruits were unemployed. The picture is far more complex than suggested by Wellington's assertion that the army was simply composed of 'the scum of the earth'. Across the army's history many men did indeed enlist because they had neither a job nor the prospect of one. Yet others yearned for foreign travel, virtually out of the question for the working-class civilian before the end of the Second World War. Some thought that the army offered an easier prospect than life outside. In 1928 the miner Richard Clemens joined up because 'I was just fed up with the mines, that's all.' In 1899 T. J. Hammond enlisted under-age into the Essex Regiment because 'I'd run away from home. That's all there was to it.'[29] Thomas Pococke, born in Edinburgh in 1790, was 'tall and well made, of a gentle appearance and address', and became an actor at the age of 16. Humiliated by a dreadful attack of stage fright, he joined a party of recruits bound for the Isle of Wight, where he enlisted into the 71st Foot for seven years. He received a bounty of 11 guineas, kept £4 for himself and sent the rest to his parents – who had begged him not to go on the stage in the first place. 'I could not associate with the common soldiers,' he wrote,

> Their habits made me shudder. I feared an oath – they never spoke without one. I could not drink – they loved liquor. They gamed – I knew nothing of play. Thus was I a solitary individual amongst hundreds. They lost no opportunity of teasing me. 'Saucy Tom' or 'the Distressed Methodist' were the names they distinguished me by.

He eventually secured his position by knocking down one of his tormentors and offering to fight him, but still found his comrades an uncomfortable crew: 'Their pleasures were repugnant to my feelings.'[30]

Some young men had profitable alternatives to enlistment but signed on anyhow. Walter Mitton was born in Burton-upon-Trent in

1877, to a family that ran a large and successful plastering concern. All but one of his brothers went into the family business, but he briefly became a signwriter at a local coach-builders, and enlisted into the South Staffordshires as a drummer as soon as he was 16. His father disapproved and bought him out. As soon as he was 18, he signed on again, this time into the Royal Field Artillery, leaving a letter at home urging his parents to let him follow his chosen profession. He remained in the army for the next twenty-two years, keeping a well-written diary of his service in the Boer War, recording in May 1900 'what a glorious time I had, reading my letter and papers dad sent to me. I was fairly reconciled again.'[31] He became, in the slang of the age, 'as regimental as a button-stick', and when he married Agnes McEvoy in Kilkenny in July 1908 he had gun-horses pulling the bridal carriage and mounted gunners as outriders. Mitton's enlistment expired in 1917, by which time he had earned a Mention in Dispatches and become a battery sergeant major. However, he felt that he should see the war out, re-enlisted at once, was killed as a sergeant on the fourth day of the great German offensive of March 1918, and is buried in Noyon New British Cemetery. Whatever the period, families were often not prepared to let their young men depart without a fight, and when Benjamin Harris's recruiting party was ready to embark for England

> We were nearly pestered to death with a detachment of old Irish women, who came from different parts (on hearing of their sons having enlisted) in order to endeavour to get them away from us, following us down to the water's edge, they clung to their offspring, and, dragging them away, sent forth such dismal howls and moans that it was quite distracting to hear them … At length we got our lads safe on board, and set sail for England.[32]

Sometimes a husband would enlist during a drinking spree after a row, leaving his distraught wife to seek him at the barracks or even to follow the drum herself in order to find him. In October 1807 a Lambeth wheelwright named Pearce enlisted in the Guards because of 'a life of idleness and extravagance', and then shot himself after a row with his wife.[33]

Some men were easy targets for recruiters. John Shipp was raised as an orphan by his parish, and knew that the army was for him when he saw his first recruiting party: 'It was all about Gentleman soldiers, merry life, muskets rattling, cannon roaring, drums beating, colours flying, regiments charging and shouts of Victory! Victory!' He found the boy drummer's smart dress irresistible, and his heart kindled when he heard a band strike up 'Over the Hills and Far Away'. He enlisted in the 22nd Regiment in 1797. We must never underestimate the appeal of uniform, ritual and reputation, especially to the young. The anonymous Irish author of *Memoirs of a Sergeant* came from a Roman Catholic family beggared when his father, steward to the Nevens family of Portarlington, died. He spent a year as a servant and then, in 1806, saw the 43rd Light Infantry on the march:

> The roll of the spirit-stirring drum, the glittering file of bayonets, with the pomp and circumstance of military parade, not unmixed perhaps with undefined thoughts of ultimate promotion passed in review before my imagination, in colours rapidly changing: resistance was in vain.[34]

Timothy Gowing admitted that as a youth he had 'admired the appearance of a soldier. Little thinking of all that lay behind the scenes'. In January 1854 'I enlisted into one of the smartest regiments of our army, the Royal Fusiliers ... I selected this regiment for its noble deeds of valour under Lord Wellington in the Peninsula. They, the old Fusiliers, had made our enemies the French shake on many a hard fought field.'[35] Some thirty years before, Alexander Somerville had made the same connection between sartorial elegance and military reputation, though in his case it was the Royal Scots Greys that appealed:

> The grey horses, their long white tails, the scarlet coats, the long swords, the high bearskin caps and the plumes of white feathers encircling them in front, the blue overalls with the broad yellow stripes on the outside, the boots and spurs, the carbines slung at the saddle side, the holster pipes and the pistols, the shoulder belts and the pouches with ammunition, and, in the wet or the wintry wind, the long scarlet cloaks flowing from the riders' necks to their knees ... the trumpets sounding, the squadrons charging, Napoleon's columns broken by the charge.[36]

It may not be far wrong to take an infantry staff sergeant's 1846 assessment of motives for enlistment as having a broader validity, though there were substantial variations: Wellington's men were undoubtedly better material.

1. Indigent. Embracing labourers and mechanics out of employ, who seek merely for support – 80 in 120.
2. Indigent. Respectable persons induced by misfortune or imprudence – 2 in 120.
3. Idle. Who consider a soldier's life an easy one – 16 in 120.
4. Bad characters. Who fall back on the army as a last resort – 8 in 120.
5. Criminals. Who seek to escape from the consequences of their actions – 1 in 120.
6. Perverse sons. Who seek to grieve their parents – 2 in 120.
7. Discontented and Restless – 8 in 120.
8. Ambitious – 1 in 120.
9. Others – 2 in 120.[37]

CHAPTER 13

PRESSED INTO SERVICE

VOLUNTARY ENLISTMENT WAS unlikely ever to keep the army's ranks filled. Although, in strict terms, the British army was not recruited by conscription till early 1916, in time of war the feckless, unemployed or indebted could find themselves pressed into service. In 1695 the law relating to insolvent debtors was modified to require a man under forty to enlist in the army or navy, or to provide a substitute, before he could be discharged from bankruptcy. After Queen Anne's accession similar arrangements applied to prisoners released for debts under £100. The 1702 Mutiny Act decreed that men pardoned for capital offences were to be handed over to a recruiting officer, an arrangement which remained in force till 1814. Successive Acts of Parliament – the Press Acts, operating in the years 1701–12, 1745–6, 1755–8, and 1788–9 – ordered that 'able bodied men who had not any lawful calling or employment or visible means for their maintenance or livelihood' were subject to enforced enlistment. Detailed procedure varied from time to time, but usually the bounty that such a man might have received as a genuine volunteer was shared out between the village constables who presented him to the recruiting officer, the churchwardens administering the poor law in his parish, or his poor relations.[1] In April 1758 Corporal Matthew Todd found himself in the Berkshire town of Reading:

> We got a great number of impressed men into our regiment, for the constable brings them in every Saturday, the market day, where we have an officer and a sergeant and a corporal and 12 men waiting

at the Town Hall where a bench of Justices of the Peace sits, and any man that is so brought by the constables, if our officer approves of him, asks him to enlist. If he is inclined the officer gives him a guinea and a crown, if he won't enlist the corporal takes him to the gaol and puts him in the Black Hole and he has nothing to subsist upon but one pound of bread per day and water, a sentry being planted there to hinder any thing from coming to him. As soon as he is wearied of this confinement and will take one day's pay he is let out and if he deserts or behaves unruly he is punished the same as though he had enlisted. There is an Act of Parliament for that purpose. Any young fellow that's out of place, or has got a girl with child, or has any loose character, is sure of being brought, for the constables receive one pound for every man they take up, and several of them will take up any one, etc.[2] ...

During the Napoleonic wars the British garrison of the notoriously unhealthy West Indies – from 1793 to 1801 roughly half the 86,000 rank and file sent out died there or in transit – was partly kept up to strength by the impressment of convicted felons and prisoners who had pleaded not guilty and were awaiting trial. A man might avoid trial and the prospect of a capital sentence if he agreed to volunteer 'for general service'. Such service was for life until 1803, when it was reduced to seven years, providing the man had been of good behaviour. By 1820 over two hundred offences attracted the death penalty, although it was inflicted comparatively rarely, with transportation to Australia becoming the fate of the majority of pardoned felons in 1787–1868. Deserters, especially if they had deserted only once, and had done so in Britain, were fair game for unpopular postings. At this time deserters were rarely executed unless they had joined the enemy, made a profession of desertion, or had unwisely chosen to abscond at the very moment that the authorities were seeking examples to discourage others. In August 1813 Wellington's judge advocate general maintained 'Desertion is terrible ... We have only as yet tried five out of sixteen sent for trial: they are all sentenced to death, and all shot! This will, I think, have a good effect on our new reinforcements.'[3]

During the Napoleonic wars those deserters in Britain judged to have 'eradicable bad habits', were simply posted off to keep normal units up to strength. Units in the Windward and Leeward Islands

Command – a detachment of Royal Artillery, some Royal Military Artificers, and twelve battalions of foot – had 1,290 'criminals, culprits and deserters' amongst the 8,736 men in their ranks between January 1799 and October 1802. 1st Battalion The Royal Scots managed to collect an astonishing 223 (a high proportion of its 926 rank and file), while 2nd Battalion 60th Regiment, with 534 rank and file, had a mere seven. Two fortunate battalions had none at all.[4] In December 1783 an inspection report on 1/60th Foot, reviewed at Spanish Town, Jamaica, described the battalion as made up of 'Foreigners … Draughts received from the 92nd Regiment … [and] British and Irish sent from the jails in England.'[5]

Harder cases, including some civil prisoners pardoned for capital crimes, found themselves in units raised specifically for garrison duties in Africa or the West Indies. Sergeant Tom Morris of the 73rd Foot recalled that Private Hardy, his rear-rank man at Waterloo, had falsely reported himself wounded and, in consequence, been denied the medal for the action. He was 'ashamed to return to his quarters without the medal … deserted … and was eventually sent to a condemned regiment in Africa for life.'[6] In 1808 Fraser's Corps of Infantry was raised for the defence of the island of Goree off the coast of Senegal. It was designated the Royal African Corps in 1804, and detachments were soon deployed on the African coast. O'Hara's Regiment was stationed in Senegal from 1766 to 1784, when it was disbanded. In the West Indies, the Royal West India Rangers and the Royal York Rangers were formed out of drafts from the Royal African Corps in 1806 and 1808. The York Chasseurs were assembled from deserters corralled on the Isle of Wight and sent to the West Indies in 1814. After the Napoleonic wars the army tried to do away with 'penal corps' altogether, and all had gone by 1821. But in 1822 part of the Royal African Corps was re-embodied, brought up to strength with convict volunteers from Britain, and styled the Royal African Colonial Corps. It immediately generated a flurry of non-purchase promotions for officers who could not expect to buy advancement within their own units and were undeterred by unhealthy postings. The corps soon took to recruiting its rank and file locally, and the Ghana armed forces now counts it as one of its predecessors.

It is impossible to be sure of the proportion of criminals or deserters in the army in the eighteenth and early nineteenth centuries. J. A.

Houlding argues that insolvent debtors and pardoned felons were 'few in number' in most regiments, and the figures for the West Indies, where most of these folk were sent, do indeed bear him out. He argues that most of those impressed came from 'the next category in the current scale of values': the 'able-bodied, idle and disorderly persons'. Houlding maintained that the main purpose of this impressment was not primarily to take up these socially undesirable elements, but to persuade others to enlist (thus pocketing the bounty) for fear of being pressed.[7] In contrast, Richard Glover's *Peninsula Preparation* emphasises the number of criminals in the army, suggesting that it was full of 'appalling thugs'. Edward Coss's *All for the King's Shilling: The British Soldier under Wellington* argues cogently that the majority of Wellington's soldiers were unemployed farmworkers, tradesmen, and artisans who decided to soldier rather than starve. Arthur Gilbert maintains that our view of the rank and file is coloured by the fact that officers, most of them middle-class and, until the turn of the eighteenth and nineteenth centuries, our main source for comments on the rank and file, confused 'the economic plight of these men with depravity'. His own work on recruiting records suggests that 'the army did attract men who had identifiable trades,' and even the rapid expansions of wartime were 'not accomplished simply by sweeping the jails'.[8]

The trades and occupations of recruits were subject to wide regional variation, and enlistment was very much dependent on the prosperity of each trade at the date in question. The infantry of the Napoleonic era was highly reliant on weavers from Lancashire and the West Riding, and 'framework knitters' from the Midlands. Areas without a developed manufacturing industry tended to produce a high proportion of labourers amongst their recruits. In 1825–7, of every 1,000 men enlisted in Dublin there were 645 labourers, 65 servants, 63 weavers, 43 shoemakers, 31 clerks, 24 tailors, and eighteen each of carpenters and blacksmiths. In contrast, at Waterloo in 1815 the 23rd Royal Welch Fusiliers had 332 labourers but 100 textile workers, 39 metalworkers, 38 shoemakers, 32 clothing makers, and 19 woodworkers, a pattern reflecting unemployment in the regiment's recruiting area.[9] Although, as its title suggests, the 23rd was in theory Welsh, in 1807 only 146 of the 1st Battalion's 991 rank and file actually hailed from Wales. Its recruiting parties had been busy in

Lancashire, the Midlands and, like so many regiments regardless of their notional regional affiliation, Ireland. In 1806 the 2nd Battalion actually had more Irishmen than Welshmen in its ranks.[10]

Non-commissioned diarists, such a striking feature of the Napoleonic period, depict an army 'composed', as Sergeant William Wheeler of the 51st Light Infantry wrote, 'of men of all grades of character'. Wheeler admitted that

> Owing to the difficulty of procuring men to keep the army effective, recruiting parties attended the [quarter] sessions and received men who had committed thefts, who if they had been put on trial would have been transported. Such men when they joined the army set about their old trades and corrupt men of weak minds. If you knew but the hundredth part of the atrocities committed by men calling themselves British soldiers it would chill your blood.[11]

Regiments of the period had a hard core of 'incorrigibles', most of whom had been in trouble before they enlisted, and whose behaviour provided the advocates of corporal punishment with abundant support for their arguments. Then came a much larger quantity of labourers, often unemployed before they joined up. Next, their proportion depending on local economic circumstances, unemployed artisans and tradesmen. Any regiment could point to a small proportion of respectable men who had enlisted to make their way in the army and would work hard for promotion. In 1854 Timothy Gowing, already a corporal in the Royal Fusiliers soon after completing his basic training, departed for the Crimea 'a proud man. I felt that the honour of our dear old isle hung upon my shoulders. I pictured myself coming home much higher in rank with my breast covered with honour, the gift of a grateful country.'[12] He became a sergeant major, but declined the proffered commission on the grounds that he could not afford to live in the required style.

There were always a few 'decayed gentlemen', some of whom had enlisted because they had been beggared by ill-luck or misjudgement, or had been crossed in love. The poet Samuel Taylor Coleridge, an undergraduate of Jesus College, Cambridge, joined the 15th Light Dragoons as a private (with the unwieldy alias of Silas Tomkyn Comberbatch) in 1793, either because he was in debt or because he had been rejected by the girl he loved. He was not a natural soldier. His brother, a serving captain, managed to arrange for his discharge on the grounds of 'insanity', and he returned to Cambridge, though he never took his degree. John Harcomb was a solicitor who squandered his fortune and enlisted. When he came into some money he bought a commission in the 10th Hussars, but lost his wealth, sold out and rejoined his old regiment as a private; he died in a Portsmouth workhouse in 1814. In 1885 Wully Robertson was promoted troop sergeant major to replace an ex-medical student who was given to heavy drinking and had got the troop's accounts into a mess. The man reverted to sergeant but, well aware of what would happen when the accounts were investigated, shot himself. 'Apparently he had felt unable at the last moment to face the ruin and disgrace which confronted him,' wrote Robertson, 'and a round of service ammunition and a carbine had done the rest.'[13] In 1909 Private John Vivian Crowther of the 18th Hussars also shot himself. The inquest described him as 'a cultured and educated Oxford graduate who had inherited a large property'. We can only guess at what had brought him to lonely despair in a barrack room.[14]

Soldiers' background is not necessarily a guide to their behaviour. At the end of the nineteenth century, Wully Robertson warned that it was never wise to assume that the incorrigibles were wholly worthless, for sometimes

> the worst characters were the best workmen – the best grooms and the best riders – when money was scarce; when it was plentiful, they would fall under the spell of drink, and this would lead to absence, insubordination and other military offences.[15]

Nor, on the other hand, could officers be confident that a regiment's 'respectable' soldiers would stay steady when faced by the lure of drink. There were moments when a combination of heavy casualties and the availability of alcohol swept away all civilised restraint. The army's shocking behaviour after the storm of the Spanish town of Badajoz in 1812 is the most striking example of drink-fuelled savagery. Even the steady drinking that was a nightly feature of the 'wet canteen' in Victorian barracks could lead well-conducted men to lapses that saw them brawl with comrades, strike NCOs and resist arrest.

Lieutenant Gordon-Alexander of the 93rd Highlanders remembered a 'smart, clean and brave soldier' who developed 'a murderously violent temper' when in drink. He was arrested for returning drunk to barracks, and in the course of the ensuing fight succeeded in crowning the sergeant of the guard with a tub of slops. After receiving the fifty lashes awarded by a regimental court martial he declared 'Dae ye ca' *that* a flogging? Hoots! I've got many a worse licking frae ma mither.'[16]

Most serious of all were the 'hot weather shootings' that were a regular feature of garrison life in India. A combination of cheap and easily available rotgut drink, blazing heat and stultifying boredom led some soldiers to run amok through a barrack room or to deliberately settle old scores with musket or bayonet. In February 1848 Private James Mulcahey of 2nd Bengal Europeans stabbed his comrade Private James Rowe. Rowe died five days later, and Mulcahey was duly sentenced to death. He was hanged that May at the centre of a square formation of 1st and 2nd Bengal Europeans. He followed his coffin to the scaffold without betraying any emotion and nodding to friends in the various companies as he passed. The execution was botched, for the rope stretched as the trapdoor dropped, and Mulcahey's desperate attempts to support himself on tip-toe caused many soldiers in both regiments to faint before the hangman shortened the rope and Mulcahey quickly strangled. The troops slow-marched past the dangling body and then broke into quick time, but their bands did not strike up till they were near barracks. Corporal John Ryder of the 32nd Foot, serving in India in the 1840s, listened to Lieutenant Colonel Hill of his regiment warn the men against drunken excesses 'till tears ran down his face on the horse's neck'.[17] Robert Waterfield, of the same regiment, saw Gunner Richard Riley Atkins of the Bengal Artillery shot by a firing party of the 32nd, a process made more ghastly by the fact that the victim remained kneeling on his coffin after the volley and had to be pistolled by the provost marshal, and that he was a young man of good family and of excellent character till drink took him.

Murder by drunken soldiers is now happily rare. However, the rape and murder of Danish tour guide Louise Jensen in the Cyprus village of Ayia Napa in 1994 shows what can go wrong when soldiers have little to do but avail themselves of cheap drink. There is still abundant evidence that good soldiers can behave foolishly when drink is in and wit is out. In May 2008 a captain in the Royal Dragoon Guards, at a party held three days after returning from Iraq, asked three NCOs to hunt for officers to carry on drinking. They pulled an officer 'in a drunken stupor' from his bed, trussed him up and carried him outside naked. The captain who made the request did not face disciplinary action and later left the service. The NCOs were fined by a court martial for what one of their defence counsel described as 'a prank [that] started in good humour.'[18]

In March that year eight commando-trained Royal Engineers, products of a demanding selection system, stripped off in a bar in the Norwegian town of Harstad and were reported to have urinated on each other. One local resident complained, 'The Dutch like a drink and get a bit boisterous but they do not have that nasty edge that so many British troops display – once they have got some schnapps inside them.' Amongst the comments generated by the online version of this report was one pointing out that 'Commando forces are famous amongst the British military for "getting naked" when drunk.' This is 'strange behaviour for the average civilian to understand, but chances are these are the same men who were facing the Taliban and Al Quaida a few months ago – give them a break and don't be so quick to criticise.'[19] Criticism or tolerance apart, the point is a simple one: there is no easy connection between a man's motives for enlistment, his military performance, and his propensity for heavy drinking.

CHAPTER 14

ALL PALS TOGETHER

<hr>

Patriotism on a grand scale, and local pride on a smaller one, often played their part in encouraging men to join the army, and there are many examples of this. 'I loved the king with a veneration which has no adequate term to express it', admitted one young Georgian officer. When Colonel Alan Cameron of Erracht was raising the 79th Highlanders, a poster affirmed that he was doing so for the 'pride of commanding a faithful and brave band of his warlike countrymen, in the service of a king, whose greatest happiness is to reign as the common father and protector of his people'.[1] The connection between patriotic zeal and battle-field morale is complex, with big issues receding and smaller ones, like brave leadership and the ties of loyalty within the tribe, becoming more important as battle approaches. Even when, as Henry Newbolt was to put it, 'England's far, and Honour a name', an appeal to patriotism might be answered. Sergeant Bill Gould recalled that when Major Rowland Smyth was about to order the 16th Lancers to charge the proverbially steady Sikhs at Aliwal in 1846 he shouted:

> 'Now, I am going to give the word to charge, three cheers for the Queen.' There was a terrific burst of cheering in reply, and down we swept upon the guns. Very soon they were in our possession. A more exciting job followed. We had to charge a square of infantry … When we got out on the other side of the square our troop had lost both lieutenants, the cornet, troop sergeant major and two

sergeants. I was the only sergeant left. Some of the men shouted, 'Bill, you've got command, they're all down.'[2]

In the Crimea, Colour Sergeant McAlister was hard hit and ordered to fall out of the line; he flatly refused, saying 'I've done nothing for old England yet.'

We should never underestimate the impact of the patriotic schoolmaster. James Marshall-Cornwall, commissioned into the Royal Field Artillery on the eve of the First World War, was educated at Rugby, and remembered how

> My early schooldays were … passed in an air of patriotic fervour and martial enthusiasm. We all wore in our buttonholes little souvenir portraits of our favourite [Boer War] generals – Roberts, Kitchener, Methuen, Baden-Powell, etc. … my early enthusiasm for a military career was stimulated by the books which I used to devour. They included Rudyard Kipling's earlier works which were then appearing, G. A. Henty's historical romances and W. H. Fitchett's *Deeds That Won the Empire*.[3]

Such passions were not confined to one class or background. J. W. Milne served in South Africa with the volunteer company of the Gordon Highlanders. In an article describing his experiences he wrote

> I have been frequently asked what made me think of going out to South Africa. Well, I believe it was partly due to my being a member of the last MIA [Mutual Improvement Association]. As a member I thus had access to the shelves of the Library and I took from them such books to read as *Darkest Africa* and *Lord Clive in India*. The stirring tales of his defence of Arcot, and other thrilling incidents imbued a spirit in me to see such things as they were told in those books for myself. Ever since the Jameson raid I had watched the trend of events in South Africa. On the call of Her Majesty's Government for volunteers to serve in South Africa, I felt that now was the opportunity to see a bit of the world.

He proudly recorded the full text of Queen Victoria's last message to the troops in South Africa, and, although he had already seen more than his fair share of fighting, re-enlisted in 1914 and fought on the Somme.[4]

Yet the real picture was more complicated. After the disasters of 'Black Week', a call for volunteers was put out in December 1899, resulting in 54,000 coming forward. There was a close correlation between unemployment and working-class recruiting (as the former went up, so too did the latter) but it is also probable that, at just the same time, patriotic newspapers like the *Daily Mail* and John Robert Seeley's persuasive defence of empire, *The Expansion of England*, helped create a mood where middle-class men with secure jobs were inclined to sign up. Moreover, while organised labour was suspicious of the Boer War, the wider mass of unskilled workers, despite having no vested interest in imperialism, was easily blown by gusts of raw patriotism.

The events of August 1914 brought a wholly unprecedented challenge. This time the conflict was not far away in South Africa, but in the very heart of Europe against a foe who had violated Belgian neutrality, and whose naval, colonial, and commercial ambitions seemed to pose a direct threat to Britain. Lord Kitchener, made secretary of state for war on the 5th, warned the Cabinet that the war would last for three years. He was deeply mistrustful of the Territorials and aware that conscription was politically unacceptable, so he set about raising the New Armies. These were duration-only volunteers who largely constituted 'Service' battalions of county regiments. On 6 August he called for 500,000 volunteers, releasing Alfred Leete's drawing of the glaring field marshal, finger pointing squarely at the reader, above the legend 'Your Country needs YOU'; this became one of the century's most influential posters. On the best single day for recruiting, 3 September 1914, a staggering 33,204 men, one-third the strength of the British Expeditionary Force in France, and rather more than a third of Britain's entire regular army at the time of writing, signed on. By the end of 1915 almost 2,500,000 men had volunteered, more than the country was able to obtain by conscription in 1916 and 1917 combined.

The rush of volunteering broke many rules. Hundreds of men, not all of them young, who would never have considered joining that old, hard army of beery moustaches and stubby pipes were content to sign on as privates. R. H. Tawney, already a distinguished economic historian, had joined the Manchesters, declined a commission and was a sergeant by the time he was wounded on the Somme. The short story writer H. H. Monro ('Saki') joined the Royal Fusiliers at the age of 43, and died as a lance sergeant on the Somme, with 'put that bloody light out' as his famous last words. Some battalions deliberately attracted middle-class men. The Sportsmen's Battalion, 23rd Royal Fusiliers, included two England cricketers, the nation's lightweight boxing champion and a former lord mayor of Exeter. One of its privates described his own accommodation:

> In this hut the first bed was occupied by the brother of a peer. In the second the man who formerly drove his motor-car. Both had enlisted at the same time at the Hotel Cecil ... Other beds in the hut were occupied by a mechanical engineer, an old Blundell School boy, planters, a mine overseer from Scotland ... a photographer, a poultry farmer, an old sea dog who had rounded Cape Horn on no fewer than nine occasions, a man who had hunted seals, a bank clerk, and so on. It must not be thought that this hut was an exceptional one. Every hut was the same, and every hut was jealous of its reputation.[5]

Regiments had never been as successful in raising men within their recruiting areas as contemporary theorists or modern friends of the regimental system suggest. But the 1914 call to arms tapped directly into the bowler-hatted dignity of mock-Gothic town halls, the tight loyalties of back-to-back houses and corner shops, and the burgeoning self-confidence of workplaces at last beginning to flex their muscles. Communities raised battalions of their own. The New Army 31st Division had three brigades of infantry. The first, 92nd Brigade, contained what were, strictly speaking, 10th, 11th, 12th, and 13th Battalions the East Yorkshire Regiment, though all were raised in Hull. They were known to their many friends as the Hull Commercials, the Hull Tradesmen, the Hull Sportsmen, and the Hull T'Others. In 93rd Brigade were 15th, 16th, and 18th Battalions, the West Yorkshire Regiment, colloquially the Leeds Pals and 1st and 2nd Bradford Pals, along with 18th Battalion, the Durham Light Infantry, or the Durham Pals. The third brigade, 94th, had 12th, 13th, and 14th Battalions, the York and Lancaster Regiment, or the

Sheffield City Battalion, and 1st and 2nd Barnsley Pals. Last, but not least, the 11th Battalion, East Lancashire Regiment, whose nickname, the Accrington Pals, somehow encapsulates the agonising pride of it all.

The divisional pioneer battalion was 12/King's Own Yorkshire Light Infantry, sometimes known as T'owd Twelfth, or sometimes – because it was full of men from Charlesworth Pit who had streamed into Leeds to enlist – as the Leeds Miners. Not all Pals' battalions were from the Midlands and the North. Three battalions of Highland Light Infantry were raised in central Glasgow, and although they had official numbers, they were always the Tramways Battalion, the Boys Brigade Battalion and the Glasgow Commercials. Just where the little road from Longueval curls northwards to skirt High Wood ('Ghastly by day, ghostly by night, the rottenest place on the Somme') a simple wooden cross remembers 12/Gloucesters. Whatever successive amalgamations might have done to cap-badges and traditions, it will always be remembered, on this broad-shouldered landscape that leeched its blood, as Bristol's Own.

Other New Army units recruited, not in specified areas but, like Public Schools and Sportmen's battalions, from amongst particular interest groups. One of the most idiosyncratic was 17/Middlesex Regiment (1st Football). There had been growing complaints that football was not doing its bit for the country, and in December 1914 the flamboyant politician William Joynson-Hicks ('Jix') set about raising a battalion of footballers. On 15 December 1914 Fred 'Spider' Parker, captain of Clapton Orient, became the first to enlist. A week later Walter Tull, a mixed-race professional who had to move from Tottenham Hotspur to Northampton Town because of racist abuse, joined the battalion. Tull rose to the rank of sergeant and was commissioned in May 1917, becoming the army's first black officer. Attached to 25/Middlesex, he was killed on 25 March 1918; his body was never found, and he is commemorated on the Arras Memorial to the Missing. The battalion suffered appallingly on the Somme, losing over 500 officers and men between 24 July and 11 August, and another 300 in the autumn. Somehow it managed to retain its identity, until it was disbanded in early 1918 as the army simply ran out of men to maintain its existing infantry structure. In 1917 Captain Percy Barnfather had played for Croydon Common, making more appearances and scoring more goals than any other player in the club's short history. In May 1917 he reported:

> We have a big match on. We are still unbeaten, and likely to remain so, although we lost a good many of the old boys in this last attack ... They are all heroes, every one of them, and we realise it more every day. I saw plenty of men knocked out in this last affair, but I never heard one word of complaint, they were simply glorious.

As was often the case in Pals' battalions, discipline in 17/Middlesex owed at least as much to the bonds of mateship in the old world as the letter of the law in the new. In July 1916 Clapton Orient forward, Private William Jonas, was trapped in a trench with his CSM, Richard McFadden. The two were childhood friends and had played for the same club: there was no nonsense about rank:

> Willie turned to me and said, 'Goodbye Mac. Best of luck, special love to my sweetheart Mary Jane and best regards to the lads at Orient.' Before I could reply to him he was up and over. No sooner had he jumped out of the trench, my best friend of nearly twenty years was killed before my eyes.

Sergeant Major McFadden – 'this fine soldier-player' – had already received civilian awards for saving two boys from the River Lea and a child from a burning house. He was awarded the Military Medal in October 1916 but was mortally wounded soon afterwards. Sergeant Fred Parker, his club captain, admitted

> It is a terrible blow to all the boys who are left. I could not believe it at first, but it is too true. Mac feared nothing. All the boys are going to visit his grave as soon as they get the chance ... We have had a splendid cross made with a football on top of it, but that will not bring him back.[6]

CSM Richard McFadden MM lies in Couin British Cemetery, east of the Picardy town of Doullens. Its register records that he was 'late of Clapton Orient Football Club'.

In the summer of 1914 recruiting had been so buoyant that mounted policemen had been required to hold the crowd outside the Central London Recruiting Office in check. Latecomers sometimes discovered that, for the moment, there were no vacancies in that most voracious of all arms, the infantry. But not all volunteers had been fired by patriotic motives. There was some moral blackmail. Harry Ogle remembered how 'young men not in uniform were presented with white feathers by young women (also not in uniform),' and older men 'thinking themselves safe behind "important jobs" urged those to enlist who had nothing to lose but their lives.'[7]

It was evident that many of the first to sign up had volunteered because they were out of work. Rory Baynes, adjutant of 9/Scottish Rifles, thought that

> the first lot ... were a pretty rough crowd. The next lot were rather better. They'd had jobs and given them up and joined the army. Then later a superior class came down. These were all very well dressed, with a couple carrying suitcases, and later on came an even smarter variety.[8]

Captain C. E. Jesser-Davis found that his company of 11/Rifle Brigade consisted of 'three hundred and twenty men and boys in every variety of civilian attire, mostly rather shabby (although one man was in possession of a white collar) waiting in the road with their newspaper parcels under their arms'.[9] There was widespread agreement that men filled out with army food and profited from physical training in the open air. The Oldham Pals were soon sent off to Llanfairfechan, and one of them reported on a 'wonderful ... change ... they are looking splendid. There are no pale faces as one saw in Chadderton.'[10] In sharp contrast to pre-war recruitment patterns, huge quantities of men with steady jobs, many of them in industries with a tradition of militancy, joined the army. By mid-1915 over 230,000 miners, about one-quarter of the entire workforce, had volunteered. A man could be a trade unionist and a patriot too.

Nevertheless, for many men of 1914, military service represented, as it has since 1660, a real improvement on the lives they left behind. Adrian Gregory is right to observe, in his important study of British society in the war, that 'No view of the horrors of the First World War can be complete without a sense of the horrors of the pre-war peace.' The death rate amongst the children of 'generally sober, thrifty and generally employed' working-class families was one in four, and this was 'roughly double the death rate of adult males in the armed forces 1914–1918.' The mining village of Sengennydd lost 440 men and boys, almost 10 per cent of its population, in a pit disaster in 1913. No British community suffered loss on this scale during the war.[11]

Yet there was a sense that, thanks to improvements in food, housing and sanitation, this was better than what had gone before, and perhaps it was, after all, worth fighting for. Moreover, officers and men in the battle zone often wrote of their horror at the destruction they witnessed, and the importance of preserving their own country from a similar fate. 'Great Britain is fortunate', wrote a Sengennydd man in France. 'It pains one to note the havoc in this country. This was an industrious place and now the work of ages lies wrecked around us.'[12] At the other end of the social scale Captain John Norwood told his wife

> I have a very fond spot for the Germans whom I regard as our natural allies and I dislike the French … I must say the way the Germans have burnt whole villages and turned out the women has made me quite sick. I have time after time stayed in a perfect little village, with good hospitable souls … and before the day was over seen the whole valley and plain burning for miles.[13]

In 1914 the *Manchester Guardian* journalist C. E. Montague dyed his hair black to enlist, to hide his 47 years. He later accepted a commission, but his *Disenchantment* marks an important point of departure in criticism of the war. Nevertheless, even he affirmed

> The war had to be won: that was flat. It was like putting out houses on fire, or not letting children be killed; it did not even need to be proved; that we had got to win was now the one quite certain thing left in a world of shaken certainties.[14]

Early in 1915 the government recognised that it needed a manpower strategy to help meet the demands of the army and war industry. So it introduced a National Registration Bill in June, requiring men and women aged 15–65 to register details of employment and skills. Lord Derby, director of recruiting, asked all men of between 18 and 40 to register voluntarily: they would then be called up by age batches, single men first. Thousands of men, who could see the way things were going, decided to jump before they were pushed. Many 1915 volunteers used the opportunity to slip into the cavalry or garrison artillery, hoping that by doing so they would escape disappearing into the infantry's maw. K. J. Fenton, an 18-year-old living in Watford with his widowed mother, could not get his employer to release him for service, but as more and more friends joined up 'I felt left entirely in the cold.' He decided to attest once the Derby scheme came into force:

> So one evening in November when I was on my way home from the station, I suddenly decided to call in at the Clarendon Hall recruiting station and present myself for enrolment. I was medically examined and passed as fit. Having taken the oath together with a few other men, I was handed a shilling and a khaki armlet …
>
> For six months I heard nothing, then on Monday May 6th 1916 the expected notice came, I was ordered to report to the Queen's Road Recruiting Office the next day. Although it was more or less expected, the summons came as a bit of a blow, this sudden order, breaking off home ties, however such things were common occurrences in those days.

He was sent to Bedford by train, and on arrival told that 'any of us who were under nineteen could go home and wait for another calling up notice.' Although he had five months to go before his birthday he reported: 'I did not avail myself of the offer, for, having taken the plunge, I decided to go through with it.' He knew one or two other Watford men by sight, and 'we contrived to keep together as much as possible. In this manner I kept the close companionship of three Watford fellows, Oatley, Randall and Dean throughout our period of training. Of the three, Oatley was killed, Dean missing, Randall got through alright.'[15]

Overall, though, the results of the Derby scheme were disappointing, for almost half the single and rather less than half the married men failed to register, persuading the government that it had no alternative to conscription, and the first of the Military Service Acts became law in January 1916. Thereafter, legislation bit ever harder by extending age limits, and as enlistment standards were progressively lowered, medical boards came under increasing pressure to send men to the front. In March 1918 one platoon commander admitted that 'in one of my sections the lance corporal was the only fit man – of the three privates one was deaf, one was almost blind and one mentally sub-normal.'[16] In 1917 James Dunn's 2/Royal Welch Fusiliers received a man who had been torpedoed four times and was so badly shocked by the experience that he had been invalided out of the navy.

Many of the men conscripted in the last eighteen months of the war would, in normal times, have had nothing whatever to do with the army. Alfred M. Hale, living a gentlemanly existence on investment income was called up in 1917 at the age of 41, and found himself as an officer's servant in the Royal Flying Corps. He was deeply resentful that he was carrying out, for others, tasks that had once been done on his behalf, and constantly terrified that a medical board would propel him into the infantry. Frank Gray was 37 and a successful solicitor conscripted into the infantry in 1917. His chauffeur drove him to the recruiting office, and thereafter he endured the 'terribly hard' life of an infantry private in the year of Passchendaele. He had no use whatever for the army's ironbound old ways, but found his anguish redeemed by the bravery and generosity of his officers. At the other extreme, young Fred Hodges, called up at 18, was anxious to do his bit, and at the war's end was proud to return home with the badges of a good battalion and two stripes on his sleeve.

There was something distinctively British about manpower policies in the First World War. Before the war, the government had slipped into an informal agreement that would, in the event of a Franco-German clash, be likely to involve Britain in a large-scale continental war. And yet her army was not a mass force designed for such a conflict. Lord Kitchener's formal instructions to Field Marshal Sir John French at the very start of the war warned him

> The numerical strength of the British force and its contingent reinforcement is strictly limited, and with this consideration kept steadily in view it will be obvious that the greatest care must be exercised towards a minimum of loss and wastage …

The high courage and discipline of your troops should, and certainly will, have fair and full opportunity of display during the campaign, but officers may well be reminded that in this their first experience of European warfare, a greater measure of caution must be employed than under former conditions of hostilities against an untrained adversary.[17]

Within a matter of weeks it was evident that it was simply impossible to fight an industrialised war at the beginning of the twentieth century without incurring 'loss and wastage' on an enormous scale. For all the urgings of the compulsory service lobby, no British government could hope to introduce conscription until the voluntary principle could be shown to have run its course. Thereafter, sustained by its conviction that this was indeed a war fought to avenge unprovoked aggression and to achieve a lasting peace, it applied a 'terrifying single-minded-ness' that was eventually to smash all those barriers that had for long stood between British men and compulsory military service.[18]

CHAPTER 15

FOREIGN FRIENDS

THE ARMY HAS used foreigners for centuries in an effort to reduce its demands on native-born manpower. The rules for the enlistment of foreigners, like their motives for joining, have varied widely across three centuries. At one end of the scale there have been mercenaries in the most literal sense of the term, joining primarily to make money, while at the other, there have been those motivated by genuine enthusiasm for the British cause or, more often, hatred of a common enemy. Foreigners fought on both sides of the Civil War, sometimes because of deeply held political or religious conviction, but as often because there was money to be made. The Croatian Captain Carlo Fantom, 'very quarrelsome and a great ravisher', according to John Aubrey, announced 'I care not for your cause ... I fight for your half-crowns and your handsome women.' No sooner was there a British army than it enlisted foreigners, chiefly Dutchmen and Germans, like Melkar Gold who was trumpeter to the King's Troop of Life Guards throughout the reign of Charles II.[1]

In addition to formally enlisting foreigners into her own army, Britain contracted with friendly states in order to lay hands on more ever-elusive manpower. Sometimes these arrangements comprised the direct subordination of foreign units to British command, as was the case with the so-called 'Hessian' battalions in the American War of Independence. In fact, of the 30,000-plus German soldiers in North America (about one-quarter of the entire British force) just under 13,000 actually came from Hesse-Kassell; states like

Anhalt-Zerbst, Anspach-Beyreuth, Brunswick-Wolfenbüttel, Hesse-Hanau, and Waldeck providing the remainder.

John Peebles rather admired them, despite their occasional weakness for marauding. Their officers were 'jovial companions' at dinner, and in November 1779 he attended a multinational parade where 'The Highlanders looked very well and in good clean order, the Hessian grenadiers dressed up and powdered, the Anspachers the finest looking troops and tallest I ever saw, and in high discipline.'[2] The perceptive Captain Johann Ewald of the Hesse-Kassell *Feldjäger* corps thought that British officers, like his own countrymen, travelled rather too heavily with hair powder, playing cards, and light reading. He believed that his young soldiers, who did not yet understand the dangers of war, did better than veterans who knew them too well and decamped in his hour of need.[3] In contrast, Private Johann Döhla of the Bayreuth Regiment thought that his British comrades travelled commendably light, though he was shocked by their behaviour: they 'have only the vices of cussing, swearing, drinking, whoring, and stealing, and these more so than almost all other peoples'. Not that his own mates were perfect, for in August 1782 'Private Fichtel, of Quesnoy's Company, was put in jail because, while drunk, he punched a hole in Private Klügel's head.'[4]

The Germans who fought in North America have had a bad press, written off by historians who ought to know better as 'mercenaries'. Individual soldiers had nothing more to gain from their service than men who enlisted into other armies of the period: financial arrangements concerned their sovereigns and not them. They were, properly speaking, auxiliaries, and the use of foreign auxiliary units was commonplace in Europe. Here lies part of the problem. Americans regarded Britain's use of foreign troops as wholly inappropriate, and the mere presence of the Hessians ratcheted up the hostility with which the war was fought. This did not, however, prevent the patriots from trying to induce Germans to desert and serve in the Continental Army. Private Döhla's account of his time as a prisoner of war (he went into captivity after Cornwallis's surrender at Yorktown) is punctuated by the frequent departure of comrades who had concluded that service with former enemies was better than captivity. Just over 17,000 Germans returned home at the end of the war. Over a thousand had been killed in action and more than 6,000 had died of illness or in accidents. Almost 5,000, many of whom had served with the patriots, settled in North America.

The German impact on the British army in North America is more complex than the story of the Hessians. During the Revolutionary War most German units fought in line with musket and bayonet, differing little from their redcoated allies. But there were some, like Ewald's *Feldjäger*, who carried rifles and specialised in the skirmishing tactics that played such an important part in the conflict. From the 1740s European armies had begun to use small numbers of foresters and gamekeepers, dressed in sombre, practical uniforms and armed with hunting rifles, to protect reconnaissance parties and guide regular troops through difficult terrain.[5] Armies that expected to find themselves facing the cunning and resourceful Croatian light infantry used by the Hapsburgs needed to take *jäger* seriously. It was typical of the way that military fashion aped that of the dominant practitioners of a particular style of warfare that *jäger* soon began to resemble Croats, with moustaches and lovelocks, and a fondness for tight trousers and fur caps. In the British case the prime impulsion for light troops came from North America, and Major General Edward Braddock's defeat on the Monongahela River in July 1755 was a graphic demonstration of what could go wrong when volley-firing regulars met light troops in the woods.

At the start of the Seven Years War the British army had taken its first steps towards the creation of light troops intended for use in wooded and broken countryside. In 1755 the Swiss James Prevost proposed that a regular regiment should be raised in North America, manned largely by German and Swiss settlers, with both British and foreign officers. The result was the 62nd or Royal American Regiment of Foot (soon renumbered the 60th). Its two battalions were commanded by Henry Bouquet and Frederick Haldimand, both Swiss, with some of its officers and soldiers recruited in Switzerland or Germany, and others volunteering from other British regiments. At first the 60th dressed in red, and its only visible concession to bush warfare was the absence of lace on its uniforms, although from the very start some officers and men carried rifles rather than muskets. The 60th fought in North America during the Seven Years War and the War of Independence, and by the 1790s part of the regiment dressed in dark 'rifle' green and was armed with rifles. During the

Napoleonic wars it had a substantial foreign component. In 1804, for instance, the 5th Battalion mustered 585 foreigners and a lone Irishman, and the 7th Battalion was raised in Guernsey in 1813 from German prisoners of war. In 1814 the whole regiment, which had by then served with distinction in Spain, Portugal, and North America, was directed to wear green uniforms with red facings. The regiment's wholesale conversion into a rifle corps saw it formally renamed 'The 60th; The King's Royal Rifle Corps' and it soldiered on as the KRRC until its 1966 amalgamation into the Royal Green Jackets.[6]

The other British rifle regiment, perversely styled the Rifle Brigade, had a parallel line of development, beginning as the Experimental Corps of Riflemen at Shorncliffe in 1800 and taking its place in the line as the 95th three years later. In 1966 it too became part of the Royal Green Jackets, themselves swept up in another major amalgamation in 2007 into The Rifles. The new regiment's German ancestry may be long forgotten, but the red facings worn by its buglers in their green full dress is an echo of the old 60th, and somewhere the shades of a moustachioed Croat may be smiling wistfully at their busbies.

It would scarcely have been possible for Britain to have fought the Revolutionary War without the use of Germans, just as foreign troops in British pay had played such a fundamental part in the army commanded by the Duke of Marlborough: slightly more Danish than British soldiers were killed at Blenheim in 1704. Often, in addition to paying for foreign auxiliaries that came directly under her command, Britain gave subsidies to friendly powers to help them fight a common enemy on the continent. Indeed, it was precisely by adopting arrangements like this that Britain was able to avoid conscription for so long. Moreover, it is impossible to consider Britain's imperial achievement without reflecting on the indispensable contribution made by locally recruited forces of which the Indian Army is the most notable example.

Sometimes foreign units were not auxiliaries at all, but were actually embodied within the army's structure. Britain's forces in the first Gulf War in 1990 were commanded by General Sir Peter de la Cour de la Billière, whose name gives a clue to his origins. Even before Louis XIV revoked the Edict of Nantes in 1685, which had given freedom of worship to his Protestant subjects, some Huguenots had seen the way the wind was blowing and departed abroad. After the Revocation over a quarter of a million Huguenots fled abroad, where there were already Huguenot communities in England and elsewhere. Early on around 175,000 Huguenots left, with more following as Louis' cruel policies of enforced conversion took hold. Many had already served as officers or soldiers in the French army; the most senior of the exiles was the Duke of Schomberg, Marshal of France. Even those without prior military experience were tempted to join the armies of those states at war with France. William of Orange was especially eager to encourage Huguenots and there were some Huguenots in the army that invaded England in 1688. As soon as William was secure, he raised four wholly Huguenot regiments, three of infantry and one of cavalry. In 1690, shortly before the Battle of the Boyne, where Schomberg was killed, they contained some 2,600 officers and men.

By the time that the Treaty of Ryswick ended the war against France in 1697 there were over 4,000 Huguenots serving in the British army, and William was reluctant to disband them largely because he could not afford to pay off their arrears. As they were now largely 'landless refugees and exiles' William knew that they were 'the easiest of his soldiers to whom he could delay payment', and packed them off to Portugal.[7] Many of them subsequently fought in the Iberian peninsula during the War of Spanish Succession, and at least one wholly Huguenot regiment was raised in Portugal. Major General Theodore Vezey's 40th Foot came into being in 1708, with Simeon Descury as its lieutenant colonel. A list of its officers suggests that all but one (Charles Keightley, the quartermaster) were Huguenot, with nineteen of them still awaiting naturalisation as British subjects. The regiment was reduced in 1712, but was called out from half-pay in 1715 and 1718.[8]

The 40th eventually came under the command of one of the most distinguished of the Huguenot exiles, Henri de Massue, Marquis de Ruvigny, created Viscount Galway in 1692 for his services in Ireland and advanced to an earldom in 1697. He had effectively been William's viceroy in Ireland and was in retirement when sent to the Peninsula in 1704. On 25 April 1707 he attacked a superior force commanded by the Duke of Berwick, one of James II's illegitimate sons, at Almanza, near Albacete. Galway, who had already lost a hand in battle, was cut across the head while leading a cavalry charge, and his Portuguese horse broke down under Berwick's counter-attack. Galway was roundly defeated, losing some 5,000 men killed or wounded, and another 12,000 captured. Almanza – every quiz-master's favourite battle, for the British army was commanded by a Frenchman and the French by an Englishman – marked the collapse of Allied fortunes in Spain, and many of those killed there were Huguenot.

The remaining Huguenot regiments were disbanded after the Treaty of Utrecht ended the War of Spanish Succession in 1714, and no new regiments were raised subsequently. Huguenots, by now spread across the wider army, continued to play a notable part in British military history. In the 1740 *Army List* forty-nine out of fifty-seven English regiments, and eleven out of twenty Irish regiments contained at least one officer of Huguenot descent – all of them directly connected to officers who had served under William of Orange. The Huguenot military tradition is exemplified by the descendants of Samuel de Pechels, Seigneur de La Boissonade. Pechels, his family typical of the *petite noblesse* that produced so many French officers across the generations, hailed from Montauban in France's Protestant heartland, and had been imprisoned and then deported to San Domingo when he refused to abjure. He escaped to England, took service with William in the Netherlands, and was pensioned in 1692 after being wounded as a captain in Schomberg's Horse. His son Jacob received a captain's commission in Stanhope's regiment in 1707, was a major in Handasyde's in 1737, its lieutenant colonel two years later, and a colonel the following year. Jacob de Pechels married Jeanne Elizabeth Boyd, daughter of Jean Boyd of Bordeaux, a Scottish merchant. Their son, Lieutenant Colonel Sir Paul Pechel, created a baronet in 1797, was the father of Major General Sir Thomas Brooke Pechel, who in turn sired Rear-Admiral Sir Samuel Pechel and Admiral Sir George Richard Brooke Pechel.[9]

It is hard to overstate the importance of Huguenots in the British army of the early eighteenth century. Their doyen was Field Marshal Jean Louis, Earl Ligonier, born to a Huguenot family at Castres in 1680, who was engaged in nearly every important action in the War of Spanish Succession. This included the shockingly bloody battle of Malplaquet, where he was unhurt despite receiving twenty-three bullets through his clothing. George II knighted him on the field of Dettingen, and in 1757 he replaced the Duke of Cumberland as commander-in-chief of the army. A baron in 1763 and an earl three years later, he died unmarried at the age of 89, leaving behind a harem of young girls. One of his brothers was killed in action and the other, Edward, also an army officer, succeeded to his viscountcy. Although the earldom was revived for Edward, he died without issue after a messy divorce in which his wife Penelope was found to have had an affair with the Piedmontese Count Vittorio Alfieri.

Huguenot names ripple like an alphabetical *feu de joie* through the *Army Lists* of the eighteenth century and beyond. Major John André was hanged in North America in 1780; Isaac Barré was Wolfe's adjutant general at Quebec in 1759; Jean Antoine de Bernières' son became a captain in the 30th Foot; and both grandson and greatgrandson were major generals. The Champion de Crespigny family spread out to Australia, with H. V. Champion de Crespigny returning to command fighter squadrons on the Western Front, and then serve as an air vice marshal in the Second World War. Colonel Scipio Duroure was killed at Fontenoy. At the far end of the line, James Villettes soldiered on from ensign to captain in the 10th Foot. William Anne Villettes, perhaps his nephew, was commissioned into the 10th Light Dragoons in 1775, commanded the 69th Foot during the siege of Toulon, and was described by Nelson as 'a most excellent officer'. He became a general, died of yellow fever (no respecter of rank or ancestry) while serving as lieutenant governor and commander of the forces in Jamaica and is commemorated in Westminster Abbey. Henry Clinton Villettes was named for General Sir Henry Clinton for reasons that remain obscure, and enjoyed a comfortable career in the Household Cavalry, retiring as a captain in the Life Guards in 1789.

The visible Huguenot impact would be even greater but for the fact that names were often anglicised: Bourgeois became Burgess, Boileau de Castelnau simplified to Boileau, and de Foix to Defoe. The actor David Garrick's father was a captain in the Buffs, and his grandfather had changed the family name from de la Garrigue. Some Huguenot officers tried hard to preserve their ancestral names and seigneurial pretensions. In 1697 Colonel Chalant de Romaignac optimistically bequeathed his fief in Burgundy to his grandson Charles Pierre d'Arassus with the stipulation that he should take the name and arms of Romaignac, but soon his soldier grandsons were spelling their name Darassus, and Burgundy was a forgotten dream. Over time the Huguenots integrated, and 'by the turn of the nineteenth century their manners, speech and appearance were indistinguishable from that of their brother officers. Only their names continued to remind them of their origins in France.'[10]

By this time there were a good many more French names in the *Army List* and on regimental muster-rolls. From 1789 French opponents of the Revolution had begun to flee abroad, and by 1793 perhaps a quarter of a million French subjects had become émigrés. Some had already been officers or soldiers. Indeed, one of the reasons for the relatively large artillery of the new republic's armies was the fact that, with a smaller proportion of officers from the old nobility, it had been less damaged by emigration than the infantry and cavalry. Although the British government was at first uncertain about the émigrés, it soon identified them as a source of manpower. In 1794 parliament passed a bill 'to enable subjects of France to enlist as soldiers' or to accept commissions without suffering 'pain and penalty' for 'professing the Popish religion'.

When the first phase of the long war against France concluded with the signing of the Peace of Amiens in 1802 there were some 17,000 foreign troops in the British army, constituting about 11 per cent of its total manpower. A few were 'white cockade' regiments, who wore the Bourbons' white cockade on their hats rather than the black British equivalent, like Castries' Regiment and the Choiseul Hussars, officered and manned by royalist Frenchmen. There were six 'cadre corps', all made up of former French officers who were to regain their commissions to command insurgents in the event of a landing in France. Each of the infantry cadres consisted of 319 gentlemen, each enjoying double rank. The captains commanding companies would be colonels in France, the corporals would be captains and the privates would become ensigns. Dozens of other units flickered into life and often flickered out again as suddenly, with Ceylon Regiments, Corsican Chasseurs, Hector's Royal Marine, Hompesch's Mounted Rifles, the Maltese Chasseurs, and Waldstein's Light Infantry. Not all attempts at securing foreign troops worked. In 1799 William Villettes was sent to Corfu to raise a corps of Albanians, but the project foundered.

Some units did well, such as the Corsican Rangers, who looked rather like a British rifle regiment with slightly swarthier soldiers, and fought bravely in Egypt in 1801. The York Rangers, mostly Germans with some Franco-Irish officers, earned distinction in Flanders and Holland in 1793–5 and its survivors finished up being incorporated into the 60th Foot in 1797. Others never amounted to much. The 'white cockade' regiment mustered by Comte Charles du Houx de Vioménil in 1794 could only boast 266 men in 1795, and was promptly disbanded. Still others were brave but unlucky. The Comte d'Hervilly's regiment, recruited up to 900 officers and men from émigrés, Germans, and some prisoners of war, took part in an ill-starred expedition to Brittany in 1795. It fought well at first, but some deserters guided republican troops into its position and the regiment eventually collapsed, only 30 officers and 177 men escaping. The 22 captured officers were promptly executed as traitors taken in arms against the republic, and d'Hervilly himself died of wounds.

Of the many foreign units raised between 1793 and 1802 most were disbanded after the Peace of Amiens. It was, after all, axiomatic that the army was reduced on the outbreak of peace, and foreign units had the most slender claim to national gratitude. When war resumed in 1803 the process of raising foreign units began again. This time there were far fewer émigré regiments, with French officers being scattered more widely across the board, and the main emphasis was on red-coated infantry rather than dressy but under-recruited cavalry units. Some contingents, like those raised in Calabria, Sicily, Malta, and Greece were at least partly officered and manned by patri-ots who hoped not simply to expel the French from their homeland but to influence post-war politics too. The most striking of the foreign corps was the Greek Light Infantry, whose members sported the engaging combination of short red jackets and the white *fustanella* kilt. The men warmed to their standard-issue British muskets, but although they were meant to have pistols too the men were believed to be rather volatile and it was 'thought prudent' not to issue the weapons.

A few units looked and behaved much like regiments of the British line. Watteville's Regiment was raised in 1801 from other Swiss regi-ments in British pay. It was part of Sir John Stuart's little force that trounced General Reynier at Maida in Calabria in 1806, in a crisp demonstration of the efficacy of close-range volleys. After seeing further service in southern Italy and Spain, Watteville's was sent to Canada, where it was roughly handled in the siege of Fort Erie, losing

278 of its soldiers. It was disbanded in Canada in 1816 and although they were offered land grants to stay on as settlers, most officers and men decided to return to Europe.[11]

Most foreign units fought at the war's periphery. The Chasseurs Britanniques, however, formed part of Wellington's Peninsular army. The regiment had been raised in western Austria in 1801 from a mixture of émigrés, and was sent to the Mediterranean almost immediately. In late 1810 it was dispatched to Cadiz, and soon sailed thence to Lisbon, moving up to join Wellington's field army. In his dispatch for Fuentes de Oñoro in May 1811 Wellington noted approvingly, 'I particularly observed the Chasseurs Britanniques under Lieutenant-Colonel Eustace as behaving in the most steady manner.'[12] The regiment was arguably less steady in the attack on Fort San Cristobal at Badajoz the following month, with Lieutenant William Grattan of the Connaught Rangers maintaining that the party of Chasseurs carrying the scaling ladders had simply slung them into the fort's ditch. In July 1812 the regiment, as William Wheeler put it, 'dropped for it pretty tidy' at the Battle of Salamanca, advancing in the centre of its brigade under a heavy fire, though it lost only fifteen officers and men killed and wounded and another fourteen missing. In June 1813 it was the hardest-hit unit in its brigade at Vittoria, with 140 killed and wounded. It lost another 45 officers and men at Sorauren in the Pyrenees that July, and another 72 on the Bidassoa in August. The regiment was disbanded from the Foreign Depot at Lymington in Hampshire.

Although administratively the Chasseurs Britanniques behaved like an infantry regiment of the line, it retained strong links to émigré families in north-eastern France. Most of the first batch of officers had served in the French royal army, and many of the young officers commissioned to make good losses in the Peninsula came from the French school at Penn in Buckinghamshire. There were also a few British officers. Some, like William Cornwallis Eustace, who purchased the lieutenant colonelcy in 1810 and commanded the regiment for much of its time in the Peninsula, were long-term members: he was swept onwards by the inexorable laws of seniority and died a general in 1835. Others simply used the regiment for bureaucratic convenience. Robert Arbuthnot exchanged into it as a captain from the 20th Light Dragoons in March 1809 and departed as an unattached major the following month. The Hon John O'Neill, promoted as a lieutenant colonel in April 1808, never actually joined, but left for his former regiment two years later.

Most French officers were commissioned and promoted without purchase, and a free commission in the regiment was a typical reward for a young man who, like Edward Richard Dalton, appointed ensign in 1812, was worthy of an ensigncy but could not generate sufficient interest to gain one in a British regiment. Dalton went on to half-pay when the regiment was disbanded and died in Brighton in 1877. NCOs were sometimes commissioned, just as they would have been in the British army proper. Both Antoine Servais and Francis Kander rose through the ranks to become sergeant major and were alike commissioned. Désiré Lernon, a native of Marcoing, was appointed quartermaster sergeant in 1809. He married the daughter of Jean Frédéric Wolf, sometime bandmaster of the Ancien Régime's *Dragons de la Reine* (Queen's Own Dragoons) and Lisbon-based composer-musician, and joined the Chasseurs when the regiment broke its voyage from Jersey to Malta in 1804. Lernon was commissioned in 1811, but died of sickness less than two years later. Pietro Santocolumbo, not a common name in the *Army List*, had served in the Calabrian Free Corps and was given his ensigncy as a reward for recruiting. Wounded at Sorauren, he retired when the regiment was disbanded and enjoyed half-pay at Milazzo in Sicily till he died in 1852.

The officers evidently spoke French amongst themselves. In August 1813 when Lieutenant William Thornton Keep of the 28th Foot, thoroughly exhausted, and drenched with sweat and rain, saw a convenient campfire on the heights above Maya he crawled towards it in the hope of drying out. He was not alone, for a

group of finer officers, about twenty, I never saw. They were attired in handsome uniform, and appeared quite unfatigued. At first the extreme exhaustion of my bodily powers led me to suppose my mind was disordered, and that this was a mere fantasy ... My companions were all French ... our bugle sounded, which gave me strength to jump up. I rushed to the tree from whence I had proceeded ... [and] met my sergeant, of whom I immediately learnt that these were the Chasseurs Britanniques ...[13]

The regiment's soldiers were a mixed bag. In its earliest days a majority of French, Germans, and Swiss served in its ranks. After Maida, Poles became the largest single nationality, and they were joined by other Eastern Europeans, notably Hungarians and Austrians, many of whom had served in the French army. There were always several Russians, rather more Italians, and even the occasional American. Amongst the casualties at Fuentes were the Polish Private Nicolas Yetchinchen, 'supposed dead', the German Private Conrad Shybell, who had a leg amputated, and Private Casimir Seresniack, another Pole, who was left wounded in the field and escaped from French captivity to turn up of his own free will at the Foreign Depot at Lymington over a year later. The authorities evidently believed him, for he received his arrears of pay.[14] Even the regiment's warmest advocate, however, cannot deny that its men deserted on an almost migratory scale, with 224 making off in 1813 alone. Wellington attributed the 'disposition of all foreign recruits to desert from our armies to the regularity of system and to the strictness of discipline which exist, and which must be upheld, in order to keep a British army in the field in a state of efficiency for any length of time'.[15] Yet despite the fact that so many soldiers had already deserted from other armies, throughout the regiment's history only two faced general courts martial for crimes other than desertion. In 1809 Private Bernard Durcurzel was sentenced to death for theft from an officer and desertion 'towards the enemy'. He was reprieved and sent off to serve in the Royal African Corps. In 1813 Corporal Francis Oddo was tried for stealing two mules from officers and selling them to Spanish civilians. He was acquitted on one count but found guilty on the other, and was sentenced to lose his two stripes and get 500 of another sort.

Most of the Chasseurs disappear from history after their discharge from the regiment, but Lewis Foghell, a musician born in Palermo, immediately enlisted into the 40th Foot and fought at Waterloo. After a stint in the 66th Foot he slipped into that green-coated refuge of foreigners, the 60th Rifles, being promoted sergeant in 1835 and taking his discharge in 1842 – far from the Piazza Pretoria. His long service in the British army underlines an important point. At a time when notions of nationality were less rigid than they became as the nineteenth century wore on, there were many soldiers who served their paymaster loyally, whoever he happened to be. Corporal James

Aldenrath of the 24th Foot died in March 1804, having served the Dutch, French, and Austrian monarchs before completing more than twenty-eight years service in the British army.[16] Before 1789 most European armies maintained foreign corps of one sort or another, and Napoleon's army was indeed multinational. Napoleon's Polish lancers gained undying glory in a desperate charge at Somosierra in 1808 and a crueller reputation for finishing off British wounded at Albuhera in 1811. He also had some 35,000 Germans from the Confederation of the Rhine serving in almost every corner of the Iberian peninsula apart from Andalucia.[17] There were inevitably family tragedies: one German soldier in British service found 'mine own broder' amongst the enemy dead.

In 1812–13 the British, hard pressed to sustain units in the Peninsula at workable strength, actually recruited a small number of Spaniards directly into British regiments. Recruits swore a modified version of the usual oath of attestation – they were bound to serve only 'during the existing war in the Peninsula' – and regiments were authorised to take on up to a hundred men apiece. Recruits were not to be under 5ft 6ins tall, 'strongly made', and 19–27 years old. They were to be allowed 'to attend divine service according to the tenets of the Roman Catholic religion', and to receive normal pay and allowances, though no bounty.[18] Harry Smith of the 95th had a high opinion of the Spanish soldiers in his regiment. Many became 'the most daring sharpshooters of our corps', and 'I never saw better, more orderly, perfectly sober soldiers in my life, and as vedettes the old German Hussars did not exceed them.'[19] Ned Costello thought them 'generally brave', adding that Rifleman Blanco was 'one of the most skilful and daring skirmishers we had in the battalion'. But a French foraging party had murdered his father and brother, and he responded by 'mercilessly stabbing and mangling' wounded Frenchmen until a comrade knocked him down with the butt of his rifle. When the Spanish contingent was discharged in May 1814 there was regret on both sides, and 'even Blanco, the sanguinary Blanco, actually shed tears.'[20]

More homogeneous than the Chasseurs Britanniques but sharing some of their polyglot characteristics was the Brunswick Oels Corps. In 1806 Charles William Ferdinand, Duke of Brunswick, was mortally wounded commanding the Prussian army in its catastrophic defeat at

Jena–Auerstadt, and his duchy was incorporated in the new kingdom of Westphalia, ruled by Napoleon's brother Jerôme. When the fifth coalition against the French was formed in 1809 the new duke, Frederick William, mortgaged his little principality of Oels to raise a 'free corps' of 2,300 horse and foot. The corps wore black uniforms with a white metal skull and crossbones badge – arguably in mourning for Charles William Ferdinand – and was known as the *Schwarze Schar* (Black Horde) in German and the Black Brunswickers in English. Frederick William briefly regained control of Brunswick in 1809 but soon found himself in exile in England. His corps, its infantry component now called the Brunswick Oels Jaeger and the cavalry the Brunswick Oels Hussars, came under British command, and the jaegers arrived in Portugal in 1811. Like the Chasseurs Britanniques they were compelled to take recruits as they found them, and their German component was soon diluted by the addition of prisoners of war and deserters from across Europe. Some of the jaegers served as light companies in Wellington's 4th and 5th Divisions, while the remainder were grouped together in the 7th Division.

The Brunswickers fought in most of the major battles in the Peninsula, and although they were looked on with the same suspicion as the Chasseurs Britanniques their desertion rate was never quite as high. Sergeant Edward Costello of the 95th Rifles thought them good soldiers, but lamented that they were 'gifted with a canine appetite that induced them to kill and eat all the dogs they could get hold of'. The 95th had a pet dog named Rifle that rather enjoyed battles, barking at passing cannon-balls, but eventually it fell victim to 'the insatiable jaws of the Brunswickers'.[21]

Frederick William was able to reclaim his duchy in 1813, and he placed his corps under allied command when Napoleon escaped from Elba in 1815. On the eve of Waterloo it numbered 5,376 infantry, 912 cavalry, and 16 guns. Wellington grouped it with Thomas Picton's 5th Division and Lowry Cole's 6th, in his own reserve. On 16 June Napoleon attacked the Prussians at Ligny and sent Marshal Ney to deal with Wellington at Quatre Bras. Thanks largely to the 'intelligent disobedience' of an allied staff officer, Ney's first attack was checked, and Wellington was just able to shuffle enough troops into position astride this crucial crossroads to win the day. When the Brunswickers arrived, about mid-afternoon, Wellington sent their infantry forward to support his own, and Brunswick led his hussars in a charge against the advancing French. As his horsemen swirled back, Brunswick rallied them south of the crossroads, but was hit by a stray musket ball and died within minutes. When Wellington deployed his army on the Waterloo position he put the Brunswickers to his right rear, but as the long and terrible day of 18 June wore on, he sent them forward piecemeal to buttress his line.

Some Brunswick battalions were visibly shaky. Captain Cavalié Mercer, commanding a troop of horse artillery in Wellingon's right centre, thought that the battalions on either side of his guns were 'perfect children' and so decided not to pull back when the French cavalry prepared to charge. The steadiness of his own men gave him confidence, and: 'The Brunswickers partook of this feeling, and with their squares much reduced in size – well closed, stood firmly, with arms at the recover, and eyes fixed on us, ready to commence their fire with our first discharge.'[22] As darkness fell, the Brunswick cavalry, with their own scores to settle, joined the Prussian cavalry in its pursuit of the French. At Quatre Bras and Waterloo the Brunswickers lost 1,556 officers and men, 27 per cent of their strength, a proportion that put them narrowly behind the 31 per cent casualties sustained by British troops and the 28 per cent suffered by that other idiosyncratic organisation, the King's German Legion.

The death's head was not new in German military iconography, for it had been used by Prussian hussars from the 1740s. In 1914, though, little Brunswick supplied the 92nd Infantry Regiment, the 17th Hussars and an artillery battery to the Imperial army. The infantry's spiked helmet bore an eagle with outstretched wings, had the Brunswick death's head and the battle honour 'Peninsula' superimposed upon it: the hussar busby's honours included both Peninsula and Waterloo. The ironies of former friendship ran deeper still. When the British army went to war in 1914, three of its infantry regiments – the Essex, Devonshires, and Northamptons – bore a representation of the castle of Gibraltar on their cap-badges. The Suffolks went even further by adding Gibraltar's motto, 'Montis Insignia Calpe'. There were to be times when they found themselves facing Hanoverian soldiers of the 73rd and 79th Infantry Regiments and the 10th *Jäger* battalion, all of whom wore a 'Gibraltar' band around their right cuffs, commemorating their service, under British command, in the Great Siege of the 1770s. From 1714 to 1837 British monarchs were also electors of Hanover, so there was good reason for British and Hanoverian soldiers to fight side by side on so many battlefields of the eighteenth century.

In July 1803 the Convention of the Elbe surrendered the electorate of Hanover to Napoleon. The treaty was never ratified by George III and so many Hanoverians, who might otherwise have been prohibited from taking up arms against France, felt justified in fleeing to Britain. Major Johann Friedrich von der Decken of the 60th Foot was ordered to raise a corps of light infantry called the King's German Regiment, with a lieutenant colonelcy as his reward for success. Major Colin Halkett, then in the Dutch service, was to raise a unit styled the Foreign Levies.

The royal proclamation authorising the raising of the King's Germans was circulated in Hanover and, despite French occupation of the electorate, large numbers of recruits travelled to Britain by way of Denmark. That December von der Decken's and Halkett's commands were reconstituted into an all-arms force known as the King's German Legion. The Germans were initially based in the Foreign Depot at Lymington, but the infantry soon moved on to Hilsea Barracks in Portsmouth. They then moved to Bexhill on Sea, which remained the KGL's depot for the rest of its existence, though the cavalry was often stationed at Weymouth in Dorset, one of George III's favourite spots for royal visits. The KGL eventually included two regiments of dragoons, both converted into light dragoons in 1812; three of hussars; two light battalions, both dressed and equipped as Rifles; and eight battalions of line infantry. The King's German Artillery comprised two Horse and three Foot batteries, and there was a small all-officer engineer detachment. The KGL peaked at 14,000 in 1813, but over its lifetime perhaps 28,000 men served in its ranks.

The KGL was qualitatively different from other foreign units raised during the period. Its combat record was consistently first-rate. It took part in an expedition to Hanover in 1805-6, and served in Pomerania, at Copenhagen and on Walcheren. The KGL not only fought in Sir John Moore's Corunna campaign, but in most of the major actions of the Peninsular War. Its hussars helped redeem a difficult battle at El Bodon on 25 September 1811, and Hanoverian hussars bore it as a battle honour until 1918. On 23 July the following year – the day after

Wellington's great victory at Salamanca – Major General George von Bocks' brigade, 1st and 2nd KGL Dragoons, came round a shoulder of high ground above Garcia Hernandez at a cracking pace to find the infantry of the French rearguard forming up in squares on rough terrain above the village. The leading squadron commander saw that if he carried on as ordered he would be exposed to heavy fire from a flank, and decided to charge the nearest infantry without delay. Two companies of the French 6th Light Infantry, bravely buying time for their comrades to get into square, held their fire till the last moment. German casualties of 54 killed and 62 wounded were attributed to the 'deadly effect of musketry at the closest possible quarters'. A horse was brought down right onto the French, and Captain von Uslar Gleichen, one of the troop leaders, immediately forced his way into the gap it made: troopers spurred in after him, laying about with their sabres. The first of the 6th's proper squares, shaken by the sight, gave way almost at once, and a second followed suit. Around 1,600 French prisoners were taken, amongst them Colonel Molard of the 6th Light Infantry. Count Maximilien Foy, the defeated French commander, thought it 'the boldest charge of cavalry in the whole war'.

Edward Costello of the 95th Rifles saw some of the French wounded from the action, shockingly cut about. 'The escort consisted chiefly of the Germans that had taken them prisoners,' he wrote, 'and it was pleasing to behold these gallant fellows, in the true spirit of glory, paying the greatest attention to the wants of the wounded.'[23] British officers reckoned that German cavalry was so good because of the quality of its horsemastership. The KGL trooper, thought Lieutenant George Gleig of the 85th Foot, 'dreams not, under any circumstances, of attending to his own comfort till after he has provided for the comfort of his steed.'[24] Captain Mercer agreed, saying that while the German trooper 'would sell everything to feed his horse', his British comrade 'would sell his horse for spirits, or for the means of obtaining them'.[25]

Although the KGL was in the early stages of disbandment when the campaign of the Hundred Days began in 1815, it fought at Waterloo, where the defence of the farm complex of La Haie Sainte by Major Guy Baring's 2nd Light Battalion KGL was one of the most remarkable exploits of the entire day. The buildings, alongside the main Brussels road, stood like the cutwater of a bridge dividing the French torrent. Baring, reinforced as that long day ground on, by elements of other KGL units, steadily repulsed repeated attacks. But his men's Baker rifles used ammunition not readily available, and although Baring repeatedly asked for more, none ever arrived. 'He would be a scoundrel that deserted you, so long as his head is on his shoulders', a twice-wounded rifleman assured him. Eventually ammunition ran out, but even then the Germans would not give up, hurling bricks and tiles at the French and fighting with butt and bayonet when their enemies came within reach. Eventually Baring's battalion lost 16 officers and 132 men who were killed, wounded, or captured – from an original total of 33 and 398; a loss rate of 47 per cent.[26]

The brothers Charles and Victor von Alten, who anglicised when they wore King George's scarlet, were ex-Hanoverian officers who had served in the KGL from the outset, and both became major generals in British service. Wellington described the former as 'the best of the Hanoverians', though he had a very literal – some maintained Germanic – cast of mind. He commanded the Light Division in the Peninsula after Robert Craufurd was killed in the great breach at Ciudad Rodrigo, and then led the 3rd Division at Waterloo, where he was severely wounded. Fighting under him that day was Major General Sir Colin Halkett, promoted to command 2nd Light Battalion KGL in 1803 and a brigade commander in the Peninsula. At Waterloo, Halkett had already been hit twice when he was shot in the face by a ball that broke his teeth and palate, which took three years to heal. The Altens went back to Hanover at the war's end. Charles became minister of war and foreign affairs and was made a field-marshal. Colin Halkett stayed on in Britain. He was lieutenant governor of Jersey from 1821 to 1830, and served as governor of the Royal Hospital Chelsea from 1849 until his death in 1856.

Most KGL officers were upper- or middle-class Hanoverians who would have held commissions in the elector's service. There were also several military dynasties, with fourteen von der Deckens, ten each of von Dürings and von Brandis, nine von Linsingens, and Guy Baring's nephew Lewis served as an ensign at La Haye Sainte. When Colonel Friedrich Wihelm von Ompteda, commanding one of Charles Alten's brigades, was ordered by the inexperienced Prince of Orange to launch an immediate counter-attack on the farm, he agreed to carry out what he rightly knew to be a suicide mission, but he asked Colonel von Linsingen 'try and save my two nephews' who were serving in his old battalion.

The original warrant for the raising of the King's Germans had specified that no French, Spanish, Italians or British were to be recruited. Although this might have applied to soldiers it certainly did not limit the appointment of officers. By 1815 there were 689 KGL officers with German-sounding names, 81 apparently British, 31 French, and 7 Italian. There are cases when a name gives little real clue as to origin. What are we to make of Ensign F. von Robertson, killed at Waterloo? Lieutenant Thomas Cary was certainly British, though Ensign George Frank was Hanoverian. And then there is Ole Lindam, who had joined the Legion as an NCO in 1810, was commissioned, went on to become a brevet major, and retired to Devon.

Most British officers appointed to the KGL were, like their country-men commissioned into the Chasseurs Britanniques, given free ensigncies. Edmund Wheatley, a Hammersmith man of modest means, was gazetted without purchase to 5th Line Battalion KGL, commanded by Colonel Ompteda, in 1813. Ensign Llewellyn was his only real friend in his battalion, but he soon came to admire the men he commanded. Although they spent so much of their time 'cooking, smoking, eating and drinking', they also

> bear excessive fatigues wonderfully well, and a German will march over six leagues [eighteen miles] while an Englishman pants and expires before a labour of twelve miles; but before the enemy a German moves on silent but mechanically, while an Englishman is all sarcasm, laughter and indifference.

German officers 'do not hesitate to accompany a reproof with a blow', but Wheatley could not 'imagine any man so dejected in situation as to patiently bear corporal chastisement'. The first time he came under fire, hearing the 'hissing and plaintive whistling' of roundshot about his ears, he jumped back 'against a tall Polack who, good natured and smiling, pushed me back saying, "Don't flinch, Ensign".' Captain Lucas Bacmeister, his company commander, at once demanded

'Vall, Veatley, how you like dat?'

'Bad for the kidneys,' I said.

That very moment another volley came and cut a fellow to pieces
before my face.

At Waterloo, Wheatley saw Ompteda receive the fatal order from the
Prince of Orange:

Colonel Ompteda ordered us instantly into line to charge, with a
strong injunction to 'walk' forward until he gave the word. When
within sixty yards he cried 'charge'; we ran forward huzzaing … I
ran by Colonel Ompteda who cried out 'That's right, Wheatley'.

Captain Charles Berger watched Ompteda ride up to the French line,
and although its soldiers aimed at him, the officers courteously used
their swords to push up the mens' muskets so as to prevent them from
shooting. But when Ompteda jumped his horse over the garden
hedge and Berger 'clearly saw his sword strikes smite the shakos off'
chivalry had run its course. He watched the colonel 'sink from his
horse and vanish'. A concussed Wheatley regained consciousness to
see him lying flat on his back, hatless, and open-mouthed, with a
bullet-hole in his forehead. When the KGL was disbanded after the
war, with most of its officers and men returning to Hanover, Wheatley
had no option but to go onto half-pay. He duly married Eliza Brookes,
who had never been far from his mind. The couple had four daughters before Wheatley died at Trèves in 1841.[27]

By September 1813 the British army included some 54,000 foreigners, nearly one in five of its strength. In the post-Waterloo rundown,
foreign units were disbanded first but British-recruited regiments
followed suit, so when the army faced its next major challenge, the
Crimean War, it was predictably short of soldiers. It fell back on the
customary expedient of recruiting foreigners, and in 1855 began to
raise the British German, British Swiss, and British Italian Legions.
The German Legion, some 10,000 strong, had four regiments, with a
little over 1,000 men apiece, stationed on the Bosphorus when the
war ended, and the Swiss Legion, which raised just over 3,000 men,
had a brigade at Smyrna. The Italians recruited over 3,500 men but,
having been formed six months after the other two legions, never

reached the theatre of war. As soon as the war was over the government was anxious to dispose of the legions as quickly as possible. Retaining them for garrison duties was politically unpopular, and the East India Company, which already included European regiments on its military establishment, declined to have them. There were also difficulties over repatriation: some governments were reluctant to re-admit men who had sworn allegiance to a foreign power.

Eventually many legionaries were settled in the colonies, and 2,362 officers and men of the German Legion accepted an offer of land in what was then called 'British Kaffaria', on the borders of Cape Colony. Baron Richard von Stutterheim, a professional soldier with a weakness for gambling, had already served in the British Legion in the Carlist War in Spain, having left Germany after killing a brother officer in a duel. He accepted command of the British German Legion, as a major general, in 1855, and agreed to command it in the Cape. Those of his men with families were allowed to take them. They were liable to serve 'as military settlers' for seven years, had to carry out a limited amount of military training, and were paid (at reduced rates) for three years. Every man received a plot of land, with allocations based on rank. The experiment was not a success. Stutterheim lasted six months before going back to Germany, citing family obligations as his reason for departure: bankrupted by gambling debts, he eventually shot himself in 1872.

Few of Stutterheim's men were farmers by profession, and although more families from Germany were imported in an effort to reduce their disaffection, there were frequent desertions. When the outbreak of the Indian Mutiny offered a fresh opportunity for military service almost half the settlers went to India and served in the East India Company's army. The 1858 Government of India Act transferred the company's European establishment to the Crown, and a few of them became regular soldiers in the British army. The government had learnt little by its experience. When it was considering the size of the British garrison of post-Mutiny India, there were 'several bizarre and barren proposals, that Maoris, Malays, "Tartars", Italians, Arabs or Albanians would be recruited as mercenaries'.[28] The Crimean legions have disappeared almost as if they had never been. In the cemetery at Alexandria, now part of Johannesberg, lies William Henry Gibbon, born at Acklington Park, Northumberland in 1832 and educated at the English school at Heidelberg. He joined the Austrian army as an ensign in 1848, fought with distinction against the Piedmontese at the battles of Custozza and Novara, was promoted captain and decorated. He became a captain in the German Legion in 1855, settled in the Cape, and styled himself 'late Captain, German Legion' for the rest of his life, dying in 1894. Although Baron von Stutterheim did not remain in South Africa for long, the town of Stutterheim in the Eastern Cape was named for him, and still proudly recalls its connection.

At the time of the second Boer War of 1899–1902, the army was again faced with the need to expand quickly. It buttressed its ranks, not by traditional foreign enlistment, but by the use of British volunteers like the City Imperial Volunteers and the Imperial Yeomanry and, no less to the point, by accepting contingents from Australia, Canada, and New Zealand, as well as pro-British South Africans. Although colonial units were valued because they could 'shoot and ride', not all their soldiers conformed to the classic image of the sturdy frontiersman, and officers were often poorly trained. Nevertheless, without the 83,000 men from the colonies who served as part of a total British force of 448,435, it is difficult to see how the army could have coped. Colonial contingents were integrated within the British chain of command, and despite occasional friction over minutiae of dress and behaviour, or muttering about 'colonial scally-wag corps', the experience of the war helped reinforce the image of sturdy offspring coming to the mother country's aid in her hour of need.

There was already an early warning of trouble to come. In February 1902, when peace negotiations were under way, two Australians, Lieutenants Harry 'Breaker' Morant and Peter Handcock of the Bushveldt Carbineers, were shot by firing squad after being convicted of murdering Boer prisoners. The issue is not whether the prisoners had been shot, for both men admitted this, but whether the court martial was properly conducted and whether the policy of taking no prisoners had actually been approved by Lord Kitchener, the commander-in-chief. In 2002 an Australian group travelled to the men's graves in South Africa, emphasising that no Australian soldiers should ever be left to a foreign power for justice. What was a source of disgrace for Australia in 1901 has come to reflect a growing conviction that dominion troops serving under British command were not mere auxiliaries, but soldiers of an independent nation with its own distinct identity.

The issue is too complex to be dealt with in detail here, but the major lines of departure are clear enough. During the First World War both the Australian and Canadian corps in France, contained, by common consent, some of the very best troops in the allied armies. They started off being commanded by British officers, but ended under the command of native-born officers. Dominion governments made it clear that controversial military issues were to be referred to them, and the Australians resolutely refused to execute soldiers for military offences. By the Second World War the process had accelerated still further. When General Sir Claude Auchinleck, Commander-in-Chief Middle East, ordered Lieutenant General Sir Leslie Morshead of 9th Australian Division to break up his division into brigade groups and send one to the front immediately, there was an unedifying spat. Not for nothing was Morshead, a schoolmaster by profession, known as 'Ming the Merciless'.

AUCHINLECK: I want that brigade right away.

MORSHEAD: You can't have that brigade.

AUCHINLECK: Why?

MORSHEAD: Because they are going to fight as a formation with the rest of the division.

AUCHINLECK: Not if I give you orders?

MORSHEAD: Give me the orders and you'll see.[29]

On 11 November 2004, New Zealand became the last of the dominions to bury an unknown warrior in home soil, selecting the body from the windy Caterpillar Valley Cemetery on the Somme, making the point that the soldier resting alone with his glory in Westminster Abbey could no longer represent the rest of the Empire.

The First World War did not simply present the British army with an unprecedented demand for fighting men, but with an unyielding requirement for the labour associated with industrialised war. A Military Works Corps had been formed for service in the Crimea, but it did not enjoy a good reputation and soon disappeared. Much local labour had been used in the Boer War, and Mohandas Gandhi, the conflict's most famous stretcher-bearer, came from the Indian community in Natal. During the First World War labour came from a variety of sources. Some infantry battalions were converted into pioneers, retaining their small arms and their regimental identity. For example, the Oldham Pals (24/Manchester) was raised, albeit with some difficulty, in and around Oldham. Of the first 625 men to enlist about a third came from the cotton industry, with a sprinkling of labourers, some from the textile mills, but as many from the building trade. There was a handful of skilled men – joiners, plumbers, and painters – and rather more clerks, insurance agents, and shop assistants, 8 per cent of the whole. There were fewer foundry workers than might have been expected (9 per cent) and just 5 miners, possibly reflecting the fact that they had signed on in other regiments, while 27 recruits came from the local tram company.

Oldham had already provided two Territorial battalions and, like so many New Army units, the Oldham Pals were desperately short of trained men. RSM Arnold Gartside, a 25-year-old fruiterer from the Mumps area of Oldham, had never served before, but had a brother who was a regular warrant officer; this may have helped him get promoted. The RQMS, Frank Entwistle, had been parcels superintendent at the post office. Senior NCOs were promoted for qualities noticed by their officers in the first days of the battalion's existence. They would need a mixture of 'tact and coercion', for their men were 'volunteers and many … would have been active trade unionists, used to disputing with those in authority.'[30] The Oldham Pals began as a standard infantry battalion, and soon had their introduction to the trenches, losing a subaltern (a nephew of the borough coroner), the RSM, a company sergeant major and three privates to a single trench-mortar bomb on their first tour of trench duty. In early 1916 the Oldhams were told that they were to become a pioneer battalion, carrying out such tasks as trench-digging and road-making as the pioneer battalion of 7th Division. The Oldhams served in France and then accompanied the division to northern Italy, and were there when the war ended.

Pioneer battalions like the Oldhams were the thin end of the wedge. Amongst the perspiring order of battle of army workers came Army Service Corps labour companies; infantry labour battalions recruited from amongst the medically downgraded; the Entrenching

Battalions; and eventually the Labour Corps itself, which numbered 395,000 officers and men in December 1918. It was in the recruitment of foreign labour that the army reverted to type. There were Canadian forestry battalions; African, Chinese, Egyptian, Fijian, Indian, Macedonian, Maltese, and Serbian Labour Corps; and a sprinkling of idiosyncratic units like the Mauritius Labour Battalion, the Zion Mule Corps, and Russian labour battalions. In addition, German prisoners of war were formed into labour companies – there were 372 in France, with an establishment of 400 men apiece, by the Armistice. Some units contained properly enlisted soldiers, others comprised indentured labourers on a variety of terms of service.

The Chinese Labour Corps, with nearly 96,000 labourers in France at the time of the Armistice, was the largest. Around 2,000 of its members died of sickness (Spanish Flu was a real killer), were killed by shelling or died of wounds. They lie buried beneath Commonwealth War Graves Commission headstones, each of which bears the labourer's name and one of four set proverbs. The cemetery at Noyelles sur Mer, the little town that housed the Chinese base depot, contains 838 Chinese graves. What was, to Chinese, an insistence on the terms of their contracts, was sometimes construed by their British officers and NCOs as 'mutiny', and there were a number of incidents where labourers were shot at. In December 1917 armed guards fired on members of 21 Company Chinese Labour Corps, killing four and wounding nine. Gambling was rife amongst the Chinese, and fifteen were sentenced to death for murder during a robbery or an argument over money. At the other extreme First Class Ganger Liu Dien Chen of 108 Company was recommended for the Military Medal in March 1918. He had been in charge of a party of 60 coolies at a goods yard, and repeatedly led them back to work during German shelling. Although it was decided that Chinese were not eligible for MMs, Liu Dien Chen was eventually awarded the Meritorious Service Medal, one of five given to Chinese labourers.[31]

Labour units, uniformed or contract, all disappeared after the First World War, though not before 68 Company Labour Corps had produced the textbook procedures for the grim but necessary task of finding and exhuming the remains of men strewn about the battlefields. In 1939 the demand for a disciplined military labour force re-emerged, and the Auxiliary Military Pioneer Corps was formed, its title stemming from the fact that a revival of the term Labour Corps would have political implications. The corps soon had a striking cap-badge of crossed shovel and rifle and the more resonant name Pioneer Corps (later Royal Pioneer Corps), surviving until its amalgamation into the Royal Logistic Corps in 1993. During the Second World War over 10,000 'enemy aliens', most of them Jewish refugees from Italy or Germany, served with the corps. From 1942 they were allowed to enlist in the combat arms, and amongst these men was the future Sir Ken Adam, the Berlin-born Klaus Hugo Adam, who served in the Pioneer corps before becoming an RAF pilot.

Few careers were, however, more poignant than that of Herbert Sulzbach, born into a wealthy Jewish family in Frankfurt-on-Main in 1894 and commissioned into the kaiser's artillery during the First World War, winning the Iron Cross first and second class. He fled abroad in 1937, just two years after the appearance of his memoirs that were eventually published in English as *With the German Guns: Fifty Months on the Western Front 1914–1918*. When war broke out in 1939 Sulzbach and his wife were interned, like many other aliens, on the Isle of Man. He volunteered for service in the Pioneer Corps, and spent three years building defences against German attack until he transferred to the interpreters' pool and was posted to a prisoner-of-war camp at Comrie in Scotland. On 11 November 1945 he persuaded most of the 4,000 men in the camp to turn out for a ceremony of remembrance, and they stood to attention on the freezing football field as the 'Last Post' was sounded. Sulzbach received a British commission, and had British decorations to add to his First World War Iron Crosses.

The contemporary army still recruits foreigners; given its history it would be surprising if it did not do so. Most noticeable are the Gurkhas, retained as part of the British army after the partition of India in 1947. Successive restructurings have reduced them to 3,760, mainly constituting the two-battalion-strong Royal Gurkha Rifles. Recruiting Gurkhas has many attractions. Not only are they fine natural soldiers, with a formidable record of service to the Crown, but they have always proved easy to recruit at times when British-born soldiers might be hard to come by. Moreover, Gurhkas could be used for tasks that might fit uncomfortably into the army's pattern of postings. One of the Royal Gurkha Rifles' battalions is permanently based in Brunei.

Successive governments have profited from the fact that Gurkhas received neither pensions on the scale awarded to British soldiers nor right of abode in the United Kingdom once they had completed their service. In 2009 the actress Joanna Lumley, whose father served with the Gurkhas during the Second World War, was instrumental in forcing changes of policy that substantially improve the Gurkhas' lot.

In addition to the Gurkhas, there were over 6,600 soldiers from forty-two countries serving in the British army in 2010, constituting almost 7 per cent of its strength. The largest contingent, over 2,000 strong, hails from Fiji; Jamaica and Grenada produce over 600 each. Lance Corporal Johnson Beharry, at the time of writing the only serving holder of the VC, was born in Grenada in 1977. He came to Britain in 1999 and enlisted into the army in 2001. On the London Underground he spotted an advertisement in a discarded newspaper: 'Recruits don't have to be British to apply; Foreign and Commonwealth applicants will be selected on their merits.' He was sent away the first time he went to the recruiting office because the sergeant on duty spotted his marijuana leaf ear-stud, asked him if he smoked, and urged him not to return until 'you … get yourself sorted out, stop smoking that shit … and get yourself fit …'. When he reappeared the sergeant introduced him to a Grenadian who was already serving, and Beharry decided to join the same unit, the Princess of Wales's Royal Regiment: 'If it's good enough for you it's good enough for me.' Cutting off his dreadlocks was a visible sign of departure. 'Now I *know* you're joining the fuckin' army,' said his cousin Gavin.[32] He earned his VC while driving a Warrior armoured vehicle in the Iraqi town of Al Amarah in 2004, saving the lives of his comrades in spite of personal injury and under intense direct attack. The Warrior's gunner was the Jamaican Private Troy McNeill Samuels, who always called Beharry Paki.

CHAPTER 16

WOMEN SOLDIERS

As we shall see in the stories of enterprising women that follow, no eighteenth- or early nineteenth-century army could have survived without women. Apart from bearing and rearing their children, washing and cooking, they helped carry and care for the sick and wounded at a time when nursing had neither the rudiments of respectability nor more than the thinnest veer of professionalism. Some women even went to war dressed as men, because it was only by looking male that they could go undetected and survive in a man's world. In the haunting folk song 'Polly Oliver', the heroine decided to 'list for a soldier and follow my love,' using 'my dead brother's clothes' as disguise. She was duly enlisted and was at her drill when her sergeant asked: 'Now who's good for nursing? Our captain, he's ill.' She cured him, and married him to return home to what nature always intended her to be, a nice young lady with a martial cut to her rig.

The story of Kit Davis ('Mother Ross') is more complex. She was a Dublin woman, born in 1667 to a father who had been killed fighting for James II at Aughrim. She inherited her aunt's pub, married Richard Welsh, one of the waiters, had two children and was pregnant with another when, in 1691, he disappeared. It transpired that he had joined the army under circumstances that remain unclear, and she left her children with her mother, disguised herself as a man and enlisted. Wounded in 1694 while serving in the infantry as Christopher Welch, she was exchanged by the French, discharged after a duel, and then re-enlisted in the Scots Greys. It was to take her thirteen years to find her husband. Although the marriage was decidedly unconventional, she seems to have been genuinely upset when he was killed at Malplaquet. By this time she had lived with male comrades in camp and field, using 'a silver tube with leather straps' to enable her to pass water standing, and it was only a breast wound at Ramillies that broke her secret. Her CO, Lord John Hay, interrogated her bedmate (for soldiers slept two or more to a bed at a time) and was wholly persuaded of her innocence. She became a sutler, selling general necessities like beer and baccy within the regiment and was buried in the Royal Hospital at Chelsea in 1739. Hers is a more complex tale than that of Polly Oliver. She was initially looking for her husband, but soon discovered that she enjoyed being a soldier, and soldiered on long after she could have become a civilian.

Hannah Snell, born in Worcester in 1723, married a Dutch seaman James Summs, and although he deserted her when he discovered that she was pregnant, after the death of their infant daughter she determined to track him down. She maintained that she served in Guise's Regiment of Foot in 1746 during the Jacobite rising, and received 500 lashes without her gender being discovered, but this part of the tale may well by apocryphal. It is certain that she enlisted in Fraser's Regiment of Marines at Portsmouth, and sailed for the East Indies with Admiral Boscawen's fleet. She was wounded several times in the fighting on the Coromandel Coast of India, and on one occasion a native woman helped her treat a groin wound. She then became a sailor, at first nicknamed 'Molly' because her face was so smooth, and later, after her good-natured ways had made her popular with her fellow sailors, 'Hearty Jemmy'. While at Lisbon on the fleet's return to Britain she heard that her husband had been executed for murder in Genoa, and when her man-o'-war paid off at Gravesend in 1750 she resumed her female identity. Hannah made much of her military service, appearing in London theatres in uniform, running through her drill-movements, and singing ballads. The Duke of Cumberland agreed that she should become an out-pensioner of Chelsea Hospital, and for a time she ran a Wapping pub called The Female Warrior. She married twice more, bearing two sons; lived in Berkshire and the Midlands; and eventually settled with one of her sons in Stoke Newington. Afflicted by mental illness, she died in Bedlam Hospital in 1792, and was buried at the Royal Hospital.

James Miranda Barry was appointed assistant surgeon in 1813 and eventually rose to become inspector of the Army Medical Department, dying in 1858 after lengthy colonial service and, allegedly, fighting a duel. It was only after she had died that it transpired that she was actually a woman, and had borne a child. It would have been much easier to conceal her gender than it was for Kit Davis or Hannah Snell, for her officer status offered more privacy. It would have been impossible to practise as a military doctor had it been known she was a woman. Perhaps the adoption of gender was the price she had pay to live on the terms that she chose.

It took another half-century for women to serve as soldiers in their own right. After the Boer War, the First Aid Nursing Yeomanry was developed to help well-to-do women provide nursing support. The FANY was not strictly speaking part of the 'armed forces of the Crown'; Its most junior officer rank was 'ensign', and in the Second World War when members of FANY served in the Special Operations Executive (SOE), appointing a woman an ensign gave her better protection if captured – as so many were. When war broke out in 1914, FANY women got to France quickly, helped by the fact that they were actually unofficial. The army concluded, however, that it did not require up-market young ladies driving generals or whizzing about as dispatch riders. It wanted women to work in a variety of jobs so as to free up fit men for front-line service. Not that those thus liberated were always delighted at the prospect of going to the front: one assistant forewoman, working in Aldershot, recalled 'some hostility from the men we were releasing'.[1] The army was not quite sure that it wanted women to be soldiers and was worried about the impact of thousands of young working-class women upon the brittle morality of young officers. But it did want them. In France 1917 Helen Gwynn-Vaughan, a former head of department at Birkbeck College, London, was appointed to command the Women's Auxiliary Army Corps (WAAC) in France. Her chief in England, Miss Watson, emphasised that all women appointed 'officials' – the term officer was not yet used – should have done regular work of some kind: there were to be no Lady Bountifuls. Ranks and their badges were always a difficulty – should they look like 'real' officers' badges, or not? On 9 April 1918 the corps' title changed to Queen Mary's Auxiliary Army Corps. This was welcomed by many women who had felt 'the WAAF and WRNS had put us in the shade – the WAAF had a much smarter uniform, and the WRNS were the senior service'.[2]

Gwynn-Vaughan's sister was commissioned, and 'we were carelessly formal in our official behaviour ... with "Yes, Ma'am" and "No, Ma'am"'. She insisted on the rule that all women should be able carry their own baggage. All grades should be referred to by their rank, and the most junior – 'workers' – by their surname. There were untold difficulties for women who had joined in the hope of being snappily turned out in smart boots and Sam Brownes, only to discover that their uniforms were utilitarian and most of their jobs seemed anything but war-winning. And there was no escaping deep-seated sexism. When Marjorie Mullins went to Devonshire House for her army medical in early 1917 she reported that 'The doctor mentioned my lovely legs, commenting on the dreadful condition of those of some of the volunteers.'[3] The Hon Dorothy Pickford arrived in France as a WAAC official in January 1918, and in late March was deeply worried by the progress of the German offensive:

> It has been a grisly week but today things seem a bit better. Hard work has been our salvation, and that is why you have so few letters, by the time we have knocked off at supper my brain has been too utterly addled to string two words together. I was doing inventory all Good Friday, yesterday was ration returns and more nominal rolls, and today we were hard at work all morning and again this evening ...

However, she had time to tell her sister:

> Your new dress sounds absolutely 'it'. I wonder if I shall yearn for clothes or be bored to tears with them, but it will be such years before I wear anything but khaki that it's not much good thinking of them. I raised a new collar and tie for Easter day and feel quite 'Knutty', but my stockings are pale green and my shirts are becoming a peculiar pink, and Grace has lost my very best new silk handkerchief which I lent her.[4]

Sex was generally less of a problem than had been feared, possibly because it was made a court-martial offence for a male officer to speak, unchaperoned, to a female worker. Assistant Forewoman Mullins recalled two girls being sent back from France for going out with male officers to whom they were not related. Out of a total of 230,240 women who served, less than 200 became pregnant. Helen Gwynn-Vaughan recalled:

> Our first baby in May, 1918, came ... as a bit of a surprise. Worker X had been on duty with a comrade all morning. When they broke off for elevenses she did not return and was discovered in her bed with a baby.[5]

Women who were found to be pregnant or who gave birth were discharged from the corps. Worker Olive Taylor, who 'had always wished to be a boy ... I really wanted to be a soldier', admitted that when she lived in a hutted camp at Aldershot

> There were trenches all around the huts and we quickly learnt the geography of all three. They were excellent hiding places and some of the more daring girls would take a chance and meet boy friends there. We who remained in the huts at night kept watch for them and when an officer made a spot check to see if any girl was missing, we would say that she had gone to the toilet and one of us would nip out quickly with a warning signal. The officer always came round again after a ten minute interval and of course every girl was present.

Girls were not allowed to speak to soldiers within three miles of camp: 'This was a very serious offence, and repetition of it could get a girl dismissed the service ...'

Worker Taylor was irritated to discover that men of the Irish Guards at Pirbright

> would even threaten to throw us into the Brookwood Canal if they couldn't have their way with us and they seemed to have only one thought in mind. What did it matter to them if a girl lost her character and ended up in the workhouse with a baby?[6]

By 1918 nocturnal air raids on British base areas in France and Belgium were frequent, and WAAC accommodation was sometimes hit; nine women were killed in this way. Worker Dalgliesh remembered the fine example shown by her officers during one air raid:

> For a time pandemonium reigned, shells bursting, shrapnel falling and the rattle and roar of the bombs contributed to the noise or not, but we kept our spirits up by attributing most of it to our own guns. Through it all our lady officers walked up and down, looking in at intervals, talking and advising without betraying the slightest anxiety. It was impossible to feel anything but stimulated by their demeanour, a feeling amounting almost to absolute trust, and whatever our individual feelings might be one and all seemed determined to show themselves not unworthy of the example the officers set.[7]

Despite the solid progress made during the war, there were no wholehearted attempts to take the scheme forward into peacetime, and it was not until 1938 that a rough equivalent, the Auxiliary Territorial Service (ATS), was set up as a part-time corps. This subsumed the other women's military organisation which then existed, including the FANY – which soon re-established its independence. Helen Gwynn-Vaughan was the director of the ATS in the rank of chief controller, equating to that of major general. Although the army was still sensitive about officer grades (a system of parallel ranks made an ATS second subaltern equate to second lieutenant, and a chief commander to a lieutenant colonel) non-commissioned ranks eventually went all the way from private to warrant officer. At first, members of the ATS were classified into five trade groups: cook, clerk, orderly, storewoman, and driver – though more soon followed, with telephonists becoming increasingly important.

The adjutant general was very clear that women were auxiliaries and not soldiers. 'Once we take the step of enlisting women for army service,' he wrote in July 1940, 'there will no longer be any bar to the employment of women for definitely combat duties. Apart from the Russians, no civilised power has yet resorted to the practice.'[8] Nevertheless, in April the following year, members of the ATS were made fully subject to military law. They were obliged to salute all officers, not just their own, and badges of rank at last became the same as those for servicemen. However, they received only two-thirds the pay of a male soldier of the same rank. At the beginning of the war the ATS was maintained by voluntary enlistment, and had 65,000 members by September 1941. In December that year the National Service Act authorised the call-up of unmarried women aged between 20 and 30, and its application was later widened to include married women, though those with young children were exempt.

General Sir Frederick Pile, head of Anti-Aircraft Command, had long argued that women could carry out many of the duties initially performed by men in the heavy anti-aircraft batteries that had become such an important feature of the war. As long as the disciplinary structure of the ATS was different from that of the army, however, it was effectively impossible to establish mixed units. One senior ATS officer warned that 'women might smash valuable equipment in a fit of boredom'. Another observed 'Care should be taken that restriction of privileges should involve punishment. For instance, stoppage of smoking should only be given to smokers and extra knitting to a proficient knitter is no punishment.'[9] However, in May 1941, a month after the ATS had become subject to military law, the formation of mixed anti-aircraft batteries was authorised. The government stressed that women could not actually fire the guns, for they were 'life givers not life takers'. Instead, they spotted and identified incoming aircraft, operated height- and range-finding equipment, worked the predictors that enabled shells to be fused so as to burst among the stream of incoming aircraft, and operated and repaired radars.

Marjorie Inkster, then an ATS private, remembered that working as a radar technician on an all-male gun site was

> most trying for us girls because the battery commander was such an old woman ... He obviously hated the idea of two women on his site and made life as difficult as possible for us. There were no 'ladies' loos and although some simple precautions could have meant this was no problem, he made it one. He would not have the girls sleeping anywhere in the quarters, although there was a medical sickbay: so we were told we had to sleep in the radar transmitter ... It was all right while the Lister generator was still running, but after it was turned off for the night it was beastly cold.

She was commissioned after attending 'a thoroughly boring' OCTU at Windsor, and was anxious to 'be involved in the gun sites in retaliation for what the German bombers had done to my home'. After attending a radar maintenance officers' course she ran the REME detachment responsible for the repair and maintenance of radars on six north London gun sites. This time

> I found at Easy 22 [Hampstead] a very friendly and helpful Royal Artillery battery. There was a Battery Commander in his 40s (ex-London Scottish), a splendid character with just the right mixture of informality and discipline. There was a Junior Commander (female equivalent of a captain) who was in charge of all the ATS personnel on the sites, including two or three ATS officers of the mixed battery … By the time I arrived in site the ATS officers were taking their turn as Gun Position Officers.[10]

Milly Le Vesconte came from a big family in Manchester's Moss Side, 'eldest of 10, often misused and abused', and volunteered in early 1942 'to do my bit towards the war'. She completed her basic training at Oswestry.

> There we trained and marched, learned to take orders, be smart and don't complain. After six weeks we were piped out. How I loved that feeling – it was wonderful to be marching behind Scotsmen in all their paraphernalia, kilts and pipes. Super. I shall never forget that wonderful feeling.

She eventually found herself with 577 (Mixed) Heavy Anti-Aircraft Battery in Kent.

> One night I was on fire picket duty walking round the camp … I heard a strange noise and looked up in the sky and saw a long trail of light. I immediately reported this – no one knew what it was – so the message was sent to HQ. It was the first ever doodle bug.
>
> Sometimes it was very cold standing at our posts in the Command Post, especially if the alarm went in the early hours of the morning. We had to remain on duty until the 'All Clear' was sounded. When this happened the duty cooks had to go to the cookhouse and make

hot sweet cocoa for us when the air raid was over. Nothing ever tasted so nice or was so welcome after perhaps a couple of hours shivering during the early morning winter. Often we would not be long in our beds before the alarm would go again.[11]

Lance Corporal Doreen Goodman, serving in a mixed battery near Portsmouth, remembered that

In times of heavy enemy air activity we could conceivably be in the command post for many hours straight – but regular shifts plus taking post when action bells sounded. On one such occasion I actually fell down asleep when running between the guns to the command post. My partner dragged me up to complete the trip. I was always a very heavy sleeper, so when we went to new camps my 'friends' insisted that I take the bed right under the action bells – and even then they would often have to drag me out of bed, throw my clothes over my pyjamas and push me out of the door when the bells sounded …[12]

In mid-1942 ATS personnel were posted to searchlight units, and in October that year 93rd Searchlight Regiment Royal Artillery was formed, with more than 1,500 women and less than 200 men. Some searchlight troops in isolated locations were allocated a single 'token man' to start the cumbersome Lister generator, but there were ATS girls who could muster the required upper body strength to swing the beast into life, and who were known as 'Lister twisters'. Anti-Aircraft Command at its height had a strength of 350,000 with 76,000 provided by the ATS. Women wore the ATS cap-badge, but had white gunner lanyards on their right shoulders and wore the Royal Artillery grenade badge above the left breast pocket. The success of mixed batteries went a long way towards establishing women's ability to carry out complex tasks in dangerous situations, and 335 members of the ATS were killed during the war. Most actually carried out more traditional tasks: Staff Sergeant Susan Hibbert typed the English version of the German surrender document at Rheims in May 1945.

The ATS became the Women's Royal Army Corps (WRAC) in 1949, partly because it was felt that adding 'Royal' to ATS would produce an unfortunate abbreviation. Not that WRAC was necessarily a more comfortable designation, for pronouncing it as 'wrac' caused its members much irritation. Women were 'badged' WRAC, but grew increasingly close to the corps with whom they spent most of their time. The issue of the carriage of arms was a lively one, with the WRAC hierarchy generally reluctant to see women armed, though accepting that there would be circumstances in which they might need to defend themselves. Brigadier Eileen Nolan, the corps' director from 1973 to 1977, was responsible for moving the WRAC forward to be recognised as a combatant but non-belligerent corps. It was as a result of her initiatives that the WRAC's officer-training college moved from Camberley to amalgamate with Sandhurst. In 1982, women were permitted to carry arms – initially the 9mm Browning pistol, rapidly followed by the Sterling sub-machine gun – for personal defence.

In 1992 the WRAC ceased to exist, with its serving members being transferred into the appropriate corps – one of the reasons why the Adjutant General's Corps was nicknamed All Girls Corps. Many officers and soldiers felt that they would be competing with men on a very uneven playing field and, while the WRAC had its own brigadier, it took seven years for another woman to reach that rank. But there is now no doubt that women are combatant soldiers, and they carry arms at the Sovereign's Parade at Sandhurst, passing-out parades in training regiments, and, of course, on operations.

Women served alongside men in mixed units long before the disappearance of the WRAC, and inevitably both sexes took advantage of the relaxed climate in some units. One contributor to the Army Rumour Service remembered that

> the 68 Squadron R[oyal] C[orps] of T[ransport] lines were like a knocking shop, in particular block 14 … (More shacked up couples in block 14 than the married quarters). As the block NCO for block 14 I had to ensure each Thursday morning that the 'ladies' were removed to their own accommodation prior to the block inspection. I remember one morning WO1 (RSM) Carl King**h RCT carrying out the block inspection and all was going well until he opened the door to the drying room/kitchen and found one of the 68 Squadron girls dressed only in a very short dressing gown collecting all her dry bits and bobs from the tumble dryer. When questioned by Carl she said that block 14 had a more relaxed regime

than the 68 Squadron blocks and she didn't think anyone would mind and her boy friend who lived in the block at the time allowed her to visit his room any time she wanted and she had been in earlier and hoovered his bunk floor, etc. etc.

Another agreed: '68 Sqn accom 1987 ... brilliant. I copped off with a WRAC and on the Sat morning went for a shower and was joined by another WRAC who chatted as she showered.'[13]

The spread of women across the army did not produce unparalleled lechery on exercises or operations. I commanded a unit with a small WRAC detachment and although there were undoubtedly romances, the rustling in the bushes was never audible. I imagined that I knew precisely what was going on, but when one of the company sergeant majors announced his engagement to a WRAC private (who resigned instantly) I was wholly surprised, though I admired his judgement. The army's *Values and Standards* pamphlet makes it clear that 'social misbehaviour' can include 'displays of affection which might cause offence to others' as well as more obvious things like 'taking sexual advantage of a subordinate'. When judging the impact of such behaviour, commanders are directed to apply 'The Service Test'. This asks 'Have the actions or behaviour of an individual adversely impacted or are they likely to impact on the efficiency or operational effectiveness of the Army?'[14] Few would object to a sexual relationship between equals, although publicly sustaining such a relationship on operations might, because of the jealousy it could arouse, fail the service test. Similarly, a relationship (be it heterosexual or homosexual) between say, commissioned and non-commissioned personnel could easily fail the same test because of perceptions of unfairness that it might arouse.

In my experience male soldiers behave differently when women are around. They swear less, boast less and (sometimes but not always) drink less too. Two female medical orderlies, one a soldier and the other from the Royal Navy, have now won the MC for courage in treating wounded men in combat. It is probably too early for the British army to put women into the collective close-combat group where dynamics are so complex, but using women to support battle or employing female 'singletons' as fighter pilots does not raise the same concerns. I cannot say what Captain Plume might make of it all. He would probably prefer 'to raise recruits the matrimonial way', but I think that he would be wrong. Women have now proved that they can fight: they may not need to do so always, but fight they can.

IV

TRIBES AND TOTEMS

CHAPTER 17

THE REGIMENTAL LINE

T HE ARMY IS still regimental, three hundred and fifty years after its birth. Officers and soldiers join a regiment or corps and most of them remain in it for the whole of their careers. Its off-duty iconography, as distinctive as the plumage of tropical birds, has become less common as the proportion of the population with army service shrinks. But it is still visible, from a striped tie here to lapel badge there, and on to the beret-and-blazer ensemble that has now become a route-marker along the road from RAF Lyneham, whence the bodies of repatriated personnel begin their journey to Oxford. These markings are sharply defined and jealously guarded. The Household Division tie, its broad navy blue and magenta stripes symbolising the royal family's blue blood and the red blood shed on its behalf by the Guards, is worn by Foot Guards so that the upper half of the knot shows blue, and by the Household Cavalry in the reverse order.

Where else in the world would there be a website debate about the right of individuals to wear a particular tie? Happily the 1966 England World Cup footballer Jack Charlton (Coldstream Guards, National Service) the comedian Tommy Cooper (Royal Horse Guards in the Second World War), the cricket commentator Brian Johnston (who earned an MC with the Grenadiers), the photographer Patrick Lichfield (a Grenadier officer, 1959–62), the jazz musician Humphrey Lyttelton (who landed at Salerno with the Grenadiers, pistol in one hand and trumpet in the other), and newsreader Kenneth Kendall (Normandy with the Coldstream) all properly pass muster as legitimate wearers of this most iconic piece of silk.

The army of Charles II followed the pattern of the armies, royalist and Parliamentarian, that had fought in the Civil War. Regiments of horse and foot were named for their proprietary colonels, or 'regimental colonels' as I often call them in these pages. These gentlemen might have obtained regimental command in a number of ways. There was 'raising for rank', usually at the beginning of a war, when a colonelcy was given to an individual or city corporation that undertook to raise a regiment according to specified arrangements. Successful senior officers might hope for colonelcies as a reward for their work to date and, all things being equal, could move steadily up the *Army List*, towards 'older' and more distinguished corps as they went. It was once possible for an officer's political attitude to lose him his colonelcy: in 1710 Marlborough's supporters major generals Meredith, Macartney, and Honeywood were dismissed for drinking damnation to the new ministry. A colonelcy stood to make a man a reasonable income, largely by pocketing the difference between the government grants received for various regimental expenses and the money actually spent, but Wellington maintained, rather frostily, that his colonelcies had never been much use to him.

But throughout this process the government took great care to ensure that colonels were up to the job. There was no point in lavishing its patronage on incompetents, or in giving boobies influence, cascading down through their own regiments, that they could promptly misapply. Of course there were officers, with the full blast of patronage behind them, who scudded along merrily. Lord George Lennox, second son of the Duke of Gordon, got his first full colonelcy at the age of 24 in 1762. Most colonels were serious and experienced folk. The age at which a man might expect to be promoted depended on the size of the army. Of the 293 colonels appointed between 1714 and 1763 more than half had served for a quarter of a century before attaining colonelcies, and none had served for less than fourteen years. Nor was the post a sinecure. One colonel, warned by an inspecting team that his regiment was in an appalling state, agreed that he must take instruction from a sergeant major.

Naming regiments after their colonels – a common practice in continental armies – remained the practice in Britain until 1751, when numbers replaced names, partly because a rapid turnover of colonels could cause confusion. In 1702 Peter Drake was in the Duke of Marlborough's Regiment of Foot, which 'had been commanded by the Marquis [de Puisan], who in coming from Ireland to join his regiment was lost at sea: upon which it became General Seymour's, and soon after Lord Marlborough's; so that in less than five months we had three colonels'.[1] A regiment's seniority, stemming from the date of its raising, had always been clear, with 'older' units less likely to be disbanded on the outbreak of peace and therefore giving safer billets for the career-conscious. Many historians understandably simplify the business by giving regiments numbers from the outset, but contemporaries were forced to remember that my Lord Tintinhull had been succeeded in his colonelcy by Sir George Baskingshark, on whose unexpected demise the regiment had gone to the Earl of Bosham, who now seemed to have developed a worrying cough.

A few regiments, early in their lives, adopted a name that set them apart from their fellows. In at least one case this reflected the danger of misunderstanding. The 3rd Foot had worn coats of stiff buff leather when in Dutch service in Queen Elizabeth's time, and on joining the British army had ochre-coloured facings and unwhitened buff leather equipment. The regiment styled itself the Buffs early on in its history, and when, in 1743, George II saw a regiment with buff facings marching briskly onto the field of Dettingen he called out 'Bravo! Bravo Buffs!' An aide helpfully pointed out that this was actually Lord Henry Beauclerk's Regiment (31st Foot) that also wore buff facings, and the King at once corrected his mistake, now crying 'Bravo, Young Buffs!' Thenceforth the 3rd styled itself Old Buffs to avoid confusion, and the 31st was nicknamed the Young Buffs. The following year the Buffs, whose colonel was then Lieutenant General Thomas Howard, were fighting alongside the Hon Sir Charles Howard's Regiment (19th Foot) so that there were actually two Howard's Regiments in the field. Each regiment unofficially defined itself by its facing colour, with the latter becoming the Green Howards and the former Howard's Buffs.

The Earl of Dumbarton's Regiment was soon termed the Royal Scots, and when the English and Scots armies were amalgamated with the Act of Union in 1707 it was indisputably the First of Foot, the British army's senior line infantry regiment. The 2nd Foot, formed in 1661 to garrison Tangier, quickly took to styling itself the Queen's Royal Regiment, and the 1st Royal Dragoons, formed the same year, were the Royals from the very start. In 1685 – the year of Sedgemoor – George Legge, Lord Dartmouth, formed a regiment based on two companies of the Tower of London Guard. It was originally designated the Ordnance Regiment, and was intended to guard the Tower-based train of artillery when it took the field. At this time infantry carried the matchlock musket, whose power-charge was ignited by a length of burning cord. This was an obvious hazard if there were barrels of gunpowder about, and so the Ordnance Regiment was issued with fusils, an early form of flintlock musket, whose charge was fired by the spark produced when flint struck steel. Regardless of its colonel's name this new regiment was soon known as the Royal Fusiliers.

The fusilier title rapidly became honorific: the 23rd Foot emerged as the Welsh Regiment of Fusiliers in 1702 and, after distinguished performance under Marlborough, the Royal Welsh Fusiliers in 1712. It eventually took to styling itself Royal Welch Fusilier. The archaic spelling of its name was officially approved in 1920 but had been used within the regiment for very much longer. The 21st Foot became the Royal Scots Fusiliers in the 1680s; the 87th, raised in 1793, became the Royal Irish Fusiliers in 1827; and the 5th Foot became the Northumberland Fusiliers in 1836. Other fusilier titles appeared with the 1881 amalgamations: the 20th became the Lancashire Fusiliers; the 27th (Innsikilling) was united with 108th Madras Infantry to emerge as the Royal Inniskilling Fusiliers. The integration of four more of the former East India Company's European battalions into the British army saw the creation of two more Irish fusilier regiments: the Royal Munster Fusiliers, formed from two regiments of Bengal fusiliers; and the Royal Dublin Fusiliers, formed from a Madras and a Bombay regiment. All these regiments were trained and equipped as line infantry, though they enjoyed dress distinctions – notably a fusilier cap, a fur or fabric cap often confused with a similar item worn by grenadiers – that set them apart from other regiments.

Just as the name fusiliers originated in a technical specialism, so the development of light troops, horse, and foot, saw title changes. We have already seen how green-clad rifle regiments, first the 60th and then the 95th, sprang up in response to the demands of North America and the development of Swiss-German expertise within the

army. There were always suspicions, on the part of more convention-
ally minded officers, that issuing men with rifles, encouraging individual initiative, and putting them in green 'jack-a-dandy' uniforms,
would see them – as Wellington put it acidly, 'running about like
lamplighters'.

The foundation of light infantry was a half-way house, with regiments retaining the red coats of the line but emphasising skirmishing
skills. Though they still carried the infantry musket, it had the helpful
addition of a backsight. The 43rd and 52nd Foot became light infantry when they were brigaded with the 95th Rifles at Shorncliffe in
1803 to form the Light Brigade that was to expand into the Light
Division in the Peninsula. The 68th and the 85th became light infantry in 1808; the 51st and the 71st in 1809; and the 13th in 1822.

These reclassifications as light infantry reflected a regiment's reputation and influence. For instance, the 51st had fought well in the
Spanish Corunna campaign and Sir John Moore, doyen of light
troops, had been a previous commanding officer. When the colonel
of the regiment, Lieutenant General Morshead, asked that 'in the
event of any addition being made to the number of light battalions,
the 51st might be included in that number,' the adjutant general told
him that the king 'approved of the 51st Regiment being immediately
formed into a Light Infantry Corps in all respects upon the same plan
as the 43rd, 52nd, 68th, 71st, and 85th Regiments'.[2] The one remaining conversion to light infantry, however, reflected exceptionally
distinguished conduct in the field. In 1857 the 32nd Foot was in
garrison in Lucknow, and was to be knocked about in the badly
handled Battle of Chinhat. They lost the battle, newly married
Lieutenant Colonel William Case ('as fine an officer as ever stepped')
and about a third of his men. As the little force fell back on Lucknow,
one of the 32nd's privates, hit in the leg, told his mates not to bother
with him. 'I shan't last long,' he said, 'and I would never be able to
reach Lucknow.' He loaded and fired steadily, one man against an
army, until he was overwhelmed. The 32nd lost 11 officers and 364
men killed and another 11 officers and 198 men wounded at Chinhat
and in the subsequent siege of the Residency at Lucknow, one of the
epic deeds that helped avert the collapse of British fortunes in India.
In May 1858 the regiment was informed that

Her Majesty, in consideration of the enduring gallantry displayed in the defence of Lucknow, has been pleased to direct that the 32nd regiment be clothed, equipped and trained as a Light Infantry Regiment from the 26th February last.

Her Majesty has also been pleased to command that the word 'Lucknow' shall be borne upon the Regimental Colour in commemoration of the enduring fortitude displayed in the defence of the Residency for 87 days.[3]

The most recent example of a tactical function naming a regiment came in 1942. In June 1940 Winston Churchill, impressed by the achievements of German parachutists, demanded the raising of 'a corps of at least 5,000 parachute troops', and so the Parachute Regiment came into being on 1 August 1942. Not all new wartime structures survived peace. Back in October 1915 the Machine Gun Corps had been raised to ensure the better handling of medium machine guns; previously these had been issued on a scale of two per infantry battalion or cavalry regiment. By the end of the war the Corps comprised over 6,000 officers and 118,300 men, but it was disbanded in 1922 and machine guns reverted to being a regimental asset. Part of the Corps' problem was that it had no network of influential supporters who might have spoken on its behalf, and so it perished unlamented when retrenchment was at hand. It is best remembered today by Francis Derwent Wood's nude statue, *The Boy David* – too close to the homoerotic for some tastes – at Hyde Park Corner, commemorating the Corps' 13,791 killed.

In contrast, after 1945 the Parachute Regiment had well-placed friends. 'Every man an Emperor', proclaimed Field Marshal Montgomery, one of the dominant figures in the postwar army and colonel of the regiment from 1944 to 1956. Its battlefield performance in North Africa, Sicily, Normandy and the Rhine was distinguished, with Arnhem becoming a classic example of a heroic failure whose lustre did much to obscure errors in the operation's planning and execution. The Parachute Regiment survived post-war reductions, although for some years it had no permanent officer corps of its own. Like the modern SAS it took officers temporarily posted into its battalions from outside. Its position in the infantry's formal hierarchy (midway between the Royal Irish Regiment and the Royal Gurkha

Rifles) reflects its seniority in the line, but not its place in public affection. Ironically, it may very well be that large-scale parachuting into battle – the core skill around which the Second World War regiment was formed – no longer has much validity today. However, the regiment draws much of its *esprit de corps*, and at least a modicum of its fine combat performance, from a selection and training process that emphasises common challenges for all ranks. It provides a palpable sense of unity between past and present.

Just as the infantry defined some of its regiments by titles that reflected royal or regional connections, or the development of a particular skill – from skirmishing to parachuting – so the cavalry too, soon became less homogeneous. The regiments of horse that fought under Marlborough were cavalry proper. They carried a pair of pistols and a carbine, but saw mounted action – coming on sword in hand at a pretty round trot – as their real raison d'être. Dragoons, in contrast, began as mounted infantry, their name (indistinguishable from the word for dragon in French) probably deriving from the 'fire-breathing' musket they carried. In 1625 the musket was described as 'a short piece with a barrel sixteen inches long of full musket bore, fitted with a snaphaunce or firelock'. Their horses were smaller (and thus cheaper) than those of conventional horse regiments, and their NCOs and men were paid less. In 1746 Britain began to convert her eight regiments of horse into dragoons to save money. To save their self-respect though, they were given the title 'dragoon guards' to make the downgrading less uncomfortable. Thus the King's Own Regiment of Horse became the 1st King's Dragoon Guards; the Princess of Wales's Own Regiment of Horse converted to the 2nd Queen's Dragoon Guards; and the 4th Regiment of Horse ended up as the 3rd Dragoon Guards; and so on until, in 1788, the 4th Irish Horse at last became the 7th (Princess Royal's) Dragoon Guards.

Dragoon guards had nothing whatever to do with guarding the monarch, and the title's introduction was no more than a sop to regimental pride. Dragoon guards were given precedence over other mounted units and their numbering was separate. Household troops, naturally enough, stood icily aloof from all this. In 1748, just after the conversion process had begun, there were three regiments of dragoon guards, four of horse – now a threatened species – and fourteen of dragoons. The same pressure that encouraged the infantry to look afresh at speed and mobility affected the cavalry too. This process began with the formation of a light troop in each regiment. The first full regiment of light dragoons, the 15th, was raised in 1759, wearing sombre blue uniforms as opposed to the red traditionally worn by horse and dragoons. Other light dragoon regiments quickly followed, including the 18th and 19th Light Dragoons. The wars of the second half of the eighteenth century suggested that light dragoons were more useful than their heavy cousins, and in 1776 the 8th and 14th dragoons were converted, with the 7th, 9th, 10th, 11th, and 13th following suit in 1783. Higher-numbered light dragoon regiments were raised subsequently, but, on the 'last in, first out' principle, did not have long lives.

The process did not stop there. British light dragoons combined new tactics with dressing down. This had some parallels elsewhere, for example in the French army where the *chasseurs à cheval* were clad in what their enemies would have called rifle-green. The overwhelming trend was to dress light cavalrymen up, not to dull them down. The hussar, originally modelled on the light horseman of the great plain of Hungary, quickly became the *beau idéal*. The British, ever sensitive to the demands of military fashion, changed the 7th, 10th, and 15th Light Dragoons to hussars in 1806 and converted the 18th the following year. For several years the titles of these new regiments were a mouthful – in 1815 they included the 10th (or Prince of Wales's Own) Royal Regiment of Light Dragoons (Hussars) – and it took some of them a little time to convert from their workmanlike light dragoon garb to the full majesty of hussar kit, with short, braided, jackets, barrelled sashes, slung pelisses, and tasselled Hessian boots.

Just as the idea for hussars had come from Hungary, so too the craze for lancers spread from Eastern Europe. In the mid-eighteenth century Polish lancers in Saxon service had worn a square-topped national cap called the *czapka*; the *chevaux-légers-lanciers* of the French Imperial army, based on the Polish-recruited Lancers of the Vistula, followed suit. As early as 1811, just after the lance had done such damage at Albuhera, some British light dragoons were instructed in the use of the lance. Interestingly, in view of the German contribution to light infantry tactics, the adjutant of the 15th Light Dragoons noted that Cornet Baron Leon, 1st Dragoons KGL, would attend for the purpose of teaching the exercise. In 1816 fifty men of the 9th Light Dragoons were selected to demonstrate the use of the lance to an invited audience, and that September the 9th, 12th, 16th, and 23rd Light Dragoons were converted into lancers. The new regiments wore a 'lance cap' based on the *czapka*, and even today officers and men of the two surviving lancer regiments wear piped 'quarter welts' on their forage caps. Those Lancers of the Vistula cast a long shadow.

By the 1850s the distinctions between heavy cavalry (dragoons and dragoon guards), and light cavalry (hussars and lancers), were no longer practical, but they account for the cavalry division sent to the Crimea constituting two brigades. There was a heavy brigade of red-coated dragoons and dragoon guards with metal helmets, and a light brigade of lancers and hussars, as well as the sole surviving light dragoon regiment (the 4th) still wearing its old-fashioned blue faced with white, to be converted into hussars in 1861. At Balaklava in 1854 there was little real difference in their tactics: both charged shoulder to shoulder in the old style, although the Heavy Brigade taking on Russian cavalry, had a much easier time of it than the Light Brigade, with its long and costly ride for the Russian guns.

The absorption of the East India Company's European regiments after the Mutiny brought the 19th and 20th Hussars and the 21st Lancers into the British army, taking the line cavalry to the twenty-eight regiments it would field in the First World War. To simplify recruiting and training, cavalry was grouped into four corps from 1893 – Household, Dragoons, Hussars, and Lancers. Regiments serving abroad were kept up to strength by transferring soldiers from British-based regiments of the same corps. The cavalry's First World War performance was a good deal more creditable than was once suggested. The British Expeditionary Force could not have held the line at Ypres in 1914 had it not been for the Cavalry Corps, fighting dismounted on Messines Ridge. We also now know that the cavalry's role in trench warfare was by no means insignificant. David Kenyon suggests that cavalry was indeed 'effective in combat at the tactical level', but that it was unable to mint operational currency from this tactical success, largely because of the unrealistic expectations of senior commanders and the communication difficulties that dogged operations on the Western Front.[4] In Palestine and Syria, the cavalry was altogether more successful, involving not just British, but also Australian, New Zealand, and Indian troopers too. Lord Wavell, in his biography of Allenby, writes of the final advance on Damascus:

The greatest exploit in history of horsed cavalry, and possibly their last success on a large scale, had ended within a short distance of the battlefield of Issus (333 BC), where Alexander the Great first showed how battles could be won by bold and well-handled horsemen.[5]

Whatever the cavalry's supporters said, there was evidently too much of it after the war. The first batch of cavalry amalgamations, in 1922, brought together regiments of the same type to create units like the 17th/21st Lancers. Shortly afterwards the cavalry began to convert from horsed to armoured regiments, a process beginning with the 11th Hussars in 1928 and ending with the 2nd Dragoons (Royal Scots Greys) in 1941. There was already a specialist tank unit on the scene. In 1916 the new-fangled tank had been given to the Heavy Branch, Machine Gun Corps, which became the Tank Corps the following year, the Royal Tank Corps in 1923, and then the Royal Tank Regiment in 1939.

When the army raised new armoured regiments in the Second World War it did not simply increase the size of the Royal Tank Regiment, but dug more deeply into its past to discover the 22nd Dragoons, 23rd Hussars, 24th Lancers, 25th Dragoons, and even a short-lived 26th Hussars. Prime Minister Winston Churchill, himself a former 4th Hussar (though at Omdurman in 1898 he had actually charged with the 21st Lancers), was not amused, and in 1941 he told the CGS:

> Surely it was a very odd thing to create these outlandish numbered regiments of Dragoons, Hussars and Lancers, none of which has carbines, swords or lances, when there exist already telescoped up the 18th, 20th and 19th Hussars, 5th and 21st Lancers. Surely all these titles should have been revived before creating these unreal and artificial titles. I wish you would explain to me what was moving in the minds of the War Office when they did this.[6]

In fact the decision was a very sensible one, for 'disamalgamating' the 1922 regiments would have created difficulties, because they would inevitably have been re-amalgamated after the war. For a while some of the amalgamations had worked very well, others had not been comfortable. The union of the 15th and 19th Hussars had begun as an 'amicable arranged marriage', but when, thanks to the influence of Field Marshal Lord Chetwode, it was decided in 1932 to call the regiment '15th The King's Royal Hussars', there was an immediate petition for divorce. Chetwode had assured the king that this was the regiment's wish. In fact it was certainly not the wish of the former officers of the 19th Hussars, and when Chetwode, by then commander-in-chief India, went into the Cavalry Club, its genial members threw things at him just to make the position crystal clear. A petition was sent to the king and a question asked in the House of Commons, after which in 1936 the regiment was redesignated 15th/19th King's Royal Hussars, and soldiered on happily under this name for nearly sixty years.

The new regiments did not survive the war, and it is beyond doubt that any 'disamalgamated' ones would also have perished. Indeed, some that had survived the 1922 unions were culled by new amalgamations in the late 1950s. In 1992–3 a further round of mergers reduced the cavalry of the line to eight regiments: three of dragoon guards; two apiece of lancers and hussars; and the Light Dragoons; an amalgamation of two 1922 hussar regiments (13th/18th and 15th/19th Hussars), whose name is a delightful revival of a time-honoured title. Nicknames reflect regimental recruiting areas – the Queen's Dragoon Guards, with its emphasis on Wales, Shropshire, and Herefordshire, is the 'Welsh Cavalry'; and the Light Dragoons, 'England's Northern Cavalry'.

For all the occasional unhappiness over enforced unions, the cavalry has managed to contract without too much misery, partly because it is swept up within the wider Royal Armoured Corps, which also subsumes the Royal Tank Regiment and the yeomanry regiments of the Territorial Army, and partly because the Council of Cavalry Colonels, an unofficial forum of the colonels of all the regiments, has been able to make common sense prevail. The infantry has been less fortunate. To understand why, we need to consider the most significant of the infantry restructurings, the Cardwell Reforms of 1881. These created the pattern of county regiments that just survived until the first decade of the twenty-first century. When the Cheshire Regiment (the 22nd Foot) was amalgamated into the Mercian Regiment in 2007 it proudly maintained that it was one of only five regiments that had never ever been amalgamated. The four others were the Royal Scots, the Green Howards, the Royal Welch Fusiliers, and the King's Own Scottish Borderers. The Cheshire's own history had begun in 1689, and the Royal Scots in 1660. Whatever the merits of this most recent bout of amalgamations, it represented a major break with the past.

To understand the mechanism of 1881 we need, first of all, to grasp the relationship between battalion and regiment. The regiments raised since 1660 were owned by a regimental colonel, with a lieutenant colonel doing most of the practical work, and a major assisting him. The companies, eight or ten in number, were commanded by captains. It was easy, when expanding the army in time of war, to avoid creating new regiments by simply doubling up the fighting element of existing ones. This meant that instead of consisting of a single battalion – its fighting companies under the lieutenant colonel – it now consisted of two battalions, still with a single regimental colonel, but now with two distinct lieutenant colonels' commands. Sometimes these second battalions broke away from their parent regiments to become regiments in their own right, which is what happened, for example to 2nd Battalion the Buffs when it became the 61st Foot in 1758. More usually, extra battalions disappeared in peacetime, leaving the regiment in being, but reducing its manpower and thus (no surprises here) its cost. To take an extreme example, the 60th emerged from the Napoleonic wars with eight battalions, but by 1819 it was down to two.

In France, Germany or the United States it was the normal practice for battalions of the same regiment to serve together, and for rank structures to reflect this. From Napoleon's time, a French regiment would have been commanded by a colonel. This colonel would be a hardworking officer, not the noble proprietor that we might have expected as regimental colonel under the old regime, and he would have a lieutenant colonel as his second in command. Each of his three battalions would have been commanded by a major; his rank, in the French infantry, the wholly descriptive *chef de bataillon*. In contrast, in the British army it was unusual for different battalions of the same regiment to serve together. But, being the British army, it was not unknown. During the Second World War the Queen's Royal Regiment (West Surrey) uniquely produced two homogeneous brigades, 131 Queen's Brigade containing 1/5th, 1/6th, and 1/7th Queens, and 169 Queen's Brigade with 2/5th, 2/6th, and 2/7th Queens. Both fought in North Africa and Italy, and 131 Brigade went thence to North-West Europe.

On the eve of the Cardwell Reforms the regular army contained 110 line infantry regiments, whose first twenty-five contained two battalions each. All the rest had a single battalion, apart from the King's Royal Rifle Corps and the Rifle Brigade, which had four apiece. Regiments retained the cumbrous county titles they had received in 1782, like '6th or The 1st Warwickshire Regiment'; '20th or The East Devonshire Regiment'; and '77th or The East Middlesex Regiment'. Bennett Cuthbertson thought that regional recruiting made very good sense, for youngsters were 'most desirous of enlisting into a corps, where they are certain of meeting many countrymen, and perhaps relations'.[7] Regiments did not have a permanent foothold in their counties, and took their recruits wherever they could find them, though there were indeed many who were able to establish a solid local recruiting base. In 1782 Lord Cornwallis obtained the title 'West Riding Regiment' for the 33rd Foot, because it 'has always recruited in the West Riding of Yorkshire, and has a very good interest and the general good will of the people in that part of the country'. When John Shaw, a Bradford lad who joined the 33rd in 1777, reached London he met 'a Yorkshireman ... who made it a constant rule to treat all the Yorkshire recruits enlisted for the 33rd Regiment, having himself been an old soldier, and served the King in that regiment formerly in Flanders'.[8]

Although Irishmen were disproportionately represented in the British army of the eighteenth and early nineteenth centuries there were occasional perversities. In 1775 the 27th Foot (Inniskilling) actually had only 175 Irishmen amongst its 374 soldiers – but twenty-five of the thirty officers were Irish. A century later emigration to the United States had replaced enlistment into the British army as the first choice of young Irishmen anxious for a better future, but the infantry, whatever its regional affiliation, still relied heavily on Irish recruits. Forbury Gardens in Reading is home to George Blackall Simonds' sculpture, the Maiwand Lion, commemorating the 11 officers and 318 men of the 66th (Berkshire) Regiment killed in Afghanistan in 1879–80. The names of the dead are on panels around its plinth, and looking at them it is evident that more of the 66th's soldiers hailed from distant Cork than from nearby Caversham.

The Crimean War and the Indian Mutiny had shown how hard it was to suddenly expand the army to meet a crisis. Although the success of the 1860s volunteer movement had suggested that it was possible to persuade middle-class men and artisans to wear their county's uniform, it was evident that they did not want to serve as regulars. Moreover, at any one time a large proportion of the regular army served abroad, especially its infantry. In January 1840 twenty-nine British regiments of foot were stationed in India, constituting about a third of all troops in overseas garrisons and just under a quarter of the infantry as a whole. Thirteen regiments had been there for over fifteen years: the 6th and 49th had been there since 1819 and 1843 respectively. Service in India left its mark on regimental symbolism. Colonel Adlercron's Regiment (39th Foot), with the sickly and unhappy Lieutenant Colonel Samuel Bagshawe in it, was the first British regiment to serve in India. This earned it the motto *Primus in Indis*, which then featured on the cap-badge of the Dorsetshire Regiment, along with the castle of Gibraltar and a sphinx with the battle honour 'Marabout' commemorating its 1801 service in Egypt. The Devons amalgamated with the Dorsets in 1958, and formed a regiment that radiated a quiet, unstuffy competence throughout its too-short life; *Primus in Indis* survived onto the new regimental badge.

Just as a sphinx pays tribute to achievements in Egypt at the turn of the eighteenth century, long service in India is normally marked by the appearance, on a regiment's 'colours and appointments', of the Bengal tiger. The 67th or South Hampshire Regiment was there from 1805 to 1826, and when Cardwell brought it together with the 37th or North Hampshire Regiment the tiger was added to the Hampshire rose to give them their 'cat and cabbage' cap-badge. When the Hampshires were amalgamated with the Queen's in 1992 the tiger became an arm badge, and gave the Princess of Wales's Royal Regiment its nickname, the Tigers. At the time of amalgamation there had been some thought of adopting the original Queen's badge, the paschal lamb, which would have been familiar to Percy Kirke's men in the Tangier garrison, for they had worn it there in the heat and stink. Discussions with the regiment's soldiers, however, made it very clear that a tiger, red in tooth and claw, had merits that a gentle herbivore did not. The charming simplicity of the old Queen's badge might induce members of other regiments to venture on easily misunderstood bleating. The Hampshires' tiger was certainly not unique. Both the Royal Leicesters, tracing their origins to Colonel Solomon Richards' Regiment, raised in 1688, and the York and Lancaster Regiment, dating back to the 1758 65th Foot, bore Bengal tigers on their cap-badges. This was supplemented for the Leicesters by the word 'HINDOOSTAN'. In 1880, even as Cardwell was at work, the 5th Foot was sent off to India. It returned in 1894, now styled the Royal Northumberland Fusiliers, and contained only eleven of those who had made that original journey. Most of the men had returned to Britain when their time with the army expired, and had been replaced by new drafts; 232 had died in India.

Cardwell's infantry was not simply alienated from the counties it pretended to belong to, but was heavily preoccupied with furnishing colonial garrisons and was by no means balanced enough for the sort of conflicts that had recently marked the continent. In contrast, Prussian success in the Franco-Prussian War of 1870–71, demonstrated just how easy it was to generate a large and effective army through conscription and regional organisation which brought conscripts and reservists together in the same framework. In March 1870 Cardwell explained that he proposed 'in time of peace to maintain a force which shall be moderate in amount and susceptible of easy expansion, and the reserve of which shall be so within reach as to be immediately available on the occurrence of any public emergency.'[9]

The process embodied a whole series of reforms, of which the abolition of the purchase of commissions, implemented in 1871, was one of the first. It outlasted Cardwell's time as secretary of state for war (1868–74) and was concluded by Hugh Childers, who held the office from 1880 to 1882. As far as regimental restructuring was concerned, Cardwell began, in 1872–3, by joining the single-battalion regiments into pairs so that they retained their identity but their soldiers could be posted, as required, within the pair so as to reinforce the linked battalions. Next, the country was divided into sixty-six sub-districts, each of them allocated to a two-battalion regiment or a pair of linked battalions. These regular regiments would now have a depot within the sub-district, and a colonel as its commander. This colonel would also be responsible for the local militia and volunteer battalions, who would train alongside regulars and, Cardwell hoped, be more likely to opt for full-time service. This service was intended to be less onerous than it once was, for the Army Enlistment Act of 1870 had reduced the normal period of service from twenty-five years. Now recruits would sign on for twelve years, but would go into the reserve after spending only six years with the colours, and would remain liable to recall for another six years. The pension bill would be reduced because most soldiers would leave when still in their twenties and able to get another job, and the army would at last have the flexibility to meet major crises.

Short service was not an immediate success. The annual requirement for recruits rose from 12,500 to around 28,800 a year, and although recruiting did indeed improve, it did not enable the army to cope with annual wastage, now swollen because desertion increased, thanks to the influx of young soldiers who found it hard to cope with army life. Moreover, the small wars of the 1870s and 1880s – the Ashanti War, the Zulu War, the second Afghan War, and the first Boer War – placed Cardwell's new regimental system under severe pressure; in 1870 there were 59 battalions at home providing drafts for 82 abroad. Calling up the reserve was no answer. However, this was done on a limited scale in 1878 when there was a risk of war with Russia, and also for the invasion of Egypt in 1882. Cardwell made it clear that this would be only done in grave national emergency – something the Zulu War, say, could scarcely be deemed to constitute. Soldiers feared that by overdoing the call-up of reservists the government was simply making them an unattractive prospect for employers.

Many reservists found it heavy going outside and, like Kipling's 'William Parsons, that used to be Edward Clay', soon re-enlisted under an assumed name.

> I done my six years' service. 'Er Majesty sez: 'Good-day –
> You'll please to come when you're rung for, an' 'ere's your 'ole back-pay:
> An' fourpence a day for baccy – an' bloomin' gen'rous too;
> An' now you can make your fortune – the same as your orf'cers do.'

[...]

A man o' four-an'-twenty that 'asn't learned of a trade –
Beside 'Reserve' agin' him – 'e'd better be never made.
I tried my luck for a quarter, an' that was enough for me,
An' I thought of 'Er Majesty's barricks, an' I thought I'd go an'
    see.[10]

Edward Roe, from Castlepollard in County Westmeath, joined the army in 1905. Dead set on the cavalry, he was told that although both the 16th and 5th Lancers were full up, there was happily a vacancy in the 'East Lancers'. He briefly thought it odd that, although a great cavalry aficionado, he had not heard of the regiment. He duly signed on, was sent to Preston to draw his kit, and only then discovered that he was in the East Lancashire Regiment. After serving his time with the colours he was discharged from 2/East Lancashire in March 1914, then stationed in Wynberg, just outside Cape Town, and

> soon regretted leaving the army. Every weekend my mind was in Cape Town, Adderley Street, the Grand Parade, Buitengraft Street, Mick O'Grady's pub of jovial memories, the Ancient Order of Hibernians, the races at Newlands every Saturday, the first class rugby and cricket matches and other forms of amusement, I could visualise Mick Cunningham, 'Spike' West, 'Paddy' Wade, 'Snowy' Parsons and the 'Bullock' Masterson walking down Adderley Street, Yes! They've turned to the left on passing Van Riebeck's statue, they're making for 'Mick' O'Grady's. I can imagine the night they will have.

Instead, he found himself 'on the borders of the Great Bog of Allan', with nobody of any military experience to talk to apart from police-men, of whom he was not fond. He had decided to enlist in the American army (although he knew that he risked arrest as a deserter if he emigrated while still a reservist), but proposed to enjoy the perch-fishing season first. In the event, his mobilisation order arrived on 5 August, and he set of for his regimental depot in Preston.[11]

When Childers came to office in 1880 he first increased Colour service to seven years and reduced reserve service to five, thereby establishing the terms of service that were to take the regular army through to the First World War. He improved pay and prospects, making it easier for NCOs to extend their service to pension. In 1881, he formalised the rank of warrant officer with 'rates of pay ... such as will give adequate remuneration for the very important duties performed'.[12]

As far as regiments were concerned, Childers pushed the system introduced by Cardwell to its logical conclusion. Had he been starting with a clean sheet of paper he might have concluded that a regiment with two regular battalions was actually too small, and that the four-battalion rifle regiments, the 60th and the 95th, actually had the flexibility to keep battalions abroad topped up from those at home. But Cardwell's scheme was now frozen in brick, asphalt, and wrought iron as the redbrick buildings with their great square mock-keeps – like Roussillon Barracks in Chichester, Stoughton Barracks in Guildford, Le Marchant Barracks in Devizes, and Brock Barracks on Reading's Oxford Road – formed the new sub-district depots. In 1881 Childers accordingly converted the linkages of 1872 into regiments with two regular and two militia battalions, and also designated volunteer infantry units within the area as volunteer battalions. The senior twenty-five regiments who had started with two battalions found this relatively straightforward. For instance, the most senior regiment of foot, the Royal Scots, with its depot in Glencorse Barracks, swept up the Edinburgh (or Queen's) Regiment of Militia Light Infantry as its militia battalion along with an assortment of volunteer units which became its volunteer battalions. These volunteers included the City of Edinburgh Rifle Volunteer Brigade and the 1st Linlithgowshire Rifle Volunteer Corps. The Queen's (Royal West Surrey) Regiment, 2nd of Foot and the senior *English* line regiment, based at Stoughton Barracks, took on the 2nd Royal Surrey Militia and four battalions of the Surrey Rifle Volunteer Corps.

The process was more complex elsewhere. There were many apparently natural alliances. The 37th (North Hampshire) and 67th (South Hampshire) came together in Lower Barracks at Winchester to form the Hampshire Regiment. They swept up the Royal Hampshire Militia and five battalions of the Hampshire Rifle Volunteer Corps, including one on the Isle of Wight. Even then, when bidden to the new regiment's first dinner, a furious lieutenant colonel of the 67th, his face no doubt the colour of the table's polished mahogany, declared that 'damned names mean nothing' because 'from time immemorial regiments had been numbered to reflect their status in the line.' He refused 'to come to anything called a *Hampshire* Regimental dinner. My compliments, Sir, and be damned.'[13] Although the 43rd Foot was in theory attached to Montgomeryshire and the 52nd to Oxfordshire, their old Peninsula association made them happy bedfellows in the Oxfordshire Light Infantry, soon to be rechristened the Oxfordshire and Buckinghamshire Light Infantry. Elsewhere, some arranged marriages settled down to happy relationships: the 35th (Royal Sussex) and the 107th (Bengal Infantry) – formerly a regiment of the 'Company's Europeans' – became the Royal Sussex Regiment, while the 39th (Dorsetshire) and the 54th (West Norfolk) materialised as the Devonshire Regiment.

There were some shotgun weddings too. Victorian Britain's enthusiasm for all things Scots had led to the progressive tartanising of the Scottish infantry, first as Lowland regiments (hitherto largely indistinguishable from the rest of the line), with adopted pipers and tartan trews, and then on to pursue the coveted designation Highlanders. When the 74th became Highlanders in 1845 the adjutant general warned its commanding officer that the Duke of Wellington wondered if the change would really work. 'His Grace cannot keep out of view,' he wrote, 'the fact that it is found very difficult to complete the Highland regiments already on the establishment of the army with Highland or even Scottish recruits.' He was cautiously confident, though, that the regiment's 'local influence in Scotland' would enable the 74th to transform itself.[14] In 1881 there were not enough genuine Highlanders to go around. When the 75th (Stirlingshire) Regiment merged with the 92nd (Gordon Highlanders) the latter scooped the pool of kudos and the resultant Gordon Highlanders were glorious in kilt, sporran, and feather bonnet. One Scots officer saw what was now officially 1st Battalion The Gordon Highlanders, in action at Tel-el-Kebir in Egypt in 1882, and admitted, 'the 75th, a good regiment, were handicapped ... by having just been turned into Highlanders. The battalion was full of Englishmen, and was the subject of much merriment.'[15] Unusually, the 79th Cameron Highlanders soldiered on as a single-battalion regiment. They raised a second battalion in 1897 and moved into a new depot, Cameron Barracks, in Inverness.

It is easy enough to point out the anomalies in the Cardwell–Childers regimental system. It affected only the line infantry. The Foot Guards and rifle regiments recruited nationally rather than regionally, and while the latter (with their depot in Peninsula Barracks, Winchester, just up the hill from the Hampshires) had associated militia and volunteers, the Guards did not. Unrest in Ireland meant there were no Irish volunteers, leaving Irish regiments without volunteer battalions. The descendants of the 'gentlemen of the ordnance' – the Royal Artillery and the Royal Engineers – lay outside the system, and recruited men for general service, posting them to units as the needs of the service dictated. Until 1920, the Royal Artillery did distinguish between the Royal Garrison Artillery who manned heavy guns, and the mounted branch, the Royal Field Artillery and the Royal Horse Artillery, who were trained separately. Then there were the Departmental Corps, which had come into being in the nineteenth century as the army's supporting services were militarised. The biggest of them, the Army Ordnance Corps and the Army Service Corps, did not coalesce until 1896 and 1888 respectively. The Army Medical Corps, its physicians and surgeons now holding homogenised military ranks, followed in 1898. All recruited nationwide, although many of their soldiers transferred across from other arms, and trained their recruits centrally.

It is also true that the relationship between counties and their regiments was not straightforward. Large counties like Lancashire and Yorkshire, as well as the teeming capital, had several regiments within their boundaries. Smaller counties were swept up in regiments named for larger ones: Cambridgeshire was regimentally part of Suffolk. The responsible committee had concluded that a community needed an adult male population of 200,000 to sustain two regular battalions and two militia battalions, and counties that fell below this total – like little Dorset, with 95,500 – had to recruit elsewhere such as London. Likewise, the King's Own Scottish Borderers (its district comprising Berwickshire, Dumfriesshire, Selkirkshire, and Roxburghshire) took many Irish recruits who had enlisted in Glasgow.[16] Between 1883 and 1900, just 19 regiments had more than half their recruits born in the regimental area.

The infantry as a whole was usually under-recruited. In order to keep battalions on service abroad up to strength, home battalions often became little more than processing units that trained recruits fresh out of the regimental depot, and then drafted them off overseas. When Fritz Ponsonby, later to become private secretary to Edward VII and George V, joined 2/Duke of Cornwall's Light Infantry in the Citadel at Plymouth in 1888 he found it

> An ideal regiment. It had practically no men. There was an officers' mess, a band, some charming officers, a certain number of excellent NCOs and a sprinkling of old soldiers, but otherwise nothing but recruits. It was what Lord Wolseley described as a 'squeezed lemon'. As soon as a recruit was sufficiently trained, he was packed off to India to feed the other battalion. Of course, I had to spend the first few months doing recruits' drill, but after that I had a wonderful time and was away practically every day merely attending a parade on Saturdays.[17]

The 1881 system formed the basis for the structural changes introduced when R. B. Haldane reformed the army after the Boer War. Most regiments retained two regular battalions, apart from the two rifle regiments, as well as the Royal Fusiliers and the Middlesex Regiment – both recruiting in populous London – which had four. In other cases a regiment's third battalion was now termed the 'Special Reserve' battalion. It was commanded by a regular lieutenant colonel based at the depot, and his soldiers, as we have seen in the case of George Ashurst of the Lancashire Fusiliers, signed on for six months' full-time service. They would have a fortnight's top-up training each year, a liability for call-up when the army was mobilised, and would be posted as required to the regiment's regular battalions. Its Territorial battalions took seniority thereafter, sometimes retaining individual quirks that harked back to their days as volunteer units.

In August 1914 the Hampshires had two regular battalions: the 1st at Colchester, ready to take the field as part of 11th Brigade in 4th Division; and the 2nd sweltering at Mhow in India. The 3rd (Special Reserve) battalion trained its recruits at Winchester, and the six Territorial battalions were scattered around the county. Of these, the 6th Battalion, from beery Portsmouth, was the Duke of Connaught's Own. The cap-badge of the 7th, from the New Forest, depicted a 'dog gauge' – a stirrup-shaped device originally used by the king's foresters to measure the paws of dogs coming into the Forest: those big enough to pull down the monarch's deer would be killed. The 8th Battalion, The Isle of Wight Rifles, Princess Beatrice's Own, perversely wore rifle green and sealskin busbies in full dress and drilled at a rifleman's quickstep. And so, when the Isle of Wight Rifles were formed up to attack on Gallipoli in August 1915, it was Bugle Major Peachey (not the drum major, as he would have been in a line battalion) who sounded the charge. The ensuing battle cost them eight officers and more than 300 men killed or missing. The small town of Newport lost 32 of its boys that day: little Orchard Street alone lost four. The Hampshires had even raised a cyclist battalion, its companies spread out across the regimental area, just before the war. Adolphus 'Dolph' Jupe, then a Romsey Post Office clerk on 18s. a week, thought that it would be a better bet than the nearby 4/Hampshires ('roguish characters'), and so duly joined the 9th Cyclist Battalion.

During the First World War the system proved readily expandable. Wartime-raised 'service' battalions were added to the regiment although, as we saw earlier, these occasionally emphasised local identity by bearing their own insignia, like the four New Army battalions of the King's Liverpools raised by the Earl of Derby. They wore the Earl's 'eagle and child' crest – 'bastard and bustard' – as their capbadge. In 1914 Territorial battalions were duplicated, with each sending a first-line battalion (say 1/4th Hampshires) to the front, while a second-line battalion (2/4th Hampshires) formed up in its place, and even a third-line battalion (3/4th Hampshires). When the war ended, service battalions were quickly disbanded and Territorial battalions demobilised. Dolph Jupe, called up with 9th Hampshires in August 1914, had risen to the rank of sergeant and was with his battalion in Siberia when the war ended. He did not leave Vladivostok till 1 November 1919, and got home to be demobilised over a year after the war had ended.

The Commonwealth War Graves Commission headstones, speckling the Western Front in bone-white rank and file, bear the capbadges of the men lying beneath them. The column after column of names on the memorials to the missing, like those at the Menin Gate, Tyne Cot, and Thiepval, are laid out by regiments, with the names taking stone by seniority as they would have taken ground when forming up on parade. At the top left of each memorial comes 'Commands and Staff': there are two generals on the memorial at Dud Corner at Loos, and the list at the Menin Gate is headed by Brigadier General Charles Fitzclarence VC, nicknamed 'General Officer Commanding Menin Road'. Then comes the Royal Navy, because of the Royal Naval Division's contribution, and then the army – Household Cavalry, Royal Artillery, Cavalry, Royal Engineers, Foot Guards, Infantry, Services, and then units that existed only in the Territorial Force, like the London Regiment. Within the infantry of the line, regiments are listed by their 1881 seniority. The visitor at the Arras Memorial searching (as so many do) for Second Lieutenant Walter Tull of the Middlesex, footballer turned well-regarded platoon commander, needs to remember that his regiment stood fifty-seventh in infantry seniority. 'Die hard, 57th, die hard,' its commanding officer had called across the smoky carnage at Albuhera in 1811, and the Middlesex, nicknamed the Die Hards, duly bore the battle's name on their cap-badge.

A man's number also appears on his headstone, and is added to memorials when needed to differentiate those with the same surname and initials – like Jones J, not uncommon in a Welsh unit. When a signaller in 2/Royal Welch Fusiliers told Private Morgan Jones that he had a premonition of death, he began: 'Look here, '95 …'. And, so Private Jones told Captain Dunn: 'When HQ Company led the way into the line next day one of the first to be killed was '91 Davies.'[18] Until 1920 these were numbers, issued to a man when he enlisted and then changed if he moved, voluntarily or not, to another regiment. The notion of an army number, attached to a soldier throughout his service, came later. Tracing a man's enlistment date through his number is a dark art, but some regiments added an 'S' prefix to those joining service battalions and 'TF' to those signing up for their Territorials. The practice of giving blocks of regimental numbers to particular recruiting offices means that men with adjacent numbers had usually enlisted together. The brothers Privates Ernest and Herbert Philby lie in the same row in Flat Iron Copse Cemetery, in the lee of Mametz Wood on the Somme. Though they died with 1/Middlesex, they both enlisted in 1/8th Middlesex in Ealing, and their regimental numbers, TF5290 and TF5291, tell us that they joined on the same day.

Yet the logic is not infallible. A few miles to the north two French Canadian soldiers in the Royal Fusiliers, Lance Corporal Charles Guy and Private Pierre Jean Destrubé, lie in the same grave in Serre Road Cemetery No 1. The family inscription on its stone tells that they were united in death as they were in life, for their bodies were found arm in arm – but their numbers, K/24 and 1236, suggest separate enlistment. A hint of the complexities of regimental numbering can be seen from the case of William Bedford. In March 1915 he arrived in France as 91613 Corporal Bedford of 19/Yorkshires. In July 1915 he became 573779 Corporal Bedford of the Labour Corps, posted to 151 Prisoner of War Company. He was demobilised in February 1919 but finding life outside hard, re-enlisted for a year that May. Bedford volunteered for exhumation and burial duties, duly receiving the new Labour Corps number 690692 and retained it till he was released due to ill health in November 1919.[19]

This everlasting association of man and regiment veils the fact that the system broke down under war's pressure, and that many a soldier lies beneath a cap-badge he might scarcely have worn. Even in the first heady flush of recruiting some New Army and Territorial battalions could not find enough local men: 9/Devons had only eighty soldiers from Devon, while the remainder came from London and Birmingham; there were 460 kilted Manchester men in 2/4th Seaforth Highlanders. Private Percy Holmes died of natural causes at home, and the seasons roll over his grave outside the church of St Michael and All Angels in the Hampshire village of Cheriton. His graven badge shows that, though he lies many miles from the county boundary, he was in the Dorsets. Initially, the army strove to send men wounded in action back to their own battalions as soon as they were fit, and to post recently trained recruits to the front in drafts commanded by officers of the regiment. But by the middle of 1916 it had little time for such niceties. Both returning wounded and newly arriving drafts destined for the Western Front arrived at Le Havre or Harfleur – Calais and Boulogne were too close to the line to serve as major logistic bases, and were used largely for leave and liaison traffic. They were then sent to the uncomfortable world of base depots centred on Etaples (inevitably Eat-Apples in soldier slang) in the estuary of the River Canche.

Between June 1915 and September 1917 over a million officers and men passed through Etaples on their way to the front, receiving training intended to prepare them for battle. It was delivered to rookies and veterans alike, by staff known from their yellow arm-bands as canaries, most of whom were anxious to remain at Etaples rather than go to the front. The place was extremely unpopular. Trained soldiers were posted up to the front in drafts under officers, but soon they were simply sent where they were needed, without much regard for those well-polished badges they had worn on arrival. I. G. Andrew, who had fought at Loos as a corporal in a New Army battalion of the Cameron Highlanders, was commissioned into the Cameronians (Scottish Rifles) and blew his £50 uniform allowance on a fine khaki doublet and a smart pair of Douglas tartan trews made by the best tailor in Glasgow. After his stint at Etaples he and some fellow Scots were posted to a Staffordshire battalion that had been lacerated on the Somme. They demurred when the colonel ordered them to dress as Englishmen, but agreed to do so when the adjutant asked them politely. Fred Hodges had attended Northampton Grammar School and enthusiastically joined the Northamptons in 1917. But when he arrived in France his draft was lined up and sent to different battalions:

> Friends who stood in line next to one another were parted by a hand and an order, and marched off to different Regimental Base Headquarters. There were bell tents in a long line, where particulars were taken and, to our surprise, new regimental numbers were given to us ...
>
> In this preremptory way, I and about 300 others suddenly became Lancashire Fusiliers, while some of our friends became Manchesters or Duke of Wellington's or East Yorkshires.[20]

He was young and eager, and was well received in 10/Lancashire Fusiliers by Company Sergeant Major Doolan, and was soon delighted to be in a new unit, proudly calling it 'T'owd Tenth' and behaving like a proper Lancashire lad.

Some soldiers coped well enough with rebadging, and simply got on with whatever the army asked them to do, for theirs was an enduring generation. By and large old sweats did not. Sergeant Major Shephard of the Dorsets dreaded the prospect of even changing battalions: 'I am particularly anxious not to get ill, or slightly wounded,' he wrote, 'as nearly all NCOs and men going home now get pushed out to the 5th and 6th Battalions and I want to soldier on with the 1st Battalion.'[21] There is good reason for this. A private soldier may stand at the very bottom of the army's formal hierarchy, but he is not necessarily a man of no consequence. What the army now calls the 'senior Tom' had a status all of his own. He may have lost a stripe or refused to accept one, like Frank Richards of the Royal Welch Fusiliers, doyen of the war's everlasting privates, but he was a known quantity within his company, a useful barometer of opinion, and an invaluable steadier of the young. Sergeant Major Shephard's diary laments the passing of men like 'Pte Hoskins No 6591, a good fellow all round'.[22] Yet all this status is unofficial. Snatched from his habitat the man is another name on a list, a body to be delivered to sergeant majors for fatigues. Some old soldiers found rebadging so painful that they simply deserted and found their way back to their former battalions, quietly trusting (with a confidence that was rarely misplaced) that a decent adjutant would square the system for them. Second Lieutenant G. F. Maclean joined 1/Argyll and Sutherland Highlanders in France in 1915:

> The first man I saw wounded was an old soldier called Black Jock, he was carried off and I never expected to see him again. After a month he arrived back in the company. After a few days a note arrived saying that Black Jock had been posted as a deserter. I spoke to him and after some thought he said, 'Oh! That. They put me in one of those convalescent camps. You never know where they will send you to from there, so I just came back up the line to the battalion.'[23]

Sergeant Major Shephard found rebadging exasperating. In August 1916 his battalion, shot to tatters on the first day of the Somme, was in billets near Béthune:

> In the evening a lot of old hands now attached to 2nd Wilts (who are in billets just over the bridge) came to see us. They are terribly upset on account of having to serve with the Wilts ... and they went to see our Adjt to ask whether they could not come back to their own regiment. Adjt promised to apply for them, but it will be useless. Why the responsible authorities do these things I cannot imagine. If a certain Regt is required to be reinforced quickly and

none of their own available, the matter is explained. But we well know that after our smash on 1 July strong reinforcements were sent for us, and on arrival at the Base they were diverted, some to 2nd Wilts, some to Hampshires, etc. and we received men of the Hampshires for reinforcements instead of our own. And so the merry game goes on. Some big pot is drawing a large salary for such muddling work as this, ruining the one thing which has kept our army going so well, i.e. 'Pride of Regiment'.[24]

Shephard was in no position to know that the army was now very concerned at the local impact of heavy casualties on the civilian population, and had concluded that there was much merit in spreading the burden of loss more widely.

A few of the men shot by firing squad had been recently transferred from regiments in which they had enjoyed good reputations, to one where, friendless and under pressure, they failed. In July 1916 Private James Anderson had been in 8/Loyal North Lancashire for just five days when he told the officer commanding a working party 'I am going out. I can stick it no longer. My nerves have gone.' An officer who knew him might have cajoled, pressed, or even turned a blind eye. This one did not. Had he known the other men on the working party Anderson might have felt inclined to stay with them. But he went back to his billet and was later found there, fast asleep. When court-martialled Anderson asked for two officers from his old battalion, 12/King's Liverpool, to speak on his behalf, but one had been killed and the other wounded. The brigade commander, recommending that the death sentence passed by the court should be confirmed, wrote 'The Commanding Officer has no personal knowledge of this man, but he is of the opinion that the man was so frightened of shell fire that he deliberately preferred to take his chance of the consequences rather than remain under it.' The fact that Anderson had volunteered in 1914 and fought at Loos, had two brothers killed in France and another wounded in Gallipoli, did not incline the authorities towards clemency, and he was duly shot.[25]

One of the more recent First World War memorials, the Irish Peace Park near Messines, was opened on 11 November 1998. Its tall round tower, looking out towards Ploegsteert Wood and the valley of the little Douvre, is made of stone from a British army barracks at

Tipperary and a workhouse near Mullingar. It commemorates all Irishmen who died in the First World War, regardless of political persuasion, and in particular celebrates the three Irish-recruited divisions, 10th Irish, 16th Irish, and 36th Ulster. It is impossible to consider the British army's history without acknowledging the Irishmen who fought in it – either in Irish regiments or in those that were, at least in theory, recruited elsewhere. With the partition of Ireland in 1922 the regiments from the south were disbanded, their colours laid up in a moving ceremony at Windsor Castle, and the Royal Irish Regiment, Royal Dublin Fusiliers, Royal Munster Fusiliers, the Connaught Rangers, the Leinster Regiment, and the South Irish Horse – the latter a Special Reserve cavalry regiment – passed into history. The Royal Irish Rifles were renamed the Royal Ulster Rifles, and the Royal Irish Fusiliers and Royal Inniskilling Fusiliers came together as a single corps with one regular battalion each and a common depot.

After the war the southern Irish regiments went, but the system itself soldiered on with little change, apart from the disappearance of Special Reserve battalions and some renumbering of battalions when the Territorial Force was revived, this time as the Territorial Army. During the First World War the army had found it hard to cross-post territorials without infringing its commitment that they should serve only in their own units. At the beginning of the Second World War it quickly decided that all recruits, regular or Territorial, must enlist for general service without any guarantee of the cap-badge they might eventually wear. The adjutant general, Sir Ronald Adam, would have gone a step further and created a Corps of Infantry to 'allow administrative flexibility and economy of personnel, and permit the simplest arrangements to be made for the distribution of reinforcements'.[26]

The project foundered for two reasons. First, it aroused much military opposition; second, David Margesson, the Conservative secretary of state for war, was not prepared to risk the political explosion he knew would result. Although Adam failed to create a corps of infantry, the establishment in July 1942 of the General Service Corps enabled all recruits to be given basic training and assessment before they were posted onward to their regiments or corps. Their destinations were determined by four criteria: suitability as demonstrated by assessment tests; the requirements of the various arms; their nationality; and only last 'the need for fostering the county, TA and regimental spirit'.[27] This was wholly in accordance with the recommendation of the Committee on Skilled Men in the Services chaired by Sir William Beveridge.

> Men should be enlisted not for this or that Corps, but into the Army as a single Service. On being received, examined and sorted at centres common to the whole Army, they should be posted from those centres to a definite Corps only when it is clear that they fit the requirements of those Corps and that any scarce skill possessed by them will be turned to full account.[28]

The benevolent impact of the new policy was arguably most evident in the case of the Royal Electrical and Mechanical Engineers. Its formation was authorised by a Royal Warrant of 19 May 1942, and it came into being on 1 October that year. By May 1945 the corps was 160,000 strong, and it is hard to overstate its impact on an army proceeding inexorably towards mechanisation. But its reverse effect was scarcely less striking. The infantry found itself at the very bottom of the manpower pile. It was first deprived of recruits with the education or aptitude that would enable them to prosper elsewhere as artificers, mechanics, tank crewmen or clerks. And then it was raided for volunteers for those 'mobs for jobs' like commandos (not confined, as they are now, to the Royal Marines), airborne troops, and other special forces.

Although General Adam was well aware of the problem, he was unable to solve it. In 1943 a War Office observer of the fighting in Sicily reported:

> Every platoon can be analysed as follows: six gutful men who will go anywhere and do anything, twelve 'sheep' who will follow a short distance behind if they are well led, and from four to six ineffective men who have not got what it takes in them ever to be really effective soldiers.[29]

It was inevitably the 'gutful men' that incurred the heaviest casualties. Martin Lindsay's account of the infantry battle in North-West Europe emphasises how the 'lions of the desert' in his own 2/Gordons were progressively killed or wounded, and the battalion's line of advance was charted by the graves of the bravest and the best. The platoon of 4/King's Own Scottish Borderers commanded by Peter White on the Dutch–German border in the winter of 1944–5 included Private Jones 'a really extraordinary chap'. This 'tall, keen-faced' ex-para-trooper was known within the company as 'the one man army,' and he had 'the closest approach to complete immunity from fear or nerves that I had so far met'. The description continued: 'The rest of the Platoon looked on in amazement at the appetite, efficiency and system shown in his soldiering.' Jones was killed by a direct hit on his truck, and it emerged that he was a skilled looter as well as a valiant warrior. White found the ravaged vehicle strewn with 'valuables remi-niscent of a jeweller's shop. Among this collection was Sgt Godfrey's GS watch which had been "lifted" off him when he was killed at Ibbenburen.' The loss of Corporal Parry and Private Byles soon after-wards left 'the very heart and dynamo of the Platoon gone'.[30]

Geoffrey Picot, had commanded a mortar platoon with 1/Hampshires in Normandy, and became an infantry platoon commander with 7/Hampshires after his old battalion was broken up for reinforcements. He was pleased to find that a few of his men

were really tough chaps! One or two were regular soldiers who knew they were in the army to fight and made no bones about it. Some conscripts, too, had plenty of battle fury. The majority would follow a strong lead, whether it came from me, from the NCOs or from their pals. A few would be weak sisters. The rest of us would have to carry them.

(This can be regarded as the normal make-up of most platoons. A few strong toughies influenced a lot of others. The formation of airborne forces and commandos took a great many toughies away from the infantry of the line, who were thereby seriously weakened. It must have been judged by the War Office that what a handful of all-tough soldiers could accomplish together outweighed the conse-quent weakening everywhere else).

He reflected that 1/Hampshires, one of the original D-Day battalions, whose fighting strength was usually between 500 and 600, had lost 231 killed and about 1,050 wounded between June and October

1944. It was 'effectively twice wiped out' with a casualty rate exceeding that of many battalions on the Somme a generation before.[31] A. P. Herbert had served in the Royal Naval Division – part of the 'Poor Bloody Infantry' – in the First World War and, just before D-Day, wrote feelingly of how

> New men, new weapons, bear the brunt;
> New slogans gild the ancient game:
> The infantry are still in front,
> And mud and dust are much the same.
> Hail, humble footmen, poised to fly
> Across the West, or any, Wall!
> Proud, plodding, peerless PBI –
> The foulest, finest job of all.

Poor indeed: doing what was proverbially the hardest job in battle with men selected primarily by their unsuitability for employment elsewhere.

The War Office policy on recruit selection meant that even fewer men served in their local regiment in the Second World War than had in the First, and both wars saw 'a waning local connection' as they went on. In 1/Hampshire (recruiting heavily from the great, if mutually hostile, conurbations of Southampton and Portsmouth), some 78 per cent of 1914 fatalities came from the county, but only 34.5 per cent by 1918. Of 8,304 men killed in seven different regiments in the Second World War, only 43 per cent were in a unit with which they had 'a close territorial connection'; by January 1944 only 34 per cent of the dead had a close link to their regiment. Rebadging was rife. In 1940 a brigade consisting entirely of Highland Light Infantry was told to expect a draft of 200 Royal Irish Fusiliers for one of its units. 'Jocks and Irish tend not to mix,' recalled its brigade major, 'but when these men arrived they all spoke with Yorkshire accents.'[32] By October 1943 battalions on overseas operations could expect that only twenty reinforcements a month would come from their own regiment, and the rest would be drafted in from across the infantry.[33] In Italy, a battalion of 56th London Division received reinforcements from fourteen different regiments just before it went into the attack. Its commanding officer urgently asked for a supply of cap-badges, 'so that at least the men could have with them the badge of the regiment in which they had to be prepared to die'.[34] As the war neared its end, the infantry found itself reinforced with redundant anti-aircraft gunners, while a large and resentful RAF contingent became Scots Guardsmen by the stroke of an unforgiving pen. In late 1944 Jim Bellows was a platoon sergeant in a Hampshire battalion, brought up to strength by drafts from all three services.

> Our trainees arrived, sailors in Navy uniforms which were quickly changed to Army uniform. The Royal Artillery became Infantry and none of these lads were used to Army discipline. The Navy lads had all been in small units with various types of assault craft, the RAs had all come from Bomb Alley where they had been shooting down flying bombs and, as this threat was over, they became redundant. I never realised what a challenge it would be to turn these lads into Infantry but what a shock I had when they took to their training like ducks to water, especially the Navy lads ... They said they liked the training and the comradeship. In the Navy they were in small messes and the atmosphere was different.[35]

General Adam was a gunner by cap-badge, and may perhaps (or perhaps not) be forgiven for not understanding how strongly infantry officers and regular NCOs were bound by regimental ties. When Brigadier Robert Bridgeman was promoted major general in 1941 he reluctantly decided that he ought to swap his Rifle Brigade black buttons for a general's brass ones, but his world was still shaped by the black and the green. He would have liked a rifleman as his military assistant, 'but after the destruction of the 1st Battalion at Calais I could see nobody who looked likely to fit the bill.' When, a month or two later, he was made director general of the Home Guard, he selected Colonel John Longmore as his deputy, giving him lunch at the Carlton Club before offering him the job with the words 'You're a Harrovian and a guardsman, I'm an Etonian and a rifleman. I'll take the risk; will you?'[36]

In 1941 Major Bernard Fergusson of the Black Watch, serving on the staff in Cairo, heard that his regiment's 1st Battalion had lost over 300 officers and men in an attack pressed with characteristic determination at Tobruk. General Sir Archibald Wavell, Commander-in-Chief

Middle East, had been commissioned into the regiment in 1901. Fergusson had served him as aide-de-camp in 1935–7, and never forgot being told that 'the Regiment is the foundation of everything'. He at once waylaid the great man's chief of staff, Major General Arthur Smith, and told him what had happened. Smith gave Fergusson a written order 'to collect all officers and men of the Black Watch, whatever their duties, who are fit for active service and take them up with him to rejoin 2BW in Tobruk ... Major Fergusson and his party will be given top priority for all transport necessary to get them to Tobruk as soon as possible.' 'I'm sure the Chief will want to say good-bye to you', added Smith. Within three days Fergusson was off with six officers and 64 men of the regiment in the overloaded and slow *Chakdina*. He found a battalion dreadfully wounded but still on its feet.

Two of the companies had no officers at all; one had fewer than ten men and was being commanded by its CSM, who had been a lance-corporal in my original platoon ten years earlier.'Big Jim' Ewan, one of my corporals in those days, now a captain and a company commander, was one of the unwounded: his company and a hand-ful of sappers took over the left flank; my first cousin Richard Boyle and the remnants of the other three rifle companies the right; HQ Company under Gerald Barry (a former Coldstreamer with a Military Cross from the First World War who had joined us from Rhodesia) the centre. Roy the Pipe-Major, my former platoon piper, had played the battalion into action, continuing to play despite three wounds. He had already been wounded and taken prisoner in Crete, but had escaped through Greece and Turkey and rejoined, refusing an offer to be repatriated to Britain ... His younger brother Neil, also a piper, was to be killed with the 1st battalion in Korea in 1952.

Fergusson was given command of D Company, and stood-to on its position at dawn, 'with two officers who had come up in the *Chakdina* with me; I was glad to find that I knew two of the NCOs of old. Among the killed was a Kilkerran man, Sergeant Andrew Scobie, with whom I had enlisted in 1932.'

There are few universally valid generalities. Thus far we have seen how the regimental system bent under the strain of major war, but

Bernard Fergusson and 1/Black Watch show us, conversely, just how resilient it could be. If we look hard at the metallurgy we can see good reason for this. When Fergusson met five Eton friends at Waterloo station in January 1930 for the journey to Sandhurst, the party included 'Patrick Campbell-Preston, destined like me for the Black Watch and to become by far my closest friend. Years later we were to marry sisters; he was to be my second-in-command and my successor in command in the Regiment.' Fergusson's father had been a Grenadier, but he had decided against the Foot Guards because of 'the prospect of doing all my soldiering in or near London' and when he joined 2/Black Watch at Colchester, although he began less than confidently by saluting the RSM and wearing his spats on the wrong feet,

> there couldn't have been a more welcoming family to join. We new boys were at once made at home in the mess, and within two weeks we had lunched or dined with every married officer. Patrick and I were appalled when we went to look up two Sandhurst friends who had joined an English Regiment in the same garrison, whose reception had been very different from ours, despite the fact that one of them had been brought up in that Regiment.

He thought that 'three quarters of the fun of all regimental soldiering derived from the Jocks. Most of them were either farm-servants from Perthshire or Angus, or miners from Fife, and they were a constant joy: sometimes exasperating, always stimulating. And they would stand by "the officer" through thick and thin.' Once, when Fergusson collected his company's weekly pay, most of it in 10s. notes, he picked the tartan bag up by the wrong end and the money fell out and was blown away, across the parade ground and football field of Maryhill Barracks, Glasgow, in the high wind. 'One by one the Jocks came back, each with a fistful of soiled or screwed-up paper: some had picked them off the windward wall of the officers' mess,' wrote Fergusson. 'Jocks from every company in the Battalion filed into the company office, and laid their findings on the table.' Eventually the colour sergeant reported that every penny was accounted for. And then the company soldiers, many of them married 'off the strength', and so drawing no marriage allowance but 'living in penury' came in to draw their pittance. 'There was and is no possible comment for me to make,' said Fergusson with justifiable pride.[37] When he was ennobled, as Lord Ballantrae, in 1972, he chose, for one of the supporters to his arms, 'a soldier of the 42nd Highlanders, the Black Watch'.

For all the smoke and mirrors that had helped to defend the system in the First World War, most senior infantry officers were convinced that there was real merit in it. The future Field Marshal Lord Slim had begun his working life as a primary school teacher and clerk, but was able to get a temporary commission in 1914 because he had been a member of Birmingham University OTC. He fought through the First World War as a junior infantry officer on the Western Front and knew, better than most, how the realities of rebadging affected the infantry. Just after giving up the post of CIGS in 1952 he reflected on the qualities that had defined the army of his day, concluding that they were discipline, comradeship and regimental pride.

The soldier's pride and loyalty are not, first, to the Army as a whole, but to his own Corps or Regiment – to his own immediate comrades. The moral strength of the British Army is the sum of all these family or clan loyalties. They are the foundations of the British soldier's stubborn valour. They hold him when more distant, wider loyalties could not. The Guards held Hougoumont at Waterloo, the Gloucesters stood on a hill in Korea, because in the last resort they remembered that they were the Guards, they were the Gloucesters.

In the First World War, with a battalion of the Royal Warwickshire Regiment, I took part in an assault on an enemy position. We advanced across the open, one long line behind the other, suffering heavily as we plodded forward. As we neared the enemy wire, salvos of shrapnel bust in our faces, blasting great gaps in our ranks. Men bowed their heads under this iron hail; some turned back; the leading line faltered. In another moment we should have broken. As we wavered, a private soldier beside me; a stolid man, whom one would have thought untouched by imagination, ran forward. In a voice of brass he roared, 'Heads up the Warwicks! Show the blighters your cap badges! Above the din, half a dozen men each side heard him. Their heads came up. They had no cap badges – they were wearing steel helmets – but they had remembered their regiment. That one little group plunged forward again. The movement spread and, in a moment, the whole line surged through the broken wire and over the enemy parapet.[38]

It was not just senior officers who supported the system. John Masters was a regular Gurkha who, though strictly speaking its brigade major, commanded a Chindit brigade in Burma and then went on to be a best-selling novelist. He agreed that the regiment bound men where other ties might not. His history may be wrong but his sense of regimental focus is wholly right.

> But in war it is necessary that all should pull together, and fight with a will, whatever their opinions of the rights and wrongs of the case. So, in the King's armies men were shielded from disturbing doubts by the interposition of a smaller cause, which no one could cavil at, between themselves and the great national cause. The spirit was and is built in the regiment.[39]

Charles Wilson won the Military Cross as an infantry regimental medical officer in the First World War, and was ennobled while serving as Churchill's doctor in the second. He believed that 'Loyalty to a fine battalion may take hold of a man and stiffen his purpose,' and many men found the regiment 'the source of their strength, their abiding faith ... the last of all the creeds that in historical times have steeled men against death.'[40] A Second World War commanding officer told Major General Frank Richardson, a senior medical officer:

> As descendants of the men who gained such splendid victories in so many battles from 1702 onwards we are simply unable to be cowardly. We've got to win our battle, whatever the cost, so that people will say 'They were worthy descendants of the 32nd,' and that's saying a hell of a lot.[41]

Martin Lindsay served as second in command of 2/Gordon Highlanders from Normandy to the Baltic. He was convinced that

> By far and away the greatest single factor in a soldier's morale is regimental pride, based on centuries of tradition ... For my part I have no doubt how the battalion faced the enemy's fire sweeping

across that wide, sullen river, the Rhine, on that dark night thirty years ago. We never wavered because, in the last resort, we were Gordon Highlanders, we were the Highland Division.[42]

These arguments owed little to those that had been used, by Edward Cardwell and Hugh Childers, to manufacture the regimental system in the 1870s and 1880s. Instead, they reflected a deep-seated human desire, arguably stronger in Britain than in some other countries, to belong to something that is not the work of a moment, but whose present performance is sanctified by the achievements of the past. When the eccentric Lieutenant Colonel Mainwaring led the 51st Light Infantry into action on Walcheren on 1 August 1809,

> He told us that all the pleasure and happiness he had ever felt fell short of the pleasure he now felt at being at the head of that Corps, who on that day fifty years before had by their native valour repulsed and defeated the whole body of the enemy's cavalry before Minden. He showed us the word Minden on our colours, and reminded us how it was inscribed on our belt plates. He said it was probable we should fall in with the enemy that day, and if we did not give them a good drubbing, how could we ever return home to our fathers, mothers etc. Our country expected much from us, the Regiment in its infant state had performed prodigies of valour in its day, and … would it not be expected we should eclipse them in their glory … In the course of this address he returned to his old maxim of firing low, you will then hit them in the legs and there will be three gone, for two will pick him up and run away with him.[43]

At Alexandria on 21 March 1801 the 28th Foot, in line two-deep, had come under attack from both sides and had been ordered: 'Front rank stand fast, rear rank about turn.' As a reward for its conduct that day the regiment was awarded a 'back badge', worn in miniature on the back of the headdress. This term has, over the years, defined things from a regimental club and journal to a Gloucester-based taxi company. At Quatre Bras, two days before Waterloo, history came close to repeating itself, and the 28th, this time in square, was under heavy attack. Its divisional commander, the scruffy and foul-mouthed Sir Thomas Picton, feared it might break. He roared 'Twenty-Eighth,

remember Egypt!' Very few of those present at Quatre Bras had actually been at Alexandria, but the appeal to ancient valour was well
understood, and the battalion braced up. When the attacks had been
repulsed, the brigade commander, Sir James Kempt, rode into the
centre of the square, doffed his hat, and said 'Bravo 28th. The 28th
are still the 28th and your conduct this day shall never be
forgotten.'

Robin Schlaefli was trained in the Essex Regiment, despite hailing
from Croydon, and was given an emergency commission in the
Queen's Royal Regiment in May 1941. When he arrived at Stoughton
Barracks it was made clear 'that we were no ordinary English Line
Regiment, but were the oldest and without doubt the greatest'. RSM
Tasker warned new officers 'Salutes is a two-way courtesy. If I see any
of you tapping your 'at with your swagger stick, or a-scratching your
eyebrow like the Wavy Navy, you'll wish you'd joined the 'ome Guard.'
Schlaefli later mused that

> Regimental pride has always been of enormous importance in the
> British army, and still is, despite the ravages of amalgamation. It was
> even – I might say particularly – true for wartime soldiers. We were
> therefore given a comprehensive and inspiring picture of the
> Regiment's history. I knew some of it from the OTC at school, but
> in the Depot, there were still old soldiers around telling tales of
> Mons, Ypres and the Somme ...
>
> Within the bounds of loyalty to his Regiment in the Army is
> always the feeling of belonging to and identity with the smaller
> formations within it. So far as the infantry soldier is concerned, this
> means being part of his Battalion, his Company, his Platoon, and
> finally his Section of ten or so men with whom he eats, drinks,
> moves and fights alongside in battle.
>
> From the soldier's worm's eye view, this could be like an upturned
> pyramid with him at the bottom; but like a man dangling beneath
> a parachute, everything above him is actually a support. And by
> turning the pyramid the right way up again, the chain of command
> from the Colonel downwards shows that the base of it – containing
> the soldiers who in the end win or lose battles – is the most import-
> ant part.[44]

In both world wars the regiment helped prove the moral cement that held men together, however slender their initial connection with it. Lieutenant Colonel A. P. B. Irwin commanded a New Army battalion of the East Surreys. Although he thought that the huge drafts that arrived to replace casualties in 1917 were far inferior to the volunteers of 1914, he took the trouble to greet each new batch – the product of the dehumanising rebadging at Etaples – with a lecture on the regiment's history and traditions, and of the battalion's own achievements. In this way they 'all became East Surreys in no time at all', proud of their battalion and of the very good 18th Division, of which it formed part.[45] John Lucy, a pre-war regular in the Royal Irish Rifles, was shocked to see how old standards were changed by the promotion of NCOs who called their men by their first names. What he called 'We remnants' held firm in 'a form of freemasonry,' that 'preserved and passed on the diluted *esprit de corps* of our regiment.'[46]

James Jack was a regular Cameronian who commanded 2/West Yorkshire in 1916–17. Sidney Rogerson, commissioned into the West Yorkshires in 1914, was one of his company commanders, and wrote admiringly of how

> so completely had he identified himself with us and incidentally endeared himself to us that his alien origin had been completely and quickly forgotten ... As punctilious on the parade ground as he was regardless of his safety and unsparing of his energy in action, he had other and rarer qualities ... In all ways he set us an example ... No matter what the circumstances he was always spic and span, and it was typical of him that before any big attack he would be careful to see that his boots and buttons were polished, explaining with a slow smile that one could 'always die like a gentleman – clean and properly dressed'.[47]

Jack's parent regiment wore black buttons, so the shining-up would not have come naturally. Recognising just what a mixed bag his officers were, he made a point of presenting each newly arrived subaltern with a regimental swagger cane. During the ten days of trench-holding that Rogerson describes so well, his company was a 'mixed Yorkshire-Northumbrian contingent' that owed little to pre-war regimental logic. But when, soon after coming out of the line, they met a guards battalion – 'fine and soldierly they looked, all big men, carrying their marching order with an enviable ease, and with their khaki new and clean,' the West Yorkshires at once braced up, 'determined to uphold the prestige of a line regiment in the face of these picked troops'. Even the iron-hard Jack confided to his diary:

> Passed Guards battalion on way to front. Very clean and smart. But 2 W. York. had got themselves marvellously straightened up in the two days of semi-peace under bad conditions. Very fine fellows indeed.[48]

This process of cultural transference was not confined to the infantry. An artillery officer described how his battery, originally a Territorial Force unit recruited in Yorkshire, had suffered a casualty rate of 250 per cent for officers and 100 per cent for men in twenty-two months in action, but although replacements came in from all over Britain, they 'assumed a Yorkshire defiant and stubborn quality that characterised the 62nd Division from its earliest days, and were proud of it. D/310 Battery, never with more than twenty Yorkshire born men, had now become Yorkshire to the core.'[49]

There was a similar process in the Second World War. For instance, Martin Lindsay thought that by the summer of 1944 perhaps one-third of 2/Gordon Highlanders actually hailed from Scotland, but most of the battalion's soldiers urgently sought that most essential element of walking-out dress: a kilt. 38th Infantry Brigade comprised 1/Royal Irish Fusiliers, 6/Royal Innisikilling Fusiliers, and 2/London Irish Rifles. Its losses in Tunisia were so heavy that London argued for the disbanding of the London Irish. The brigade commander, however, argued successfully that the battalion should be retained and the brigade kept up to strength by drafting in Irishmen. They did not need to be very Irish: an Irish stepfather would be good enough, and the spirit of his three wonderful battalions would do the rest.[50] Peter White's 4/King's Own Scottish Borderers retained its Scottish character, although he himself was an Englishman brought up in South Africa. His platoon sergeant Sergeant Dickinson was a London docker and Taffie, also in platoon headquarters, was a 'mature Welshman'. Corporal Parry was a Scot, but, as a Glaswegian, came from well outside the regiment's home patch. It took White some time to find out that when he said 'Th'onny-guid-yin's-a-deed-yin' he meant 'The only good one's a dead one.'[51] A fellow platoon commander had been a regular officer in the Buffs, a regiment recruiting in theory from East Kent, but he had been cashiered after knocking his commanding officer though a plate-glass window on a lively mess-night, and then, as wisely as surprisingly, re-commissioned.

Major John Hill was a company commander in 2/Royal Berkshires in Burma. At the start of the war his was still a homogeneous Berkshire battalion.

> Many were farm-hands or working in associated agricultural fields; a few were from small service trades in the towns. They came from Reading, Windsor, Maidenhead and Wokingham; from Aldermaston, Theale, Thatcham and Newbury; from the north Berkshire Downs, Lambourn, the Ilsleys, Buckelbury and Beenham; from Pangbourne and Twyford. In 1944 the Royal County of Berkshire also included Wallingford, Abingdon, Didcot and Wantage, now all parts of Oxfordshire.

In 1944 the battalion received a major reinforcement

> from all parts of Great Britain: Geordies from the north-east, Yorkshiremen, Sherwood Foresters from Nottingham, and Scotsmen. We came to value their resilient and sterling qualities: humour, toughness, a spirit of comradeship and a will to work, especially from among those who had been miners ... In a few months the regimental system began to make its value felt. We achieved as close a knit team of 'Royal Berkshiremen' as one could wish for. Teaching regimental history and past achievements to the newcomers, allied to the expected higher standards of soldiering, produced stalwart and staunch 'regimental enthusiasts' with a high degree of comradeship to stand us in good stead for the future.[52]

Hill took stock of his company in March 1945. It had left Imphal the previous November with 196 men, all ranks, and now had only 23 of these originals left; Hill was the sole surviving officer. It had lost five officers, a warrant officer, and 96 men to enemy fire. By this time only about 10 per cent of the company were Berkshire men, and it was not until the war's end that 'drafts of Royal Berkshire soldiers began to arrive. It was good to see Reading, Maidenhead, Newbury and other Berkshire towns represented as they had been at the beginning.' Hill, a regular officer, firmly believed

> it was the regimental tradition ... that kept us going when times were hard ... The knowledge that throughout the ages – at Maiwand, at Tofrek in Egypt in 1885, at Bourlon Wood in France in 1917 and at Kohima in 1944 – the regiment had, before the eyes of the world, fought according to the highest traditions of the service, both in victory and in defeat, was our foundation and inspiration.[53]

Yet there were certainly limits to a regiment's ability to cope with waves of outsiders. Major D. A. Philips of 7/Oxfordshire and Buckinghamshire Light Infantry told his mother in March 1944,

> I wish we could be reinforced by officers and men from the Regiment; there must be plenty of Regimental Officers who could be sent out to us. I know that regimental *esprit de corps* is of tremendous value in keeping up the morale of the troops when they are tired and conditions are not too good; but the policy of treating officers and men like so many numbers and posting them hither and thither at random makes the task of keeping alive a regimental spirit well-nigh impossible. Some of the new officers do their best to conform to our habits and customs; others seem to make no efforts at all. Perhaps they are not to be blamed; they did not ask to leave their parent regiments.[54]

Indeed they did not. Also in March 1944 Raleigh Trevelyan, with a wartime commission in the Rifle Brigade, found himself posted to 1/Green Howards in the Anzio beachhead. He was not received with much cordiality: 'Oh, hallo. Good show. You've arrived', said an officer. A Rifle Brigade comrade was soon 'string-pulling to get me back to my own regiment', a process that was eventually successful. In the meantime he was disgusted by what had happened to him:

When I originally joined up, straight from school and therefore impressionable, I had it dinned into me day and night that I now belonged to a crack regiment; only Guards regiments and one or two others in the cavalry could be tolerated. As soon as I went abroad, what happened? Without the smallest apology I and a lot of my contemporaries were doled out as cannon folder to any mob that happened to be short of platoon commanders. No wonder at first we were unhappy, and no wonder that we are now bitter with the people that taught us that iniquitous rubbish.

After recovering from a wound he was sent to the Infantry Reinforcements Training Depot – 'the depot for lost souls' – but when he eventually joined his own battalion he found that

After so much string-pulling, so many hopes and fears, it is nothing but an anti-climax. Only the senior officers are at all congenial; the others are inconceivably stuffy and grand – mostly made up from sergeants in the Desert, and therefore jealous of their status. I have also been fobbed off with the dregs of the battalion for my platoon, one or two of the men being old sweats just out of the glasshouse.[55]

Norman Craig also passed through the IRTD on his way from 4/5 Royal Sussex, where he had been an acting captain, to being a subaltern in 1/East Surreys. Although he was made very welcome to his new company's mess in a big whitewashed Italian farmhouse, a spaghetti and vino dinner party depressed him: 'something in the very conviviality of the occasion made me miss the old battalion more keenly than at any time since I had left, and nothing had quite the same sparkle anymore.'[56]

CHAPTER 18

IMPONDERABLE ENTITIES

Trevelyan touched a great truth when he wondered, at Anzio, if 'my ties with the blokes in this platoon don't outweigh any nebulous loyalty I may have felt towards the traditions of the regiment'.[1] Real loyalty was to people – not to shapes or constuctions, stamped metal or embroidered cloth. There is widespread agreement that the primary group – infantry section, gun detachment or tank crew – lies at the very heart of motivation in combat. Charles Carrington hit the nail on the head:

> A Corporal and six men in a trench were like shipwrecked sailors on a raft, completely committed to their social grouping, so that nobody could have any doubts about the moral and physical failings of his pals since everyone's life depended on the reliability of each.[2]

C. E. Montague, who served, hopelessly over-age, in the ranks of the First World War infantry before he was commissioned, saw things just the same way:

> Our total host might be two million strong, or ten millions; whatever its size a man's world was his section – at most his platoon; all that mattered to him was the one little boatload of castaways with whom he was marooned on a desert island making shift to keep off the weather and any sudden attack of wild beasts.[3]

There are certainly national variables, and both Russian and German soldiers in the Second World War were more influenced by both indoctrination and sheer compulsion than we sometimes recognise. This does not mean that the primary group and the larger regimental identity in which it nested were unimportant, simply that the precise mix was different. For armies sharing at least part of the cultural DNA of Marlborough's redcoats, though, the links between man and man remain fundamental. Canadian Lieutenant Farley Mowat's thoughts on his relationship with his own platoon in Second World War Italy could have been written by either a British or American officer:

> Leaving Seven Platoon in order to return to the intelligence officer's job was a considerable wrench. The two months I had spent with the platoon seemed like a lifetime. Although I knew very little of the past lives and inner beings of those thirty men, I had been more firmly bound to them than many a man is to his own blood brothers.

Mowat was surprised to discover that once he was away from his old platoon this loyalty faded:

> I was slow to comprehend the truth; that comrades-in-arms unconsciously create from their particular selves an imponderable identity which goes its own way and has its own existence, regardless of the comings and goings of the individuals who are its constituent parts. Individuals are of no more import to it than they were in the days of our beginnings when the band, the tribe, was the vehicle of human survival.[4]

Between them, Trevelyan and Mowat describe what we might call the endpapers of regimental identity. As Trevelyan suggested, loyalty to immediate comrades – vertically, with relatively little regard for rank, within the section or platoon, and horizontally, amongst the members of the officers' or sergeants' mess, or between mates who swigged tea at the same end of the cookhouse – formed a network of close relationships that said more about human nature than about the bigger constructs of regimental identity. Sensible officers had known this for years. The charming and witty Patrick Ferguson was born in Edinburgh in 1744, and knew many of the important figures in the Scottish enlightenment. He served in the Scots Greys before buying a captaincy in the 70th Foot in 1768, and not only took a serious interest in light infantry training but also developed a successful breach-loading rifle. He became a major in the 71st in 1779, served as inspector-general of militia in South Carolina, and was probably the only British soldier killed at the Battle of King's Mountain in 1780, fought between loyalists and a band of 'over-the-mountain' men whose behaviour in victory (they stripped and urinated on Ferguson's corpse) tells us that not all 'patriots' were reluctant heroes in homespun. In the orders Ferguson wrote for his provincial unit, the American Volunteers, he recommended to the officers

> to promote among the soldiers of the several detachments a free choice of comrades, who ought never to be separated when it can be avoided; but ... [who should instead] compose one file, to assist and defend each other, in action ... to share in hardships as well as in danger for their mutual advantage and relief; to sleep and mess together; to take care of each other in sickness, and of one another's arms and necessaries during absence. Three of these files, if afterwards so [fused] into one mess, would at all times easily rally and stand by each other, so as to add much to their own safety and increase the strength of the detachment. This fellowship will naturally be agreeable to men of good disposition and much increase their confidence in action. The man who at any times behaves unfaithfully by his comrade must be despised, and he who abandon[s] his friend in danger [must] become infamous.[5]

These arrangements were echoed in the *Regulations for the Rifle Corps* prescribed by Colonel Coote Manningham in 1800 and published the following year. It was not until much later that the platoon was finally established as the standard subdivision of the company, although the term had long been used to describe the small fire-units into which a battalion might be divided before it fell to the smoky and dangerous business of volley-firing. Manningham told his company commanders to divide their commands into two equal parts (platoons), and then to split these into two again (half-platoons, or squads), spreading officers and NCOs equally between them.

Although he recognised that subalterns might occasionally have to serve away from their companies, they should return to them as soon as possible. Once a captain had divided up his company, he

> will arrange comrades. Every Corporal, Private and Bugler will select a comrade of the rank differing from his own, e.g. the front and rear rank, and is never to change him without the permission of his Captain. Comrades are to have the same berth in quarters; and, that they may be as little separated as possible in either barracks or the field, will form the same file on parade and go on the same duties with arms ... After this arrangement is made the captain will then establish his messes, which are to be invariably by squads. Ten is the best number for a mess to consist of; from that number to 18 the squad will still consist of but one mess. But whenever it amounts to that number it will be divided into two messes, at the head of one will be the Corporal, and of the other the acting Corporal or Chosen man ...

Officers were to mess together: anyone who objected was suggesting that he did not really wish to live with his brother officers, and ought to leave the regiment at once. Sergeants too were to mess together, and the commanding officer was to ensure that their mess was 'as comfortable and economical as possible'.[6]

This sort of formalised stability was an ideal that was rarely attained. In the eighteenth and early nineteenth centuries, regiments in Britain were regularly 'drafted', that is, raided for men who were packed off to reinforce regiments that were either on active service already, or about to embark. In September 1760 Lieutenant Colonel Edward Windus told our harassed friend Colonel Samuel Bagshawe that the men of his newly recruited regiment were beginning to grasp their trade. 'I am teaching four pretty large squads, and the grenadiers, the method of firing, advancing and retreating,' he wrote, 'one in the rear of the other, with the officers superintending, and the sergeants and corporals paying attention to their own squads. So that, by this means, every squad is sure to do alike, to step together, and all must do it with the same signal of the drum, and keep the same time.' They were even beginning to present a uniform appearance: 'We begin to get their hair in tolerable order, which I see every morning that it be well combed, tied and oiled to make it look smooth and well, and before next review it will all be long enough to plait and turn up under their hats.' But in November almost a hundred of the regiment's best men were drafted into the Royal Scots and Handasyde's, 'which has indeed effectively demolished us.' The recruiting officers toiled manfully, and in late March 1762 Windus reported that they were now 'only one man wanting to complete to 630 rank and file.' At the beginning of April, 297 men were drafted out to reinforce Colonel Armstrong's Regiment, and Samuel Bagshawe, already mortally ill, died with his regiment under strength, worried about whose clothing account would bear the cost of the uniforms sent off with the drafted men.[7]

The process did not merely play havoc with regimental identity, infuriating the officers who had tried so hard to recruit up to strength, but it also smashed the smaller loyalties forged amongst messmates and the broader bonds of regionality that played their own part in maintaining cohesion. Rebadging in two world wars had very much the same effect. So too, of course, did the losses that regiments suffered in action and through postings to unhealthy stations. The First World War provides enough dramatic examples of what might happen to battalions in battle. In the London-raised 56th Division, whose military identity was still heavily overlaid with peacetime allegiances, the Queen's Westminster Rifles lost all its 28 officers on 1 July 1916 as well as 475 of 661 men; the London Scottish, in its hodden-grey kilts, 14 of 28 officers and 602 of 847 men; and the London Rifle Brigade 19 of 23 officers and 535 of 803 men.[8]

But butcher's bills had sometimes been as high in the past. When Marlborough stormed the Schellenberg, dominating the Bavarian town of Donauworth, in 1704, 1st Foot Guards lost 12 officers and 217 men, killed and wounded; two battalions of Orkney's Regiment 30 officers and 418 men; and Ingoldsby's Regiment 16 and 228 respectively. At Albuhera in 1811, the Buffs, caught by that 'storm of lancers' emerged with 7 officers and 85 men still standing in a battalion that had mustered 755 all ranks at the start of the day. The 48th was left with 109 of its initial strength of 452; the 66th lost 272 of its 441 men; and the 57th, soon to be nicknamed the Die-Hards, started the day with 647 all ranks and ended it with just 219. Officer casualties were so bad that one of the British brigades was brought off the field by a French émigré with the grimly appropriate name of Captain Cimetière.[9]

The 24th Foot took 31 officers and 1,065 men into action against the redoubtable Sikhs at Chilianawala in 1849, and saw 13 officers killed, 9 wounded, and 255 men killed, 278 wounded: 525 in all. The day was all the more shocking because Brigadier John Pennycuick, commanding the brigade, and his son Ensign Alexander Pennycuick were both killed. The 24th had managed to take its 39-ft officers' mess table on campaign with it, and Lieutenant McPherson recorded 'In our mess tent, on the table at which they had so often sat in mirth and merriment, were reverently laid the bodies of 13 of our officers, together with the remains of Sergeant-Major Coffee (commissioned in death).'[10]

Battles this costly were the exception rather than the rule, though as far as the Sikh Wars were concerned, General Sir Hugh Gough's predilection for frontal attacks on strongly held positions tended to produce more dead redcoats than was strictly necessary. Across most of the army's history microbes killed more soldiers than bullet or blade, and disease played its part in the erosion of military communities, big and small. The 68th Foot put a total of 2,330 men through its ranks from 1801 to 1806, when it was garrisoning St Lucia, and 1,588 of them died: the regiment did not fire a shot in anger. Lieutenant General Sir William Myers died as governor of the Windward and Leeward Islands in 1805. He had taken eighteen members of his family with him, and fourteen of them died there. His eldest son, William James Myers, inherited the family baronetcy, only to be mortally wounded commanding the Fusilier brigade at Albuera. One newly arrived young officer, chatting to a comely Barbadian lady (who was, though he did not yet know it, the town's most notable madam) was nonplussed when she seized his regimental button to check its number, and cheerily assured him that he had plenty of comrades in the cemetery. In India, cholera slew more British soldiers than bearded Sikh or clattering Maratha: the 86th Foot had 410 cases of cholera and 328 deaths at Karachi in 1845; and in 1853 the 70th Foot lost two officers, 344 men, 37 wives, and 99 children to the same disease.

Nevertheless, it was – and remains – the soldier's nature to rebuild his little world as best he can, however outrageous the treatment it receives. Bernard Livermore, posted to 2/20th London in 1916, saw how the process worked in a battalion that had begun life as a Territorial unit recruited in Blackheath and Woolwich, but was now an almost classless, nationwide amalgam of conscripts. In his case, loyalty to 2/20th London began with the small group. He

> wondered if it was just a lucky chance that my bivvy mates were such fine friends – or whether a kindly Providence arranged things so expertly. Throughout my army life I was continually brought into contact with men who became very dear friends and very close companions. Considering the fact that they all hailed from many parts of the British Isles and were derived from all manner of classes, labourers, business men, clerks, professional men, they formed a true cross-section of the population. It was a very real privilege to have enjoyed their friendship.[11]

Captain Anthony Farrar-Hockley was adjutant of the Glosters, containing a mixture of regulars and National Servicemen, preparing to make what was to prove their last stand on the Imjin River in Korea in 1951. 'I look round the small body of men in the trenches,' he wrote,

> Some of them are young men, hardly more than boys; some of them in their late thirties; most of them are somewhere inbetween. I see that it is a good lot of faces to be in a tight corner with; reliable faces, the faces of old friends.

He was touched to hear two signallers argue the merits of different beers: 'A voice that surely came from Bristol was declaring: "I don't care what you say about your fancy London beers, John. As far as I'm concerned, there's no beer in the world like George's Home Brewed."'[12] Sometimes it is the accent that strikes a chord, like a creamy West Country voice assuring a First World War officer 'Doan e worry, zur, usn'll beat they', or a Scots Guards company commander, asking his company in the dangerous darkness of Tumbledown Mountain in 1982, whether it was still with him, only to hear an NCO roar back 'Ay, Sir, we're fuckin' wi' you!'

All manner of subtleties affected these relationships and the way they sat within broader loyalty towards the regiment. Comradeship rippled outwards. In both world wars infantry platoons might feel that company headquarters was remote. Norman Craig, preparing for what was to prove his last attack in Italy in 1944, recalled

> I was suddenly angry and intolerant of all this safe, smug pressure from behind, urging my platoon on to destruction. It was always the same. They were in such a hell of a rush to write you off. I felt irrationally contemptuous of everyone in the army who was not taking part in this particular attack.[13]

From company headquarters, though, the commanding officer could seem a distant figure and battalion headquarters a source of fury sometimes laced with merriment. Captain Alexander Stewart was commanding a Cameronian company on the Somme in November 1916, and although his commanding officer was a man of 'common sense and moral courage', without which 'he would have got his Brigade very much sooner than he did', his headquarters was exasperating.

> I am very much annoyed by the memos sent round by Headquarters that come in at all hours of the day and night; they stop me getting a full night's rest and some of them are very silly and quite unnecessary. When I am very tired and just getting off to sleep with cold feet in comes an orderly with a chit asking how many pairs of socks my company had a week ago; I reply '141 and a half.' I then go back to sleep; back comes a memo: 'Please explain at once how you come to be deficient of one sock.' I reply 'man lost his leg.' That's how we make the Huns sit up.[14]

Alan Hanbury-Sparrow was a regular Royal Berkshire lieutenant in 1914 and was commanding a battalion, as a temporary lieutenant colonel, at Passchendaele three years later. He was only too well aware of the impact of rebadging on the infantry, and the fact that it finished up with hopeless cases like Private Ailey, 'Feeble in body, he was feebler still in mind', who lost touch with the man in front during a night move, splitting the battalion as it moved up to the line. Hanbury-Sparrow argued that what he called 'regimental will' held units together, bridging the crosscurrents of smaller loyalties. For him the regiment's impact was partly ritualistic, for 'The real enemy was

Terror, and all this heel-clicking, saluting, bright brass and polish were our charms and incantations for keeping him at bay.'[15] By this argument the costume jewellery of the regimental system – its buttons, collar-dogs, lanyards and patches – all played an important part in a process that was never wholly logical.

At its best the regiment met a man's need for a sense of belonging, which helps explain its success in appealing to those who brought so little into the army with them. An extreme example of the way the process can work is the French Foreign Legion's Max Mader, who emerged from the First World War as its most highly decorated NCO, although his military service had begun in the German army, whence he deserted after hitting a bullying NCO. When the golden thread of history and tradition shone bright, then a man could easily find himself seduced by the knowledge that he was very lucky indeed to have managed to become a member of such a club. When Robert Bridgeman was posted to 3/Rifle Brigade in 1914 he was conscious of having joined 'a first-class battalion of a first-class regiment', whose commanding officers were to prove 'outstanding men, in whose hands the traditions of the regiment laid down in 1800 by Coote Manningham and William Stewart were entirely safe'. All four company commanders were regulars, who 'knew their job perfectly, though the idea of being described as professionals ... would have filled them with horror'. 'So for most of us,' he wrote,

> our outlook was a simple one. We had our duty to do as good rifle-men, we trusted and liked those who told us what it was, we had their example to follow, and we were there to do our best and in the words of the original regimental standing order, to do it first and complain, if need be, later.[16]

Although the term 'battalion' was not used in the cavalry, cavalry regiments behaved much like single-battalion infantry regiments. Francis Hereward Maitland, describing life in the ranks of the hussars in the early 1900s, maintained that regimental spirit was as much about comradeship as competence.

> There is a clear *esprit de corps*, a great mutual admiration between commissioned and non-commissioned ranks. The men looking up

to their officers, as epitomising everything meant and implied by the stock phrase 'an officer and a gentleman', the officers holding their men in esteem as the finest soldiers in the world ... We are aware that many of our officers – recruited from the hunting shires and county families – lack military genius. We are aware that in the field-day they show more dash and courage than actual knowledge of tactics. But wasn't it always so?[17]

For fellow cavalryman Spike Mays, there was the unifying discipline of mucking out – 'a smelly and revolting way to begin each day' – and grooming. Lieutenant Whittle, his troop leader, mucked out with the men, and in the process 'commanded from us common soldiers admiration and respect for a real man, which developed to that unsentimental affection known only to soldiers'. 'Cavalry officers are the best in the world', thought Mays. 'They always inspired respect and confidence in their men, although in some cases courage exceeded wit and knowledge ... There was friendship as well as discipline, and both were sure and certain.'[18]

In 1936 Bruce Shand, with two fellow cadets, was about to be commissioned from Sandhurst into 'a certain well-known cavalry regiment'. Unfortunately, the regiment had an officer on the Sandhurst staff, and he, 'for reasons only partly understandable, took a dislike to all three of us'. Because they were nearing the end of their last term, there was 'some panic and confusion' before they could be found places, but the system looked after its own.

Kim Muir, charming, dashing and far too rich, went to the 10th Hussars to be killed in France in 1940. He was a great steeplechaser and there is a race in his memory at Cheltenham. Tim Llewellen-Palmer, the youngest of four splendid brothers, two of whom were also to be killed, joined the 7th Hussars, where he had a very distinguished and highly individual career before too early a death.

Shand was told that Lieutenant Colonel Dick McCreery of the 12th Lancers would come to interview him, and after a conversation 'which included a question from him on the delicate subject of "means" it was settled that I should join the regiment at Tidworth early in the New Year (1937) subject to my passing out adequately.'

Although many officers were on leave, as the regiment had just returned from six years in Egypt, Shand found that everyone 'was very welcoming'. He was particularly grateful to the adjutant, Frank Arkwright, 'as nice a man as ever lived and a quietly efficient soldier,' who 'not only pulled me out of various scrapes ... but also judiciously handed me over to certain senior NCOs who took my education in hand and tactfully but firmly directed my floundering steps.' The quartermaster, Uncle Lawrence, had won a DCM on the retreat from Mons, and was 'deeply versed in regimental history'. He was succeeded by the then regimental sergeant major, Mr Mabbott, who 'was to be a godsend to the regiment and its commanding officers'. Shand quickly discovered that the regiment had become 'a highly efficient entity' after converting from horses to armoured cars in 1928, but it had previously been through 'a bad patch'.

This 'had been rectified when "Bloody" Mike Blakiston-Houston was brought in from the 11th Hussars, making Dick McCreery his adjutant and sacking half a dozen over-lighthearted officers.' A decade on from mechanisation, horses still played a large part in the lives of the officers, who were still provided with two chargers at government expense. Although the regiment had not served in India since the beginning of the century, a corruption of *jaldi* (to hurry), lived on in its vocabulary as: get a 'jillo on', meaning that soldiers were to move rapidly in whatever they were doing. And so, as the last months of peace spun by, the regiment soldiered in its comfortable, understated, self-assured way. A couple of nights before it went to France in 1939 one young officer invited his father, himself a distinguished 12th Lancer, who recalled his departure to the South African war, from the same Aldershot barracks, in 1899. He had been at a party in London and missed the last train home, and so

he had gone to the nearest hansom-cab stand, which was apparently in Park Lane, and found a driver with a good horse to take him back to Aldershot for a fiver, provided that the horse could be put up until the next day. There had been no problem and he had bowled into barracks in a tailcoat as the dawn was coming up and first and second servants had horses and baggage and uniform ready for the march out an hour or two later.[19]

When Bruce Shand was given temporary command of a squadron after his predecessor was accidentally killed he was comfortable, because 'All the subalterns and most of the senior NCOs I already knew, as I had started my service in C Squadron five years before.' Wounded and captured as a major after Alamein, he suffered from 'appalling remorse' because the two NCOs in his armoured car, Sergeant Francis and Corporal Platt, had both been killed. 'They had both been with me for some months,' he wrote, 'and we had lived intimately as one did in the desert. Obviously they had considerable trust in me, a trust that had been betrayed even if their deaths were blessedly instant ... They are not forgotten by me.' A prisoner of war, he was sitting on a bollard on Derna quay, awaiting the boat that was to take him to Greece, when a German major 'disporting one of the higher grades of the Iron Cross and ... yellow cavalry shoulder badges' – a fellow warrior across the chasm of hostility – took him under his wing, ensuring that he sailed in the same vessel as wounded from the major's own regiment. He shared a cabin with a German lieutenant who lent him washing gear. Later, when he was recovering in hospital, the officer, whose arm had by then been amputated, dropped in to bid him farewell, leaving him with several cartons of cigarettes. There was something international about the cavalry spirit. And, for all the ebb and flow of war, the regiment was still a recognisable entity. While Shand was in a prison camp in Germany,

News filtered in of the 12th Lancers and I was able to obtain a fair idea of where everyone was and what had happened to them ... it ended the war in a blaze of glory and excitement when, in its true armoured car role, it was pushed far ahead of the 8th Army, now commanded by Dick McCreery, to liberate and occupy Venice and Trieste ... Most of my friends and companions were still there, though [Lieutenant Colonel] George Kidston, who had done outstandingly well, had been invalided home after the German defeat in Tunisia, to be succeeded by Kate Savill who commanded with equal panache until the end of the war.[20]

The 12th Lancers had avoided cataclysms like the fall of Singapore or, on a smaller scale, the loss of Tobruk. Although the regiment experienced a busy war, it was never shot to pieces and reconstituted, and retained sufficient pre-war officers and NCOs to maintain its character and identity. Its First World War story had been much the same: it had 166 officers and men killed from start to finish. In contrast, the Royal Berkshire Regiment, without as populous a recruiting area as many line regiments, lost 353 officers and 6,375 men killed in the first war; 93 officers and 974 men died in the second. Many infantry battalions were repeatedly hollowed out and rebuilt. Sometimes, when brigades reduced from four battalions to three in the winter of 1917–18, or divisions had to be broken up in 1944 because there was not enough manpower to keep them in being, battalions were disbanded altogether and their officers and men posted elsewhere. This is what happened to Geoffrey Picot when 50th Division was disbanded, and 1/Hampshires with it. The disappearance of a particular battalion did not mean the end of its parent regiment, and a wise commanding officer might succeed in using regimental spirit, as expressed through its signs, symbols, and traditions, to infuse a reconstituted unit.

But it was seldom easy, and there were sad failures as well as heartening successes. Amongst the former is the case of 1/6th Duke of Wellington's Regiment. Their commanding officer, Lieutenant Colonel A. J. D. Turner, himself posted in from the Suffolks, reported that its losses in the grim bludgeon-work of Normandy in late June 1944 – 23 officers and 350 men were killed or wounded in fourteen days – made the battalion unmanageable. His blunt report went straight to the desk of Montgomery, who sacked him at once. The battalion was brought back to England and disbanded; its officers and men posted off as drafts. Although Turner had acknowledged that such honesty would be fatal to his career, he was soon promoted and awarded the DSO, and died a brigadier. Whatever Montgomery's view of the business, it is clear that there were many experienced staff officers who knew that there were moments when all the traditions in the world would not stop terrified youngsters from running away.

The system based on county regiments was at its best in peacetime, when the primary groups within it, those that formed the immediate focus of men's loyalties, were not subjected to the disruption that came from 'a bloody war or a sickly season'. In the two major wars of the twentieth century it quickly lost much of the sense of regionality that had helped sustain it, but was still often capable of fostering that sense of what Farley Mowat called 'imponderable identity' that helped strangers to knit together. By and large it mattered more to regulars, officers, and NCOs alike, than it did to temporary soldiers. Donald Featherstone, a wartime Royal Tank Regiment NCO, certainly put the regiment into his own hierarchy of duty and obedience, and there were many like him:

> Consciously, I kept a low profile, did not project myself into any situations I considered dangerous or foolhardy – while admiring and envying those who were able to perform more creditably. At the same time I obeyed orders, did what I was told, and never ran – although often tempted! Conscious of being a minute cog in a huge wheel, I tried in my own timid way to do my duty, support my comrades and, through them, the regiment and the country.

He added that he fought,

> Certainly for my country – a deep sense of patriotism and chauvinism has always sustained me. I was immensely proud and sustained by being in the Royal Tank Regiment, and my own group were good. The lads around me – with whom I am still in regular contact – were first class.[21]

Jack Chaffer, who won the MM with the Grenadier Guards at Anzio thought that 'I was fighting for my country, and always doing the best of my ability not to let down my Regiment and Comrades.'[22]

CHAPTER 19

THE REGIMENTS DEPART

M OST THINGS ARE much clearer in retrospect than they are at the time. Britain's post-1945 recession from waning imperial power to dignified penury may now seem predictable, but the scale and pace of her military run-down against a background of small wars, with the constant risk of a major war against the Warsaw Pact, was never simple. In the process the army shrank, and the regimental system that emerged from the Second World War was soon forced, contraction by contraction, into offspring that are never far from our television screens. The second battalions of line regiments disappeared soon after 1945, though the Foot Guards hung on to theirs until 1993. It was evident that single-battalion regiments of the 1950s had all the weaknesses that had marked them a century before. They were rarely strong enough to go on active service without being reinforced by other regiments, and it was seldom easy for them to replace, from within the regiment, gaps torn by combat or sickness.

Yet, in many cases, they retained the characteristics that had made the regiment such a powerful unifying force in the first place. When Bernard Fergusson took command of 1/Black Watch at Duisberg in March 1948 he found that

> The senior officers were all friends of pre-war days, and many others were sons of officers whom I had known in the past: indeed, at one time in my three years in command out of the thirty-two officers in the battalion seventeen were 'sons': and much the same applied in

the Sergeants' Mess … I was delighted to find the names of the
eight most senior officers formed … into an elegiac couplet:

Campbell-Preston, Rose, Rowan-Hamilton, Burnaby-Atkins
Fortune, Wingate Gray, Sutherland, Pollok-McCall.

No fewer than five of these were 'sons', and Rowan-Hamilton,
whose father had been my first Commanding Officer, had two
brothers in the Regiment as well.[1]

Fergusson resolutely opposed cross-posting within what was then
called the 'Group System'.

At one moment I was told that three of my company commanders
would be posted away, and three from other regiments posted in to
replace them. I said I would accept one and no more: Dugald McFie
of the Camerons, who I knew would fit in, as he did: I had to invoke
[Field Marshal Earl] Wavell to avert the other two. Later I was told
to give command of a company to an officer who had been reported
on adversely *by his own regiment*: he was to be given another chance
at our expense. He was a nice enough chap, but not company
commander timber. I employed him in some other way, and in due
course received the written 'displeasure' of the Army Council.

We can begin to see why, as Fergusson admitted, with regard to
another episode 'Not many people have been put under arrest as a
brigadier, and I take a twisted pride in being one of them.'[2] When he
told his fifty-two warrant officers and senior NCOs that it might be
necessary to post some of them to other regiments of the Highland
Brigade, forty-eight affirmed that they would rather drop a rank than
be posted. When two sergeants, one a bachelor and the other a
married man with two children, were indeed posted against their will,
both bought their discharge from the army and re-enlisted in the
Black Watch as private soldiers.[3]

Change was never going to be easy. This was partly because senior
officers were reluctant to murder their darlings, and partly because
the two world wars had left county regiments deeply entrenched in
popular consciousness. Although regional links had never been quite

as robust as Cardwell and Childers had hoped, they were certainly strong enough to ensure that the Britain of the 1950s and 1960s was full of men who had worn the local regiment's cap-badge. Not all the support for a particular regiment was necessarily local, for sometimes, as evidence of durable loyalty to a distant unit, stalwarts steadfastly maintained a branch of the regimental association many miles outside its recruiting area. For instance, in 2010 the Black Watch association had branches in London, Birmingham, Newcastle, and Stoke on Trent – to say nothing of those in Scotland. There was still a visible military presence in the land. Most county towns housed a regimental depot, still in those redbrick Cardwell barracks, with all its comforting undergrowth of a bugler and wreath party on Remembrance Day, officers' balls, raffles in the sergeants' mess, jollifications on great regimental anniversaries, and 'freedom parades' when the regiment exercised its right to march proudly through the town with bayonets fixed, drums beating and colours flying. Time gilded the military experience, and middle-aged men gathered to talk about their times in the 'old mob', compare the ferocity of sergeant majors and beerily assure balding ex-platoon commanders that they had been the finest officer a man could have. Politicians of all persuasions were caught up in the process, and even if there were no votes to be won in defence, there were certainly plenty to be lost by tinkering with sacred icons.

It was characteristic of successive army boards to seek compromise rather than to press for radical solutions. As a consequence of the 1957 Defence Review which reduced the size of the army, as such reviews generally do, numerous single-battalion regiments were amalgamated with a neighbour to form a new single-battalion regiment. In 1958, for instance, the Devonshire and Dorsetshire Regiments amalgamated as the Devon and Dorsets; in 1959 the Queen's Royal Regiment (West Surrey), merged with the East Surreys to form the Queen's Royal Surrey Regiment; the Wiltshire Regiment and the Royal Berkshire Regiment, became the Duke of Edinburgh's Royal Regiment (Berkshire and Wiltshire); in 1961 the Buffs and the Queen's Own Royal West Kent, came together into the Queen's Own Buffs; and the Seaforth Highlanders and the Cameron Highlanders became the Queen's Own Highlanders. This process met the desired aim of scaling-down the army by a battalion every time it occurred, but it did nothing to remedy the inherent weaknesses of single-battalion regiments. In the 1960s there was an attempt to restore a measure of flexibility in posting officers and NCOs by grouping regiments into administrative brigades, like the Home Counties Brigade, comprising all the infantry regiments of the south-east, and the Fusilier Brigade, with all the English fusilier regiments. For a period officers and men wore the brigade, rather than a regimental, cap-badge, and I well remember what resentment that caused.

The Army Board suggested that these brigades might wish to become large regiments, adding helpfully that those who chose to do so would be looked upon favourably in future reorganisations. Some agreed to amalgamate, and the first 'large regiments' were children of the sixties. In 1964 the four battalions of the East Anglian Brigade became the Royal Anglian Regiment. In 1966 the Royal Green Jackets were formed from the two rifle regiments and the Oxfordshire and Buckinghamshire Light Infantry – less perverse than it might seem, for all had served in the Light Division in the Peninsula. The Queen's Regiment in the same year merged the four regiments of the Home Counties Brigade; in 1968 the Light Infantry swept the four remaining regiments of light infantry into a single regiment; and the Royal Regiment of Fusiliers was created from the four English fusilier regiments.[4] Bringing together the regiments of the Ulster Brigade was a taxing business, for there were two fusilier regiments (the Inniskilling Fusiliers and the Royal Irish Fusiliers) as well as the Royal Ulster Rifles; one battalion would have to disappear, whatever the mixture. A far-sighted committee decided to create a new regiment, The Royal Irish Rangers. Its bracketed title – (27th (Inniskilling) 83rd and 87th) – was long-winded, but the new regiment, with its green-hackled caubeens and its saffron-kilted pipers, was an engaging and idiosyncratic mixture of old and new.

The process was made less painful because, except in the case of Ulster, the individual battalions of the new large regiments retained part of the identity of the old regiment from which they were descended. Thus in the Queen's Regiment each battalion bore a bracketed title – like 3rd Battalion The Queen's Regiment (Royal Sussex) – that reinforced its old allegiance, and retained the old regiment's distinctive lanyard, of a striking orange in the case of the Royal Sussex. The comfortable feeling that nothing had really changed did not last for long. When it was time for further reductions of the infantry, the army board of the day did not consider itself bound by the promises of its predecessors, and it was easier to trim a battalion from a large regiment than to grasp the nettle of amalgamation elsewhere. Fourth battalions went quickly: 4th Battalion The Queen's Regiment (Middlesex) was reduced to Albuhera Company in 1971, and disbanded altogether in 1973.

The 'Options for Change' defence review of 1990 led to the Grenadier, Coldstream and Scots Guards losing their second battalions – those of the Irish and Welsh Guards had gone already – with The Royal Regiment of Fusiliers, Royal Anglians, Light Infantry, and Royal Green jackets losing their third battalions. The Queen's Own Highlanders (Seaforth and Cameron) were amalgamated with the Gordon Highlanders to form The Highlanders; the Gloucesters and the Duke of Edinburgh's Royal Regiment came together in the Royal Regiment of Gloucestershire, Berkshire, and Wiltshire. The Royal Irish Rangers not only lost a regular battalion, but subsumed the full-time elements of the Ulster Defence Regiment to emerge as the Royal Irish Regiment.

Most controversially, the Queen's Regiment was amalgamated with the Royal Hampshires to form the two-battalion Princess of Wales's Royal Regiment. For some officers and men this could mean a third change of cap-badge within a long career, and it was noticeable that although the young embraced change with enthusiasm (as they generally do), there were those, grown grey in the monarch's service, who saw the whole business as a monstrous betrayal. It is painful to recall that the colonels of the Queen's and the Royal Hampshires, distinguished and widely admired officers, were no longer on speaking terms by the time of amalgamation. Major General Mike Reynolds of The Queen's made his own position very clear:

> To the utter disbelief of the Regiment we learned that not only were we to lose a battalion but, in addition, we were to be amalgamated with a single battalion regiment with which we had nothing in common and no associations. Despite many requests to ministers, including the Prime Minster, the Chief of the General Staff and other members of the Army Board, no explanation was ever given for this unwarranted treatment … At the stroke of a pen the vision

and faith of our founding colonels had been betrayed and the agonies endured over a quarter of a century to create one regiment from four had proved in vain. The older members of the Regiment realised that we would have been no worse off, and probably much better off, to have remained 'small' in 1966.

He concluded that his regiment had been sacrificed simply 'so that others should survive and a government and an army board could claim that no regiment had been disbanded.'[5]

This latest battle in the long war of administrative attrition meant that large regiments, founded with such innocence in the 1960s, were now rather small. A two-battalion 'large' regiment representing, as it might, at least four old regiments of the line, was bound to look askance at a single-battalion regiment that had declined the army's board's amalgamation suggestion and soldiered on with an unbroken thread to Cardwell and beyond. The Cheshire Regiment still saw itself as the 22nd Foot, and the equally pure-blooded Royal Welch Fusiliers recalled following Colonel James Webster over the first rail fence at Guilford Court House in 1781 ('Come on, my brave Fusiliers') and arriving with the fusilier brigade just in time to snatch victory from the jaws of defeat at Albuhera.

This account necessarily marches briskly past some of the more complex twists and turns in the story. There were brief reprieves as some regiments were reduced to company strength, reconstituted as regiments, but then amalgamated anyhow. In 1968 the Cameronians (Scottish Rifles), product of the 1881 union between the 26th Cameronian Regiment and the 90th Perthshire Light Infantry, chose disbandment rather than amalgamation with another regiment in the Lowland Brigade. The York and Lancaster Regiment similarly decided to disappear rather than amalgamate. The infantry was now grouped into administrative divisions – Guards, King's, Prince of Wales's, Queen's, Scottish, and Light, each composed of regiments with regional or historical links. In the Queen's Division, for instance, were the Queen's Regiment, the Royal Regiment of Fusiliers, and the Royal Anglian Regiment.[6] Within these divisions a good deal of effort was made to cross-post officers and warrant officers between regiments, to ensure that vacancies that could not be met by a particular regiment were filled from within the division. This process meant there were no log-jams of talent or, for that matter, black holes of inadequacy. Regimental depots, for so long a visible link between regiment and community, disappeared to be replaced by divisional depots, and then in turn by army training regiments. Then finally, in 1995, they were replaced by the Infantry Training Centre at Catterick in North Yorkshire, which trains all adult infantry soldiers in its two infantry training battalions, each of them containing companies aligned with the divisions of infantry, the Foot Guards or the Brigade of Gurkhas. Colonels of regiments, such significant figures at the beginning of our army's history, had been gradually losing their importance, although they remained influential, chairing the boards that interviewed potential officers at Sandhurst and keeping a watchful eye on officers' careers. They did their best to raise the regiment's profile within its area, worrying about recruiting (for the sounder a regiment's manning the greater its chance of survival), and in the great tradition of tribal chieftains, congratulating, commiserating, lamenting, applauding, advising, and warning. They were almost always senior officers, serving or retired, of the regiment concerned, appointed for a five-year period. The regiment's council made its recommendation, and the officer concerned was notified by the military secretary once his appointment had been approved by the queen. In my own case the military secretary emphasised that

the Army Board recognises the need to foster the regimental system to ensure that it remains robust and secure to face whatever the future holds; and the Army Board appreciates the contribution made by Colonels of Regiments who provide such valuable guidance, support and continuity.[7]

A regimental colonel had to appreciate that he had substantial influence, but little real power. In the not too distant past, if the regiment's preferred candidate for command of the 1st Battalion scored badly on the Command Board – which graded officers for appointments at this level – then the colonel might wear out goodwill in pressing well-placed senior officers (who were likely to be old friends) to ensure that his paragon got command despite the blip. He would be rash to try that now, although if there was no suitable candidate for command within the regiment, he could certainly expect to interview candidates from outside it who had scored highly on the Command Board. Though it would be made very clear that the ultimate decision was the military secretary's and not his, there might well be a pleasing congruence between the colonel's views and the eventual outcome.

The colonel of a regiment worked through his Regimental Headquarters. This was run by the regimental secretary (typically a retired colonel), and contained a small staff, usually a handful of retired officers with a little clerical support. They would look after the colonel, develop his policies, plan and run regimental events, dispense charity, publish the regimental journal, and maintain contact with museums and old comrades' organisations.[8] RHQs were also part-responsible for recruiting. Regiments were formally established to provide Regimental Information Teams, busy at shows and public events in the home area. Most also had a 'black economy': NCOs filched unofficially from the regular battalions. It made a real difference if RHQ could, by fair means or foul, get an NCO into every Army Careers Office in its area. Recruits are famously suggestible, often showing a mysterious preference for the cap-badge of the first man to interview them.

RHQs were also responsible for finding officers, and the best (the Winchester-based Royal Green Jackets had few equals) had long adhesive tendrils running deep into the community, and into schools with a tradition of helping to officer the regiment. Regimental officers were expected to keep their eyes and ears open, and tell RHQ if they found a suitable candidate. In 1969 Richard Dannatt, of Essex farming stock and with a loose preference for the Royal Armoured Corps because he had a school friend destined for the cavalry, was asked by a brigadier at the Regular Commissions Board whether he would like to know more about the infantry. He said that he would, and the Green Howards, conveniently stationed in Colchester, duly invited him to visit the battalion. Shortly afterwards he was told by RHQ 'that if I would like to join the Green Howards then they thought they could find me a place'.[9]

Headquarters were co-located with regimental depots and then, as these closed, scratched a living as best they could in a climate where it was increasingly hard to persuade officials bent on savings that there was any value added by what they did. They are now usually isolated, with no serving elements of the regiment at hand, striving to maintain those local contacts upon which so much still depends. In 2009–10 the process of drawing together most of the British-based units into 'super garrisons' – in Aldershot, the east of England, North Yorkshire, and Salisbury Plain – was completed. As Bob Ainsworth, Minister of State (Armed Forces) put it in 2009, these were to provide 'a sustainable military community better integrated with the local civilian community and the local civilian authorities. These will be places where people will want to work and live.' When asked whether this structure 'broadly reflects' where the army was recruited, he acknowledged, in the finest minster-speak:

> It can never do that in its entirety. The garrison in this country reflects historic decisions that have been made and facilities that have been located in different parts of the country. Of course it would be sensible, to the degree that is practical, to align the garrison of the army in Great Britain with the locations in which its members are recruited, and we should try to do that. However, we cannot simply change our footprint and an extensive estate that has existed for a long time.[10]

The truth is blunter. The super-garrisons are generally not where soldiers come from. The government's respectable desire to make economies of scale and to establish robust military communities pulls in precisely the reverse direction to maintaining a wider military presence in the country as a whole. RHQ the Royal Anglian Regiment shares the last remaining building of Gibraltar Barracks in Bury St Edmunds with the Suffolk Regiment Museum and an Army Careers Office. This building was once the Suffolk Regiment's depot and, predictably, one of those Cardwell keeps. RHQ The Princess of Wales's Royal Regiment is in Howe Barracks, Canterbury, though there has not been a battalion of the regiment in the barracks for many years and is not likely to be one in the foreseeable future. The regiment has a regular battalion in Woolwich, and another in Paderborn, Germany. Neither is deep in the regimental heartland.

The regimental system that existed in 2004 was no system at all. There were large regiments, like the Royal Anglians and the Royal Regiment of Fusiliers, now down to two battalions apiece;

amalgamated single-battalion regiments like the Devon and Dorsets; and those last four unadulterated line regiments. Links between regiments and their recruiting areas had been progressively weakened, though by dint of hard work and good local contacts a regiment could still tap profitably into traditional strengths, as the Worcestershire and Sherwood Forester Regiment demonstrated in the late 1990s.[11] Sometimes a distinguished regiment found itself with a recruiting base that could no longer sustain it. In 2004 the Black Watch affirmed that it welcomed applicants 'from the UK and across the world. We currently have soldiers from Texas, Canada, New Zealand, Australia, England, Wales, Gibraltar, and Fiji.'[12] It was not just the Black Watch that welcomed Fijians. These big, good-natured men were widely represented across most of the infantry. In 2004 the Princess of Wales's Royal Regiment drew about 75 per cent of its strength from within the regimental area of south-east England. Around 10 per cent of its soldiers were 'Foreign and Commonwealth,' including Fijians, Africans, South Africans and men from the Caribbean, like the Grenadian Private Johnson Beharry, who was to win the Victoria Cross on the 1st Battalion's Iraq deployment that year.

It was rare for a battalion to be so well up to strength that it could go on operations without being reinforced by men of another regiment, and sometimes there were crippling shortfalls. An under-recruited unit often became worse recruited by the minute, for any battalion in barracks had to find the manpower for certain 'fixed costs' in terms of guards and other duties. The smaller its numbers the more often such tasks came round, and the more frustrated soldiers became. When Richard Dannatt was commanding the Green Howards in 1989, on the eve of the 'Options for Change' or 'cull', he was

asked to supply thirty soldiers to reinforce the King's Regiment in Northern Ireland and was happy to do so, but was less happy when I was ordered to send another ninety to reinforce 3rd Battalion The Royal Anglian Regiment back in Londonderry. Chancing my arm a little, I refused to send ninety soldiers but offered to send a fully-formed rifle company instead, complete with its own officers, sergeants and corporals. There was some tooth-sucking at Headquarters Infantry before my offer was accepted ... I knew I would lose some Royal Anglian friends, but it was a case of survival of the fittest. As it happened we supplied three companies for six months each over an eighteen-month period.

The fact that the Green Howards were so comfortably up to strength told heavily in their favour, and when the decision was announced,

Sadly, and inevitably, 3rd Royal Anglian who we were reinforcing in Londonderry, were to be disbanded, together with the other two infantry battalions with us in 24th Airmobile Brigade – The Glosters and the Duke of Edinburgh's – who were to be amalgamated with each other.[13]

The 'Options for Change' amalgamations did not solve the problem of undermanning in the infantry, and the need to top up battalions with officers and soldiers from other units, or with mobilised reservists – a process that became common after the passing of the Reserve Forces Act 1996 – damaged one of the traditional arguments in favour of the regimental system. There were other issues too. Infantry battalions, like regiments of the Royal Armoured Corps, were posted wholesale from garrison to garrison in a process called 'arms plotting'. This meant that, at any given time, part of the infantry was 'in baulk' because it was preparing for, or recovering from, a move. Since changing garrisons usually involved a change of role – there is armoured, mechanised, light, and air assault infantry – some skills were lost and others had to be built. It was argued that the process ensured freshness and provided a constant challenge, but it was expensive: about £1 million to convert a light-role battalion to armoured infantry. Furthermore, when a battalion changed garrisons it dragged behind it a comet's tail of unhappiness as wives sought new jobs and children were put into new schools. This instability tended to worsen as one became more senior. An officer, who would be likely to alternate staff or instructional postings with regimental duty, could find himself an eternal bird of passage. When Richard Dannatt left the army as CGS in 2009 he and his wife had lived in twenty-three houses since 1977. In contrast, the Royal Artillery, the Royal Engineers, and the logistic corps practised 'trickle posting', rotating individuals between their more static regiments, and although some seasoned infantrymen maintained that this process diminished cohesion, there was little real evidence for this.

When the gravelly-voiced Mike Jackson became commander of the Allied Rapid Reaction Corps in 1997, he and his wife had moved seven times in twelve years of marriage, so he was well aware of the instability of army life. Although he had transferred to the Parachute Regiment as a captain in 1970, he had been commissioned into the Intelligence Corps and was a Russian linguist – and a member of MENSA. He felt that his predecessors had been reluctant to grasp the nettle of infantry structure on their watch; indeed, one of his most single-minded predecessors, General Sir Nigel Bagnall, had been 'seen off' by the Director of Infantry of the day when he had proposed a similar reform in the mid-1980s. So no sooner had Jackson become CGS in early 2003 than he made it clear that he would address it. He produced a list of criteria that should be embodied in any future structure, and it could be seen, early on, that he tended towards the 'large regiment' solution. It was to be tempting for those who would be infuriated by his eventual recommendations to maintain that he came to the issue *parti pris*, had done too little regimental duty to understand the real strength of the regiment, and lacked the combat experience that might have shown him the error of his ways. But there was a strong swell of opinion, certainly amongst junior and middle-piece officers, in his favour. In July 2004 a large group of infantry officers attending the Joint Service Command and Staff College wrote to tell him of their wish to

> see a system that fits the demand of the present day and future so that we deliver the most effective possible level of fighting capability. We anticipate that the initiative proposed achieves this, and trust that the implementation will be sensitive to all, swift in execution and bold in scope. We respect the legacy of our forebears which will always be enshrined in any Regimental System, but hope that they will support us in making these changes that we believe are crucial to the infantry's ability to fight and win in the conflicts of today and tomorrow.[14]

The decision was complicated by the belief that the infantry could manage with four fewer battalions, largely because the situation in

Northern Ireland had improved. This was certainly a contentious view, and Richard Dannatt thought that it reflected Whitehall's failure to 'appreciate the value of well-trained infantry, especially in the type of warfare with which we had been engaged since the end of the Cold War'.[15] The Treasury, with its unerring knack of gauging the price of everything and the value of nothing, had initially demanded a reduction of at least ten battalions. In the spring of 2004 General Jackson tasked the adjutant general, Lieutenant General Sir Alistair Irwin, with writing a paper on the strengths and weaknesses of the regimental system. General Irwin had read history at St Andrews before going to Sandhurst. He was the third generation of his family to join the Black Watch in modern times – 'more like a religion than a regiment,' wrote Bernard Fergusson – taking command of its 1st Battalion in 1985.[16] The Irwin paper was wholly honest and objective. On the credit side, it affirmed that 'the best of the current regimental system is a sense of belonging to an entity which has an existence, a past, present, and future of its own ... all our officers and soldiers acquire a sense of belonging when they join.' It provided continuity, ensuring 'the ability of individuals to keep returning to the regiment or corps in which they began, to their individual benefit and the benefit of their units'. General Irwin argued that regional connections helped provide a focus for recruiting and, though the evidence was equivocal, 'those examples of where regional connections are strong represent part of what is best in the current regimental system.' He emphasised the importance of names and traditions, and of *esprit de corps*.

He also acknowledged that there was a debit side too. There was a risk of inflexibility: 'The talents and the skills of the best officers and NCOs are often ignored and their ambitions thwarted,' he wrote, 'by keeping them with their own regiments, regardless of where those regiments might be stationed.' He admitted that 'the main, perhaps the only reason that we continue to arms plot is to ensure that the current ... system is preserved.' Furthermore, 'by tying individuals to particular units ... we ensure that when the unit moves they move too, regardless of whether it is convenient or desired.' And he feared that units would find it hard to generate 'critical mass, because authorised strengths were already too low,' and simply recruiting up to that strength 'gives no room for manoeuvre; it has excluded the human dimension from the numbers equation'. In consequence, 'today's single-unit regiments struggle on a daily basis to make ends meet in manpower terms, regardless of their role or readiness state.'[17]

The Army Board decided to recommend the adoption of a system based wholly on large regiments. Arms plotting would disappear, and instead battalions would be based in one location for the long term, and individuals could expect to be posted between their regiment's battalions as required. While the changes were warmly welcomed by some, they were catastrophic for others. 'It had a devastating impact on my own regiment,' said Richard Dannatt,

> as it meant the end of the Green Howards after 318 years of loyal service to the Crown. The Green Howards became part of the much larger Yorkshire regiment. To be specific, 1st Battalion, The Green Howards (Alexandra Princess of Wales's Yorkshire Regiment) became 2nd Battalion The Yorkshire Regiment (Green Howards).[18]

On the day in 2004 that the crucial decision was taken, General Dannatt was commander of NATO's Allied Rapid Reaction Corps, and not a member of the Executive Committee of the Army Board (ECAB). Once the board had finished the day's work he joined its members as they reconfigured into No 1 Board, the group that decides senior officers' promotions and appointments.

> As I went into the meeting room I saw … Alistair Irwin … with his head in his hands. 'What's up?' I asked, knowing Alistair pretty well. 'This is the worst day of my life,' he replied, explaining how the ECAB discussion and decisions had gone. I felt for him. At the time he was the only born and bred infantryman on ECAB, and as a fellow infantryman I could understand his anguish. The logic of the situation was clear, but logic and emotion and history do not always go hand in glove … Of course on the day of the decisive meeting Alistair could have resigned in protest, but to what point? The decisions would still have been taken in the army's wider interests, and his resignation would not have changed the outcome. Instead, he nobly continued, working to secure the best outcome for his Regiment, Scotland and the Army.[19]

In its original form the new structure left The Princess of Wales's Royal Regiment, the Royal Regiment of Fusiliers, the Royal Anglian Regiment, the Light Infantry, and the Royal Green Jackets as they were, with two regular battalions apiece. In the Scottish Division, the Royal Scots and King's Own Scottish Borderers became The Royal Scots Borderers (1st Battalion, the Royal Regiment of Scotland). The Royal Highland Fusiliers, the Black Watch, the Highlanders, and the Argyll and Sutherland Highlanders took seniority thereafter, as 2nd to 5th battalions, the Royal Regiment of Scotland. The King's Division now comprised two battalions of the Duke of Lancaster's Regiment (King's, Lancashire, and Border) and the three-battalion Yorkshire Regiment (14th/15th, 19th, and 33rd/76th Foot). The Prince of Wales's Division also comprised two new regiments, the three-battalion Mercian regiment – 1st Battalion (Cheshires), 2nd Battalion (Worcesters and Foresters), and 3rd Battalion (Staffords) – the two-battalion Royal Welsh Regiment. The Parachute Regiment retained three battalions, but one of these was to form the core of the new Special Forces Support Group and was removed from the infantry order of battle. Territorial units were wisely aligned with the new structure, so that each regiment had at least one Territorial battalion.

After the main decisions had received ministerial approval, The Light Infantry and The Royal Green Jackets announced their intention of amalgamating as The Rifles in 2007. In the process, and after some hard-headed negotiations with both regimental councils, they caught up both the Devon and Dorsets and the Royal Regiment of Gloucestershire, Berkshire, and Wiltshire, who were originally to have been amalgamated into a battalion of Light Infantry. There was particular grief about the disappearance of the title Light Infantry; the move was indeed both swift and bold. It left The Rifles with five regular battalions, including one in 3 Commando Brigade, and thus unrivalled opportunities for service in various roles. Within three years of its formation, three battalions of the new regiment had served with distinction in Afghanistan, and the regiment had become the most sought-after amongst Sandhurst cadets.

In sharp contrast, changes within Scots regiments caused very serious dissatisfaction. Alistair Irwin initially threw his full weight behind them, arguing that the new regiment would

Preserve those things that we all hold most dear in Scotland, while at the same time providing for our people a very attractive combination of increased personal and family stability and a much wider career choice for all our officers and men within the same regiment … I regard the preservation of real and meaningful links with the past as being particularly important.

These 'overt and strong' links would be fostered by the policy of naming battalions, with the battalion name followed by its regimental bracketed title. He was also happy that links with the past would be maintained by battalions continuing to wear specific items of uniform: 'So the Black Watch battalion will continue to wear that famous red hackle, and The Highlanders their blue hackle.' We have already seen that there was a close relationship between successful recruiting and regimental survival, and General Irwin pointed out that

> The reason that we have been required to lose a battalion from Scotland is that for many years now we have been the worst recruited division in the whole of the infantry … In fact our figures are so bad, with four of our six battalions in the top 10 worst recruited battalions in the whole army, that we very nearly lost two battalions.

He was concerned that opposition to the changes would 'dispirit the serving community', and called for support for young men who wished to join.[20]

The discussion swiftly slipped beyond logic. A vociferous 'Save the Scottish Regiments' campaign assailed the government's decision, with well-attended public meetings in Scotland containing be-medalled veterans, and in one case a youngster bearing a placard announcing that he wanted to join his grandfather's regiment. A fiercely critical website listed the Scottish regimental colonels, noting that all but one had voted in favour of what it called 'disbandment and amalgamation', although it did not speculate how they might have been lured into acting against their consciences. 1st Battalion the Black Watch, serving in Iraq for the second time in two years, had been deployed, at American request, for a difficult tour of duty to Camp Dogwood, near Baghdad. Scots Nationalist MP Annabelle

Ewing called Secretary of State Geoff Hoon 'nothing but a back stabbing coward' for agreeing to the regiment's merger after it had
performed with such distinction. In Edinburgh, Scots Nationalist
leader Alex Salmond blamed the Scots Labour MPs who had
supported the government: they were Scotland's 'parcel o' rogues'.

Things went from bad to worse when it became clear in 2005 that
the regiment would wear a new cap-badge on the fore-and-aft
Glengarry in its most formal uniform, with the insignia of the separate
regiments worn on other occasions. General Irwin had by then retired
to Scotland, where the *Herald* quipped that the name of his new house,
Drumuaine, might have been prefaced by 'Should've'.[21] He told *The
Times* that he had learnt of the decision 'with the utmost dismay', and
had written to General Jackson, urging him to reverse it, for

> This will make the task of building up the new regiment more diffi-
> cult … Up until now we have been doing quite well, bringing every-
> one along with the plans. We had a kilted regiment, the red hackle,
> and we retained our local links which are so important to us … The
> decision has overturned all the good work that had led to support-
> ive hinterlands and serving battalions keen to get on with the
> change and make the best of it. Of course, we shall press ahead, and
> the serving men will do their duty, but this decision makes it all the
> harder. The sense of gloom that has fallen on us is palpable. People
> feel let down.[22]

Jeff Duncan, of the 'Save Our Scottish Regiments' campaign, was
fiercely critical of General Irwin. 'Alistair Irwin, who is universally
accepted as having written a paper which was the blueprint advocat-
ing the creation of a single super regiment, has for the past 16 months
stressed that the golden threads that bind the regiments together
would be retained by the individual Scottish regiments … Alistair
Irwin's final chance to do the right thing has arrived.'[23] This was
published *after* Alistair Irwin had 'most passionately' urged General
Jackson to adhere to what he saw as the original cap-badge agreement, and we might wonder what options were now available to him.
Few who read the Irwin paper would deduce that it was a blueprint
for the creation of anything – still less of a large Scottish regiment.
The discussion had now become so rancorous that the Royal Regiment

of Scotland's cap-badge, a thoughtfully designed lion rampant, surmounted by a Scots crown, on a St Andrew's saltire, was described by some of the scheme's opponents as 'a crucified pussy'. Lieutenant Colonel Stuart Crawford thought that 'a better and more appropriate badge might be a dagger in the back, superimposed on a white flag.'[24]

The fundamental issue of under-recruiting in the Scots infantry was rarely addressed by supporters of the status quo, and many who sympathised with those so deeply hurt by the changes found it hard to see how the fragile business of recruiting would be improved by wholesale criticism of the new structure. Some of the English and Welsh regiments amalgamated at this time were older and not a jot less distinguished than similarly affected Scots regiments. It was no less of a painful wrench for the Green Howards to become 2 Yorks; the Cheshires to become 1 Mercian; and the Royal Welch Fusiliers to become 1 Royal Welsh. There was much private grief and a smattering of public protest south of the border, but ultimately change was accepted more positively than it was in Scotland. Richard Dannatt had no doubt that it had been an extraordinarily painful process, for, as he saw it,

> the history of the British Army invariably points to the strength of the Army being the strength of the Regimental System. We tinker with it at our peril, and just got away with it between 2004 and 2005. Later, as Chief of the General Staff, it was up to me to own and implement those earlier decisions, and in the frenetic world of the Army in recent years I believe we have come through this re-organisation intact. For some it has gone better than others, but the future is in front and the past behind. We have always adapted and must continue to do so.[25]

Scotland's turmoil emphasised that local connections were still important, even if it was not always easy to translate them into serving soldiers; that veterans, proudly wearing badges and medals, attracted public sympathy; that politicians would be quick to engage, often as part of a wider battle; and that the media was unlikely to let lack of knowledge prevent it from entering the fray. Also, in a much broader sense, it hammered home yet again the point that the regimental system is at least as much about emotion as about logic. As the date of the Army Board's eventual decision approached, colonels of regiments strained every nerve in order to ensure a favourable outcome, marshalling their supporters, military, civic, and political, while leaking like sieves to an attentive press. I myself had become convinced that, although with two well-recruited regular battalions my regiment should, in logic, emerge intact – as indeed it did – its survival was now the single most important thing to me. A few months before I was standing steady for demographic logic and workable compromise. Now, suddenly, that turbulent undertow of collar dogs and stable belts, facing colours, and goose-necked spurs had tugged me off my feet.

CHAPTER 20

TRIBAL MARKINGS

N O SOONER DID the army dress in uniform than the centrifugal
pressures of the regimental system strove to make it as far from
uniform as possible. Regiments developed their own particular quirks
of dress to distinguish themselves from each other; some subtle, some
less so. As a 1645 description of Parliament's New Model Army noted
'The men are redcoats all, the whole army are only distinguished by
the several facings of their coats.'[1] There was no regular army before
the Restoration, but both the Yeomen of the Guard and the Yeomen
Warders (founded by Henry VII in 1485) wore the Tudor livery of
red. After 1660, horse – with the exception of the Blues – and foot
alike dressed in red. Artillery, light cavalry, and logisticians wore blue,
and rifle regiments green. Logisticians came into being after the
army's transport, supply, and medical services were fully professional-
ised in the nineteenth century. Uniform coats were 'faced', usually in
a contrasting colour, although the 33rd Foot obstinately wore red
faced with red.

The long coats of the eighteenth century were lined in the facing
colour, which showed to good effect on the wide, buttoned-back
lapels, the turned-up cuffs and the garment's inside where it was
folded back across the thigh. In the eighteenth century coats were
'laced' with broad worsted ribbon of regimental pattern that stretched
from the inner edge of the lapel to each buttonhole, where it might
end square or in the arrowhead called a 'bastion-end'. Practice varied
greatly – some regiments paired their buttons and so doubled up the
lace – but cuffs, pocket edges, and coat turnbacks were all suitable

candidates for the application of lace; drummers were smothered in it.

Red coats were last worn in battle in the Sudan in 1885. By 1902, when the last pattern of red tunic was authorised, facings simply appeared on collar and cuffs. The War Office had made an earlier attempt to standardise by ordering that all royal regiments should wear blue facings, and all non-royal regiments white. The scheme soon foundered with the Buffs arguing it was absurd that they should lose a facing colour that defined them. By 1914 regiments had facing colours that, in many cases, dated from the 1748 regulations. There was indeed a good deal of blue and white, but amongst the more vivid exceptions the Royal Northumberland Fusiliers wore gosling green, the Norfolks yellow, the Devons Lincoln green, and the Middlesex lemon yellow. The Duke of Wellington's Regiment, naturally enough, followed the precedent of the 33rd Foot and wore red facings, just as the 33rd had done in 1748. The Queen's Own Royal West Kent, a Cardwell merger of the 50th and 97th Foot, had the black facings that had earned the 50th its nickname 'the dirty half-hundred'.

Facing colours marked a man to his regiment as surely as a distinctive cowhide shield linked one of Shaka's Zulu warriors to his. When Sergeant Ned Botwood of the 47th Foot wrote the words of the song 'Hot Stuff' before he embarked for the attack on Quebec in 1758 he made much of the fact that his regiment's spare clothing had been taken by a French privateer, and the best they could do was to buy the redundant coats of Shirley's Foot. In consequence the Marquis de Montcalm, to whom Botwood attributed encyclopaedic knowledge of British regimentalia, would be sadly confused.

> When the Forty-seventh regiment is dashing ashore,
> When bullets are whistling and cannons do roar,
> Says Montcalm 'Those are Shirley's, I know their lapels.'
> 'You lie,' says Ned Botwood, 'We are of Lascelles!
> Though our clothing is changed, yet we scorn a powder-puff;
> So at ye, ye bitches, here's give you Hot Stuff.'[2]

Facing colours were also used for the fronts of grenadier caps, the shells of drums, bells of arms (the bell-shaped canvas covers used to protect stacked muskets), and the broad shoulder-belts worn by drum majors. Each company in the infantry battalions of Charles II's army carried its own colour and each troop of horse its own standard. During the Civil War, infantry colours had been carried on short staves and flourished enthusiastically by their bearers. Captain Thomas Venn had seen plenty of service, and devoted several pages to 'Postures and Flourishing' in his 1672 manual. By about 1700 there were just three colours in each battalion, one for the small body of pikemen in its centre, and the other two for the two 'sleeves' of musketeers on their flanks. In 1743 battalions were ordered to carry only a pair (properly a 'stand') of colours. The Sovereign's Colour of an English regiment was originally 'the standard of St George', a red cross on a white ground with the regiment's distinctive motif, usually derived from its colonel's arms, in the centre. Scots regiments bore the white-on-blue saltire. After the 1707 Act of Union brought England and Scotland together, the Sovereign Colour became the Union flag, and these new colours were first carried in a general action at Oudenarde on 11 July 1708. What was at first called the 'Second Colour' – eventually known as the Regimental Colour – was usually of the regiment's facing colour, with its motif or device in the centre and the Union in its upper canton. Regiments with red or white facings bore a red cross on a white field, with a Union in the upper canton, though in 1881 they adopted the regiment's facing colour, and the Union disappeared.

Between 1743 and 1751 Horse Guards stamped out the practice of colonels using personal devices on colours, and a 1743 warrant specified the badges that 'old corps' were allowed to use. From 1751 the regiment's number, in Roman numerals, appeared within a laurel wreath in the centre of both colours. In 1760 the first battle honour, Emdsorf, was formally granted to the 15th Light Dragoons, although some regiments had unofficially adopted battle honours before this. In 1784 the 12th, 39th, 56th, and 58th Foot were allowed to bear 'Gibraltar' on their colours, and the practice soon became more widespread, with 'Minden' granted to the appropriate regiments in 1801. A committee was set up in 1882 to regularise the business, and regiments now bear a selection of their world-war battle honours on the Queen's Colour and a selection of others on the Regimental Colour: all have far more than can be accommodated on a stand of colours. Colours were initially made of painted silk, but were then embroidered from the early nineteenth century. The size altered too: in 1747 the orders were given to stick to 78 ins long by 74 ins deep. They were steadily reduced thereafter, to 48×42 ins in 1858 – when they gained a two-inch gold and red silk fringe – and then 45×36 ins in 1865. The staff was reduced from 118 ins, including its ornamental spearhead, to 105 ins in 1873, by which time a gilded lion and crown had replaced the pointed finial.

For many years cavalry flags – square-ended standards for horse and dragoon guards, and swallow-tailed guidons for dragoons – were more numerous than infantry colours, for individual troops retained their own. However, the tactical role of light cavalry meant that it was inappropriate for them to carry guidons in the field. They were not taken to the Peninsula, and were abolished in 1834, reappearing only in 1959. Heavy cavalry bore troop standards until the early nineteenth century, and then carried two, Sovereign's and Regimental, till 1858 when they were ordered to retain only the Sovereign's standard. Just as the campaign role of light cavalry made guidons an encumbrance, so rifle regiments, from their foundation, had no use for colours. Neither did the Royal Artillery, though its battle honour 'Ubique' (everywhere) testified to its wide-ranging achievements.[3] We should not, however, expect too strict an application of logic as the Parachute Regiment bears colours, and the Army Air Corps a guidon.

Colours were presented to a regiment at a formal parade where they were consecrated before being handed over by an appropriate dignitary. They were then 'trooped' in slow time down the battalion's ranks, traditionally so that men should recognise their colours so as to defend them or rally on them in time of need. The process now forms the central part of the annual Queen's Birthday Parade when the colours of a Foot Guards battalion are trooped. Lieutenant Gordon-Alexander of the 93rd Highlanders tells us,

> The old colours of the 93rd, which had been presented by the great Duke of Wellington in the year 1834, and had been carried throughout the campaign in the Crimea, were replaced on May 22, 1857, by new colours received at the hands of His Royal Highness the Duke of Cambridge, who had but recently been appointed Commander-in-Chief.[4]

The old colours were marched off parade, to be laid up in a church or cathedral: the 93rd's were placed in Glasgow Cathedral above the monument to the regiment's Crimean dead. Traditionally both the presentation and laying up of colours strengthened a regiment's links with its recruiting area, and persuading a notable figure to preside over the ceremony gave extra *éclat*. On Minden Day, 1 August 1986, the Royal Hampshires received new colours from their colonel-in-chief, the Princess of Wales, in the brilliant sunshine of the cricket ground at Tidworth (in the county by a hair's-breadth), and the old colours were later laid up in Winchester Cathedral, a short walk from the old Royal Hampshire depot.

Colours spent much of their lives in cases made of black oiled canvas with a brass cap. In peacetime they would be accommodated in the commanding officer's lodgings or in the mess once these were in general use. They were borne, in battle or on the march, by the battalion's junior ensigns, and passed up amongst the subalterns by reverse seniority as the need arose, from tiredness on the march or casualties in action. A colour belt, passing over the wearer's left shoulder, housed a socket into which the butt of the colour-pike could be slotted, taking much of its weight, and cased colours might be sloped across the ensign's shoulder on the march. Colours were not uncased without reason – when action was evidently imminent, for instance, or when the regiment was on parade, or was about to make its formal entry into a town or garrison.

Even if the colours were already uncased, the ensign would keep them secured by holding them against the staff with his right hand, letting them fly only on appropriate occasions. The etiquette was elaborate. For instance, if the battalion was quick-marching past a senior officer, then the ensign to the Regimental Colour would slip the silk from his hand to let it fly on the order 'eyes left' or 'eyes right', deftly snatching it back on 'eyes front', while the ensign to the Sovereign's Colour kept a haughty grip on his colour, letting it fly only for the monarch or their representative. If the battalion, drawn up in line on the very best of its behaviour, delivered a general salute, with the band thumping out 'Point of War', the ensigns slipped their colours from their belts, extended them out to the right and then, in one of the most elegant of drill movements, swung them gently downwards and to the left, ending with the gleaming silk laid out before them. However, the Sovereign's Colour remained stock-still unless the recipient of the salute enjoyed the required royal status.

Regiments would carry their colours uncased through British cities, and ensigns were careful not to let their colours fly. The exception being if they had been granted the Freedom of the City, which gave them right of entry 'with bayonets fixed, colours flying and drums beating'. Here again there was a close relationship between recruiting and identity, for a regiment might expect to enjoy the freedom of the cities and major towns within its area, and to hold 'freedom' parades from time to time, capitalising on the appeal of music and spectacle to pick up recruits. Colours were received on, or marched off, parade with the battalion at 'present arms', and were saluted as they passed. The Royal Artillery extended similar honours to its guns. Because rifle regiments never bore colours, after the Devon and Dorsets had been transformed into 1/Rifles their colours were laid up, on 27 June 2007, in Exeter Cathedral.

The word ensign referred to the colour's bearer regardless of his rank, though for a long time it also defined the junior commissioned rank in the infantry. An ensign might well be in his late teens and carrying the colour was a practical problem, because even at the best of times it was heavy, and unwieldy if allowed to fly. On the battlefield it was a natural magnet for hostile fire and physical attack. A stand of colours would be protected by a small group of dedicated NCOs (now constituting two sergeants and a warrant officer) known collectively as the 'colour party'. Carrying or defending the colours was a dangerous business, as Sergeant William Lawrence of the 40th Foot knew when, on the afternoon of Waterloo, he was ordered to take his place in the colour party:

> This ... was a job I did not like at all, but still I went to the work as boldly as I could. There had been before me that day fourteen sergeants already killed and wounded while in charge of the colours, and officers in proportion, and the staff and colours were almost cut in pieces.[5]

Colours were last carried in battle at Laing's Nek in 1881, when the 58th Regiment had 74 men killed, including its commanding officer, and 101 wounded while attacking the Boers. Lieutenants Peel and

Baillie set off up the hillside with the Queen's and Regimental colours under a scorching fire. When Baillie was hit, Peel picked up his colour, and struggled on with both until he tripped in an ant-bear hole and was knocked unconscious. Thinking him dead, Sergeant Budstock took both colours to the rear. Lieutenant Hill carried Baillie to safety but the wounded officer was hit again, this time mortally.

It was already evident that colours were very vulnerable in irregular warfare. The Regimental Colour of the 1/24th Foot was lost when the Zulus overran the British camp at Isandlwana, and the Queen's Colour, carried off by Lieutenant Teignmouth Melvill, was found in the Buffalo River ten days later, as Captain Charlie Harford tells us. He

> stumbled on the Colour case mixed up with a host of other things and picking it up I said to Harber, who was closest to me, 'Look, here's the case! The Colours can't be far off!' Then ... I noticed a straight piece of stick in the middle of the river, almost in line with us ... He waded straight in, up to his middle, and got hold of it. On lifting it out he brought up the colour still adhering to it, and on getting it out of the water handed the standard to me, and as he did so the gold-embroidered central scroll dropped out, the silk having more or less rotted from the long immersion in the water.[6]

Both colours of the 66th Foot were lost at Maiwand in Afghanistan in 1880, and neither has ever been recovered.

Colours were emotive enough even in peacetime, and the composition of colour parties, bringing together as they did young officers and older sergeants, symbolised the battalion's internal cohesion. An ensign had much to learn, not least about the way that the same NCOs who got you out of trouble on parade, might very well get you into it when champagne and bitter were involved at celebrations afterwards. One of the most evocative acts of regimental symbolism commemorates Sergeant Bernard McCabe of the 31st (Huntingdonshire) Regiment. In the attack on the Sikh entrenchments at Sobraon in 1846 Lieutenant Tritton and Ensign Jones, carrying the Queen's and Regimental Colours of the 31st, were shot down. Lieutenant Noel recovered the Queen's Colour and carried it with the main assault along the line of the Sikh earthworks, while Sergeant

McCabe seized the Regimental Colour and clambered right up to plant it atop the rampart, rallying the attackers. He was commissioned in the field and died bravely as a captain in the 32nd Foot at Lucknow. On 10 February each year, the anniversary of the battle, the Regimental Colour of 1/Queen's was marched from the Officers' Mess, through the ranks of the battalion, to the Warrant Officers' and Sergeants' Mess, where it was held for the day and eventually recovered, at great peril to his liver, by a subaltern. That day the ensign was not an officer, but a sergeant specially selected for the honour of being 'Sobraon Sergeant' for the year. The tradition is today upheld by the Princess of Wales's Royal Regiment.

Several regiments had unofficial colours, both the Seaforth Highlanders and the Highland Light Infantry owing their single extra colour to distinguished performance at Major General Arthur Wellesley's victory over the Marathas at Assaye in 1803. The Royal Northumberland Fusiliers had a third colour in memory of the 5th Foot's conduct at Wilhelmstahl in 1762, and it was carried on St George's Day by a drummer. 2/Duke of Wellington's Regiment had an extra stand of colours, presented to the regiment by the Court of Directors of the Honourable East India Company as a reward for the 76th Foot's conduct in India.

The 2nd Foot (The Queen's) retained a third, or colonel's, colour – allegedly presented by Catherine of Braganza – until 1750, when the regiment carried it into Dublin, and its colonel, well aware that the rules were being broken, ordered it to be laid up in the chapel of the Royal Hospital at Kilmainham. In 1824 the Queen's was granted royal permission to carry a third colour and, even though this authority was soon revoked, managed to retain one, provided it did not appear on parade. The original colour had grown very shabby by the time it was replaced, and over the years some replacements have owed much to lively imaginations: one bore the words 'From the Queen 1661', a year before Catherine married Charles II. The design eventually reverted to the 'traditional' sea-green sheet bearing Catherine's crowned cipher. The final version was presented to 1/Queen's at its Jubilee parade in 1977, although production in Pakistan had led to compromises: the colour was in two joined sections, and 'it could not be described as sea green'. However, as one of the battalion's subalterns put it 'The main thing ... was that the tradition of the

Colonel's Colour, which dates back to the pre-Restoration regiments of Harley, Fitzgerald and Farrell, had been maintained for another generation.'[7] It had been carried, quite illegally, on the King's Birthday parade in Hong Kong in 1927, appeared again at 1/Queen's disbandment parade in 1992, and is now in the hands of 1/Princess of Wales's Royal Regiment.

Once men saw their colours regularly. Victorian soldiers knew them so well as to be able to stitch them, in long hours in a numbingly cold barrack room, onto the fabric panels that still emerge from junk shops and attics. It is no coincidence that the charity, Fine Cell Work, currently teaches embroidery to prisoners. Soldiers saw them stiffly trooped in their first crisp splendour, trudged behind them in the dust of India's Grand Trunk Road, glimpsed them wreathed in powder-smoke on the field, and might eventually peer up at them, skeletal and dusty, when they themselves were old men gathered in the hush of a cathedral. The Victorian general, Edward Hamley, was a gunner, but when he saw the laid-up colours of the 43rd Foot he wrote:

> A moth-eaten rag on a worm-eaten pole
> It does not look likely to stir a man's soul,
> 'Tis the deeds that were done 'neath the moth-eaten rag,
> When the pole was a staff, and the rag was a flag.

The battle honours and regimental devices on colours, standards and guidons rippled out to colour the wider tapestry of regimental tradition.

Every regiment celebrated special days, some of them with echoes of Sobraon. The Royal Berkshires commemorated the 62nd Foot's participation in the Anglo-Sikh War at the Battle of Ferozeshah, by entrusting the colours to the sergeants on 21 December, Ferozeshah Day; the custom was carried on into the Duke of Edinburgh's Royal Regiment. The South Staffordshires celebrated the 80th's perform-ance in the same battle by handing the colours over to the sergeants. Colour Sergeant Kirkland of the 80th captured a Sikh standard in the battle, and it is still in the Staffordshire Regiment Memorial Chapel in Lichfield Cathedral. The 10th and 29th Regiments had fought alongside one another at Sobraon. The officers of their lineal descendants, 1/Royal Anglian and 2/Mercian, are honorary members of one another's messes, and the adjutants of the two battalions refer to one another in correspondence as 'My Dear Cousin'. 2/Mercian celebrates Alma Day on 20 September by having its Regimental Colour trooped through the ranks by a private soldier. When the 95th Foot ascended the slope above the River Alma in 1854 both ensigns were felled by Russian fire, and Private Keenan picked up the colour and planted it in the Great Redoubt.

Most regimental days mark victories. The Cheshires celebrated the 22nd Foot's part in the defeat of the amirs of Scinde at Meanee on 17 February 1843; the Prince of Wales's Own Regiment of Yorkshire held Quebec Day, 13 September, sacred because the 15th Foot helped Wolfe win his battle on the Heights of Abraham; and the Durham Light Infantry marked the 68th's role in the foggy slaughter of Inkerman on 5 November 1854. When the British stormed Badajoz on 6 April 1812, Lieutenant MacPherson of the 45th Foot, having no Union flag to hand, ran his short scarlet coatee up the castle's flag-pole to show that the place was taken. The Sherwood Foresters duly celebrated Badajoz Day each year, sending a red coat up the flagstaff of Nottingham castle, a practice continued today by 2/Mercian. There were relatively few British cavalry regiments in India, but the 16th Lancers charged Sikh squares at Aliwal on 28 January 1848, giving the 16th/5th Lancers its regimental day, and initiating the regimental practice of pleating lance-pennons to mimic their creasing with blood.

Although the charge of the light brigade at Balaclava on 25 October 1854 was at best a pyrrhic victory, it gave regimental days to both the 13th/18th Hussars and the Queen's Royal Irish Hussars. Maiwand was anything but a triumph, but the Royal Berkshires were to recall the last stand of the 66th with justifiable pride. The Cheshires celebrated Mons, although their battle, fought on 24 August 1914, was the day after the main action. 1/Cheshire held the long, gentle slope above the village of Audregnies on the left flank of the retreating British army. It was effectively wiped out, losing 771 officers and men, but managed to keep the flank covered. The officers' wives had embroidered a quarter-scale regimental colour that was awarded to the best shooting company, and Captain Shore of B Company decided to take it to France in August 1914. It was carried by Drummer

Charles Baker, who, with the collapse of the position imminent, managed to hide it. Private Harold Riley told the nun nursing him what had happened, and eventually, thanks to priest, schoolmaster, and village secretary, the colour was rolled into a length of pipe and hidden in a bricked-up attic. The Cheshires sent a colour party back to the village to collect it on 17 November 1918.

The Royal Scots emphasised their antiquity by having 28 March as their regimental day. It was on 28 March 1633 that the Privy Council of Scotland, under the authority of Charles I, issued a warrant for the raising of the regiment. The Black Watch allegedly won the right to its wholly distinctive red hackle for bravery at the battle of Geldermalsen in 1795, although there is some evidence that the regiment had already worn the hackle in North America. Officers and men were presented with their red vulture feathers on the king's official birthday that year, though it was not until 1822 that formal permission for the wearing of the hackle was given. In 1919 the central committee of the Black Watch Association resolved that Red Hackle Day would be celebrated on 5 January, and this continues.

The days of national patron saints were celebrated with appropriate enthusiasm. Irish regiments made much of St Patrick's Day, 17 March, and in North America Captain John Peebles saw that his fellow Scots also did their best for the old gentleman. In 1777 Peebles was adjutant to a battalion of grenadiers, made up by combining the grenadier companies of individual battalions. He and his men lived on transports and went ashore when the chance offered.

> Monday 17th March. Ushered in with St Patrick's Day in the morning. At 'Reveille' beating, parade ashore at the usual hour, the Shamrock mounted by the Hibernians who dedicate the day to the saint and the bottle or rather to the saint for the sake of the bottle, we drank to his memory at dinner in the cabin, but was more amply sacrificed to between decks.

Peebles was in Philadelphia in the following year, when

> the Hibernians mounted the Shamrock and an Irish grenadier personated St Patrick in a procession through the streets with a prodigious mob after him – the friendly brothers [of the Order of

St Patrick, an admirable anti-duelling society whose regimental branches were called 'Marching Knots'] and several other Irish Clubs dined together and dedicated the day to the saint and the bottle.

He was back in his own battalion in 1781, when he saw that celebrations started before the usual time: 'several men drunk on parade this morning, no keeping them sober when they get money.'[8] Things were more decorously observed on St Andrew's Day, 30 November. On the evening of 29 November 1799 Peebles 'gave out a dollar a man and two to the sergeants to keep St Andrew's'. On the great day itself, he

Went to Town to celebrate the day with his Excellency [General Sir Henry Clinton] where the field officers and captains of the 42nd were invited, the admiral [Arbuthnot] there the officers of the Royal Highland Emigrants and some others, about 24 in all. Major Small personated the saint, who gave good toasts and apropos for the occasion. The admiral very chatty and entertaining. Major [Adam] Hay sang some good songs and spouted a prologue very well, a good dinner and drink till 10 o'clock. A numerous party of the Sons of St Andrew dined at Hicks' above 60, among whom were the subs of the 42nd. Exchanged a compliment, and some of our company joined them after we broke up, and made a night of it.[9]

St David's Day – *Dydd Gwyl Dewi Sant* – falls on 1 March, and was the subject of particular attention from the Royal Welch Fusiliers. On 1 March 1808 Captain Thomas Henry Browne found himself aboard ship on the Atlantic, but that did not stop the festivities.

This being St David's Day and mine a Welsh regiment, we did honour to our tutelary Saint, in the best manner that our station would permit. The custom of the corps is, that on that day, immediately after dinner, when we are in barracks, one of the little drum-boys rides a large goat, with which the regiment is always provided, round the mess-room, carrying in his hand a dish of leeks. Each officer is called upon to eat one, for which he pays the drummer a shilling. The older officers of the regiment, and those who have seen service with it in the field, are favoured with only a small one, and salt. Those who have before celebrated St David's Day with the regiment, but have only seen garrison duty with it, are required to eat a larger one without salt, and those unfortunates, who for the first time, have sat at the mess, on this their saint's day, have presented to them the largest leek that can be procured, and unless sickness prevent it, no respite is given, until the last tip of the green leaf is enclosed in the unwilling mouth; and day after day passes before the smell; and taste is fairly got rid of. This may be a nasty way of making a Welsh Fusilier – and so it is, but not much worse than making a man pass though a dirty horse pond, in order to become a freeholder of Berwick. We could not, of course, on board our little ship, render all the honours due to the day, but we had every thing dressed in onions, and drank an extra glass of grog on the occasion.[10]

Captain James Dunn proudly records how 2/Royal Welch Fusiliers kept up the tradition, regardless of circumstances, on the Western Front. On 1 March 1918, with the great German offensive palpably on its way, the battalion in the line and the officers' mess corporal arrested by Military Police (it was just one glass, his chums maintained, but he had no head for drink), the mess staff achieved a miracle.

The only possible hut ... was occupied until after dark by Englishmen who knew not David and didn't want to hear about him ... only the largest of the holes, through which a raw cold wind swept, could be closed. At half-past eight it was not known where plates, glasses and cutlery could be got; however, one of the remaining estaminets in Erquinghem was persuaded to lend what had been packed for removal, to eke out the contents of the company boxes, and clean bed linen to serve as table cloths. Midnight was near when the CO invited our old-maidish Brigadier to be seated. [Cook Sergeant] Parry, as ever, sent in first-class fare in the most adverse conditions. The menu, in the French of Kitchen cum Orderly Room: 'Consumme of Gallos; merlan Duglers; Escallops de Veau Vilanairese; Gigot de Mouton Roti, pommes Rissoles, Choux Bruxelles; Pudding au Chocolat; Scotch Woodcock; Dessert; Café; Veuve Cliquot, Benedictine, Kümmel. At Gris Pot.' Only port was wanting, even the Portuguese canteen had none – or said so. Of 31 at table 23 ate the Leek in the odour of the Goat and to the roll of the drum. The toasts were proposed by the CO – 'St David,' 'The King,' 'Other Battalions': [Major] Cuthbert 'Toby Purcell and his spurs'; [Captain] Moody – 'Shenkin ap Morgan'; [Lieutenant] French 'The Ladies'; [Captain] Radford – 'The Guests.' As usual I had to reply for The Guests, though I'm responsible for the dinner and pay my whack. After the Brigadier and the CO had gone the younger members of the Mess resumed, and made merry … until near daylight. A biting wind, some snow in it; thaw later. Digging is to be got on with, everyone at it.[11]

The Royal Northumberland Fusiliers, with St George and his steed curvetting on their cap-badge, naturally celebrated his day, 23 April. In 1951, 1/Royal Northumberland Fusiliers found themselves holding the line of the Imjin River in Korea as part of the British 29th Brigade. Despite the unpropitious conditions, beer (albeit at the dismal rate of two bottles per man) had been stockpiled and the cooks stood ready to produce a turkey lunch. Because red and white roses were traditionally worn behind the cap-badge but were not readily available on the Imjin, hundreds of Japanese-made imitations had been issued. However, on the night of 22–23 April the Chinese mounted the largest offensive of the war, and by its end the brigade had been driven back after a formidable defence, with 1/Glosters, one of its battalions, effectively destroyed. Amongst the thirty Northumberland Fusilier dead was the CO, Lieutenant Colonel Kingsley Foster, who had declined promotion to take his battalion to war. More fusiliers would have died had it not been for the support provided by the 25-pounder guns of 45 Field Regiment Royal Artillery. Lieutenant George Truell, his battery under attack by Chinese infantry in the pre-dawn darkness of St George's Day, ordered a single gun to take them on with direct fire at a range of 150 yards. The Chinese scattered and the battery was saved. Truell, awarded an MC for his bravery that day, had a rose tucked into his service dress cap. But while the fusiliers were sporting fabric flowers, the gunners had managed to obtain real ones.

The Royal Regiment of Fusiliers was formed from the four English fusilier regiments on St George's Day 1968. The new regiment celebrated St George's Day, and in 2009 the fact that its second battalion was on its third operational tour of Afghanistan did not stand in the way of tradition. Men were awakened that morning by the rattle of a side-drum beaten by the drum major, and then served 'gunfire' – tea laced with rum – by the officers. In happier times there would have been a battalion parade in the morning, with sports in the afternoon, and parties in the evening.[12] The Queen's Royal Irish Hussars had celebrated both St Patrick's and Balaklava Day in much the same way, with 'gunfire' first thing, sporting activities all day, and celebrations in the evening. When the QRIH amalgamated with The Queen's Own Hussars in 1993 to form The Queen's Royal Hussars, the new regiment added the anniversaries of Dettingen (27 June) and El Alamein (2 November) to its regimental days, and continued to pay homage to St Patrick.

The pattern of activities on regimental days across the army is very similar: a formal parade, perhaps with caps and colours suitably embellished, sports, and then parties in canteens and messes. The process is part historical commemoration, part tribal ritual leavened with family bonding and, given that attempts are usually made to mark the occasion even in the midst of operations, an affirmation that the exigencies of the moment must not weaken ties to the past. In 1944 Captain A. G. Oakley of the Hampshires recorded in his diary

> *1st August* ... Hell of a sports programme today for Minden Day
>   ... What a day, I am half gone as I write this.
> *2nd August* ... Well, we have recovered from Minden Day apart
>   from a slight headache.[13]

CHAPTER 21

FULL OF STRANGE OATHS, AND
BEARDED LIKE THE PARD

LANGUAGE, LIKE MUSIC, costume, shared history, and even hairstyles, helps groups – national, social, and professional – define themselves. Military English remains a distinctive mixture of professional jargon laced with rank-and-file bluntness, dotted with slang, and foreign words or expressions acquired on overseas campaigns or garrison duty. It has long separated those who could penetrate its thorny thickets from those who could not, and by doing so has helped to mark out the military tribe.

Not all British soldiers, even those born in the United Kingdom, actually spoke English. Scots and Irish soldiers of the eighteenth century and the first half of the nineteenth were often more comfortable in Gaelic. During the Peninsular War a general inspecting the Connaught Rangers asked a private

> to whose squad he belonged. Darby Rooney understood about as much English as enabled him to get over a parade tolerably, but a conversation such as the General was about to hold with him was beyond his capacity, and he began to feel a little confused at the prospect of a *tête-à-tête* with his General: 'Squidha – sqoodha – *cad dershe vourneen?*' said he, turning to the orderly-sergeant, Pat Gafney, who did not himself speak the English language as correctly as Lindley Murray. '*Whist, ye Bostoon,*' said Gafney, 'and don't make a baste of yourself before the General.' 'Why,' said General Mackinnon, 'I believe he don't understand me.' 'No sir,' replied Gafney, 'he don't know what your honour manes.'[1]

Soldiers across the ages have had technical preoccupations that inspired in-house jargon. *Tristram Shandy*'s Uncle Toby, a veteran of the 1695 siege of Namur, could not describe his experiences without becoming mired in the minutiae of fortification and siegecraft:

> my uncle *Toby* was generally more eloquent and particular in his account of it; and the many perplexities he was in, arose out of the almost insurmountable difficulties he found in telling his story intelligibly, and giving such clear ideas of the differences and distinctions between the scarp and counterscarp, – the glacis and the covered way, – the half-moon and ravelin, – as to make his company fully comprehend what he was about.[2]

The words to 'The British Grenadiers' refer to the defining role of a grenadier in the fortress warfare of late seventeenth and early eighteenth centuries.

> When ere we are commanded to storm the palisades
> Our leaders march with fusees, and we with hand grenades.
> We throw them from the glacis about our enemies' ears,
> With a tow row row row row row row for the British Grenadiers.

The palisades were the sharpened stakes that lined the edge of the covered way, an entrenched walkway running along the outer side of the ditch surrounding a fortress. Fusees were not 'fuses', for every grenadier carried his own 'match' – a length of smouldering cord – to light his grenades. Fusils were light muskets that enabled officers to lend a little fire support to their men, whose own muskets were slung across their backs, leaving their hands free to light and throw grenades. The glacis was the open, gently sloping landscape in front of a fortress. When British tank designers were seeking a word for the sloped armour on the front of a tank they borrowed from the seventeenth century to come up with glacis plate.

Veterans of the First World War found it very hard to discuss their experiences with those who had not shared them. Part of their problem stemmed from the sheer difficulty of describing that juxtaposition of horror and normality, comradeship and obligation that had characterised their wartime existences. Part, too, arose from the way in which their language had been so coloured by jargon as to be almost unintelligible. A code of abbreviations confused outsiders, and sometimes insiders too: what was a GOC, BGRA, BGGS, GSO1, or an ADC to the CCRA?[3] Where might one find a bomb stop or a bomb store, a hay box or some elephant iron, a Bangalore torpedo or a bearing picket? The phonetic alphabet in use at the time gave 'Ack Emma' for a.m. and 'Pip Emma' for p.m.; an observation post was an 'O Pip', and Talbot House, the all-ranks club at Poperinghe, was 'Toc H'. The Distinguished Conduct Medal was a 'Don C Emma', and a machine gun an 'Emma Gee'. Place names were mercilessly anglicised: Ypres was Wipers, Auchonvillers was Ocean Villas, Monchy Breton emerged as Monkey Britain, and Ploegsteert as Plug Street.

The language of Racine and Molière was tortured to death. *Il n'y en a plus* (there is no more), too often heard by eager soldiers in search of home comforts in French villages, became the universal negative *napoo*. It was applicable to commodities, as in *napoo* rum or *napoo* jam, or to almost anything else: an exhausted man might grunt '*napoo* breath', and a dead man was plain *napoo*. *Ça ne fait rien* (it doesn't matter), became 'sana fairy ann', and *tout de suite*, immediately, was 'toot sweet'. The German soldier, *l'Allemand* to the French, was soon the 'Alleyman' to the British. Bully beef (corned beef), one of the soldier's main rations, had long been corrupted from the Napoleonic *boeuf bouilli*. Bombardier Fritz was not a German artillery NCO but *pommes de terre frites*, chips, ideally served with 'erfs' and a glass or three of 'van blong'.

And then there was slang. Senior officers were brass hats, from the gold-braided peaks of their caps; the deeply unpopular training ground at Etaples was the bull ring, and the yellow armbands of the staff who worked there gave them the nickname canaries. The long-handled German grenade's visual similarity to a humble kitchen tool earned it the name potato-masher or, more simply, stick bomb. A large trench mortar bomb was a flying pig, a high-velocity German field gun a whizz bang, and the shell of the German 15cm heavy gun, which burst with a cloud of black smoke, was a coal-box or (from the black world heavyweight boxing champion), a Jack Johnson. To 'funk' a task was to shrink from it, to be in a funk (or, more seriously, in a blue funk) was to be in a state of panic, and so a funk hole was a small personal shelter scraped in the front wall of a trench. The music hall comedian Fred Karno lent his name to Fred Karno's Army, first applied to Kitchener's New Armies but soon part of the popular song, wrung out, as lugubriously as possible, to the tune of 'The Church's One Foundation'.

> We are Fred Karno's army
> The ragtime infantry
> We cannot shoot, we cannot fight,
> What bloody use are we?
> And when we get to Berlin,
> The Kaiser he will say,
> Hoch hoch! Mein Gott, what a bloody rotten lot,
> The ragtime infantry.

Something not quite up to scratch might be termed 'a bit Fred Karno'.

Soldiers of previous generations had larded their conversation with words or phrases acquired in India, and many of these survived into the world wars and beyond. I remember the kindly CSM Fred Burrows, as late as 1969, warning the company, hard at work on rifle-cleaning after getting back from exercise: '*Jildi, jildi*, it's your own time you're wasting.' 'You put some *juldi* in it,' shouted Kipling's soldiers to the regimental water-carrier, Gunga Din, 'Or I'll *marrow* (hit) you this minute.' Even in the late 1960s men might still refer to a rifle as a *bundook* (indeed, the word is currently experiencing a revival, alongside *gat* and *bang-stick*) and a bed as a *charpoy*, though those who called a cell in the guard-room *chokey* had little idea that it derived from *cauki*, a lockup. But the heyday of military Hindustani had been a century before. When Edwin Mole joined the 14th Hussars in 1863, he found that

> There were fifteen men in my mess, fourteen of whom wore three or four medals. They were good-natured fellows in the main, though a little short-tempered; and all bore signs of their long residence in India, where the regiment had been for nineteen years without coming home. They used many queer Hindustan names and terms, which it took me some time to get the hang of. For instance, they never spoke of knives, or salt, or bread, but always 'Give me a *churrie*!' 'Pass the *neemuck*!' or 'Sling over some *rootee*!'[4]

Rootee, or bread, gave its name to the *rootee gong*, the long service and good conduct medal, awarded before 1870 for eating army bread for 21 years in the infantry or 24 in the cavalry, though the qualifying period was reduced to a uniform 18 years in 1870.[5]

The bukshee was a paymaster or military officer in Mogul India. 'The *bukshee* is an awful *bahadur*, but he keeps a first-rate *bobachee*': tells us that this gentleman was 'a haughty or pompous personage', but had a good cook.[6] The anglicised word buckshee – 'something in addition to the usual allowance' is actually a corruption of *baksheesh*, tip or bribe.

> Fourteen annas, one rupee,
> Fifteen annas, one buckshee.

Even today a wise Company Quartermaster Sergeant will keep a buckshee store of items that do not feature on his official ledgers but can be deployed to alleviate individual misfortune or avert collective disgrace when kit is being checked. *Pani*, water, produced not only *brandy-pani* for the stout-hearted, and *limbu-pani*, lime juice, for the less resolute, but furnished a nickname for anyone with the surname Waters. *Mufti* or plain clothes, derives from a Muslim scholar and official, informally clad 'in dressing gown, smoking cap and slippers', though the best-known glossary of Anglo-Indian terms generously admits that 'the transition is a little obscure.'[7]

The *dam* was a small copper coin, and the Anglo-Indian equivalent of 'I don't care a brass farthing' was 'I don't give a *dam*.' The change in spelling and implication came later, although the phrase 'twopenny damn' (a favourite of the Duke of Wellington's) emphasises the word's numismatic origins. *Burra* (great) gave not only *burra sahib*, for the most important individual in a station or garrison; *burra khana*, for big dinner; *burra din* for great day (Christmas Day in particular); and *burra peg*, for a large measure of spirits. *Chota*, in contrast, meant small, and *chota hazri* was an early morning cup of tea and biscuit, and *tiffin* a light lunch. *Dekko*, a look or a peep, sprang from *dekh-na*, to look, and although *ramsammy* had begun life as a collective noun for Indians, it was enlisted by the army to mean a fight or wild gathering. Ernest Shephard recalled that on 14 March 1915:

In the evening we were expecting to be called up for the trenches, and to break the monotony we (the Sgts) had a ramsammy with sawdust and jam. We all agreed after that it was the best laugh we have had for ages. We were smothered in sawdust and jam all over, and to cap it all could not get water to wash after the hour's horseplay.

The following morning he was still 'Roaring at last night. I feel ten years to the good.'[8] A madman was *fanti* or *doolally*, the former springing from the Urdu and the latter from Deolali, a military hospital just outside Bombay, where men worn out by long service in India (and copious libations of locally distilled *arrack*) awaited the boat home, their twitchy symptoms known as the *doolally tap*.

The suffix *wallah* derived from *wala* and, just as Indians added it to other words to produce compounds like *attar-wallah* for perfume seller, so the British applied it widely. As far as private soldiers were concerned, the *dhobi-wallah* was a laundryman, the *char-wallah* dispensed tea, and the *nappy-wallah* crept into early-morning barrack rooms to shave recumbent men. To officers, a *competition-wallah* had gained admission to the Indian Civil Service by the competitive examination that was introduced in 1856; and a *box-wallah*, an itinerant pedlar to the Indians, was any European engaged in trade or commerce. *Wallah* was added to military terms to produce compounds like *transport-wallah* and *machine-gun wallah* for a battalion's transport and machine gun officers and *amen-wallah* for its chaplain. A trench mortarman might simply be a *trench mortar wallah*, or, in a mixed marriage with the phonetic alphabet, a *Toc Emma wallah*.

The British soldier in India prized his ability to 'sling the bat' (speak the language) but a popular couplet was not far from the truth in suggesting that

His Hindustani words were few – they could not very well be fewer
Just idharao, and jaldi jao and khabadar, you soor.

Which translates as 'Come here, go quickly, and take care, you swine.'[9] 'Bat' was often curt and imperative. When Private Frank Richards reached France with 2/Royal Welch Fusiliers in August 1914 one of his comrades persisted in calling for drinks in bat, and assured Richards that the only way of dealing with foreigners was to shout the order as loudly as possible, and to reward non-compliance with a prompt thrashing. 'Soldier bat' did not just provide men with a *lingua franca* that enabled them to communicate around the cantonment, but marked them out as veterans, and many soldiers who had never served in India gleaned enough bat to sling it convincingly about a Portsmouth pub.

It is the most extreme example of the word-borrowing that has added another page to the addenda of the military vocabulary after each successive campaign. In the Second World War *bint*, Arabic for daughter, became a general (and at best slightly derogatory) term for women in general, while soldiers who fought in Italy called the Germans *Teds*, from the Italian *Tedeschi*, though the word never gained wider currency. Malaya brought *ulu* – remote, rural, out of the way – into the vocabulary, and soldiers of my generation might describe trudging out onto Salisbury Plain as 'shagging off into the *ulu*'. The army's long tour of garrison duty in Germany left a surprisingly small linguistic mark, though most soldiers struggled to get their German much beyond *zwei bier bitte* and *bratwurst mit frites*, and to seek a persuasive translation of 'My friend will pay'.

Regimental nicknames littered military English. The Gloucesters, their 'back badge' earned at Alexandra in 1801 when the rear rank faced about to repel an attack, were the 'Back Numbers'. The Queen's were either the Mutton-Chop Lancers, from their paschal lamb cap-badge or, in rhyming slang, the Pork and Beans. Both the Leicesters and the Hampshires, with their Bengal tiger badges, were Tigers, and the Middlesex, thanks to the 57th Foot's performance at Albuhera, were the Die-hards. The Norfolks were the Holy Boys, apparently because a Spanish soldier mistook the figure of Britannia on their badges for the Virgin Mary. The ability of men of the Northamptonshires to tolerate flogging gave the regiment its nickname the Steelbacks. The York and Lancaster Regiment was the Twin Roses, the Young and Livelies or, more contentiously, the Cork and Doncaster. The Gaelic war-cry *Faugh-a-Ballagh*, clear the way, led to the Royal Irish Fusiliers being the Faugh-a-Ballagh Boys or simply the Old Fogs. The Royal Signals, who originated in the Royal Engineers Signal Service and became a corps in their own right in 1920, were Scalybacks, probably because the batteries of early man-pack radios leaked acid and scarred their users' backs.

Organisational abbreviations offered wide opportunities for abuse. RAOC, Royal Army Ordnance Corps, was transliterated as Rag and Oil Company. The First World War Army Service Corps (ASC) took on the name of a comic-strip character to become Ally Sloper's Cavalry, and after the corps had gained its royal title in 1918 there were those who maintained that the initials now stood for Run Away, Someone's Coming. It was cheaper for officers to serve in the Indian than the British army, and an officer with neither private income nor social pretensions might finish up in the Royal Indian Army Service Corps, only to discover that brother officers in smart cavalry regiments maintained that the corps' initials stood for Really I Am So Common. Wounded soldiers whose kit mysteriously disappeared somewhere down the painful line of medical evacuation subscribed to the notion that RAMC stood, not for Royal Army Medical Corps, but for Rob All My Comrades. Matters have not much improved recently, with the Royal Logistic Corps (RLC) becoming the Really Large Corps, and the Adjutant General's Corps (AGC) the All Girls' Corps.

The alphabet soup has thickened since 1945, with a rich stock of abbreviations for organisations, individuals, and objects. An AFV is an Armoured Fighting Vehicle, the ARRC is the Allied Rapid Reaction Corps (its commander COMARRC and his chief of staff COSARRC), while the FEBA is the Forward Edge of Battle Area and the FLOT the Forward Location of Own Troops. POL stands for Petrol, Oil, and Lubricants, and has spawned its own verb, as in: 'Get those vehicles polled up'. A TCP is a Traffic Control Point, and a TCV a Troop Carrying Vehicle. Many abbreviations are most frequently pronounced as words: Supreme Headquarters Allied Powers Europe (SHAPE), is shape and to be Absent Without Leave (AWOL) is to be awol. The 7.62mm General Purpose Machine Gun (GPMC) is a gimpy, and the 84mm Carl Gustav anti-tank weapon (a beastly thing to carry, and now happily obsolete) was a Charlie Gee.

Recent slang includes its own derogatory asides, like blanket stacker for a storeman or logistician of any sort; dropshort for a gunner; donkey-walloper for a cavalryman. Craphat ('Harry the Hat, or 'hat' *tout court*), is used by members of the Parachute Regiment to describe anyone who does not wear their distinctive maroon beret. A cunt cap, however, is altogether different: it is the flat sidehat with a distinctive fold along its top. Guardsmen are woodentops, and the black-buttoned Royal Green Jackets were known as the Black Mafia. The term shiny-arse reminds us that the seats of polyester barrack-dress trousers grew glossy after repeated application to an office chair, while a REMF (Rear Echelon Mother-Fucker) is any individual who, in the speaker's highly subjective opinion, lives a comfortable life, out of danger. The heavy wool jersey was a woolly pully; drawers cellular (standard-issue army underwear) were simply drawers Dracula; and the zip-fronted Norwegian shirt was a noggie. A bed is a scratcher and a sleeping-bag a green maggot or doss-bag. Food is scoff or scran, and a knife, fork and spoon can be KFS or noshing-rods. Something unspeakably grubby (say a rifle, barrack room, or woman of doubtful habits) is gopping, and rubbish is gash, best entrusted to a rubbish sack or gash-bag. Rhyming slang still puts in an appearance, perhaps most frequently as cream-crackered for knackered.

'The army passed over into Flanders and swore horribly,' complained a seventeenth-century commentator. It has never really stopped. In 1939 Fitzroy Maclean abandoned a colourful diplomatic career to join the Cameron Highlanders, his father's old regiment, as a private soldier. He arrived at the depot at Inverness with several hundred other recruits, and they hung about the barrack square in the drizzle until they were pounced on by half a dozen NCOs:

> And given numbers. And divided up into squads ... And issued with things ... And told not to ——— lose them. And told to look out and look sharp and use our ——— initiative. And given mops and pails and scrubbing brushes and told to ——— scrub the ——— floor.

The process of recruit training changed men physically and mentally.

> We ceased to be recruits and became trained soldiers. Effortlessly, we fell into the linguistic habits of the army; every other word in our conversation was the same meaningless and monotonous, yet some-how satisfying, expletive.[10]

Stephen Graham served as a private in the Scots Guards during the First World War, and thought that once a man 'begins to use the army's language wishing it he has ceased to be an individual soldier, he has become *soldiery*.'[11] There were many who found military language not a source of unifying strength but a constant reminder of their own debased status. Alfred M. Hale was a middle-class, middle-aged man conscripted in the summer of 1916. Hale hated every moment of his time in the army, and found its language especially wearing. 'One got so very wearied of hearing everything being described as f-cking this and f-cking that,' he wrote, 'the very word, with its original indecent meaning, being at length a mere stupid and meaningless vulgarity.'[12]

Stupid perhaps, but infinitely variable. To fuck might indeed mean to engage in sexual intercourse, but it also means to cheat or victimise, and to kill or destroy. To be fucked about is to be set onto nugatory tasks. The expression features in a song once popular at 'smokers', all-male concerts where humour was very blunt. It should be sung in a falsetto, with the singer in as much drag as circumstances permit.

> My husband's a corporal, a corporal, a corporal,
> My husband's a corporal, a corporal is he.
> All day he fucks men about, fucks men about, fucks men about
> And then he comes home and fucks me.
> *Chorus*
> Singing hey jig-a-jig fuck a little pig, follow the band
> Follow the band all the way
> Singing hey jig-a-jig fuck a little pig, follow the band
> Follow the band all the way.

A task or project can be simply fucked up, or right royally fucked up. An exhausted man might describe himself as fucked, and to be down on one's luck with little prospect of immediate remedy is to be fucked up and far from home. An unserviceable weapon or vehicle is fucked. One can be told to fuck off, generally, though not always, by a superior, and might report the peremptory dismissal of a subordinate by saying: 'I fucked him off at the high port'.[13] Almost anyone can be spoken of as a fucker, usually in a perjorative sense: 'Ee were a reet miserable fooker'. Fuck intensifies an enquiry, as in 'What the *fuck* was that?' The word forms a key part of more complex phrases, like that used to describe taking on a complex task on the spur of the moment: to take a running fuck at a rolling doughnut. When I was a young private, I attracted the unfavourable attention of a sergeant who informed me with some asperity that I was 'a four-eyed fuckpig'.

The charades that often formed part of smokers brought that art form to a new low ebb. A man might wear a red tracksuit, rouge his face and fill his bulging cheeks with custard, jetting it out at a suitable moment to reveal that he was a pustule. A soldier might shuffle on stage naked apart from an army boot held steadfastly against his private parts. 'What the fuck are you?' yells an accomplice in the audience. 'Nothing,' he replies. 'I'm just fucking aboot.'

The cliché 'swear like a trooper' is soundly founded on fact. In the early eighteenth century there were few gentlemanly constraints against using fuck. The word gained ground steadily as swive ('Thus swived was this carpenter's wife', wrote Chaucer) fell into disuse. Sarah, Duchess of Marlborough, who admittedly prided herself on plain speaking, agreed with her son in law the Duke of Montagu that his wife was indeed 'F[ucking] with Mr Craggs'.[14] Georgian plain-speaking was followed by Victorian primness, and by 1850 there were two distinct forms of military English: a suitably bowdlerised officers' version, and a soldier's brand alive with earthy Anglo-Saxon. Even the latter, though, lost ground thanks to the influence of Methodism and the temperance movement, both of which identified swearing as one of the perils of army life. Some officers found soldiers' cursing genuinely unsettling. Lieutenant Colonel the Earl of Airlie was killed commanding the 12th Lancers in a charge at Diamond Hill near Pretoria in June 1900. His last words, to a battle-maddened sergeant, were reported as: 'Pray moderate your language.' Officers were indeed expected to mind their language. Even bloody was too strong for some stomachs, and bally became an acceptable substitute.

First World War soldiers might swear horribly but would not tolerate blasphemy. An army chaplain recalled

There was a certain word which to the soldier of those days was an everyday adjective. It was frequently heard in the barrack room and no person seemed to be annoyed. However, should anyone use a blasphemous term half a dozen comrades would immediately tell the offender to shut up ... and as likely as not in telling him off the adjective referred to above would be used. 'Stop your ——— blasphemy.'[15]

The First World War saw significant erosion of officers' English, and the Second World War continued the process. Just as schoolchildren often have two vocabularies, one used at home and the other at school, so many officers developed two distinct styles of speech, one laced with epithets and used with the military community, and the other for family and civilian friends. Senior officers addressing groups of soldiers sometimes sought to increase the impact of their words by deliberately including vulgarities to show that they were in contact with the common man. Soldiers often found it embarrassing, and an officer who heard General Sir William Slim addressing troops in Burma reported that his speech was all the more effective because he made no effort to curry favour with his audience, but spoke with palpable honesty using moderate language. Since 1945 the gap between officers' and soldiers' English has narrowed to the point where it exists only as a matter of degree: officers use just the same words, though they tend to be more restrained in their frequency and application.

I cannot leave this discussion of military English without reflecting on Lord Raglan, commander-in-chief of the British army in the Crimea. Raglan had not only served throughout the Peninsular War and so knew just how soldiers talked, but spoke good French into the bargain. So when he found himself speaking to the French general, Pierre Bosquet, in the early stages of the battle of Inkerman, when things looked bleak for the Allies, he was caught in a gentlemanly bind. 'Nous sommes ... Nous sommes ...' he said, hesitating about that dreaded word. 'Vous avez un mot d'argot qui exprime bien ce que je veux dire.' 'Nous sommes foutus, milord?' said the helpful Bosquet. 'J'espère que non.'[16]

Hair – on the head and face – like language, helps identify soldiers. For the first four decades of the army's existence, officers sported great full-bottomed peruques, and their soldiers either wore shoulder-length hair loose, or in a short ponytail. By 1710 officers' wigs were becoming less elaborate, and soldiers' hair was worn in the

'Ramillies tie', combed to a straight pigtail and bound with leather, or clubbed – with the pigtail doubled up and held in place by a leather strap. As the century wore on, gentlemen, and so army officers, wore tie-wigs with a fabric ribbon around the short pigtail; or bag-wigs, with the pigtail vanishing into a black taffeta bag. Wig styles defined professional status. The Marlburian veteran, 'Captain' Peter Drake, kept the Queen's Arms tavern near St Clement Danes in the 1720s. He 'provided bob-wigs, blue aprons etc. proper for the business of a vintner; these I wore at home, but could not yet leave off the tie-wig and sword when I went abroad.'[17]

Members of conservative professions, like lawyers and doctors, retained the wig after it went out of fashion at the end of the eighteenth century. Within the army a similar process was at work. George Augustus, 3rd Viscount Howe, eldest of a trio of talented brothers, was commissioned into the decidedly traditional 1st Foot Guards in 1745. He played an important part in the development of light infantry in North America. On campaign there he wore a simple uniform, slept in a blanket, and wore his own hair cut short, rather than a wig. James Wolfe thought him quite simply 'The best officer in the British army', but he was killed as a brigadier general in 1758, while taking part in Sir James Abercrombie's failed attempt to take Fort Ticonderoga. With the gradual disappearance of wigs, officers wore their own hair, pomaded and powdered, with the side-locks curled – or 'frizzed and rubbed up with the palm of the hand' in fusilier regiments – and hair at the back plaited into a shoulder-length pigtail.

Pitt's 1795 hair powder tax struck a fatal blow at powdering in the civilian community, but the army did not formally abolish it till 1808. Lieutenant Colonel Charles Donnellan of the 48th Foot was mortally wounded at Talavera in 1809 dressed, for all the world, like an eighteenth century officer in white buckskin breeches, tricorne hat, and powdered hair. Hard hit, he handed over to his second in command with a courtesy as old-fashioned as his dress: 'Major Middlemore, you will have the honour of leading the 48th to the charge.' There were some merits to the wig. Hair could be kept short, and louse free, beneath it, and at the end of a long day it could be jettisoned in tent or quarters. It was not always easy to keep wig and headdress firmly anchored. When the Marquess of Granby led the cavalry charge at

Warburg in 1760 he lost both hat and wig, originating the term 'going at it bald-headed'. The portrait by Sir Joshua Reynolds shows him, as colonel of the Blues, proudly shiny of pate.

Private soldiers and NCOs, however, did not enjoy the comparative luxury of the wig. For most of the eighteenth century their hair, allowed to grow about a foot long, was greased thickly with tallow or lard, and tugged back into a queue held in place by a polished leather strap: fusiliers adorned theirs with a silver grenade. The whole ensemble was then powdered – often with flour. In 1741 a German author complained that the practice constituted an avoidable waste of foodstuff. It is impossible to be sure quite how much flour the average soldier used, although in the 1790s officers of the 10th Light Dragoons each got through a pound of powder a week. A man could not dress his own hair, and so soldiers paired off to help one another, working in barrack rooms if the weather was cold or wet, or sitting astride benches outside and perhaps enjoying a pipe of tobacco if it was sunny. Married men had their hair dressed by their wives, and a woman who was adept at her clubbing and powdering would not lack for suitors if she was widowed. Regiments often gave up powdering when they went on active service. Queues needed up to an hour's treatment two or three times a week; it was not easy to lay hands on sufficient tallow and flour in the field, and vermin, especially rats, were attracted by the smell.

Captain Thomas Browne of the 23rd Royal Welch Fusiliers told his readers that they might imagine that clubbing and powdering was 'a tedious and troublesome operation, and how much of the Soldiers' time was needlessly occupied in this formidable preparation for parade'. Yet when his regiment received the order 'for the discontinuance of the use of powder in the hair … and directing that … heads should be closely cropped', neither officers nor men were pleased about it. The commanding officer, with his 'luxuriant plait', was particularly vexed. The officers discussed the matter over dinner,

> and having perhaps taken an extra glass, by way of softening our
> vexation, one of the Officers proposed, that we should, then and
> there, cut off each other's plaits with a carving knife, and make a
> grand friz of them, in the fire. The first part of the proposition was
> acceded to, and I can vouch for it's having been a rough and

painful operation. The question of burning and frizzing our precious locks, was off a much more serious nature, and acceded to only by one or two old Subalterns whose heads time had taken its usual liberties of thinning and bleaching. The rest of us wrapped up our discarded tails in pieces of brown paper or pocket handkerchiefs, and carried them to our barrack rooms.

When word reached the men the result was 'very little short of mutiny'. Wives announced that 'they would murder the first operator who dared touch a hair of their husband's head,' for 'this cruel docking innovation' would inevitably damage the 'caste of wives'. The commanding officer ordered the battalion to form up, a company at a time,

> and sending for benches from the barrack rooms he had them placed behind each rank, and commanded the men to sit down. This they did in perfect silence, he then ordered off their foraging caps, and sent for half a dozen hair cutters … They were set to work and in less than ten minutes, nothing remained but the stump of the favourite club.[18]

The officers decided to retain the ribbon with which their pigtails had been tied, and the distinctive 'flash' of five black ribbons sewn into the collar, worn at first by officers and senior NCOs and latterly by all ranks of the Royal Welch Fusiliers, was the result.

The end of powdering did not mean that officers and men could do as they pleased with their hair. Most regiments, especially on active service, took a practical view, insisting only that hair should be clear of the collar and not visible beneath the front of a shako or forage cap. Officers with sufficient hair sometimes teased locks over the forehead, and sideburns began their steady advance towards the bottom of the ear and then onto the cheek. But there were martinets for whom this was not enough. General Prince Edward Augustus, Duke of Kent, was the fourth son of George III and father of Queen Victoria. He was appointed Governor of Gibraltar in 1802, with orders to restore discipline, and produced a 300-page set of *Standing Orders*. These decreed that no officer or soldier could disembark until they had received the duke's regulation haircut, and the first man aboard a newly-arrived troopship was his personal barber. Kent's rigidity provoked a mutiny on Christmas Eve 1802, and when the Duke of York heard of it he summoned his brother back to England. Kent characteristically refused to leave until his successor arrived, and he remained titular governor until his death in 1820, although he was never allowed back.

Thin moustaches were fashionable in the 1660s, but for most of the eighteenth century the army was clean-shaven, although it was rare even for officers to shave every day, and most soldiers got by with two shaves a week, one of them on Sunday. As the century wore on there was a close connection between facial hair and broader military fashion. Light dragoons had originally been clean-shaven, but soon their officers and men took to wearing their sideburns well below the ear, jetting forward towards the mouth, with substantial moustaches. Captain the Hon Charles Somers Cocks, Eldest son of John, Lord Somers, arrived in the Peninsula with the 16th Light Dragoons and showed great aptitude for reconnaissance work, serving as one of Wellington's intelligence officers and becoming his particular favourite. In 1812 he bought a majority in the 79th Highlanders, and assured his mother 'I shall make a very respectable figure with the bonnet and tartan.' He told his brother 'I have shaved off my moustaches and most of my beard and turn out a smooth regular infantryman.'[19] Wellington attended Cocks's funeral when he was killed at Burgos that year leading the light companies of the Highland Brigade in an assault, and was evidently so over wrought that nobody dared speak to him.

By the 1830s cavalrymen, heavy and light, were fiercely hairy. When young Buck Adams joined the 7th Dragoon Guards in 1843, his first mentor was a giant Irishman, 'not a particle of the upper part of whose face was distinguishable for the amount of hair which covered it'.[20] Elsewhere chins and upper lips were shaved, but sideburns had now matured into substantial mutton-chops. In 1843 the shaving of the upper lip was forbidden, and the army took on the hirsute appearance that was to characterise it for much of the century. Although hair had become shorter, and sideburns much more restrained by the time of the First World War, the ban on shaving the upper lip remained in force and all regulars, officers and men alike, were expected to have at least the makings of a moustache. Many NCOs favoured the lion-tamer look with pomaded moustaches curled horizontally into sharp points.

The army did not enforce the no-shaving rule strictly as far as the Territorials and New Armies were concerned, although many officers and men experimented with new suitably martial growths. These were not always a success. Alan Sugden volunteered for the Royal Garrison Artillery in 1914, and that autumn, while stationed at Newhaven, he grew a moustache. In a letter that included complaints about the tea ('there is some stuff in it that makes men so that they do not want women') he declared:

> My tache is a swanker now dear. I am going to be photographed with it on. I want you to see what you think about it. If you say it has to come off then I shall shave it off.

Every picture tells a story. The new growth evidently did not meet with Amy's approval, for a photograph of a moustachioed Gunner Sugden is followed by one of a clean-shaven lance bombardier.[21] Captain Bruce Bairnsfather's cartoon character 'Old Bill', profane and lugubrious, sported a great soup-straining walrus moustache, but 'Young Bill', his nervous and gullible comrade (Q. 'What made that 'ole?' A. 'Mice'.) was smooth-faced. And that, in its way, had always been what the moustache was about: it marked its wearer out as veteran and warrior.

In mid-1916 an officer was court-martialled for shaving the upper lip. He argued, not wholly persuasively, that he was an actor in civilian life, and if he grew a moustache its removal at the war's end would leave a rash that would make it hard for him to get work. He was convicted and sentenced to lose his commission. When the findings passed through the hands of the adjutant general in France, Sir Nevil Macready, on their way for confirmation, Macready – who had never liked his own moustache – not only suggested to Haig that the business was absurd, but got the rules changed. However, almost all generals remained moustachioed, and amongst the corps commanders of 1918 only one, Sir Arthur Currie of the Canadian Corps, an insurance broker and estate agent in civilian life, had a clean-shaven upper lip. Most officers and men wore their hair in short-back-and-sides, but there was a fashion, especially among infantrymen, to have back and sides viciously clipped but to leave a bushy forelock: on the march the steel helmet could be pushed back to reveal it.

The half-century following 1918 saw little change in military hairstyles. Many regular officers and NCOs were moustachioed, and short back and sides remained the rule for hair, as National Servicemen remembered. Just as military hairstyles tended to reflect, albeit with a time-lag, civilian fashions, so the longer hair of the 1960s made its presence felt in the army. There was a period of stiff competition between adjutants and RSMs, and young officers and soldiers who fancied themselves more Sergeant Pepper than sergeant major. By the mid-1970s there was a comfortable compromise, with the army accepting longer styles provided they were off the collar. A Northern Ireland veteran recalled 'outrageous sideburns and long hair' in the province in the 1970s, and a distinctive image created by 'NI boots, skin tight lightweights, and short 68 pattern smocks and the lovely S[elf] L[oading] R[ifle]'.[22] Photographs and newsreel clips of the Falklands show a bushy-topped army, with moustaches, sometimes with a 'Mexican Pete' downturn, popular amongst NCOs of the Parachute Regiment.

In the first decade of the twenty-first century the urgings of civilian fashion and the demands of operational service in hot climates, where tightly-fitting steel helmets were worn for much of the time, encouraged short hair-styles, with buzz-cuts or shaven scalps increasingly widespread. The young, whether commissioned or not, might indulge in streaks or gel off duty. There remains one clear line connecting the facial appearance of the army of 2010 with that of Marlborough's day. Each infantry battalion had a section of pioneers, charged with clearing obstacles in the field and with a variety of tasks requiring simple engineering skills about camp. Pioneers had leather aprons to protect their uniforms and carried axes, picks, billhooks, and shovels – the tools of their trade. In 1856 they gained their own pattern of sword, with a brass stirrup guard and a double row of saw-teeth along the back of its blade: it was eventually declared obsolete in 1904.

In the early eighteenth century, the pioneer sergeant wore a beard and bore an axe on parade, and once NCO stripes were in use he had a badge of crossed axes above his chevrons. There is no wholly persuasive explanation for the beard. It is sometimes said that it originated in the pioneer sergeant's duties as the battalion's blacksmith, and was intended to protect his face from the heat of the forge. That logic would have led to farriers in the cavalry being bearded, but they were not. The detailed structure of pioneers within the infantry changed over the years, and the term 'assault pioneers' is now used to describe them. Members of a modern assault pioneer platoon provide an infantry commanding officer with in-house engineering, and their skills include wiring, explosive demolitions and basic carpentry. The pioneer sergeant is still allowed a beard, and most units expect him to avail himself of the privilege. In the Coldstream Guards 'The Pioneer Sergeant may wear a full set beard and is encouraged to do so,' while in the Irish Guards 'The Pioneer Sergeant is permitted to grow a full beard if he so wishes, and he invariably does.'[23] Many commanding officers set much store by having a suitably hirsute pioneer sergeant. In Second World War Italy Sergeant Roscoe, pioneer sergeant of 3/Grenadier Guards, burnt his face in an accident with a cooker and so could not sport a beard. The commanding officer, Lieutenant Colonel A. G. W. Heber Percy, directed his deputy, Lance Sergeant Alf Peters, to wear it in his place.[24]

CHAPTER 22

TUNES OF GLORY

MUSIC PLAYED ITS own distinctive part in the bonding process. From the very beginning, regiments of horse had trumpeters and infantry regiments, drummers. These were properly enlisted soldiers who did duty alongside their comrades in peace and war. Both fulfilled important functions, transmitting and relaying calls in the field, and, in an age when clocks and watches were rare and telephones unknown, they regulated life in camp and barracks with routine calls and specific orders. Where drummers were concerned, the early seventeeth-century soldier Francis Markham tells us

> Valour and courage is necessary in all their employments, for the Drummer's place is ever at his captain's heels. It is he that brings the battles to join, he that stands in the midst when swords fly on all sides; he that brings them to pell mell and the fury of execution; and it is he that brings them both on and off, when they are either fortunate or abandoned and forsaken.[1]

Captain Thomas Venn emphasised that a soldier needed to understand 'the several beats of the drum, or he may often fall short of the captain's commands', and it was part of the captain's duties to make sure his men knew what the different drumbeats meant.[2] At this time drummers were also used for parleying with the enemy, and needed to be discreet and resourceful.

In 1665 1st Foot Guards had a drum major and 36 drummers, but the Buffs had only one drummer for each of their twelve companies when they went to Flanders in 1692. The Buffs gained an extra drummer per company on active service but lost him when they came back to England six years later. Soon, however, two drummers were allotted to each company of infantry and troop of dragoons; it was not until 1765 that dragoons gained trumpeters instead. Cavalry regiments also had a pair of kettle-drums, cauldron-shaped instruments slung across the shoulders of a large and steady horse. They were covered with embroidered drum-banners, except in the 3rd Hussars, who were uniquely allowed to carry silver French drums captured by their ancestors, the King's Own Dragoons, at Dettingen in 1743. From 1689 the Master General of the Ordnance had a pair of kettle-drums mounted on a carriage drawn by four grey horses and this extraordinary vehicle accompanied the Duke of Marlborough's campaigns.

During the eighteenth century only the Foot Guards and Royal Artillery had drum majors financed by the public purse, other regiments paid for theirs from company funds. The post of drum-major was eventually established, but as an appointment, rather than a rank: today it can be held by a soldier holding the rank of sergeant, colour sergeant or Warrant Officer Class 2. Opinion varied as to whether the squealing of flute and fife were fitting accompaniments to the noble thudding of the drum, but woodwind music was widespread from early in the army's history, whether played by drummers, as part of their normal duties, or by fifers. In 1753 ten drummers and five fifers of the Royal Artillery headed a royal review in Green Park.

> See drummers with the fifers come,
> And Carter with the massive drum;
> The grand drum-major first doth stalk
> With gold-knobbed stick and pompous walk,
> And as he marches o'er the ground
> He thinks he turns the world around.[3]

Highland regiments, the oldest of them, the Black Watch, dating from 1739, had pipers as well as drummers from their foundation but it was not until 1854 that the pipers and a pipe major were made part of a battalion's establishment. Until then vacancies for pipers were created by misemploying drummers or private soldiers.

European military music owed a substantial debt to developments in the Middle East. The English word tabor and the French *tambour* both derive from the Persian *taburak* drum, and the Turkish janissary band has good reason to be seen as the grandfather of modern bands. When the Sultan of Turkey gave the King of Poland a janissary band in full fig in 1730 it gave new impetus to the fashion for making drummers look as Turkish as possible. In 1750 Sir Robert Rich's Regiment of Dragoons had a black drummer called Toby Gill, 'a very drunken and profligate fellow', who was eventually hanged for murder. Because genuine Turks or Moors were hard to come by, many British regiments compromised by recruiting drummers in the West Indies. In 1759 Admiral Edward Boscawen brought ten boys back from the West Indies and presented them to his soldier brother Colonel George Boscawen of the 29th Foot, who took them on as drummers. The 29th continued to have some black drummers till 1843. In the 1820s 1st Foot Guards' bass drummer wore a huge turban topped with a gilt crescent and red plume, with a short gold-laced red jacket and a scimitar at his side. The Royal Fusiliers went one better by giving their exotically dressed bass drummer strings of cowrie shells hanging from his ears, that rattled when he beat the drum.

There were also negro drummers in the Peninsula. Nicolas Thorp, son of a wealthy Lancashire merchant, had run away from home to enlist in the army. By 1809 he was drum major of the 88th Foot – the Connaught Rangers – whose Lieutenant William Grattan thought him 'quite a lad'. He fell in love with a Spanish girl, whose rich and influential father objected to the match and was permitted to inspect the regiment before it left town to ensure that she had not been hidden in its ranks. Thorpe had in fact slipped her into the band, blacked up as a negro cymbal player. The 88th set off to a quick march with Thorp flourishing his baton at the head of the band and his lover clashing her cymbals behind him. When the sergeant major was killed at Busaco in 1810 Thorp replaced him, and, although wounded four times, enjoyed a successful career and a happy marriage. He was recommended for a free ensigncy, but it had not arrived when he was killed at Toulouse in 1814 by a cannon-ball that took him squarely in the chest and 'whirled his remains in the air'. The commission appeared the next day, and the fact that Mrs Thorp was now an officer's widow was 'the means of reconciling her father to the choice she had made'.[4]

There was a distinction between infantry drummers and cavalry trumpeters, enlisted to carry out military functions, and other musicians, hired by the regiment's officers. True, drummers and trumpeters had always been able to do more than just play routine calls: at Dettingen a trumpeter in the Earl of Crawford's Troop of Life Guards stood up in his stirrups and sounded the popular Purcell tune 'Britons Strike Home' before the troop charged. But their repertoire was necessarily limited, and so regiments that sought more elaborate music employed civilian musicians. The Royal Artillery had the earliest British ensemble (pre-dating the London Philharmonic by half a century), formed at Minden in Germany in 1762, and shifting to the Royal Artillery's depot at Woolwich the following year. It was small at first, with ten musicians playing trumpets, French horns, bassoons, oboes, and clarinets, with violins, cellos, double-bass, and flutes for use when the band played at dinners or receptions. Other regiments followed suit – the Royal Scots was reported as having 'fifers and a band of music' as early as 1763 – and, like the Royal Artillery, they favoured German or Italian musicians.

It was not until the early nineteenth century that a 'Band of Musick' at last became part of a regiment's establishment. Its size varied from time to time. In 1830 it numbered a bandmaster and fourteen musicians, though officers continued to pay for extra men, and soldiers were illicitly drafted across from the companies to increase the size of the band. An inspection report of 1813 on 4/Royal Scots affirmed that although the band played 'very correct marching time', its personnel 'rather exceed the limited numbers'. There was still a preference for employing foreign civilian bandmasters. In 1847 Bandmaster Paolo Castaldini of 1/Royal Scots, noted for his intemperate treatment of bandsmen, was attacked by his subordinates, who first threw a sheet over him so that he could not identify any individuals, and then gave him a sound beating. Although sixteen bandsmen were court-martialled and imprisoned, it transpired that Castaldini had been driven out of three previous bands, and when he moved on to the 63rd Foot its band resigned en masse rather than put up with him. In 1857 the band of the 61st Foot struck up the Victorian favourite 'Cheer, boys, cheer', when it marched into the British camp on

Delhi Ridge. A couple of days later Lieutenant Charles Griffiths was sitting in a tent with the bandmaster, Mr Sauer, when

> We were saluted with the sound of distant music, the most discordant I have ever heard. The bandmaster jumped up from his seat, exclaiming: '*Mein Gott! Vat is dat?* No regiment in camp can play such vile music.' And closing his ears immediately rushed out of the tent.

The Kashmir contingent was arriving in camp, and although its tough soldiers aroused admiration, 'the shrill discord of their bands created great amusement among the assembled Europeans.'[5]

It was not just the Kashmiris who could make a din. In 1854 the British army of the east, shortly to embark for the Crimea, held a grand review at Scutari, just across the Bosphorus from Constantinople. The troops looked splendid and drilled marvellously, but when it came to the National Anthem, the twenty or so bands played simultaneously in different arrangements, pitches and key signatures, and the result was a shocking cacophony. In 1857 the Duke of Cambridge, who had been dismayed by the Scutari debacle, set up the Royal Military School of Music at Kneller Hall, in Twickenham, London. Kneller Hall was responsible for training bandmasters, who were now increasingly soldiers, as the practice of recruiting civilians was discouraged. This established a common standard in military music and, more recently, provides training for all the army's musicians.

The late Victorian army had one band for each regular infantry battalion and cavalry regiment, and their marches became part of the texture of a soldier's life. Some regimental marches were ancient. The quick march of the Royal Scots, 'Dumbarton's Drums', harks back to the days when the regiment's colonel, Lord George Douglas, was created Earl of Dumbarton in 1675, and may very well be the same as the old Scots March that long pre-dates the regular army. When Samuel Pepys met Lord George in Rochester in 1667 he noted that 'here in the streets I did hear the Scots March beat by the drums before the soldiers, which is very odd.' Others were deeply fashionable. When the 11th Light Dragoons became the 11th (Prince Albert's Own) Hussars in 1840 they adopted Joseph Haydn's stately 'Coburg' as their slow march. The regiment also took the cherry-red of Prince Albert's livery for their trousers, a sartorial distinction now perpetuated by the King's Royal Hussars. No sooner had Johann Strauss composed the 'Radetzky March' in 1848 than the Austrian Bandmaster Schramm of the Queen's Dragoon Guards took it up as a regimental march. The Emperor Franz Joseph became colonel-in-chief of the regiment in 1896, giving it permission to adopt the Austrian double-headed eagle as its cap-badge.

There was the occasional compromise. The Queen's Royal Regiment's quick march, 'The Old Queen's', incorporated the National Anthem, and when it was played in the presence of Queen Victoria in 1881 she frostily enquired whether special permission had been given for its use, adding that unless such permission had been granted the practice must cease. The Queen's, much piqued, grimly marched past without a regimental march for the next few years, earning the nickname 'The Silent Second'. The regiment made much of the fact that it had been formed to garrison Tangier, Catherine of Braganza's dowry, and eventually discussions with the Portuguese embassy led to the adoption in 1903 of 'Braganza', itself a free arrangement of 'O Patria', the Portuguese National Anthem at the time.

Regimental marches often pointed to a unit's recruiting ground. The Irish Guards, the 8th Hussars, and then the Queen's Royal Irish Hussars had the rollicking 'St Patrick's Day'. General John Reid's fine 1770 composition 'The Garb of Old Gaul' was popular with Scottish infantry regiments and with the 7th Hussars, which had begun life as a Scots-raised dragoon regiment. Reid himself was a proficient flautist who left his substantial fortune to Edinburgh University to endow a chair of music. The Black Watch, the Royal Scots Greys and the Scots Guards swung along to the stirring 'Hielan Laddie', and the traditional 'Brian Boru's March' was a favourite with the Connaught Rangers and, from their formation in 1900, the Irish Guards. When the Connaughts were feeling the strain after a 'hot and heavy march' the commanding officer would order the band to play 'Brian Boru', and the sergeant major would order a 'Connaught Yell' at appropriate moments, after which the band would pause for a beat or two. This practice continued into the rumbustious 'Killaloe', written around 1887, and developed by Lieutenant Charles Martin of the Connaughts. It became very popular with them, and went on to be the regimental quick march of the Royal Irish Rangers and then, on its formation in 1992, the Royal Irish Regiment. Welsh regiments were fond of 'Men of Harlech', used as both a quick and slow march. But (despite the best endeavours of the film *Zulu*) it is unlikely that soldiers of the 24th Regiment sang it at the battle of Rorke's Drift in 1879 because, although there were indeed five men named Jones and four named Williams in B Company 2/24th that held the little outpost on the Buffalo River, the proportion of Welshmen there was only marginally higher that was usual in the army at the time. Until Cardwell transformed the 24th into the South Wales Borderers it still bore the bracketed title 2nd Warwickshire, and its regimental quick-march was 'The Warwickshire Lads'.

Many English county regiments had versions of folk songs as their regimental marches. The Wessex Regiment marched past to 'The Farmer's Boy', whose words tell the story, so common in folk songs, of a poor but honest lad who eventually marries the farmer's daughter and inherits the farm. It has a remarkable poignancy.

> The sun had set beyond yon hill,
> Across yon dreary moor.
> When weary and lame, a boy there came,
> Up to the farmer's door,
> 'Can you tell me where ere I be,
> And one that will me employ,
>
> To plough and sow, to reap and mow,
> And be a farmer's boy,
> And be a farmer's boy?'[6]

Officers might sing these words after dinner in the mess, but there was (as is so often the case) a less polite version, beginning

> The vicar of a country church
> One Sunday morning said,
> Some dirty bastard's shat himself,
> I'll punch his fucking head …

> Jolly Jack got up, walked down the aisle,
> With his organ on his back,
> And the vicar from the pulpit said,
> 'You can walk that bastard back,
> You can walk that bastard back, Jack'.

The Staffordshire Regiment, a 1959 amalgamation of the North and South Staffordshires, brought both ends of the county together with 'Come Lasses and Lads' and 'The Days We Went a-Gypsying'. The Wiltshire regiment had the definitively rustic 'The Vly', properly 'The Vly be on the Turmut' or 'Turmut Hoeing':

> 'Twas on a jolly summer's morn, the twenty-first of May,
> Giles Scroggins took his turmut hoe, with which he trudged away,
> For the vly, the vly, the vly be on the turmut
> And it's all my eye for we to try to keep vly off the turmut …

The Border Regiment had the measured 'John Peel', with the lively 'Corn Rigs are Bonnie' tucked into it, and the Green Howards celebrated the white rose of Yorkshire with 'Bonnie English Rose'. The West Yorkshires banished gentle airs from home with 'Ça Ira', the only regimental march to be 'won' in battle. 'Ça Ira – It'll be fine' – was a dance air that became the signature tune of the French Revolution, and versions of its lyrics ranged from the piously patriotic:

> Pierrette and Margot sing the guinguette
> Let us rejoice, good times will come

To the decidedly bloodthirsty:

> Aristocrats to the lamp-post …
> If we don't hang them,
> We'll break them,
> If we don't break them,
> We'll burn them.
> Ah! It'll be fine, It'll be fine, It'll be fine.

On 23 May 1793 an Allied army attacked the French at Famars, near Valenciennes. The 14th Foot, in one of the main assaulting columns, was checked by French infantry whose drummers were thumping out 'Ça Ira'. 'Let's beat them at their own damned tune', said the 14th's commanding officer. His own drummers at once took up the rhythm and the battalion pressed on to victory. The 14th bequeathed the march to the West Yorkshires, and today it lives on as the regimental quick march of The Yorkshire Regiment.

The Foot Guards tended towards the stately, with 'The British Grenadiers' as quick march and Handel's 'Scipio' as slow for the Grenadier Guards, and Johann Valentin Hamm's elegant 'Milanollo' for the Coldstream's quick march and the matchless aria 'Non pui andrai', from Mozart's *Marriage of Figaro* as its slow march. It was as well not to stray too far from familiar musical paths where royalty was concerned. Just before the First World War Mr Williams, bandmaster of the Grenadiers, made an arrangement of Richard Strauss's *Electra* for use during a long interval in the Changing of the Guard. The band was suitably elated 'at their own audacity and the success that had crowned it', when a red-coated page emerged from the palace with a personal message for Bandmaster Williams from King George V. 'His Majesty does not know what the band has just played,' it ran, 'but it is never to be played again.'[7] Rifle regiments needed marches that could accommodate their quickstep, and the 60th Rifles' 'Lutzow's Wild Hunt' nodded towards the influence of those German *jäger* on British light troops.

New regiments and corps often found something wholly appropriate. The Royal Army Medical Corps, founded in 1898 when the army's medical services were brought together, their officers at last holding formal military rank, had the old royalist air 'Here's a Health Unto His Majesty' as its march. The Royal Army Veterinary Corps traces its origins to the commissioning of the first vet in 1796, although an Army Veterinary Department was not formed till 1889, and has 'Drink Puppy Drink' and 'A Hunting We Will Go' as its marches. 'The Village Blacksmith' commended itself to the Royal Army Ordnance Corps. The Royal Tank Regiment, emerging from the Heavy Branch, Machine Gun Corps, which had manned the first British tanks in 1916, chose the old Worcestershire folk song 'My Boy Willie' because the first prototype tank to be completed was called 'Little Willie'. This was spliced with 'Cadet Rousselle', a folk song from the area of Cambrai, where the first major tank battle took place in 1917. I am not sure what Richard Wagner would make of the march version of 'Ride of the Valkyries', but it serves The Parachute Regiment well and has the merit of being wholly unmistakable. Then there were some oddities. The Cheshire Regiment's quick march was the Jacobite 'Wha Wadna Fecht for Charlie', and 2/Queens, despite its Surrey connection, had 'We'll Gang Nae Mair to Yon Toun'.

The drummers of Guards and line regiments, and the buglers that had existed in rifle regiments from their origin, had always been serving soldiers, although the early practice of giving drummers a short sword with the point broken off suggested that they were not expected to engage in hand-to-hand fighting. The cruciform-hilted pattern introduced in 1856, which remained broadly the same as that now in use, cannot be regarded as a serious weapon. Though that did not prevent an instruction of 1901 requiring all swords, including drummers', to be sharpened when a regiment went on active service. An English or Welsh battalion's drummers, under their drum major, constituted its Corps of Drums, while Highland regiments had Pipes and Drums under a pipe major. Although they might find themselves marching on parade at the head of the band, they were wholly distinct from it.

These were certainly not the beardless lads of popular fiction and sentimental imagery, not least because a drummer needed to carry a regulation side-drum and look after himself in the field. Lady Butler's 'Steady the Drums and Fifes' shows the Corps of Drums of the 57th Foot drawn up under fire at Albuhera. It is full of youngsters: one little chap, boldly standing bareheaded to await whatever fate has in store, cannot be more than 10. In fact, the average age of drummers of the 57th in 1811 was a respectable 26.

In Kipling's short story 'The Drums of the Fore and Aft', Jakin and Lew, young drummers who were always being birched by the drum major for fighting or smoking, were too young to accompany their battalion to the North West Frontier as company drummers but, on their earnest entreaties, followed the band as supernumeraries. When the untried unit was attacked by Afghan *Ghazis* the men bolted, leaving Jakin and Lew sheltering behind a rock. On Lew's suggestion they marched out of cover with fife and drum, picked up from instruments discarded by the band, mangling 'The British Grenadiers' but beginning to rally the battalion before 'Jakin halted and beat the long roll of the Assembly, while Lew's fife squealed despairingly.'A mullah amongst the Afghans shouted for the boys to be spared and raised as Muslims, it was too late, for

> the first volley had been fired and Lew dropped on his face. Jakin stood for a minute, spun round and collapsed as the Fore and Fit came forward, the curses of their officers in their ears and in their hearts the shame of open shame. Half the men had seen the drummers die, and they made no sign. They did not even shout. They doubled out straight across the plain in open order, and they did not fire.

The battle was won and the brigade commander saw his knighthood glittering:

> But some say, and amongst these be Goorkhas who watched on the hillside, that the battle was won by Jakin and Lew, whose little bodies were borne up just in time to fill two gaps at the head of the big ditch-grave for the dead under the heights of Jagai.[8]

My eyes are damp as I write these words, but there is no evidence that these drummer boys are anything but the products of Kipling's gloriously fertile imagination.

Youngsters, frequently the sons of serving soldiers, were indeed recruited as drummers, often between the ages of 10 and 12, but generally this was little more than a device for getting them pay and rations, though Samuel Potter, in his 1810 *The Art of Beating the Drum*, maintained that it was 'of the utmost importance' that drummers were taught during boyhood 'whilst the muscles of the wrist are supple.' John Shipp, who joined the 22nd Foot as a drummer in 1797, was anxious to exchange his drum for a musket as soon as he could, precisely because he feared that he would be known as a drummer boy whatever his age. As soon as he turned 18:

I then begged the captain that I might be removed from the drum-mers to the ranks. I did not like the appellation drum-boy. As I have seen many a man riding post, who was at least sixty years old, so if a drummer attained the age of Methuselah, he would never acquire any other title than drum-boy.

He was quickly given 'three steps in one day! From drum-boy to private, from a battalion company to the Light Bobs; and from private to corporal!'[9] One survey of the 304 British drummers in units engaged at Quatre Bras and Waterloo, suggests that only 10 per cent of them were between 16 and 17, with the average age of around 25, the same for soldiers in the ranks. The oldest drummer was John Leeds of the 23rd Foot, who had enlisted in 1802 aged 49, and was 62 at Waterloo.[10] There were persistent stories that two boy drummers of the 24th Foot had been 'hung up and gutted like sheep' at Isandlwana in 1879, but Ian Knight has recently shown that 'of the twelve 1/24th drummers killed … the two youngest were eighteen and the oldest was in his late thirties.'[11]

The fate of the drummers of the 24th demonstrates that, whatever their age, drummers and buglers did not enjoy a risk-free existence. Bugler Robert Hawthorne, of the 52nd Light Infantry, was a native of Maghera, County Londonderry and 35 years old when he accompan-ied the British attack on the Kashmir Gate at Delhi on 14 September 1857. He was with the party of British and Indian engineers under lieutenants Duncan Home and Philip Salkeld that crossed a damaged bridge under heavy fire to lay powder bags against the gate: six of the thirteen were killed or mortally wounded. Not only did Hawthorne sound the charge so that the assaulting column would know that the gate had been successfully blown in, but he then helped the mortally wounded Lieutenant Salkeld. Both Home (killed the following month) and Salkeld were 'provisionally' awarded the VC by the force commander, Major General Sir Archdale Wilson, 'for their conspicu-ous bravery in the performance of the desperate duty of blowing in the Cashmere Gate of the Fortress of Delhi under a heavy fire of musketry … [and] would have been recommended to Her Majesty for confirmation in that distinction had they survived.'[12] Hawthorne, too, was awarded the VC, and died in his bed in Manchester in 1879. On 1 July 1916, the first day of the Somme, Drummer Walter Ritchie of

2/Seaforth Highlanders, carrying a bugle, as most infantry drummers in battle had done since the 1850s, took part in the assault on Redan Ridge. His VC citation tells how he

> stood on the parapet of an enemy trench and, under heavy machine-gun fire and bomb attacks, repeatedly sounded the 'Charge' thereby rallying many men of various units who, having lost their leaders, were wavering and beginning to retire. He also, during the day, carried messages over fire-swept ground.[13]

Pipers, too, were very much in harm's way. At Sir Arthur Wellesley's first Peninsular victory, Vimiero, Piper George Clarke of the 71st piped his comrades into battle despite being wounded. At the time, there were no gallantry awards for private soldiers, but the Highland Society of London presented him with a fine set of silver-mounted pipes. Piper George Findlater was more fortunate. When the Gordons attacked the Dargai Heights on the North-West Frontier in 1897 he was shot though both feet and crawled to a rock, whence he piped his battalion forward. Officially he played its march, 'Cock o' the North', but he later admitted that he found the pace of the strathspey 'Haughs of Cromdale' more appropriate to a charge. On 25 September 1915, with the British assaulting in dismal weather into their own gas-cloud at Loos, the 40-year-old Daniel Laidlaw of 7/King's Own Scottish Borderers stood up on the parapet and piped his company out of its trench. He chose the regimental march 'Blue Bonnets Over the Border', continuing to play even after he was wounded. Both Findlater and Laidlaw were awarded the VC.

By the Second World War, although pipers might still play men into battle – on D-Day Lord Lovat's piper, Bill Millin, famously piped his commando brigade forward from Sword Beach to Pegasus Bridge – drummers and buglers were combat soldiers first and musicians second. Many battalions kept their Corps of Drums together by using them as the defence platoon for battalion headquarters, but they were often broken up. However, in the Italian campaign the battalions of 38th Irish Brigade (Royal Irish Fusiliers, Royal Inniskilling Fusiliers, and London Irish Rifles) retained their pipes and drums, and on 12 June 1944 they swaggered, caubeened and saffron-kilted, into St Peter's Square, Rome playing the 1798 street ballad 'The

Wearing of the Green', serenading Pope Pius XII with 'The Minstrel Boy', and then beating the 'Retreat', an event 'enjoyed immensely by the many Irish priests present who were mad with excitement shouting out their favourite tunes. The tune 'The Boys of Wexford' seemed to be their favourite.[14]

The postwar army, under the dual pressures of financial retrenchment and successive operational tours, found it increasingly hard to sustain its Corps of Drums. An enthusiastic commanding officer could make a real difference, but while piping always attracted the interest of officers (many of whom played the pipes themselves) there was infinitely less concern with drumming. A forceful drum major might both attract and train drummers and protect his Corps of Drums from the adjutant's desire to post drummers off to the rifle companies. Bernard Lively joined The Buffs as a boy drummer in 1958, became drum major of 2/Queens in 1967, and finished his service as RSM of 6/7 Queens. He did much to uphold the old standards of Corps of Drums.

But it was an unequal struggle. In 1977 a group of enthusiasts formed the Corps of Drums Society in order 'to preserve the Corps of Drums style of music as a living thing before it is too late'. The first issue of its newsletter *The Drummer's Call* lamented

To-day it is not even necessary for the routine barrack calls to be sounded (though this is still done in many battalions) and the Corps of Drums is an entirely ceremonial body whose primary task must be their allotted military function within the battalion. On a ceremonial parade however many Corps of Drums have become merely an extension of the regimental band and very rarely parade on their own ... The Royal Military School of Music have stated that they have no jurisdiction or authority over the training or establishment of drummers, fifers, buglers, trumpeters, etc.[15]

Thanks to the initiative of Warrant Officer Class 2 Mike Hall and Major Jack Barrow of the Duke of Edinburgh's Royal Regiment, *The Drummer's Handbook* was published as an infantry training manual in 1985. Major General Colin Shortis, Director of Infantry, affirmed in its foreword that

It was felt that with the more rapid turnover in personnel in Corps of Drums, particularly in the Infantry of the Line battalions, the customs, traditions and the music too, which had been passed on among the long serving drummers, would have become lost and distorted because so little had been put to print over the years.

The Army School of Ceremonial, part of the Infantry Training Centre at Catterick, now trains drummers and buglers and the Army School of Bagpipe Music and Highland Drumming provides the Royal Regiment of Scotland, and the handful of other units that maintain pipes and drums, with qualified musicians. The Royal Scots Dragoon Guards, which as a cavalry regiment would traditionally have had trumpeters rather than pipers, took on pipers in 1946. Its pipes and drums went to the top of the British pop chart in April 1972 with 'Amazing Grace'. The album *Spirit of the Glen: Journey*, was recorded when the Scots DG were serving in Basra in 2008. The regiment's pipers and drummers are trained as crewmen on the Challenger 2 main battle tank, and are expected to maintain their skills as armoured soldiers whilst maintaining high musical standards. Elsewhere the picture is more patchy. The Foot Guards, with their emphasis on ceremonial parades, maintain strong Corps of Drums, and both The Royal Green Jackets and their successors The Rifles, have seen the advantages that accrue from having buglers available (even on operations) to sound appropriate calls. After the painful formality of seeing off a dead comrade on his way home, it is wholly appropriate for a bugler to sound the advance; there can be tears and beers later, but for now there is a job to be done. Sadly, the line infantry struggles, and in most battalions the *Drummer's Handbook* recommendation that a Corps of Drums should consist of a drum major and sixteen drummers is an ideal that is seldom achieved.

In contrast to members of the Corps of Drums, who were fighting soldiers, for years bandsmen were in a more anomalous position. In the eighteenth century they were civilians, paid for by the regiment's officers, and might accompany it on campaign. The band of the 52nd Light Infantry played the regiment into the assault on the Mysore town of Savandroog in 1791 with the evergreen 'Britons Strike Home', and when the French were repulsed from Tarifa in 1812 the band of the 87th Foot saw them off with the lively 'Garryowen'. This had started life as an Irish drinking song: 'Let Bacchus' sons be not dismayed/We'll break windows, we'll break doors/But join with me each jovial blade/The watch knock down by threes and fours'. It was to cross the Atlantic with Irish immigrants to become the regimental march of George Custer's 7th Cavalry. Major George Simmons of the 95th recalled that when the regiment crossed the Ebro in June 1813 'Our band struck up "The Downfall of Paris", we were amused at their wit on this occasion, and we had it followed by a national tune or two to remind us of Old England and absent friends.'[16]

By this time the army was making determined efforts to ensure that bandsmen were enlisted soldiers. In 1803 a general order declared:

> It is His Majesty's pleasure that in regiments having bands of music not more than one private soldier of each troops or company shall be permitted to act as musicians; and that one Non Commissioned Officer shall be allowed to act as master of the band. These men shall be drilled and instructed in their exercise, and in the case of actual service are to fall in with their respective troops or companies completely armed and accoutred – soldiers first, bandsmen second.[17]

This order was not generally obeyed, in part because commanding officers saw the advantage of taking their bands on campaign with them, and in part because the allocation of enlisted bandsmen was so stingy that officers hired extra musicians. The last civilian bandmasters did not disappear until the twentieth century, and they were common in the nineteenth. William 'Billy the Bugler' Miller was born in 1815, son of a soldier in the Rifle Brigade. He enlisted in 1/95th in 1828 and became a bugler in the band, then numbering fifteen musicians led by a sergeant. Miller became bandmaster in 1842 and gained a Greek licentiate of music when the battalion was stationed in Corfu. He bought his discharge from the army in 1854 and was immediately employed by the officers of 1/95th as civilian bandmaster. Miller went to the Crimea with his battalion, and his bandsmen were used as stretcher-bearers, work so arduous that the band was reduced in strength from forty-five to sixteen men in a year. He handed over the remnants to Bugle-Major Peachey, who took responsibility for bandsmen and buglers alike, and set off home to raise a new band. When 1/95th returned to England with just twelve bands-men and a handful of buglers Miller had trained forty new bandsmen. He later boasted 'My turn with the 1st Battalion was from '28 to '80, that was 52 years service; never away from the green jackets, at home or abroad.'[18]

Despite the intention of the 1803 order, it took some time for the army to develop a comprehensive policy on the employment of bandsmen when their regiments went on active service. When the 75th Foot was ordered to join the attack on Delhi in 1857 Colonel Herbert wanted to leave his bandsmen behind, but as Captain Richard Barter, the adjutant, discovered, 'the men came up in a body and pleaded so hard to be allowed to go with their comrades as duty soldiers in the ranks' that the colonel gave way, and 'all the best play-ers were killed or disabled'. One bandsman, with his right hand shot off, begged to be allowed to soldier on: 'I could play the trombone, sir. I could fix a hook to my stump and play it first rate.'[19] For the second half of the nineteenth century bandsmen were taken on campaign to play music when they could, but to act as stretcher-bearers in action. By 1914 however, policy had changed once more, and on mobilisation bandsmen over the age of 18 were posted to squadrons or companies, and the bandmaster remained behind at the regimental depot to supervise the band boys. However, some regiments, not content with the music provided by their Corps of Drums, tried to create small bands in France where, whatever the miseries of trench warfare, men spent longer out of the line than in it. In Quarry Cemetery, just below Montauban ridge on the Somme, lies the German-born Sergeant Major W. G. Kleinstuber of 9/Cameronians, killed on 14 July 1916, and perhaps the last example of a foreign bandmaster.

There is another irony. Edward Thomas was born in India, where his father was serving in the Durham Light Infantry. He joined the Royal Horse Artillery as a trumpeter at Kirkee at the age of 14, and transferred to the band of the 4th Royal Irish Dragoon Guards two years later. In the summer of 1914 he was a corporal of 29, but already had fifteen years' service. He knew

> every bandsman has got to do his military duties in addition to his
> musical ones, and the moment war comes he has to turn from his

musical instrument to his weapon of battle. It was a big change for me and my pals of the band ... who were playing at Southampton on August 4 1914, when we suddenly had to return to headquarters and prepare for the stern business of war.

Thomas was posted to his regiment's C Squadron, commanded by Major Tom Bridges. On the morning of 22 August 1914, the day before the battle of Mons, Bridges had posted two of his troops in ambush on the Brussels road with the remaining two, mounted, out of sight behind them. When an approaching German cavalry patrol smelt a rat before the ambush could be sprung one of the mounted troops charged – one German was wounded by a sword thrust and others were captured – and then Thomas's troop galloped up and was sent into action on foot. Thomas ducked into some cover behind a wall. 'I could see a German cavalry officer some four hundred yards away, standing mounted in full view of me,' he remembered. 'Immediately I saw him I took aim, pressed the trigger, and automatically, almost instantaneously, he fell to the ground.' The British army's first shot of the war had been fired by a bandsman.

Bands are best known for their contribution to military spectacle. Cornet Sir William Fraser of the Life Guards describes the Duke of Wellington's last appearance at the Queen's birthday parade.

No military spectacle ... has equalled that of the Duke's coming on to the Parade ... on the morning of the Queen's birthday ... At the first stroke of the Horse Guards' clock, the Duke appeared on the left flank of the line. At the moment that his horse passed the extreme left, the word was given by the Commanding Officer to stand to 'Attention', then 'Present Arms'; instantly the magnificent band of the three Regiments of the Guards, with their drums and fifes, numbering together 200 instruments, played the first note of Handel's glorious air ('See the Conquering Hero Comes') ... The Duke, on arms being presented, instantly and slowly raised his right hand, nearly touching the lower right edge of his bearskin with two fingers. He rode slowly across the parade; and the ceremony of 'Trooping the Colours' was gone through. During this time some well chosen air, not infrequently the 'Benediction des Poignards' from 'Les Huguenots', was played. The March Past followed. The united bands played Mozart's noble 'Non pui andrai', the finest march for slow time that was ever composed.

Afterwards the Guards marched past in quick time; the Grenadiers playing 'The British Grenadiers'; the Coldstream Guards a beautiful march known as 'The Milanollo', the most perfect in as regards time that I have heard; the Scots Guards the national, but mediocre melody 'Will ye go to Inverness?' The line then advanced and presented arms; the Duke again saluted, leaving the ground amidst tumultuous cheering.[20]

Bands played at all sorts of other military events, sometimes fielding smaller ensembles when the full majesty of drum and brass was too much, weaving a bright braid into the texture of life. They were busy in the summer months at the covered bandstands that formed a distinctive feature of London's parks, British cities, and seaside towns. In the pre-radio era they provided listeners with a welcome repertoire, from martial airs to operatic favourites and music-hall hits. There were now opportunities for successful bandmasters to move on to the commissioned post of director of music (this can at present take a musician as far as lieutenant colonel), but many bandsmen grew grey in the service, with slow promotion tempered by the comfortable routines of regimental life.

New intakes of teenage 'band rats' were taught their trade by the bandmaster, a process that sometimes shunned the best in musical pedagogy, as a Rifle Brigade bandsman of the early twentieth century remembered:

Unfortunately I found that I had bound myself to a man, who, as bandmaster, was to dominate my life for quite a long time to come. To my mind, he was nothing less than a criminal brute to Band Boys. He had one method of instruction only: bash it into them.

His name was Mr Chas H. Barry.[21]

In the 1920s bandboy Spike Mays of the Royal Dragoons occasionally received 'a cut across the backside' from the bandmaster's stick. Like most soldiers he particularly appreciated a well-sounded 'Last Post', the call that brought the long military day to its end: 'and the repetition of the penultimate notes, "Sleep on, sleep on", was followed by his top note. One which trailed away into the nothingness that all men die in.' The first time he put on his full dress – plumed helmet, scarlet tunic, tight 'overalls', boots and spurs, he thought that 'king-fishers are drab compared with me'. But his real admiration was reserved for Coronet,

> our magnificent drum horse … Seventeen and a half hands, as proud as the proudest Royal Dragoon, Coronet was a sight to behold when dressed for ceremonials, with silver kettledrums, all the trappings and drummers Simpson or Barnes aboard, he would lift up his forelegs to prance and dance along as if to say, 'Just look at me'.[22]

There was the glory of formal parades, and the pride that came with lifting a weary battalion along its line of march with those tunes of glory, even if musical logic was not clear to all listeners. Sergeant Shawyer was with the Rifle Brigade band in Mesopotamia (modern Iraq) in 1920.

> Change of routine when the Band headed the battalion on a route march for two hours. I spent most of the journey, inbetween playing marches, trying to explain to CSM Tom Selway MC DCM, why that I, a six foot man, plays a small instrument like a clarinet, whilst bandsman Brown, several inches shorter, plays a huge brass bass. I doubt if I succeeded in persuading the CSM who forwarded the policy of the biggest men playing the heaviest and largest instru-ment, in which case I should be the bass drummer.[23]

Until the army began its slow post-1945 recessional there were bands aplenty, with one for every line infantry battalion and cavalry regi-ment. There were also staff bands for the departmental corps like the Royal Army Ordnance Corps, Royal Army Medical Corps, and Royal Army Service Corps; a Chatham-based Royal Engineers band (with a second band at Aldershot from 1949–1985); and large 'State Bands' for the regiments of Household Cavalry, Foot Guards, and for the Royal Artillery. Bands, so easy to cost and so hard for outsiders to value, were steadily reduced. In 1994, after the 'Options for Change' defence review had announced the reduction from sixty-nine to twenty-nine regular bands, the Corps of Army Music was formed. Centred on Kneller Hall, it is the corps into which all bandsmen and women now enlist. The traditional cap-badges and full dress associated with their regiment or corps are still worn. Their musicians – around 1,100 all told – are all members of the Corps of Army Music. There are twenty-three regular army bands at the time of writing, the most recently formed the Band and Bugles of the Rifles that replaced the Light Division Band in 2007. It consists of a band of thirty-five musicians reinforced with a platoon of buglers drawn from the five regular battalions of The Rifles.

There can be few better examples of the links between ancient and modern than its recent recording of the haunting eighteenth-century air 'Love Farewell'.

> I thought I heard the colonel crying
> March brave boys there's no denying
> Cannon roaring – drums a-beating
> March brave boys there's no retreating
> Love Farewell.[24]

The song was 'extraordinarily well received' by soldiers awaiting departure for Afghanistan or returning from operations there. 'It's by soldiers and for soldiers', thought Captain Mark Purvey, the Rifles' director of music. 'It's about the horrors of war but it's also about leaving the people you love behind, and looks at both sides.'[25]

Bandsmen have seen horrors of their own, and on two occasions have been bombed by the IRA whilst giving a recital. In 1921 the band of 2/Hampshires was at Youghall in Ireland, playing the march 'Lord Nelson' when a bomb went off, killing seven members of the band and wounding seventeen: the march was never again played by the Hampshires. The Green Jackets band was bombed in 1982 at Regent's Park when seven bandsmen were killed. Shortly before this another bomb exploded alongside a mounted detachment of the Blues and Royals in Hyde Park: three cavalrymen were killed and a fourth died later.

When I was visiting 1/PWRR in the Iraqi town of Al Amara in 2004, I poked my head into soldiers' accommodation – transport containers, roofs reinforced with sandbags, and mercifully fitted with air conditioning. The place was silent but for the subdued hiss of pop music from a dozen iPods: the soldiers, knackered and comatose, were young men with modern tastes. Two months earlier I had attended the repatriation of Private Chris 'Ray' Rayment at RAF Lyneham. He had been the best sort of South London soldier. He never let the fact that he was a private deter him from forcefully advising his commanding officer on how to run the battalion. His comrades were anxious to know how the ceremony had gone. Who was in the bearer party that brought him, alone with his glory, out of the C 17 transport aircraft that had flown him home? Who had sounded the 'Last Post' for him? I said that 2/PWRR had provided bearer party and drummer, and that the veteran RAF Warrant Officer in charge of the event said that he had rarely seen things better done. I told them that I will always remember that 'Last Post', eased out with lots of lip and spit to hold that last high note. Accountants can say what they like about military music, but it goes straight to a man's heart.

V

HABITS AND HABITAT

CHAPTER 23

THE RAMBLING SOLDIER

THERE HAS ALWAYS been something of the smoky whiff of the nomad about the soldier. His life alternates between the measured routine of barracks and the jolting transfer from one garrison to the next; the urgent demands of an unexpected campaign or the long, dour slog of major war. In one sense he is defined by what General Sir John Hackett called 'the contract of unlimited liability', for he is bound to kill or be killed for a purpose in which he may have no personal interest whatever. In another way, though, soldiers are moulded by their world: collective, structured, and introspective; comfortably habit-forming for some and infuriatingly intrusive for others. Alfred de Vigny, an early nineteenth-century French soldier and man of letters, believed that 'regiments are moving monasteries', with their colours as objects of devotion and a daily routine as rigidly prescribed as the liturgy of matins, terce, vespers, and compline, with drum or bugle replacing the great bell or the monophonic rhythm of plainsong. Osbert Sitwell, an officer in the Grenadiers on the eve of the First World War, thought that after the daily Changing of the Guard at Buckingham Palace:

> The performers in this ceremony cease to exist when they have marched away; and so I propose to give ... an account of the very individual life led by officers on this duty who, after the manner of monks ... are immured in the seclusion of a brick building from which, though situated in the very centre of the capital, you can scarcely hear the passing of the traffic.[1]

There is, of course, at least one striking contrast between monk and soldier: the latter rarely embarks willingly on sexual abstinence, although its enforcement sometimes becomes a salient feature of his life. The analogy hints at deep truths, not least in the way that fraternal terminology so often describes the relationship between soldiers. Shakespeare put 'band of brothers' into the mouth of Henry V, Horatio Nelson used it to define his relationship with his captains, Stephen Ambrose took it as the title of his 1992 story of an American parachute infantry company that in turn went on to become the subject of Steven Spielberg's television series. The Confederate song 'The Bonnie Blue Flag' catches the phrase in its own jaunty way.

> We are a band of brothers
> Native to the Soil
> Fighting for the property
> We gained by honest toil ...

In 1763 the diarist James Boswell went off for a rowdy night on the town dressed in shabby-genteel costume topped by an officer's round hat with tarnished braid, and found a young prostitute who charged him sixpence and 'allowed me entrance ... but refused me performance.' When Boswell pressed the issue she called for help, and in the ensuing fracas he gained the support of nearby soldiers by shouting 'Brother soldiers ... should not a half-pay officer r-g-r for sixpence?'[2]

The paternalistic streak so often present in trusted commanders is remembered in nicknames like Daddy Hill for Wellington's lieutenant and Daddy Plumer for the painstaking commander of Second Army on the Western Front. In 1870 Emily Wonnacott, whose husband William was schoolmaster to the 8th Foot, then serving in India, wrote 'Dear old Col Woods is coming back on Sunday. We are all so glad. He is like a father to the regiment.'[3] Major General James Wolfe described himself as a 'military parent'. When he was commanding the 20th Foot in 1750 and one of his grenadiers was suspected of murder, he wrote to the Lord Justice Clerk, the second most senior judge in Scotland, saying that he had 'not been able to observe either in his look, conduct or demeanour, any symptom of so black a villainy'. Moreover, he had recently undergone 'a very violent remedy' for venereal disease, and Wolfe was sure that 'he could never have borne it if the guilt of murder had hung upon him.'[4]

Field Marshal Lord Wolseley fondly recalled General Sir John Lysaght Pennefather, the Irish-born 'swearing general' who had held his division together at Inkerman by sheer strength of leadership. As the historian A. W. Kinglake wrote, even when his rubicund countenance could not be seen there was comfort in his voice, with 'the "Grand Old Boy's" favourite oaths roaring cheerfully down through the smoke.' 'Blood and 'ounds, boys, blood and 'ounds' was his favourite expression. Pennefather had transferred to the 22nd Foot as a captain in 1826, made his way by seniority, and finished as colonel of the regiment. 'His regiment was his love,' wrote Wolseley, 'and all ranks in it were to him as his children.'[5] A regimental family might have black sheep and prodigal sons, wayward teenagers, randy uncles and scatty aunts, but family it was, its behaviour powerfully influenced by the circumstances of its collective life.

Today's public house may be anything from a spit-and-sawdust bar with the Gents' making its subtle presence felt, through a beamed tribute to Merrie England, and on to a low-lit gastropub. But for the first half of the army's life its officers and men lived in the public houses that were precisely what their names implied: houses, big and small, where food and accommodation were at least as important as drink. They had originated in the alehouses of Saxon England, and became increasingly important after the dissolution of the monasteries deprived travellers of monastic hospitality. Public houses provided travellers with small beer with a low alcohol content, little more than water brewed sufficiently to make it safe to drink, with stronger ales like porter becoming more popular, for those who could afford them, from the eighteenth century. Private Thomas Thetcher of the grenadier company of the North Hampshire Militia died in 1764 'of a violent Fever contracted by drinking Small Beer when hot' and lies buried just outside Winchester Cathedral, his headstone urging:

> Soldiers be warned by my untimely fall
> And when ye're hot drink Strong or not at all.

When an infantryman, standing on that low ridge at Waterloo, told his mate that he did not much like to see their own cavalry scurrying back with the French in hot pursuit, he was told not to worry his head about it. 'We must blow the froth away before we come to the porter.' The French would soon find that a solid square had rather more weight than a scampering hussar.

Gin-shops became popular when cheap gin was introduced to England after 1688 – the use of *genever* as a pre-battle stimulant had already spawned the expression 'Dutch courage'. These were never the same as alehouses, and even some temperance movements did not regard sipping small beer as drinking at all. In 1392 Richard II ordered those who brewed with the intention of selling to hang a sign outside their premises, and the early symbols of brewing – like a bunch of hops or a malt-shovel – gave illiterate customers a firm steer towards the available product. The painted inn-sign, its symbolism often reflecting the heraldry of prominent local families, came later. When ex-sailors bought pubs they often named them after the commander whose success had brought them the prize-money that made the venture possible, and portraits of white-wigged, blue-coated admirals still swing outside many a pub. John Manners, Marquess of Granby (1721–1770) combined military virtue – when he led the charge at Warburg in 1760 hat and wig blew off, leaving him 'going at it bald-headed' – with genuine concern for the private soldier. Edward Penny's painting *The Marquess of Granby Relieving a Sick Soldier* helped the Marquess into a political career that proceeded to go badly wrong. Many grateful subordinates set up alehouses that still, from London's Shaftesbury Avenue to Waltham on the Wolds, from Hoveringham to Knaresborough, testify to his liberality.

Soldiers' close acquaintance with public houses was only partly linked to their search for drink or their interest in congenial civilian employment. As R. E. Scouller observes in his magisterial *The Armies of Queen Anne*, 'the government had to make shift for their dangerous charges by visiting them on the other criminal class – inn-keepers.'[6] The practice of billeting troops on private houses, such a hated feature of the Civil War, was declared illegal in 1679 and again outlawed by the 1689 Bill of Rights. That year the second Mutiny Act recognised that because there was so little barrack accommodation, available soldiers would have to be housed somewhere. Because there was occasion for 'the marching of many regiments, troops and companies in several parts of this kingdom towards the sea-coasts and otherwise,' local constables and magistrates were authorised to billet the army in 'inns, livery stables, ale houses, victualling houses, and in all houses selling brandy, strong waters, cider, or metheglyn, by retail, to be drank in their houses, and no other, and in no private houses whatsoever'.[7]

Even after most soldiers were housed in barracks the law still permitted them to be billeted in public houses when they were on the line of march, and they were 'frequently billeted after they had arrived at their destination under a presumption that they were still on the march, and that the route authorising them to be billeted was still in force'. The 'route' – from the French *feuille de route* – was a document signed on behalf of the Crown by the secretary at war and then by the secretary of state for war, with regiments being issued with sufficient blank forms for their use. The 1914 *Manual of Military Law* noted proudly that 'billeting is now hardly ever resorted to by regular forces, except when actually moving, and the introduction of railways has greatly diminished its necessity even on these occasions.'[8] The rules in Scotland and Ireland were different: in Scotland soldiers could be billeted on private houses till 1857, and in Ireland till 1879.

Although it was recognised that billeting was 'oppressive and generally unpopular, as well as detrimental to the soldier', opponents of the standing army maintained that putting troops in barracks not only institutionalised a force that ought to be dispensed with, but provided the government with a ready means for oppressing the people. There was certainly a grain of truth in the latter argument, for some of the earliest barracks were built in Scotland and Ireland, where governments needed military force readily to hand and it was either impractical or downright dangerous to billet soldiers. The first purpose-built barracks, at Berwick-upon-Tweed on the Scottish border, were built in 1717 to the design of Nicholas Hawksmoor. They could accommodate 600 men in what was, by the standards of the age, reasonable comfort. Ruthven Barracks, sited on top of an old castle mound in the Highlands, was built in 1719, just after the Jacobite rebellion of 1715. It had two three-storey barrack-blocks within an enclosing wall, with bastioned towers on two of its corners, and both barracks and wall were loopholed for defence. Fort William, Fort Augustus, and Fort George picketed the Great Glen. Fort George, Ardersier, not far from Inverness, was built in 1748 to replace an earlier structure. It is a formidable star-shaped fortress, the best example of Vauban-style 'artillery fortification' in the British Isles.

Neither scattered inland barracks nor the limited accommodation within the elderly fortifications of great seaports were sufficient to house the army of the Georges. It was in a state of constant movement, as regiments marched to and from the harbours that connected Britain to her burgeoning empire and the seats of war in Europe, North America, and India. There were the West Country ports of Plymouth, Bristol, and Bideford; mighty Portsmouth on the south coast; Greenwich, Woolwich, Dartford, and Gravesend on the lower reaches of the Thames; Chatham and Rochester on the Medway; and occasionally Newcastle upon Tyne. Troops sailing to and from Ireland used the River Dee, near Chester, Liverpool, and the Clyde. Within Britain there were established corridors of military movement. These tended not to be in bleak and exposed countryside with little in the way of towns for billeting troops. So Wales or the extreme south-west would be avoided. Billeting cavalry brought the added complication of feeding and watering horses. On three of the four occasions that cavalry was sent into Wales to support the civil power, it went dismounted. In Scotland regular soldiers did not stray far from fortified barracks or large towns, and the policing of the Highlands was left largely to independent companies of locally raised infantry, in whom the Black Watch has its origins.

If some regimental peregrinations were dictated by the demands of foreign service, others reflected the army's frequent employment in aid of the civil power. Cavalry and dragoon regiments patrolled the coast and sent detachments inland to cut routes used by smugglers. Horse and foot alike were stationed in areas where riots and other disturbances were common. Seaports were troublesome, for these towns often bent under the strain of industrial expansion. Gloucestershire had unruly weavers, and there were areas of persistent agricultural unrest like Northumberland and Durham. Ireland was particularly taxing. In November 1753 Corporal Todd found himself in a subaltern's party sent by sea from Cork 'to take Murphy O'Sullivan, a great smuggler, who was outlawed for killing an officer of the customs'. They surrounded Sullivan's hut and the lieutenant ordered him to surrender. When there was no response they tried to fire the place, but at first it would not burn, for it was a rainy day.

Three women emerged and were spared, and the men inside fired through the windows until the roof was well alight, then ran out and were shot. O'Sullivan was the last to appear: his blunderbuss missed fire, and he was shot dead at the door. The soldiers found some silver spoons and other valuables in the hut 'which was divided amongst us', and sewed O'Sullivan into a piece of sail cloth to take him back to Cork. There was a reward of £500 for taking him dead or alive, and the soldiers happily pocketed £4. 12*s*. apiece.[9]

Not all excursions in aid of the civil power ended as happily. The Bristol riots of 1831 saw three days of serious unrest, in which the bishop's palace, mansion house, and much of the prison were burnt. Isambard Kingdom Brunel halted his work on the Clifton suspension bridge to become a special constable. The 3rd Dragoon Guards charged the mob in Queen Square with drawn swords. Officers were usually concerned about being accused of over-reacting, and would take no action until an hour after a sheriff or magistrate had read the riot act. On this occasion, though, the Irish-born Lieutenant Colonel Thomas Brereton – as Inspecting Field Officer, Bristol Recruiting District, he found himself in command – was court-martialled for neglect of duty. He had tried to persuade the crowd in Queen Square to disperse, and had ordered the troops to use swords rather than firearms. He shot himself while his trial was in progress.

A soldier in 1/Cameron Highlanders remembered a Belfast riot in 1907 that might have been familiar to men of his regiment eighty years later.

> The scene that followed must have closely resembled the night before Quatre Bras ... our services were called for the 11th and 12th August, when the natives of the 'Falls' district entered into a nut-cracking competition with the police, and several of the military had the opportunity of experiencing what it was like to be struck with a 'Belfast Kidney' (a paving stone) and also of listening to the elocutionary power of the 'Falls' damsels.[10]

Soldiers were regularly used to contain or disperse riots, to patrol the countryside at times of agricultural unrest and, increasingly, to intervene during strikes. In the Featherstone colliery riot of 7 September 1893 two bystanders were killed when troops opened fire, and thereafter the military authorities sought to intervene in maximum strength so as to deter the crowd without the need to use firearms. The need to provide aid to the civil power disturbed regimental deployments in the eighteenth century, making it harder for battalions to train together. Thereafter, there were occasions on which the army's whole pattern of life was disrupted by the need to maintain essential services: the fire service disputes of 1977 and 2002–3 had a major impact on training.

Keeping troops in volatile urban areas was believed to be harmful to discipline. In 1771 Major General James Murray reviewed the 35th Foot in Bristol. It was packed with recruits, and he reported that the city was 'a very bad quarter for so young a regiment. It is productive of all the vice, and bad consequence, which Wapping would be.'[11]

The Foot Guards were more static, marching into central London for parades or inspections or less frequently going off on campaign. In 1726 1st Foot Guards had nine of its companies billeted about Holborn and the parish of St Andrew Holborn, with two each in Clerkenwell and St Giles Cripplegate, one apiece in Spitalfields, Whitechapel, and St Sepulchre without Newgate, a company in Shoreditch and Folgate, and one in East Smithfield and St Katherines. A further ten were across London Bridge, in the Borough of Southwark.[12] With companies of around 100 men apiece and an abundance of alehouses – more than 7,000 in the whole of London – such arrangements worked well enough. But when the 20th Foot marched from Canterbury to Devizes in May 1756, it did such damage that Lieutenant Colonel Wolfe feared 'We have ruined half the public houses upon the march, because they have quartered us in villages too poor to feed us without destruction to themselves.'[13] In order to avoid swamping local accommodation, regiments customarily marched in two to four 'divisions', each a day ahead of the next, and all observing two 'halting days', usually Thursday and Sunday each week. In consequence a battalion covered the ground far more slowly than an individual traveller. In May 1738 the 11th Foot set out from Exeter for Berwick, marching in three divisions and observing the usual halting days. It was quartered at twenty-nine towns on its route, and rested a full week at Newcastle and Gateshead, taking 51 days to cover about 430 miles.[14]

In October 1756 William Todd's 12th Foot was on the move in the south east. On the 24th he was on baggage guard, marching with the wagons behind the regiment. These held the officers' baggage, and such of a soldier's possessions as he was not wearing about his encumbered person or carrying on his broad back. From 1729 an infantryman received

A good full-bodied cloth coat, well lined, which may serve for the
waistcoat for the second year
A waistcoat
A pair of good kersey breeches
A pair of good strong stockings
A pair of good strong shoes
Two good shirts and two good neckcloths
A good strong hat, well laced.

For the SECOND YEAR:

A good cloth coat, well lined, as for the first year
A waistcoat made of the former year's coat
A pair of new kersey breeches
A pair of good strong stockings
A pair of good strong shoes
A good shirt, and a neckcloth
A good strong hat, well laced
For the Fusilier regiments, caps once in two years
The new waistcoat in the first year, is only to be given to regiments
new-raised, and to additional men, who are likewise to be
furnished with two pairs of stockings and two shirts.[15]

William Todd would have worn a broad leather belt for sword and bayonet over his right shoulder, although by now swords were not worn by privates and corporals except in grenadier companies, whose men affected natty hangers, not much use in battle but comforting in a Dartford tavern. Over his left shoulder went another belt, this one supporting the cartridge box. Both were coloured buff in his regiment, and Todd, a reliable handyman, was allowed 4½d. to make each man in his company a ball of yellow clay, ochre, and tragacanth gum so that soldiers could buff up their belts before an inspection. He may still have been carrying most of his belongings in a large cow-hide knapsack slung across his right shoulder, but oblong packs were increasingly popular: the government paid for canvas ones, but generous regimental colonels might run to the more durable goatskin. A water bottle and light knapsack completed Todd's equipment. On the march he might have slung his musket across his back to keep both hands free to help with the wagons along their rutted way.

Much as the details of dress and equipment were to vary over the centuries, Todd's own problems would change little. He might, with luck, discover that arrangements had been made for his large pack to travel in a baggage wagon, but soldiers were often unhappy, not without reason, about letting their kit out of sight. Also on the baggage wagons were a variety of 'camp necessities', like hatchets, tin kettles, blankets, 'bells of arms' to cover piled muskets, and tents – 14-man tents for the men, and privately purchased ones for the officers.

With its patient oxen hauling the creaking wagons, the baggage train of the 12th Foot lumbered along.

We marched to Dartford but the regiment crossed the river Thames at Gravesend and the next day we marched and quartered in London, and the next day we marched to Romford, the next to Chelmsford and the next to a village, and on the 30th instant we marched into Colchester. The Regiment had got in two days before us, our comrades had got a very good billet for me at the sign of the Crown in the market place.

On 23 December they trudged off again.

Marched from Colchester for Canterbury in the County of Kent, the same road the regiment marched from Chatham camp, only we had two days more marches from Chatham to Sittingbourne, and from thence to the city of Canterbury. I was quartered at William Badcock's at the sign of the Cold Bath as he rented the bathing house for the quality, they paying so much for the season … My old comrade Sergeant Merrin got in with Mrs Cooper at the sign of Lord Marlborough's head … I very often visited them and was made one of the best, as he was made paymaster sergeant and could not make up his accounts without me.

In March 1757 the regiment left Canterbury briefly to help make space for seven Hanoverian regiments on their way to Dover for transport home. When it returned Todd found that the influx of troops had had a serious effect on the local prices:

> Everything is unreasonable dear and it is said several poor people eat grains, potatoes is 3½d. per pound. Here I sent for ½ a guinea which was sent me under seal of a letter but I never received it. John Freeman of our company stole a silver tankard from his quarters for which he was transported for 7 years. All our Regiment was put into stoppages [of pay, to recompense the owner for it]. Here the officers could not live upon their pay, etc. ... Men live very hard.[16]

The military authorities paid publicans to supply soldiers on the march with breakfast and dinner, washed down with small beer. Wise men kept sufficient bread, and cheese too, if they could salvage any, in their 'snapsacks' to sustain them at the midday halt. Publicans were also required to provide men with straw and candles, arrangements which were as much honoured in the breach as the observance, and soldiers quipped 'The Angel treats us like devils, and the Rising Sun refuses us light to go to bed by.' In Scotland men quartered on private householders supplied their own food for the landlady to cook, as James Anton of the Black Watch, in garrison in Edinburgh in 1804, tells us:

> I shall mention here our usual meals (with which we were perfectly contented) during the time we were in quarters, as they differ so widely from what soldiers now-a-days are accustomed to; premising, that we had our provisions, without contract, at our own purchasing. We breakfasted about nine in the morning, on bread and milk; dined at about two in the afternoon, on potatoes and a couple of salt herrings, boiled in the pot with the potatoes: a bottle of small beer (commonly called swipes) and a slice of bread served for supper, when we were disposed to take that meal, which soldiers seldom do. On the whole I am certain our expenses for messing, dear as markets were, did not exceed three shillings and sixpence each, weekly; and to do our landlady justice, she was not anxious to encourage extravagance in preparing and cooking our meals,

particularly as they required fuel and attention; and, in these matters, we were far from being troublesome or particular. Our obliging landlady would, when requested, bring us a pennyworth of soup, called *kale*, for our dinner, instead of herring; and if we had a little cause to remark on the want of cleanliness in the dish, or its contents, she jocosely replied, 'It tak's a deal o' dirt to poison sogers.'[17]

Officers paid for their own food, though they received an extra daily allowance to help them to do so, and could generally afford a convivial dinner, though local shortages of provisions might limit their menu and drive up its price.

Although the billeting system was well regulated and familiar, it was fraught with hazards. Sergeant Ned Botwood of the 47th Foot advised his listeners that there was much to be said for settling tavern debts by 'giving leg-bail', simply failing to pay when the detachment moved on. Before a detachment departed its drummers would beat the 'General Call to Arms' around the town, telling soldiers to prepare to fall in under arms (the next call would be the 'Assembly' which brought the companies together), and coincidentally warning tradesmen that this was their last chance to get their bills paid. Soldiers brawled with civilians and one another, led youths astray, and seduced local girls. Regiments passed from town to town leaving a trail of broken hearts and broken pates, unpaid accounts and raided orchards. James Anton recalled three girls from Hamilton who had been induced, 'by promises of marriage', to follow their soldier lovers to Edinburgh, where they scratched a living by walking barefoot to Leith to unload colliers. 'These poor girls were sensible that they had acted wrong in leaving their home,' he wrote, 'relying on the faith of worthless lovers, but they were still honest, and as yet had not been under the necessity of throwing themselves upon the town.'[18]

There were, though, times when the inhabitants of a town might sympathise with the men quartered there. In about 1776 an Irish regiment was billeted on private houses in Perth 'and in most cases were wretchedly lodged; often in open tiled garrets with an unglazed window, or in dismal vaults fit for only for pigs.' The men had just 3*d.* a day for food, and their 'common breakfast was a half-penny roll, and half-penny worth of Suffolk cheese.' Those who spent the rest of their allowance on 'a glass of spirits' to 'alleviate their sufferings' could afford nothing more to eat that day. In consequence the men 'were driven to commit petty depredations', and the regiment responded by flogging those who were caught, so that 'the North Inch became a scene of continual barbarity. It was no uncommon thing to see six, or even ten of these unfortunate wretches suffer from 100 to 500 lashes each.' Eventually a married soldier with four children was sentenced to 500 lashes for stealing potatoes from a field. The regiment's commanding officer turned away the man's wife when she begged for mercy, and the minute the flogging was over

> a general attack was made upon the officers. The adjutant was less fortunate than some of the others in escaping. He got a terrible mauling from the women, who laid him down on his belly, in which position he was held by some scores of vigorous hands, till he got a handsome flogging on the bare posteriors, in the presence of thousands, inflicted with an energy that would remain imprinted on the memory till the day of his death.[19]

The unpredictable pattern of movement made it hard for commanding officers to get companies together for training, and while recruits could be trained well enough in billeting areas, collective exercises were well-nigh impossible. In consequence the authorities established 'camps of instruction' in wartime, with troops concentrated under canvas and able to learn the collective grammar of their trade. In August 1757 William Todd's regiment marched to Portsmouth to prepare for the Rochefort expedition, and was shipped to the Isle of Wight where it encamped with ten other battalions of foot, two recently formed battalions, and a company of the train of artillery – the whole under Lieutenant General Sir John Mordaunt. The cavalry destined for the expedition trained separately at Salisbury. The infantry was divided into two brigades under major generals Conway and Cornwallis, and 'we were frequently exercising by bushfighting, street firing, etc.' Todd added, 'We had our guards round the island to stop any man from deserting, and no man was allowed to pass above a mile from camp without a passport.'[20]

Desertion, the wasting disease of eighteenth century armies, was encouraged by billeting. Men sloped off to home when their regiment's route took them close to it, or ran rather than embark for a campaign or foreign posting. Some disappeared without apparent reason, although the frequency with which several deserted from the same troop or company suggests that harshness or poor leadership made its own contribution. The pages of the *London Gazette* are speckled with notices describing deserters and advising 'the diligent subject' how to claim money for apprehending them. On 21 December 1728 the *Gazette* announced:

> Deserted Nov 30 1728 from His Majesty's third Regiment of Foot Guards, commanded by the Right Honourable the Earl of Dunmore, and out of His Lordship's own Company, John Eidis, aged 27 Years, five foot, 11 inches and a half in his shoes, a tailor by trade, thin faced, staring full eyes, dark brown hair and eye brows, but wears a fair bob wig, a white set of teeth, wide mouth, thin lips, thick spoken, round body, good cleaver legs, stoops forward with his head when he walks, born in Guildford in Surrey, and says his mother keeps the White Hart Inn or ale-house, went away in his regimental clothes with white lace.

Private Alexander McLeod and Drummer Philip Longbon of the same company had also deserted. They were told that if they returned to the regiment within 21 days of the *Gazette* 'they shall be freely pardoned, as if no such misfortune had happened.' Otherwise anyone who apprehended any one of them and lodged him in a town or county jail could, on application to the regimental agent, Captain Edison, 'at his house in the Savoy, Strand, London,' receive five pounds reward from the regiment for each of the privates (but only two guineas for the drummer) together with 'the King's Bounty Money' of twenty shillings a head. John Williams, who had deserted from the Coldstream Guards, must have been the answer to a thief-taker's prayer, for he cannot have been difficult to spot: he was 'short and bald on the crown of his head, with a large scar on his right cheek and a small one on his left, a large mole with white hair on it growing on the right side of his head.'

Officer deserters were infinitely more rare. The *Gazette* for 11 May 1805 appointed Quartermaster Robert Russell of the 18th Light Dragoons to be adjutant of his regiment, with the rank of cornet, 'vice

O'Donnell, deserted'. Despite the detailed descriptions of deserters and the substantial rewards on offer for catching them, many slipped back into civilian society or struggled for an existence on its margins. Eighteenth-century *Gazettes* often warn of deserters who 'are now supposed to be guilty of ill practices on the highway'. Many re-enlisted under an assumed name, pocketing, as we have seen, a fresh enlistment bounty. The *Gazette* repeats offers of pardon to re-enlisted deserters in terminology that changes little over the years. In April 1742 they were 'to continue in the same regiments they now are, without being molested or claimed by the officers of the respective corps to which they did formerly belong'.[21] In October 1805, with the army urgently short of men, there was a general pardon for all deserters from the regular army provided they surrendered to a magistrate, commanding officer or senior officer of the recruiting service. Once established in new regiments 'they shall not be liable to be claimed by any other corps to which they might formerly have belonged.' Those who failed to return to service within the prescribed deadline of a month would be 'proceeded against with the utmost severity'.[22]

Few deserters voluntarily returned to service, and throughout the eighteenth and nineteenth centuries desertion remained a running sore. In the 1780s one soldier in every six deserted from the army in Ireland, and from 1796 to 1825 desertion comprised between 14.3 per cent and 77.4 per cent of all military crimes, with an annual average of around 33 per cent. In 1875 the radical MP John Holms pointed out that recent attempts to make the army fully recruited had 'utterly failed'; over the past five years desertion had run at an average of 5,516 men a year, most of them coming from the home-based army of around 90,500 men. Soldiers escaped easily enough from an army that circumnavigated the land, but potential deserters were surprisingly undeterred by a combination of well-guarded barracks and draconian punishments. Wully Robertson reported that it was easy enough to escape from his own barracks in 1870s Aldershot, but added that most had high walls, tipped with broken glass. It was not until 1871 that the practice of branding deserters with the letter 'D' at last stopped. True, by that time the process involved administering a tattoo with a spiked stamp, an improvement from the brutality of needles and black powder, but it was an index of the army's fear of this debilitating illness.

The steady increase in barrack accommodation from the late eighteenth century helped reduce the frequency of regimental moves, but they never wholly ceased. As early as 1840 the War Office shifted the 20th Foot from Manchester to Liverpool by rail, demonstrating that the railway could be used to move troops more quickly and with less attendant disorder than was entailed in long marches. In 1858, North Camp station – its four broad platforms designed to help troops entrain and detrain – was opened to serve the new camp at Aldershot. The big redbrick barracks at Tidworth were served by a station that opened in 1900. In 1907 the army opened its own railway line, the Longmoor Military Railway, to connect the barracks and training camps in the Bordon area. Thenceforward the railway would remain the preferred method of moving troops until the internal combustion engine supplanted it in the second half of the twentieth century. Indeed, the worst rail disaster in British history involved a troop train, and took place on 22 May 1915 at Quintinshill, near Gretna Green in Scotland, on what is now the West Coast main line. 1/7 Royal Scots, a Territorial unit raised in the Leith area, was on its way to Gallipoli, and lost 210 men killed and 224 injured, making up the majority of the 473 casualties.

Long after the railway hissed and smoked its way across the landscape, small military parties still moved by road. In 1879 Corporal Robertson was ordered to take three troopers as mounted orderlies from his regiment's barracks in Brighton to headquarters Chatham district, and on the way he encountered a problem that would not have surprised his ancestors:

> The only available accommodation was occupied by an old lady who flatly refuse to take us in, and consequently I had to ride on for another two miles to a police station and obtain the requisite authority compelling her to take us in. This brought her to her senses, and by the time we had groomed our horses and made them comfortable for the night, about ten o'clock, she had prepared for us an excellent supper to which we did full justice.[23]

In February 1881 his regiment moved from Brighton to York by road in 'exceptionally severe' winter weather which meant that the horses had to be led for much of the way to prevent them from slipping.

However, in the process the regiment marched the 26 miles from Chatham to Woolwich, the next 18 miles to Edmonton, and the next 16 to Ware in a day apiece.

In 1914 both regular battalions of Royal Welch Fusiliers were so close to Southampton, their port of embarkation for France, that they marched part of the way in the old style. A coal merchant in Lyndhurst remembered 1/Royal Welch Fusiliers as

> the last of the Old Contemptibles, were these soldiers. The finest body of men I ever saw. Drunk as lords every night, but each one as fresh as a band box the next morning. They marched out of here on October 4 1914. I saw them go. All those proud men. They marched out of here to Southampton Docks and got caught in the First Battle of Ypres.[24]

When told to prepare for mobilisation, 2/Royal Welch Fusiliers were training at Bovington Camp in Dorset and marched, on the night of 30–31 July, to their home barracks at Portland.

> For the main body the march was long and dreary. The Band and Drums were unable to play the whole night without their music, but they put up a wonderful show. Day was breaking as we came down the hills to Weymouth, and, as daylight increased, the awful sleepiness always associated with night-marching wore off and the march became less irksome … The Band and Drums started to play again, and the good folks of Weymouth were roused about 6 o'clock by the Band playing 'I do like to be beside the seaside'.

A rail move from Portland to Dorchester was something of an anticlimax, and on arrival the battalion was sent into billets,

> Which was a new experience for us. It was not real billeting, however, for the officers went into one or another of the hotels, HQ was in the King's Arms, and the men were in various public buildings. A Company's first billet – Infant School, block floor with a pack for a pillow. B Company, in the Corn Exchange, were also able to test the discomfort of sleeping on the hard wooden floor.

On 10 August the battalion was taken by train straight to Southampton Dock. The optimistic Major Williams opined that 'we should be lunching on a sumptuous Cunarder, with unlimited Champagne at the government's expense.' Unfortunately they were destined for MV *Glengariff*, 'a wretched pig boat ... She was not very clean, and, since there was no food whatever on board, we subsisted on the ration we had with us – bully-beef, biscuits and water.'[25]

CHAPTER 24

BARRACK-ROOM BLUES

SOCIOLOGISTS CLASSIFY BARRACKS with boarding schools, warships, prisons, monasteries, nursing homes, and some hospitals, as total institutions where the lives of individuals are dependent upon the organisation's authorities, and a clear sense of hierarchy prevails. Stanley Goffman, who identified the total institution, wrote of

> Mortification processes … A privilege system of rewards and punishments … house rules … institutional lingo … social formalities and informalities [and the] phenomenon of engaging in forbidden activity.[1]

British army barracks were traditionally designed as much to keep their occupants in as to hold the unauthorised at bay. A process of gradual liberalisation that had begun to see barracks built without external walls and might well have seen the development of ungated military communities was curtly ended by the IRA's bombing campaign in the 1970s.

John Lucy enlisted in the Royal Irish Rifles in early 1912, spent six months at the regimental depot in Belfast and then joined the 2nd Battalion at Dover. He thought that a battalion in barracks was like being in

> a little town, and viewed in this way has many attractions. The seven or eight hundred men and the thirty or so officers are not solely and at all times engaged in training for war. Working hours are not

long, and holidays are numerous. A duty soldier, that is, one fully trained, may ease his boredom by finding employment in various stores and workshops, by looking after horses, making himself expert in specialised jobs like machine-gunnery or signalling, or by educating himself in the regimental school. While still in the army he may become, among other things, a cook, a waiter, a valet, a clerk, a butcher, an armourer or a storekeeper, if he so wishes. He may also compete for promotion.[2]

Just as the inhabitants of other total institutions can become wholly absorbed with their surroundings, so too soldiers could find barrack life reassuringly absorbing. Spike Mays of the Royals thought that 'there was something almost sacramental about daily turnout and the wearing of uniform, and to us professional soldiers this became an end in itself; a strange combination of regimental and personal pride, an art, ritual, ceremony, almost a religion.'[3]

It was not until 1793, with the war against revolutionary France in full swing, that barrack-building began in earnest. Until then there had been some purpose-built accommodation at Chatham, Tynemouth, Plymouth, Liverpool, and the notoriously unhealthy Hilsea barracks at Portsmouth, alive with smallpox when the Norfolk Militia were housed there in 1759. Ireland was better provided with barracks than either England or Scotland, but many were very small, and one penalty paid for a more settled military life in Ireland was the barracking of many regiments in small detachments. Dublin, however, housed 'the largest peacetime concentration of regular regiments of infantry and cavalry in the British Isles', and Phoenix Park was the largest exercise-ground at the army's disposal. However, Irish barracks were not necessarily an improvement on their counterparts in England, and in 1774 Lieutenant General Lord Blayney, inspecting the 27th Foot at Limerick, reported

The Lower Barracks of Limerick which now contains 7 companies of this regiment, have been condemned near twenty years. The stairs, floors, windows and doors very bad, officers were obliged at their own expense to plaster the ceiling, as the Barrack Master would not do it without an order from the [Irish] Board [of Ordnance], the building being condemned.[4]

The construction of new barracks was not trouble-free. The Royal Artillery Barracks at Woolwich were begun in 1774, after a false start when an inconvenient pond imperilled the new foundations. The buildings were almost ready for occupation three years later, but there were the usual unedifying squabbles between the Board of Ordnance – responsible for the construction, maintenance, and equipping of barracks – and the contractor and the building's occupants. Rooms were not aired before occupation, and so 'through the inclemency of the weather continued extremely damp'. The Board would not pay for stables to prevent the adjutant's horse 'standing out in all weathers when he has business at the barracks', and although it generously agreed that the orderly room could have a chimney, it directed that old timber 'where salvageable' should be used for work in the barracks. Soldiers' bedding arrived before there was anywhere to store it, and no sooner were the 'dust holes' in the barrack yard roofed than the lead was stolen.[5]

There was also accommodation in fortresses like the Tower of London, the Royal Citadel at Plymouth and Dover Castle, but much of it was in decidedly poor order, for the Board of Ordnance had other things to spend its money on: some things never change. As late as 1785, the 64th Foot complained that Dover Castle lacked

> all kinds of barrack utensils and [had] a very small allowance of wood and candles, the men not having a sufficient quantity to dress their provisions. No pump for the tank, for getting water ... [and men are] obliged to draw water from a well 350 feet deep, with very great labour.[6]

The barrack construction of the Napoleonic era left a lasting legacy. Brompton barracks, the largest of the new constructions, sat within the defences of Brompton Lines, overlooking Chatham. It was built to house 1,300 artillerymen, with stables and gun-sheds at hand. The architect James Wyatt drew up three blocks to frame a quadrangle on which parades took place, in a pattern than was familiar elsewhere. An infantry barracks was built at Colchester in 1794, and by 1805 there was accommodation there for 7,000 officers and men. It was also in 1794 that work began on new barracks on the site of the King's House in Winchester, a palace once intended by Charles II (his regal vision characteristically blurred by lack of funds) to rival the Versailles of Louis XIV. The complex was able to house 3,000 troops, and in 1872 the upper barracks, now named Peninsular Barracks, became the Rifle Depot, for the Rifle Brigade and the King's Royal Rifle Corps. This started a long association that ended only when the Light Division Depot left the site in 1986. At the end of the nineteenth century the barracks was badly damaged by fire, and the rebuilt structure, bright brickwork faced with quoins and pediments in white ashlar, has few rivals. It is now divided into luxury apartments, and the old parade ground, for so long the delight of riflemen, is a parterre that might have gratified Charles II's architect, Sir Christopher Wren.

The need for larger training areas and, as weapons shot further and marksmanship became so important, more rifle ranges, inspired the next burst of barrack-building. In 1854 the army bought land on the sandy heath at Aldershot, conveniently situated midway between London and Portsmouth. 'What Pompey is to the sailor, the 'Shot is to the soldier', thought Francis Hereward Maitland.[7] First troops were accommodated in bell tents in North and South Camps on either side of the Basingstoke Canal. Wooden huts soon replaced tents, and were themselves succeeded by barracks made of ochre brick, with the first permanent structures called Wellington Lines. Stanhope Lines, its barracks named for battles in the Napoleonic wars (and with one commemorating Wellington's surgeon-general, James McGrigor) replaced South Camp. Marlborough Lines, its barracks names celebrating battles of the War of Spanish Succession, replaced North Camp.

One of the most striking edifices in the whole complex was 'the Glasshouse', the three-storey Aldershot Military Detention Barracks, built from 1870 to house 165 inmates in individual cells designed, as penal theory then demanded, to 'prevent the evils of association'. The building earned its nickname from its great glass roof, and 'glasshouse' was to become synonymous with a military prison of any sort. The building was no longer used as a prison after it sustained heavy damage in a spectacular riot in 1946 and was dismantled in 1958. The army's only 'glasshouse' is now the Military Corrective Training Centre at Colchester.

Cardwell's reforms inspired the building of regimental depots in county towns, but however useful these structures were as links between regiment and community, they were often badly placed for access to training areas. Though they were able to house 'miniature' ranges on which troops could fire subcalibre or 'tubed down' versions of their service rifles in .297/.230 and later in .22 calibre, it was often a brisk tramp to the nearest full-bore shooting range. The army had begun training on the rolling expanse of Salisbury Plain in 1898, and just after the Boer War – which had so effectively illustrated the need for individual marksmanship – it built new barrack complexes at Tidworth and Bulford on the plain. The barracks at Tidworth, approached via the Grand Trunk Road, its name echoing that of the great lifeline of British India, are named after battles fought in India and Afghanistan, like Aliwal, Bhurtpore, Delhi and Lucknow, with Candahar (despite its unfamiliar spelling) as evidence that if history does not actually repeat itself it sometimes rhymes. The attraction of open countryside also encouraged the army to build a new set of barracks at Catterick in North Yorkshire just before the First World War. This now constitutes the largest barrack complex not only in the United Kingdom, but probably in the whole of Europe.

It was ironic that barrack accommodation across the empire was often a good deal better than it was in the United Kingdom. Billeting was rarely an option, and disease spread so quickly that crowded and insanitary barracks dramatically lengthened the sick-list. An official report on Up Park Barracks, Jamaica, in 1806, warned that the soldier's

situation is particularly distressing, far different from anything he experiences in any other countries; the soldier here is debarred from the common indulgence met with in other barracks; he is left exposed to the necessity of sleeping on damp fixed platforms, or more generally damp floors, which must almost constantly be the case in the rainy seasons (when fevers are most prevalent) without a bed to lie upon, consequently must have increased the dreadful mortality so lately experienced in this island ... The Board inspecting the construction of the new barracks regret that they had not been erected on arches at least six feet from the ground, which would have afforded a free circulation of air attended with the advantage of a comfortable shade during the day. Under these arches the soldiers' arms and accoutrements might have been cleaned without occasioning filth in the barracks, or any unnecessary exposure to the sun ...

The Board on minutely inspecting the barracks find that they cannot accommodate the number of men for which they were originally intended. Each barrack is to contain ten rooms, each room supposed capable of accommodating 50 men, but after the hammocks are hung it is found that they can only contain 36 men ... Each room is 50 feet in length and 24 in breadth ... In consequence of the confined manner in which the rooms are built, being not more than 10 feet in height including joists and beams in the lower apartment, and 9 to the pitch of the roof in the upper, the Board cannot think considering the health of the soldier, that the two feet allowed in the estimate under so low roof, sufficient to accommodate each man.[8]

In contrast, barracks built in India after the Mutiny paid careful attention to the soldier's well-being, with the new cantonment at Jakatalla in the Nilgiri Hills in Madras presidency looking 'more like a health resort than a military camp'. John Fraser thought that the barrack blocks at Agra had

> a certain affinity in size and shape to a cathedral. One for each company. Long and wide and spacious, they were cut off in the middle by a transept-like messroom fitted with tables where the whole company could sit down at table at one time. The two halves for sleeping accommodation consisting each of an airy, high space, forty feet to the roof and twenty feet wide, the walls interspersed with aisles. The stone slabs of the floor added to the effect of cloistered coolness. The necessary shelves, cots and kit-boxes were fitted between an arch at the side.

A wide verandah, where men could chat and smoke on tropical evenings, ran right round the building.[9]

The two world wars saw huge increases in military population but most of the accommodation built to house it was intended to be temporary. The breeze-block sheds and Nissen huts thrown up to supplement existing barracks or create new camps on training areas like Salisbury Plain or the Yorkshire moors proved to have a longer life than had ever been intended. In 1942 the army took over 30,000 acres of breckland around Stanford, near Thetford in Norfolk, and the camps built to house the troops training there will still be familiar to Second World War veterans. Hawksmoor's rustic stonework at Berwick, and Wyatt's elegant façades at Brompton, both demonstrate that the design of barracks had always reflected the architectural ideals of the age. It was inevitable that that the 1960s would leave their mark on barrack construction. Montgomery Lines in Aldershot was built to accommodate an airborne brigade, with its barracks – Arnhem, Bruneval, Normandy, and Rhine – commemorating airborne actions. The complex was opened by Field Marshal Montgomery in 1965 but soon began to show its age: its flat roofs leaking, with concrete walls taking on a fungal hue. The Royal Military Academy Sandhurst comprises three large buildings built to accommodate officer cadets: Old Building, completed in 1812; New Building, finished a century later; and Victory Building, opened in 1970. I have worked in all three, and it always struck me that their attractiveness and utility alike were in direct proportion to their age – the older the better.

Shortage of barrack accommodation within the United Kingdom is a major reason for so many British troops remaining in Germany so long after the end of the Cold War. One way of making more military housing available was for the army to take on redundant RAF stations. Thus RAF Swanton Morley, near Dereham in Norfolk, is now Robertson Barracks (named for the Wully Robertson who features so often in these pages) and houses the Light Dragoons. RAF Tern Hill in Shropshire now incorporates Clive Barracks, and is home to 1/ Royal Irish. Stoke Heath Young Offenders Institution is within sight of the barracks, and when a battalion of my own regiment was stationed there, one senior Tom, rightly dissatisfied with his own accommodation, jerked his thumb in its direction. 'If I was over there,' he told me, 'I'd have a room to myself and there'd be hot water in the showers. Tell me, sir, where did I go wrong?'[10]

Whatever the face they showed to the outside world, barracks could lour, grim-faced, upon their occupants. From the eighteenth century onwards private soldiers and NCOs lived in long barrack rooms, often part of a block that could house a whole company, with stores and offices on the ground floor and accommodation above. Sergeants had partitioned-off 'bunks' at one end of the room, though as part of deliberate attempts to improve the NCOs' lot they were gradually given separate quarters and their bunks were taken over by corporals. This process did not encourage philosophical reflections after lights-out.

> Shut up, out there! Ow many more times do you want telling! If I 'ave to come out there I'll 'ave a few names an' numbers. Why don't you let decent soldiers sleep? Another word and I'll put some of you on a crime sheet.[11]

Initially soldiers slept in straw-filled wooden cribs, sometimes with four men to a crib, or on straw-filled palliasses on the floor, but by the 1820s single beds, with palliasse, bolster, and two blankets, were more usual. There was often as little as five inches between beds, and not much more between the foot of the bed and the communal table that ran down the length of the room. Until the advent of dining rooms towards the end of the nineteenth century men did 'everything but drill' in their rooms. These were proverbially overcrowded. In 1858 it was said in the House of Lords that the average allowance of air for a convict was 1,000 cubic feet but only 400 for a soldier, and some barracks and five military hospitals managed a mere 300. A private in the 15th Hussars maintained that in the cavalry barracks at Maidstone men were 'packed … so closely that I have seen them sleeping on the tables used for dining, under the tables and in the coal-boxes. This in the middle of the summer.'[12]

A row of outside privies served each barrack block, but for overnight sanitation men relied upon the latrine tub or 'sip pot'. This receptacle, a two-man lift when full to the brim, as it so often was after liberal consumption of swipes, was carried off first thing in the morning and scrubbed out, whereupon it became a wash-basin: the only alternative was to wash directly beneath a pump. One sergeant spoke of a promising recruit as 'a smart, active boy, always first in the urine-tub in the morning'.[13] It is small wonder that a sergeant, giving evidence to a commission reviewing the state of barracks in the 1850s, admitted that he found it impossible to enter a barrack room first thing in the morning, until the room orderly had thrown open the windows. 'The air was offensive both from the men's breath and from the urine tubs in the room; and, of course, some soldiers do not keep

their feet very clean, especially in the summer time.'[14] During the nineteenth century pipe-smoking became increasingly popular amongst
soldiers, and in 1842 an officer who entered a room 72 ft long by 36
wide could not see any of its 48 occupants because of the smoke. Nor
did the practice of quartering cavalrymen directly above the stables
improve matters, and Hulme Cavalry Barracks in Manchester had the
additional disadvantage of having the privies and middens of a closely
populated neighbourhood right up against its walls.

There were substantial improvements in the second half of the
nineteenth century. Ablution blocks were added to barracks, and in
1874 the modern Anglesey Barrack in Portsmouth had a handsome
wash-room, as that unlikely private soldier, John Acland-Troyte tells
us,

with stone slabs all round, and also down the middle. Large tin
basins were supplied in quite sufficient quantity, and water pipes
running all round, just above the stone slabs, with taps at intervals,
and always a good supply of water.
    Besides this 'Ablution Room' there was a bath-house with four or
six baths, in which a man could lie at almost full length. Cold water
was laid on as a permanency, and in the winter hot water also.[15]

There had been a short-lived attempt to replace urine tubs with chamber pots in 1858–61, but it was not until water urinals were eventually
installed that the problem was at last solved. Cardwell barrack blocks
had four, eventually converted to proper WCs, on each landing. Yet
even the close proximity of urinals has never quite prevented bed-
wetting, where drunken men simply fail to make it to the lavatory. In
my time the 'urinated mattress' always featured on the list of 'barrack
damages' that had to be paid for by a departing unit.

Private Acland-Troyte goes on to tell us about his barrack room.

The walls were whitewashed, and the floor, bare boards; there were
[trestle] tables in the centre sufficient for all the occupants of the
room to sit down at once, and wooden forms to correspond.
Generally a hanging shelf over the table, on which are kept all the
plates and basins, one of each being provided for each man in the
room. The iron bedsteads are arranged all round, the heads against

the wall, and they are made in two parts, so that during the day one half can be run in or closed up under the other, thus giving much more free space to move about in. The mattress is rolled up, pillow inside, and kept fastened with a strap, the two blankets and the two sheets folded up very neatly, and placed on top of the rolled mattress, which is stood against the head of the bed, occupying about half the bedstead when closed up. The remaining half (on which the rug or counterpane is laid) serves for the men to sit on. As a rule there is a space of about three or four feet between the bedstead, and a man next a window is generally best off.

All round the room, over the heads of the beds, are iron shelves, and hooks just below, each man having that part of the shelves immediately over his own cot. All the soldier's worldly possessions are kept on these shelves, and have to be arranged with scrupulous tidiness. The knapsack and other accoutrements are put up on the hooks … Very often if a man has near his cot a piece of spare wall he will hang up pictures or photographs, which gives the room a more comfortable appearance, and provided it is done tidily, it is never objected to. The other articles of common property in the room are a hair broom, mop, long-handled scrubber (for cleaning the wood floors), a hand scrubbing brush (for cleaning tables and forms), two tin dishes, on which the dinner is brought in, two tin pails, two wooden buckets and a big iron coal box, also two coal trays, i.e. square wooden boxes used for carrying coal about in, but generally kept in the room for throwing any litter into.

Despite hard scrubbing it was difficult to keep the tables clean, and so the men generally used one side for eating and writing on, and reversed it to show the 'extra clean' side for inspections.[16]

This barrack-room organisation would change comparatively little over the next century. The precise form of kit layout was determined by regimental regulations, and as late as 1929 the sliding bedframe was still in use, so that the Royal Army Ordnance Corps standing orders could specify that for room inspections

The bedstead will be drawn out to the full extent, and at a distance of nine inches from the wall, the bed made up so as to form a seat, a blanket folded and placed over the bedirons from the lower mattress to the foot. The soldier will then stand one pace from the foot of the bed, at the right-hand side.

Labelled photographs now replaced the illustrative diagrams of yesteryear, showing exactly how each of the soldier's forty-one items of equipment should be laid out, from mess-tin cover, drawers, woollen, and drawers, cotton, through to boot polish and dummy ammunition, and on to medals.[17] A regimental bedplate, made of brass, stamped with its owner's name and highly polished, marked a man's ownership of his territory when he was away on duty. There had long been complaints that a soldier had nowhere secure to store his personal belongings, and by this time a padlocked barrack box, sliding neatly under the foot of the bed (thus footlocker in American English), was issued to soldiers.

The system was intended to ensure that all a man's kit was present and in good order, but this was often counter-productive. Many soldiers 'won' extra personal equipment by fair means or foul, kept a show set of key items 'gimped up', pressed or polished to perfection, and actually used another set. Horace Wyndham recalled that an inspection shirt was not a wearable garment at all, but actually consisted of 'about a square foot of grey flannel, with a collar band attached thereto with a couple of pins.'[18] Commanding officers generally inspected their unit lines on Saturday mornings, and this gave rise to what 2/Argyll and Sutherland Highlanders, in garrison at Maryhill Barracks in Glasgow in 1911, called

the barrack sports – get down on your knees and scrub the place out. And the floor had to be snow white. And to keep it snow white you used to put a blanket from your bed down on the floor so that the floors wouldn't get dirtied.[19]

Soldiers often slid about in slippers made of loose blanket so as not to injure the floor, and it was sometimes most convenient to get one's bed suitably arranged for inspection and then sleep on a blanket on the floor.

The military day was regulated minutely. The daily routine of cavalryman or gunner was defined by trumpet calls, while line infantry used drum-beats until the 1820s and 30s, when the bugle replaced them. For most soldiers the day began with 'Reveille', generally sounded at 6.00 a.m. in the summer and 7.00 a.m. in the winter, followed by 'Rouse', the last warning to get up. Men were taught words that rhymed with the most common calls. The first bars of 'Rouse' were meant to bring to mind the phrase 'Come, make a move! And show a leg! Why dil-ly da-ly? Now don't you hear? Get out of bed, It's past re-veil-le.' But other words came to mind more easily 'Get out of bed, Get out of bed, You lazy bug-gers; Get out of bed, Get out of bed, You lazy bug-gers.' The orderly sergeant, coming to the end of his 24-hour period of duty and thinking of his breakfast, would stride amiably through the room, full of the gentle aphorisms of his breed: 'Hands off cocks and grab your socks, the sun's burning your eyes out.' If he was in a room full of recruits he might cheerfully defenestrate any stray items of clothing, promoting tidiness and keeping the men on their toes, but it was not always advisable to treat old soldiers like that, for scores might well be settled later.

Until the 1870s soldiers ate in their rooms, and soon after 'Reveille' the room's mess orderly-men would cut away to the cookhouse and return with tea and bread, the latter known as 'Tommy' or 'Pong'. First parade might be at 7.30 or 8.30 a.m. often with a half-hour bugle warning – 'Just half an hour they give us all to dress: Lots of time to turn out a-fresh! Things will be bad if you're not there just the same – The Ord'-ly Sergeant, he will dot down your name.' The 'Quarter Call' gave a final warning before the bugles blared the 'Fall In': 'Fall in A, Fall in B, Fall in every companee', or 'Soldiers all, great and small, don't you hear the bugle-call?' Summoned by the bugle soldiers stood easy, in company groups, at the rear of the parade ground. Then the regimental sergeant major called for right markers, who slammed to attention, strode out to the spot marking their company's right front, and halted. Then, on the sergeant major's command, the companies fell in and the unit was ready for the day's work.

Daily routine varied greatly. Recruits would be drilled from dawn to dusk, and in the 1870s it took a cavalryman about nine months to be 'dismissed recruit drill'. In the nineteenth and early twentieth centuries many regiments expected newly-joined officers to drill with the men until they had 'passed off the square'. In the early nineteenth century Lieutenant John Cooke wrote that he was expected

To drill with a squad composed of peasants from the plough and other raw recruits, first learning the facings, marchings and the companies' evolutions. That being completed, the officer put on cross-belts and pouches and learnt the firelock exercises; then again he marched with the same; and when it was considered that the whole was perfect, with and without arms, they began to skirmish in extended file, and last of all learned the duties of a sentry, and to fire ball cartridge at a target.[20]

Once a man had passed off the square his life became very much easier, not least because he could now be out of barracks after work and before Last Post, always assuming that his standard of dress was high enough for him to 'pass the guard' at the barrack gates. Soldiers leaving barracks were, by definition, in uniform, for it was not until the 1930s that they were allowed civilian clothes, and even then might not be permitted to walk out in them. By Victoria's reign they left barracks in the full majesty of best uniforms, brushed and polished within an inch of their lives, natty caps replacing full-dress helmets, and carrying the riding whips or swagger canes without which, somehow, their military identities would have been incomplete. Unless a man had a pass to enable him to remain out longer or, better still, to 'sleep out' of barracks, he was expected back by 9.30 p.m., when the main gate was closed. The small wicket gate would be opened for late arrivals.

Learning how to manage the finery of walking out was no easy task. In 1850 the men of the 74th Highlanders were advised that their carriage and gait off duty 'required constant attention', and in 1906 men of the Royal Fusiliers were enjoined to 'at all times walk in that light and airy manner that distinguishes the fusilier'.[21] R. G. Garrod, who joined the 20th Hussars before the First World War, remembered that the braces holding his overalls tight against the straps that ran beneath his instep had to be cushioned with cotton-wool to prevent him from chafing his shoulder, and he was not allowed near the barrack gate until he had mastered the art of picking up a dropped whip or glove. If cavalrymen made a magnificent sight striding out two by two, spurs tinkling on the cobbles, then they certainly paid for it. The repetitive demands of his steed meant that the cavalryman had a long day, with morning stables, mucking-out, generally at 6.00 a.m.,

SOLDIERS

followed by breakfast, another round of stables mid-morning and third stables after tea. The words for the cavalry trumpet call 'Hay up', or 'Litter down', sounded for third stables, ended on a hopeful note: 'Soon as the Off-'cer's been a-round boys, Then we can go to town.' There was horses' tack to be cleaned in addition to personal equipment, and the price a cavalryman paid for his elegance was a working day that might not end till perilously close to 'Last Post'.

However, Sergeant John Pearman, in India with the 3rd Light Dragoons in the 1840s, admitted that

> Our time was spent very idly, as all our drill was in the morning and dismounted drill in the evening. As it was very hot in the day, we sat on our charpoys and played at cards, backgammon or chess or anything that took our taste. At other times I would read books or sit at the needle.[22]

Thanks to locally employed grooms he was spared the drudgery of looking after his horse. Infantryman John Fraser, serving in India forty years later, remembered that his day began when the nappy-wallah appeared and whispered 'Shave, sahib?' 'We felt like lords,' wrote Fraser, 'for all of the interior tasks, sweeping out the rooms and verandahs, and carrying water from the well, was done for us by the natives.'[23]

The end of the day was marked by the calls of 'Last Post' and 'Lights Out'. The music bringing the army's day to its end had originated in the seventeenth-century 'tattoo', the word deriving from the Dutch *doe ten tap toe*, directing sutlers and innkeepers to turn off the taps of their beer-kegs and soldiers to make their unsteady way homewards to camp or barracks. A party of drummers beat about the town, following a prescribed route from first to last post. As late as 1914 *Trumpet and Bugle Sounds for the Army* still contained the tune for 'Tattoo' (1st Post), although by then it was not always sounded, and the haunting 'Last Post', played at about 10.00 p.m., was followed, half an hour later by the brief lights out. The soldier was then confined for the night in the indescribable and subtly all-pervading aroma of pipe-clay, damp clothes, lamp oil, dish cloths, soft soap and butter and cheese suppers – for the soldier's food is kept on a shelf in the same apartment in which he eats and lives. By this arrangement, his single apartment answers the purpose of dining-room, smoking-room, sitting-room, and bed-room combined.[24]

During the day buglers would sound routine calls, like *Men's Meal*, with the familiar refrain 'Oh, come to the cook-house door, boys! Come to the cook-house door.' That soldiers were bidden to the building's door shows that the words pre-dated the construction of dining rooms in barracks from the 1870s. Until then mess orderlies – a mess consisted of about sixteen men from the same company – would report to the cookhouse and collect the cooked rations for their comrades, which were distributed and devoured at the barrack-room table. Because the quality of meat was variable, in some messes the orderly, standing with his back to the mess, would dole out a portion and ask 'Who will have this' to ensure pot-luck fairness. In 1863 Private Edwin Mole of the 14th Hussars saw how things were done in his mess:

> there came a shout of 'Look out for scaldings!' and a man ran up with a large dish of meat and a small tin of potatoes. Lumping them down on the table, he cried: 'Come on; bring your *churries*!' whereupon some of the soldiers produced knives and began to cut up the meat into lots according to the number in the mess. Then each soldier took the portion that suited his fancy; but at least half-a-dozen men, after a look at the dish, lit their pipes and went off to the canteen … The meat and potatoes were both bad and I made my dinner off bread …
>
> After a bit the men who had gone to the canteen began to return, a few not quite so steady as they might be, and by three o'clock all the room was asleep except myself.[25]

The main meal of the day was known as dinner, but it was generally eaten between 1.00 and 2.00 p.m., and there was usually nothing but the 'tea-meal' of bread and tea between 5.00 p.m. and lights out unless the soldier chose to pay for it. The Napoleonic soldier had a daily ration of 1 lb bread, 1 lb beef, 1 oz butter or cheese, 1 lb pease pudding and 1 oz rice: pork might be substituted for the beef. By 1914 diet was only slightly more sophisticated, and a man was entitled to 1¼ lb meat, 1¼ lb bread or 1 lb biscuits, ¼ lb bacon, 3 oz cheese, tea, sugar, jam, salt, pepper, and mustard, with ½ lb fresh vegetables when available or 2 oz dried vegetables in lieu.[26] Until 1873 these 'commissariat rations' were funded by stopping 4½d from a man's daily pay, and thereafter soldiers were still required to pay 3d for their 'regimental rations', things like the potatoes, and extra vegetables and bread, that had always been required to eke out the basic ration.

The quality of the food was not improved by the fact that meat often arrived on the hoof, to be butchered regimentally and then issued to messes on the bone. In 1859 an officer thought that once meat and gristle had been removed a man actually received six or seven ounces of meat from a daily allowance that then amounted to ¾ lb. Each mess had two large coppers and food was boiled in them, usually meat in one and potatoes in the other, so there was little variety. Meat bones and off-cuts with vegetable trimmings, sometimes with oatmeal added, were boiled to make soup. Suet and raisins, given as 'commissariat issue' to embarked troops, might be purchased as regimental rations and, steamed in a cloth, made a very tasty 'figgy duff'.

As dining rooms were established in barracks, and cookhouses were equipped with better ovens, food could at last be roasted or fried as well as simply boiled. The messing-group largely disappeared, so cooking was now the responsibility of regimental cooks, under a sergeant, often called the 'master duff' just as the unit's sergeant tailor was the 'master stitch'. Cooks came under the control of the quartermaster, who was answerable to the commanding officer for the provision and preparation of rations. There were times, when it was not actively engaged on operations, when a battalion might not be able to eat centrally. In 1915 1/6th King's was at HQ Third Army, and reverted to the old mess system, with each fifteen-man mess providing a cook each day. Private Norman Ellison recalled that rations were lavish, as was often the case for units living in the world of the rear.

Every morning we open the ball with porridge, bacon and fried bread, honey or jam and tea. Luncheon mid-day: steak and onions or mutton chops. Dinner 6.30 p.m.: soup, roast beef or mutton, potatoes and another vegetable, milk pudding and jam, coffee and cigarettes.[27]

By the middle of the nineteenth century quartermasters had inevitably passed through the ranks to their commissions, and, in the process, had learnt a good deal about how extra rations could be procured and how small improvements could make a real difference to the men that ate them. All-in stew, that great military staple, could be much enhanced by big suet dumplings ('babies' 'eads') and extra onions. The addition of curry powder delighted old India hands, and a splash of paprika might persuade the uninitiated that they were eating goulash. Army biscuits, pounded to crumbs in a cloth, could make a savoury topping or, with 'liberated' apples, a fruit crumble. There was no pleasing everyone. One soldier exulted: 'Today we have stew – and a rattling good stew. Followed by my favourite currant duff – spotted dog.' However, a comrade opined 'What! Stew again? Can't that perishin' *bobadhji* cook anything but stew?'[28] Soldiers craved bulky food with a bit of bite to it, and there was no check on unhealthy practices. When the cooks had finished frying bacon they would yell 'Gypp-oh!' and soldiers would rush up to dip their bread gleefully in the hot fat. Most recruits were so badly fed outside the army that the first six months of their service changed them physically and psychologically. The food filled them out, and physical training toughened them. 'Our bodies developed and our backs straightened according to plan' wrote John Lucy.

> We marched instead of walking, and we forced on ourselves that rigidity of limb and poker face that marks the professional soldier. Pride of arms possessed us, and we discovered that our regiment was a regiment, and then some.[29]

On campaign, if fresh vegetables were not at hand, lime juice might be given on the recommendation of the unit's medical officer with the approval of the general officer commanding. Both these worthies had to agree to the issue of spirits, ½ gill of rum per man, and up to 2 oz of tobacco for smokers. Needless to say, most doctors and generals did indeed conclude that rum and tobacco were wholly essential for the well-being of their soldiers. A notable exception was Major General Reginald Pinney, who commanded 33rd Division on the Western Front in the First World War, 'a devout, non-smoking teetotaller who banned the rum ration in his division'. Private Frank Richards of 2/Royal Welch Fusiliers thought him 'a bun-punching crank ... more fitted to be in command of a Church Mission hut at the base than a division of troops'.[30] In contrast, Douglas Haig, though his family fortune was founded on whisky distilling, thought him one of the most reliable of divisional commanders, and 33rd Division's fine performance in checking the German offensive of April 1918 certainly seemed to bear this out. Cigarettes and pipe tobacco were issued free to troops during both world wars, and although the rum ration is no longer routine issue for troops on operations, it can still be given, on medical advice, in quite exceptional circumstances. In the whole of my time I never managed to encounter circumstances that were exceptional enough, though I lived in hope.

From the end of the nineteenth century bully beef and tinned meat-and-vegetable stew, often called Maconochie's from its original manufacturer, were an essential part of the preserved rations eaten on manoeuvres or campaign. Corned beef often made its appearance in barracks, perhaps fried up into a hash with onions and potatoes (luxurious when topped with a fried egg and lubricated with brown sauce) or carried out to the ranges in thick doorstep sandwiches. Composite ('Compo') rations, issued during and after the Second World War, were tinned or packaged food that arrived in wooden crates or cardboard boxes, with a number of menus (initially A to G) to ensure variety. It might be cooked, with the heartening roar of the petrol-fired, and occasionally lethal, No 1 burner, by a company's cooks under the forceful direction of the colour sergeant, or simply issued to platoons to be divvied up amongst the sections and cooked under local arrangements. Armoured vehicle crewmen, likely to be given a big box to last them for several days, grew expert at heating tins on exhaust grilles.

If tactical circumstances made collective cooking impossible, then troops lived on the tinned 24-hour ration packs. There are ten different menus: 'Menu 1' has bacon, omelette and beans for breakfast; tomato soup and lamb curry with rice for dinner; a tuna in mayo snack; and both an isotonic lemon drink and the powder for a chocolate drink. All packs contain a sundries wallet with a chocolate bar, oatmeal blocks, fruit biscuits, hard-tack biscuits, boiled sweets, jam, the makings for tea and coffee, Tabasco sauce, chewing gum, a natty folding can opener, water purification tablets, all-weather matches, and toilet tissue. Both compo rations and 24-hour packs contained individual favourites, and barter was rife within the subtribe as one tin of the ever-popular beans and sausages was traded for several of the salty bacon grill. Processed cheese issued with it was not much liked and could usually be cadged easily. Yet there were worse things, at the end of a long and wearing day, than a thick slice of cheese on a hard-tack biscuit, or a good squeeze of tubed apricot jam on an oatmeal block.

In an effort to improve the standards of army cooking, cookery schools were established in home commands during the First World War. It was not until 1941 that the Army Catering Corps was founded, initially as part of the Royal Army Service Corps. It became a corps in its own right in 1965, and was subsumed within the new Royal Logistic Corps in 1993. Warrant officers, NCOs, and men of the catering corps were posted to units, where they worked alongside regimental cooks. When the call for the men's meal was blown, soldiers took mess tins or plates (local arrangements varied), together with their 'noshing rods' – to a long counter where food was ladled out, and to a table where they ate it. As they left the cookhouse, they washed and rinsed their utensils by plunging them into two tubs of water, one soapy and the other (in theory) clean. Over the past quarter-century the old-style cookhouse has disappeared, to be replaced by a restaurant or cafeteria, often sympathetically decorated, serving wholesome food with healthy options available. One of the services' most controversial recent decisions has been the partial adoption of 'Pay as You Dine'. The logic was that soldiers paid, by deductions from their pay, for food that they often did not eat, and it was fairer to allow them to opt out of eating army food, and to spend the money on things they preferred. Some of the many critics of 'Pay as You Dine' maintain that it is 'Save to Starve', for many soldiers pocket the extra pay but eat inadequately, or live on burgers, chips, and fizzy drinks. Other critics have argued that it has destroyed the social function of the cookhouse, which formed part of the wider apparatus of corporate control.

The eighteenth-century soldier had ready access to small beer in his billet, and to porter or spirits if his purse allowed him that luxury. From the start, barracks included canteens, bleak rooms with tables and chairs where men could buy drink. The Board of Ordnance soon let the contracts for canteens to the highest bidder, and by 1847 it was making an annual profit of almost £54,000 from canteen lettings. Horace Wyndham's description of a night of entertainment in a Victorian canteen catches the mood of the place perfectly. 'It is about as much as one can do, at first, to see more than a dozen yards into the interior of the room,' he wrote. There were perhaps 300 men in a space designed for 150. The two dozen tables and benches housed 'schools' of three or four men, drinking from a single half-gallon jug: it was a point of honour for each man to pay for a round before leaving. There was a low stage at one end of the room, with a piano, played by a 'professional gentleman [in this case Professor Guillaume, known to most of his listeners as Bill 'Iggins] who, for a small pecuniary consideration, and as much beer as he can take without getting unduly intoxicated, presides at the instrument for two hours every evening.' A soldier acted as chairman, and performers from the body of the canteen were invited up.

> 'I 'ave much pleasure, gents ... in inviting our well-known friend
>   Ginger Jackson to oblige us with a song an' dance.'
> 'Wot's it goin' to be, mates? Give it a name.'

Eventually the familiar bugle sounded outside:

> 'First post, gents,' announces the chairman, descending promptly
>   from his rostrum.

The sergeant on canteen duty rapped his stick on the door, so as to be able to report 'canteen closed and correct' to the orderly officer at tattoo-parade at 10.00.

This, at least, was the theory. But when drink was in, wit was too often out. Francis Hereward Maitland thought that by halfway through the evening soldiers had drunk themselves into 'a sort of twilight between sobriety and near-drunkenness ... The men are not quite lit up enough for the raucous songs which will follow, they are not quite sober enough to drink quietly.'[31] First came the impromptu recitals, with:

> There's a one-eyed yellow idol
> To the north of Kathmandu ...
> But, for all his foolish pranks,
> He was worshipped in the ranks ...

Morphed into:

> There's a cross-eyed yellow bastard
> Who fought at Waterloo ...
> 'Cos of all his foolish frolics
> 'e 'ad crabs upon 'is [dramatic pause] ear-'oles ...

Then came the songs. Spike Mays, writing of the 1930s, remembered a classic, 'the old song sung by ex-India wallahs in canteens the world over, and on Old Comrades' nights in British pubs.' It laces soldiers' Indian (*bobaji* is a cook, *pani* is water and *atcha* OK) into general nonsense, and there are many versions of its words.

> Sixteen annas one rupee,
> Damn and fuck the bobaji.
> Sergeant major, hollow-ground razor,
> Queen Victoria bloody fine man.
> Sixteen years you've fucked my daughter,
> Now you go to Blighty, sahib.
> May the boat that takes you over,
> Sink to the bottom of the pani, sahib.
> Tora tini, tora char,
> Bombay bibi bohet atcha.[32]

By the time the sergeant arrived to close the canteen a well-oiled customer might decline to leave. The guard was called out, and the offender was 'at length borne to the guard-room, happy in the consciousness that it has required the united efforts of at least half a dozen men to get him there.' In addition to his hangover he would face charges of 'Drunk and disorderly in the canteen, and violently resisting the escort' when brought before the commanding officer. A man might easily worsen his plight by assaulting an NCO, and in 1835 the adjutant general of British troops in India specifically prohibited NCOs 'from taking any other part in the confinement of drunken privates than ordering an escort of privates to place them into restraint'. If an NCO became involved then 'violence is generally the consequence and the offence of the culprit swells to so great an extent as to demand the sentence of a General Court Martial.'[33] It was important that the orderly officer kept himself well out of the way, for striking an officer was an offence that could bring a man the death sentence.

Regiments tried hard to reduce the perils of the canteen. In October 1809, 1/30th Foot, then in garrison in Gibraltar, issued fresh standing orders. The canteen's good order was the responsibility of 'a respectable sergeant'. It was to be open from an hour after guard mounting in the morning to 'the drumbeat for tattoo' at night. No spirits were to be sold, wine was not to be adulterated in any way, and there was to be no gambling. Drinks were to be paid for on the nail, according to a fixed price, and were not to be consumed off the premises. Only NCOs and men of the regiment, and their families, were to use the canteen. At the first sign of drunkenness the offender was to be sent back to barracks. The sergeant in charge had the power to call out the guard if required, and the captain of the day and orderly officer should both make regular visits to the canteen.[34]

Field Marshal Lord Hardinge was past his best when he served as commander-in-chief of the army from 1852 to 1856, but with the active assistance of his military secretary, Richard Airey, he succeeded in altering regulations so that regiments were allowed to run 'Regimental Institutes' to sell non-alcoholic drinks, some food, and a variety of necessaries like polish and pipe-clay, cigarettes and tobacco, paper and envelopes. The 'dry canteens' created by this regulation were not universally popular. Spike Mays' troop leader warned his men

Do not ever let me catch you in a dry canteen eating sticky buns or drinking hog-wash tea. From now on I strongly advise [you] to eat bread and cheese and drink beer. You'll need them, for you are about to become soldiers.[35]

However, the best dry canteens included reading rooms where men could write letters or read newspapers, and their creation coincided with a wider campaign for temperance within the army.

There were regimental and garrison temperance associations from the 1850s. General Sir Frederick Roberts, commander-in-chief India 1885–93, maintained that 'serious crime in the army is almost entirely due to the effects of drink'. Troops in India not only received a daily issue of spirits, for it was believed that this helped them withstand the rigours of the climate, but had easy access to 'country spirits', usually arrack, made from fermented palm-sap, rice or molasses. In 1833, the 710 men of the 26th Foot in garrison at Fort William, Calcutta, drank 5,320 gallons of arrack, 209 of brandy, and 249 of gin, with 207 2½ gallon hogsheads of beer. Drink was associated with many crimes in India, especially 'hot-weather shootings' where a drunken man grabbed his rifle (weapons were then held in barrack rooms) and shot a man with whom he might have had no real quarrel. Kipling's poem *Danny Deever* is probably based on the hanging of Private Flaxman of the Leicesters at Lucknow in 1887. In 1888 Roberts was instrumental in forming the Army Temperance Association by merging two existing associations. It had 23,000 members by the time he left the country. The Army Temperance Association (Home Organisation) soon followed, becoming the Royal Army Temperance Association in 1902. It was finally disbanded in 1958, by which time there were many alternatives to drinking in the canteen.

Some of these were private. Elise Sandes was born comfortably off, in Tralee in 1851, and in the late 1860s invited young soldiers to her house for Bible study, hymns, prayers and lessons in reading and writing. The first proper 'Sandes Soldiers' Home' was set up in King Street, Cork in 1877. Others followed in garrison towns across Ireland, and in 1899 she opened a home in that 'most delightful station' the great camp on the Curragh of Kildare, not far from Dublin. Temporary homes were established under canvas in South Africa during the Boer War, and permanent homes in India and Singapore followed. The Singapore home, in service 1948–1975, consisted of

> several curved, terraced, tiled and brightly painted blocks situated on the top of a hill and nestled amongst lush greenery. Two of the

blocks were sleeping quarters which could accommodate fifty men each. The outdoor amenities included a swimming pool, tennis courts, and a putting green, and the home also had a canteen, a lounge, a dining room, a billiard room, a gift shop, and a huge reading and games room stocked with periodicals, jigsaws, chess, draughts, dominoes, and ping pong tables. The bedrooms came with built-in wardrobes, drawers, a wash-basin with hot and cold water, and a writing-cum-dressing table with long mirror ...

The home had strict dormitory-like regulations ... [but] was a good place to stay in and was popular amongst soldiers.[36]

During the First World War, Miss Sandes and her supporters sent parcels to soldiers at the front, and went aboard troopships to give men pencils and postcards to write a last letter home. Elise Sandes died in 1934, and her headstone, at Tyrella in County Down, reads 'For 66 years the friend of soldiers'. The last of the Sandes homes in Eire, at the Curragh, closed in the 1980s. Although he thought that it was 'essentially British', a senior Irish officer had reported

In justice, I must say that Sandes Home is well run and fills a real need. Young soldiers are made to feel at home and not faced with the cold commercial atmosphere of the canteen. A good feminine influence meets a real need where young soldiers are concerned, and the only place here some of the young recruits that I obtain, receive anything approaching a motherly care is a Sandes home.[37]

Today there are still Sandes Soldiers' and Airmen's homes in Ballykelly, Ballykinlar, and Holywood in Northern Ireland; and Pirbright and Harrogate in Britain.

During the First World War the YMCA, Church Army, and the Salvation Army were amongst the voluntary organisations that opened huts to serve food and non-alcoholic drink to soldiers and provide them with books and writing materials. Some set up hostels where the relatives of the wounded could stay. In 1915 the Revd Philip 'Tubby' Clayton, an army chaplain, set up Talbot House in the Belgian town of Poperinghe, not far behind the front line. This was a place 'where friendships could be consecrated, and sad hearts renewed and cheered, a place of light and joy and brotherhood and peace'. It was named for a Rifle Brigade officer killed outside Ypres, and known, from the phonetic alphabet then used by the army, as Toc H. A sign above its front door warned 'Abandon rank, all ye who enter here', for it was open to men of all ranks, who could drink tea in the kitchen, sit in the walled garden, or attend church services in the 'Upper Room'. Toc H survived the war and prospered in the inter-war years, becoming a spiritual movement that went well beyond heartening soldiers. During the Second World War it opened servicemen's clubs both at home and abroad, and afterwards it developed in many ways: the Revd Chad Varah, a Toc H padre, went on to start The Samaritans. After the Second World War it provided canteens to some British barracks in Germany, as a trooper in the Royal Hussars, stationed in Munster in the 1960s, recalls.

> The Toc-H which was a canteen, was set in the wall of the camp and we would go there to have a tea or coffee and something to eat, also to read the daily papers and chat up the girls who work there ... We spent a lot of time there during the day time when we weren't at work and in the evenings we would go into Munster itself ... Either to eat and drink and sometimes to the Army Cinema or the S[ervices] K[inema] C[orporation] which was just past the railway station on the right.[38]

The biggest change, however, was the establishment in 1921 of the Navy, Army and Air Force Institutes, abbreviated to NAAFI, although these letters were thought, by an unkind few, to stand for 'No Ambition And Fuck-all Interest'. Previously, regimental institutes had had a mixed reputation. Some sold inferior goods to a captive audience at too high a price; there were great opportunities for profitable dishonesty. In 1894 three officers formed the Canteen and Mess Co-operative Society, buying goods wholesale and selling them on to canteens. This was absorbed during the First World War by the Expeditionary Force Canteens, run by serving members of the Army Service Corps. In 1917 the Army Canteen Committee was set up to take over canteens at home, and this committee eventually absorbed the Expeditionary Force Canteens and formed the nucleus of the NAAFI. By April 1944 the NAAFI ran 7,000 canteens and had 96,000 personnel.

In peacetime its employees are civilians, but on mobilisation those going overseas take on military ranks as part of the Expeditionary Forces Institute (EFI), to ensure that they are governed by appropriate legislation. The equivalent for the navy is the NCS, the Naval Canteen Service. In May 1982 when HMS *Ardent* was under air attack off San Carlos in the Falklands, its canteen manager was John Leake, transformed into a petty offer when the ship sailed for war. He had used the General Purpose Machine Gun when he was in the army, and volunteered to man a gun taking on the attacking Skyhawks; he damaged one so badly that it had to land at Port Stanley and he was awarded the Distinguished Service Medal.

Today the NAAFI has 500 stores and entertainment facilities in seventeen countries, providing servicemen and their families with many of the goods and services that they might expect to find at home. The NAAFI's reputation wavered substantially ten years ago, and it remains vulnerable to comparison with cutting-edge organisations that operate more widely. However, on operations it provides a service that few others might wish to duplicate. A recent advertisement for staff, headed 'Serving Private Ryan', sought personnel who would be prepared to sign on for six months in Afghanistan followed by six months rotation in a non-operational posting. In 2004 the small garrison at Camp Abu Naji, just outside the Iraqi town of Al Amarah, contained a small EFI that did a roaring trade in cold drinks, chocolate bars, and Pringles, usually clearing $5,000 a week. One NCO thought it 'basic but a godsend when its shelves were stacked', and a soldier thought that Pot Noodles were 'morale in a container'. Major James Driscoll explained:

> Even though you knew what was on sale from the last time you were in the NAAFI people still enjoyed wandering around this little shop – I believe it was the association with doing something 'normal'. Sometimes people would buy things not because they really wanted them but because they could afford that and it was nice to own something new like a CD player or a camera, almost like a toy to a child, difficult to describe but I've seen it on all operational tours.[39]

Within the barracks from 1921, the NAAFI took over the running of what had been the dry and wet canteens, and provided a refuge for those personnel who were not members of the officers', sergeants' or, for those units that ran them, the corporals' mess. The NAAFI bar was out of bounds to officers and senior NCOs so that junior ranks would not find their spare time intruded upon. The one exception was the nightly procedure of closing the NAAFI, when the orderly officer and orderly sergeant would visit the place to ensure that all customers were out at closing time. This presented many of the hazards of closing the dry canteen, and was one of those many moments when a young officer would profit from the guidance of an experienced sergeant.

Arrangements for the supervision of barracks varied over the years, but most of the work was done by an orderly officer and orderly sergeant who did a twenty-four hour period of duty, beginning when the bugle sang out 'Parade for Guard' or 'Picquet' at about 9.00 in the morning. Neither was allowed to leave barracks during their tour of duty, and both had to remain in uniform. Orderly officers were found, by rotation, amongst the subalterns, though awarding extra tours of duty to young officers guilty of minor infractions was a popular sport for adjutants, whose efforts were warmly appreciated by the law-abiding, or undetected, majority. In all units orderly officers were required to visit the men's meals and ask if there were any complaints. This procedure could vary from the wholly ritualistic to the genuinely helpful, with much depending on the common sense and moral courage of the officer. The orderly officer was also to inspect the barracks' guard once every night. The time of this inspection was usually allocated by the adjutant, although in some units the orderly officer might be invited to throw a specially made die which had 'lucky bastard' on one of its faces, sparing him from duty that night. An early inspection meant that the officer could fulfil his obligation not long after dinner and, with luck, enjoy an undisturbed night. With a late inspection he would not have long to wait till breakfast. An adjutant who wanted to make a point would have the youngster visiting the guard between 2.00 and 3.00 every morning.

There might be a captain of the day providing the orderly officer with immediate support, and a field officer of the week, one of the unit's majors, who maintained an overview. The guard (sometimes called quarter-guard or picquet) was generally commanded by a sergeant, with a corporal, drummer, bugler or trumpeter, and up to eight men. When the guard was inspected by the orderly officer after coming on duty it was customary for the most smartly turned out private to be made 'stick man', or orderly to the commanding officer for the day, which freed him from standing guard. In the Royals, as Spike Mays tells us, he was

> maid-of-all work for the guard; he carried their meals, washed up, lit fires ... carried messages to squadron, regimental and brigade headquarters at the gallop – regarded as the stick orderly's privilege.[40]

Most barracks had several sentry posts that would be manned, after dark, by members of the guard, usually on two-hour 'stags', with reliefs being marched from post to post by the guard commander. Cavalry regiments also had to provide stable guards, who went on duty at 5–6.00 p.m. and came off at 'Reveille', to see that no horses got loose in the night. Stable guards were on duty for two hours at a time with four hours off, and in the 1870s sleeping at post inevitably brought a prison sentence of two months. Wully Roberston remembered being on stable guard, armed with an empty carbine, on Christmas Day 1877, and his loyal comrades brought him 'a huge plateful of miscellaneous food – beef, goose, ham, vegetables, plum-pudding, blanc-mange – plus a basin of beer, a packet of tobacco, and a new clay pipe.'[41]

When the orderly officer visited the guard-room the sentry outside it would challenge 'Halt! Who comes there?' The officer would reply 'Roving Rounds', the sentry would yell 'Guard, turn out!' and the guard, awakened from sleep or disturbed at cards, would come clattering out under the lantern beneath the guard-room verandah. If the field officer of the week chose to visit – he might do so once or twice during his tour of duty – he would reply 'Grand rounds' to the sentry's challenge, for while a subaltern or captain was owed a butt salute, with the soldier slapping the butt of his sloped rifle, a field officer was entitled to a full present arms. The East India Company's armed forces were not legally part of the British army at all, but followed most of its procedures. However, the very high proportion of rumbustious Irishmen and a rather *laissez-faire* style in its European regiments led to a blurring of the proper formalities, as an officer of

2nd Bengal European Fusiliers discovered in 1856 when he came upon Private Poynard at sentry-go and rather expected that he might call out the guard.

SENTRY: 'Who comes there?'
CAPT A. F.: 'Officer of the Day'.
SENTRY: 'Arrah, *major* jewel, go home again, the boys are all tired & fast asleep.'

They say that the officer *did* pass on without turning out the guard, and I know that Poynard was not confined or reported for neglect of duty to which he was liable or for insolence.[42]

The guard commander would compile a guard roster, listing the names of his men and the posts they were to patrol, as soon as he came on duty, and ensured that prisoners in the cells adjacent to the guard-room were present and as correct as their situation allowed. Wully Roberston remembered the cell area in his Aldershot barracks as 'about fifteen feet square … and with the most primitive arrangements for sanitation. No means of lighting it after dark was either provided or permitted.' Prisoners were provided with no mattresses or bedding, and slept on a platform covered with their cloaks. There were single cells for the drunken or violent. Soldiers returning to barracks after a night out had to ensure that the guard commander had no reason to doubt their sobriety, or they too would find themselves enjoying his hospitality for the night.

By the 1880s garrison towns outside barracks were patrolled by military policemen. In the Peninsula Wellington had been supported by a provost-marshal and twenty-four assistant provost-marshals, supported by members of the Staff Corps of Cavalry. This organisation had not survived the war, and there had been another short-lived body of military police during the Crimean War. In 1877 the Military Mounted Police were formed and the Military Foot Police joined them in 1885. The two bodies were unified in 1926 as the Corps of Military Police, and renamed the Royal Military Police in 1946. Like many other small corps, in 1992 they were swept up into the Adjutant General's Corps. The military police dealt, within the military community, with the tasks carried out by civilian police forces outside it. They also had numerous operational tasks. Today, they are at their most visible dealing with route signing and traffic control. They wore red brassards with the letters MP in black, and the red covers on their khaki field-service caps gave them the affectionate nickname 'redcaps', the origin of their less pleasing sobriquet 'monkeys' is less clear.

At first MPs were selected from soldiers with previous exemplary service, and all held the rank of at least lance corporal. They rarely appeared within barracks, however, because the commanding officer had his own police force, the Regimental Police. These were regimental soldiers, half a dozen or so, commanded by the Provost Sergeant, assisted by a corporal. They wore RP brassards, often carried canes of office, and were widely regarded as the RSM's myrmidons. Yet a good provost sergeant was very valuable, as James Dunn was reminded when both RSM and provost sergeant were splashed by the same shellburst.

> [Sergeant] Butcher looked his part; and he was poacher turned gamekeeper. To his eye for useful things, and to his skill in fixing-in a window or building-in a good-drawing grate, HQ officers had owed much comfort. His personality, rather than character, made him eminent in the battalion, apart from his office. He never had to officiate at an execution, though it is easy to think of him reporting, as did another Provost Sergeant, 'It went off champion, sir.'[43]

At one level this process of social control reduced desertion, went some way towards reducing drunkenness, and ensured compliance with formal regulations and the unwritten codes of the clan. In a regiment whose officers took their responsibilities seriously it would go a great deal farther than that. Captain Cyril Wedderburn of the Royal Fusiliers, at Chatham Barracks before embarking for the Crimea, was wholly committed to his job.

> When not on guard or piquet, and when captain of the day, he had to make incessant inspections of the barrack-rooms, to see that the iron beds are turned up in the morning, and the ventilators open; also before and after, and at every meal, to ascertain that the messes were in order, wholesome and sufficient. Then came visits to the

patients in hospital, to prisoners in the cells and the guardroom, the children in school, for the numbers of each and all were to be entered in his daily report. There were courts-martial and enquiries, committees of all kinds, mess and band; the foreign outfit for his company to be provided.[44]

Indeed, it was precisely this sort of paternalistic supervision that was encouraged by Field Marshal Sir Garnet Wolseley, one of the dominant figures in the late Victorian army. The muscular Christianity of the same era encouraged some officers to take a deeply personal interest in their soldiers. Henry Havelock, whose lack of means left him under-promoted until general's rank and a knighthood caught up with him shortly before his death in the Mutiny, set up an all-ranks Bible class ('Havelock's saints') as soon as he arrived in Burma with the 13th Foot in 1823. He told his missionary father-in-law that 'instances of insobriety or neglect of duty amongst this body in the course of a year are very rare. The frequenters of the chapel are reckoned among the best behaved men in the regiment.'[45]

CHAPTER 25

BULLIES AND BEAST-MASTERS

WE ARE ENTITLED to wonder how deeply the officer's authority extended into the barrack room. While there can be no doubting that officers are superior to NCOs within the military hierarchy, crossing an NCO could have worse consequences than displeasing an officer, as helpful hints for soldiers in a 1918 diary observed:

> To drop your rifle onto foot of Second Lt
> Is bad luck – for him.
> To drop ditto onto foot of Sergeant Major
> Is bad luck – for you.[1]

For most of the time, certainly after corporals replaced sergeants in those partitioned-off bunks, barrack rooms were actually run by junior NCOs or forceful private soldiers. Soldiers accused of offences against the group, such as dishonesty, or carelessness which had subjected the group to collective punishment or other inconvenience, were subjected to barrack-room courts martial, which meted out summary corporal punishment, like the whipping with a musket-sling described earlier. Officers certainly knew that such things went on. Indeed, our best description of the unofficial punishment of 'cobbing' comes from the pen of Captain Thomas Browne, who described what happened to a cook who had allowed his mess's food to become tainted with smoke.

The cook ... throws himself on the mercy of the court. Feelings of mercy are out of the question, and show themselves only in sentencing the cook to be cobbed. This ceremony is performed by soldiers forming two ranks, facing inwards, and making the cook pass between them, cobbing him well about the head with their foraging caps; he is not allowed to run through them, but to march in slow time, and if he attempts to hurry his pace he is made to begin again.[2]

There were other punishments, one levied when a man was accused of being dirty and helped into the 'regimental bath'. 'When a trooper got a bit on the smelly side,' wrote Spike Mays,

we took him to account in the cleaning water of a horse-trough; there to scrub his nakedness – good and hard – with body-brushes and dandy-brushes. Sometimes for good measure we cut his hair close to his scalp with manually operated horse-clippers. Ever afterwards he would remain clean and dragoon-like.[3]

'Practical jokes' abounded. The ever-enthusiastic John Shipp enjoyed 'a good many tricks with my friends, such as filling their pipes with gunpowder, tying their great toes together and crying fire, sewing their shirts to their bedding when asleep, and fifty more'.[4] The novelist Tom Sharpe, who went straight from Lancing College to do his National Service with the Royal Marines at Lympstone, recalled:

There were a good number of Glaswegians in our squad ... One of their favourite pranks was to fill a condom with water and put it down the top bunk of a bootneck [marine] who'd 'gone on the piss' in Exeter. The thing would burst when he climbed in, dripping on the fellow below, who would go out of his mind with rage.[5]

Some of these jests were potentially lethal. Alexander Somerville, who joined the Royal Scots Greys in 1831, recounts how arriving late for first stables brought a recruit no end of trouble.

If the recruit has not been active in getting downstairs to have his turn on the limited space, others will be there before him [and] if he be not yet beyond the point of having tricks played on him, he may be seen laying out his plaited bands and fancy straw on the stones, horses on each side kicking with their hindfeet within a yard of his head ... A man tickles one of them to make him prance and strike the stones, or to toss back his litter on the recruit. As if in a rage, the man commands the horse to stand still, and asks if it means to knock Johnny Raw's brains out?[6]

Riding instructors could be guaranteed to behave more responsibly, and would sometimes whip a horse so that a recruit was thrown, to much mockery.

Did you ever see such a sight! Leaving the bloody *maidan*! I told you 'e came off a farm – 'e's looking for taters. I bet if I looked at the back of 'is neck I'd find some taters all right! Ride – 'e couldn't ride a button-stick.[7]

At the close of the nineteenth century, Horace Wyndham attacked the 'popular fiction' beloved of contemporary authors. A young man of good family joins the army as a private, thrashes the barrack-room bully in a fair fight, distinguishes himself in battle and is then, to universal applause, commissioned, marries the colonel's daughter and lives happily ever after. Although many regiments did indeed allow supervised fist-fights between soldiers, more often than not the barrack-room bully won them, and the process simply upheld existing unofficial power-structures. Wully Robertson's first night in a brawling barrack room was so utterly shocking that he seriously considered desertion. He thought that he still had his civilian clothes (they were to be parcelled up and sent home the following day) but a comrade promptly stole them, legged it, and was never seen again. The future broadcaster and author Ned Sherrin was much more fortunate: with the engaging whisper 'Race yer, Ginge' he was simply challenged to a first-past-the-post wanking contest by the soldier in the next bed. There was a certain amount of twanging and a satisfied grunt before Sherrin realised the rules of the game.[8]

Educated men could find the whole process of barrack-room control exasperating because it turned their world upside down, leaving them at the mercy of the lords of misrule. 'Look at us all,' said one National Serviceman,

A painter, four plumbers, a carpenter, two motor mechanics, a plasterer, two shopkeepers! ... And what do we do? March about the square, stand in queues for kit every day, obey orders from stupid bastards who couldn't get by in civvy street ... walk round that rope, don't trip over it, stamp your number on the lower left hand brace of your braces, not the right hand ... We're here saluting smartly idiots who don't know whether their arsehole's bored or punched.[9]

A Royal Signals soldier found that his accent attracted an NCO's hatred.

The lance corporal in charge was a sadist and picked on me from the start in particular because I spoke nicely. I could do nothing about it and he harried me from pillar to post for about nineteen hours a day. I think that is the nearest I have even been to being a murderer.[10]

Some men were indeed pushed over the edge by this sort of behaviour. Brigadier General Frank Crozier, author of hard-hitting (but not wholly accurate) accounts of his service in France in 1914–18 tells of a bullying NCO who was murdered by a small group of conspirators who shoved a hand grenade, pin duly withdrawn, down the back of his trousers and blew him to tatters. In February 1915 a private and a lance corporal of 2/Welch were executed for murdering their CSM, The poet Robert Graves, acknowledging that it was not his own battalion but 'the story is true as the telling is frank', blamed it on a conflict between the CSM's 'old army humour ... so well-spiced and hearty that one poor sod shot himself and another lost his wits'.[11]

Soldiers were frequently punched by comrades and NCOs. James Dunn, medical officer of 2/Royal Welch Fusiliers, had served in the ranks (albeit the atypical ranks of a yeomanry regiment in the South African War) and knew perfectly well what went on behind the stables, but also knew that soldiers would never speak of it. In May 1917 a groom had a badly-marked face. Before Dunn could raise the issue, the man immediately blamed an officer's charger: 'You know, sir, that Dolly kicks sometimes.' At the same time another groom told his company commander 'why his face was askew', a horse had walked over him in his sleep.[12] The kick of horse or rifle was as familiar an excuse for barrack-room injury as the unseen door edge or the missed stair is for the results of modern domestic violence.

Roberston admitted that merciless men would use any opportunity to make strength and cunning count. Soldiers 'classified' by firing their personal weapons to gain an official ranking – marksman, first class shot, and so on. Lancers also 'classified in the use of sword and lance'. Although whacking one another with the single-stick that represented a sword apparently caused little harm, when charging

with a stout ash pole nine feet in length ... the case was different. For the rider and his horse to be ridden down or rolled over was a common occurrence, and it was seldom that one or more of the competitors was not carried off to the hospital ... [This] afforded a certain class of individual an opportunity of paying off old scores against any non-commissioned officer against whom he had a grudge.[13]

He defended himself by being tougher and more adroit than his enemies.

There were times when unofficial punishment met formal discipline head-on. Captain Dunn knew X, a private soldier who was 'a dirty and unhopeful recruit,' but in the line 'showed he had a great heart in his small body.' In contrast, Corporal Z, once a champion boxer, was a 'smart-looking man but a poor NCO'. A company quartermaster sergeant 'found the boxer knocking X about, told him to stop it, got some "lip" from him, so he laid him out.' Corporal Z 'reported, whining, that the QMS had struck him ... Under Military Law ... the QMS could not well escape a court martial. It was decided, however, that if he knocked Corporal Z down again, round the corner, justice would be done – and was.'[14] The application of what can so easily seem natural justice takes officers onto dangerous ground when they condone, for reasons they think are perfectly valid, acts that they know to be illegal. The issue of 'beasting' highlights the question of officers' responsibility for illegal acts carried out, perhaps without their formal knowledge, but certainly within their real cognisance.

A contemporary, and decidedly unofficial, definition describes 'Motivational Beasting' as a process in which:

A group or individuals are pushed to their limits or to see how far they go before they jack. Not always nice to watch and a real bummer if you are the beastee. One reason for Beasting is to make sure that the person or group will be able to carry out a harder than usual task and it sorts the men out from the boys.

A group that has been Beasted and survived will have developed a comradeship between them, morale will be high.

Beasting or to Beast is probably not PC in the forces anymore.

One who administers Beasting is known as a Beast Master.[15]

Putting military groups under pressure during training can indeed have a beneficial effect, binding them together and often showing that they can achieve things that they might never have believed possible. Amyas Godfrey, a Royal Welch Fusilier officer who spent two years training recruits at Harrogate and then served on a trying tour in Iraq, argued that beasting

> was simply a term for being pushed, pushing oneself, very hard. It's often misused, it really has to be separated from the criminal act which is bullying ...
>
> The Army, if anything, is extraordinarily strict in what rules it follows and you are not allowed to give any physical punishment. The old classic like 'get down and give me 10 press ups' can be used in training, but the officer giving that out as sentence has to record the reason and pass it to the next up commander ... You might feel like you are being punished when you are told, 'that wasn't good enough, do it again', it's part of the training package.[16]

One prominent anti-bullying campaigner recognised that 'The training has to be robust because their lives will depend on it at some point. There's such a fine line between that and abuse – beastings are not part of training.'[17] A former National Serviceman argued that kit inspections, bearing down most heavily upon the maladroit, ensured that the group swung in to support a man who was in difficulties:

> Did someone have to 'show clean'? Then we cleaned his boots or his small pack for him. If the room's total incompetent ... could not lay out his kit in other than a jumble, we all rallied round to make

sure he passed muster when our troop sergeant came prowling.[18]

In November 2005 a former Royal Marine NCO, who had served in the Falklands and the Gulf, described the brutality shown in a controversial video of training on the Green Beret course at Lympstone as an extreme form of 'beasting'.

There is a fine line between character-building and humiliation. This video seems to have crossed the line and appears to be more gladiatorial.

The officers go through even harder training than the ordinary guys when they join up so they know what the NCOs dish out and how far it goes. But you always have one or two people who take things too far and that's what has happened here. There have been court martials in the past involving NCO trainers who were found out taking things too far.

But a lot of that sort of thing happened in the past before society became much more politically correct and bullying was not under such constant focus. Having said that, recruits and marines have to be pushed to the extreme because the corps wants to stay the best, the elite, and you cannot do that with kid gloves. We have all dished it out and been on the receiving end of stuff which would make civilians cringe.[19]

If motivational beasting already risks blurring a fine line, what the same contemporary source calls 'Punishment Beasting' begins on the wrong side of it. This is

A punishment ritual, usually involving physical violence to some degree but can be verbal, carried out by one person or more and used to intimidate or reinforce hierarchical status within a group. Can be anything from a Regimental Bath to a good shoeing.

Beastings do not go on in today's Armed Forces of Her Majesty ... much.

The third form of beasting is 'Contact Counselling, normally administered on a one to one basis in order to re-educate a cnut[sic].'[20] Spike Mays has already shown us the regimental bath. For the avoidance of doubt, shoeing is described as 'a well administered and carefully conducted physical assault on the enemy', much on the lines of the beating with a musket-sling mentioned earlier. A 'right shoeing' has to be defined by 'milky handed 250K a year lawyers', and 'excessive shoeing is still being debated ... by a bunch of Chardonnay drinking, bree [sic] munching guardianistas ... so expect a decision that a slap on the wrist is too much fairly soon.'[21] The author of these words evidently regards beasting as an inherent part of army life, albeit one that is officially disapproved of, and that is criticised by exactly those elements of society least likely to understand the role it plays in the creation of robust morale.

In July 2006 Private Gavin Williams of 2/Royal Welch died of heat stroke leading to a heart attack, after being made to carry out physical exercise on one of the hottest days of the year. He had returned to barracks drunk – the post-mortem also found traces of Ecstasy in his body – and set off a fire extinguisher at a guest at the officers' mess ball. Although Private Williams could have been formally charged for this breach of discipline, Captain Mark Davis, the adjutant, ordered him to be brought in 'hot and sweaty', after a work-out. The three NCOs involved (one of them the provost sergeant) were tried for manslaughter and acquitted. The trial judge asked the jury to consider whether the NCOs had been 'hung out to dry' while Captain Davis was not prosecuted, although we might note that as this was a criminal trial rather than a court martial, the decision not to prosecute Captain Davis had been made by the Crown Prosecution Service, not the military authorities. The judge went on to say, 'The practice of beasting, which clearly falls outside appropriate military discipline, was going on openly and must have been known to senior officers.'[22] The Ministry of Defence, straight-batted as ever, affirmed, 'The Army does not allow or condone any form of physical activity to be used for disciplinary purposes. Commanding officers are made fully aware of their responsibility to protect their soldiers from all forms of physical or mental harassment, and any suspicion of bullying is dealt with immediately.'[23]

Private Williams' father set up a petition to 'Stop Beastings in the Army', and an angry mother joined the correspondence initiated by the trial. Her son was serving in Afghanistan, and his unit had taken with it the shell used for beasting: 'the sad thing is that this punishment is given out for the smallest misdemeanour and is used on a regular basis ... I remember the day my son passed out with such pride, however now I count the days until he can get out.' But another correspondent echoed an old, hard logic.

Of course Williams told the officers and NCOs that he'd been E'd up to the eyeballs as well as drunk on the night in question? NOT likely! So his probable silence contributed to his own sad end. And as for the hour and a half beasting. Does anyone seriously think the Taliban fight only in short hourly sessions? Of course not ... The army was giving him a chance to redeem himself without getting a disciplinary record by giving him the exercise that a normal soldier would just have sailed through. A bit of the dreaded 'beasting' to more of our young people who stray would do them all more good than a thousand probation and welfare officers.[24]

Many of the army's professional and political heads, across the years, have made it clear that beasting will not be tolerated. Indeed, even in 1906, when we might have expected more blind-eye tolerance, Second Lieutenant Clark-Kennedy of the Aldershot-based 1/Scots Guards complained that he had been given a 'subalterns' court-martial' followed by a guardee version of the regimental bath. There was an immediate Court of Enquiry, presided over by Lieutenant General Sir Gerald Morton. Clark-Kennedy said that on 15 March he had been:

stripped. He was put into the bath, water was poured over him as though he were verminous, and a grey mixture, motor oil, he thought, was poured on him, strawberry jam being rubbed in his hair. Then a pillow of feathers was put over him.

He eventually locked himself in his room, then escaped through the window to the Queen's Hotel at Farnborough, wearing pyjamas, Wellington boots, and greatcoat.

Colonel G. J. Cuthbert, the commanding officer, told the enquiry that Surgeon-Major P. H. Whiston had come to him on 8 March and warned him that he had recently examined Clark-Kennedy, finding him 'in a very dirty bodily condition, and his teeth and mouth in a very filthy condition.' He added that in November 1905 Clark-Kennedy had presented with itch, although that was now cured. General Morton informed the court that: 'Itch might be contracted by going with a dirty woman, putting on some dirty clothes, or coming in contact with some person who had it.' He added helpfully that in this case the aggrieved had picked it up from a brother officer in the Bedford militia, though he gave no further details. Colonel Cuthbert,

> expressed his unqualified disgust that such a thing should be possible in a man brought up at Eton and in such a path of life as he. It was not a military offence, and he expressed the opinion that it was a matter for the subalterns. He meant that moral pressure should be brought upon him to become clean. He made these remarks to the adjutant. This officer might have been foolish in repeating the words, but he could not blame him.

The adjutant had indeed 'conveyed the colonel's opinions to the senior subaltern,' and the subalterns had, predictably, we might think, taken the matter forward in their own way. It transpired that Clark-Kennedy had been so ill as to be unable to wash himself or clean his teeth, and his private servant testified that 'bathing and shaving was a pretty regular custom with the young officer [and] his master did clean his teeth regularly.'

The court was not favourably impressed by what it heard. Colonel Cuthbert was immediately stripped of command and placed on half-pay. Captain Stracey lost the adjutancy and was severely reprimanded, and fourteen subalterns suffered a variety of punishments, mostly by being severely reprimanded, having their leave stopped and being superseded for promotion. Surgeon-Major Whiston, by no means the last doctor to confuse duty to regiment with responsibility to patient, had 'an expression of the displeasure of the Army Council' conveyed to him. One subaltern was a peer, another a peer's son, and amongst the guilty officers' surnames were some well-known in society – Dalrymple-Hamilton, Jervoise, Orr-Ewing, Liddell-Grainger, and Ballantine-Dykes. *Sheldrake's Aldershot Military Gazette* reported 'a general feeling of regret' for the loss of Colonel Cuthbert. He was 'a strict disciplinarian, but no martinet ... Not only was his word law, his every wish was in itself a command. But his methods were paternal

– punishment where punishment was deserved …' yet he strove to avoid formality.[25]

The Victorian army called it ragging, but beasting in its many forms is so deeply embedded in the gnarled load-bearing timbers where officers' mess, sergeants' mess and barrack room meet that it is part of the tribe's fundamental structure. It is neither always good nor always bad. Although it can often be deliberate cruelty or thoughtless brutality, it no less often reflects a genuine desire to use informal sanction to avoid an interminable or career-stopping process of law. It has helped gear the extraordinary power of common identity to serve the organisation's wider purpose, has buttressed the ancient against the pressures of the modern (sometimes wisely and sometimes not), destroyed and created self-regard, and aroused hatred, contempt, and sometimes even gratitude. It has both wrecked lives – and saved them.

CHAPTER 26

OH! WHAT A TIME THOSE OFFICERS HAVE

TRUMPET AND BUGLE sounds, our trusted pilot across the long army day, suggests that when the 'Officers' Dinner' blares out at about 7.30 p.m. the men, their own tea-meal long behind them, intoned; 'Oh! What a time those officers have – I'd like to have their din-ner … Just give me theirs and let them have mine: I bet they'd get much thin-ner.'

Officers' messes, buildings where the officers of a regiment could live and eat together, were generally included in fortresses and barracks built from the seventeenth century onwards, both in the United Kingdom and abroad. In the forts on the American frontier of 1758–78, officers might be allocated a block of their own, sub-divided into rooms, or have separate chambers in the corner bastions flanking the barrack rooms. Field officers were allocated two rooms, captains a room each, and subalterns were two to a room as 'the army reinforced the social hierarchy on which good order and discipline were thought to depend.' At Fort Niagara officers lived in the 'Great House', a self-contained fortified manor-style house that had been the original French fort, pleasantly reflecting the 'good order and elegance' that a gentleman holding King George's commission might hope to encounter, even on the wildest margins of that monarch's expansive domains.[1]

Within Britain, however, most officers lodged and ate in public houses until the barrack-building of the Revolutionary and Napoleonic wars. Like the men they commanded they perambulated about the country. In the infantry only captains and field officers were entitled to horses and forage allowance, subalterns often procured nags to ride on the line of march, and all officers expected their baggage to be carried in wagons. Their requirements were a good deal more substantial than those of the private men they commanded. One newly commissioned ensign recalled the long-awaited arrival of his uniform:

> Never did I behold so beautiful – so ravishing a sight! The coat like silk – scarlet silk; the pantaloons as blue as the sky – ethereal blue; the epaulettes and lace as bright as the sun – or 20 suns! Price! What was the price to me? ... It would be endless to describe the evolutions, the marches, and the countermarches, which I performed before the looking-glass that day. I nearly wore out my scabbard by drawing and sheathing my sword; I absolutely tarnished my epaulette by dangling the bullion of it, and the peak of my cocked hat was very much ruffled and crushed by practising my intended salutes to the ladies. I dined – in full uniform, and unshackled by my admiration of strangers to interrupt my admiration for it ... This was the climax of my hopes.[2]

Then there were swords, dress and undress; pistols nestling in their mahogany cases; civilian clothes for town and country; boat-cloaks and reefer jackets; riding gloves and dress gloves; sporting guns and fishing rods; horse furniture, and all those things a man wanted but was not yet experienced enough to know that he did not need.

Demands that regiments should reduce their baggage trains to regulation scales (or worse if it was to be a demanding campaign) produced howls of misery. However, most young gentlemen eventually rubbed along well enough, as Captain William Dansey of the light company of the 33rd Foot, writing from North America in 1778, assured his father:

> after procuring a horse I have [spent] this month past in contriving what things to carry on him that will be most comfortable and convenient and not to overload him. My first thought was a comfortable tent which I have been lucky in contriving and executing one that is admired by everybody for its convenience, elegance and lightness ... Now for furniture, first a floor cloth which serves as a

bedstead and also to cover my baggage when loaded, a palliasse weight about two pounds to stuff with leaves, straw or grass for a bed ... Two blankets and my Portugee cloak, my bed clothes, a small portmanteau holding a change of necessaries is my pillow, a pair of canteens holding liquor and provisions and a small writing trunk holding paper and some knick-knacks is the whole of the baggage that I expect to see before Christmas next and these are great comforts and conveniences to what I had last campaign.[3]

Perversely, though, an officer often discovered that his home kit was not up to the demands of foreign service. When Lieutenant Walter Campbell reached Madras with his regiment in 1830 he found that he was hopelessly ill-equipped for India. He needed a tent, camp-table, chair and basin stand, a light camp-cot whose cotton mattress fitted into the chair. And then there was the small matter of

> A good horse – or two of them if you can afford it – with his
>   attendants ...
> A sufficient number of bullocks to carry your baggage.
> Two servants; a *doobash* or head man and a 'matey-boy'.
> Two 'cowrie-baskets' containing a sufficient stock of tea, sugar,
>   coffee, brandy and wax candles, carried by a 'coolie',
>   suspended from the end of an elastic slip of bamboo.
> A couple of hog-spears ...
> A hunting-knife ...
> A hunting cap, strong in proportion to the respect you have for
>   your skull ...
> A good stock of cheroots and ammunition – it being taken for
>   granted you are already provided with a gun, a rifle and a
>   telescope.
> Some men, who study their comfort rather than their purse,
> indulge in a palanquin, a Chinese mat, a tent carpet, and many
> other little luxuries; but the fewer things of this kind a man
> hampers himself with the better.[4]

Lieutenant George Gleig of the 85th Foot had two portmanteaux that could be slung on either side of a mule's back.

In one portmanteau … I deposited a regimental jacket with all its appendages of wings, lace, etc.; two pairs of grey trowsers; sundry waistcoats, white coloured and flannel; a few changes of flannel drawers; half a dozen pairs of worsted stockings and as many of cotton. In the other were placed six shirts, two or three cravats, a dressing case completely filled, one undress pelisse. Three pairs of boots, two pairs of shoes, with night-caps, pocket-handkerchieves etc. in proportion.[5]

An officer could live out of portmanteaux like this in taverns or on campaign.

The whole brown-wood-and-brass world of campaign furniture lay ripe for exploration by a man with funds behind him. The two-part teak chest with recessed handles and brass-bound corners, often with a cunningly-fitted secretaire top drawer, could sit on either side of pack-saddle or be stacked in the back of a wagon or in a vessel's hold. With its big bun feet screwed in to lift it above the damp it would look well in a tent. Before officers' rooms had much issued furniture, the chest made a good start for the whole panoply of rattan chairs, 'Brighton bun' candlesticks and collapsible bookshelves, squatting beneath walls that groaned under the weight of big game heads, native weapons (as likely to be the booty of bazaar as battlefield) and paintings that sometimes showed mama but sometimes did not.

Not all officers could afford such luxury, and in 1808 an old captain in the Royal Welch Fusiliers, his 'many singularities' attributed to a blow on a head during a shipwreck, eschewed furniture. He spread out all his belongings on the floor – 'a curious piece of mosaic work, composed of coats, waistcoats, fishing rods and stockings, boots and swords, shoes and sashes', leaving 'a sort of alley' between door and bed, and reckoned that he could count all his 307 worldly possessions in just fifteen minutes. He was 'as correct as any officer of the corps, and exceedingly beloved by the soldiers of his company'. He kept his accounts by making appropriate notes in red chalk on the wall of his room in large characters: 'I have just lent Browne a shilling.'

As on leaving barracks, officers are obliged to pay for any damage they may have done to their rooms. My friend the captain always had a bill to discharge for the fresh white-washing of his room, which he did without the least dispute.[6]

Browne's comment on prompt payment for damages raises a wider point. At this time a barracks was the responsibility of its barrack master, usually a regular captain or major posted there from his regiment, an ideal appointment for a man whose days of active soldiering were over. He was assisted by a small staff of sergeants, who were eventually to become the barrack-wardens, almost always retired NCOs, who remained an immutable part of this dusty, fly-blown, blocked-drains world. Officers and soldiers – and families in married quarters – were obliged to pay 'barrack damages' for damage incurred during their occupation. The system was bound to cause disputes, for it was easy to ignore what seemed trivial knocks and scratches on 'marching in' when one was late and tired, and the warden all courtesy, only to be charged handsomely for serious structural defects when 'marching out'. Moreover, it was often not clear what barrack damages actually paid for. Our sour acquaintance the urinated mattress, for instance, with the evidence of successive mishaps ringed, dated and initialled by 'barracky-bill's' marker-pen, rarely showed a sign of the 'special cleaning' for which successive beery miscreants had been forced to pay. Those mattresses were steady little earners.

So too were broken windows. Ensign Garnet Wolseley reported to Chatham Barracks in 1852 to await his passage to India.

Like all other ensigns, I was allotted one very small room as my quarters. It had the usual barrack table and two chairs: the rest of the furniture, as is usual in all barracks, I had to find myself. The officers' quarters were very old and abominably bad. An old great-uncle had told me that he had towards the end of the previous century occupied a room in the house where I was now lodged. It was, he said, even then generally understood that these quarters were so bad that they had been condemned as unfit for use.

Wolseley thought that the barrack-master and his underlings charged young officers, those inexperienced birds of passage, for damage done long before: 'A cracked pane of glass was a small silver-mine to these men. Fifty ensigns may have occupied the quarter with the cracked pane in it, and all had to pay for a new one.' Wolseley was billed for a latch key just before he sailed. He had it in his pocket, and duly gave it to the sergeant. This worthy, true to his colours, refused to accept the key and continued to demand payment: Wolseley, never a man to cross, even as a subaltern, hurled it into the river.[7]

With their regiments on the march, officers moved from King's Head to Queen's Arms, usually dining together at the best local public house and settling their bills as their division marched on. They ate in uniform, and, for it was not until the end of the nineteenth century that mess kit was officially prescribed, took easy and often casual steps towards informality. They had already hung up their gorgets, the fat half-moon of silver or gilt, a symbolic remnant of throat-armour, in their rooms. These, like his broad sash of netted scarlet silk, denoted that an officer was on duty. Gorgets were worn till 1830, and today the cord and button on an officer cadet's white collar tab or a colonel's red one are their palimpsest. Sashes, having migrated, with the ebb and flow of fashion, from waist to shoulder and back to waist again, are still worn with No 1 Dress, the elegant 'Blues'. The sash is now so attenuated, though, that you would never know that it had once been huge, with a channel stitched into both long edges so that two half-pikes could be slipped into them to make an instant stretcher for bearing its wounded owner from the field,

Even in Britain on a Georgian summer's evening, short white jackets in nankeen, linen or cotton often replaced scarlet broadcloth. Boots and breeches, redolent of a long days's road, might yield to the knee-breeches, silk stockings, and pumps of the night, and then from the 1820s, to comfortably cut pantaloons. Officers naturally wore knee-breeches and stockings to the Duchess of Richmond's ball at Brussels in 1815 and, with no time to slip into anything more uncomfortable, wore them at Waterloo as well. It was tempting for an officer to get too relaxed on a warm evening. Senior officers in India tried hard to get the boys out of their *chummeries*, the multi-occupancy bungalows that housed three or four officers in delightful chaos, and into the mess for dinner. There was every danger that they would take to wearing carpet slippers in the evening, thus becoming *slip-shod.*

Officers were reluctant to lay aside their blades. For the first century of the army's life, gentlemen habitually wore swords: slender, straight small-swords were worn about town, and little hunting swords often in the best of Georgian taste, in the countryside. Beau Nash banned swords from Bath in the 1770s, and in 1795 Horace Walpole complained that he would have to be sworded to receive royal ladies at Strawberry Hill, and much dreaded tripping up. The 1796 pattern infantry officer's sword, or its cousin the heavy cavalry dress sword of the same date, were closely modelled on the civilian small sword. Although neither was much use in battle, both would see off footpads in Piccadilly or the Steyne. As damage to the scabbards of surviving examples often shows, they could also easily come to grief in doorways or sedan chairs. In 1743 the 29th Foot, then serving in Canada, was warned of an insurgent attack at dinner. Thereafter its officers wore swords in the evening, earning the regiment the nickname 'eversworded 29th', until 1850 when the practice was restricted to the orderly officer and captain of the week. Today, when the officers and RSM of 2/Mercian wear their Sam Browne belts they also wear their sword frogs, the leather sockets that house the scabbarded sword.

The close proximity of swords, pistols, and alcohol, entwined with a strong sense of gentlemanly honour, meant that duelling was common. Some officers of Lord Berkeley's dragoons were enjoying a convivial evening in Captain Edward Mortimer's lodgings in Louvain in 1692 when Captain Thomas Lloyd, who had lately left the regiment in disgrace, arrived in drink. As they walked out across the square he blamed Major Giles Spencer for his misfortunes: both men lugged out their swords, and Lloyd was mortally wounded in the thigh. Spencer was court-martialled and acquitted: although this encounter had not met the rules of duelling, it was clearly a case of self-defence. Neither military rank nor social status prevented duelling. In 1711, General the Duke of Argyll heard that Colonel Court of the Foot Guards had refused to drink his health because Argyll was a prominent member of the anti-Marlborough faction. Argyll at once asked him whether this was true. Court replied that it might well have been, although he added that, in fairness, he had been too drunk to remember. The men fought in Hyde Park, and Court was deftly disarmed.

The Whig grandee Lord Mohun, who had already been tried twice for murder by his peers, met the high Tory the Duke of Hamilton in Hyde Park in 1712. Both men – regimental colonels and figures of the highest political importance – were mortally wounded in an exceptionally savage encounter. The Duke of York duelled with Colonel Lennox; and the Duke of Wellington – when prime minister – took on Lord Winchelsea. Lord Cardigan wounded Captain Harvey Tuckett, late of his own regiment, the 11th Hussars. The conduct of Lieutenant Colonel Hervey Aston of the 12th Foot had so vexed his officers that he agreed to let them challenge him in turn: the major's pistol missed fire, but the senior captain duly killed him. The duel between Lieutenant Munro of the Blues and his brother-in-law Lieutenant Colonel Fawcett of the 55th Foot in 1843, originating in high words in the presence of a servant, saw Fawcett shot dead and Munro forced to flee abroad.

By this time neither the military authorities nor civilian lawyers were inclined to look favourably on duelling. To kill a man in a duel had always been murder, and simply to fight one was attempted murder. If participants were gentlemen, then juries (in their perverse way) might refuse to convict, or a literate man might be given 'benefit of clergy' for a first offence. The House of Lords traditionally showed remarkable benevolence towards duelling peers. In 1813 four subalterns of the 100th Foot were found guilty of the murder of a fifth during a minor disagreement. They were sentenced to be cashiered, although the proper rules had been obeyed and those involved were gentlemen. The Prince Regent actually pardoned Ensign McGuire, who had fired the fatal shot, presumably on the grounds that he had no alternative but to fight, and the seconds should have done more to settle the quarrel sooner.

In the early eighteenth century officers tended to fight with 'sharps' (swords) rather than 'snaps' (pistols) and well on into the nineteenth century many an officer had a cased pair of Joe Manton's finest duellers ready for that fatal morning, competing for space in his already-overloaded quarters. When Georgian barracks were constructed, an officers' mess formed an integral part of them, perhaps closing one side of the square of buildings round the parade-ground, or standing apart from a row of company blocks. The design of a mess changed little over the years: although the description that follows summarises the messes of my own day, officers returning from, say, Martinique in 1808 with the familiar thud of jettisoned kit and pleas for a cleansing ale would not have found this layout puzzling. The front door, usually up a few steps, would open into a hall containing some of the best furniture and pictures that the regiment could muster. Officers were sometimes discouraged from chucking caps, swords, sticks, and belts onto the hall furniture, or abandoning Jezebel the lurcher there to defend her virtue against Archie the terrier, but messes, then as now, were as idiosyncratic as the rest of the tribe's stamping-ground.

On one side of the hall was the ante-room, furnished with sofas, armchairs, and tables, with enough space for all officers to gather for drinks before lunch or dinner, read newspapers and magazines, and chatter. On the other was the dining room, with polished mahogany tables that could be arranged to cope with everything from everyday breakfast to a formal dinner night. A long corridor ran along the back of the mess, with the kitchens at one end, and the usual administrative and sanitary offices at the other. A staircase, curved and sweeping for many Georgian barracks, but rectangular and vitreous-tiled for the Victorians and Edwardians, led up to two floors of accommodation, with single rooms for most officers and perhaps a small suite at the end of each floor for visiting dignitaries. Plumbing was once primitive, with washstands and chamber pots in some Georgian messes, but from the 1850s there were big bathrooms with duck-boarded floors. En-suite arrangements are comparatively recent, and even today it is easy to forget that to be comfortable in a mess as a visitor you need to take towel, soap and dressing-gown – there are limits to the absorbent qualities of curtains. Officer cadets' rooms at Sandhurst are very like rooms in messes, containing just a washbasin, with baths and lavatories down the corridor. Male cadets are sweetly asked by jutting-jawed colour sergeant instructors 'There are two sorts of officer cadet, ones that piss in the basin – and liars. Which sort are you, sir?'

The mess was run by a small committee – wines, food, games members, and so on, with a president, universally abbreviated to PMC, and almost always as universally, the unit's second in command. At the end of dinner the PMC initiated the loyal toast by asking the vice-president (traditionally the most junior member dining) to propose it. An officers' mess was an association of gentlemen (and latterly of ladies too) with regimental rules to define behaviour and War Office regulations intended to ensure probity. A mess was not the commanding officer's in any proprietorial sense. At mess meetings his vote counted for no more than anyone else's, but it would be a rash

PMC who did not pay attention to his wishes. In an age of forceful commanding officers plying huge patronage the PMC could become a simple appendage to a commanding officer who saw the mess as a symbol of his regiment's cachet and his own good taste, and even now a CO might need to be reminded that although subalterns would not wish to furrow his brow by saying as much, formal dinners might not feature as high on their list of priorities as they do on his.

Lord Cardigan bought command of the 15th Hussars in 1832, apparently paying a non-regulation excess of £35,000. Removed by the king's direct order because of his bullying ways, he was given command of the 11th Hussars, and proceeded to turn it into the most stylish regiment in the army. He banned porter from the mess table at dinner, and when Captain John Reynolds ordered a bottle of Moselle for his guest, Cardigan promptly confused one black bottle with another and duly put Reynolds under arrest, launching another of the scandals that laced his career as gold braid embellished his pelisse. In sharp contrast, when the surviving officers of the 28th (North Gloucestershire) Foot dined together after the Battle of Barossa in 1811, the president rose and made the customary request for the loyal toast: 'Mr Vice, the King.' Mr Vice, painfully aware that only two of them were still on their feet, knew that the customary 'Gentlemen, the King' would not be appropriate, and so, reflecting, no doubt, on those gallant and convivial friends who were supping on a more distant field, replied 'The King, Mr President.'

Given that there was no specific career path designed to produce a mess sergeant – a twentieth-century one might have been promoted from platoon sergeant and have CSM in his sights – it is perhaps surprising that so many mess sergeants were so good. The best were a cross between omniscient *maître d'hôtel* and Jeeves, with dashes of indulgent uncle and stern father. Georgian gentlemen had been breezily encouraged to retire to a nearby sideboard to avail themselves of an array of chamber-pots, but in Victorian times dinners became formidably starchy, with nobody allowed to rise, however pressing the reason, until the loyal toast was safely drunk. Many young officers came to regret their pre-prandial libations, appealing at 8.00 p.m. but appalling three hours later as the PMC's gavel seemed rooted to its base. The actor David Niven was commissioned into the Highland Light Infantry in 1930, and maintained that he had actually requested 'anything but the Highland Light Infantry'. At his first dinner night catastrophe seemed close when the mess sergeant materialised to whisper that an empty champagne bottle stood ready beside his right foot.

Behind the scenes in the mess kitchen, up to half a dozen cooks would normally be working. Early on, these would have been civilians privately employed by the officers, but by the end of the nineteenth century they were replaced by army cooks. Talented chefs, like skilled bandmasters, were lured from one regiment to another. Generals ran their own little households, and Wellington, cooked for by James Thornton in the Peninsula, switched to French chefs when he went to the Paris Embassy in 1814. He re-employed Thornton for the Hundred Days, and wrote 'Cole gives the best dinners in the army; Hill the next best; mine are no great things; Beresford's and Picton's are very bad indeed.'[8] Many officers brought private servants with them (some regiments insisted on this), and were also entitled to a soldier-servant, paid for by the army but with his income reinforced by his master. Private servants would often wait at table, and it was customary for them to wear a simple regimental livery when they did so. The mess sergeant had a small team of full-time military mess-waiters, but for a large dinner night he would have to trawl for volunteers or pressed men from the battalion at large.

Volunteers could be attracted by extra cash and rumours of food and wine. Many a slab of Beef Wellington was slapped between thick slices of bread and carried off for private consumption, and many was the bottle of Dow's '27 that slid unheralded into a barrack room, its drinkers muttering unkindly about a certain sludginess towards the end. There was the sheer bloody pride, even for private-soldier-turned-waiter, of seeing the old mob quite simply excel itself. The band, perhaps sitting towards the back of the hall, for it needs to be audible but not numbing, strikes up 'The Roast Beef of Old England' after the mess sergeant announces that dinner is served, and keeps at it, bar after rolling bar, as the myopic or idle shuffle around and peer, with growing hopelessness, for their place-card.

It can now be seen how Knacker Knight the silver-man's grubby fingers are rewarded by those bowls, statues, and centrepieces glistening in the candlelight, and how the uncased colours look so glorious on their stand behind the commanding officer's chair. One's own officers are in their well-brushed best, middle-aged tums cinched in and youthful thatch damped down. There are the tacksmen of allied clans, the brigade major, a pug-faced Coldstreamer with little curls of gold lace on his cuffs downplaying his rank, and a scattering of officers from other battalions in the brigade, green-jacketed riflemen who show no rank at all (why advertise what insiders already know?), and Highlanders with broad buff turnbacks to their scarlet. Difficult soldiers, mind you, with reports of another downtown punch-up and attendant 'Glesga' handshakes' smouldering in the brigade commander's in-tray, but big, bonny officers. Here is a gunner or two in blue faced with red, there a sapper in his red and blue (his presence generally presages loud bangs, though we may hope that tonight will be different), and there a cavalryman, floppy of hair and so easy of manner that he seems more host than guest. On top table sits an ordnance officer from the brigade staff, again in blue and red, here tonight because we can all blot our equipment ledgers but cannot always find somebody to help us as readily as this kindly friend at court.

There are other distinguished guests on top table, a lord-lieutenant here and a peer there – an officer of the regiment in his youth, who may yet be transformed into a defence minster and remember his friends – and the last but one commanding officer, now a full colonel in the rather ordinary staff mess kit, with something new and shiny at his neck. It evidently makes him happy, for he as frequently as discreetly reassures himself of its continuing presence, and so it makes his old friends happy too. Then there is an ancient gentleman in a lumpy black jacket with a splash of ribbon on his lapel, bright colours fading into the quiet purple of the VC. His knighthood came, much later in life, from a different profession altogether, and tonight, when he would happily drop such nonsense, the young could not be more assiduous in reminding him of it, for on this of all nights they share his lustre and he their pride.

Soldiers pressed into service for a night's work in the mess, especially in the days of National Service, often wrote to their MPs about the sheer rotten archaic class-ridden irrelevance of it all, and loudly objected to being cast as extras in some Jane Austen drama. Some occasionally managed to get their retribution in early: 'Waiter, your thumb's in my soup!' 'That's all right, sir, it's really quite cool.'

Ghosting in the dreary drizzle behind the kitchens in their denims and plimsolls, fags on and fingers crinkly, are the stagehands, the GD (general duties) men, 'bodies' hauled in from the rifle companies for mass washing up and humping bins of pig-swill. Nobody can leave the ante-room before the last guest and the commanding officer have departed, and from before midnight there is a lengthening queue of cars in front of the building, once largely official, but after successive defence cuts, now largely minibuses ('Anyone else for the King's Royal Hussars?') and taxis, and private cars driven by wives or girl-friends. For some there is something uniquely romantic about the imminent struggle with skin-tight overalls, spurs and mess Wellingtons. But for others, retrieving one's man, bat-faced, rich-breathed, and already somnolent, is not a good end to a day with its own uncharted minefield of grumpy children, bank statements, and biopsy results. Livers-in, and married officers who have taken the precaution of booking a room for the night, now stay on as the evening changes key.

The official departure of guests (some of whom, having left formally now creep back by arrangement, amongst them, alas, a Highlander with his pipes) warns a wise mess sergeant that this is the moment to begin damage limitation, although the best that he will manage, these days, is clearing away colours and silver. Things were different when Second Lieutenant Francis Yeats-Brown joined his regiment on the North-West Frontier in 1906 and managed to pick a dinner night to arrive on. After the meal

> Well-trained servants appeared by magic to remove all the break-able furniture … replacing it with a special set of chairs and tables made to smash. Senior officers bolted away to play bridge; the rest of us, who were young in years or at heart, began to enjoy ourselves according to the ancient custom.
>
> Somebody found an enormous roll of webbing and swaddled up a fat gunner subaltern in it. A lamp fell with a crash. Wrestling matches began. A boy in the Punjab Frontier Force brought in a little bazaar pony and made it jump sofas …
>
> Hours afterwards, I left the dust and din and walked back under the stars to the bungalow in which I had been allotted a room. I was extraordinarily pleased with myself and my surroundings. Everyone in my regiment was the best fellow in the world – and that first

impression of mine has not been altered by twenty years of intimacy.[9]

This is just the love at first sight that the regimental system could so easily produce. There were also different currents of emotion, with their own complex expressions, and many misunderstandings, especially in a mess that housed officers from different units within the same garrison. In 1959 Freddie Rawding was a captain in the Royal Army Education Corps. His own mess-kit was dark blue brightened with Minerva-blue facings, although in 1992, after he had retired, the RAEC was absorbed into the Educational and Training Services branch of the Adjutant General's Corps and took on the AGC's high-collared red mess jacket faced with dark blue. The RAEC had originated in 1848 as the Corps of Army Schoolmasters, with a few officers as inspectors or headmasters, and more numerous warrant and senior non-commissioned officers. In 1859 its duties were extended from teaching within the regiment to wider functions, including running army libraries, and in 1920 it became the Army Educational Corps. Its role broadened hugely during the Second World War, and critics maintained that as part of its efforts to prepare soldiers for post-war life, it had warmly encouraged them to vote Labour, and it was this, so they waspishly alleged, that had gained the corps its royal prefix in 1946. You will already have guessed the Corps' quick-march – why, 'Gaudeamus Igitur'.

Towards the end of the Corps' independent life its rank-rich structure attracted envy, for there was a major general as Director of Army Education, backed by one brigadier in Britain and another in Germany, and colonels and lieutenant colonels to match. Many officers and soldiers in other regiments and corps owe their subsequent success in life to the painstaking work of RAEC officers, but it was never easy for the latter to strike a happy balance between the military and academic aspects of their lives. Some strove, not always convincingly, to become every bit as exquisite as the officers in the (sometimes very up-market units) to which they were attached as Education Officers. Others, in contrast, retained an unpolished practicality that left some brother officers feeling uneasy.

Sometimes the relationship got the best out of neither of those involved. I recall a College Commander at Sandhurst, a charming

Foot Guards colonel (we all spoke of him as 'father'), conspiratorially catching my eye before he walked across the ante-room to greet the day's senior visitor, the Director of Army Education. It was clear that they did not share the same tailor, or indeed identical views on the Sam Browne belt. 'Ah,' the colonel whispered sideways. 'It is indeed the schoolmaster-general. Why, I believe that his belt is made of – of – *linoleum.*' As their hands clasped in the slanting sunlight of Topper's Bar, above Old Building's grand entrance, each would have had his preconceptions reinforced. On the one side: 'old army ... anti-intellectual streak ... courteous but so slow-moving ... really does think that the company drill competition is more important than getting more graduates into the army.' On the other: 'clever, and knows it too ... encourages discussion when the youngsters need to believe ... thinks that intellect trumps character.'

During National Service the RAEC had taken suitably qualified men and promoted them to sergeant in the corps after basic training, thereby causing irritation in sergeants' messes of the more traditional stamp. Freddie Rawding, called up into the Rifle Brigade, duly passed WOSB and was sent to Eaton Hall where

> My company commander ... presided over a regime where Sergeants and Sergeant Majors, drill instructors, bullied, shouted, swore and screamed and went berserk in front of young men who had recently shown that they were competent, smart and eager to do well.
>
> Our collective morale, high when we arrived, was systematically destroyed by blundering fools who, if they had been any good at all, would not have been released by their regiments for duties they so obviously hated ... I learned nothing at all at Eaton Hall except the certainty that for an officer or NCO to bully and ill treat subordinates who are bound helpless under military law is inexcusable cowardice.[10]

Rawding left the army after National Service but took a short-service commission in 1952 and expanded it to a regular commission the following year. In 1957 he was posted to Malaya to help teach English to Gurkhas, and lived in the mess at Sungei Patani. The messes of depots and training establishments often lack the sense of corporate identity enjoyed by regimental messes, and Rawding was soon struck by the 'directness, lack of subtlety and overweening self-confidence' of some of his brother officers. Life in the mess was made pleasant by the high standard of Chinese cooking and the

Gurkha component of Mess Sergeant and three mess orderlies [who] kept the ante-room in pristine condition and served drinks quickly and accurately which took some effort of memory when fifteen or so officers came in about the same time to assemble for dinner … There was inevitably an atmosphere of rivalry and competition between officers in charge of recruits. This was usually good-humoured. The only sour note was produced by some of the senior majors, pre-war or Emergency Commissioned in the 1940s, passed over for promotion, who tended to be liverish in the mornings. One of these would be aggressively rude to the younger officers at breakfast without any reason; the other, a self-appointed *jongleur*, would make offensive remarks about junior officers' civilian clothes at lunch or teatime.[11]

Rawding was posted, as Brigade Education Officer, to the Mercian Brigade Training Centre at Whittington Barracks, Lichfield, where the three regiments of the brigade – Cheshires, Staffords and Worcesters – trained their recruits. Here he found none of the 'supercilious exclusivity' that had so annoyed him at Sungei Patani. The majors all set a good example, and young officers, 'polite and considerate in their conduct', were never picked on. And it was a proper, old-fashioned mess.

We had a formal mess night on Thursdays when all appeared in their expensive mess kit and after a most decorous meal and the Loyal Toast, all hell broke loose. Various, rowdy 'indoor games' were played like 'high cockalorum', 'Where's Moriarty', and 'breaking the wall'. The first, like the others, was like a team game where the losers had to buy drinks, Depending on how many wanted to play, it was not compulsory; two equal teams were self-selected. One man from each team got onto his back on the floor to be joined by his opposite number lying head to foot, grasping him close with arms linked at the elbow. On the command 'Mount!' each competitor raised the nearest leg to the other and attempted to overturn him. Each couple had the best of three throws to decide the winner. My long legs and superior weight usually prevailed but I was frequently overthrown.[12]

Mess kit included spurs for officers who would have gone to war mounted in 1914, but they were not strapped on, as they would have been across a riding boot, but 'boxed', with an oblong bar that was shoved into a spring-loaded slot in the heel of a mess Wellington or ankle-height George boot. It was as well to slip them off before mess games – though they gave good guarantee of lock-on for 'breaking the wall' – and to remember their step-catching propensities when walking downstairs.

In command at Lichfield was the 'universally popular' Colonel Lough, who, following a bad head wound, had a steel plate riveted under his scalp, invisible beneath his hair.

At some lull in the proceedings after the usual games had begun to pall, he would call the mess sergeant to produce half a dozen old dinner plates. Since Lichfield market was near the potteries, crockery was cheap and we suspected him of having a stock of imperfect plates bought and kept for these occasions. He would call for attention and challenge those 'not in the know' to follow his example and crack a plate on their heads. One plate shattered on the colonel's head with a loud metallic clang, the volunteer would produce a dull thud on his own head with the next and, no doubt, a headache.[13]

There is a world of difference between the officers' mess of an infantry battalion or a regiment of royal artillery, royal engineers, royal signals and say, that of an ordnance, transport or medical battalion. It reflects not simply varying technological specialisms, history, and tradition, but the specific composition of a mess (even of a different battalion of the same regiment) at a given time. Change any tiny part of the mixture, and much else is altered too. A proficient and upwardly mobile CO has just taken over from an officer who never ever wanted to do more than lead his own clan – probably because it was his father's too. He will set a different style, showing perhaps, that a modest ambition fully attained can be more satisfying than a breath-catching pirouette on each ascending step. There will be any number of personal or professional rivalries and ripples, as lieutenants and captains weigh love against career, juggle the chances of a tour in the special forces against something 'sensible'.

The members of a mess are subjected to constant pressure, almost invisibly discreet at one extreme or crashingly obvious at the other, sometimes welcomed and occasionally resented. It is not just about the quest for superficial conformity in appearance. There is much more to military fashion than the way a man dresses in uniform or in plain clothes. In 1956 the army told its officers that for off-duty wear they must (and one can almost hear Mr Cholmondeley-Warmer's crisp voice-over) 'avoid buying flashy or highly coloured clothes'. It was naturally a good deal more specific about what officers should wear in uniform in 1796 when the officers of the 25th Foot were told that 'they were to wear their coats hooked up in front, facings buttoned back, and the sash ... tied around the body, over the coat, the knot on the left side, except for the flank officers, who tie theirs on the right side.'[14] Military fashion reflects official regulations, regimental customs, and the way that young men who spend so much of their time together actually like to dress. The confident and self-assured set one style, the more reserved embrace another, and the naturally disorganised (not all of whom are deflected from the profession of arms) select what is apparently cleanest in a room that might give Attilla's Huns pause for thought, to create style by ambush. Even if you had no idea of a man's unit or rank, then a glance at half a dozen officers in plain clothes at the Hatchet at Chute on Salisbury Plain, a Sunday curry lunch at the battalion second in command's, or a memorial service in a darkling cathedral would tell you much. These days it's not all *Sloane Ranger* – and none the worse for that.

Styles of dress are one thing, styles of address are another. I was brought up to believe that within a regimental mess officers were all on first-name terms, apart from the CO, who was 'colonel'. Rising to one's feet as he entered the ante-room was as much deference as was required. In contrast, I have known messes where field officers expected to be sirred by subalterns at all times: 'You'd think they wore those bloody crowns on their heads, wouldn't you?' The young take time to learn, and it is not only their peers that teach them. Let us say that you have just joined your battalion, and on your first night have discovered that your immediate master, the relaxed officer command-ing A Company, is happily known as 'Dozy' in the mess. You may not, though, be aware that of the three Oxbridge entrants to the regiment in his year he was the only one not to emerge with a First. It was an amusing jest at the time, but has become a little over-used since. If, the following morning, you herald your arrival at your first Orders Group (a sort of company planning meeting) with him, making free of your new status by a casual 'Mornin' Dozy', then the CSM – who knows, officially, about none of these things, but, unofficially, under-stands them all – will, just a little later, put you in what is called the picture – 'The Big P'. There is one way of behaving in the mess and quite another of behaving outside it. Although the CSM may not be the sort of man who naturally uses the phrase *formal command structure*, at this stage in your life he knows a good deal more than you about what it actually means.

CHAPTER 27

THE SERGEANTS' MESS DINNER IS WORTH PUTTING DOWN

O FFICERS' MESSES HAVE had a far longer existence than those used by warrant officers and sergeants. But it was recognised very early on that discipline could be better preserved if there was some distance to it, and that distance said a good deal about the behaviour of, say, rifles NCOs on the one hand and the Guards NCOs on the other. In April 1756 Corporal Matthew Todd was told

> that no sergeant should drink with the corporals nor corporals to drink with the private soldiers nor soldiers to drink with drummers neither to keep company with each other but the sergeants and corporals to carry sticks and beat the soldiers but as they so occasion to keep them at a distance in not making things so free with them, so as soon as these orders were out I proposed to the rest of the corporals that we would have a club or meeting every Thursday at night after roll calling at first at the oldest corporal's quarters so on by seniority and to spend 3 d. each and any corporals neglecting coming to be fined 3 d. upon duty or sick, etc. and we all signed a paper.

The plan was immediately applauded by the officers, and the sergeants at once established a similar mess, with its 6 d. subscription reflecting their status.[1]

Permanently-established sergeants' messes were rare in the Napoleonic era, save in the sense of the temporary messing groups just described by Todd. Although some of the newly built barracks did indeed have sergeants' messes, the majority put sergeants in enclosed bunks in barrack rooms, or partitioned up whole rooms so as to give more space and privacy. As the nineteenth century went on, purpose-built sergeants' messes were at last included in barrack design. In India unmarried officers would eat and socialise in their mess, and sleep in rented bungalows within the military cantonment, while sergeants would use their mess in the same way but live in what they called 'cabins' in a barrack room behind it. Communal eating was regarded as important by COs and RSMs alike, and members of both messes were expected to turn up at the appropriate hour, washed, shaved, and sober. Protocol varied hugely. There were commanding officers who expected nothing more than a quiet 'good evening, colonel' as another scapegrace slipped in seconds before dinner was called. Some RSMs required every sergeant entering the mess to do themselves the honour of buying him a drink – and not to leave for the evening until they had asked his permission to fall out.

No sooner had officers acquired a regulation mess kit than sergeants had one too. Their mess committee had its PMC and Mr Vice, and the sergeants' mess caterer did, for his mess, just what the mess sergeant did for the officers. Their watch chains might be silver rather than gold, just as in their mess the best silverware might be EPNS rather than hallmarked. If the officers had a ball, the sergeants must have one too, usually with suitable title like the 'Albuhera' or 'Lucknow' Ball. A stiff invitation card from 'The Warrant Officers, staff sergeants and sergeants of the – Regt' invited guests for 10.00 p.m., and attentive hosts, already warned that one-third of the costs of the evening will be met from mess funds and the remainder pro-rata, with the RSM contributing £1. 10s. and the lance sergeant 12s. knew that they were to be in the hall at the appointed hour 'in their best tunics and new pumps'. Versailles could not have shown better *ton.*

First-Class Staff-Sergeant and Foreman of Works Simpson, Royal Engineers, requests the favour of a dance with you, Miss Robinson … Thus, while the colonel dances with the sergeant-major's wife, that excellent warrior pilots his commanding officer's 'good lady' though the maze of the cotillion.

The first sitting of supper was at 12.00 midnight, and the colonel and senior officers had mostly flown by 1.00 a.m. Subalterns were expected to be away by 'Reveille', indeed, most had left long before, ducking beneath that penumbra of disappointed hopes, with a lance sergeant asking a friend whether those new pumps had really been a wise investment.

> She said she loved me, Jim, this very afternoon ... and I saw her a squeezing the hand of the Rifles' master-tailor in the corner of the supper-room only an hour ago.[2]

It is quite as misleading to speak of a British NCO corps as of an officer corps, for we have already seen that the real complexities of social structure make these terms the most unreliable of guides. But, like it or not, from 1800 the expression sergeants' mess meant a good deal more than four brick walls and a tiled roof.

In one sense the burgeoning of the sergeants' mess was as much about social class as military discipline. Attempts to improve the sergeant's lot and reinforce the status of the warrant officer by the creation of what we might call an artisan class gave rise to a social life that half-mirrored that of the officers' mess. Success was increasingly dependent on mastering basic skills of literacy and numeracy and moving on to a system of tiered educational qualifications. The mess that housed John Fraser and the sergeants of 5th Fusiliers at Agra, had a dining room, billiard room, and 'refreshment bar'. There was a 'quadrille party' once a month, and sergeants were encouraged to entertain members of nearby sergeants' messes and, of course, guests of suitable status from the civil lines. A more subtle change of status than the acquisition of those three broad white stripes on one's upper arm was eating the main meal of the day a little later than corporals and privates, almost as if a man became more respectable the later he dined. In 1900 one military writer thought that the process was satisfactorily complete, with three natural levels of military-social structure, so that 'no sergeant now has to go to the canteen for a glass of beer; in fact, such an action would lead to trouble, as great store is laid on the regulations forbidding non-commissioned officers to associate with private solders.'[3]

Yet, in many regiments, there was almost as much contact as separation. Reciprocal mess visits on national and regimental days brought officers and sergeants together. There were company or battery 'smokers', informal concerts that might be held in barracks, camps or on the line of march to give the naturally talented, or the eternally optimistic, the chance to sing, recite or play an instrument. They were certainly not events to which women were invited, although their style, to us at least, looks comparatively innocent. In India soldiers enjoyed collecting butterflies and selling the carefully mounted results to officers on the way back to England. Some soldiers there shot game on their own account, and others might set off with an officer or two in a little group where, listening to the sounds of an Indian night around the camp fire, it did not much matter whether a man was smoking Navy Cut or a Jermyn Street cheroot. 'Gurning', or face-pulling, was a popular party act, although there were complaints that nature had given some men an unfair advantage.

Freemasonry was strong in the army, although it is difficult to be sure of its practical effect on promotions and appointments. I read about the way that Freemasonry had the Territorial Army of my time in its grips. But I managed to become its professional head without ever having been a mason, and so am inclined to suspect more smoke than fire. In 1810 there was a British Freemasons' procession through Lisbon, causing much local offence. Wellington at once issued a general order saying that Freemasory was 'an amusement which, however innocent to itself, and allowed by the laws of Great Britain, is in violation of the law of this country'. In 1838 the members of a Dublin lodge asked his permission to call themselves the Wellington Lodge, and he told the master

> The Duke of Wellington presents his compliments to Mr Carleton. He perfectly recollects that he was admitted to the lowest grade of Free Masonry in a lodge which was formed at Trim in the county of Meath. He has never since attended a lodge of Free Masons.
>
> [It] would be a ridiculous assumption of the reputation of being attached to Freemasonry, in addition to being a mis-representation.[4]

A provincial grand lodge was established in India in 1728, and regional lodges soon followed, with growing numbers of regimental or 'ambulatory' lodges following fast. Freemasonry in India peaked towards the end of the nineteenth century, but even by 1919 there were eighty lodges in Bengal, forty-one in Bombay, thirty-one in Madras and another thirty-one in the Punjab.

Military men played a notable role in Indian Freemasonry. A succession of commanders-in-chief India were masons, amongst them Kitchener, O'Moore Creagh, and Power Palmer. Of the twenty-nine officials of the District Grand Lodge of the Punjab in 1914 eight were officers, five warrant officers or NCOs, and four were Indian. Sergeant Major George Carter records the first meeting of his lodge on 11 August 1856:

> Present Bros Wood, Carter, Monk, McDowell, Lake and Guthrie; joining members balloted for successful Bros Lord Wm Hay, Graham and Tapp of Simla, and Harding and Campbell of Kussowlie.[5]

As far as the army in India was concerned, Freemasonry helped, in its small way, to blur the rougher edges of an unthinking racism. It brought together the military and the civil, especially in the weary circles of tiny communities deep in the hinterland, And, within the army, as Kipling, a Freemason himself, argued so sonorously, its own oblique formality helped blend other rigidities.

> Outside – 'Sergeant!' 'Sir! Salute! Salaam!'
> Inside – 'Brother', and it doesn't do no 'arm.
> We met upon the Level and we parted on the Square,
> And I was Junior-Deacon in my Mother-Lodge out there.[6]

At a regimental level, Freemasonry added another shade to the *chiaroscuro* of influence, patronage, and understanding that gave sensitive officers and NCOs the chance for informal discussion where stripes and stars mattered less than they did outside the Lodge.

So too did sport. There was a general agreement that football was *the* soldier's sport. James Jack complained that, wherever one went on the Western Front, soldiers claimed to be exhausted, and yet there was a kick-about at the first opportunity. Many officers loved the game, and the eccentric Lieutenant Colonel Mainwaring of the 51st encouraged robust tackles, assuring his men that there was no rank on the football field. A Norfolk lad who joined the cavalry told a comrade that he had no family or regional connection with his new regiment, but 'when you were at Norwich I played football agin you, so when I thought o' takin up sodgerin' I found out where you was and here I be.'[7] Percy Wyndham thought that soldiers enjoyed watching officers playing cricket because it gave them the opportunity to lament, in mock-genteel, the drop of another catch. When the 68th Light Infantry on its way to the Crimea played in what the scorebook calls 'Sultan's Valley, Varna' there was a creditably hard-fought match, with Private Fossy taking four wickets and Corporal Jester another three, including that of Lieutenant Barker, caught and bowled.

Regimental policies varied a good deal. In the 1920s the junior officers of 1/King's Own Scottish Borderers were told that, once parades were complete, their first duty was to play sports with their men, but ten years before an officer in another regiment discovered that he was one of only two officers who regularly played team sports. Many regiments cultivated expertise in a particular sport. The Duke of Wellington's was a famously hard rugby-playing tribe, while the officers of the Durham Light Infantry took on the cavalry at polo and very often won. During the National Service years some regiments took infinite care in getting suitable sportsmen posted to them, 'packing' high-quality teams and ensuring that a successful sportsman was not over-burdened with military duties. 'The CO was boxing mad', wrote Henry Cooper, called up into the Royal Army Ordnance Corps. 'He kept an eye peeled for likely looking fighters coming up and wangled them. In two years our battalion never lost a match.'[8]

Keeping men fit and busy was now an important element in barrack design. Tipperary Barracks, begun in 1874, housed an infantry battalion, initially the 1/East Yorkshires, who arrived in 1879. It was

A self-contained installation with accommodation for over 500 officers, NCOs and men. For the welfare of its military personnel and their families, the barracks had an officers' mess, sergeants' mess, canteen and recreation establishment, chapel, hospital, teacher's quarters and school house, soldiers' quarters, married quarters, washing establishment, bath house and cook house. All three buildings were equipped with the most modern conveniences of the period. Other buildings within the confines of the barracks included the regimental office block, band room, warrant officer's quarters, guard-room, detention barracks, stores, magazine, stables, water tower and latrines. Sporting and recreational facilities such as a fives court, skittle alley, sports green and a fully equipped gymnasium were available.[9]

The Army Gymnastic Staff came into being in 1860, became the Army Physical Training Corps in 1918, and a corps in its own right in 1940. Soldiers were introduced to scientific physical training by 'muscle benders' who ran unit gymnasia and larger complexes in major garrison towns like Aldershot. A man could join the ranks, show aptitude as a fitness instructor, and eventually, just as a bandmaster might become a director of music, a skilled gymnast could move to commissioned rank as a master at arms. None of this overturned the army's social structure overnight, but it made another of those little differences. The names of sportsmen and women in the army now come to our attention more easily than many of the great and the good: Kriss Akabusi MBE had been a warrant officer in the APTC, and Kelly Holmes DBE a sergeant in the same corps.

So, as the band plays us in to dinner, we cross that richly textured rug of communal life, with its dress, phrases, and behaviour – learnt, borrowed or stolen – reflecting the weft and warp of four structures so well identified by Charles Kirke, gunner colonel turned academic. Firstly there is the *formal command structure*, embedded in hierarchy and discipline; next, the *informal command structure*, that network in which unwritten behaviours – friendships and associations, nicknames and sharing – are fundamental. Third comes the *functional structure*, the attitudes and expectations concerned with carrying out military tasks – really the whole nature of being soldiers. Finally the *social structure* of the army (to which so much of this book is devoted) is about belonging and group identity. None of these structures is distinct: indeed, even during our short walk to the table we will unconsciously weave from one to another.

CHAPTER 28

CAMPAIGNERS
STRAIGHT AND GAY

THE BROADER RELATIONSHIP between men and women within the army was not primarily about sex, but constituted another of those informal structures that had a disproportionate effect on the way the army really worked. For most soldiers sex was indeed a serious preoccupation. For many, indeed, it was intimately linked with alcohol so as to constitute a man's major interest in life. Through the army's history, a far smaller proportion of soldiers than civilians was able to marry, and by no means all wives accompanied their husbands on active service, so that there was a constant shortage of women. Sometimes soldiers had affairs with comrades' wives, often with fatal results. In 1756 Drummer Lewis of the 30th Foot cut his wife's throat with his razor – 'this rash action he confessed to us all that he was jealous of Sergeant Hemmington of their company.' He tried to drown himself in the Medway, but was caught and tried: 'The next day he was sent to Gaol at Rochester where he was hanged and gibbeted.'[1] A century and a half later a cavalryman warned rookies that a young soldier could easily catch the eye of Potiphar's wife, and get sent up to do a little light duty at his married quarters. 'Hey, you, will you go up to my quarters and help my missus give the place a dig out?' he asked. 'She'll give you a good supper and a glass o' beer. And draw my ration o'coal while you're at it.' The lady in question had other ends in view. 'I've seen you,' she said. 'I've taken a likin' to you ... Don't you be afraid o'me ... I'm a sport, I am. I'll give you a good time.'[2]

Officers and soldiers alike availed themselves of prostitutes who varied in wit, appearance, aptitude, cleanliness, and potential lethality from 'All Night Miss from Boarding School, Chelsea', who cost Lieutenant Lord Alvanley £5. 5s. in 1808, to the sixpenny tart pursued by James Boswell disguised as 'a half-pay officer', and on down to Portsmouth's 'fireships of the sally-port' who might give a man what he sought (and much, much else besides) for a tumbler of gin. Some women started in the officers' mess and crashed down to behind the barrack wall. By no means all of them had intended to become prostitutes. Many a woman enjoyed an honest and monogamous relationship until her man's regiment went abroad and she could not follow it. Another might have a series of long-term relationships with men in the same unit but, as one told Henry Mayhew, collecting material for his book *London Labour and the London Poor*, 'If I have a row with a fellow he's always the first to taunt me of being what he and his fellows have made me.'

In many parts of the Empire there were women who were less than wives but a great deal more than prostitutes. It was far easier for officers to maintain ladies like this than it was for soldiers; and practices that Georgian Britain tolerated happily enough soon raised Victorian eyebrows. Lieutenant Thomas St Clair was shocked to discover, on arrival in the West Indies, that

> Two of our officers were living in barracks with two of these girls, one in Demerara, Lieutenant Myers, had a beautiful young mulatto, and Lieutenant Clark, in Berbice, had with him a fine handsome black woman. Though I disapproved of the system, which, on first arrival, appeared to me an outrage on common decency and propriety … yet I was at last obliged to alter my opinion, as I saw both the above-mentioned officers saved from certain death by the uncommon care and attention which these two girls paid to them during a violent attack of fever.[3]

British India eventually took to calling women like this *bibis*, but it was a cruel gibe, brought about in part by the jealousy of *memsahibs* and partly by the pious mutterings of missionaries. You must forgive me for manoeuvring the following lady into these pages, for her husband did not hold a regular commission in the British army, though he died fighting the Queen's enemies, commanding a well-equipped local regiment, 'having its own band and colours'. She was Moslem, and regarded herself as his wife, and the things that made this Scots professional proud made her proud too, as she tells us on his headstone.

> Hamish McGregor McPherson of Scotland
> Killed in battle at the head of his Regiment
> While fighting against the Dewan Mool Raj
> At Siddhoosam, near Multan, on the
> 1st July, 1848[4]

Around barracks and camps in Britain and the Empire, sex was largely a question of supply and demand at its most basic level. The great camp at the Curragh bred its own 'wrens', girls who lived rough in gorse huts, and in India there were whole communities devoted to servicing the troops. No sooner had Private Frank Richards arrived at Jhansi and gone to wash his feet in a nearby stream, than a local procurer arranged numerous girls at six annas apiece and several soldiers duly formed up in line, it being their nature to do so. Private Richards thought that it worked very smoothly.

> The native took the money while the girls did the work. The stream was very handy; it enabled the girls to wash themselves and they did not mind in the least who was looking at them while they were doing this.[5]

Prostitution raised practical and moral issues for army and government alike. If desertion had been the wasting disease of the eighteenth-century army, venereal disease was scarcely less damaging to the Victorian army. In the middle of the nineteenth century about one-quarter of its strength was infected at some point in the year. In 1864 the Contagious Diseases Act established compulsory medical inspection for prostitutes in garrison towns, and infected women were confined in 'lock hospitals' until they were 'cured'. The unreliable nature of treatment together with the harsh and intrusive nature of inspection, all brought the scheme into disrepute. Some zealots believed that by reducing the risk of the disease, medical inspections would actually 'make sinning safe', and by becoming a practical success this could be a moral disaster; policy soon changed. The encouragement of prophylactic treatment went some way towards reducing the risks of infection, but in 1890–93 VD rates had risen to 438 admissions per 1,000 men in India, double the ratio for the British army at home and almost six times as bad as in the German army.

Lord Kitchener, as commander-in-chief India, introduced a number of effective reforms. First, more wives were allowed to go out to India. Next, VD returns were now required with other statistics at a unit's annual inspection, and so a wise commanding officer could see the potential impact of a high rate of VD in his battalion on his own career. Making the issue one of command responsibility had much in common with the practice in the Second World War army of disciplining COs whose units had an unacceptable rate of malaria, revealing that men were not taking the anti-malaria drug mepacrine. In India regiments had long maintained *Lal Bazaars* (Red Bazaars), where a procuress ('the old bawd') dealt with recruitment and pay while the military authorities tried to reduce brawling and theft. I can already glimpse the provost sergeant engaged in some delicate quid pro quo manoeuvres. Officers also became involved, particularly in ensuring that there were enough girls to keep pace with demand and to prevent soldiers from taking their pleasures elsewhere. There were only 30–40 girls to accommodate the 1,500 men in the Agra garrison and it was clear that this would never do. Lieutenant Colonel Parry of 2/Cheshire formally requested the cantonment magistrate at Amballa to obtain 'extra attractive women' as the six girls in his *Lal Bazaar* were worn out. Kitchener appealed to his soldiers by asking them what their mothers or sisters would make of their conduct: even in the toughest of battalions there were many soldiers for whom such an appeal to common decency would never be wholly wasted. Lastly, lurid pamphlets left men in no doubt as to the ghastly progress of the disease. By 1909 there were just 67 cases per thousand British soldiers in India per year.

In the matter of VD as in so much else, the First World War confronted the army with an old problem on a huge scale, constituting 'the greatest amount of constant inefficiency in the home commands.' Almost 417,000 men were admitted to hospital with VD during the war, and as each admission for syphilis averaged fifty days the bill for lost manpower was alarmingly high. There were occasional attempts to maintain licensed brothels, almost like the *Lal Bazaar* from Amballa somehow transported to Rouen, but now with redcaps keeping an eye on the steady pulse of trade. The evidence suggests that such establishments did indeed keep infection rates low, but there was always too much domestic political pressure for them to last for long.

Men who contracted VD were obliged to declare it, and risked two years' imprisonment for failing to do so. They were sent to special hospitals where, because their illness was deemed self-inflicted, their pay was stopped. A married man who had been making a regular 'allotment' of pay to his wife might now not be able to do so, and an ill-judged evening in Poperinghe or Amiens wrecked many a marriage. An officer might be able to persuade a kindly medical officer to treat him privately, or a member of the sergeants' mess could perhaps get the medical sergeant (not known as 'the pox-doctor's clerk' for nothing) to squirrel away an illegal prescription of what might have been the right drugs. For soldiers there was no choice between shameful hospitalisation and untreated disease. Nor would the disease remain undetected for long. Soldiers were routinely given intimate 'short arm inspections', the very depth of humiliation for many a middle-class conscript, and their 'crimes' were discovered.

Effective treatment of VD had improved by the time of the Second World War, but policy had scarcely changed. The contraction of VD remained a criminal offence, and in consequence many soldiers waited until they were caught by an inspection rather than reporting the disease earlier when they might have been cured quicker. Montgomery, very much the realist, was censured for recommending officially approved brothels. In some theatres, especially Italy, where it should have been possible to bring well-established civilian brothels under military control, they were simply placed out of bounds. Soldiers were given practical advice on prophylaxis, and condoms were freely available. When the condoms arrived at his battalion, Company Sergeant Major Stan Hollis of the Green Howards, who was to win the VC on D-Day, told his company commander that this seemed to him to be a diversion from the real war effort. 'What's to do, Sir? Are we going to fight them or fuck them?' None of this stopped soldiers from finding girls: it simply helped ensure that they did so in circumstances that minimised risk. Throughout the war the annual rate of infection ran at around 30 men per thousand, an improvement on rates of the high Victorian army, but scarcely the apogee of the successful application of what was in effect a major public health issue.

It is not unfair to classify the fight against Sexually Transmitted Diseases as the British army's longest campaign, for it still goes on. Condoms remained a free issue in the post-war army, and 'short-arm inspections' continued. Soldiers were encouraged to visit Prophylactic Aid Centres, located in garrisons and camps, receiving a chit signed by a medical orderly testifying to the fact that they had, at least, done their best to avoid infection. But it was rarely a simple matter. The forms issued in Dusseldorf included the phrase 'glans penis (knob)', because 'there were lads in the regiment who didn't understand the word penis.'[6] There remained a touching confidence in folk remedies. A soldier saw a comrade 'bollock naked ... with Old Spice poured on his tackle. You've never seen the like of the crabs on him ... I asked him why he didn't go to the MO. The gist of it was, he worked in the canteen with the German staff, could speak a bit of German, and he'd been shagging his head off. He wanted to keep it quiet.'[7] Some enthusiasts really did their best to test venereologists' skills. A doctor at Singapore remembered 'one unfortunate who had achieved the grand slam, having syphilis, gonorrhoea, and lymphogranuloma inguinale'.[8] National Servicemen were warned that they could not be discharged from the army while they were still being treated: 'Blobby Knob Stops Demob'. The development of STDs that do not respond well to antibiotics takes the campaign on, and I have no doubt that if British soldiers form a branch of the Intergalactic Spaceship Troopers three hundred years from now, there will be young men and women nervously telling their medical officer that they have not felt tip-top since that last posting to Alpha Centauri.

Sodomy, 'when a male has carnal knowledge of an animal ... or a human being *per anum*' was made a felony in England and Wales in 1533, and remained a capital offence till 1861.[9] Thereafter sodomy itself attracted a maximum penalty of penal servitude for life, and attempted sodomy for up ten years. Sexual activity between two adult males, with no other person present, was made legal in England and Wales in 1967, in Scotland in 1980, and in Northern Ireland in 1982.

Until 2000, homosexuals were not allowed to serve in the British armed forces. There are strong arguments in favour of maintaining discreet areas where military regulations circumscribe the rights that service personnel would otherwise enjoy as citizens: few would argue, for instance, that soldiers should either be permitted to withdraw their labour or to disobey lawful commands. The opponents of removing the ban on homosexuality argued that trust and confidence within the unit would be weakened if it was felt that there might be a new source of patronage, and that young soldiers would be coerced into unwanted sexual activity by predatory gays. In 1952 the adjutant general affirmed that

> Once you get it started in a barrack room you get the whole lot corrupted, and we want to protect the individual. It is an offence that we have got to stop because otherwise you get corrupt barrack rooms, just like the vicious type of public school dormitory where vice spreads widely.[10]

With the demand for change reaching the last surge of its triumphant momentum, in 1999, General Sir Anthony Farrar-Hockley argued that 'the overwhelming majority of those in military service today find homosexuality abhorrent', and it was feared that up to 10 per cent of serving personnel would leave rather than remain within an organisation that had betrayed a deeply held conviction.[11]

There had never been any doubt that there were homosexuals in the armed forces. Some officers argued that soldiers took to 'detestable practices' not because they were necessarily homosexual but because the conditions of their lives gave them no alternative to 'masturbation and mercenary love'. In practice, the army was far less zealous in prosecuting men for homosexuality than one might expect, and sentences usually fell far below the maximum available to a court martial. Between 1796 and 1825 twenty soldiers were accused of crimes ranging from sodomy itself to 'Indecent and disgusting conduct'. Four were acquitted and three were hanged: most of the remainder were given 500–1,000 lashes and discharged from the service. A soldier convicted of a homosexual act in 1863 was drummed out of the army in one of those rituals designed to show the unit's collective disapproval.

> About noon on Friday the ... battalion was mustered ... The
> sentence upon the culprit was read out aloud and he was stripped
> of his buttons, facings, etc. The battalion formed a line on the other
> side of the roadway, and, preceded by a corporal and private and
> led by a rope attached to his neck by the smallest drummer boy,
> Smith marched to the gate, the band playing 'The Rogue's March'.[12]

During the whole of the First World War, with the army at the largest
in its history, eight officers and 153 men were court-martialled for
'indecency' on service abroad. One medical officer, after hearing two
young officers on a leave train discussing the merits of 'being caught
red-handed in someone else's bunk' so as to avoid going up the line
again, mentioned it to the assistant provost marshal at Poperinghe,
who said that it was a well-known ruse. However, there was certainly a
recognition in some units that monogamous homosexuals who got on
with their lives as best they could should not be penalised. David
Jones's wonderful prose poem *In Parenthesis* tells of one of a pair of
lovers being killed on the Somme, and

> ... Bates without Coldpepper
> Digs like a Bunyan muck-raker for his weight of woe.

Subsequent politicising has not made balanced discussion any easier.
Captain Edward Brittain MC of the Sherwood Foresters, Vera Brittain's
brother, is a classic member of the sparkling generation swept away
by the war. He was killed in Italy in 1918. Although we can never be
sure of the circumstances of his death, there is at least an argument
for saying that an impossible counter-attack was suicide by proxy. Mail
was censored, and in a letter to a former officer of his company –
opened in a random check – Brittain had described homosexual relationships with private soldiers. Brittain's CO had been told that the
assistant provost martial was investigating the matter. Possibly knowing that Brittain would choose death rather that the sentence of cashiering and imprisonment that would follow conviction, he warned
him that he should be more cautious about what he wrote. Sexuality
is not a matter of choice, and we would not blame Brittain for his. Yet
relationships like this would, even today, fail 'the service test',
designed to ensure that sexuality does not interfere with the military

chain of command. Edward Brittain was a gallant officer, but his proclivities had encouraged him to impose a greater burden on the formal command structure than it could reasonably be expected to bear.

After the war prosecutions for indecency remained uncommon, and between 1920 and 1937 they averaged forty a year. Although there were doubtless zealots who pursued the crime whenever they discerned it, one RSM admitted

We knew what went on but we didn't go out to look for it. Let me put it that way. Obviously it went on. You can't have eight hundred troops living together and something of that not being practised. But so long as we didn't stumble on it then we didn't go looking for it.[13]

The tribe was, in practice, prepared to take a relaxed view of behaviour that did not, whatever regulations might say, go as deeply to the core of its being as so many traditionalists argued. But it was not prepared to tolerate caste-breaking behaviour, and an officer or NCO who made advances to private soldiers in general and 'band rats' in particular could expect not only rigorous prosecution but an exemplary sentence on conviction. The issue was not sexuality, but the abuse of power.

The legalisation of homosexuality in the British Armed Forces was not instantly followed by the blizzard of resignations as many (this author amongst them) had feared. The one brigadier who did resign is an old friend, and phoned me a few days before the news broke. He was quoted in the press as having 'strongly held moral and military convictions', about the issue. He told me that it had always been his policy not to try to explain something to the sergeants' mess if he could not do so with a clear conscience. Although, as it happens, I had concluded that the army would not be wrecked by the legalisation of homosexuality, I thought it commendable that an officer should have the moral courage to take a career-breaking path on a point of principle.

In its important 'Values and Standards' pamphlet the army affirmed 'Social misbehaviour can undermine trust and cohesion ... misconduct involving abuse of power, trust or rank, or taking advantage of an individual's separation will be viewed as being particularly serious.' The same document introduced 'The Service Test', that would enable a commander contemplating disciplinary action to ask himself whether certain behaviour had damaged the army's effectiveness. It did not talk specifically about sexuality, recognising that there would be times when either homosexual or heterosexual activity would breach the test. For a male officer to have a sexual relationship with a male or female under his command would indeed be potentially damaging, whereas for him to have a homosexual relationship with a civilian would not, all other things being equal, cause difficulties.

There will inevitably be some finely judged points. Let us return to a Ladies' night in the officers' mess, to which one male subaltern has elected to bring his civil partner, not in an effort to affront but because he cannot see why his lover should not spend an amusing evening with his friends. There may come a moment when the night is far from young, band has been replaced by disco, and couples – including the homosexual pair – are smooching closely on a darkened dance floor. Does the service test stand unbroken? The quartermaster, the straightest of men who has given his life to the regiment, is visibly infuriated by what he sees as an insult to all that glorious iconography about him: he can hardly hold his temper in check. And one of the mess-waiters, conscripted for the evening but normally a rifleman in the homosexual subaltern's platoon, takes his pleasures copiously, and whenever he can find them: he glances across to the dance floor and thinks ... now *there's* a thought.

I am, for all my earlier reservations, delighted to see that the army has at last recognised that simple sexual preference does not disqualify an individual from practising the profession of arms, and lament all those officers and men who suffered criminal prosecution for their sexuality in the past or, more recently, found their careers curtailed. Throughout this chapter there has been a braided cord of fraternity, of evolving family bonds and of legal structures moderated by informal proceedings. Ultimately 'Values and Standards' is right because it targets the abuse of power. But it will not be the work of a moment for old beliefs, however wrong, to be expunged from view, and for the army to remember that all the best families have to subsume diverse opinion – and stay a family still.

CHAPTER 29

OFFICERS' WIVES GET PUDDINGS AND PIES

THE BRITISH ARMY was anything but celibate. In H. M. Bateman's cartoon *The Second Lieutenant who joined His Regiment with His Wife* even the tiger rug on the ante-room floor is knotting its tail in sheer horror at the prospect of a married subaltern. Before the First World War it was affirmed that subalterns must not marry, captains could marry, majors should marry, and colonels must marry. When officers were granted marriage allowance in 1918 it was made clear that this would not be paid until an officer had reached the age of 30. It was common for officers to leave marriage and the raising of a family as long as they decently could: Douglas Haig married Dorothy Vivian in 1905 when he was 44, and their son and heir was born just before the great German offensive of 1918. In the past an officer or soldier required his commanding officer's permission to marry, and today an officer will often, as a simple courtesy, tell the colonel of his regiment of his impending engagement.

Many officers scraped along on private means with little margin for error, very few wives worked, and all took it for granted that the happy home would have domestic servants. Early marriage could be personally awkward and, at least in some regiments, professionally damaging. Ensuring that an officer's wife came from approved stock involved endless chatter as the commanding officer's wife interrogated members of her own social circle. Fond mamas were just as busy on behalf of their own darlings. In 1830 Captain Philip Meadows-Taylor had just been made captain and adjutant in the Nizam of Hyderabad's little army. This was not exactly the Grenadier Guards, but when he overheard a young lady ask her mother's permission to dance with him, he was delighted to hear her reply that if he was an adjutant: 'He is quite eligible *now*.'[1] The Georgian army was relaxed about the private lives of its officers – Wellington had a string of mistresses – but it was far less forgiving of officers who married unsuitably. Captain Glanville Evelyn of the 4th King's Own, took family servant Peggy Wright to North America with him. They never married, but when he made his will before Bunker Hill he left her 'all my worldly substance'. An officer committed an even worse breach of caste (we might almost add 'theft in breach of trust' to our charge-sheet) by having an affair with the wife of a soldier or NCO. In 1814 a court martial suspended an officer of the 19th Foot from rank and pay for three months for visiting a soldier's wife, and his general was furious. The sentence was wholly inadequate for a crime that went straight to the heart of the relationship between officers and soldiers.

By marrying an officer, a lady joined a community she might never have encountered before, and was dependent on the advice of senior wives. If the regiment was serving in India – where Europeans constituted such a tiny drop in a huge ocean – she had become a citizen in a world ruled by precedent. She soon became aware that there was tension between her own affection for her husband and his duty to his men. She, just like her husband, was now part of the great caravanserai pulsing its way across the globe, furniture wrecked in successive moves, treasured trinkets broken by servants, and pathetic imitations of half-forgotten English gardens withering in another scorching summer. Until the Crimean War, wives routinely accompanied their regiments on campaign. Although it was far easier for an officer's wife to secure passage and accommodation than it was for a private's, social status was little protection against the vagaries of terrain and climate, shipwreck, piracy, and the assaults of fauna from bed bugs to polar bears.

In a pre-contraception age, the Colonel's Lady was just as likely to become pregnant as Mrs Judy O'Grady. Both were at risk of a difficult confinement as the monsoon bucketed down and the regiment was suddenly ordered off to suppress a rebellious tribe, and the baby of the family already had a worrying rash. Rank was no protection against mortality. Fred Roberts, that beau idéal of British India, lost his first daughter about a week after her birth, another died soon afterwards, and a boy at the age of three weeks. Although the family's remaining son, Freddie, narrowly escaped death in 1871 he was killed in action at Colenso in 1900. When it was time for a child to be educated, off to Britain it went. Those half-embarrassed farewells, *faux*-jolly letters, and sense of incomplete lives lived half a world away were part of the price paid for a glorious empire.

On some of its 'reports and returns' the high Victorian army aligned the relative status of its members as follows: 'Officers – Ladies; NCOs – Wives; Soldiers – Women.' The process was later made marginally less offensive by designating a wife in her husband's rank, as: 'W/O Corporal' for 'Wife of Corporal.' As society became less deferential, many women could not understand why their own status was so inextricably linked to that of their husband. Why should they be expected to eschew 'officer type' interests simply because their husbands were not commissioned? Conversely, as an increasing number of officers' wives had jobs of their own (some of which paid more than their husband's) they resented the damage done to their careers by the 'accompanied postings' that compelled them to follow their menfolk about the globe. One of the great strengths of the regimental system was the creation of a parallel universe in which the regiment looked after its own, with a panoply of Wives' Clubs, Thrift Clubs, Playgroups and the like, precious little of it financed by public funds and so much of it depending on the unpaid labour of wives.

The lethal little wars of the early twenty-first century have shown just how much work is done where the formal structure of the battalion's welfare team and the unofficial network of families and friends meet. Captain Chris Wright, who dealt with much of the heavy lifting on the home front during 1/PWRR's 2004 Iraq tour, tells us about sustaining normality in a world where abnormality descends by unmarked car at an unpredictable hour. Even running a house is not simple when it is located in a complex that, just over a century ago, was chosen for its proximity to a training area.

> Many of the wives could not drive and Tidworth is no sprawling metropolis. Its high street contains a chemist, a NAAFI, an arts supply shop, a strange two-storey shop selling furniture and pornography, a tyre centre and two takeaways … The wives needed to be

able to get into Salisbury or Andover to do most of the shopping and the welfare office provided coaches at least once week. Pregnant wives needed to be taken in for scans and health checks while their husbands were away …

There would be a Sunday lunch where the wives could bring their children and chat with each other while the children ran riot in the battalion bouncy tiger, or attacked the clown. These were not only attended by the wives but by a few girlfriends and their children as well.[2]

A Ladies' night in a modern mess shows just how things have changed. There is still a uniformed mess sergeant but most services are provided by civilian contractors for whom the lustre of King Joseph's chamberpot is not a matter of family pride. Some messes, often still managed by the team that ran them before contractorisation, make an extra effort to show off the place at its very best. But running a mess is a financial venture with a bottom line, its entertainments often hamstrung by the fact that many members would rather be at home with their families. By not appearing at an event that they know the mess committee has put such effort into organising they may themselves make it less of a success. Can the commanding officer himself fail to appear? But can his wife bear another duty dinner where even the most inspired *placement* will see her revolving in a confined constellation? All these factors – the increased age at which officers join the army, the backdated seniority that whisks them on to early captaincies, the challenge of becoming adjutant of a regular battalion, of getting on the right career courses and off on the right operational tours – tends to threaten Jack getting all work and no play, emerging as a dull boy. Can the most loving husband always steer the conversation away from the next tour in Afghanistan? How do wives – their husbands commissioned into the regiment the same day and who have soldiered together for twenty years – adjust to the fact that only one of them can command it?

Across the centuries, the problems confronting officers' wives have been wholly eclipsed by those facing the wives of soldiers. Earlier we followed the orderly sergeant into a fetid barrack room, urging the orderly to open the window as soon as he could. At the far end of the room, given the slimmest modicum of privacy by blankets draped around beds, was the accommodation allocated to married soldiers, whose wives and children lived in the barrack room, taking in washing to earn a penny here and there: trying to dry a wash in barracks with small, smoky fires or stoves and no issued clothes-horses must have tried the patience of a saint. When William Lucas joined the Inniskilling Dragoons in 1846 his barrack room contained 18 bachelors, two married men and their wives, with seven or eight children. Nine years later Colonel Richard Gilpin told the House of Commons that he had just seen a barrack room with fifty men and one wife, the only concession to privacy being 'a sort of curtain' between two beds.

From 1685 a man was required to ask permission in order to marry at all. A fortunate soldier might be allowed to marry 'on the strength', with his wife allowed to live in barracks and draw a ration – she received one-half a soldier's ration and a child one-quarter. Regulations varied as to the proportion of women that a regiment might carry 'on the strength'. For much of the nineteenth century most sergeants and about 7 per cent of corporals and privates were married, with another 7 per cent or so wed, but not officially on their regiment's married roll, and in consequence not entitled to rations or accommodation. Being married on the strength was narrowly tolerable, especially (and we can scarcely overstate the case) when working-class accommodation outside the army was so appalling. But being married 'off the strength' was infinitely worse, with a husband trying to arrange accommodation for his wife when the regiment was on the move, even within the United Kingdom. Even James Wolfe, capable of showing such a regard for the soldier, thought that any man who did such a thing should be proceeded against 'with the utmost rigour'.

Even if a woman was married on the strength, there was no guarantee that she would be allowed to accompany the regiment if it went abroad. At the start of a campaign the authorities decided how many women could be taken: in 1758 ten women per company, for regiments sent to the West Indies. In 1801 the 95th was allowed only six women for every hundred men, sergeants' wives included, and no woman with more than two children would be considered. Selection of wives who were to sail with their men was generally made at the point of embarkation by some simple form of ballot, and few issues aroused greater grief and fury than to see a couple separated, probably forever, at the quayside, with the women and any children trying to find their way, usually on foot and in all weathers, to the parish of her birth in the hope that she might receive some sort of relief. Private Buck Adams of the 7th Dragoon Guards called scenes liked this 'a disgrace to the name of England', and many agreed with him. Indeed, Wellington himself averred that 'Nothing can be more disagreeable to the service than allowing the wives of soldiers to become chargeable to the parish.'³

Women were often smuggled aboard departing ships, and regimental authorities, painfully aware of the anguish of it all, were often not over-zealous in their search for stowaways. Indeed, there is clear evidence that the regiment regarded its regimental women as part of its moral responsibility, whatever the rules or regulations might say. A widow would remain 'on the strength' for up to three months after her husband's death, and a regiment that could not find her a suitable replacement within that time was failing in its duty. Some women kept a discreet list of potential husbands to hand, with suitors moving up the roll (this was, after all, an organisation that set great store by seniority and patronage) as blade or bullet struck. Of course sex was involved. But a reliable washerwoman, good cook, honest stepmother or brave nurse had much to recommend her, and many Victorian soldiers would have understood Kipling's warning that sometimes 'love ain't enough for a soldier.' Sensible commanding officers knew that, in an army whose ancilliary services were still poorly developed, well-conducted women could make a real difference to the practical everyday life and, indeed, the whole character of a regiment.

There was a similar emphasis on ensuring that regimental orphans were not turned away, although accounts of teenage girls being swept off by rubicund old NCOs are less than edifying. George Waterfield of the 32nd tells us that when Colour Sergeant Blackford and his wife died in India the regiment brought up their daughter until she was 16, when she was married off to a 34-year-old colour sergeant. Waterfield thought that she had 'always shown a preference for a smart young man in the band,' but 'I really think that some women in the army would marry the devil himself if he had a scarlet jacket with three stripes on the sleeve.'⁴ George Loy Smith, who was later to charge with the light brigade at Balaklava as a sergeant major, had just arrived in India as a young private and was taken off by a chum to

Lady Moira's orphanage, where he was 'admitted to a large room containing a dozen soldiers' orphans: "One or two of them were Europeans, the remainder half-caste, and so on, in fact there was every shade from white to nearly black."' Having obtained leave to marry, a soldier could simply make his choice. We conversed with them for a short time,' wrote Smith, 'and then left.'[5]

By the 1850s there were repeated complaints in both professional journals and the liberal press that the situation was wholly intolerable. One line was familiar: barrack life was dehumanising. A man 'who is lodged with hundreds of his comrades in a barrack ... has no family to provide for, is not in any sense his own master, is housed, clothed, fed and attended in sickness, under regulations over which he has no control' could not be expected to have any sense of self-respect. How could he, in such circumstances, hope to become a respectable husband and father? Next, given the 'inconvenience and distress' inevitably arising when troops were sent abroad, proper accommodation had to be made for wives at home and in overseas garrisons: a man would fight harder if he knew that his family was safe.[6] Until 1867 regiments were given a free hand as to the size of the married establishment at home, but thereafter this was defined centrally. By 1871, 33.5 per cent of officers were married, as opposed to 13.19 per cent of soldiers. At the same time 23.03 per cent of male civilians were married. In 1881, at the time of the short-service enlistment crisis, marriage regulations were made liberal in an effort to encourage privates to sign on in the hope of becoming NCOs, and NCOs to extend their service. All warrant officers, staff sergeants and colour sergeants, half of all sergeants over 24, and 12 per cent of rank and file over the age of 26 could now marry on the strength.

Simply changing the regulations, of course, made no difference unless married quarters were actually provided. In 1852 a group of guards officers clubbed together to built a hostel for regimental families, and from 1860 the first married quarters were built. Thereafter, although there were all the familiar problems with sub-standard accommodation and the depredations of barrack-wardens, there was at least a clear recognition that looking after the soldier meant looking after his family too. From 1871 the wives of NCOs and men were given 'separation allowance', if they could not serve with their menfolk, and although this amounted to just 6*d.* a day for a wife and

2*d.* for each child under 14 it was another leap forward. There were repeated attempts to improve the quality of regimental and garrison schools. All sorts of employment could be found within barracks, usually carefully graduated so that a husband's rank was roughly aligned with his wife's job: the colour sergeant's wife would happily see to the captain's shirts, but it would not be right for her to contend with a private soldier's flannel drawers. However, the fundamental niggle remained, as a soldier's wife complained in 1870, 'we can't help marrying soldiers,' she said, 'but it is very hard indeed to be made to work for nothing. A labourer's wife can go to church on Sunday, but the wives of a crack line regiment must go twice on a Sunday to clean barrack rooms.'[7]

AFTERWORD

As WITH ALL the pictures from military life described in this book, the frame portraying the predicament of wives and families embraces huge changes during the twentieth and early twenty-first centuries. Woven through this history are those features of army service that never change. Soldiers are still deployed on operations for long periods and, though they seem like mere interludes compared to the years of separation experienced during the two world wars, with such a small army another tour often looms on the horizon amidst the joys of homecoming. Soldiers still yearn for letters and parcels, even in these days of email, iPhones, and Skype, and what one soldier described in his diary during the First World War as the 'dumb agony' of goodbyes continues. As does the constant threat of bad news from the theatre of operations, and the consequent importance of a community spirit amongst those left behind, fostered through social and recreational activities. Paradoxically, these can be much more difficult to generate in a largely home-based army where spouses may no longer be following the drum, but pursuing careers as important to them as the soldiers', and sometimes more lucrative, too.

We have come a long way from 1907, for example, when the funeral of a Royal Artillery captain, who died from tetanus poisoning after coming off his bicycle on a Blackheath road, could be reported in tedious detail by the *Kent Argus* without a single reference to the deceased soldier's wife and three young sons. After the First World War, the Royal British Legion (RBL) was founded under the patronage of Field Marshal Earl Haig, in recognition of the enormous challenges involved in helping struggling ex-service families who had fallen on hard times. That the Legion and its fundraising is thriving in 2011 is a remarkable tribute to its founder, as well as reflecting the continuing need for such support in an era of Treasury parsimony – another striking thread of continuity, one might observe. These days, the ever generous British public could be excused for becoming frustrated by the seeming plethora of service fundraising organisations, all doing important work but sometimes needing more effective co-ordination. The Army Benevolent Fund, now retitled the Soldiers' Charity, like the RBL raises money for people rather than for buildings or facilities, as does the Sailors, Soldiers and Air Force Association (SSAFA). With other charities, like Combat Stress and the British Limbless Ex-Servicemen's Association (BLESMA), filling more specialist niches in the market, the achievements of new charities such as Help for Heroes – raising many millions of pounds to provide facilities for seriously wounded servicemen – are especially striking. Initially launched to raise funds for a swimming pool at Headley Court Rehabilitation Centre near Epsom, it is now financing further centres around the country to support wounded servicemen and women as they face the difficult process of changing direction in their lives.

Another major advance – which started in the 1980s with some government funding underpinning it – was the introduction of the Home Start concept to army garrisons. This professional support for young families relieves wives of regimental commanding officers and company/squadron/battery commanders of the sometimes awkward task of providing such advice. A young soldier or his wife is generally much more willing to approach a genuinely independent agency than to 'wash dirty linen in public' within the regimental family; the latter recourse sometimes even perceived as potentially 'career threat-ening'. Allied to this development has been the growth in importance of the Army Families Federation, an organisation that does excellent work, lobbying both government and the chain of military command on behalf of families. Their influence over matters such as the provi-sion and quality of garrison quartering, for example, has been signifi-cant. It is interesting to recall that when Brigadier and Mrs Gaffney were invited to study this whole subject in the mid-1980s, they found that those regiments most vociferously opposed to change – defend-ing the traditional 'regimental' approach to these sensitive matters – were also amongst those with the worst track-record of family welfare problems.

It would not be fair to claim that the Government and Treasury have been entirely sitting on their hands in these endeavours, but it might be reasonable to judge that without voluntary and charitable work, the casualties of modern wars would feel not unlike those returning from the trenches in 1919 to the 'land fit for heroes'. Richard's rides on his beloved charger, Thatch, raised many thousands of pounds for the Soldiers' Charity, so let him have the final word on this timeless topic, taken from his study of the British soldier on the Western Front, *Tommy*:

> T. P. Marks remembered his train journey home with veterans 'almost all of whom hoped to start a life of which they had dreamt in the trenches …' The blighting of these aspirations struck many veterans as the cruellest aspect of their service. Many of those who came to look upon the war as waste and sham did so, not at the time of the armistice, but through the lens of penury and disillusionment that characterised the post-war years for all too many of them.

Today's soldiers are professionally trained volunteers who engage in sometimes controversial wars, not volunteers or conscripts involved in wars of national survival. But a duty of care on the part of the government of the day remains unarguable. The covenant between the soldier and the nation must surely be sustained.

HEW PIKE

ACKNOWLEDGEMENTS

Richard died suddenly at the end of April 2011, and although he had finished the book, the acknowledgements were still to be written. Unfortunately, I do not know the names of many of those who may have helped him with research or expert opinions, for which he would have been so very grateful. However, I can at least acknowledge the people who helped with the production of this book. First and foremost I must thank Arabella Pike, at HarperCollins, for her expert editorial guidance, and her calm encouragement and support during what must have been an unusually difficult time for her. Also at HarperCollins, Kerry Chapple, Melanie Haselden and Katharine Reeve; and Corinna Harrod, our daughter. Furthermore I am grateful to Sonia Land, Richard's agent, and to Dr Alison Milne, his consultant, who allowed him to break out of hospital on at least two occasions in order to finish the book; and to his friends Lieutenant-General Sir Hew Pike, Major-General Sir Evelyn Webb-Carter, Stephen Wood and to Professor Hew Strachan, who so kindly helped me with corrections. Finally I would like to acknowledge the hard work and the dedication to military history of my brave and truly delightful husband Richard Holmes.

Lizzie Holmes, July 2012

ENDNOTES

Introduction

1 Antony Beevor *Inside the British Army* (London 1990) p.35.
2 Michael Yardley and Dennis Sewell *A New Model Army* (London 1989) p.65.
3 Ibid. p.59.
4 Quoted in Richard Holmes *Shots From the Front* (London 2008) p.32 from a typescript memoir in the Royal Hampshire Regiment Museum, Winchester.
5 Quoted in Lt Col J. C. M. Baynes *The Soldier in Modern Society* (London 1972) pp.66–7.
6 Ronald Skirth *The Reluctant Tommy* (London 2010) p.454.
7 Trevor Royle *The Best Years of their Lives: The National Service Experience 1945–63* (London 1986) pp.253–4.
8 Gerald Kersh *Clean, Bright and Slightly Oiled* (London 1946) pp.67–8.
9 Ken Lukowiak *A Soldier's Song* (London 1999) p.27.
10 Ibid. p.8.
11 Lieutenant Colonel Edward Windus to Colonel Samuel Bagshawe, 18 October 1761 in Alan J. Guy (ed.) *Colonel Samuel Bagshawe and the Army of George II 1731–1762* (London 1990) p.246.
12 Richard Holmes *Dusty Warriors: Modern Soldiers at War* (London 2006) p.218.
13 'Baha Mousa inquiry hears corporal accuse officer of abusing Iraqi detainees' in *The Guardian* 16 November 2009.
14 George Orwell *Rudyard Kipling: The Orwell Reader* (New York 1956) p.278.
15 *Rudyard Kipling's Verse, Inclusive Edition* (London 1933) p.397.
16 Horace Wyndham *Soldiers of the Queen* (London 1899) pp.120–1.
17 Field Marshal Sir William Roberston *From Private to Field Marshal* (London 1921) pp.3.
18 Commissioners on Military Punishments, Parliamentary papers, Reports Commissioners, 1836 Vol 1.
19 Ibid. p.11.
20 John Railton *The Army Regulator: or, the Military Adventures of Mr John Railton* (London 1738) p.17.
21 'Notes by Maj A. J. Smithers' National Army Museum 2001-01-360-1.
22 Spike Mays *Fall Out the Officers* (London 1969) p.13.
23 Beevor *British Army* p.19.
24 Ira D. Gruber (ed.) *John Peebles' American War 1776–1782* (Stroud, Gloucestershire 1998) p.368
25 *Peebles' American War* p.507.
26 Martin van Creveld 'A Short History of the Management of Violence' *The Quarterly Journal of Military History* Autumn 1988 p.56.
27 Arthur Bryant *Jackets of Green* (London 1972) p.24.
28 Richard Holmes *Dusty Warriors: Modern Soldiers at War* (London 2006) p.248.
29 Notes for 11 November 1831 in Philip Henry Stanhope *Notes of Conversations with the Duke of Wellington* (London 1886) p.250.
30 Quoted in David French *Military Identities* (Oxford 2005) p.37.

31 http://news.stv.tv/
scotland/143262-msp-under-fire-
over-army-recruit-remark/accessed
31 December 2009.

32 Stephen Wood *The Scottish Soldier*
(Urmston, Manchester 1987) p.27.

33 Alan Ramsay Skelley *The Victorian
Army at Home* (London 1977)
p.248.

34 Sergeant Major J. White
'Reminiscences of my Army Life'
National Army Museum pp.94–5,
181.

35 Robert Edmondson *John Bull's Army
from Within: Facts, Figures and a
Human Document ...* (London 1907)
p.3. Edmondson rose to the rank of
sergeant, and after his discharge
supported the Social Democratic
Foundation, which was eventually to
evolve into the Labour Party,
arguing in favour of a national
militia-style army.

36 Mays *Fall Out* p.2.

37 Joseph Gregg 'The Charge of the
Six Hundred' in E. Milton Small
(ed.) *Told from the Ranks* (London
1897) p.61.

38 Richard Holmes *Riding the Retreat*
(London 1995) p.32. Based on
unpublished questionnaires
circulated during research for *Firing
Line* (London 1985).

39 Doug Beattie *An Ordinary Soldier*
(London 2008) p.19.

40 Helen McCorry (ed.) *The Thistle at
War* (Edinburgh 1997) p.32.

41 A sangar, deriving from the North-
West Frontier of British India, is a
stone breastwork; *bocage* is the
distinctive field-pattern of north-
west Normandy, lethal to men
whose job it was to fight through it;
a Desert Rose is a field urinal; and
PIAT is the acronym for Projector
Infantry Anti-Tank, a Second World
War spring-loaded bomb-thrower
with short range and the trajectory
of a gently lobbed turnip.

42 Wyndham *Soldiers* p.8.

43 Holmes *Dusty Warriors* p.94.

44 'Row over military uniforms in
public' *The Times* 7 March 2008.

PART I

Chapter 1: Chuck Him Out, the Brute

1 Robertson *Private to Field Marshal*
p.382.

2 Kipling *Inclusive Edition* p.392.

3 Charles Carlton *Going to the Wars*
(London 1992) p.348.

4 Ibid. p.348.

5 Cromwell to Sir William Spring,
September1643, in Thomas Carlyle
(ed.) *Oliver Cromwell's Letters and
Speeches, Vol. 1* (London 1846) p.135.

6 Lois G. Schwoerer *No Standing
Armies* (London 1974) p.168.

7 Sheldon Richmond 'America's Anti-
Militarist Tradition' in *Freedom Daily*
21 March 2008.

8 Quoted in John Childs *The Army of
Charles II* (London 1976) p.8.

9 Henry Hanning *The British
Grenadiers* (Barnsley 2006) p.13.

Chapter 2: King's Army

1 Mrs Ward 'Reflections of an Old
Soldier, by his Daughter' in *United
Services Journal* 1840 Vol II p.217.

2 Samuel Ancell and 'Jack Careless', *A
Circumstantial Account of the Long and
Tedious Siege of Gibraltar* (Liverpool
1785) p.58.

3 Jolyon Jackson (ed.) *A World Apart:
The Foljambe Family at War* (London
2010).

4 J.C.M. Baynes *The Soldier in Modern
Society* (London 1972) p.50

5 Robertson *Private to Field Marshal*
p.17.

6 Ibid. p.17.

7 Peebles *American War* p.482.

8 Philip Ziegler *King William IV*
(London 1971) p.59.

9 Quoted in Hew Strachan *The Politics
of the British Army* (Oxford 1997)
pp.204–5.

10 Quoted in Strachan *Politics* pp.68–9.

11 Sir George Barrow, *The Life of General Sir Charles Carmichael Monro* (London 1931) p.47.

12 Alex Danchev and Daniel Todman (eds.) *Field Marshal Lord Alanbrooke: War Diaries 1939–45* (London 2001) p.504.

13 Typescript by Lord Selborne, Bodleian Library Selborne MSS 93.

Chapter 3: Parliament's Army

1 John Childs *The Army, James II and the Glorious Revolution* (Manchester 1980) p.xvii.

2 *Manual of Military Law 1914* (London 1914) p.14.

3 Henry L. Snyder (ed) *The Marlborough–Godolphin Correspondence* 3 Vols (Oxford 1975) II p.268.

4 Beevor *Inside the British Army* p.139.

5 The author served in the MOD for three years as a brigadier in the late 1990s. It is always dangerous to let personal experience intrude too much upon what one writes, but nothing had prepared me for the MOD. Few things have gratified me more than to stand, after a farewell lunch with my delightful colleagues, on the pavement outside a London club and to know that I would never need to enter Main Building ever again. I will long recall the Treasury's input into the Strategic Defence Review process: insufferably cocky, breathtakingly ignorant and as unstoppable as a charging rhino.

6 Childs *The Army, James II …* p.107.

7 Quoted in Childs *The Army, James II … p.47.* Being on the wrong side of James had its advantages when Dutch William arrived in 1688, and Charles Bertie found himself commissioned a captain in the Coldstream Guards.

8 Gwyn Harries Jenkins *The Victorian Army in Society* (London 1977) p.220.

9 Strachan *Politics* p.27.

10 Edward Smith *William Cobbett: A Biography* (London 1878) pp.7, 43, 47, 48.

11 Smith *Cobbett* p.18.

12 Gerald Gliddon *The Aristocracy and the Great War* (Norwich 2002) p.xix.

13 Philip Abrams 'Democracy, Technology and the British Retired Officer', in Samuel P. Huntington (ed.) *Changing Patterns of Military Politics* (New York 1962).

14 Sir Neil Thorne to Colonel Tony Scriven, 14 October 2008, on the website of Dr Julian Lewis MP, accessed 19 January 2009.

15 Star count relates to the stars worn by US generals and the 'star plates' once displayed on senior officers' staff cars. Brigadiers and their equivalents in the other services are one-star officers, major generals rate two stars, lieutenant generals three, and generals four. The rank of field marshal, now in abeyance but still held by a dwindling number of officers, is five-star.

16 Tony Hayter (ed.) *An Eighteenth Century Secretary at War: The Papers of William, Viscount Barrington* (London 1988) p.285.

17 *Barrington Papers* pp.316–17.

18 Strachan *Politics* p.28.

19 Bellamy Partridge *Sir Billy Howe* (London 1922) pp.6–7.

20 Elizabeth Longford *Wellington: Pillar of the Sate* (London 1972) p.333.

21 Quoted in Strachan *Politics* p.82.

22 William Napier *History of the War in the Peninsula* 6 Vols (London 1851) IV p.317.

23 Ibid. II p.401.

24 Harries-Jenkins p.22.

25 J. H. Stocqueler *A Personal History of the Horse Guards* (London 1873) pp.121, 156–7.

26 Harold Nicolson *King George V* (London 1952) p.226.

27 French to Stamfordham 25 September 1914 Royal Archives GV K2553.

28 Field Marshal Lord Carver *Out of Step* (London 1989) pp.230, 312.

29 *The Times* 4 August 1997.

30 BBC News Online Network 2 December 1988, accessed 20 January 2010.

31 *Independent* 14 January 1999.

32 *Hansard 9 December 1998* Cols 296–8.

33 Text of resignation letter in *Channel 4 News* 3 September 2009, accessed 19 January 2010.

Chapter 4: Brass and Tapes

1 Quoted in Smith *Cobbett* pp.44–5.

2 Alan J. Guy (ed.) *Colonel Samuel Bagshawe and the Army of George II, 1731–1762* (London 1990) p.31.

3 Lt Gen Sir John Keir *A Soldier's Eye View of Our Armies* (London 1919) pp.v, 7.

4 'Irish History is Over Now' *The Times* 24 January 2010.

5 The best study of this troublesome rank is Lt Col W. B. R. Neave-Hill 'The Rank Titles of Brigadier and Brigadier-General' in *Journal of the Society for Army Historical Research* (1969) Vol 47.

6 Marlborough to Godolphin 24 May/4 June 1704 in Snyder *Marlborough-Godolphin* I pp.310–12

7 Nigel Collett *The Butcher of Amritsar: General Reginald Dyer* (London 2005). For the contentious figure of victims see p.263, and for the honorary rank issue pp.408–13.

8 Shephard *Sergeant Major's War* p.74.

9 Ronald Skirth *Reluctant Tommy* (London 2010) pp.90–1.

10 David D. Chandler (ed.) *John Marshall Deane: A Journal of Marlborough's Campaigns …* (London 1984) pp.7–8.

11 Smith *William Cobbett* p.41.

12 Quoted in Philip J. Haythornthwaite *British Infantry of the Napoleonic Wars* (London 1987) p.98.

13 *The Reluctant Tommy* p.209.

14 Shephard *Sergeant Major's War* p.53.

15 Andrew Cormack and Alan Jones (eds) *The Journal of Corporal William Todd 1745–1763* (London 2001) p.136.

16 Holmes *Dusty Warriors* p.333.

17 William St Clair *The Road To St Julien* (Barnsley 2004) pp.186–7.

18 Beevor *British Army* p.244.

19 Richard Holmes *War Walks* (London 1996) p.176 from original text in Staff College Camberley's Arras battlefield tour notes.

20 George Hogan *Oh! To be a Soldier!* (Brancaster, Devon 1992) p.42. Once WO3s had disappeared completely, WO2s resumed the crown badge of rank, leaving the laurel-ringed crown for regimental quartermaster sergeants and some other warrant officers.

21 Captain Owen Rutter *The Song of Tiadatha* (London 1921) p.16. Tiadatha ('Tired Arthur') sent up Longfellow's *Hiawatha*, and was written during its author's service in Salonika.

22 John Jackson *Private 12768: Memoir of a Tommy* (London 2004) pp.50, 78.

23 Beattie *Ordinary Soldier* pp.61–2.

24 George Loy Smith *A Victorian RSM* (Tunbridge Wells 1987) pp.93, 152.

25 Quoted in The Marquess of Anglesey *A History of British Cavalry* 8 vols (1973–1998) II p.383.

26 'Extracts from General Routine Orders issued to the British Armies in France … Part 1 Adjutant General's Branch' 1 January 1917.

27 Jones *Companion* I p.126.

28 The National Archives WO 71/224, edited on Carole Divall's website (caroledivall.co.uk), accessed 28 June 2009.

29 Beattie *Ordinary Soldier* pp.73, 301.

30 Anglesey *Cavalry* II p.367.

31 James Churchill Dunn *The War The Infantry Knew* (London 1987) pp.32, 92, 183, 227, 468, 580.

32 J. M. Bourne *Who's Who in World War One* (London 2001) p.64.

33 'Extracts from General Routine Orders issued to the British Armies in France ... Part II Quartermaster General's Branch' 1 January 1917.

34 *Field Service Pocket Book* 1914 (with amendments to 1916) p.25.

Chapter 5: To Observe and Obey

1 William Bray (ed) *The Diary of John Evelyn Esq FRS* (London 1890) p.400.

2 Quoted in Barney White-Spunner *Horse Guards* (London 2008) p.261.

3 White-Spunner *Horse Guards* p.262.

4 Matthew Clay *A Narrative of the Battles of Quatre Bras and Waterloo, with the Defence of Hougoumont* (Bedford ND) pp.14–15.

5 'Lieutenant Colonel Sir James Macdonell' in Christopher Summerville *Who Was Who at Waterloo* Harlow 2007) pp.252–256. There are several spellings of Sir James's name: Wellington called him 'MacDonald' in his Waterloo dispatch.

6 I am indebted to Dr John Houlding not only for these two examples, but for so much other detail on eighteenth-century officers.

7 Major Charles Jones *The Regimental Companion* 3 Vols (London 1811) I p.xxvii.

8 Field Marshal Lord Wolseley *The Story of a Soldier's Life* 2 Vols (London 1903) pp.199–200.

9 Major H. Daly (ed.) *The Memoirs of Sir Henry Dermot Daly* (London 1905) p.246.

10 Quoted in Lieutenant Colonel W. B. R. Neave-Hill 'Brevet Rank' in *Journal of the Society for Army Historical Research* Vol 48 (1970) p.91.

11 Ibid. p.92.

12 Major J. A. Scouller *The Armies of Queen Anne* (Oxford 1966) p.75.

13 Quoted in Neave-Hill 'Brevet Rank' p.88.

14 Brig Gen James Edmonds *Official History of the War: Military Operations:*

France and Belgium 1914 2 Vols (London) I p.188.

15 Neave-Hill 'Brevet Rank' p.100.

16 I am grateful to my old friend Stephen Wood for early sight of a draft journal article on Pigot.

17 Carver *Out of Step* p.157.

18 Ibid. p.252.

19 Ibid. p.192.

20 Ibid.

21 Ibid. p.227.

22 Army Rumour Service 29 December 2005, accessed 21 January 2009.

Chapter 6: Weekend Warriors

1 Holmes *Dusty Warriors* pp.346–7.

2 Ibid. p.349.

3 Lieutenant Colonel J. K. Dunlop *The Problems and Responsibilities of the Territorial Army* (London 1935).

4 Ian F. W. Beckett *Territorials: A Century of Service* (London 2008) p.3.

5 Roger B. Manning *An Apprenticeship in Arms* (Oxford 2006) p.126.

6 Robert Ward *Animadversions of Warre* ... (London 1639) p.30.

7 'The Vindication of Richard Atkyns' in *Military Memoirs: The Civil War* (London 1967) pp.12, 19.

8 Manning *Apprenticeship* p.302.

9 Beckett *Territorials* p.18.

10 Quoted in Victor A. Hatley *Northamptonshire Militia Lists 1777* (Kettering 1973) p.x.

11 *Manual of Military Law 1914* p.171.

12 Detail from the admirable Worcestershire Regiment (29th/36th of Foot) website.

13 Quoted in Michael Glover *Wellington's Army* (Newton Abbot, Devon 1977) p.33.

14 Peter Dennis *The Territorial Army 1907–1940* (Woodbridge, Suffolk 1987) p.8.

15 Beckett *Territorials* p.8.

16 *The Spectator* 20 July 1711.

17 Howard Pease *The History of the Northumberland Hussars* (London 1924) p.viii.

18 W. B. and G. D. Giles *Yeoman Service* (Tunbridge Wells 1985). The Duke of Westminster wrote the introduction to this collection of yeomanry cartoons.

19 Beckett *Territorials* pp.19–20.

20 Les Carlyon *Gallipoli* (Sydney 2001) p.483.

21 Beckett *Territorials* p.72.

22 *Manual of Military Law 1914* p.208.

23 Beckett *Territorials* pp.122–3.

24 David French *Raising Churchill's Army* (Oxford 2001) p.53.

25 Quoted in Beckett *Territorials* p.124.

26 Statistics from Miles Jebb *The Lord Lieutenants and their Deputies* (Chichester 2007) passim. Jebb concludes that lord lieutenants is indeed the correct plural for these worthies, and I follow his sage advice here.

27 Jebb *Lord Lieutenants* p.150.

28 Beckett *Territorials* p.261.

PART II

Chapter 7: A National Army: 1660–1914

1 French *Churchill's Army* p.274.

2 Quoted in Joachim Stocqueler *A Personal History of the Horse Guards* (London 1873) p.120.

3 *Military History of Ireland* p.6.

4 *The Memoirs of Sir Lowry Cole* (London 1934) p.3.

5 Nigel Nicolson *Alex* (London 1973) p.12.

6 David Fraser *Alanbrooke* (London 1982) p.39.

7 B. H. Liddell Hart (ed.) *The Letters of Private Wheeler 1808–1828* (Adlestrop, Gloucestershire 1951) p.64.

8 Maj H. Daly (ed.) *The Memoirs of General Sir Henry Dermot Daly* (London 1905) p.276.

9 Paul Dukes 'The First Scottish Soldiers in Russia' in Grant A. Simpson (ed.) *The Scottish Soldier Abroad* (Edinburgh 1992) p.49.

10 Childs *Army of Charles II* p.31.

11 Ibid. p.37.

12 Ibid. p.44.

13 Latham *Pepys* p.320.

14 Alington to Lord Arlington (sic) in SP 78/137 f.142.

15 Quoted in White-Spunner *Horse Guards* p.111.

16 John Childs *The British Army of William III* (Manchester 1987) p.16.

17 William Bray (ed.) *The Diary of John Evelyn Esq* (London 1890) p.534.

18 Charles M. Clode *The Military Forces of the Crown* 2 Vols (London 1869) II p.602.

19 James W. Hayes 'The Social and Professional Background of the Officers of the British Army 1714–1763' (Unpublished MA thesis, University of London, 1956) p.61.

20 Alison McBrayne (ed.) *The Letters of Captain John Orrock* (London 2008) p.115.

21 T. A. Heathcote (ed.) *The Indian Mutiny Letters of Colonel H. P. Pearson* (Leeds 2008) pp.116, 119, 122.

22 Dr Thomas Fletcher to William Bagshawe, 7 January 1740 in *Bagshawe* p.35.

23 Samuel Bagshawe to Dr Thomas Fletcher 7 February 1746 in *Bagshawe* p.48.

24 Samuel Bagshawe to Brigadier General Edward Richbell 13 October 1747 in *Bagshawe* p.58.

25 Captain Thomas Levett to Samuel Bagshawe 3 November 1747 in *Bagshawe* p.63.

26 Lieutenant Archibald Grant to Samuel Bagshawe 4 May 1749 p.87.

27 Samuel Bagshawe to Viscount Barrington, 5 May 1758, 5 May 1758 in *Bagshawe* p.185.

28 Viscount Barrington to Samuel Bagshawe, 11 May 1758 in *Bagshawe* p.186.

29 Lieutenant Francis Flood to Samuel Bagshawe, 24 January 1761, in *Bagshawe* pp.232–3.

30 Captain Alexander Joass to Samuel Bagshawe, 25 August 1761, in *Bagshawe* pp.242–3.

31 Lieutenant Francis Flood to Samuel Bagshawe 15 October 1761 in *Bagshawe* p.245.

32 Lieutenant Francis Flood to Samuel Bagshawe 28 February 1762 in *Bagshawe* pp.251–2.

33 Lieutenant Francis Flood to the Earl of Halifax, 21 May 1762, in *Bagshawe* pp.262–3.

34 Barrington to Charles Gould, Judge Advocate General, for onward transmission to the Board of General Officers, 8 February 1766, in *Barrington Papers* pp.297–9.

35 *Orrock* p.123.

36 Quoted in Mark Frederick Odintz 'The British Officer Corps 1754–1783' (Unpublished PhD thesis, University of Michigan, 1988) p.137.

37 *Orrock* pp.55–6.

38 *Pearson* p.148.

39 The Marquess of Anglesey (ed.) *Little Hodge: Being Extracts from the Diaries of Colonel Edward Cooper Hodge* … (London 1971) p.57.

40 *Pearson* p.70.

41 *Orrock* p.85.

42 Quoted in James W. Hayes 'The Social and Professional Background of the Officers of the British Army' (Unpublished MA thesis, London University, 1956) p.42.

43 *Peebles' American War* pp.113, 220.

44 Sir William Howe's order-book, consulted when in the collection of the Joint Services Command and Staff College, now in the British Library.

45 Bryan Perrett *A Hawk at War: The Peninsular War Reminiscences of General Sir Thomas Brotherton* (London 1986) p.28.

46 Stephen Brumwell *The Paths of Glory* (London 2009) p.319.

47 Quoted in Carl G. Slater 'The Problem of Purchase Abolition in the British Army 1856–1862' in The South African Military History Society's *Military History Journal* Vol 4 No 6.

48 The best account of this puzzling period is in T. A. Heathcote *The Military in British India* (Manchester 1995) p.168. Dr Heathcote served for many years as curator of the Sandhurst Collection.

49 Quoted in Harries-Jenkins *Victorian Army* p.137.

50 Capt Gregory Fontenot 'The Modern Major General: Patterns in the Careers of the British Army Major Generals on the Active List at the time of the Sarajevo Assassinations' (Unpublished MA dissertation, University of North Carolina at Chapel Hill, 1980) pp.47–8. This survey deals with the 91 general officers whose educational background could be determined.

51 Quoted in Harries-Jenkins *Victorian Army* p.143.

52 David G. Chandler (ed.) *The Oxford Illustrated History of the British Army* (Oxford 1994) p.193.

53 Franklin L. Ford *Robe and Sword: The Regrouping of the French Aristocracy after Louis XIV* (New York 1965) p.138.

54 Christopher Duffy *The Army of Frederick the Great* (Newton Abbot 1974) p.27.

55 *Barrington Papers* pp.290–2.

56 Odintz 'British Officer Corps' p.182.

57 John Seed 'From "middling sort" to middle class in late eighteenth- and early nineteenth-century England' in M. L. Bush (ed.) *Social Orders and Social Classes in Europe since 1500* (Harlow 1992) p.115.

58 Quoted in Thomas Bartlett and Keith Jeffrey *A Military History of Ireland* (Cambridge 1996) p.7.

59 P. E. Razzell 'Social Origins of Officers in the Indian and British Home Army' *British Journal of Sociology* XIV Sept 1963 pp.248–60.

60 Hansard 3rd Series Vol 136 Col 1362, 8 Feb 1855.

61 E. B. de Fonblanque *Treatise on the Administration and Organisation of the British Army* (London 1958) pp.236–7.

62 My analysis of the officers of the 32nd Foot and of the 1858 Probate Index relies on Donald Breeze Mendham Huffer 'The Infantry Officers of the Line of the British Army 1815–1868' (Unpublished PhD thesis, University of Birmingham, 1995).

63 Gwyn Harries-Jenkins *The Victorian Army in Society* (London 1977) p.27.

64 Wolseley to Louisa Wolseley 7 February 1874 in *Wolseley and Ashanti* p.391.

65 *Wolseley and Ashanti* pp.39, 322.

66 Margaret R. Hunt *The Middling Sort: Commerce, Gender and the Family in England 1680–1780* (Berkeley and Los Angeles 1996) pp.51–2.

67 Hayes 'Social and Professional Background' p.80.

68 Houlding *Fit for Service* p.105.

69 Hayes 'Social and Professional Background' p.66.

70 Mark Urban *Fusiliers: Eight Years with the Redcoats in North America* (London 2007) pp.133, 137.

71 Major General Sir John Adye *Soldiers and Others I have Known* (London 1925) p.15.

72 Houlding *Fit for Service* p.105.

73 Hayes 'Social and Professional Background' p.101.

74 Quoted in Trevor Royle *Death before Dishonour: The True Story of Fighting Mac* (Edinburgh 1992) p.65.

75 Ibid. p.103.

76 Ibid. pp.124–6; *Manual of Military Law 1914* p.395.

77 Ibid. pp.160, 162.

78 His biographer David Rooney argues, in *Mad Mike: A Life of Brigadier Michael Calvert* (Barnsley 1997), that he was convicted by false witness.

79 Quoted in Edward Spiers *The Army and Society 1815–1914* (London 1980) p.5.

80 *Private to Field Marshal* pp.29–30.

81 Quoted in Anglesey *British Cavalry* III p.86.

82 Quoted in Anglesey *British Cavalry* IV p.473.

83 *Pearson Letters* pp.123, 131.

84 Christopher Hibbert (ed.) *The Recollections of Rifleman Harris* (London 1985) pp.67–8.

85 Quoted in Huffer 'Infantry Officers' pp.129–30.

86 *Pearson Letters* p.77.

87 W. E. Cairns *Social Life in the British Army* (London 1900) pp.xvi, 14.

88 *Private to Field Marshal* p.78.

89 Ibid. pp.36, 41.

90 Quoted in Harries-Jenkins *Victorian Army* p.98.

91 Cairns *Social Life* p.36.

92 Quoted in Anglesey *British Cavalry* p.86.

93 Mole pp.354–5.

94 Quoted in Anglesey *British Cavalry* p.86.

95 F. H. Maitland *Hussar of the Line* (London 1951) p.66.

96 Finn, Henry (Harry) (1852–1924) in *Australian Dictionary of Biography – Online Edition*.

Chapter 8: Temporary Gentlemen: *1914–45*

1 *Private to Field Marshal* p.129.

2 *Old Wufrunians Died in World War One,* accessed 20 March 2010.

3 'Herbert Victor Lee 1887–1916' privately printed booklet 2001.

4 John Oakes and Martin Parsons *Old School Ties: Educating for Empire and War* (Peterborough 2001) pp.196–7.

5 Martin and Mary Middlebrook *The Somme Battlefields* (London 1991) p.185.

6 VC Citation in *London Gazette* 18 November 1915.

7 John Jackson *Private 12768: Memoir of a Tommy* (Stroud 2004) p.48.

8 Bernard Lewis *Swansea Pals* (Barnsley 2004) pp.32–42.

9 K. W. Mitchinson and I. McInnes *Cotton Town Comrades* (London 1993) pp.39–40.

10 Second Lieutenant James Mackie to his parents in *Answering the Call* (Eggleston, Durham 1999) p.7.

11 Herbert Buckmaster *Buck's Book* (London ND) pp.25, 117–8, 120, 122, 183.

12 Cecil M. Slack (ed.) *Grandfather's Adventures in the Great War* (Ilfracombe 1977) p.13.

13 Robert Bridgeman *Memoirs* (privately printed 2007) p.31.

14 Tonie and Valmai Holt *Poets of the Great War* (Barnsley 1999) p.132.

15 John Blacker (ed.) *Have You Forgotten Yet? The War Memoirs of C. P. Blacker* (Barnsley 2000) pp.36–7.

16 Cameron Stewart (ed.) *A Very Unimportant Officer: Life and Death on the Somme and at Passchendaele* (London 2008) pp.23, 24, 25–6.

17 *Very Unimportant Officer* p.169.

18 Capt J. C. Dunn *The War the Infantry Knew 1914–1919* (London 1987) p.109.

19 Quoted in Charles Messenger *Call to Arms* (London 2005) p.321.

20 Bruce Rossor (ed.) *A Sergeant Major's War* (Ramsbury 1987) pp.136, 138, 141.

21 John Lucy *There's a Devil in the Drum* (London 2000) pp.352–4.

22 George Ashurst *My Bit* (Ramsbury 1987) pp.137, 139–40.

23 A. Duff Cooper *Old Men Forget* (London 1953) pp.63–4, 66, 69.

24 *Statistics of the Military Effort of the British Empire During the Great War 1914–1920* (London 1922) p.235.

25 *Military Effort* p.707.

26 Bridgeman *Memoirs* p.33.

27 Anne Nason (ed.) *For Love and Courage* (London 2008) pp.106–7.

28 Hubert Essame *The Battle for Europe 1918* (London 1972) pp.12–13, 107–8, 111, 179–81.

29 Sidney Rogerson *Twelve Days* (London 2006) pp.22–3.

30 Rogerson *Twelve Days* pp.60–1.

31 *Love and Courage* pp.349, 354–5.

32 Desmond Young *All the Best Years* (New York 1961) p.62.

33 Alan Thomas *A Life Apart* (London 1968) p.67.

34 Quoted in Gary Sheffield *Leadership in the Trenches* (London 2000) p.103.

35 Ibid. p.105.

36 Ibid. p.109.

37 *The War the Infantry Knew* p.309.

38 Keir *Soldier's Eye-View* pp.15, 18, 25, 131.

39 Charles Farrell *Reflections 1939–1945* (London 2000) pp.13–14.

40 Captain J. R. Kennedy *This, Our Army* (London 1935) pp.38, 87, 110, 139.

41 Bridgeman *Memoirs* p.119.

42 Lt R. D. Foster 'Promotion by Merit in the Army' *Journal of the Royal United Services Institute* No 25 (1925) p.685.

43 Mays *Fall Out The Officers* pp.51, 92.

44 Quoted in French *Churchill's Army* p.73.

45 J. D. A. Stainton *Memoirs* (privately printed 1988) pp.98–9.

46 Robin Schlaefli *Emergency Sahib* (London 1992) pp.14–15.

47 Norman Craig *The Broken Plume: A Platoon Commander's Story* (London 1982) pp.20, 4–5.

48 Kersh *Clean, Bright* p.59.

49 French *Churchill's Army* pp.73–4.

50 Kersh *Clean, Bright* p.76.

51 Geoffrey Picot *Accidental Warrior* (London 1993) p.23.

52 Stainton *Memoirs* p.100.

53 Schlaefli *Emergency Sahib* p.16.

54 Craig *Broken Plume* pp.26–7.

55 Quoted in French *Churchill's Army* p.75.

56 Picot *Accidental Warrior* pp.25, 307.

57 Picot *Accidental Warrior* p.24.

58 Stuart Hills *By Tank into Normandy* (London 2002) pp.44, 48, 54–5, 85, 242.

59 French *Churchill's Army* pp.12–13.

60 Picot *Accidental Warrior* p.11.

61 Quoted in Sidney Jary 'Reflections on the Leader and the Led' *Journal of the Royal Army Medical Corps* No 156 (2000) p.55.

62 Bridgeman *Memoirs* p.299.

63 French *Churchill's Army* p.80.

64 Sidney Jary *Eighteen Platoon* (Carshalton Beeches 1987) p.16.

65 'Corrected figures' in Brig. Gen. Sir James E. Edmonds *History of the Great War … Military Operations, France and Belgium 1916,* Vol I (London 1932) p.483. It must be acknowledged that this sort of statistical analysis is fraught with peril.

66 Farrell *Reflections* pp.152, 16–17.

67 Picot *Accidental Warrior* p.263.

Chapter 9: Sandhurst: Serve to Lead

1 R. G. L. von Zugbach *Power and Prestige in the British Army* (Aldershot 1988) p.83.

2 Beevor *British Army* p.68.

3 General Sir Mike Jackson *Soldier* (London 2007) pp.9, 15.

4 Zugbach *Power and Prestige* pp.62–3.

5 Beevor *British Army* pp.68–9.

6 Reggie von Zugbach and Mohammed Ishaq *Public Schools and Officer Recruitment in the Late 20th Century* (Paisley 1999).

7 Jackson *Soldier* p.43.

8 Zugbach *Power and Prestige* p.139.

9 Zugbach and Ishaq *Public Schools* pp.13–14.

Chapter 10: Church Militant

1 Quoted in Keith Roberts *Cromwell's War Machine: The New Model Army 1645–1660* (Barnsley 2005) p.121.

2 Firth *Cromwell's Army* p.325.

3 Ibid. p.332.

4 Quoted in Michael Snape *The Royal Army Chaplains' Department: Clergy Under Fire* (Woodbridge, Suffolk 2008) p.15.

5 Edward Ward *Mars Stript of his Armour: or the Army displayed in all its True Colours* (London 1708) p.21.

6 Stephen Brumwell *Redcoats: The British Soldier in North America* (Cambridge 2002) p.70. Cuthbertson's *A System for the Compleat Interior Management and Oeconomy of a Battalion of Infantry* (Dublin 1768, reprinted with corrections Bristol 1776) was one of the best privately produced manuals. Its author had served as adjutant in the 5th Foot in 1755–68, and he had studied the practice of several well-conducted battalions, notably the 20th Foot under James Wolfe. See Houlding *Fit for Service* pp.216–17.

7 Ward *Mars Stript* pp.60, 63.

8 Roger Hudson (ed.) *Memoirs of a Georgian Rake: William Hickey* (London 1995) pp.396–7.

9 The Marquess of Anglesey (ed.) *Sergeant Pearman's Memoirs, being chiefly, his account of service with the Third (King's Own) Light Dragoons* (London 1968) p.65.

10 Robert Graves *Goodbye to All That* (London 1929) pp.242–3. The story seems apocryphal, and reflects Graves' dislike of Anglican clergy and his admiration for Roman Catholics – 'we never heard of one who failed to do all that was expected of him and more.'

11 Personal communication from a senior chaplain 26 January 2011.

12 Todd *Journal* pp.213–14, 317.

13 Snape *Royal Army Chaplains' Department* p.25.

14 Quoted in Snape *Royal Army Chaplains' Department* pp.17, 23. Bedford refused the request, saying that every chaplain in Ireland should either do duty himself or have a properly approved deputy.

15 Ibid. p.23.

16 'The Letters of Samuel Noyes, Chaplain of the Royal Scots 1703–4' in *Journal of the Society for Army Historical Research* No 37 1959.

17 Quoted in Michael Snape *The Redcoat and Religion* (Abingdon 2005) p.25.

18 Ibid. pp.36, 19.

19 Lieutenant Colonel John Gurwood (ed.) *Selections from the General Orders and Dispatches of Field Marshal The Duke of Wellington* (London 1841) pp.429–30.

20 Quoted in Snape *Royal Army Chaplains' Department* pp.42–3.

21 Ibid. p.53.

22 George Bell *Soldier's Glory: Rough Notes of an Old Soldier* (London 1956) p.99.

23 Wheeler *Letters* pp.153, 92–3.

24 George Gleig *The Subaltern* (London 1909) p.130. Gleig's views must be taken with caution, for he had a particular dislike of Samuel Briscall, with whom he vied for Wellington's favour.

25 Snape *Royal Army Chaplains' Department* p.51.

26 Snape *Redcoat and Religion* p.191.

27 Henderson *Highland Soldier* p.217.

28 A. W. Kinglake *The Invasion of the Crimea* 8 Vols (London 1863–87) II p.427.

29 Edward Cotton *A Voice From Waterloo* (London 1849) pp.106–7.

30 Bancroft *Recruit to Staff Sergeant* pp.29, 15.

31 Fraser *Sixty Years* p.133.

32 Quoted in Philip Guedalla *The Duke* (London 1997) p.163.

33 Quoted in Snape *Redcoat and Religion* p.161.

34 Ibid. p.168.

35 Quoted in Snape *Royal Army Chaplains' Department* p.80.

36 Ibid. p.131.

37 Wyndham *The Queen's Service* pp.66–7.

38 Wyndham *Soldiers of the Queen* p.185.

39 Maitland *Hussar of the Line* p.35.

40 Wyndham *Soldiers of the Queen* p.57.

41 Maitland *Hussar of the Line* pp.65, 67.

42 Robertson *Private to Field-Marshal* p.9.

43 Richards *Old Soldiers* p.14.

44 Wyndham *The Queen's Service* p.68.

45 Evelyn Wood *From Midshipman to Field Marshal* 2 Vols (London 1906) II 265.

46 William Forbes-Mitchell *Reminiscences of the Great Mutiny* (London 1894) pp.256–7.

47 Two chaplain generals were indeed bishops, but had attained this rank before their military preferment.

48 Snape *Royal Army Chaplains' Department* p.160.

49 John Bickersteth (ed.) *The Bickersteth Diaries* (London 1995) p.81.

50 Quoted in Alan Wilkinson *The Church of England and the First World War* (London 1986) p.127.

51 Stephen Graham *A Private in the Guards* (London 1919) pp.253–6.

52 Alan Hanbury-Sparrow *The Land-Locked Lake* (London 1932) p.160.

53 Guy Chapman *A Passionate Prodigality* (London 1985) p.117.

54 Snape *Royal Army Chaplains' Department* pp.11–12.

55 W. M. Nicholson *Behind the Lines* (London 1939) p.156.

56 Quoted in Mary P. Wilkinson *The Unknown Warrior: Unknown and Yet Well Known* (London 2000) p.64.

57 Citation for the MC 21 December 1944 in National Archives WO 373/9.

58 Quote in Snape *Royal Army Chaplains' Department* p.302.

59 Leslie Skinner *The Man Who Worked on Sundays* (Epsom, Surrey 1996) pp.26, 44, 48–9.

60 Snape *Royal Army Chaplains' Department* p.310.

61 Ibid. p.329.

62 Ibid.

63 Ibid. p.354.

64 'Man of God in the Line of Fire' *Sunday Times* 1 April 2007.

65 Stephen Armstrong 'The Good Fight' *The Guardian* 15 October 205.

66 *Army Rumour Service*, accessed 15 March 2011.

PART III

Chapter 11: Soldier Boys

1 *Manual of Military Law 1914* p.158.
2 Ibid.
3 John Loesberg *Folk Songs and Ballads Popular in Ireland* (Cork 1982) III p.75.
4 Andrew Cormack and Alan Jones (eds) *The Journal of Corporal William Todd 1745–1762* (Stroud, Gloucestershire 2001) pp.6–7.
5 'Recruiting Instructions for the 93rd Regiment of Foot' in *Bagshawe* pp.210–12.
6 Harris *Recollections* p.52.
7 Quoted in Matthew H. Spring *With Zeal and Bayonets Only* (Norman, Oklahoma 2008) p.30.
8 J. M. Craster (ed.) *Fifteen Rounds a Minute: The Grenadiers at War, August to December 1914* (London 1976) p.141.
9 Ray Westlake *Kitchener's Army* (Staplehurst 1998) p.137.
10 Bennett Cuthbertson *Scheme for the Interior Economy of a Battalion of Infantry* (Bristol 1776) pp.55–6.
11 Quoted in Philip J. Haythornthwaite *The Armies of Wellington* (London 1988) p.51.
12 Haythornthwaite *Armies* p.50.
13 Anglesey *History of the British Cavalry* III p.46.
14 Quoted in Houlding *Fit for Service* p.134.
15 Anglesey *History of the British Cavalry* III p.49.
16 My interest in the Sweeneys was sparked by Diana Henderson *Highland Soldier: A Social History of the Highland Regiments 1820–1920* (Edinburgh 1999) and extended into the internet's Glasgow Guide Boards.
17 Roberts *Forty-One Years in India* (London 1897) p.181.
18 A. W. Cockerell *Sons of the Brave* (London 1984) p.95

19 Ibid. p.96.
20 Ibid. p.128.
21 Ibid. p.109.
22 Ibid. p.73.
23 N. W. Bancroft *From Recruit to Staff Sergeant* (London 1979) p.4. Bancroft enlisted into the Bengal Artillery, then in the East India Company's employment, but its terms of service were not unlike those of the British army.
24 George Coppard *With a Machine-Gun to Cambrai* (London 1969) pp.6, 64–5.
25 George Adams papers, Liddell Collection, Brotherton Library, University of Leeds. Jack Badrick is almost certainly Private George Henry Badrick, killed in action on 15 September 1915 and buried in Cambrin Churchyard Extension.
26 Dunn *The War the Infantry Knew* p.579.
27 *Manual of Military Law 1914* p.18. The staff officer who used my copy of this book has underlined the 'Evidence of intention not to return' paragraph.
28 David Lister *Die Hard Aby! Abraham Bevistein – The Boy Soldier Shot to Encourage the Others* (Barnsley 2005) passim.
29 The question of under-age soldiers executed during the war is examined in Ch. 24 'Young Offenders' of Cathryn Corns and John Hughes-Wilson *Blindfold and Alone*. For further thoughts, some measured and others not, see 'Britain's Boy Soldiers' on the internet's Great War Forum.
30 Charles Kirke 'An Upstream Journey for the Military Recruit?' in Teri McConville and Richard Holmes (eds) *Defence Management in Uncertain Times* (London 2003) p.154.
31 Ashurst *My Bit* pp.19–20, 24–6.
32 Quoted in Holmes *Dusty Warriors* p.331.

Chapter 12: The King's Shilling

1 Lieutenant Colonel Edward Windus to Colonel Samuel Bagshawe 26 March 1760 in *Bagshawe* pp.219–20.

2 Lieutenant Charles Crawford to Colonel Samuel Bagshawe 31 March 1760 in *Bagshawe* p.221.

3 Haythornthwaite *Armies* p.48.

4 'Recruiting Instructions' in *Bagshawe* p.212.

5 Haythornthwaite *Armies* pp.46–7.

6 *Manual of Military Law 1914* p.190.

7 Anglesey *History of the British Cavalry* III p.47.

8 Todd pp.111–13.

9 Roy Palmer (ed.) *The Rambling Soldier* (London 1977) p.27.

10 *The Life and Diary of Lieut Col J Blackadder of the Cameronian Regiment* … (London 1824) p.236.

11 Quoted in Holmes *Riding the Retreat* pp.32–3.

12 Wyndham *Soldiers of the Queen* pp.17–20.

13 Quoted in Scott Hughes Myerly *British Military Spectacle* (Harvard 1996) p.229.

14 Anglesey *History of the British Cavalry* III p.49.

15 David French *Military Identities* (Oxford 2005) p.60.

16 William Surtees *Twenty-Five Years in the Rifle Brigade* (London 1973) p.41.

17 Quoted in French *Military Identities* p.50.

18 Anglesey *History of the British Cavalry* IV p.484.

19 Quoted in Myerly *British Military Spectacle* p.59.

20 Christopher Hibbert (ed.) *The Recollections of Rifleman Harris* (London 1985) p.109.

21 Antony Brett-James (ed.) *Military Memoirs:* Edward Costello *The Peninsular and Waterloo Campaigns* (London 1967) p.24

22 Quoted in Haythornthwaite *Armies* p.47.

23 Quoted in *The United Service Magazine*, Third Part for 1846 p.560.

24 Michael Crumplin *Guthrie's War: A Surgeon of the Peninsula and Waterloo* (Barnsley 2010) pp.157–8.

25 Lieutenant Colonel Sir Arthur Leetham 'Old Recruiting Posters' *Journal of the Society for Army Historical Research I* 1921 p.120. Leetham dates the poster between 1803 and 1812.

26 J. Paine 'Recruiting Poster: 73rd Regiment, 1813' in *Journal of the Society for Army Historical Research* XXXI 1953 p.184 and Leetham 'Recruiting Posters' p.119.

27 Lucy *Devil in the Drum*.

28 John Miller *Former Soldier Seeks Employment* (London 1989) pp.15, 20.

29 Quoted in French *Military Identities* p.39.

30 Christopher Hibbert (ed.) *A Soldier of the Seventy-First* (London 1976) p.1.

31 Walter Mitton *The Boer War: A Bombardier's Memoirs* (Knebworth, Hertforshire 1996)

32 Harris *Recollections* p.6.

33 Haythornthwaite *Armies* p.51.

34 *Memoirs of a Sergeant late in the Forty-Third Light Infantry Regiment* (London 1839) p.13.

35 Timothy Gowing *A Voice From the Ranks* (London 1954) p.6.

36 Alexander Somerville *The Autobiography of a Working Man* (London 1967) p.125.

37 Anglesey *British Cavalry* I p.115.

Chapter 13: Pressed into Service

1 Information from Andrew Cormack's ongoing doctoral research into British army pensioners in the 18th century.

2 Todd *Journal* pp.38–9.

3 George Larpent (ed.) *The Private Journal of Judge-Advocate Larpent, attached to the head-quarters of Lord Wellington* … (London 1854) p.244.

4 Table in Roger Norman Buckley *The British Army in the West Indies* (Gainesville 1998) pp.102–3.

5 Houlding *Fit For Service* p.118.

6 John Selby (ed.) *Military Memoirs: Thomas Morris* (London 1967) p.105.

7 Houlding *Fit for Service* p.118.

8 Arthur N. Gilbert 'An Analysis of Some Eighteenth Century Army Recruiting Records' in *Journal of the Society for Army Historical Research* Spring 1976 p.47.

9 Haythornthwaite *Armies* p.49.

10 Roger Norman Buckley (ed.) *The Napoleonic War Journal of Captain Thomas Henry Browne 1806–1816* (London 1987) pp.23–4.

11 B. H. Liddell Hart (ed.) *The Letters of Private Wheeler* (London 1951) p.196.

12 Gowing *Voice from the Ranks* p.12.

13 Robertson *Private to Field Marshal* p.28.

14 Con Costello *A Most Delightful Station: The British Army and the Curragh of Kildare* (Cork 1999) p.261.

15 Robertson *Private to Field Marshal* p.29.

16 Lt Col W. Gordon-Alexander *Recollections of a Highland Subaltern* (London 1898) p.6.

17 Arthur Swinson and Donald Scott (eds) *The Memoirs of Private Waterfield* (London 1968) p.xxiii.

18 'British Cavalry Officer Trussed up Naked in Drunken Prank' published 25 June 2009 on http://www.telegraph.co.uk/news/uknews

19 'Sent Home in Shame, the British Commandos who Stripped Naked for a Crass Stunt in a Foreign Bar' published in Daily Mail Online 4 March 2008.

Chapter 14: All Pals Together

1 Quoted in Myerly *Military Spectacle* p.64.

2 Quoted in Anglesey *British Cavalry* I pp.263–4.

3 General Sir James Marshall-Cornwall *Wars and Rumours of War* (London 1984) pp.1–2.

4 http:///www.jwmilne.freeservers.com/speech.htm accessed 29 May 2010.

5 Quoted in Peter Simkins *Kitchener's Army* (Manchester 1988) p.92.

6 Andrew Riddoch and John Kemp *When the Whistle Blows: The Story of the Footballers' Battalion in the Great War* (Sparkford, Somerset 2008) pp.211, 155–6.

7 Harry Ogle *The Fateful Battle Line* (London 1993) p.10.

8 John Baynes and Hugh Maclean *A Tale of Two Captains* (Edinburgh 1990) p.65.

9 Quoted in Charles Messenger *Call to Arms: The British Army 1914–18* (London 2005) pp.96–7.

10 Mitchinson and Innes *Cotton-Town Comrades* p.45.

11 Adrian Gregory *The Last Great War: British Society and the First World War* (Cambridge 2008) pp.278–9.

12 Ibid. p.280.

13 Papers of Captain John Norwood VC, Department of Documents, Imperial War Museum.

14 C. E. Montgue *Disenchantment* (London 1922) pp.33, 59.

15 Unpublished typescript memoir 'K. J. Fenton late Lance Corporal 1/7th Middlesex Regiment' private collection.

16 Quoted in Messenger *Call to Arms* pp.167–8.

17 Brig Gen J. E. Edmonds *History of the Great War Based on Official Documents … Military Operations, France and Belgium 1914* (London 1922) I pp.442–3.

18 Gregory *Last Great War* p.296.

Chapter 15: Foreign Friends

1 Childs *Army of Charles II* p.24.

2 Peebles *American War* pp.71, 311.

3 Joseph P. Tustin (ed.) *Diary of the American War: A Hessian Journal* (New Haven, Conn. 1979).

4 Bruce E. Burgoyne (transl. and ed.) *A Hessian Diary of the American*

Revolution (Norman, Okla. 1990) p.209.

5 Christopher Duffy *The Army of Frederick the Great* (Newton Abbot 1974) p.74.

6 Lt Gen Sir Christopher Wallace *The King's Royal Rifle Corps ... the 60th Rifles: A Brief History 1755 to 1965* (Winchester 2005).

7 Matthew Glozier *The Huguenot Soldiers of William of Orange and the Glorious Revolution of 1688* (Brighton 2002) p.131.

8 Stephen Wood 'A Huguenot Regiment' *Journal of the Society for Army Historical Research* 67 1989 pp.116–7.

9 Glozier *Huguenot Soldiers* p.137.

10 Ibid. p.148.

11 The most accessible studies of émigré units are René Chartrand and Patrice Courcelle *Émigré and Foreign Troops in British Service* (1) *1793–1802* (Wellingborough, Northamptonshire 1999), and (2) *1803–15* (Wellingborough, Northamptonshire 2000).

12 Alistair Nichols *Wellington's Mongrel Regiment: A History of the Chasseurs Britanniques Regiment 1801–1814* (Staplehurst, Kent 2005) p.76.

13 Ian Fletcher (ed.) *In the Service of the King: The Letters of William Thornton Keep* (Staplehurst, Kent 1997) p.163.

14 Nichols *Mongrel Regiment* p.78.

15 Ibid. p.176.

16 Haythornthwaite *Armies* p.146.

17 John H. Gill 'Vermin, Scorpions and Mosquitoes: The Rheinbund in the Peninsula' in Ian Fletcher (ed.) *The Peninsular War: Aspects of the Struggle in the Iberian Peninsula* (Staplehust, Kent 1998).

18 Robert Burnham, 'Filling the Ranks' in Rory Muir et al. *Inside Wellington's Peninsular Army* (Barnsley 2006), pp.211–12.

19 G. C. Moore Smith *The Autobiography of Sir Harry Smith* (London 1910) p.185.

20 Edward Costello pp.125–6, p.149.

21 Ibid. pp.47.

22 Mercer *Journal of the Waterloo Campaign* (1815), Vol 1. p.320.

23 Edward Costello p.108.

24 George Robert Gleig *The Subaltern: A Chronicle of the Peninsular War* (Edinburgh 1877) p.277.

25 Mercer *Journal* p.14.

26 A good deal of rubbish is written about the losses suffered by 2nd Light Battalion KGL. Forty-two of the defenders did indeed escape from the farmhouse with Baring, but others had left earlier in search of ammunition: my figure is from Baring's own return. For a helpful analysis see Gareth Glover *Letters from the Battle of Waterloo* (London 2004) p.251, and Baring's account ibid. pp.242–9.

27 Christopher Hibbert (ed.) *The Wheatley Diary: A Journal and Sketch-Book Kept during the Peninsular War and the Waterloo Campaign* (London 1964) pp. 4, 7, 8–9, 70.

28 Peter Stanley *White Mutiny* (New York 1998) p.115.

29 Quoted in Niall Barr *Pendulum of War: The Three Battles of El Alamein* (London 2005) p.101.

30 Mitchinson and McInnes *Cotton Town Comrades* p.38.

31 See John Starling and Ivor Lee *No Labour, No Battle* (Stroud, Gloucestershire 2009) for a comprehensive and long overdue history of labour in the First World War.

32 Johnson Beharry *Barefoot Soldier* (London 2006) pp.165, 169, 174.

Chapter 16: Women Soldiers

1 Marjorie Grindle née Mullins typescript memoir Department of Documents, Imperial War Museum 06/128/1.

2 Ibid.

3 Ibid.

4 The Hon Dorothy Pickford, letters in the Department of Documents, Imperial War Museum.

5 Chief Controller Dame Helen Gwynn-Vaughan *Service with the Army* (London 1952) p.50.

6 Olive Taylor, handwritten memoirs, Department of Documents, Imperial War Museum 83/17/1.

7 P. Dalgliesh, typescript account in Department of Documents, Imperial War Museum, 93/30/1.

8 Quoted in Gerald J. de Groot 'Whose Finger on the Trigger? Mixed Anti-Aircraft Batteries and the Female Combat Taboo' in *War in History* 1997 (4) p.434.

9 Quoted www.thegarrison.org/uk/ats_section, accessed 25 March 2011.

10 Marjorie Inkster *Bow and Arrow War* (Studley, Warwickshire 2005) pp.19, 31, 38.

11 ATS Remembered website, accessed 25 March 2011.

12 Ibid.

13 Army Rumour Service website accessed 26 March 2011.

14 *The Values and Standards of the Army* January 2008, paras. 22 and 32.

PART IV

Chapter 17: The Regimental Line

1 Peter Drake *Amiable Renegade: The Memoirs of Captain Peter Drake* (Stanford, Calif. 1960) p.51.

2 *Letters of Private Wheeler* p.22.

3 Hugo White *One and All: A History of the Duke of Cornwall's Light Infantry* (Padstow, Cornwall 2006) p.91.

4 David Kenyon 'British Cavalry on the Western Front 1916–18' (Unpublished PhD thesis, Cranfield University, 2007) p.294.

5 Quoted in Anglesey *British Cavalry* V p.340.

6 Quoted in Allan Mallinson *The Light Dragoons* (Barnsley, South Yorkshire 1993) pp.211–12.

7 Quoted in Spring *Zeal and Bayonets* p.112.

8 Ibid. p.113.

9 Quoted in French *Military Identities* p.13.

10 Rudyard Kipling 'Back to the Army Again' in *Barrack Room Ballads* (Second Series) (London 1896).

11 Peter Downham (ed.) *Diary of an Old Contemptible: From Mons to Baghdad* (Barnsley, South Yorkshire 2004) p.1.

12 Quoted in French *Military Identities* p.21.

13 Quoted in Richard Holmes *Shots From the Front* (London 2008) p.381 from a typescript memoir in the Royal Hampshire Regiment Museum, Winchester.

14 Quoted in Henderson *Highland Soldier* p.230.

15 Ibid.

16 French *Military Identities* p.45.

17 Ponsonby *Recollections of Three Reigns*.

18 Dunn *The War the Infantry Knew* p.393.

19 Starling and Lee *No Labour, No Battle* p.323. At this stage the Green Howards was formally known as Alexandra Princess of Wales's Own (Yorkshire Regiment).

20 F. J. Hodges *Men of 18 in 1918* (Ilfracombe 1988) p.17.

21 Shephard *Sergeant Major's War* p.69.

22 Ibid. p.38.

23 Richard Holmes *Firing Line* (London 1995) p.299.

24 Shephard *Sergeant Major's War* p.124.

25 Corns and Hughes-Wilson *Blindfold and Alone* pp.199–200.

26 Quoted in French *Military Identities* p.279.

27 Ibid. p.280.

28 Quoted in Brig B. B. Kennett and Col J. A. Tatham *Craftsmen of the Army: The Story of the Royal Electrical and Mechanical Engineers* (London 1970) p.150.

29 Quoted in French *Churchill's Army* pp.71–2.

30 *Peter White With the Jocks* (Thrupp, Gloucestershire 2001) pp.170, 303, 333.

31 Picot *Accidental Warrior* pp.282, 263.

32 Fergusson *The Trumpet in the Hall* p.24.

33 French *Military Identities* pp.280–1.

34 David Williams *The Black Cats at War: The Story of the 56th (London) Division TA 1939–1945* (London 1995) p.73.

35 Jim Bellows *When in Doubt, Brew Up* (Bradford on Avon, Wiltshire 2002).

36 Bridgeman *Memoirs* pp.210–11.

37 Fergusson *The Trumpet in the Hall* pp.11, 18, 22.

38 Field Marshal Sir William Slim *Courage and Other Broadcasts* (London 1957) pp.85–6.

39 John Masters *Bugles and a Tiger* (London 1956) p.121.

40 Lord Moran *The Anatomy of Courage* (London 2007) p.166.

41 F. M. Richardson *Fighting Spirit: a Study of Psychological Factors in War* (London 1978) p.21.

42 Martin Lindsay *So Few Got Through* (London 1946).

43 Wheeler p.28.

44 Schlaefli *Emergency Sahib* pp.17–19.

45 Sheffield *Leadership in the Trenches* p.161.

46 Ibid. p.162.

47 Sidney Rogerson *Twelve Days on the Somme* (London 2006) p.22.

48 Ibid. pp.113–14.

49 Sheffield *Leadership in the Trenches* p.185.

50 Paul Addison and Angus Calder (eds) *Time to Kill: The Soldier's Experience of War in the West 1939–1945* (London 1997) p.84.

51 White *With the Jocks* p.183.

52 John Hill *China Dragons: A Rifle Company at War, Burma, 1944–45* (London 1991) pp.22–23.

53 Ibid. pp.137, 165.

54 Quoted in French *Military Identities* p.282.

55 Raleigh Trevelyan *The Fortress* (London 1979) pp.18, 46, 202.

56 Craig *Broken Plume* p.149.

Chapter 18: Imponderable Entities

1 Trevelyan *Fortress* p.46.

2 Charles Carrington *Soldier from the Wars Returning* (London 1965) p.98.

3 Montague *Disenchantment* p.40.

4 Farley Mowatt *And No Birds Sang* (Toronto 1979) pp.109–10.

5 Quoted in Spring *Zeal and Bayonets* pp.110–11.

6 Bryant *Jackets of Green* pp.24–5.

7 *Bagshawe* pp.226, 230, 231.

8 Sir James Edmonds *History of the Great War … Military Operations, France and Belgium 1916* Vol I p.473.

9 Ian Fletcher *Bloody Albuera* (Ramsbury 2000) pp.99–100.

10 J. M. Brereton *A History of the Royal Regiment of Wales (24th/41st Foot)* (Cardiff 1989) p.122.

11 Bernard Livermore *Long 'Un: A Damn Bad Soldier* (Batley, W.Yorks 1974) p.97.

12 Anthony Farrar-Hockley *The Edge of the Sword* (London 1954) pp.37, 52.

13 Craig *Broken Plume* p.184.

14 Stewart *Unimportant Officer* pp.150–1.

15 Alan Hanbury-Sparrow *The Land-Locked Lake* (London 1932).

16 Bridgeman *Memoirs* pp.23–4.

17 Maitland *Hussar of the Line* p.22.

18 Mays *Fall Out the Officers* pp.49, 51, 92.

19 Bruce Shand *Previous Engagements* (Wilton, Wiltshire 1990) pp.13–22, 103.

20 Ibid. pp.89, 141, 143, 163.

21 Questionnaire compiled during research for my *Firing Line* (London 1985). US Edition as *Acts of War* (New York 1986).

22 Questionnaire for *Firing Line*.

Chapter 19: The Regiments Depart

1 Fergusson *Trumpet in the Hall* p.243.

2 Ibid. p.194.

3 Ibid. p.245.

4 There were particular complexities in the Fusiliers' amalgamation. The

Royal Welch Fusiliers were part of the Welsh Brigade, and the Royal Highland Fusiliers were (controversially) part of the Lowland Brigade: neither was involved in this amalgamation. The Fusilier Brigade, which was to constitute the Royal Regiment of Fusiliers, consisted of the three traditional English fusilier regiments (the Royal Northumberland Fusiliers, the Royal Fusiliers, and the Lancashire Fusiliers) together with the Royal Warwickshire Fusiliers, which had been the Royal Warwickshire Regiment till 1963 when it had been retitled to join the Fusilier Brigade.

5 Lieutenant Colonel J. P. Riley *Soldiers of the Queen: A History of the Queen's Regiment 1966–1962* (Chippenham 1993) pp.667–8. Lieutenant Colonel Riley, disgusted by his regiment's treatment, declined to join the amalgamated PWRR but transferred to the Royal Welch Fusiliers. He won a DSO commanding its 1st Battalion in the Balkans and retired as a lieutenant general in 2009.

6 The Light Division disappeared in 2007 when its component regiments, the Light Infantry and the Royal Green Jackets, amalgamated to form the Rifles.

7 Maj Gen A. S. H. Irwin to Brig E. R. Holmes 3 July 1999. The letter covered a helpful pamphlet, 'Notes for Colonels and Commandants of Regiments, Divisions of Infantry and Corps'.

8 In the cavalry, in contrast, Regimental Headquarters runs the fighting part of the regiment, with the commanding officer in charge. The cavalry equivalent of the infantry's Regimental Headquarters is Home Headquarters.

9 General Sir Richard Dannatt *Leading from the Front* (London 2010) p.28.

10 House of Commons questions 23 February 2009 in theyworkforyou. com/debates, accessed 27 July 2010.

11 This was largely thanks to Lieutenant Colonel Patrick Mercer, who was then posted, on promotion, to be Director of Strategy and Communications at the Army Training and Recruiting Agency. He became MP for Newark, in his regimental heartland, in the 2001 General Election.

12 Black Watch website quoted in French *Military Identities* p.348.

13 Dannatt *Leading from the Front* p.118.

14 Quoted in Holmes *Dusty Warriors* p.22.

15 Dannatt *Leading from the Front* p.228.

16 Fergusson *Trumpet in the Hall* p.278.

17 My digest of the Irwin paper in *Dusty Warriors* pp.18–19.

18 Dannatt *Leading from the Front* p.229.

19 Ibid.

20 BBC News news.bbc.co.uk 16 December 2004, accessed 27 July 2010.

21 Alternative Army Web Site www. arrse.co.uk, accessed 27 July 1010.

22 *The Times* 25 November 2005 in www.timesonline.co.uk, accessed 27 July 2010.

23 Alison Anderson 'Cherished Icon Lost to History' *Perthshire Advertiser* 2 December 2005.

24 *The Sunday Times Scotland* 21 August 2005 in www. royalregimentofscotland.org.uk/ comments.php, accessed 27 July 2010.

25 Dannatt *Leading from the Front* p.230.

Chapter 20: Tribal Markings

1 C. H. Firth *Cromwell's Army* (London 1962) p.233.

2 Lewis S. Winstock 'Hot Stuff' *Journal of the Society for Army Historical Research* Vol 33 (1955). It was first

published in the *New York Gazetteer* in
1774, described as being 'by Ned
Botwood, Sergeant of Grenadiers in
the 47th Regiment ... Tune: "Lillies
of France."' Botwood was apparently
killed on 31 July 1759. It is difficult
to be sure of Botwood's fate or the
song's alleged popularity in the
Seven Years War or the American
War of Independence. Its final
verse, though, must have appealed
to Thomas Atkins: 'With Monkton
and Townsend, those brave
brigadiers,/I think we shall soon
have the town 'bout their ears./And
when we have done with the
mortars and guns,/If you please,
Madam Abbess, a word with your
nuns./Each soldier shall enter the
convent in buff/And then, never
fear, we will give them Hot Stuff.'

3 This simply summarises a long and
complex history, and leaves the Foot
Guards, who characteristically had
rules of their own, out of the story.
See Ian Sumner *British Colours and
Standards 1747–1881* (1: Cavalry
and 2: Infantry) (Oxford 2001),
and P. R. Phipps 'Notes on the
Dimensions and Design of
Regimental Colours' *Journal of the
Society for Army Historical Research* Vol
XIV (1935).

4 Lt Col William Gordon-Alexander
Reflections of a Highland Subaltern
(London 1889) p.3.

5 William Lawrence *The Autobiography
of Sergeant William Lawrence*
(Cambridge 1987) p.210.

6 Quoted in Ian Knight *Zulu Rising*
(London 2010) p.557. In 1907
Lieutenants Teignmouth Melvill and
Nevill Coghill were both killed, and
were later awarded the VC for
attempting to save the colour.

7 Riley *Soldiers of the Queen* p.235.

8 Peebles *American War* pp.103,
169–70, 432.

9 Ibid. pp.312–13.

10 Roger Norman Buckley (ed.) *The
Napoleonic War Journal of Captain*

Thomas Henry Browne (1807–1816)
(London 1987) p.73.

11 Dunn *The War the Infantry Knew*
pp.449–50.

12 'Fusiliers celebrate St George's Day
in Afghanistan' 24 April 2009 on
http://www.mod.uk/
DefenceInternet/ ... accessed 6
August 2010.

13 A. G. Oakley 'Diary', Department of
Documents, Imperial War Museum.

*Chapter 21: Full of Strange Oaths,
and Bearded Like the Pard*

1 Grattan *Adventures in the Connaught
Rangers* p.126.

2 Laurence Sterne *The Life and
Opinions of Tristram Shandy,
Gentleman* (London 2003) p.74.

3 General Officer Commanding;
Brigadier General Royal Artillery;
Brigadier General, General Staff;
General Staff Officer Grade 1 (a
lieutenant colonel, often holding
the key appointment of chief of staff
to a division), and aide-de-camp to
the Corps Commander Royal
Artillery.

4 Edwin Mole *A King's Hussar, Being the
Military Memoirs for 25 years of a Troop
Sergeant Major of the 14th (King's)
Hussars* (London 1893) pp.29–30.

5 The period was further reduced in
1977 to fifteen years, and stands
there at present. The good conduct
element of the medal has always
been taken seriously, and a youthful
mishap is enough to prevent its
award.

6 Henry Yule and A. C. Burnell
Hobson-Jobson *A Glossary of
Colloquial Anglo-Indian Phrases* ...
(New Delhi 2000) pp.48, 135.

7 Hobson-Jobson p.503.

8 Shephard *Sergeant Major's War* p.27.

9 Maj Gen Sir C. E. Callwell *Stray
Recollections* 2 Vols (London 1923) I
p.255.

10 Fitzroy Maclean *Eastern Approaches*
(London 1951) pp.149, 151–2.

11 Stephen Graham *A Private in the Guards* (London 1919) p.78. During the First World War, private soldiers in the guards were styled private rather than guardsman. They were termed guardsmen from 1920 onwards, and the headstones of guards privates killed during the war bear this new rank.

12 Paul Fussell (ed.) *The Ordeal of Alfred M. Hale* (London 1975) p.43.

13 The high port is a product of the drill movement 'port arms.' The rifle is held obliquely across the body with its muzzle uppermost, and to the left.

14 Iris Butler *Rule of Three. Sarah, Duchess of Marlborough and her Companions in Power* (London 1967) p.325.

15 J. L. Findlay *Fighting Padre* (London 1941) p.133.

16 'We are … We are … You have a slang world that expresses well what I want to say.' 'We are fucked, My Lord? I hope not.'

17 Drake *Amiable Renegade* p.319.

18 Browne *Napoleonic War Journal* pp.114–15.

19 Mary McGrigor *Wellington's Spies* (Barnsley 2005) pp.168–9.

20 Anglesey *Cavalry* I p.127.

21 Pamela McCleary (ed.) *Dear Little Girl: Letters from the Front 1914–18* (Shipston on Stour 2004) p.18.

22 'The use of Beards in the British Army' in Army Rumour Service, accessed 3 December 2010.

23 http://www.shinycapstar.com and http://www.irishguards.org.uk, both accessed 3 December 2010.

24 Grenadier Guards Association, Nottingham Branch, in http://beehive.thisisnottingham.co.uk, accessed 3 December 2010.

Chapter 22: Tunes of Glory

1 Francis Markham *Five Decades of Epistles of Warre* p.59.

2 Captain Thomas Venn *Military and Maritime Discipline* (London 1672).

3 Quoted in Hugh Barty-King *The Drum* (London 1988) p.51.

4 Sir Charles Oman (ed.) *Adventures with the Connaught Rangers 1809–1814*, William Grattan Esq late lieutenant Connaught Rangers (London 1902) p.128.

5 Charles John Griffiths *A Narrative of the Siege of Delhi* (London 1910) p.136.

6 There are many versions of the words: this is from the website of the Duke of Edinburgh's Royal Regiment, www.farmersboy.com, accessed 18 August 2010. The Duke of Edinburgh's used the march until its amalgamation, and The Princess of Wales's Royal Regiment inherited it from the Royal Hampshires, with whom it had been popualr. The PWRR now marches past to a mixture of the Queen's Regiment's 'Soldiers of the Queen' and 'Farmer's Boy'.

7 Osbert Sitwell *Great Morning* (London 1948) p.197.

8 Rudyard Kipling 'The Drums of the Fore and Aft' in *Wee Willie Winkie and other Child Stories* (Calcutta 1888). The action best describes the Third Afghan War victory of Ahmed Khel (April 1880), when the 59th Foot was caught changing formation without bayonets fixed.

9 John Shipp *Memoirs of the Extraordinary Military Career of John Shipp* (1830) p.127.

10 http://theminiaturespage.com, accessed 19 August 2010.

11 Ian Knight *Zulu Rising* p.471.

12 *London Gazette* 18 June 1858.

13 *London Gazette* (Supplement) 9 September 1916.

14 'The Pope and the Warpipes' in http://st.louis.irish.tripod.com, accessed 19 August 2009.

15 *The Drummer's Call* April 1978.

16 George Simmons *A British Rifle Man* p.287.

17 Barty-King *The Drum* p.80.

18 http://military-bands.co.uk/3 rgj. html accessed 19 August 2010.

19 Richard Barter *The Siege of Delhi: Mutiny Memoirs of an Old Officer* (London 1984) p.23.

20 Sir Frederick Maurice *History of the Scots Guards* (London 1935) p.45.

21 Unpublished diary of Sergeant Shawyer 'Wanderings of a Windjammer' quoted in http:// military-bands.co.uk/3_rgj.html accessed 20 August 2010.

22 Mays *Fall Out the Officers* pp.13, 19, 23, 39.

23 Shawyer 'Wanderings of a Windjammer'.

24 'Love Farewell' was arranged from its traditional format by folk singer John Tams for the Sharpe series, and then recorded with the band and Bugles of the Rifles to raise money for the service charity Help for Heroes.

25 'Centuries old folk song re-recorded for Help for Heroes' in the *Daily Telegraph* 11 December 2009.

PART V

Chapter 23: The Rambling Soldier

1 Sitwell *Great Morning* p.195.

2 John Wain (ed.) *The Journals of James Boswell* (London 1991) p.247.

3 Wonnacott papers, British Library Oriental and India Office Collections, Mss Eur C376/2.

4 Stephen Brumwell *Paths of Glory* (London 2006) p.77.

5 Wolseley on Pennefather.

6 R. E. Scouller *The Armies of Queen Anne* (Oxford 1966) p.164.

7 *Manual of Military Law 1914* p.180.

8 Ibid. p.181.

9 Todd *Journal* pp.7, 10.

10 Quoted in Henderson *Highland Soldier* p.218.

11 Houlding *Fit for Service* p.30.

12 Ibid. p.33 fn 60.

13 Beckles Wilson *Life and Letters of James Wolfe* (New York 1909) p.292.

14 Fortescue IV pp.903–7.

15 Stuart Reid and Paul Chappell *King George's Army 1740–1793 (2)* (London 1995) p.3.

16 Todd *Journal* pp.17–18.

17 James Anton *Retrospect of a Military Life* (Edinburgh 1841).

18 Anton *Retrospect*.

19 G. Penny *Traditions of Perth* quoted in Helen McCorry (ed.) *The Thistle at War* (Edinburgh 1997) pp.48–9.

20 Todd *Journal* p.20.

21 *London Gazette* 31 May 1740.

22 *London Gazette* 25 October 1805.

23 Roberston *Private to Field Marshal* p.21.

24 Cadogan *Road to Armageddon* p.175.

25 Dunn *The War the Infantry Knew* pp.2, 6, 8.

Chapter 24: Barrack-Room Blues

1 Patrick Mileham 'Moral Component: The Regimental System' in Alex Alexandrou et al. (eds.) *New People Strategies for the British Armed Forces* (London 2002) p.73.

2 Lucy *Devil in the Drum* p.56.

3 Mays *Fall Out The Officers* p.78.

4 Houlding *Fit for Service* p.55.

5 'The Royal Artillery Barracks 1172–1803' based on research by the Revd. Dr Michael Gilman in Brigadier Ken Timbers (ed.) *The Royal Artillery, Woolwich, A Celebration* (London 2008).

6 Houlding *Fit for Service* p.40.

7 Maitland *Hussar of the Line* p.4.

8 Buckley *British Army in the West Indies* pp.329–30.

9 Fraser *Forty Years* p.80.

10 Perceptions are not always accurate, for a 2004 report by the Howard League for Penal Reform made substantial criticisms of the regime at Stoke Heath.

11 Maitland *Hussar of the Line* p.123.

12 Anglesey *British Cavalry* I p.129.

13 Ibid. I p.132.
14 Ibid. II p.315.
15 Acland-Troyte *Through the Ranks* p.38.
16 Ibid. pp.15–18.
17 'Standing Orders for the Royal Army Ordnance Corps 1929' Appendix XVI Kit Laid Out For Inspection.
18 Wyndham *Soldiers* p.174.
19 French *Military Identities* p.101.
20 Michael Glover (ed.) *A Gentleman Volunteer: Letters of George Hennell from the Peninsular War 1812–13* (London 1979) p.14.
21 Myerly *Spectacle* p.18.
22 The Marquess of Anglesey (ed.) *Sergeant Pearman's Memoirs: Being Chiefly, His Account of Service with the Third (King's Own) Light Dragoons* (London 1968) p.64.
23 John Fraser *Sixty Years in Uniform* (London 1939) p.83.
24 Wyndham *Soldiers* p.31.
25 H. Compton (ed.) *A King's Hussar, Being the Memoirs for 25 Years of a Troop Sergeant Major in the 14th (King's) Hussars* (London 1893) pp.29–30.
26 *Field Service Pocket Book 1914* (Reprinted HMSO 1916) p.168.
27 Messenger *Call to Arms* p.446.
28 Maitland *Hussar* p.61.
29 Lucy *Devil in the Drum.*
30 Richards *Old Soldiers* p.88.
31 Maitland *Hussar* p.69.
32 Mays *Fall Out the Officers* p.173.
33 General Order of 19 March 1835 in the papers of Sir William Gomm, National Army Museum 1987-11-116-143.
34 'The 30th Foot in the War against Napoleon' on Carole Divall's very useful website http://www.caroledivall.co.uk, accessed 28 August 2010.
35 Mays *Fall Out the Officers* p.53.
36 'Sandes Soldiers Home' in Singapore Infopedia http://infopedia.nl.sg.articles, accessed 28 August 2010.
37 Col O. Leathlobhair in Brian McMahon 'Endynamited by Christ' in http://www.sandes.org.uk, accessed 28 August 2010.
38 http://www.dunnings.net/barry/xrh, accessed 28 August 2010.
39 Holmes *Dusty Warriors* p.159.
40 Mays *Fall Out the Officers* pp.78–9.
41 Roberston *Private to Field Marshal* p.10.
42 Oriental and India Office Collections of the British Library, Papers of Sergeant Major George Carter, Mss Eur E262.
43 Dunn *The War* p.274.
44 Myna Trustram *Women of the Regiment* (Cambridge 1984) p.17.
45 John Clark Marshman (ed.) *The Memoirs of Major General Sir Henry Havelock* (London 1860) p.37.

Chapter 25: Bullies and Beast-Masters

1 Ilana R. Bet-El *Conscripts: Lost Legions of the Great War* (Stroud, Gloucestershire, 1999) p.147.
2 Browne *Napoleonic War Journal* p.48.
3 Mays *Fall Out the Officers* p.65.
4 John Shipp *The Path of Glory* p.15.
5 Tom Hickman *The Call-Up: A History of National Service* (London 2004) p.33.
6 Alexander Somerville *Autobiography of a Working Man* (London 1967) p.84.
7 Maitland *Hussar of the Line* p.24.
8 Ned Sherrin *The Autobiography* (London 2005).
9 Royle *Best Years* p.39.
10 Ibid. p.72.
11 Corns and Hughes-Wilson *Blindfold and Alone* p.360. Graves' poem is *Sergeant-Major Money* and he refers to the incident in his book *Goodbye to All That,* although, as is so often the case with Graves, the line between history and myth is a little blurred.
12 Dunn *The War* p.347.
13 Robertson *Private to Field Marshal* p.18.

14 Dunn *The War* pp.100–1.
15 'Beasting' in ARRSEpedia http://www.arrse.co.uk last modified 11 March 2009, accessed 31 August 2010.
16 BBC News '"Beasting" – part of army life?' 31 July 2008 on http://news.bbc.co.uk accessed 2 September 2010.
17 Ibid.
18 Royle *Best Years of Their Lives* p.46.
19 Joanna Bale 'A "beasting" can turn into humiliation' in *The Times* 28 November 2005.
20 'Beasting' http://www.arrse.co.uk
21 'Shoeing' in ARRSEpedia http://www.arrse.co.uk accessed 1 September 2010.
22 Michael Evans 'Soldiers cleared of Private Gavin Williams "beasting" death' *The Times* 1 August 2008.
23 BBC News 'Army "does not tolerate beasting"' 1 August 2008 http://news.bbc.co.uk accessed 2 September 2010.
24 Lucy Ballinger 'Army rapped over "beasting" death …' *Daily Mail Online* 1 August 2008.
25 *Sheldrake's Aldershot Military Gazette* 6 and 27 April 1906. ch. 24.

Chapter 26: Oh! What a Time Those Officers Have

1 Michael N. McConnell *Army and Empire: British Soldiers on the American Frontier, 1758–1778* (Lincoln Nebr. 2004) p.42.
2 William Maginn, *The Military Sketch-Book: Reminiscences of the Service at Home and Abroad* 2 Vols (London 1827) I pp.20–1.
3 Dansey letters, Historical Society of Delaware, Wilmington, Delaware.
4 'Lieutenant Walter Campbell' in Michael Brander *The Sword and the Pen* (London 1989) p.70.
5 George Robert Gleig *The Subaltern: A Chronicle of the Peninsular War* (Edinburgh 1877) p.3.
6 Browne *Journal* pp.112–13.

7 Field Marshal Lord Wolseley *The Story of a Soldier's Life* 2 Vols (London 1903) I pp.8–9.
8 Elizabeth Longford (Introduction) *Your Most Obedient Servant: James Thornton. Cook to the Duke of Wellington* (Exeter 1985) p.20.
9 F. Yeats-Brown *Bengal Lancer* (London 1930) pp.16–17.
10 Freddie Rawding *Life as a Curious Traveller* (Langley Park, Durham 2009) p.13.
11 Ibid. pp.168–9.
12 Ibid. pp.221–2.
13 Ibid. p.222.
14 Percy Sumner 'Regimental Orders for Dress, 25th Foot, 1796 and 1828' *Journal of the Society For Army Historical Research* 16 1937 p.148.

Chapter 27: The Sergeants' Mess Dinner is Worth Putting Down

1 Todd *Journal* p.14.
2 Wyndham *Soldiers* pp.143–56 passim.
3 Cairns *Social Life* p.118.
4 Jasper Ridley *The Freemasons* (London 1999) p.161.
5 George Carter Journal in British Library Oriental and India Office Collection Mss Eur E262.
6 *Rudyard Kipling's Verse Inclusive Edition* (London 1933) p.437.
7 Maitland *Hussar* p.85.
8 Hickman *Call-Up* p.143.
9 'British Military Garrison – Tipperary, Co Tipperary Ireland' http://tipperarybarracks.webs.com accessed 22 August 2010.

Chapter 28: Campaigners Straight and Gay

1 Todd *Journal* p.16.
2 Maitland *Hussar of the Line* pp.90–2.
3 Buckler *British Army in the West Indies* p.165.
4 Holmes *Sahib* p.438.
5 Richards *Old Soldier Sahib*.
6 Hickman *Call-Up* p.201.

7 Ibid.
8 Ibid. p.205.
9 *Manual of Military Law 1914* p.97.
10 Quoted in French *Military Identities* pp.132–3.
11 'Gays in the Military: The UK and US compared' *BBC News at Six* 2 February 2010 in http://news.bbc. co.uk, accessed 16 September 2010.
12 Buckley *British Army in the West Indies* p.233.
13 Quoted in French *Military Identities* p.133.

Chapter 29: Officers' Wives Get Puddings and Pies

1 Holmes *Sahib* p.153.
2 Holmes *Dusty Warriors* pp.311–12.
3 Trustram *Women of the Regiment* p.71.
4 Swinson and Scott (eds) *The Memoirs of Private Waterfield* (London 1968) p.107.
5 Smith *Victorian RSM* p.21.
6 Trustram *Women of the Regiment* pp.23–5.
7 Ibid. p.111.

INDEX